John J.K. Lee
636 N. 14th St.

Acquired from Prof. Marburg.

FT

INTERMEDIATE ECONOMIC ANALYSIS

INTERMEDIATE ECONOMIC ANALYSIS

BY JOHN F. DUE PH.D.

PROFESSOR OF ECONOMICS
UNIVERSITY OF ILLINOIS

THIRD EDITION

1956

RICHARD D. IRWIN, INC.

HOMEWOOD, ILLINOIS

THIRD EDITION

First Printing, January, 1956

PRINTED IN THE UNITED STATES OF AMERICA
Library of Congress Catalogue Card No. 56–5337

PREFACE

The primary purpose of this book is to provide a summary exposition of contemporary economic theory at a level intermediate between the beginning principles courses and graduate courses in economic theory. It is intended for use in undergraduate courses designed to provide a more intensive training in economic analysis than is possible in the elementary course. The emphasis, as in the previous editions, is upon value and distribution theory. The level of analysis is based upon the assumption that the students have had an elementary course in economics, but basic concepts are reviewed in order to provide a common background of terminology. The treatment is largely nonmathematical, beyond the simple geometrical tools. In order that the book may be kept within manageable length, no attempt is made to develop the historical antecedents of contemporary theory, nor to analyze in detail the current controversies in the field, although the more important of these are pointed out.

The general level of analysis in this edition is comparable to that in the previous one. However, a large portion of the material has been completely rewritten in an effort to make it more easily understandable. Several changes in terminology have been made in order to obtain greater conformity with standard usage. The term "monopolistic competition" is now used with respect to the case of differentiation and large numbers, rather than for the entire field of nonpurely competitive conditions. The term "sales schedule" as applied to the demand for the product of an individual seller has been abandoned despite its convenience, because it is no longer generally used. The term "net value of output" as applied to the figure of national income obtained by the product approach has likewise been abandoned.

The most important changes made in the revision involve reorganization of material and recognition of recent developments in the field of economic theory. The first chapter is now devoted entirely to the basic concepts of economics, while the second is concerned with the nature of economic analysis. A new third chapter deals with the units of the economic system and the goals of the various units. The chapters on nonpurely competitive conditions have been completely reorganized, with a separate chapter now devoted to oligopoly. The material contained in Chapter 11 of the previous edition has been integrated into other chapters.

Significant changes have been made in the material dealing with factor pricing. The analysis of factor demand has been removed from the chapter on the theory of production and incorporated in the introductory chapter to the analysis of factor pricing. The material on wage theory has been modified in terms of recent contributions to the literature in the field, and has been expanded into two chapters, with additional emphasis on the theory of marginal productivity as applied to wage determination. The old Chapter 14 has been broken down into three parts. The portion dealing with investment decisions has been expanded and now comprises a separate chapter; the portion on goals of business firms has been introduced into Chapter 3; and the section on profits, in greatly expanded form, now comprises a separate chapter. The theory of interest has been completely rewritten in terms of the loanable funds approach. General equilibrium analysis now is allocated a separate chapter, which includes the basic equations, and a description of input-output analysis.

The chapters on national income have been brought together by the moving of the material on national income concepts to Chapter 21. The two chapters presenting the analysis of national income determination have been greatly modified, particularly in light of recent work in the field, with reference made to such developments as the theory of growth. The concluding chapter, which presents a summary of welfare economics, has been reorganized.

As in the previous editions, the references at the ends of the chapters are selective, and are not intended to be exhaustive. The questions, which are similar in type to those of the previous edition but have been rewritten, are designed to facilitate study of the material on the part of the student. If time permits, a course of the type for which this book is intended can be improved by the inclusion of problem material. Unfortunately, compilations of such material are limited. The book by W. C. Bradford and R. M. Alt, entitled *Business Economics: Principles and Cases* (Chicago: Richard D. Irwin, Inc., 1951) contains some useful cases. Some of the best case material is to be found in such sources as the *Wall Street Journal* and *Fortune.*

The task of revision has been greatly facilitated by the comments of numerous persons. I am indebted to the three reviewers, whose identity is unknown to me, who supplied detailed comments at the request of the publisher; to my colleague Professor J. Fred Bell; and to the three members of the Editorial Committee of the Irwin Series in Economics: Professor Malcolm M. Davisson of the University of California, Professor E. S. Shaw of Stanford University, who read the revised chapters on investment, interest, and profits, and Professor Lloyd Reynolds of Yale University, particularly for his suggestions with respect to the material on wage theory. In addition great assistance has been provided by the various persons who have sent in suggestions on the basis of their experience in using the book as a text. I wish to thank the students in the Economics 300 course in the University of Illinois during the past several years for their comments on various sections. Finally, I should like to acknowledge the assistance given by my wife, Jean Mann Due, for her assistance in the preparation of the revision, and to the art and editorial staffs of Richard D. Irwin, Inc., for their work in getting the manuscript and charts into final shape.

Acknowledgment is made to Harcourt, Brace & Company for permission to quote a short section from J. M. Keynes, *The General Theory of Employment, Interest and Money,* and to Harper & Brothers for permission to use a quotation from K. E. Boulding, *Economic Analysis,* 3rd edition.

JOHN F. DUE

URBANA, ILLINOIS
September 1955

TABLE OF CONTENTS

PART I. INTRODUCTION

PART II. THE THEORY OF COMMODITY PRICE AND OUTPUT DETERMINATION

PART I

Introduction

Chapter 1: NATURE AND FUNCTIONS OF THE ECONOMIC SYSTEM

The complex society in which we live today is characterized by the importance of extensive social institutions which greatly influence the behavior of individuals, and insure co-ordinated operation of the society. The very high degree of interdependence, the constant contact of various individuals with one another, and the extent to which the welfare of each person is dependent upon the action of others have resulted in the growth of a very elaborate organization which insures the integration of the actions of the various persons. The elaborate structure of modern society stands in sharp contrast to the situation in a primitive society, in which each family or small group is largely self-sufficient in all respects, and the welfare of one group is completely independent of the action of other groups. Despite the apparent freedom of choice of action which the individual has in countries such as the United States, his behavior is greatly conditioned by the existing institutions. For example, while no law compels a person to work for a wage, the only way in which he can make a living in a manner compatible with existing institutions and social pressures is to do so, if he does not have other sources of income. These social institutions are, in the terms of one writer, "the molds within which individual conduct is shaped."[1]

ECONOMIC INSTITUTIONS

There are several types of social institutions. There are, for example, religious institutions through whose operations man's desire for spiritual guidance is met. Political institutions provide the means through which a community determines and enforces formal rules of behavior, conducts military operations, and undertakes certain activities (e.g., postal service) the provision of which is deemed to be more satisfactory on a community basis. There are numerous other types. But one

[1] H. R. Bowen, *Toward Social Economy* (New York: Rinehart, 1948), p. 16.

of great importance—the one with which we are primarily concerned in this study—is the group of *economic institutions,* or, regarded as a unit, the *economic system, the organization through the operation of which the various resources—scarce, relative to the need for them—are utilized to satisfy the wants of man.*

In somewhat different terms, the economic system consists of the set of institutions which determine the manner in which the various resources available in the world are utilized in the satisfaction of our wants. Were all *goods*—physical objects and services capable of satisfying human wants—present in quantities in excess of the amounts which persons desire, as is air, for example, economic institutions would be nonexistent; all wants would be satisfied without effort and without interference with other persons. Increased use of a good by one person would not reduce the amounts which other persons could obtain to satisfy their wants. No organization would be necessary to facilitate use of the resources, and no control would be required over this phase of human behavior. But unfortunately the world is not of this character. So long as most goods are scarce, relative to the demand for them, conflicts of interest over possession of them must arise, and thus institutions for control are necessary. However, if each person satisfied his wants by his own activities, by obtaining directly from nature by his individual efforts the goods which he used for want-satisfaction, economic institutions would be minor influences in human life. But modern economic society is characterized by a very high degree of specialization, and extensive interdependence. Each person performs, usually, a highly specialized task in the production system and, by the use of the income received for the performance of this task, purchases goods which he desires. For such a system to function, an elaborate mechanism of economic institutions to co-ordinate the actions of the individuals is necessary. It is the study of this system which constitutes economics. Thus, more precisely, *economics* may be defined as the study of the organization through the operation of which the utilization of scarce resources in the satisfaction of human wants is directed.

Human Wants

The basis of economic activity is the existence of individual wants. Persons are born with certain basic desires. A person wishes food, in part because it is necessary for life, in part because the use of food is itself a source of pleasure. He seeks to escape unpleasant sensations, such as excessive heat or cold. He desires security—the assurance that he will be able to continue to have the means of want-satisfaction to which he has become accustomed. He desires recognition by others. These are merely examples; the list could be extended materially.

The choices which a person makes of the particular goods to satisfy these wants, however, are determined to a great extent by the customs of the society in which the person is living. Some ways of satisfying these wants are socially (and legally) acceptable; others are not. A person has a basic desire to avoid the discomfort of extreme cold; the type of clothing which he wears is dictated—except for a very narrow range of individual choice—by the customs of the community in which he is living. Selections of food are influenced greatly by the habits of the community. The type of recreation which a person seeks is particularly controlled by the current practices of the period. The manner in which a person seeks to obtain recognition by his fellow-men varies with the society in which he lives. Recognition may depend upon the number of wives which he acquires or the size of the house that he builds or the extent of the business empire which he controls. Human wants are very complex. A person is often not entirely aware of the real desires which he is seeking to satisfy when he acquires certain goods, and frequently, he does not recognize the extent to which his choices are dictated by the social institutions of the period—that the free choice which he seems to have is actually confined within very narrow ranges by custom and tradition.

Individual choices in the present-day economic society are subject not only to influences of the general cultural background of the period but also to those developed by the producers of goods, in the form of advertising and other sales effort, in order to increase their own profits. Some of this activity is designed to encourage persons to satisfy one desire instead of another or to utilize one particular method to satisfy a desire in preference to alternatives. Much advertising, however, attempts primarily to induce the buyer to use the brand of one producer in the field instead of that of another.

The Means to Satisfy Human Wants

Material objects and services which are capable of satisfying human wants are known as *goods;* the property or capacity which they have which enables them to satisfy wants is known as *utility.* A few goods, known as *free goods,* exist in nature in quantities in excess of the amounts which persons desire, even when they can get them free of charge, and exist in the form, place, and time desired for consumption. By the use of these goods, wants can be satisfied without conscious effort on the part of the individual. Thus, under ordinary circumstances, a person can acquire all the air which he desires, without effort to obtain it. But most goods are *economic goods,* which exist in quantities limited in relation to the demand for them. Most *consumption goods*—ones which directly satisfy personal wants—are not available at all in nature in the form, place, and time desired.[2] Instead, there are available *factors of production*—means which can be used to produce goods which will directly satisfy wants.

The factors of production which are provided by nature can be classified into two general groups: (1) the capacity of human beings to perform various activities and (2) natural resources—material objects which can be utilized directly or indirectly in want-satisfaction. Many of the natural resources—the better grades of farm land, for example—are scarce, relative to the demand for the goods which they can produce; others, such as coal in the United States, are not themselves scarce, for any generation at least, but, since human activity is necessary to produce consumption goods from them, the products made from them are limited in quantity.

In early societies persons satisfied their wants by utilizing directly their own activities in obtaining want-satisfying goods from the natural resources. Thus primitive man lived on fruits and vegetables which grew in nature and wild animals which he could catch. But, as time passed, man himself developed two additional aids to production: greater *skills* in carrying on productive activity and *capital goods*—material objects produced by human effort for use in further production. Thus improved techniques for performing various tasks were developed, and the skills acquired were passed on from one generation to another. And man discovered that he could obtain more goods to satisfy his wants if he devoted a portion of his activity to making various objects—capital goods—to assist him in producing consumption goods rather than devoting all his working time to direct want-satisfying activities. Thus, for example, he discovered that he could, over a period of time, catch more fish by spending part of his time in making nets and spears instead of using it all in fishing with his bare hands.

In the present-day economy, the factors of production—the means used to produce goods to satisfy wants—can be classed into three general groups:

1. Natural resources:[3] all economic goods used in production

[2] There are exceptions; the land upon which homes in a city are built may exist in the form, place, and time desired but in limited quantities relative to the demand for it.

[3] The term *land* is often used in economic analysis to refer to the entire group of natural resources, as defined.

which are found directly in nature, as, for example, land used in wheat production, coal in the veins of a mine, or a waterfall which can be harnessed to generate electric power, such as Niagara Falls.

2. Labor: all human activity utilized in production. The nature of the labor service being rendered is controlled not only by the native capacity of human beings to work but also by the skill which they have acquired. It is impossible and unnecessary, however, to separate the labor services into the parts for which each of these two elements is responsible.

For purposes of economic analysis it is desirable to distinguish activity involved in the undertaking of *business* activity and the making of business decisions in the face of uncertainty from usual *labor* activity involved in the performance of routine tasks. The former type is often called *entrepreneurial* activity. In the small owner-operated store or farm, the entrepreneurial activity is clearly distinguishable. In the large corporation the identification of entrepreneurial activity is more difficult, as outlined in Chapter 3.

3. Capital goods: all material goods produced by man which are used in production. Thus factory buildings and machinery, locomotives and trucks, tractors and horses, and industrial fuel and raw materials constitute capital goods. Some such goods have useful lives of many years, while others can be used but once in the production process. The term *circulating capital* is often used with reference to materials, fuel, and similar items which can be used only once, or over only a short period (usually within one year under usual conventional standards), while the term *fixed capital* or *capital equipment* is used with reference to capital goods used over a longer period.

Money capital is not regarded as a distinct factor of production, or a good, but as the means by which other factor units, and particularly capital goods, are acquired. The money is essential to the business firm, but in itself does not play a part in the production processes.

There has been a tendency in recent years for many writers to regard natural resources as merely one form of capital goods, and thus to classify all factor units into two classes—labor and capital goods—because of the difficulties of distinguishing, in practice, between natural resources and capital goods. However, for certain purposes, it is useful to retain the differentiation, despite the practical difficulties in identifying the two elements, because one type of factor is produced, and thus has a cost of production which influences supply, while the other is provided by nature, and thus has no cost of production.

THE FUNCTIONS OF THE ECONOMIC SYSTEM

The nature of human wants and the means which make possible their fulfilment have been described briefly in the preceding paragraphs. It is now possible to consider in detail the tasks which an economic system performs in fulfilling its general function of facilitating and controlling the use of resources in the satisfaction of wants.

Provision of Incentive

A primary function which an economic system must perform is the provision of incentive for the undertaking of the conduct of production. In a simple economy without exchange or division of labor, the incentive problem is a minor one; since all persons are producing goods for their own direct consumption, they obviously have incentive to carry on the production. In a complex society characterized by extensive specialization, the problem of incentives is more difficult; there must be some inducement offered in the operation of the economy which will lead persons to take the initiative in undertaking production which does not directly satisfy their own wants. Furthermore, there must be some inducement which will persuade factor-owners to supply units of the factors which they own to those conducting production enterprises.

Co-ordination of Economic Activity

The second primary function of an economic system is the provision of a method of co-ordination and control over the activity of the individuals in the economy. There are several aspects of this coordination. In the first place, there must be some method of determining which goods are to be produced. Most factors of production can be used to produce a wide variety of goods. From iron ore, for example, can be made automobiles or washing machines, railroad cars or paper clips, or many other objects. The services of a carpenter can be used on house construction, the building of new service stations, or government public works. There must be some method in the economy for determining the uses to which these resources will be put or, in other words, for the selection of the goods to be produced and the determination of the amounts of output of each. Since the quantities of the factors are limited, there must be some method of allocating them among various alternate uses.

Secondly, the economic system must provide for the determination of the methods to be used in production. Since at any one time there are available a number of possible methods for producing particular goods, there must be some system for selection of actual methods to be used. Is coal to be mined by hand labor or by machinery? Are railroad trains to be operated with diesel or steam motive power? Are urban passengers to be carried by streetcar or bus? Selection must be made not only between particular techniques but also among various possible methods of organizing the conduct of production. Shall production of a commodity be centered in one locality or scattered throughout the country? Shall production be concentrated in the hands of a few large producers or distributed among many small firms? What form of administrative organization shall be utilized in a business enterprise?

Finally, there must be some mechanism for distributing the output of production among the various members of society and some system of determining the amounts of the product going to each person. There would be no problem of controlling distribution if the total output were sufficiently great that each person could obtain as much of every product as he desired. Since the products are scarce, relative to the demand for them, control is necessary.

These functions must be performed in any type of economic system. But the exact manner in which they are performed depends upon the particular type of economic system in operation. The type with which we are primarily concerned is that of capitalism; a brief description of this type is necessary as a preliminary step toward a discussion of the manner in which such a system performs the functions.

The Nature of Capitalism

Capitalism may be defined as a type of economic society characterized by private ownership of the factors of production and by private initiative, guided by the profit motive, in the conduct of production. More specifically, the major social institutions to be found in capitalism include the following:

1. The legal institution of private property: in consumption goods, such as houses; in the factors of production, such as capital equipment and land; and in money capital, the means by which producing units obtain physical goods and human services needed to carry on production. The concept of private property is that of the right of ownership, use, and employment of wealth to gain an income.

2. Private enterprise: the conduct of production by privately owned enterprises. Except for a limited number of governmentally rendered services, goods are produced by businesses owned directly or, in the case of the corporation, indirectly, by individuals. The firms are free to acquire the necessary means of production by purchase or hire

and to dispose of the products as they see fit. The motive to carry on production is the desire of the owners of the business units to gain greater income in the form of profits.

Because of private ownership of the factors of production and private initiative in production, the capitalist economy is characterized by a very large number of independently reached individual decisions and an equally large number of exchange transactions. Individual decisions are made by factor-owners with respect to hiring or selling units of the factors of production to business firms; they are made by business firms with regard to determination of products and volumes of output, selection of methods of production, acquisition of factor units, and, in many cases, setting of price. Consumers make numerous decisions with regard to the purchase of goods. There are transactions between factor-owners and business firms, among business firms themselves, and between business firms and consumers.

3. Control of the functioning of the economy by the price system: The control functions which an economy must perform, as described above, are carried out primarily by the operation of the price system. The services of the factors of production[4] and the products of production are exchanged for money; the relationships of the prices—the amounts of money for which the goods exchange—provide the mechanism for the determination of the uses to which the resources are directed, the methods of production, and the pattern in which the output of production is distributed.[5] The price system provides the means for co-ordination of the individual decisions and transactions discussed in the previous paragraph. The operation of the price system will be discussed in detail in subsequent sections.

4. Importance of competition: The force which is expected to prevent exploitation of some groups in the economy by others is competition—the struggling of various individuals against one another to increase their own economic well-being. Thus, if firms seek to raise prices of their products in order to gain profits higher than the average, new firms will enter the industry and reduce prices and profits. In practice, in present-day capitalism, competition does not work with complete effectiveness, but it still serves as a force of great importance. Interferences with competition will be discussed in later chapters.

[4] And, except in the case of labor, the units of the factors themselves.

[5] The fact that, in present-day capitalism, individual sellers have considerable influence in setting prices does not destroy the importance of the price system as the coordinating mechanism of the economy. The sellers, in setting prices, are guided by their costs and the demand prices of their customers.

5. Limited role of government: Capitalism is characterized by the relative absence of government control over economic activity, particularly over prices and production. In the laissez faire capitalism of the last century, governmental interference was extremely limited. Virtually no control at all was exercised over private production, and governmental production itself was held within a narrow scope, limited to such areas as national defense and police protection. In the economic system which we regard as capitalism today, the extent of government control is greater, yet relatively small compared to the sphere of private initiative. Some of the government controls regulate the conduct of private economic activity, presumably in the interests of society as a whole. For example, the government seeks to prevent monopoly, and thus to insure more fully the protection of particular groups from exploitation by others. Some governmental measures are designed to improve the relationships between business firms and persons supplying labor services to them. Others are intended to prevent the sale of goods regarded as detrimental to the welfare of the community.

In addition to these regulatory actions, governments in all countries have undertaken some direct production of goods and services themselves. This is confined, primarily, to the provision of "social" goods—ones which benefit the members of the community as a whole, but which do not provide direct separable benefits to individuals, and thus cannot be produced on a profit-making basis. National defense is the traditional example of this type of good. In other cases governments have taken over because of the costs involved in selling the services to the users (as is true in the case of highways), or because the production tended to pass into monopoly control. But despite these actions, the governmental sector is relatively small compared to that of private enterprise in the United States. Our economy is still primarily one of free enterprise and private initiative. Today a person is legally free to start any business he desires, provided that the product is not considered harmful and the business is not in one of the few industries, such as the public utilities field, in which the number of firms is restricted. He can use any method of production he desires and, with certain exceptions, set prices as he sees fit. He can obtain units of the factors of production from any supplier and pay for them the amount that he and the supplier agree upon, subject to certain restrictions in regard to wages. He can produce any quantity of goods without restrictions on quality, if the product is not considered harmful and is not misrepresented. He can cease production whenever he pleases, unless he operates in the public utilities field.

These five features are usually regarded as the basic characteristics of capitalism. It must be recognized, however, that the exact nature of capitalist systems varies with time and place. The American economy has undergone marked changes in the last century, in the extent and nature of competition, the degree of governmental interference with the price system, the conduct of production and the amount of direct governmental production. Nevertheless, the economy is still regarded as capitalistic in nature. Among the capitalist countries of the world today, wide variations are to be found in the exact nature of competition, in the functioning of the price system, and in the role of government in the economy; these variations inevitably affect the manner in which the system operates. In the analysis to follow, primary emphasis is given to the present-day economy of the United States. But much of the analysis, developed in terms of the general characteristics of capitalism, is applicable to any capitalist society.

Earlier in the chapter the functions which any economic system must perform were outlined. It is now possible to consider the way in which they are performed in capitalism. This question will be discussed in summary fashion in the remainder of the chapter and will be considered in greater detail in subsequent chapters.

Incentives in Capitalism

Since the initiative to undertake production in capitalism rests with individuals, the system must provide some incentive to these individuals to induce them to carry on production. This incentive is provided primarily by the opportunity which capitalism offers for the earning of profits from the conduct of business—profits which enable the recipients to increase their own material well-being. Not only does the possibility of making profits encourage persons to undertake production, but the desire to maximize profits guides their actions in the conduct of production. In the choice of products, levels of output, methods of production, and forms of organization, the action of the producer is guided by the possibility of greater profit from some choices than from others.[6] The profit incentive is particularly important in encouraging the development and introduction of new methods of production,[7] which, by

[6] Other considerations besides profit maximization play a part in business decisions, as explained in Chapter 3. The assumption of profit maximization, however, can be regarded as the best single assumption that can be made about motivation of business behavior.

[7] There are some exceptions in the present-day economy; monopoly power occasionally restricts the introduction of new techniques until existing investments are liquidated.

allowing lower cost or better quality of product, will enable the producers to increase their net incomes.

The inducement to factor-owners to allow producers to use their factor units is provided by the prices which the producers pay for the use of the units, since these prices constitute incomes for the factor-owners. The factor-owners, in seeking to maximize their incomes, will provide their factor units to those producers who will offer them the highest payments.

Control of the Operation of the Capitalist Economy by the Price System

The controlling mechanism of the capitalist economy—the instrument which co-ordinates the actions of the individuals in the economy and provides a method of attaining performance of the necessary control functions of the economy—is the price system. In the first place, the price system determines the selection of goods to be produced and the quantities of output of each good; thus it determines the manner in which the available factors of production are allocated to the production of various articles and services. Business firms can succeed in making profits only if they are able to sell their products at prices in excess of the contractual costs of producing them, that is, in excess of the amounts which must be paid for the means of production. Thus production will be limited to those goods which can be sold for prices which cover contractual costs and yield at least an average rate of profit to the firms. The output of each good will tend to adjust to the amount which can be produced and sold at an average rate of profit.

The contrast between the direction of the economy by the functioning of the price system and that exercised by governments in non-capitalist economies is very sharp. In the latter the decisions with respect to output are made directly by governmental agencies, and necessary materials are allocated to the production regardless of the relative desires of consumers, and relationships between prices and costs. The contrast between normal operation of capitalist economies and wartime operation is also significant; in World War II, government found it necessary to interfere drastically in the operation of the price system, and to control directly the levels of output in many lines. But these controls were removed shortly after the end of the war.

The price system in capitalism likewise controls the selection of techniques of production and methods of organization of producing units. From the choice of various possible techniques, the producers, in attempting to minimize cost, will select those methods which allow the most efficient (lowest cost) production of the desired quantity of output. If the quality of output depends upon the choice of techniques, the firm must attempt to estimate the relative profits from various combinations of techniques and product-qualities, and select the combination which offers the best profit.

The size of the producing unit also is determined by the functioning of the price system. If the size is too small or too large, costs will be high relative to price.[8] The size which will allow low cost is determined by the techniques of production in the industry; maximum efficiency requires larger steel mills than bakeries. Likewise, through the operation of the price system, there will occur a selection of firms which will remain in production. Those firms which have relatively high cost, due, for example, to inefficient management or poor location, will be unable to continue.

Finally, the price system serves as the mechanism for the distribution of goods among the various members of society. The owners of the means of production—including, of course, the workers—sell the services of their factor units to the business enterprises for prices (wages, rent, etc.); with the money received, they purchase the goods forthcoming from production. The relationship of the prices paid for the services of the factors determines the manner in which the total output is distributed among the various factor-owners. If, for example, the price paid for a certain type of labor is high compared to that paid for other factor units, a relatively large share of total income will go to these workers.

The Economic System of Socialism

Although this study is primarily concerned with the functioning of the capitalist economy, it is desirable to note briefly the characteristic features of the socialist form of economic society.[9] As distinguished from capitalism, the basic feature of socialism is the conduct of all or most production activity directly by the government rather than by private business. In addition, under the usual concept of socialism, private ownership of the factors of production (other than human services) would be replaced by government ownership, and thus property would cease to be a source of individual income.

[8] This statement must not be interpreted to mean that all firms will attain optimum (low-cost) size; this problem will be discussed in subsequent chapters.

[9] There are, of course, many possible forms of socialism. The characteristics indicated in this section are those generally regarded as fundamental features of any socialist system.

When ownership and control of production rests in the hands of the government and individual freedom in the conduct of production is eliminated, the price system ceases to provide an automatic control mechanism over the operation of the economy. The government—or, more specifically, those in control of the government—can determine the commodities to be produced and the techniques of production on any basis that they desire to use and can allocate the output of production on some arbitrary standard. Actually, however, if reasonable efficiency in production is to be obtained and production is to be directed toward those goods for which there is greatest desire, the price system must be retained in a socialist economy and allowed to perform functions almost as important as those which it has in capitalism.

Under the usual concept of a socialist society, persons would be paid money wages for their services. Since other factor units would be owned by the government, these money wages would be the sole source of individual income. The persons receiving wages would use them for the purchase of government-produced goods, which would be sold for money prices, just as is the output of business firms in the capitalist economy. Prices would be set by the government at levels which would insure that the total purchases would equal the total supply being produced, and production would be adjusted to such figures that the costs of production would equal the selling prices. Only by this means could the government insure that production was being directed to those goods most desired by the consumers. For the selection of the most efficient methods of production and types of organizational structure, the costs of the various methods would be determined. Thus the government would utilize the price system in controlling production and as the device for distribution of income. But the importance of the price system in socialism would not be an inevitable consequence of the form of the economy, as it is in capitalism, but rather the result of deliberate choice on the part of the government—a choice which must be made, however, if the economy is to operate with maximum efficiency and resources are to be used in the production of the goods most desired by consumers.

The Activities and Magnitudes of the Economic System

Economic activity may be classified into two general forms, namely, production and consumption. *Production* may be defined as activity which increases the ability of goods to satisfy wants, or, in other words, creates utility. Some types of production, such as manufacturing and agriculture, result primarily in creation of *form* utility, that is, in the changing of the physical form of goods in such a manner as to increase their ability to satisfy wants. Other types, such as transportation, result primarily in the creation of *place* utility, that is, the movement of goods to locations in which they can more easily be obtained to satisfy wants. Other types, such as the work of wholesalers and retailers, warehouses, etc., result in the production of *time* utility—the storing of goods from the time of production to the time at which they are most wanted. Finally, the work of wholesalers, retailers, brokers, etc., also results in the creation of *exchange* utility, that arising from the transfer of goods from some persons to others. Actually, of course, most all types of business firms create more than one form of utility; the examples given refer merely to the primary type of activity carried on by the particular form of business.

Consumption activity, on the other hand, consists of the utilization of goods in the satisfaction of personal wants. The term is not used in reference to the utilization of goods by business firms in further production, but solely to the use of the goods in the satisfaction of personal wants directly.

The net contribution of production activity during a given period of time toward goods available for consumption, or for a net increase in accumulated wealth of society, is known as *national income.* This may be measured as the sum of all factor incomes received during the period from the provision of factor units to business firms, that is, the sum of wages and salaries, rent and interest, and the net profits of business firms. Or, the magnitude of national income may be measured as the sum of the values of all finished goods produced during the period, including both consumption goods and finished capital goods, in excess of the figure of the decline in value (depreciation) of capital goods existing at the beginning of the year.[10] The values of intermediate goods, such as flour produced and used in further processing during the year, are not included, since their values enter into the values of the finished products. The two approaches to the measurement of the magnitude of national income must yield the same figure, since factor incomes are obtained only from the values of products produced, and every dollar of the value of output becomes, directly or indirectly, an element in factor incomes.

Further attention will be given to the magnitudes of income and output in Chapter 21.

[10] As explained in Chapter 21, indirect business taxes are also subtracted from the total value product (gross national product) in calculating national income, since these taxes do not become factor incomes.

SELECTED REFERENCES

BOWEN, H. R. *Toward Social Economy,* chap. 1. New York: Rinehart, 1947.

STIGLER, G. J. *The Theory of Price,* chap. 1. rev. ed. New York: Macmillan, 1952.

QUESTIONS

1. How do economic institutions differ from other institutions in society?
2. What is the economic system?
3. In what sense is scarcity the basis of economic activity?
4. Distinguish between the terms utility and good.
5. What is the distinguishing characteristic of economic goods?
6. Distinguish between consumption goods and factors of production.
7. What are the three major classes into which factors of production are classified?
8. What is entrepreneurial activity?
9. Distinguish between fixed capital and circulating capital.
10. Explain the major functions which the economic system performs.
11. What are the principal characteristics of capitalism?
12. What are "social" goods? Why have governments undertaken their production?
13. How does the capitalism of the present-day United States differ from that of 100 years ago? From the present-day economic system of Great Britain?
14. What is the basic regulating mechanism of capitalism? How does it function?
15. Contrast the role of the price system in socialism and capitalism.
16. Explain the four types of utility.
17. Distinguish between production and consumption activity.
18. What is national income?
19. Define economics.

Chapter 2 THE NATURE AND SCOPE OF ECONOMIC THEORY

Economics has been defined in the previous chapter as a study of economic institutions, which comprise the organization through the operation of which scarce resources are utilized in the satisfaction of wants. Economic theory, in turn, is that portion of the general study of economics which explains the relationships existing between various sets of data in the economy. It is the purpose of this chapter to examine more carefully the nature, scope, and methods of economic theory.

The Nature of Economic Theory

It it the purpose of economic theory to develop knowledge of the relationships among various phenomena in the economy, in order to provide tools for analyzing and explaining the behavior of the various elements. Economic theory thus seeks to explain causal relationships, in order to provide a guide for the selection of data which will allow the development of an explanation of various events, and the prediction of the reactions which will occur in response to particular changes. For example, in the early months of 1954, coffee prices rose sharply. The theory of price determination does not in itself explain why this rise occurred. But by indicating the various forces which influence the prices of commodities, it provides a guide to the selection of the data (such as ones of changes in supply) which will allow an explanation, and facilitates the formulation of the explanation by demonstrating how changes in the various determinants of price will affect the price level.

The relationships which are established by economic analysis may be called *economic principles.* These consist of generalizations which express the relationships between the behavior of various elements in the economy. Thus, for example, the principle that over a long-run period in pure competition, price tends to equal average cost expresses the relationship between price, on the one hand, and cost on the other, under the assumed conditions.

There are two types of such generalizations. The first or *analytical* type expresses conclusions which follow logically from certain assumptions. In the example given in the previous paragraph, under certain assumptions with regard to motivation of human behavior and the nature of pure competition, the principle that price will equal average cost follows as a matter of logical necessity. It is this type of generalization with which we are primarily concerned in this study. The second type of generalization is that of an *empirical* nature, a statement of relationships between observed data. Thus if a large number of observations show that price reductions lead to increases in consumption and if a logical explanation of such a relationship can be discovered, the empirical generalization may be advanced that price reductions lead to increases in consumption. But, unlike the analytical generalization, in which the conclusion follows as a matter of necessity from the assumptions, the empirical type is merely a statement of a tendency which may or may not be valid in particular instances.

Generalizations of the empirical type, which are direct products of inductive study of actual conditions, are often reformulated into analytical principles, by selection of appropriate assumptions and determination of the logical conclusions which follow. Thus the price-consumption relationship expressed above, as an empirical generalization, would not necessarily apply in all particular cases. But, if it is reformulated into an analytical principle, by selecting certain assumptions about the motivation of human behavior, the reactions of individuals to consumption of successive units of a good, and of given income levels and by developing the conclusions which follow logically from these assumptions, the conclusions become necessarily valid (provided that the logic by which they are obtained is correct) in all cases in which the assumed conditions are found.

Analytical Principles

Formulation. The first step in the formulation of an analytical principle is the determination of the problem, that is, the selection of the question with which the principle is to deal. If economic analysis is to be of any use beyond providing an exercise in logic, the problems selected must be ones of significance for the actual world. For example, there would be little gained from developing a theory of possible causes of unemployment if no one had ever been unemployed.

The next step is that of selection of the assumptions from which the conclusions will be derived. If the principles are to be of any significance in guiding further empirical research, in explaining actual relationships in the economy, and in providing a basis for economic policy, the assumptions must agree so far as possible with the actual conditions present. If the relationship of price and cost in certain industries is to be explained, for example, assumptions must be made about the nature of competition in the industries; it is essential that these assumptions agree as closely as possible with actual conditions in the industries, or the principles will not be applicable.

This rule must often, as a matter of necessity, be tempered by the need for simplification. The economic system is a very complicated mechanism; if economic analysis is to be manageable and is to provide generalizations which are significant in any substantial number of cases, rather broad assumptions must be made, ones which recognize the major characteristic features of a number of situations but ignore individual variations in particular cases. As a result of this procedure, the principles cannot offer very detailed conclusions. The alternative—the selection of very detailed assumptions—would allow more detailed conclusions but would necessitate an extremely large number of principles, no one of which would be significant in a substantial number of cases. In Boulding's terminology, economic analysis thus presents a "map" of reality rather than a perfect picture of it: "Just as we do not expect a map to show every tree, every house, and every blade of grass in a landscape, so we should not expect economic analysis to take into account every detail and quirk of real economic behavior."[1] Thus, in development of analytical principles, a compromise is necessary between the use of assumptions which resemble actual conditions as closely as possible, on the one hand, and the need for simplification and the development of generalizations of reasonably broad scope, on the other.

Once the assumptions have been selected, the final step is the development by a process of logical reasoning of the implications of the assumptions, that is, the determination of the logical relationships between the elements involved in the problem and the expression of them in the form of an economic principle. Thus, given the assumptions of pure competition and of the action of businessmen on the basis of profit maximization, the generalization can be developed by a process of logical reasoning that, in the long-run period, price will come to equal average cost.

Validity. As implied in the definition of an analytical principle given above, the sole test of the *correctness* of such a principle is that of logical consistency: Does the conclusion follow logically from the assumptions? But the *applicability*—that is, the validity of the use of the

[1] K. E. Boulding, *Economic Analysis* (3rd ed., New York: Harper, 1955), p. 13.

principle in a particular situation—depends upon agreements between the assumptions of the principle and the conditions of the actual situation. Regardless of its logical consistency, a principle is useless in a particular case if its assumptions are not in adequate agreement with the conditions present, and an attempt to apply it will lead to erroneous results. For example, the theory of price-cost relationships in pure competition is based upon certain assumptions (to be discussed in later chapters) with regard to the nature of pure competition. If in a particular industry conditions are such that one or more of these assumptions are not realized in practice, the principle—that price will equal average cost in the long run—will not necessarily be valid; in other words, price will not necessarily tend to equal average cost. The general usefulness of a principle depends upon the number of situations in which the actual conditions agree with the assumptions of the principle.

The most frequent source of error in the use of economic analysis, as well as in government policy based upon economic principles, appears to be the failure to consider carefully whether or not the principles are applicable to the particular situation. In many cases the exact nature of the assumptions has not been realized, while in others, too little attention has been paid to their relation to actual conditions. The subsequent misapplication of the principles has served to discredit economic analysis, since the conclusions developed from the misapplied theories are so obviously contrary to what is observed to occur. Such procedure promotes the popular statement that economic principles are "fine in theory, but don't work in practice." A principle is not "fine" for a particular purpose unless its assumptions agree with actual conditions. If they do, the conclusions advanced by the principle will be realized (granted its logical correctness). Apparent discrepancies between theory and practice arise from misapplications of the theory, of using it in situations for which it is not relevant.

As indicated above, if economic principles are to be of significance for any substantial number of situations, the assumptions must involve some simplification of reality. As a result, when the attempt is made to apply a principle to a particular situation, usually no precise answer to the problem can be given directly by use of the principle because of the generalized nature of the assumptions. Thus the principle of incidence of taxation cannot provide directly the answer to the question of the actual incidence of the federal excise tax on luggage. For such problems the general principle indicates which facts in the case must be collected and studied (for example, those relating to the exact nature of competition in the industry) before any specific answer to the question is possible. Then, by the process of application of the portion of the general analysis whose assumptions are as nearly as possible in agreement with the facts of the case, it may be feasible to reach a provisional conclusion. But in all likelihood the assumptions are still too generalized to allow precision in the conclusions; the varieties of competition, for example, are too numerous to make it possible for a general theory of tax incidence to cover all of them. As a result, to obtain greater precision, it is necessary to refine the general principle in terms of the particular situation, to consider the significance of the actual facts in the situation, and to modify the more general conclusions of the theory in terms of the particular characteristics of the case.

The Relationship between Empirical Studies and Economic Analysis

Earlier in the chapter, the distinction was made between empirical generalizations and analytical principles. Controversy has existed for many years in the field of economics over the relative desirability of the two general approaches to the furtherance of economic knowledge. The institutionalist school of thought has emphasized the importance of the development of empirical studies and empirical generalizations, while the classical tradition has stressed the importance of analytical tools. To an increasing extent, however, it has been recognized that the furtherance of economic knowledge requires use of both empirical and analytical studies, each being necessary if successful use is to be made of the other. Today the disagreement is mainly over the relative importance of the two, rather than over the desirability of the exclusive use of one approach or the other. Empirical studies undertaken without an analytical framework to guide the selection of relevant data are completely futile; analytical studies made without reference to empirical data are mere exercises in logic, without possible significance or usefulness.

The Functions of Empirical Studies for Analytical Work. More specifically, empirical studies serve several important functions for the development of analytical principles. In the first place, such studies indicate the problems which warrant the development of economic principles to facilitate an analysis of them. For example, if studies show that a significant portion of the labor force is unemployed, or that farmers' incomes have been dropping steadily, development of tools to analyze the reasons for these changes is clearly warranted.

Secondly, studies of the actual data of the economy suggest the assumptions upon which the analysis must be based if it is to be useful. All economic analysis must be based upon certain assumptions about actual behavior, whether the theorist realizes this or not. The more closely these assumptions agree with actual conditions, the more useful is the analysis in interpreting the facts in particular situations and explaining the behavior involved. For example, if a theory of price and output determination is to be developed, it is essential that the assumptions with regard to the character of competition agree as closely as possible with conditions in the markets to be analyzed with the use of the principles.

Finally, empirical studies provide a check upon the validity and applicability of particular principles. If studies of actual reactions to a particular change show responses which differ from those anticipated on the basis of the theoretical analysis, a review of the analysis is necessary. For example, suppose that the particular principle of price determination leads to the conclusion that an increase in demand will raise prices. However, empirical studies of the actual response of prices to demand changes show that prices do not increase when demand increases. Re-examination of the principles and their applicability to the particular case is obviously necessary. If the principles are found to be logically correct, the difficulty lies in the relation of assumptions and actual conditions. Careful re-examination of the assumptions of the theory may show that the assumptions were not clearly understood. Or it may show that the principle was not applicable because there was not a sufficiently close similarity between the assumptions and the conditions, perhaps because of the great degree of simplification in the assumptions. In this case, further refinement of the principle may be desirable. Or further consideration may show that an entirely new theoretical approach to the problem, with a completely new set of assumptions, is desirable.

While disparity between expected and actual results indicates that the principle is not valid for the particular case, similarity between the two does not "prove" that the principle is logically correct and applicable to the situation. In the first place, there may be accidental mutual offsets; for example, an error in the logic may be offset by a difference between the conditions and the assumptions of the principle. In the second place, there is always the possibility that there may be a better principle, in the sense of more universal validity, or the provision of more precise statement of relationships. For example, suppose that there is developed a principle that a flow of gold into a country will cause a rise in the general price level by increasing the total money supply. A flow of gold into the country occurs, and the general price level rises. But a far more satisfactory explanation of the rise might be one which attributes it to the increased demand for goods coming from foreign buyers, the gold flow being regarded merely as an indicator of the excess of exports of goods over imports. Furthermore, the correlation may be purely accidental; the rise in price and the gold flow may have occurred in the same period due to completely unrelated causes. If the correlation is found to exist in a large number of cases, the chances of accidental correlation are of course slight.

The Contributions of Analytical Studies for Empirical Work. So far as empirical research itself is concerned, analytical studies are of the greatest importance. In the first place, some theoretical framework is needed as a guide to the selection of facts; without it the investigators would be lost in a sea of completely unmanageable individual occurrences. Just as all analytical work is based upon certain assumptions about actual behavior, likewise all empirical work is guided by an analytical framework, which may be simple or elaborate. Moreover, the development of empirical generalizations itself requires some analytical work. No matter how carefully data are collected, generalizations do not "leap out" of them; the generalizations can be derived only by a careful study of the relationships which appear.

Further advancement in knowledge of the functioning of the economy requires extensive use of both empirical and analytical studies, in close co-operation with one another. Empirical work will suggest further problems for analysis and will test present hypotheses, many of which are built upon rather flimsy assumptions which have not been carefully tested empirically. On the other hand, additional analytical work is required to guide the collection of significant facts, and to develop generalizations on the basis of the facts uncovered by the empirical work. The development of all knowledge of social institutions is hampered by the inability to conduct experiments, because of the impossibility of holding constant the variables other than those which are under study. But careful collection of data, the study of it by advanced statistical techniques, and further development of analysis on the basis of more realistic assumptions can allow substantial progress.

The Use of Mathematics in Economic Analysis

Mathematics has come to play an increasingly important role in economic analysis in recent years. The use is not new; the simple geometry of supply and demand curves has been employed for many decades, and even the use of calculus dates back for a century. But the relative role has become greater in recent years, and the increased use has been responsible for the development of a major controversy. It is argued that the use of mathematics allows more precise statement of relationships than purely literary methods, and is particularly advantageous in handling various deductive inferences, especially when a large number of variables is involved. Mathematical analysis is also useful in compelling persons to make their assumptions precise.

The critics of the use of mathematics in economic analysis emphasize the fact that mathematics is merely another language, which provides no answers that cannot be obtained by literary means and no principles that cannot be expressed in nonmathematical terms. The critics stress the danger that mathematical analysis in the field tends to divert the efforts of the scholars to the development of complex theoretical systems which may have very little significance in application. Furthermore, it suggests a preciseness and degree of validity for the results which may not be warranted. The fact that the results are valid only to the extent to which the original assumptions agree with actual conditions can too easily be ignored. The elaborate mechanism and the preciseness of the results attained by the mathematical tools are likely to cause persons to attach too much significance to the results. Mathematical research is often criticized for giving precise symbols to concepts whose meaning is not at all precise.

There is obviously a place for both mathematical and nonmathematical expositions in economic analysis: they essentially represent alternative techniques of exploration and alternative languages of explanation of relationships. In some instances one may be preferred to the other; each encounters certain dangers. In the succeeding chapters primary use is made of the nonmathematical exposition, apart from the use of simple geometry. For the reader who wishes to pursue the mathematical approach more completely, other studies are available.[2]

Mathematical economics as a tool for deducing and explaining relationships between various elements in the economy must not be confused with the use of mathematical techniques in statistical work. These techniques make possible the determination of relationships in observed data, from which empirical generalizations may be developed, and which may be used in verifying analytical principles. Mathematical economics, on the other hand, is employed in developing the analytical generalizations from certain assumptions.

In recent years, statistical analysis of empirical data and the use

[2] Somewhat greater use of mathematics is made by K. E. Boulding, *Economic Analysis,* 3rd ed. (New York: Harper, 1955), S. Weintraub, *Price Theory* (New York: Pitman, 1949), and G. Stigler, *The Theory of Price,* rev. ed. (New York: Macmillan, 1952). At a much higher level is P. Samuelson, *Foundations of Economic Analysis* (Cambridge: Harvard University Press, 1947).

of mathematical techniques in abstract analysis have been co-ordinated together in the field of *econometrics.* In this field, statistical and theoretical treatments of a problem are integrated and combined, as a means of insuring that the theoretical analysis is established in such a manner that empirical testing is facilitated and that the collection of data is directed along the most useful lines. Thus econometrics essentially combines the statistical and analytical work into an integrated whole, with extensive use made of mathematical techniques. The emphasis in the work of the econometricians has been upon the development of extended hypotheses in terms of accepted concepts and assumptions of economic theory, and the empirical testing of these hypotheses. They have given relatively little attention to initial exploration of empirical data as a basis for discovering more suitable assumptions upon which to build the hypotheses. Critics of this approach argue that more extensive preliminary investigation of empirical data to develop more satisfactory assumptions is to be preferred to the extensive elaboration and statistical testing of principles built upon rather casual empirical assumptions.

The Usefulness of Economic Analysis

Apart from the desirable accomplishment of providing increased knowledge of the world in which we live, economic analysis is of primary significance in indicating the consequences of various alternative actions and thus in providing an intelligent basis for choice among the possible actions. To the businessman, the consumer, the worker, and the union official and to those responsible for governmental policy, economic analysis provides the guide to logical behavior; given the desired goals of the individuals concerned, the utilization of economic principles suggests the policies which are most likely to allow optimum attainment of the goals.

Closely related to the function of guidance of choice is that of providing a basis for the prediction of future events. Only by careful application of economic principles in terms of existing circumstances is there made possible any reasonably satisfactory estimate of the future. A business firm is interested in future trends in costs of goods which it purchases and in the prices of its products. A study of price-determining forces in the type of industry in which the firm operates and utilization of these principles to analyze the facts of the particular situation provide the soundest basis available for prediction. Almost all persons in the economy are interested in the trend of the general price level. If, on the basis of economic analysis, we know that a general increase in demand for goods, not accompanied by a comparable increase in supply, will lead to price increases, we can expect the general price level to rise during a war period, in which this type of imbalance of supply and demand forces develops.

Knowledge of the principles is particularly important as a basis for governmental (or other community-action) control over economic activity. If in some manner the operation of the economy is failing to produce the desired results (from the standpoint of accepted goals of achievement), the establishment of satisfactory governmental control measures to produce more efficient operation requires knowledge of the principles of operation of the economic system. Thus, to continue the example of the preceding paragraph, if during a war period the general price level is rising rapidly and such a rise is considered to be undesirable, some knowledge of the causes of the increase is essential if effective control measures are to be introduced. The importance of economic analysis as a basis for selection among various alternative policies is substantial; only by the use of economic analysis is it possible to predict the consequences of the various policies and thus to select the one which is most likely to yield the results desired in light of the assumed goals. Policies which appear superficially to offer satisfactory remedies may in practice produce highly objectionable results, which can be foreseen only by the use of economic analysis.

Finally, economic analysis provides a basis for judgment of the efficiency of particular economic systems, or various phases of them, for accomplishing the ends assumed to be desirable. For example, if one aim of the economic system is assumed to be the maximization of want-satisfaction, it is essential that all persons seeking employment be able to find jobs. If at any time many persons are found to be unemployed, a knowledge of the principles which control the determination of the level of employment is necessary in order to decide whether the unemployment is due to an inherent weakness in the economy or to some minor maladjustment in its operations, such as unwise union or government policy.

But care must be taken not to expect too much of economic analysis. The economic system is too complex to allow explanation of its operation by a few absolute truths. The principles are primarily tools of analysis, to be applied in particular cases to provide aid in determining which facts in the situation require study, and in developing a solution to the problem. In the terms of J. M. Keynes, "The object of our analysis is, not to provide a machine, or method of blind manipulation, which will furnish an infallible answer, but to provide ourselves with an organised and orderly method of thinking out particular problems; and, after we have reached a provisional conclusion by isolating the complicating factors one by one, we then have to go back on ourselves and allow, as well as we can, for the probable interactions of the factors amongst themselves. This is the nature of economic thinking."[3]

The Terminology of Economic Analysis: Definitions and Classifications

Confusion in terminology has long been a source of serious difficulty in the understanding and development of economic analysis. As the study of economics developed, the terms adopted for various phenomena were ones in general everyday usage. But refinement of the analysis, with greater precision in definition, resulted in the development of meanings for these terms which differed somewhat from those of common usage. For example, the term "investment" in the business world is usually used in reference to the purchase of securities, while in economic analysis it refers to the acquisition of new capital equipment by business firms. If economists had followed the practice of botanists and had developed an entirely new terminology, by the use, for example, of Latin, much confusion would have been avoided.

The confusion in terminology has been furthered by the failure of economists themselves to use particular terms in the same manner. Thus the term "capital," for example, means something quite different for one writer than it means for another. This diversity of usage is a product of the nature of the subject matter of economics, but nevertheless it is an unfortunate source of confusion. Many of the controversies in the field of economic analysis have had their origins in differences, often not realized, in the meanings given to various terms.

The criterion of *correctness* cannot be applied to a definition; it is impossible to say that a particular definition of a term is "right" or "wrong." A person is entitled to define a term in any way that he desires, provided that he makes his definition clear. The only criterion of a definition is that of usefulness for purposes of analysis, and thus the most satisfactory definition of a term is the one which facilitates to the greatest extent the clarity of exposition. There is, of course, obvious merit in using definitions which are consistent with general usage in the field (if there is any), when this procedure does not interfere with exposition, since the reader is spared the inconvenience of reorienting him-

[3] *General Theory of Employment, Interest and Money* (New York: Harcourt, Brace, 1936), p. 297.

self to the new meaning of the term, and chances of confusion and misunderstanding are lessened.

Just as definitions are neither "right" nor "wrong," there is no "right" or "wrong" classification of data. In order to facilitate analysis, it is often desirable to classify material into certain groups. There may be a large number of ways in which the classification can be made, no one of which is the sole "correct" classification. The criterion of a classification is the same as that of a definition: Does the classification best facilitate the analysis for which it is developed? For some purposes one classification of certain data may be better; for other purposes, another.

Positive versus Welfare Theory

The body of contemporary economic analysis may be classified into two general types, according to the purpose involved. The first type, the *positive* theory, attempts to develop the principles of operation of the economy, without regard to the desirability or undesirability of the results in terms of goals. The second type, the *welfare* theory, is concerned with the evaluation of the operation of the economy in terms of assumed standards. Thus the positive theory of monopoly explains the principles of price and output determination under conditions of monopoly, whereas welfare theory, as applied to monopoly, evaluates the price-output levels which exist under monopoly in terms of their desirability from the standpoint of an assumed goal of society.

The goals in terms of which welfare theory seeks to evaluate the functioning of the economy are not themselves derived by economic analysis. Selection of goals is essentially an aspect of ethics, not of economics. There are certain goals, outlined in Chapter 24, which have come to be regarded as generally accepted, or in other words, to represent the consensus of opinion in present-day society. But we must not lose sight of the fact that these are merely assumptions of an ethical character, and not products of scientific analysis; any evaluation of various phenomena in the economy is valid only in terms of the particular goals which are assumed.

The role of welfare economics has been one of increasing importance, although welfare considerations have played a part in the writings of economists for centuries. Nevertheless it is sometimes argued that welfare theory has no part in economics as a scientific study, the appropriate scope of economics being solely that of analyzing the adjustments involved in the adaptation of scarce means to given wants. This point of view, however, has been one of declining importance as welfare theory has come to be recognized widely as a legitimate element in the field of study. But there is substantial merit in distinguishing clearly between the positive and welfare portions of the body of theory.

Closely related to the controversy over the appropriate scope of economics is the controversy over the desirability of the making of policy recommendations by economists. On the one hand, it is argued that policy considerations are beyond the scope of economics as a scientific study, since they can be made only in terms of goals which must be assumed, rather than determined by scientific analysis. On the other hand, it may be argued that persons who are trained in economic analysis are in a particularly advantageous position to make policy recommendations. As a practical matter few economists have ever refrained from dealing with policy questions. However, it must be recognized that the making of policy recommendations is not a part of scientific economic analysis as such, since such recommendations must be based upon value judgments with respect to desirable goals. But there is no reason why a person who is engaged in scientific study of economics should not be free to make such judgments and policy recommendations.

The Major Segments of Positive Theory

Contemporary positive economic theory may be divided into two major segments, value theory and national income theory. The former is concerned with the functioning of the price system in the determination of the output of various commodities, and thus the allocation of resources among the production of various goods, and in the determination of the incomes of the owners of factor units. The segment of value theory which is concerned with the determination of the prices of the factors is known as distribution theory.

The theory of national income, or employment theory, as it is often called, seeks to explain the level of national income, in both real and monetary terms, and thus the level of employment. It is also concerned with changes in the real level of output, and with changes in the general price level. The two segments of economic theory overlap in analyzing the role of money in the economy, the determination of the interest rate, and the general price level; this sphere of the over-all body of theory is often known as *monetary* theory.

There are two general approaches to the explanation of price and output levels, and thus resource allocation. The first, *partial equilibrium* analysis, stresses the determination of prices and outputs of particular commodities, the prices and outputs of other goods being assumed as given. In contrast, the second approach, known as *general equilibrium* theory, is concerned with the price and output structure as a whole, with stress upon the interrelationships among the prices and outputs of various goods and factors. These two approaches are not mutually exclusive, and can be integrated together; the difference between them is primarily one of emphasis.

The earlier chapters in this book are devoted to the partial equilibrium approach, with a survey of general equilibrium theory presented in Chapter 20. Chapters 21, 22, and 23 present a relatively brief analysis of national income theory, while the final chapter contains a survey of contemporary welfare theory.

SELECTED REFERENCES

RUGGLES, R. "Methodological Developments," *Survey of Contemporary Economics* (B. F. HALEY, ed.), Vol. II. Homewood, Ill.: Richard D. Irwin, Inc., 1952.

SAMUELSON, P. "Economic Theory and Mathematics—an Appraisal," *Proceedings of the American Economic Association,* 1952, pp. 56–66.

ELLIS, H. S. "The Economic Way of Thinking," *American Economic Review,* Vol. XL (March, 1950), pp. 1–12.

ROBBINS, LIONEL. *The Nature and Significance of Economic Science.* New York: Macmillan, 1935.

KEYNES, J. N. *The Scope and Method of Political Economy.* 4th ed. London: Macmillan, 1930.

LANGE, O. "The Scope and Method of Economics," *Review of Economic Studies,* Vol. XIII (1945–46), pp. 19–32.

HUTCHISON, T. W. *The Significance and Basic Postulates of Economic Theory.* London: Macmillan, 1938.

WALKER, E. RONALD. *From Economic Theory to Policy,* chap. iii. Chicago: University of Chicago Press, 1943.

HARROD, R. F. "Scope and Method of Economics," *Economic Journal,* Vol. XLVIII (September, 1938), pp. 383–412.

ADAMS, W., and TRAYWICK, L. E. *Readings in Economics,* chap. i. New York, Macmillan, 1948.

FRASER, L. M. *Economic Thought and Language.* London: Black, 1937.

QUESTIONS

1. What is the purpose of economic theory?
2. What are economic principles?
3. Distinguish between analytical and empirical principles.
4. What considerations influence the selection of the assumptions upon which an analytical principle is based?
5. What compromise must be made in the selection of the assumptions?

6. Distinguish between the test of *correctness* of a principle and the test of *applicability* of a principle.
7. If the results anticipated from the use of an economic principle in a particular case do not occur, what is likely to be the source of the difficult?
8. Explain the statement: "Economic theory does not provide the answers to a particular question, but rather serves as a guide to the facts necessary to obtain an answer."
9. In what respects do empirical and analytical studies complement each other?
10. In what sense can empirical studies show that a principle is not applicable in a particular case, yet never prove that a principle is applicable?
11. Why is empirical work completely futile without some analytical framework?
12. Discuss the relative merits and limitations to the use of mathematics in economic analysis.
13. Distinguish between statistics, mathematical economics, and econometrics.
14. Of what use is economic analysis?
15. Economists have debated for years the question of whether there are 2, 3, 4, or some other number of factors of production. Is there one correct number which careful analysis can discover? If not, what is the correct criterion of evaluation of a particular classification?
16. Can a definition be "right" or "wrong"?
17. Distinguish between positive theory and welfare theory.
18. Can economic analysis alone be used as the sole basis for making policy recommendations?
19. Distinguish between value and distribution theory; between value and employment theory; between partial and general equilibrium theory.

Chapter 3 THE UNITS OF THE ECONOMIC SYSTEM AND THE MAXIMIZATION GOALS

Before the task of explaining the price system and the allocation of resources is undertaken, some attention must be given to the basic units of the economic system, the goals which they are presumed to follow, and the nature of their market relationships with other units. This chapter will consider the first two questions, and the following chapter the market relationships.

THE BASIC UNITS

Three basic units are involved in the conduct of economic activity. In the first place, the units which carry on consumption activity are known as *households* or *consumers.* These consist of single persons, or, more commonly, families, which utilize the funds obtained from current or past income to acquire consumption goods and utilize them in the satisfaction of their personal wants. The expenditures made by consumers are known as *consumption expenditures.*

The second basic units are the *factor-owners,* the persons possessing factor units (or money capital) which they can make available for use in production. Each household ordinarily possesses at least one factor-owner, whose activity in providing factor units to business firms yields the income necessary for the conduct of consumption activity. The factor units may be the labor services of the person, or land or capital goods which are leased to others or used in the person's business, or money capital loaned out.

The third unit is the *business firm,* or, more commonly, the *firm,* the enterprise which undertakes and carries on production activity. The firm may consist of a single person, as a dentist, or a large corporation owned by thousands of individuals. The expenditures of money by firms for the use of factor units constitute cost expenditures, or *costs,* in contrast to the consumption expenditures made by consumer units.

These cost payments constitute incomes for the ultimate recipients. The concept of the firm must be distinguished clearly from that of entrepreneurial activity. The former is the enterprise—as a unit—which carries on production; entrepreneurial activity consists of the work involved in the control of the operation of the enterprise by those individuals who are in a position to exercise such control.

For purposes of analysis it is desirable to classify firms on the basis of type of product into *industries*—groups of firms producing commodities which are identical or are close substitutes for one another. Thus the retail grocery industry consists of the various firms operating retail grocery stores; the steel industry consists of the various steel-manufacturing enterprises. Some difficulty is encountered in determining exactly the boundaries of an industry when the products of the firms are not identical, since the products of one industry may shade off gradually into those of another, and the brands at each end of the quality scale may be poorer substitutes for one another than each is for some other commodity.[1] Sellers of low-priced cars may compete more directly with bus companies than with the sellers of the most expensive cars. However, in most cases the coverage of an industry is relatively clear-cut, on the basis of ease of substitution. For example, various brands of washing machines are substituted for one another much more readily than they are substituted for other products.

The Functions of Business Firms

The business firm, considered for the moment as a separate unit distinct from the individuals who own and manage it, performs several functions. In the first place, it acquires ownership of the various factor units, and owns the products until it disposes of them in the market. With respect to workers, only their services, rather than the workers themselves, are acquired; but in the case of capital goods, and often land, the physical units themselves are purchased by the firm. In order to acquire the units of the factors prior to the sale of the products, the firm must have units of money capital, which may be obtained from the owners of the firm, from profits earned, or from borrowing.

In the second place, the business firm performs the function of management by co-ordinating the activities of the various factor units. In capitalism, only within the firm is production activity subject to

[1] Some writers have urged the abandonment of the concept of the industry in economic analysis because of the difficulties involved in defining and delimiting an industry. See R. Triffin, *Monopolistic Competition and General Equilibrium Theory* (Cambridge: Harvard University Press, 1940).

planned control. In the enterprise decisions are made in regard to the choice of type and quality of product, the methods of production (and thus the types of factors to be used, the relative proportions of factors, and the volume of investment), the volume of output, and in most cases the price of the product. The enterprise initiates production, and suspends it if profits are not earned. The decisions of the enterprise are conditioned by price relationships or, more specifically, by the relationships between various sets of cost and revenue data; it is nevertheless significant that these decisions are not made automatically but by deliberate action of those managing the enterprises.

Thirdly, the business firm, in a dynamic economy, must estimate future conditions in a situation of uncertainty, and base its present decisions upon its expectations of the future. In a static society, the management functions of the firm would consist of the making of routine decisions; once a satisfactory program of products, factor combinations, outputs and prices had been attained, decision-making would be of the most elementary sort. But in the actual dynamic economy, the firm must constantly make estimates of future conditions, and adjust its policies in terms of the uncertainties of the future. These decisions must be made in terms of the best expectations of the future, but the firm can never be certain about the validity of the expectations.

As a consequence of the role which the firm plays in undertaking production and making decisions in a dynamic economy, it bears the largest share of uncertainty of financial loss. Because the firm contracts to pay for the other factor units, and in fact makes most of its payments prior to actual sale of the goods produced, it runs the greatest chance of loss in case operations are not successful—that is, if they were based upon wrong expectations about future conditions. Even the lenders of money capital have prior claim to any earnings made before they are available to the firm, as such. Of course, other factor-owners run some chance of loss; workers may not receive their full pay and bondholders may not be paid their interest if the business is unsuccessful. But the greatest chance of loss is incurred by the firm itself—the co-ordinating unit in the conduct of production.

The Performance of the Functions within the Firm

In the preceding section the functions of the business firm were discussed in terms of the firm itself, as an entity distinct from the individuals who comprise it. But the functions, or at least most of them, must actually be performed by individuals within the firm. Analysis of this aspect requires the classification of business firms into two groups, those in which the owners and the managers of the firm are the same persons, and those in which the two groups are at least in part separate.

The first group includes proprietorships and partnerships, and the majority of small closely held corporations, plus a very few large corporations owned and managed by a small group of persons. In these enterprises, regardless of the legal form of organization employed, the same persons who own the enterprise constitute the entrepreneurial group; that is, they, themselves, undertake the making of policy decisions, and thus perform the functions of management and estimating future conditions. Since they are the owners and directly control the disposition of the earnings, they obtain the profits in case of success, and, personally, bear the greatest risk of loss in the case of failure. With the proprietorship and partnership forms of organization, even their personal property may be taken to satisfy the debts of the enterprise.

The second group of firms is characterized by a separation, at least in part, and often almost completely, between ownership and management. The typical large corporation is owned by large numbers of small stockholders, who are not in a position to exercise any influence over the policies of the enterprise, and are not, as a rule, interested in doing so if they could. Even the holders of relatively large amounts of stock are often not interested in management decisions, but only in the rate of return and increase in the market price of their stock. The typical part owner of a large corporation performs no entrepreneurial functions beyond the purely technical one of ownership, plus the provision of money capital; his position in fact differs very little from that of the bondholders, except that he runs a somewhat greater risk of loss. The stockholder does, of course, receive a share of the earnings, provided that the persons controlling the enterprise decide to make dividend payments; the profits earned by the enterprise do not accrue directly to the stockholders.

The primary functions in the large corporation are performed by the executive group—the top management officials, or business leaders of the enterprise. These persons are usually not major owners; while they often own some stock in the corporation, the amounts are typically not large.[2] Accordingly, they receive relatively small amounts of the profit of the enterprise, most of their income being derived from salaries. While technically these executives are responsible to the stockholders, as a matter of practice the influence exercised by the latter, even as a

[2] R. A. Gordon, *Business Leadership in the Large Corporation* (Washington: Brookings, 1945), pp. 23–45.

group, is often very limited. If a few persons hold relatively large amounts of stock they will be able to influence the executives, but this is often not the case. Even the boards of directors are frequently, in practice, really selected by the executives, and the selections merely ratified by the stockholders.

THE GOALS PURSUED IN THE CONDUCT OF ECONOMIC ACTIVITY

The development of a coherent system of economic theory requires the making of assumptions with respect to the goals pursued by persons and groups of persons in their economic activities. It must be recognized initially that no assumption of a single goal pursued by each type of economic unit can be entirely satisfactory as an explanation of motivation. But some assumption about goals is necessary; the most satisfactory procedure involves the selection of the goal which appears to be most commonly pursued, and the subsequent introduction of modifications into the analysis in cases in which there are obvious deviations from this goal.

The primary assumption with respect to goals pursued by the units carrying on economic activity which serves as the basis of most economic analysis is the *maximization* assumption, that each unit of the economic system seeks to maximize its own economic well-being. The application of this assumption to consumers and factor-owners encounters relatively few difficulties; its application, however, to business firms is somewhat complicated, especially with the present-day large-scale business organization.

Maximization of Consumer Satisfaction

As applied to households, the maximization assumption involves the pursuit by each consuming unit of the goal of obtaining maximum satisfaction from the use of the funds available for saving and consumption. In a given period of time each household has available, from income received and past accumulations, a certain sum of money. It is assumed that the household seeks to allocate this money between savings and consumption, and among the purchases of various consumption goods, in such a manner as to maximize satisfaction. It is not assumed that satisfaction from the use of the income is actually maximized, but merely that households attempt to do so. It is recognized that lack of adequate knowledge of the satisfactions to be gained from various goods makes the realization of the optimum position impossible.

It is sometimes argued that persons buy primarily from habit, without any careful effort to balance gains from the consumption of various goods, and that they make, on the average, no serious effort to maximize satisfaction. The force of habit is without doubt important in influencing actual purchase patterns. But it does not contradict the assumption; it may be presumed that persons would adjust their purchase patterns if they believed that a different one would actually increase their satisfaction; so long as they adhere to a routine pattern, it may be assumed that they regard this as the optimum. It may, of course, be true that persons could actually gain greater satisfaction if they were less dominated by habit in their purchasing. But this does not demonstrate that the assumption is unsatisfactory.

Maximization of Factor Income

Secondly, with respect to factor-owners and holders of money capital, under the general maximization assumption, it is assumed that they make available such a number of factor units, and in such a manner, as to maximize the net gain which they receive from the units which they own. Maximum net gain does not necessarily mean maximum dollar income, as examination of the application of the assumption to various types of factor units will show.

If workers are to maximize satisfaction from the provision of their services, they must provide such a number of labor hours that the marginal gain from the provision of additional hours just equals the marginal disutility of additional labor. Since the provision of labor hours (at least beyond a certain point) involves increasing disutility of work, eventually a point will be reached (short of the maximum number of hours the persons could possibly work) at which the additional gain just balances the additional disutility, and the person will supply no additional units of work. Thus it cannot be assumed that the worker seeks to maximize his income, but rather that he will work such a number of hours as to maximize relative gains from both work and leisure. Attainment of this adjustment, however, is restricted by the fact that many workers have little discretion about numbers of hours worked. Since standard work periods must be set for various groups of workers, it is not possible for each person, individually, to strike an optimum balance between work and leisure. It is merely assumed that each attempts to do so, as far as is possible. Furthermore, the maximization assumption requires that each worker supply his services to the business firm which offers the highest reward, taking into consideration not only wages, but other conditions of work, such as prestige, job security, and working conditions.

In the case of money capital, the assumption requires that the holders of wealth will allocate it between liquid (monetary) holdings and various forms of loans and other uses in such a manner as to maximize gain from it. Since the holding of wealth in liquid form in itself offers certain advantages (discussed in Chapter 17), the quantity made available will not necessarily be the amount which will maximize dollar income, but the amount which will allow the optimum balance between money income gains from making the funds available to business firms and the liquidity advantages of keeping it in monetary form. It is also assumed that the money will be made available to those users who will offer the maximum return, with appropriate allowance for different degrees of risk.

In the case of the owners of land and existing capital goods, however, maximization of net gain does require simply the maximization of monetary income received. The owners of these factors will make available the number of units which will yield them the greatest income (which, under pure competition, will be the entire number of units which they have, as shown in later chapters) and will make them available to the business firms which will pay the highest return.

MAXIMIZATION OF BUSINESS PROFITS

As applied to business firms, the maximization assumption, in unmodified form, requires that firms seek to maximize the net income—the profits—of the enterprise. In a sense this rule is merely an extension of the maximization-of-factor-income rule. However, careful examination of its application suggests that certain modifications are necessary if the rule is to reflect satisfactorily the actual goals typically pursued by firms. The first source of modification arises out of the fact that, just as in the case of labor, the earning of additional profits may result in additional disutility. The second relates to the uncertainty of future conditions. The third pertains to the fact that in larger enterprises the persons receiving the profits may not be the same as those making the decisions of the business. Finally, it may be argued that in some instances it is obvious that other goals exercise substantial influence on business policy. Each of these will be considered briefly.

Disutility Incurred in the Gaining of Additional Profits

In the proprietorship, partnership, or closely held corporation, the gaining of additional profits may necessitate additional personal effort on the part of the owner-managers of the enterprise. If, in order to gain maximum dollar profit from the business, the owners must devote more time to the business and less to leisure than they would prefer, they will attempt to obtain a balance between additional money income, on the one hand, and gains from additional leisure, on the other. Thus they will not necessarily maximize dollar profit. This modification of the maximum-profit rule is less significant in larger businesses, as additional managerial activity may be delegated to other persons.

Uncertainty and Profit Maximization

Under conditions of uncertainty about the future, the concept of maximization of profit is by no means entirely precise. It is obvious that the enterprise is not concerned merely with the maximization of the current profit rate, since pursuit of this objective might result in failure to maximize gains over a longer period of time. Rather, the firm is assumed to attempt to maximize the sum of profits over a period of time, the various segments being discounted to the present. However, the firm cannot be certain of the gains from various policies. Not only will expected profit from these policies differ, but also the expectations about the likelihood of actually earning the profit. One policy, for example, may offer a chance of a very high gain, but little certainty that it will be obtained. Another policy may offer chances of a much lower profit, but a high degree of certainty that it will be earned. The firm must balance the considerations of gain expectations and certainty of the receipt of the gain, as well as the effects upon the firm if the policies fail.[3]

Separation of Ownership and Management in Large Enterprises

The two modifications noted in the preceding paragraphs do not seriously lessen the significance of the profit-maximization assumption. Much more important is the effect of the separation of ownership and management in the large corporation. As explained earlier in the chapter, most large corporations, which are dominant in many lines of production, are characterized by separation of ownership and management, the typical owner—the stockholder—having no voice in the making of decisions, and the typical executive owning little or no stock in the enterprise, and thus receiving relatively little of the profit earned. The primary income of the executives consists of salaries, while the profits

[3] The most complete analysis of the definition of profit maximization in conditions of uncertainty is to be found in the book by G. L. S. Shackle, *Expectation in Economics* (Cambridge: Cambridge University Press, 1949).

accrue initially to the corporation, and may ultimately be paid out as dividends to the stockholders. The question of the extent to which this separation of ownership and management affects the applicability of the profit-maximization assumption must be considered.

Continued Importance of the Profit-Maximization Goal. It is widely believed that the profit-maximization assumption is still applicable in large measure to the corporation, despite the fact that the persons who make the decisions may not receive the profits earned. In the first place, there is a tendency on the part of corporation officials to regard the corporation as a separate entity, distinct from the stockholders who own it, and to identify their own welfare with that of the corporation, even though they do not receive the profits earned. It is almost universal in the business world for management officials to regard the profits earned by the corporation as the best measure of their professional success in the management of the enterprise. Profits represent the objective criterion of skill in management. Furthermore, in a more direct way the attainment of a high rate of profit may affect the economic position of the executives. Continued failure to earn as good a rate of return as the informed stockholders believe to be possible may lead to a revolt by the stockholders, which will result in replacement of top management personnel.[4] Failure to earn profit may endanger the continued existence of the firm, or at least lead to bankruptcy and reorganization. Moreover, a good rate of profit is essential for continued expansion of the firm; the profits directly provide funds for expansion and facilitate the acquisition of additional capital. Growth of the enterprise not only increases the income of the executives but also raises their prestige and power, as discussed below.

Business leaders may be much more likely to strive to obtain the absolute maximum figure of profits when the actual rate being earned is below a figure regarded as "satisfactory" than when the current rate earned exceeds this figure. So long as a rate of profit as good as, or better than, the average return is being earned, the position of the management is likely to be secure, and expansion is possible if the firm wishes to undertake it. Any attempt to push profits still higher, to the actual maximum figure, may be regarded as being more troublesome than it is worth, particularly because it may result in additional competition or governmental interference. If profits are less than the figure regarded

[4] For example, in the last year the managements of two railroads, the New Haven and the Minneapolis and St. Louis, have been ousted on this basis, and a strong but unsuccessful effort was made to oust the management of Montgomery Ward.

as satisfactory, a strong effort will be made to restore them to this level, particularly because failure to do so may endanger the position of the management, and possibly the continuation of the firm itself.

Conflicts between Maximization of Profits and the Interests of the Executives. While profit maximization may be regarded as the primary goal of management in large corporations, despite the separation between ownership and management, this goal is likely to be pursued only so long as it is consistent with the interests of the management group. When divergencies arise, the executives are likely to follow policies which will maximize the gains to themselves rather than those of the enterprise. Several examples of such divergencies of interest can be noted. A projected expansion—though obviously profitable over a period of time—may imperil the solvency of the firm in temporary depression periods by increasing fixed charges, or it may bring in new dominant stockholders who may gain control and eliminate the present management. As a consequence, the expansion will not be undertaken, or at least will be postponed until funds becoming available from earnings make it possible without sacrificing future solvency or control. In other cases, also, profits may be sacrificed to solvency; current assets may be disposed of at a heavy loss or maintenance postponed in order to obtain funds to meet pressing obligations. Finally, complete liquidation of a business may be delayed by the management long beyond the point at which it should be undertaken in the interest of the stockholders. The managers not only dislike seeing the disappearance of the firm to which they have long been attached but also seek to avoid the loss of their positions. Accordingly, they are likely to continue operation through dissipation of the firm's capital, perhaps for a long period of years. Through undermaintenance, depletion of inventories, failure to cover depreciation charges, and sale of assets they may be able to continue to operate until the equity of the owners is completely destroyed, whereas earlier liquidation might have preserved a substantial portion of their money capital.

Rigorousness in the Pursuit of the Goals. In the large-scale business organization, the rigorousness with which the goal of profit maximization is sought may be less than that in the small owner-managed enterprise. Management of a large-scale business can easily become overcautious; the desire to maintain the status quo—to protect the positions of the executives—may encourage the managers to avoid changes which appear profitable for fear that the expected gains might not be realized. Since profits do not accrue to the executives to any extent, the dynamic qualities of management characteristic of smaller enterprises may be overwhelmed by the desire to avoid disturbance of conditions which are "satisfactory." As a consequence, possible readjustments in the conduct of the business, especially ones not involving growth, may be avoided.

The very complexity of the structure of the large corporation in itself slows down readjustments. Since changes in policy may require the approval of a number of persons, speed of action is inevitably lessened, and the chance of rejection of the change greatly increased. The initiation of new policies must to a large extent originate in the lower levels of management. There is danger that the persons in these levels in the best position to see desirable changes may be unwilling to take the initiative in suggesting them, partly because they fear to disturb the routine of operations and to imply that the old policies developed by their superiors are not satisfactory, and partly because of sheer inertia. In some cases their own welfare may be affected adversely. A person is not likely to suggest any change which will reduce the number of personnel under his jurisdiction, as his own prestige will be reduced if the change is carried into effect. Foremen who realize, for example, that more men are being utilized for a task than are necessary are likely to be reluctant to suggest reducing the working force; the number of their subordinates will be reduced, and the persons laid off are likely to be their personal friends. Even when suggestions for change do originate in the lower levels of management, a long delay is likely to result before action is taken; meanwhile, conditions may change materially. Final decision must be made on the proposals by persons out of touch with the situation.

The Goal of "Satisfactory" Profits

In some instances it appears that business firms aim primarily for a "satisfactory" rate of profit rather than for the maximum figure; not only do they strive more diligently for profits when the earnings figure is less than satisfactory than they do when it is higher, but they actually, from all indications, in some instances come to regard the "satisfactory" goal as the dominant one.

However, acceptance of the goal of "satisfactory" profits from a short-run standpoint does not necessarily involve actual failure to seek the maximum return over a long-run period. The importance of this goal may result simply from the belief that, over a long-run period, profits are likely to be greater if the firm avoids full exploitation of all the temporary situations which might allow high profits for a time, but would encourage the development of new firms. However, emphasis upon "satisfactory" profits does affect the reactions of firms in the short-run period. An increase in demand will almost of necessity lead to a price increase if firms are to maximize profits. But if they are temporarily seeking only "satisfactory" profits, they may leave prices unchanged.

Nonpecuniary Goals

In both the small owner-managed enterprise and the large corporation, the persons making the decisions are without doubt in some cases influenced by nonpecuniary motives, which take precedence over profit maximization in these instances. For example, the prestige of the business leaders may be very important to them; they may thus undertake policies which will increase their prestige in the community or in the industry even though the policies do not insure profit maximization. Closely related is the desire of business leaders for power over as large a "business empire" as possible; while in many cases profit maximization is the best path to expansion, in other cases it may not be. History offers many examples of business firms which undertook unprofitable expansions merely because the executives wished to build a larger empire. Some firms appear to strive for maximum gross sales or a higher share of the market, instead of for the maximum net return. Such policies are more likely to be followed in the large corporation, in which the executives do not directly benefit from the profits, than in the small enterprises, but they are not absent in the latter. It is likewise apparent that in some instances new capital equipment is acquired primarily because the officials of the firm enjoy the possession and use of ultramodern facilities, even though they may not insure profit maximization.

As another example, large firms sometimes follow policies which they regard as best serving the interests of the community or nation as a whole, even though they may interfere somewhat with profit maximization. Thus firms may be reluctant to cut wages or lay off men in a depression, in the belief that such action aggravates the decline in economic activity. Or officials of firms or small business operators may be reluctant to fire aged employees for purely humanitarian reasons. Such policies can be followed only within limits, or they may endanger the financial position of the firm.

Businessmen also operate within the framework of legal and social institutions. They will not, except in rare instances, seek to maximize profits by taking illegal action, such as the murder of a competitor or the theft of secret formulas! Furthermore, they are likely to avoid certain practices which, although legal, are contrary to the accepted ethical standards of the business community. Thus they may avoid price-cutting if this practice is generally frowned upon by the other firms, or the hiring of certain racial groups.

SUMMARY

These various qualifications suggest that for a more rigorous analysis, the profit-maximization assumption should be replaced by one of preference maximization, in which the various goals, including profit maximization, could be integrated. Such an assumption would be particularly desirable in the case of uncertainty, in which the profit-maximization rule is inadequate because the executives are confronted by a group of possible outcomes, with different degrees of uncertainty, rather than a single profit-maximization potentiality. Further progress in economic analysis may require such an assumption. But the complexity of the over-all analysis will be tremendously increased by replacement of the profit-maximization goal by a broader one. For purposes of the present analysis the assumption of the profit-maximization goal must be retained, in the interests of simplicity, but recognition will be given to the effects of major cases of deviations from the assumption.

SELECTED REFERENCES

GORDON, R. A. *Business Leadership in the Large Corporation.* Washington: Brookings Institution, 1945.

An excellent study of policy determination and goals in the large corporation.

PAPANDREOU, A. G. "Some Basic Problems in the Theory of the Firm," *A Survey of Contemporary Economics* (B. F. HALEY, ed.), Vol. II. Homewood, Ill.: Richard D. Irwin, Inc., 1952.

A high-level discussion of the nature and goals of the firm.

REDER, M. "A Reconsideration of the Marginal Productivity Theory," *Journal of Political Economy,* Vol. LV (October, 1947), pp. 450–58.

A review of the sources of deviation from the profit-maximization goal.

LAUTERBACH, A. *Men, Motives, and Money,* chaps. i and ii. Ithaca: Cornell University Press, 1954.

An analysis of business motives and decision-making.

CHAMBERLAIN, N. W. *A General Theory of Economic Process,* chaps. ii–v. New York: Harper, 1955.

A study of motivation of the various units in the economy.

HICKMAN, C. A. "Managerial Motivation and the Theory of the Firm," *Proceedings of the American Economic Association,* May, 1955, pp. 544–54.

The importance of social psychology in further study of the motivation of business firms.

QUESTIONS

1. What are the basic units of the economic system?
2. Distinguish between the concepts *firm* and *industry*. In terms of this definition, is General Motors a firm or an industry? When would a particular firm constitute the industry?
3. What are the primary functions of the business firm?
4. By whom are the functions of the firm performed in a large corporation?
5. Explain the maximization assumption, and apply it to consumer behavior and factor-owner behavior.
6. Why does the application of the maximization assumption to workers not require that each worker seeks to maximize his money income?
7. Why does uncertainty complicate the application of the maximization assumption to business profits?
8. Why may a business firm still follow the goal of profit maximization despite the separation of ownership and management?
9. Give two examples of conflicts between the interests of the executives and profit maximization on the part of the firm, other than those given in the chapter.
10. Give examples with which you are familiar of actions by business firms which are obviously contrary to the goal of maximization of profits.
11. Why is the profit-maximization goal usually retained in economic analysis, despite its obvious deficiencies?

Chapter 4 MARKET RELATIONSHIPS

The determination of prices and outputs of various commodities and of the prices paid for the various factors is affected by the market relationships prevailing in the particular economy. The price and the output of a commodity will obviously be different if the entire supply is controlled by one firm than it will be if it is supplied by a large number of small sellers, all acting independently of one another. The number of buyers and the relationships prevailing among them will likewise affect price and output. The nature of the markets for the factor units will affect the prices paid for them, and thus the costs of producing the products made with them and the distribution of the income among the various factor-owners. Accordingly, attention must be given to major types of market relationships. Furthermore, not only will prices and outputs depend upon the competitive relationships among the sellers and buyers, but also upon such considerations as the knowledge of market conditions on the part of the various buyers and sellers, and the mobility of factor units from one employment to another. These considerations will be reviewed in the last section of the chapter.

The Concept of a Market

The term *market* requires clarification before further consideration is given to the various types of market relationships, since price and output are determined within particular markets. A market consists of a group of buyers and sellers in sufficiently close contact with one another that exchange takes place among them. In the sale of some commodities there are large numbers of more or less isolated markets; in the sale of gravel, for example, markets are essentially local. Buyers are in contact only with local producers, since transportation costs, relative to selling prices, are so high that the commodity cannot be shipped any substantial distance. Thus price and output are determined in each of a number of small markets, and total national production of gravel is the summation of the amounts of output determined separately in each of the markets. It should be noted that the local markets are not completely isolated from one another; if price differences between previously separate markets exceed transportation costs, goods will commence to move from one to the other, and the two will become a single market. In other industries markets are nation-wide; automobile manufacturers, for example, sell to dealers throughout the country and determine prices and output on the basis of considerations relating to the entire economy.

TYPES OF MARKET RELATIONSHIPS

Various possible market situations differ from one another primarily on the basis of the extent to which individual buyers and sellers can by their own separate action influence price. The extent of such influence, in turn, depends primarily upon four considerations: the homogeneity of the product, the number of sellers, the number of buyers, and the extent of co-operative action or interdependence among the various buyers and sellers. Homogeneity—the extent to which buyers regard the products of all sellers as being identical, and sellers have no preferences in regard to the buyers to whom they sell—is of primary importance in controlling the degree of freedom which firms have in acting independently of their competitors. The development of differentiation—that is, of preferences on the part of buyers and sellers concerning particular varieties of the product and the firms with which they deal—increases the freedom of firms to act independently and thus increases the control which they have over their own prices. The greater the differentiation, the less is the ease with which customers will shift from one firm to another in response to price changes.

The numbers of buyers and sellers determine the extent to which each buyer and each seller is aware of the effects of his own policies on those of his competitors and thus the extent to which each expects his action to affect the prices and outputs of the competitors. If sellers are numerous, for example, they will not expect their own policies to have sufficient effect upon their competitors to affect the policies of the latter; if the number is small, each firm knows that competitors will inevitably react to its policies. The numbers of buyers and sellers also affect the extent to which certain standard practices (cost accounting methods, for example) will be adopted by the firms, as well as the likelihood of outright agreements on price and output. When such collusive policies are followed, their exact nature is of primary importance for the nature of the market relationships and thus of price and output determination. Collusive policies depend not only upon the number of competitors but also upon the nature of the product, the attitudes of the officials of the competing firms toward co-operative action, the relationships of the firms in past years, and government antitrust policy.

The Major Classes of Markets

The number of possible types of market relationships is almost infinite, because of the large number of possible degrees of differentiation of product and of numbers of buyers, sellers, and relationships among them. For purposes of analysis, however, the various possible situations will be grouped into two general classes, the first consisting of the cases in which neither individual buyers nor sellers have any control over prices, and the second including all possible cases in which individual buyers, or sellers, or both, do exercise such control. The first general class is known as *pure competition;* the second may be called *nonpure competition.*

The case of pure competition is a useful model for purposes of analysis, although actual conditions may approximate it in only a relatively few industries. It is a simple, clear-cut case, the analysis of which will serve to clarify various basic relationships more easily than analysis of the more complex cases.

Nonpurely competitive markets actually consist of a heterogeneous collection of various situations, differing substantially from one another. This general case will be subdivided into four major models, distinguished from one another by the exact relationships among buyers and sellers:

1. Monopolistic competition, characterized by differentiation of product, but with a sufficiently large number of sellers so that each determines its policies independently of any effects which they may have upon the policies of competitors.

2. Oligopoly, a situation in which the number of firms is sufficiently small so that mutual interdependence exists among them; that is, each firm, in determining its own policies, takes into consideration the possible effects which these policies may have upon the actions of the competitors. The products of the various firms may be either homogeneous or differentiated.

3. Complete monopoly, a situation in which there is only a single seller.

4. Monopsonistic markets, characterized by the exercise of influ-

ence upon price by individual buyers. This influence may arise because of the smallness of the number of buyers, or because of the development of preferences on the part of sellers for dealing with particular buyers. Markets which contain monopsonistic elements may be purely competitive on the side of the sellers, or contain any of the forms of nonpure competition noted above.

Since deviations from purely competitive conditions appear to be more common on the sellers' side than on the buyers' side, primary attention will be given to cases 1 to 3 above, with the assumption that individual buyers are unable to influence price, except where noted specifically to the contrary.

It must be emphasized that these various cases are simplified analytical models, based upon various assumptions of exact market relationships prevailing, and the analysis of price and output determination in the various models must not be regarded as an exact description of actual conditions. For the price and output analysis to be manageable, it must be developed in terms of a relatively small number of simple models, the assumptions upon which each is based being derived from studies of actual competitive relationships in various markets. A particular model will be useful for purposes of analysis in those cases in which the actual conditions bear a sufficiently close relationship to the assumptions upon which the model is based. The models must be regarded as analytical tools, not as precise descriptions of actual conditions.

Pure Competition

Pure competition is a relatively simple, clear-cut case. As indicated above, the characteristic feature is the lack of control by individual buyers or sellers over price; each seller adjusts his output and each buyer his purchases, without consideration of any possible effect of these actions upon the market price. Thus, for example, a wheat farmer knows that he can sell as much as he can produce (within practicable limits) without in any way affecting the price which he receives; he can sell 10 bushels or 100,000 bushels at the current market price without affecting the price. Accordingly, he determines his output of wheat in the light of expected market prices. The flour miller who is buying wheat likewise knows that the volume of his purchases will not alter the price of wheat.

Conditions of pure competition can prevail only if two requirements are met:

1. The numbers of buyers and sellers must be sufficiently large, and the volume of business handled by each must be sufficiently small,

that changes in sales or purchases by any one seller or buyer will not perceptibly affect the price. It is impossible to state exactly how many sellers and buyers there must be for the effect of the action of any one of them to be imperceptible. It is obvious, for example, that with 10,-000 sellers, no one of whom produces a substantial percentage of total output, no individual seller will be aware of any effect of his actions upon price; if there are 10 or even 100 producers, it is clear that each will realize that he can affect the price. With successively larger numbers, eventually a figure is reached at which the effects of the actions of any one firm become imperceptible. It is essential that the various sellers and buyers act independently of one another if the market is to be purely competitive. If firms agree upon policies, the effect on competition is the same as that of smallness of numbers of sellers or buyers.

2. The product must be homogeneous, in the sense that buyers regard the products of all sellers as identical, and have no preferences for dealing with any particular firms. Likewise sellers must have no preferences for dealing with particular buyers. If any preferences, and thus differentiation of product, exist, individual firms will have some control over prices.

Conditions approaching those of the model of pure competition are found today in the wholesale markets for staple agricultural commodities. For example, there are many thousands of wheat farmers, producing wheat of a relatively small number of standard grades. There are likewise thousands of buyers, who have no preferences for wheat grown by particular farmers, but merely wish to obtain wheat of a given grade. Similar situations are found in many other lines of agricultural production. The individual farmer has no control over price; he can sell as much as he can possibly produce without affecting price in any perceptible way,[1] if he tries to obtain more than the current market price, he can sell nothing at all. In recent years some interference with the purely competitive nature of agricultural markets has developed from the government price-support programs. When prices fall below certain figures, purchases are made by governmental agencies to restore the higher prices, and thus one buyer is perceptibly (and deliberately) affecting the price. But, nevertheless, from the standpoint of the sellers

[1] This is not true, of course, when a farmer is selling through a roadside stand or in a local market with limited demand for a specialized farm product. In some agricultural industries (oranges or walnuts, for example), strong co-operatives provide co-ordinated action for the small producers and thus eliminate the purely competitive nature of the markets.

essentially pure competition remains. Outside of agriculture, markets approximating the situations of pure competition are rarely found.

Monopolistic Competition: The Case of Differentiation and Large Numbers[2]

The case in the nonpurely competitive class most closely resembling pure competition is that of monopolistic competition,[3] a situation in which, (1) the number of sellers is sufficiently large that each acts independently of one another, with no consideration of the effects of his policies upon those of his competitors, but (2) the products of the various sellers are differentiated. No longer do the purchasers regard the products of the various firms as identical, but instead have definite preferences for particular products. Thus, in a sense, each seller has a monopoly over his own product, but is subject to competition from other firms selling products which are very close substitutes. Accordingly, any changes in price by the firm will have very significant effects upon sales, since customers will shift from one seller to another as the relative prices charged change. The extent of the shift will depend upon the strength of the consumer preferences for the various products.

Product differentiation develops in a number of ways. Differences in store location, which affect the relative convenience to the customers, are important in retailing. The personalities of clerks and their attitudes toward their customers, and the effectiveness of the work of salesmen create preferences. Physical differentiation of product may be possible; in some cases differences are created solely for the purpose of distinguishing the product from those of competitors. Changes in automobile body design and in styles of women's clothing are examples. In other cases differentiation involves nothing more than packaging in a distinctive style and the application of a brand name. Regardless of the physical basis of the differentiation, extensive advertising and other sales activity are usually employed to impress the significance of the differences upon the purchaser. Thus most differentiation is the result of deliberate effort on the part of the seller—effort designed to protect the latter from the rigors of intensive price competition, with its inevitable periods of losses,

[2] The theory of monopolistic competition, although suggested in the writings of earlier economists, was first developed by E. H. Chamberlin, in *The Theory of Monopolistic Competition* (Cambridge, Mass.: Harvard University Press, 1933).

[3] In the previous editions of this book, the term "monopolistic competition" was used in a much broader sense, to cover all cases of deviations from pure competition on the sellers' side. But to an increasing extent the term is now confined to the situation of differentiation and large numbers, and thus the terminology has been modified to conform with this usage.

and in many cases to allow the seller to obtain a higher price than he could obtain in a purely competitive market.

Elements of differentiation are very widespread throughout the economy, and customers are rarely completely indifferent about the products of the various firms. The degree of differentiation varies widely, however, in large measure depending upon the nature of the product and of the wants which it satisfies. Such commodities, such as salt, sugar, or cement, are by their nature difficult to differentiate. Capital goods, including materials, are typically less subject to differentiation because they are purchased for the performance of particular tasks in production by persons who are specialists in the art of buying.

While differentiation itself is very widespread, the case of differentiation and large numbers is of doubtful usefulness as a model for economic analysis; there appear to be relatively few markets in which the actual conditions approach those assumed in the model. Most industries in which differentiation is present are characterized by interdependency of the firms. The best examples of situations approaching those of monopolistic competition are to be found in certain lines of retailing in large cities, in which there are numerous firms, determining their policies in large measure independently of one another. The analysis of price and output determination under conditions of monopolistic competition, presented in subsequent chapters, is of greatest use in showing the extreme limiting case in the field of nonpure competition, the one most closely resembling pure competition, and as a basis from which to develop an analysis of price and output determination in other fields. The analysis itself is of little assistance in studying actual price and output determination in significant segments of the economy.

Oligopoly

The model of economic analysis which is of greatest use in an analysis of the functioning of the present-day economy is that of oligopoly, a situation in which the number of sellers in a particular market is sufficiently small that their actions are interdependent. Each seller shapes his policy in terms of the policies of the other firms in the industry, and takes into consideration the effects which his own policies may have upon the policies of the competitors.

In general, oligopoly arises whenever the number of firms become sufficiently small that any change in output or price by one firm will materially affect the sales of competing firms. In this situation, it is inevitable that the competitors will react to changes made by each firm and that the firms will commence to expect these reactions and take them into consideration in determining their own policy. Thus, for example, if a service-station operator considers reducing prices in order to increase sales, he is almost always aware that his competitors are likely to reduce also and he will take this reaction into consideration in deciding whether or not to make the price reduction.

Oligopoly is very widespread throughout the American economy. In manufacturing, many major industries are dominated by a few firms operating in typical oligopoly situations. Tin-can production is dominated by two firms; copper refining and automobile production by three; cigarette and rubber production by four—these are merely representative examples.[4] In retailing, in any particular market, there is usually only a limited number of stores; there may be 500 grocery stores in a large city, but considerations of convenience usually limit any particular group of consumers to a relatively small group of stores.

What is responsible for the widespread occurrence of oligopoly elements? Fundamentally, the situation is an outgrowth of the relationship between technological conditions of production and the potential sales volumes in the markets. With many products, reasonably low cost of production cannot be obtained unless a firm is producing a large volume of output; if this constitutes a substantial percentage of the total potential sales in the market, the number of firms will necessarily be small. Automobile and steel production require large volumes of output for low cost and thus the total number of firms is small. Even though bakeries or theaters require relatively small volumes of business for low cost, only the largest cities can provide a sufficient number of customers to allow a large number of competing firms.

Decreases in the number of firms in an industry may also result from the desire of firms to increase profits by consolidation with competitors, even though cost is not reduced as a result. Such consolidations may lessen the severity of competitive pressures. They also allow individuals to control larger business empires, and may offer substantial profits for the promoters of the consolidation. It is likely that in some industries today firms have grown beyond the size necessary for low-cost operation because of these considerations.

Pure versus Differentiated Oligopoly. Situations of oligopoly can be classed into two general groups on the basis of the presence or absence of differentiation. If the products of the various firms are identical,

[4] For further discussion see *United States vs. Economic Concentration and Monopoly: A Staff Report to the Monopoly Subcommittee of the Committee on Small Business* (Washington: U.S. Government Printing Office, 1947), pp. 100–38; see also W. Fellner, *Competition among the Few* (New York: Knopf, 1949), p. 18.

the term *pure oligopoly* is applied; this situation is approximated in some of the capital goods industries, such as cement production. When products are identical, the mutual interdependency will be greater, other things being the same, than when differentiation exists, since any price change by a firm is certain to produce substantial effects upon the sales of competitors, and reactions by competitors are therefore almost inevitable.

On the other hand, in *differentiated oligopoly,* in which products are not homogeneous, price changes will have somewhat less direct effect upon competitors because the partial isolation of the market for the product of each firm makes the reactions of the competitors less certain. In general, the stronger the differentiation, the weaker is likely to be the feeling of mutual interdependence. Differentiated oligopoly is characteristic of a very large portion of the total economy. Most manufactured consumers goods are differentiated, and the markets are dominated by a few firms; retailing in most areas is characterized by the same features. Even many of the capital goods industries have some differentiation of product, and frequently contain only a few firms. The exact degree of differentiation and the exact strength of the feeling of mutual interdependence, however, vary widely among the industries, a fact which greatly complicates the development of a usable analysis of price and output determination.

Collusion versus Spontaneous Co-ordination. Oligopoly situations may also be classified on the basis of whether the mutual interdependence manifests itself in outright *collusion* or merely in *spontaneous co-ordination* of the policies of the various firms through the recognition by each firm of the effects of its actions upon those of its competitors. Collusion involves direct negotiation among competitors and the making of agreements, of necessity informal in countries such as the United States which prohibit outright price and output agreements. Without such collusion oligopoly situations may be unstable, since firms will base their actions in some cases upon mistaken estimates of their competitors' behavior. The making of the agreements is facilitated by the smallness of the number of firms.

The coverage of agreements made with collusion varies widely. The agreements may extend to both price and output, prescribing both the price to be charged and the volume of sales which each firm can make.[5] More frequently they apply only to price. In other cases merely the method of price determination is agreed upon. The firms may accept

[5] Agreements on sales volume are difficult to carry out without encountering danger of antitrust-law prosecution and therefore are probably relatively rare.

the principle of following prices set by one firm recognized as the price leader or agree to use certain pricing methods which will produce substantial price uniformity. Acceptance by firms of standard cost accounting procedures for allocation of overhead among various products, for example, will reduce price differences.

Frequently, however, oligopoly involves *spontaneous co-ordination* rather than outright agreement. Each firm simply takes into consideration the expected responses of competitors to its own action and determines its policies accordingly; with each firm following similar practices, price and output levels will eventually adjust to figures which are acceptable to all firms. Spontaneous co-ordination may involve adoption by various firms, without outright negotiation and agreement, of pricing practices comparable to those agreed upon in situations of collusion. The firms may come, quite independently of any outright agreement, to accept the prices of one firm and adjust their own prices to figures set by this firm, or to adopt methods of price-setting—such as the markup system common in retailing—which lessen effective price competition.

Complete versus Partial Oligopoly. If the feeling of mutual interdependence among oligopolists is sufficiently strong, maximum profits for the group as a whole may be attained; such a situation is known as one of *complete oligopoly,* and the effects are much the same as those of complete monopoly. It is at least theoretically possible that completeness of mutual interdependence might be attained without collusion; if each firm is convinced that any price change which it makes in either direction will be accompanied by more or less comparable changes on the part of competitors, this result may be approximated. But such situations are unlikely. Price-leadership cases, in which the leader knows that all other firms will follow any price changes which it makes, also may allow complete oligopoly, whether collusion is involved in the establishment of the price-leadership situation or not. But most likely complete oligopoly will arise only with outright negotiations among competing firms. As will be explained later, even with such agreements total profits are seldom actually maximized. The concept of complete oligopoly is of more significance as an analytical case, which indicates the extreme limiting situation of mutual interdependence, than as a tool of analysis for use in particular cases.

It is likely that in most cases oligopoly takes a partial form. Firms are conscious of the effects of their policies upon those of other firms, but the feeling of mutual interdependence is not sufficiently strong to allow action which will maximize profits of the firms of a group. When agreements are made, they may involve nothing more than the acceptance of pricing methods which will lessen the degree of price competition. If prices are actually agreed upon, the divergent interests of the various firms may prevent the acceptance of the group profit-maximization figure. Without agreements, firms may be aware that competitors will make some price changes in response to changes which they make, but they are uncertain about the exact extent of the responses. In most oligopoly situations one of the major characteristics is the presence of great uncertainty on the part of the firms about competitors' responses to their policies.

One case of partial oligopoly which may be of importance is that in which firms expect that competitors will follow price reductions which they make, but not price increases. Reductions will be followed because the lowering of the price cuts seriously into the sales of the competitors and forces them to change their own prices, while increases will not be followed because the competitors prefer to benefit from increased sales volumes at the expense of the firm which raises its price.

The wide variety of cases of oligopoly makes the development of a satisfactory analysis of price and output determination in this field difficult. A broad theory, with assumptions so general that they cover all possible oligopoly situations, can offer very little in the way of aid to analysis of particular situations. To develop separate theories of all possible cases of oligopoly is an impossible task. At present, all that can be done is to develop the analysis of those cases which appear to be of paramount importance; additional empirical work of actual behavior in oligopoly situations is necessary to determine which cases are of sufficient importance to warrant further attention, and to provide the precise generalizations to use as assumptions in these cases.

Monopoly

When a product is sold by only one firm in a market, the situation is one of *monopoly,* a situation in which total supply is controlled by one seller. In the particular market area, the firm and the industry are identical. Since there are substitutes for all products, even a monopolist is not free from the effects of the actions of other producers. But when one firm is the sole seller of a particular product, in the usual sense of the term the firm can determine its policies without fear of reactions from other firms, and it does not need to fear substantial losses in business as a result of actions of other groups of firms.

Monopoly is not widespread in American industry, in part because of the antitrust laws, which usually operate to check complete domination of an industry by one firm. Examples are most common in the public utilities industries; firms in these fields are, as a rule, allowed (and often insured) monopoly positions in their market areas but are subject to close regulation by government agencies. Outside the utilities industries, examples are infrequent. In the past aluminum and nickel production have been major examples. In small communities, individual retailers may possess a monopoly position in the sale of certain commodities. However, principles of monopoly price and output determination are of greater significance than would be expected from the scope of actual monopoly situations. Monopoly price and output levels represent goals for which firms are striving (if they are seeking to maximize profits) in situations in which the number of sellers is small—goals which they may attain if co-ordinated action among them is adequate.

Monopsonistic Influences

The types of markets discussed in the previous paragraphs have represented deviations from pure competition on the sellers' side of the market. As deviations of this type are of greater consequence than those on the buyers' side, they warrant more complete attention. But nevertheless the deviations on the buyers' side are not negligible.

It is possible to conceive of a situation in which there are a large number of buyers, but the various sellers have preferences for dealing with particular buyers. This case of *monopsonistic competition,* the corollary of monopolistic competition, is not of sufficient importance to warrant consideration. Much more significant are the cases of *oligopsony,* or smallness of numbers of buyers, in which each buyer has direct influence on price, and is aware that his actions will affect the price which he pays, and the policies of his competitors as well. Thus, for example, an oil refinery is well aware that any increases in the purchase price paid for crude oil will cause competing refineries to raise their prices as well. Oligopsony, just as oligopoly, may take the collusive form, as buyers agree upon purchase prices, or it may take the form of spontaneous co-ordination.

If there is but one buyer, the term *monopsony* is applied; this is the corollary of complete monopoly on the sellers' side. Various forms of monopsonistic influences may develop in an industry characterized by a homogeneous product and a large number of sellers. In this situation, the market is essentially one of pure competition from the standpoint of the sellers, since no one seller can influence price, but price determination is actually dominated by the buyers. Examples of this situation are to be found in the market for crude oil, in which a few refineries buy a standardized product from many small producers. The same is true of the wholesale markets for tobacco and sugar beets. More commonly, however, oligopsony elements exist in conjunction with differentiation and oligopoly on the sellers' side. Such situations are found in several capital goods markets; many types of specialized machinery, for example, are produced by a few firms and are used by only a few buyers. The labor market is frequently influenced by labor union action, and thus co-ordinated control of supply, on the sellers' side, and by a few large dominant employers on the buyers' side. While monopsonistic competition is not common in the final markets for consumption goods, it occasionally exists in the wholesale markets for such goods. Three large automobile manufacturers buy approximately half the annual output of tires, produced by a small number of firms. Large department stores, mail-order houses, chain stores, and co-operative buying organizations (IGA, for example), frequently dominate wholesale markets for consumption goods.

Summary

From the foregoing discussion, it is apparent that the number of possible market situations is almost infinite. There is the possibility of one buyer and one seller confronting each other (monopsony-monopoly or bilateral monopoly) and various possible situations of a few buyers and few sellers (oligopsony-oligopoly, or bilateral oligopoly). There may be many sellers and many buyers, with or without differentiation of product; many sellers and few buyers, and many buyers and few sellers, with various possible degrees of differentiation. And in the different situations involving small numbers, there is a wide range of possible situations according to the exact manner in which competitors are expected to react to one another's policies. It is misleading to regard market relationships as consisting of a few well-defined cases, such as monopoly, oligopoly, etc.; actually, there is a great range of possibilities, each individual situation being only slightly different from another. But a relatively small number of models, based upon assumptions which reflect reasonably well the actual conditions in major segments of the economy, will provide the tools of analysis. The simplifications involved in developing these models must be recognized, and taken into consideration when the models are used in selecting relevant data and analyzing relationships among them in particular cases.

The succeeding chapters dealing with output and price determination will cover the cases of pure competition, monopolistic competition, oligopoly, and monopoly, with recognition given to the wide variation of possibilities within the oligopoly category, which, unlike the other situations, is not a simple clear-cut case. Finally, some attention will be given the significance of monopsonistic elements.

PERFECTION IN MARKET CONDITIONS

Price and output determination are affected not only by market relationships prevailing among various buyers and sellers, but also by the absence or presence of other institutional factors which affect the actions of various units in the economic system.

One important set of such factors consists of those relating to the knowledge possessed by various persons relative to the actions necessary to attain the desired goals, and to the mobility or adjustability of the various factor units. Deviations away from perfect knowledge and perfect mobility are known as *imperfections.*

A market characterized by complete absence of imperfections, as well as by purely competitive market conditions, is known as one of *perfect competition.* In such a market, all sellers and buyers have perfect knowledge of market conditions, and frictions checking immediate adjustment of price and output to the equilibrium level are completely absent. Producing units have complete knowledge of costs and market price conditions, so that they are able to maximize profits at all times. Factor units are freely mobile, so that they will always move to the most remunerative employments.

The concept of perfectness in markets may be applied to nonpurely competitive markets as well. In monopolistic competition, for example, perfectness requires complete knowledge on the part of sellers about cost and demand conditions, so that they may set optimum prices, and perfect factor mobility. In oligopoly, perfectness requires that the firms know the reactions of their competitors to their own policies, as well as other data pertinent to profit maximization.

The assumption of perfectness is necessary as a first approximation in the development of the analysis, in order to make it sufficiently simple to be manageable. Actually, of course, all markets are characterized by substantial imperfections which interfere with the attainment of the goals of business firms, households, and factor-owners. The major imperfections are described briefly in the succeeding paragraphs.

Imperfect Knowledge

A major source of imperfection is the lack on the part of factor-owners and business firms of information necessary to succeed in attainment of maximization goals. Workers, for example, may be unaware of alternate employment possibilities. Persons contemplating the establishment of new business enterprises have only very limited knowledge of profit possibilities. Despite improved techniques, sellers have inadequate knowledge of potential sales at various price levels and often imperfect knowledge of cost behavior. As a consequence, actual attainment of income maximization is extremely difficult. The degree of knowledge of income possibilities, sales, and costs depends to a great extent upon the institutions of the period—the education of the persons involved, the state of market-research and cost-analysis techniques, the activity of government agencies in preparing and distributing information in regard to job and profit possibilities, trends in national income, etc. As a consequence of imperfect knowledge, outputs of various goods are different than they would otherwise be, and both resource allocation and income distribution are affected. Too many producers may enter some lines of production, for example, and others may make unwarranted plant expansions or fail to make ones which would be profitable. Prices may be set at levels which do not maximize profits, and production may exceed the quantities which can be sold at profitable prices.

Mobility of Factor Units

A second major imperfection is the existence of interferences with movement of factors of production from one use to another. There are two major classes of such interferences, namely, restrictions upon the entry of new firms into an industry, and the nonadaptability of specialized resources to new uses.

Restricted Entry. Restrictions on entry of new firms into an industry are widespread. Some are due to natural conditions relating to factor supply or conditions of production, some are created deliberately by individual producers, and some arise as a result of governmental action. The major examples are noted briefly below:

1. Limited raw-material supplies. When necessary specialized resources, such as ores of a certain type, are to be found only in limited areas and existing firms control the entire supply, it is impossible for new firms to commence operation. Entry into nickel production and diamond mining, for example, is severely restricted by this consideration.

2. Difficulties in obtaining money capital. The ability to obtain money capital depends primarily upon a satisfactory credit standing; new firms, whose credit position is not established, often have great difficulty in obtaining the necessary capital, even in periods in which money capital is generally plentiful. Typically, new businesses must be developed

primarily with the capital of the promoters plus reinvested earnings; thus persons lacking adequate resources of their own find the establishment of a business extremely difficult, regardless of profit prospects and their own management abilities. This type of restriction is particularly serious for lines of production which require heavy initial capital investment, such as steel production.

3. Legal restrictions. Governmental activity frequently restricts entry of new firms. Patent rights may interfere with the ability of new firms to develop competing products. Trade-marks protect various differentiation devices. Tariffs interfere with the entry into domestic markets of foreign competitors. Cities and towns may limit the numbers of certain types of enterprises (taverns, for example) or prevent peddlers from operating. Licensing requirements for various trades are often used to restrict numbers. The most severe legal restrictions are applied to the public utilities industries; new firms are not permitted to enter without approval of regulatory agencies. In general, sanction will not be given unless substantial proof can be presented that the service of existing firms is inadequate.

Some of these legal restrictions are established in the interest of the welfare of the economy. Control of entry into public utility industries is necessary to prevent excess plant capacity and higher rates, for example. But many of the restrictions, such as most tariffs and many licensing requirements, result from the political activity of the interested groups.

4. Established reputation. When existing firms build up strong preferences for their products by successful advertising and other sales activities, new firms will encounter difficulty in taking away substantial volumes of business. Once customers become strongly attached to particular firms, sales expenditures far in excess of those made by the original firms are often necessary to draw the customers away from the latter.

5. Technological conditions of production. In some industries technological requirements necessitate a large volume of output for the attainment of low-cost operation. Certain types of capital equipment can be used efficiently only when output is substantial. As a result, the problems confronting new firms in such industries are very serious. A large volume of sales cannot be built up overnight, especially if existing firms have well-established reputations; heavy losses are inevitable for a period of several years while customers are being obtained. Unless the owners have substantial money capital, the business is likely to end in bankruptcy before it ever gets on its feet. Fear of this serves as a serious deterrent to the establishment of new firms.

In some situations, technological conditions are such that one additional firm would result in excess capacity and losses, though existing firms are making profits higher than the usual rate of return.

Nonadaptability of Resources. Movement of resources from one industry to another in response to changing conditions is seriously restricted by the nonadaptability of specialized factors of production. The problem is particularly serious with capital goods. Machinery constructed for one purpose is frequently completely unsuited for any other use. A railroad grade, including expensive bridges and tunnels, is ordinarily useless for any purpose except railroad operation. Apple trees cannot produce anything but apples. In some instances the transfer of resources is not impossible but is not feasible because of the costs of transference; streetcar rails on abandoned lines are often left in the pavement because the costs of removal and transfer would exceed the value in another use. As a result of this nonadaptability of capital, resources will often be continued in a particular use for a long period, even though they would yield a far greater return had they been utilized originally for some other purpose.

Labor likewise is not entirely adaptable. Persons trained in certain lines of work cannot easily shift to employment requiring different skills. Geographical mobility of labor is seriously restricted by costs of moving, family ties, and preferences for living in certain areas. Workers are typically reluctant to shift away from present occupations and employers and to move to other areas.

The significance of these various imperfections will be indicated in the discussion of price and output determination in the succeeding chapters.

The Approach to Price Theory

With the survey of the nature of the units in the economic system, the goals pursued, and the nature of market relationships completed, it is possible to proceed to the analysis of price and output determination, and thus of resource allocation. The analysis will be divided into two general segments, the first portion relating to the prices and outputs of consumption goods which are produced by business firms, and the second to the prices and quantities utilized of the various types of factor units. The first segment is known as price theory; the second, as the theory of factor pricing, or distribution theory. The interrelationships of the two sets of prices and the nature of the price system as a whole will be summarized in Chapter 20.

The prices of produced commodities depend in general upon two sets of forces, those relating to the demand for the commodities, and those relating to cost of production and supply. Each of these two forces must be analyzed separately before consideration is given to the manner in which their interaction determines price and output under various competitive conditions. A similar procedure will be followed in Part III dealing with factor prices.

SELECTED REFERENCES

CHAMBERLIN, E. H. *The Decline of Competition,* chap. ix. 5th ed. Cambridge, Mass.: Harvard University Press, 1948.

MACHLUP, F. "Monopoly and Competition: A Classification," *American Economic Review,* Vol. XXVII (September, 1937), pp. 445–51.

DEAN, JOEL. *Managerial Economics,* chap. ii. New York: Prentice-Hall, 1951.

CHAMBERLIN, E. H. "Monopolistic Competition Revisited," *Economica,* Vol. XVIII (November, 1951), pp. 343–62.

BISHOP, R. L. "Elasticities, Cross-Elasticities, and Market Relationships," *American Economic Review,* Vol. XLII (December, 1952), pp. 779–803.
See also comments on this article in December, 1953, issue of the *American Economic Review.*

QUESTIONS

1. What is a market? How does the market for magazines differ in area from that for particular newspapers?
2. What are the characteristics of a purely competitive market?
3. What conditions must be present for a market to be purely competitive?
4. What are the primary characteristics of monopolistic competition?
5. Why do firms differentiate their products?
6. What is the primary characteristic of oligopoly?
7. Why is oligopoly widespread in the present economy?
8. Distinguish between pure versus differentiated oligopoly; complete versus partial oligopoly.
9. What is meant by spontaneous co-ordination? How does it differ from collusion?
10. Distinguish between oligopsony and oligopoly; between monopsony and monopoly.
11. A firm in monopolistic competition has essentially a monopoly of its particular brand. Why is its position not regarded as one of monopoly?
12. Servel is the only manufacturer of gas refrigerators. Would you regard this as an example of monopoly?
13. What is bilateral oligopoly? Bilateral monopoly?
14. Distinguish between perfect competition and pure competition.

15. Indicate three types of restrictions on the entry of new firms into an industry.
16. Why does imperfect knowledge interfere with the attainment of the results expected in terms of economic analysis?
17. What type of competition appears to prevail in the following industries (at the manufacturing level, unless otherwise specified):
    a) gasoline
    b) automobiles
    c) telephone service, in a particular area
    d) telegraph service
    e) automobile tires
    f) cement
    g) wheat (wholesale markets)
    h) eggs (wholesale markets)
    i) newspapers, Chicago or New York
    j) women's clothing (manufacture)
    k) diesel locomotives
    l) plate glass
    m) farm machinery
18. In the case of the items in Question 17 listed as oligopolies, indicate whether industries constitute pure or differentiated oligopolies.
19. Give three examples (not listed in the chapter) of monopsonistic or oligopsonistic markets.
20. Entry into the following industries is or has been restricted. What has been the source of restriction in each case?
    a) manufacture of automobiles
    b) telephone service
    c) manufacture of aluminum
    d) taxicab service
    e) manufacture of cola types of soft drinks
    f) production of helium
21. How many new companies have been successfully established in the automobile industry in the United States since 1930? How many attempts have there been? What has been responsible for the failures of new firms to become established?

PART II

The Theory of Commodity Price and Output Determination

Chapter 5 CONSUMER DEMAND

Economic activity is the activity of man in utilizing scarce means to satisfy his wants. Accordingly, the character of economic activity and the manner in which resources are allocated to the production of various goods are influenced by the relative desires of persons for various goods and the reactions of these desires to increased quantities of the various goods which become available. Particularly in a market economy, characterized by individual choice of action, consumer desires play a dominant role in guiding production. Business firms find it profitable to produce particular goods only if there exists a sufficient demand for the goods, and the total amount of each commodity which can be produced profitably depends upon the total demand for the commodity. Accordingly, an analysis of the nature and behavior of consumer demand is an essential step in the development of the explanation of price and output levels and resource allocation.

The Concept of Demand

The demand of an individual buyer for a product, known as *individual demand,* is a schedule of the amounts of the product which the person would buy at various possible alternative prices in a particular interval of time.[1] A shopper enters a store to buy oranges for use during the coming week; she finds the price to be 30 cents a dozen, and she buys four dozen. Had the price been 40 cents (for oranges of the same grade), she would have bought a certain quantity—perhaps three dozen. Had it been 50 cents she might have bought none at all; at 20 cents she might have bought five dozen. Her demand for oranges at the particular time is the schedule of these various amounts that she would have purchased at the various possible prices. The schedule is shown in Table 1. The fact that the shopper is not aware of the amounts that she

[1] Demand schedules may be considered in terms of a particular moment of time, or more realistically, in terms of a short period.

would purchase at prices other than the prevailing one does not alter the fact that she has a schedule, in the sense that she would have bought the various other amounts had the other prices prevailed instead of the actual current price. It must be emphasized that the schedule is a list of alternative possibilities; at any one time only one of the prices will prevail and thus a certain determinate quantity will be purchased.

TABLE 1

INDIVIDUAL DEMAND SCHEDULE OF A CONSUMER FOR ORANGES, WEEK OF JUNE 10–17

Price (Cents)	Quantity Demanded (Dozen)
50	0
40	3
30	4
20	5
10	7

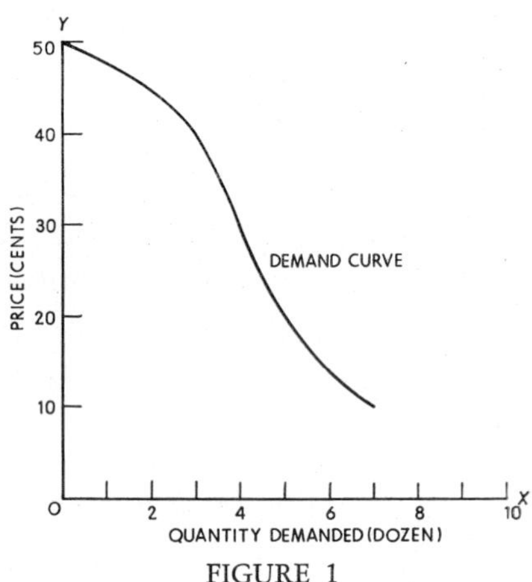

FIGURE 1

INDIVIDUAL DEMAND SCHEDULE OF A CUSTOMER FOR ORANGES OF A CERTAIN GRADE, WEEK OF JUNE 10–17

The data in Table 1 can be plotted graphically, as shown in Figure 1. The data as given provide a series of points, which, when connected by a continuous line, constitutes the demand curve. This procedure essentially provides by interpolation estimates of the quantity-demanded figures for prices between those for which information is available. In the graphs employed in price and output analysis which show relationships between quantities and prices, price is always plotted on the *Y* (vertical) axis, and quantity on the *X* (horizontal) axis, as a matter of standard practice.

In a particular market there are ordinarily a substantial number of buyers, each with his own individual demand schedule. The sum of these schedules, known as *total demand,* or, more commonly, *demand,* is thus the schedule of the total amounts that would be purchased by all of the buyers in the particular market at various possible prices, in a given time interval. The total demand for oranges in a particular market for a certain week might appear as shown in Table 2 and illustrated graphically on Figure 2. A given schedule refers, of course, to a given grade of the commodity. Although the actual quantities which would be purchased at prices other than the prevailing one may not be actually known, or easily ascertainable, the schedule is nevertheless determinate, in the sense that the total purchases would shift to various other amounts, should the price change.

TABLE 2

TOTAL DEMAND SCHEDULE FOR ORANGES IN A PARTICULAR MARKET, WEEK OF JUNE 10–17

Price (Cents)	Quantity Demanded (Dozen)
50	40,000
40	60,000
30	75,000
20	90,000
10	120,000

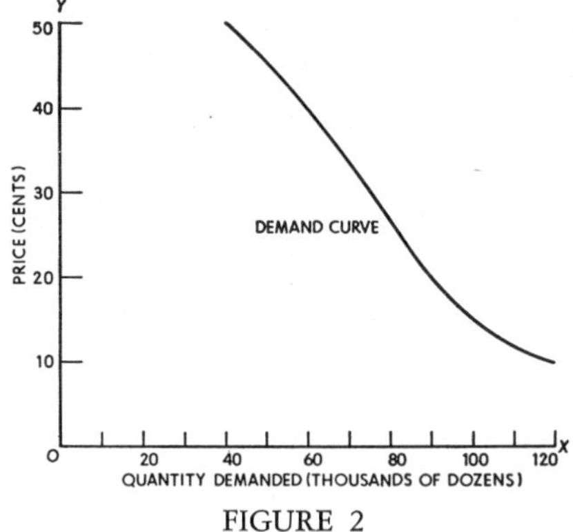

FIGURE 2

TOTAL DEMAND SCHEDULE FOR ORANGES OF A CERTAIN GRADE IN A PARTICULAR MARKET, WEEK OF JUNE 10–17

When the commodity is homogeneous, in the sense that buyers have no preferences for particular brands or makes of the commodity and thus no preference for the product of any particular seller, the concept of total demand is precise; the various individual demand schedules for the commodity can be added without conceptual difficulty. But when the product is differentiated, as is common in most markets, the concept of total demand, although still useful, becomes less precise. With differentiation, the individual buyers have preferences for the brands of particular producers; a buyer's schedule is not, for example, for "cigarettes," but for particular brands. The amount that he is willing to buy depends upon the brands available, and he may use less of the commodity if his favorite variety cannot be obtained. Likewise, with differentiation, the selling prices of the firms may not be identical; thus there may in practice be no such situation as a 20-cent price for cigarettes, but rather one situation in which some brands are selling for 20 cents, some for 25 cents, and others for 15 cents; another situation in which the three brands are selling for 18, 23, and 13 cents, respectively, etc. It is not possible, in cases of this sort, to conceive of a clear-cut total demand schedule, in which, at particular prices, certain amounts would be purchased. Instead, the schedule must be regarded as the set of total amounts of particular brands that would be purchased at various possible levels of a pattern of prices, with the fact recognized that the amounts which individuals will buy are different for the various brands. Even with these qualifications, the concept of "total demand" has significance; it is useful to be able to speak of "an increase in the demand for automobiles," for example, even though this total is actually a series of closely related demands for particular brands of cars and not a single schedule for a homogeneous commodity, as is the demand for a certain grade of potatoes.

Isolation of the Effects of Price Changes upon Quantity Demanded

The quantity of a commodity purchased is, of course, dependent upon a number of other considerations besides the price paid. The amounts which persons will buy will depend upon their incomes and accumulated wealth, upon their relative preferences, and upon the prices and quantities available of other goods, as well as upon expectations of future prices. A particular demand schedule, relating quantity purchased to price, is based upon the assumption that these various determinants are given, in order to isolate the relationship between price and quantity purchased. In other words, for the period for which a particular demand schedule is valid, it is assumed that incomes, relative consumer preferences, prices and quantities of other commodities, and expectations about future prices remain unchanged. This procedure is necessary in order to separate the effects of price changes upon quantity demanded from the effects of changes in these other considerations, all of which influence purchases. Shifts in these other determinants of demand manifest themselves as changes in the height of the demand schedules rather than as influences which affect the nature of the schedules themselves. This procedure is not at all unrealistic; it merely allows isolation of the effects of price changes from the effects of changes of the other determinants of demand.

Changes in Demand

For purposes of economic analysis, *demand* is defined as the schedule of the amounts which would be purchased at various possible prices. Thus a change in demand occurs when larger or smaller quantities than previously are purchased at particular prices. The change may affect the entire schedule or only portions of it. An increase in demand is shown in Table 3, and is illustrated graphically in Figure 3. A change in demand is reflected in an entirely new demand curve ($D'D'$ in Figure 3).

A change in demand must be distinguished clearly from a change in *quantity demanded,* resulting from a price change. The latter adjustment involves no shift in the demand schedule (or curve, in graphical terms), but merely a movement along an existing schedule, from one point to another. A change in the price of a good cannot cause a change in the demand for the good (but only a change in quantity demanded)

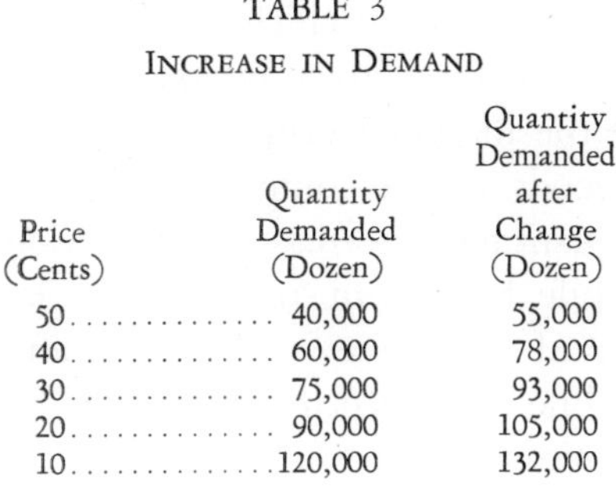

TABLE 3

INCREASE IN DEMAND

Price (Cents)	Quantity Demanded (Dozen)	Quantity Demanded after Change (Dozen)
50	40,000	55,000
40	60,000	78,000
30	75,000	93,000
20	90,000	105,000
10	120,000	132,000

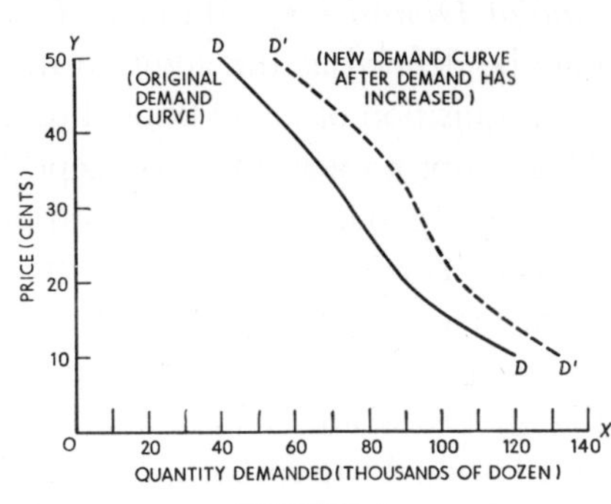

FIGURE 3

ILLUSTRATION OF AN INCREASE IN DEMAND

as the term demand is defined, since the demand is the entire schedule of the various quantities which would be purchased at all possible prices. A change in demand, that is, a shift in the entire schedule, will result from a shift in any of the primary determinants noted in the preceding paragraph, such as consumer preferences and incomes, as discussed later in the chapter.

THE NATURE OF THE DEMAND SCHEDULE: THE MARGINAL-UTILITY APPROACH

In general, demand schedules, both individual and total, will be of such a nature that larger quantities will be purchased at lower prices than at higher prices. This statement is known as the *Law of Demand.* Thus the demand curves slope downward from left to right, as the graphs are conventionally drawn. This law can be derived by logical analysis from the assumptions (1) that consumers seek to maximize satisfactions from their incomes, (2) that consuming units have limited incomes, and (3) that as additional units of a good are acquired, in a particular period of time, the power of these units to satisfy wants falls. There are two approaches to the explanation of the manner in which the Law of Demand is derived from these assumptions. The first, utilizing the concept of marginal utility, will be presented in this section, while the second, employing the indifference-curve technique, will be presented in the following section.

The Law of Diminishing Marginal Utility

The marginal-utility approach to the explanation of the nature of demand schedules is based upon the concept of marginal utility and the *Law of Diminishing Marginal Utility.* The concept of marginal utility may be defined as the addition to total satisfaction which results from the acquisition of an additional unit of a good in a given period of time. This is not a measurable concept, but the marginal utilities of various units of a good, and those of various goods, can be compared with one another. A person cannot measure in quantitative terms the satisfaction gained from acquiring another automobile, but he can compare the relative satisfaction gained from purchase of successive automobiles, and that gained from an additional automobile compared to that yielded by an additional trip to Europe or new furniture.

The Law of Diminishing Marginal Utility expresses the relationship between the quantity of a good which a person possesses and the marginal utility of each unit of the good. According to the Law, as a person obtains additional units of any good, the marginal utility declines; that is, each successive unit adds less to the person's satisfaction than did the previous unit. The Law is relevant for a particular period of time. The first automobile that a person acquires may yield him a great deal of satisfaction by providing a form of transportation more suitable for many purposes than alternative forms. If the person acquires a second car (in the same period of time), the latter will increase his satisfaction to a certain extent, because, for example, two members of the family can now use cars at the same time. But the marginal utility —the increase in satisfaction resulting from the acquisition of the second car—is likely to be far less than that resulting from the purchase of the first car. The marginal utility of a third car is likely to be very small.

The Law of Diminishing Marginal Utility may be attributed to the mutual interaction of two factors; individual wants are satiable, and different goods are not perfect substitutes for one another in the satisfaction of particular wants. As a person uses more and more units of a good to satisfy a want, the intensity of the want diminishes. But units of the good cannot be transferred to the satisfaction of other wants and produce as much satisfaction as they yielded initially in the satisfaction of the first want, because the good is not a perfect substitute (and possibly not one at all) for goods best designed to satisfy the second want.[2] For example, as a person consumes more and more salt, his desire for it on his food is eventually satisfied; additional amounts can be used for other purposes, such as removing ice from sidewalks, but will yield less satisfaction than the initial units used on food.

The Allocation of Consumer Income

Because marginal utility diminishes as additional units of a good are acquired, a person must avoid extending purchases of any one good too far, regardless of the intensity of his original desire for it, and he must exercise care in allocation of income among various commodities. More precisely, for maximization of satisfaction, income must be allocated in such a way that the marginal utilities of a unit-of-money's worth (for example, 10 cents' worth) of all commodities purchased are equal. When this situation is realized, 10 cents' worth of gasoline will yield the same increase in total satisfaction—the same marginal utility—as 10 cents' worth of bread and apples and theater tickets and soap and all other commodities purchased. If this situation is not attained, the person can increase total satisfaction by buying more of some goods and less of others; if, for example, the marginal utility of 10 cents' worth of apples is less than that of 10 cents' worth of bread, total satisfaction can be increased by buying more bread (and thus lowering the marginal utility of bread) and fewer apples (and thus raising the marginal utility of apples). The principle that income must be allocated in such a way that the marginal utilities of a unit-of-money's worth of all goods purchased are equal may also be stated in terms of the relationship between the marginal utilities and the prices of the various goods. Maximum satisfaction requires allocation of income in such a way that the marginal utilities of units of the various goods purchased are proportional to the prices of the goods; that is, if potatoes cost twice as much per pound as spinach, the consumer will adjust his purchases of the two commodities until the marginal utility of a pound of potatoes will be twice as great as the marginal utility of a pound of spinach. It must be recognized that many goods, such as pianos and automobiles, are not available in small, inexpensive units, and accordingly the making of perfect adjustments in marginal utilities is not possible.

The Relationship between Price and Quantity Demanded

It follows as a matter of logic from the Law of Diminishing Marginal Utility and the principle of income allocation outlined above that

[2] This could occur if two goods were perfect substitutes for one another, and thus, in an economic sense, essentially the same good.

a price reduction will lead to an increase in the quantity of the good demanded. The price reduction necessitates a reallocation in the use of income, since the old equilibrium has been disturbed. The price reduction has two distinct effects, both of which tend (apart from certain exceptions) to bring about an increase in the quantity purchased.

1. The income effect. Since the consumer can now buy the same quantity of goods as he was previously obtaining for less money, he has additional purchasing power available to spend on this good, or on others, or to save. The person may thus feel that he can afford to buy more of the good because it is cheaper. Suppose, for example, that the price of coffee falls from 80 cents a pound to 40 cents. If a person has been buying one pound a week, he now has 40 cents left over after making this week's purchases, just as if he had received 40 cents additional in his pay check. He may therefore buy an additional pound of coffee, or he may use this money on other goods. Whether he buys additional coffee or purchases larger quantities of other items depends of course on the relative marginal utilities. If the marginal utility of an additional pound of coffee is relatively low to him, he will spend the freed purchasing power on another commodity; hence the income effect will not in this instance operate on the demand schedule of this consumer for the particular product. If the marginal utility of an additional pound exceeds that of alternative purchases, he will buy the coffee, and thus the income effect will be significant.

2. The substitution effect. Secondly, a decline in the price of a good reduces the relative cost of this good compared to that of others, and increases the relative advantage of buying this one instead of others. Thus the price decline encourages the person to substitute this commodity for others, especially for those which are close substitutes for the satisfaction of a particular want. Since the decline in price of the good increases the quantity of the good which a unit of money will acquire, the marginal utility of 10 cents' worth of the good is increased compared to the marginal utilities of 10 cents' worths of other goods. If the price of coffee declines from 80 cents to 40 cents a pound, 10 cents' worth of coffee is now $\frac{1}{4}$ of a pound instead of $\frac{1}{8}$ of a pound, and thus may exceed the marginal utilities of 10 cents' worths of substitute commodities, which remain unchanged in quantity, since the prices are the same. Accordingly, a readjustment in the relative purchases of coffee and other goods is necessary to restore the equality of the marginal utilities of 10 cents' worths of all goods purchased.

The substitution effect will be particularly important when several goods can satisfy the same want more or less equally well. Changes in their relative prices will cause substantial readjustments in purchases. But the effect is significant even when the various goods do not satisfy the same want, as a reduction in the price of one may cause the consumer to satisfy one want more intensively at the expense of another. If gasoline becomes very cheap, a person may decide to do more traveling and spend less money on clothing.

Thus, in summary, under the assumptions employed, as the price of a commodity declines, the quantity demanded will normally increase, in part because the price reduction, by freeing purchasing power, allows the person to buy more of this good without sacrifice of other goods, and in part because the reduction encourages the person to substitute this commodity for others which remain unchanged in price.

NATURE OF THE DEMAND SCHEDULE: THE INDIFFERENCE-CURVE APPROACH[3]

In recent years[4] an alternative approach to the explanation of the allocation of consumer income and the nature of the demand schedule has been developed, one which utilizes indifference schedules and curves to illustrate consumer behavior. The use of indifference curves facilitates explanation of various demand and consumer behavior relationships, avoids the implicit assumption of the marginal utility approach that the utility concepts have quantitative measurements, and stresses the interrelationships among the demands for various articles. The basic principle in the marginal-utility explanation of income allocation—that income is allocated in such a manner that the marginal utilities of the various goods are proportional to their prices—implies that the consumer is, in some manner, measuring marginal utility, which of course is impossible.

The Indifference Schedule

An indifference schedule consists of the various combinations of two goods which will yield a consumer the same total satisfaction. For example, a household may obtain the same satisfaction from the use of

[3] This section (to p. 89) may be omitted without affecting the continuity of the remainder of the chapter.

[4] This approach is not entirely new; it was suggested in the writings of V. Pareto (*Manuel d'économie politique* [1909]) and by the Russian economist Slutzky (1915). It has been popularized, however, only in the last twenty years, commencing with an article by J. R. Hicks and R. G. D. Allen, "A Reconsideration of the Theory of Value," *Economica,* Vol. I (February and May, 1934), pp. 52–76, 196–219; see also J. R. Hicks, *Value and Capital* (2d ed.; Oxford: Oxford University Press, 1946), chaps. i and ii.

3 loaves of bread plus 4 pounds of steak a week as from the use of 1 loaf of bread and 5 pounds of steak, or 10 loaves of bread and 2 pounds of steak, etc. The person's indifference schedule for these two commodities, shown in Table 4, contains all of the possible combinations of the two commodities which will yield the same satisfaction. For another level of satisfaction there is another pattern of combinations.

TABLE 4

VARIOUS COMBINATIONS OF BREAD AND STEAK YIELDING A GIVEN LEVEL OF SATISFACTION TO A CONSUMER

Steak (pounds)		Bread (loaves)
6	plus	0
5	plus	1
4	plus	3
3	plus	6
2	plus	10
1	plus	15
0	plus	25

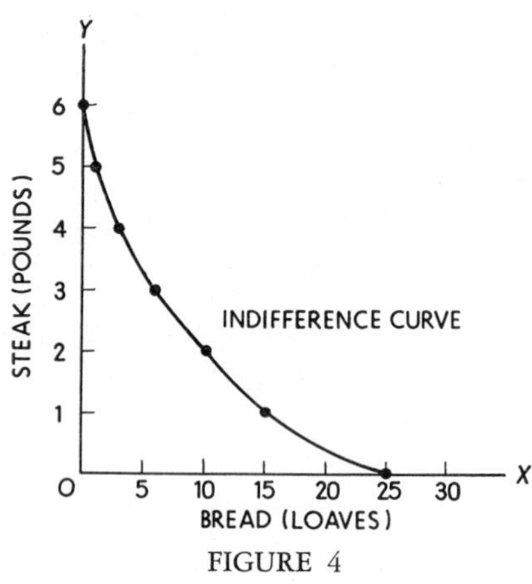

FIGURE 4

AN INDIFFERENCE CURVE OF A CONSUMER FOR BREAD AND STEAK

This schedule can be plotted on a graph, one commodity being plotted on the vertical axis, the other on the horizontal. The line connecting the various points is known as an indifference curve. The curve on Figure 4 shows the various combinations contained in Table 4. The curve shows nothing about the absolute amounts of satisfaction obtained but merely the various combinations which will yield equal satisfaction.

An indifference curve necessarily slopes downward from left to right; that is, to maintain the same satisfaction, as more units of one good are added, less units of the other will be required. The actual slope depends upon the *marginal rate of substitution* between the two commodities—the number of units of one of the commodities necessary to replace one unit of the other commodity in order to maintain the same total satisfaction. Thus the marginal rate of substitution of steak (Y on Figure 4) for bread (X) is the number of units of bread which must be added to replace a unit of steak and maintain the same level of satisfaction. Thus on Table 5, with 4 pounds of steak, 3 loaves of bread must be added if one pound of steak is eliminated, if the same amount of satisfaction is to be obtained. With one pound of steak, 10 loaves of bread must be added, if the one pound of steak is eliminated, to maintain satisfaction. When a large number of units of X (plotted on the horizontal axis) is necessary to replace a unit of Y (plotted on the vertical axis) the indifference curve is nearly horizontal; if the number of units of X required to replace a unit of Y is relatively small, the curve will be nearly vertical.

TABLE 5

THE MARGINAL RATE OF SUBSTITUTION BETWEEN BREAD AND STEAK FOR A PARTICULAR CONSUMER

Steak	Bread	Marginal Rate of Substitution of Steak for Bread*
6	0	
		1
5	1	
		2
4	3	
		3
3	6	
		4
2	10	
		5
1	15	
		10
0	25	

* The number of units of bread necessary to replace a unit of steak and maintain a given level of satisfaction.

The Convexity of Indifference Curves and the Principle of Diminishing Marginal Rate of Substitution

Under the assumptions that particular wants are satiable, and that various commodities are not perfect substitutes for one another, indifference curves must be convex to the point of origin, that is, the left-hand portion is relatively steep while the right-hand portion is relatively horizontal. In other words, the greater the number of units of X acquired, the smaller the number of units of Y that will be necessary to replace a unit of X in order to maintain the same total satisfaction. Likewise, the greater the number of units of Y, the smaller the number of units of X necessary to replace a unit of Y. The rule, known as the *Principle of Diminishing Marginal Rate of Substitution,* may also be stated in terms of the behavior of the marginal rate of substitution; as additional units of one commodity are added, the marginal rate of substitution of this commodity for the other falls; that is, progressively less of the other commodity will be necessary to replace units of the first in order to maintain the same satisfaction. The principle follows as a matter of logical necessity from the assumptions that particular wants are satiable and that various goods are not perfect substitutes for one another. As more units of one good are added, the ability of additional units of this good to satisfy wants falls because the want for which the good is best suited becomes satisfied. Thus a relatively small quantity of the other good (the desire for which is relatively intense, per unit, with few units being acquired) is necessary to replace a unit of this good and maintain satisfaction. If the consumer has relatively little of the first good and large quantities of the second, a large additional amount of the second must be added if another unit of the first is eliminated, in order to maintain the same level of satisfaction.

There is one class of exceptions to the Principle, which arises in cases in which the desires for two commodities are interrelated. If two goods are *complementary* to each other, that is, if the use of more units of one necessitates the acquisition of additional units of the other, units of one good cannot be replaced by units of the other and the same satisfaction be maintained. The use of gasoline and oil in a car or the use of bread and butter are examples of complementary goods; increased use of one necessitates increased use of the other. The case of complementarity cannot be illustrated satisfactorily with indifference curves.

The degree of convexity of an indifference curve, that is, the extent to which the curve deviates from a straight line, depends upon the ease of the substitution of the two goods for each other. If two commodities are perfect substitutes, the indifference curve is a straight line, as shown in Figure 5A based upon the data in Table 6, since the marginal rate of substitution is the same, regardless of the extent to which one good is replaced by the other.

TABLE 6

INDIFFERENCE SCHEDULE OF TWO COMMODITIES WHICH ARE PERFECT SUBSTITUTES FOR EACH OTHER

X	Y	MRS
1	6	
		1
2	5	
		1
3	4	
		1
4	3	
		1
5	2	
		1
6	1	

At the other extreme is the case of two commodities which are not substitutes at all. Since it is impossible to replace units of one by units of the other and maintain satisfaction, the marginal rate of substitution is infinite, and the indifference curve contains a right-angle turn convex to the point of origin, as shown in Figure 5B. The left portion is vertical, in the sense that an infinite amount of *Y* is necessary to replace one

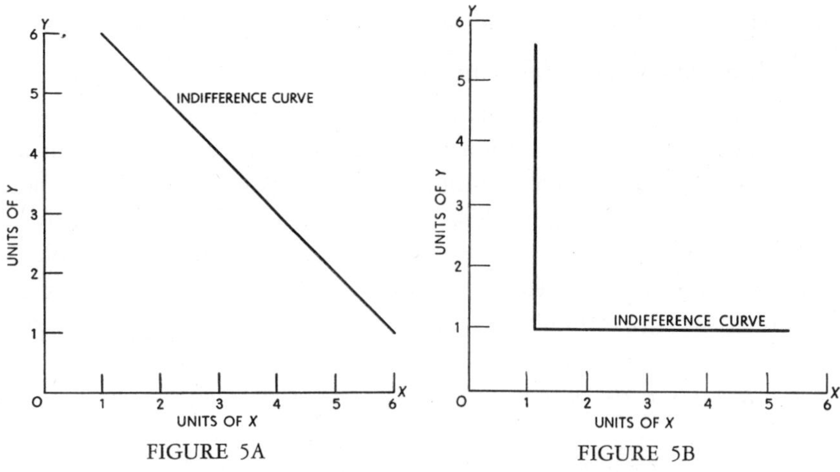

FIGURE 5A

AN INDIFFERENCE CURVE OF PERFECT SUBSTITUTES

FIGURE 5B

AN INDIFFERENCE CURVE OF COMMODITIES WHICH ARE NOT SUBSTITUTES

unit of *X;* the right portion is horizontal, since an infinite amount of *X* is necessary to replace a unit of *Y*. In more typical cases, in which the two commodities can be substituted for each other but are not perfect substitutes, the indifference line will be curved. The more easily the two commodities can be substituted for each other, the nearer the curve will approach a straight line; in other words, it will maintain more closely the same slope throughout.

The Indifference Curves with More than Two Commodities

The usual indifference curve shows the relationship between two commodities only, since the limitations of a two-dimensional surface prevent the inclusion of additional commodities. But the relationships portrayed for two commodities are valid for the relationships among all of the various commodities which a person is interested in acquiring. This can be illustrated by following the procedure of showing one commodity on the horizontal axis and all other commodities, represented by dollars of income which constitute purchasing power used to buy all other commodities, on the vertical axis.[5] The indifference curve then

[5] For purposes of explaining the allocation of income, saving may be regarded as one type of expenditure.

shows various combinations of purchases of this commodity and total expenditures on all other commodities which will yield the same satisfaction; and the slope of the curve shows the person's marginal rate of substitution between this good and all other goods, or, in other words, the person's marginal valuation of the good, relative to the money he has available for spending and saving.

The Pattern of Indifference Curves

The discussion up to this point has been in terms of a single indifference curve, representing a particular level of satisfaction. But actually, there is, for each consumer, for each pair of goods, a whole pattern or family of indifference curves, each indicating successively higher levels of satisfaction. Four schedules are presented in Table 7, plus the one given in Table 4 above, and illustrated graphically on Figure 6. Successive indifference curves never intersect, since each por-

TABLE 7

A PATTERN OF INDIFFERENCE CURVES OF A CONSUMER FOR STEAK AND BREAD

(Pounds and Loaves, Respectively)

SCHEDULE A		SCHEDULE B		SCHEDULE C		SCHEDULE D	
Steak	Bread	Steak	Bread	Steak	Bread	Steak	Bread
6	0	6	3	6	6	6	10
5	1	5	4.5	5	8.5	5	12
4	3	4	7	4	11.5	4	15.5
3	6	3	10.5	3	16	3	20.5
2	10	2	15.5	2	22	2	28
1	15	1	23	1	31	1	42.5

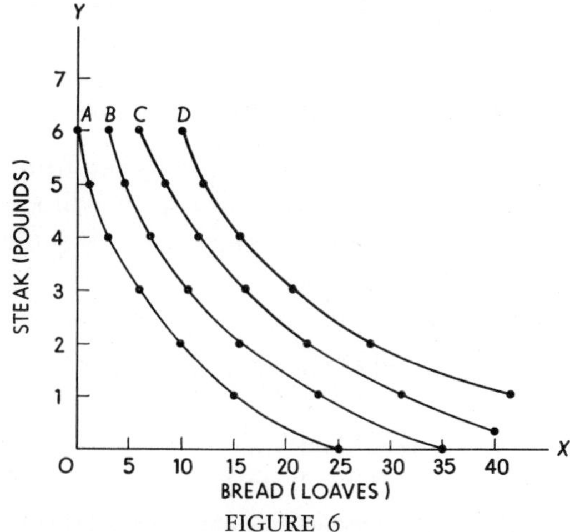

FIGURE 6

A PATTERN OF INDIFFERENCE CURVES OF A CONSUMER FOR STEAK AND BREAD

trays various combinations which yield the same degree of satisfaction. There is no way of knowing—and no attempt is made to ascertain—the quantitative differences in satisfaction yielded by the various combinations; the schedules merely show that each successive set of combinations yields more satisfaction than the previous, since it contains a greater number of units of one commodity with given quantities of the others.

The Price Line

A person's schedule of preferences, or pattern of indifference curves, for various goods, is assumed to be independent of his income. But the actual purchases which he makes—and thus the actual indifference curve which is significant—depend upon the level of his income and the manner in which he allocates the income between savings and consumption. Possible patterns of expenditures of a given sum of money on two commodities may be illustrated on the indifference graph by the use of the *price line,* a line which shows the various combinations of quantities of the two commodities which can be purchased with a certain expenditure, given the prices of the two goods. For example, if $5 is to be spent on bread and steak, and bread costs 20 cents a loaf and steak $1.00 a pound, 25 loaves of bread can be purchased if no steak is bought, 5 pounds of steak if no bread is bought; or various combinations of the two, such as 3 pounds of steak and 10 loaves of bread; 1 pound of steak and 20 loaves of bread, etc. The various combinations are

TABLE 8

EXPENDITURE SCHEDULE ON BREAD AND STEAK, TOTAL EXPENDITURE OF $5

Bread (Price 20 Cents) Loaves	Steak (Price $1.00) Pounds
0	5
$2\frac{1}{2}$	$4\frac{1}{2}$
5	4
$7\frac{1}{2}$	$3\frac{1}{2}$
10	3
$12\frac{1}{2}$	$2\frac{1}{2}$
15	2
$17\frac{1}{2}$	$1\frac{1}{2}$
20	1
$22\frac{1}{2}$	$\frac{1}{2}$
25	0

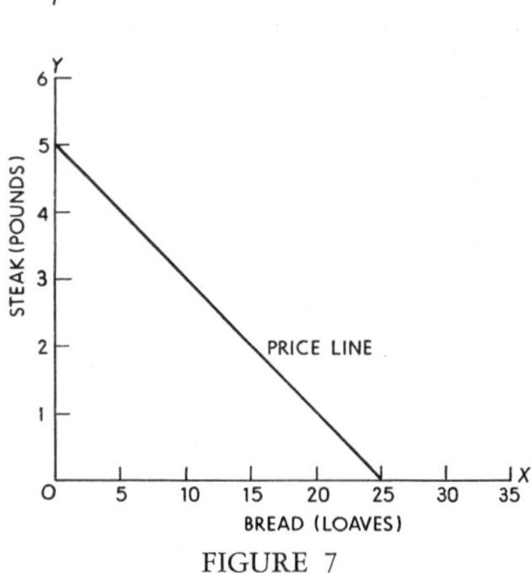

FIGURE 7

PRICE LINE, SHOWING VARIOUS COMBINATIONS OF BREAD AND STEAK WHICH CAN BE PURCHASED WITH A TOTAL EXPENDITURE OF $5, ASSUMING PRICE OF 20 CENTS FOR BREAD AND $1.00 A POUND FOR STEAK

shown in Table 8, and illustrated on Figure 7. Under the assumption that the prices of the commodities are independent of the quantities purchased, the price line will of necessity be a straight line. The slope of the curve is dependent upon the ratios of the prices of the two commodities. The same principle applies to the expenditure of a person's entire income on a wide range of commodities; for example, if a person has an annual income of $5,000, there are a large number of various combinations of different goods which could be purchased with this amount, given the prices of the goods.

The Quantities Purchased

Given the pattern of indifference curves of the consumer for two commodities, and the price line showing the various quantities of the two which can be purchased out of the expenditure allocated by the person to the two commodities, the quantities of each which will be purchased can be determined. By the same principle, given the indifference

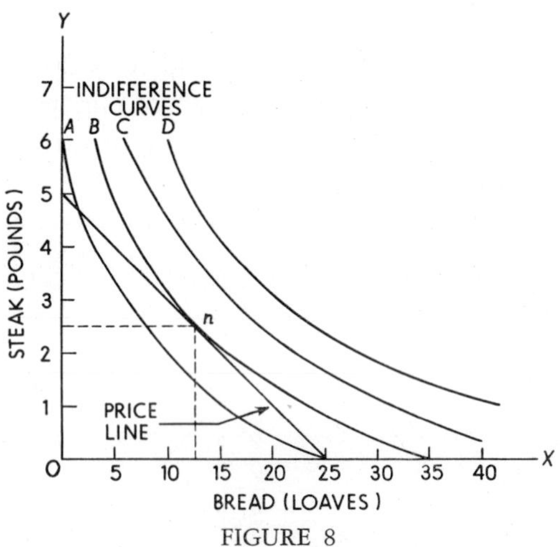

FIGURE 8

THE OPTIMUM COMBINATION OF PURCHASES OF TWO COMMODITIES

relationships among all commodities purchased and the person's income (and the prices of all goods), the total quantities of all goods purchased are determinate. The point of tangency between the price line and an indifference curve indicates the quantities of each good which will be purchased, if total satisfaction is to be maximized. On Figure 8 the price line is tangent to indifference curve *B* at point *n;* the person will acquire $2\frac{1}{2}$ pounds of steak and $12\frac{1}{2}$ loaves of bread. In order to maximize satisfaction the consumer must reach the highest indifference curve attainable with a given expenditure of money; the highest one which can be reached is that curve to which the price line is tangent. Any other possible combination of the two goods would either be on a lower indifference curve and thus yield less satisfaction, or would be unobtainable with the given expenditures. The same principle applies to all goods; there will be one combination which will allow greatest total satisfaction, given the indifference relationships, prices of the goods, and total expenditures to be made.

At the point of tangency of the price line and an indifference curve, the marginal rate of substitution of the two commodities is equal to the ratio of the price of the commodities. On Figure 8, at point *n*, the marginal rate of substitution between bread and steak is 5 to 1, that is, 5 loaves of bread must be added if one pound of steak is eliminated; this is equal to the price ratio (100/20, or 5/1). This relationship follows as a matter of mathematical necessity from the fact that since the curves are tangent at this point, they must have the same slope. If this relationship were not obtained, the consumer could gain satisfaction by purchasing more of one of the commodities and less of the other. If for example the consumer were buying such quantities of steak and bread that the marginal rate of substitution were 12 to 1, while the price ratio was 5 to 1, the addition of 1 pound of steak would necessitate the loss of only 5 loaves of bread, whereas the person would be willing to sacrifice 12 loaves in order to gain the pound of steak. Thus substitution is obviously desirable, and will continue until equality of the two ratios is obtained. The rule of equality of marginal rates of substitution and price ratios applies to each pair of commodities purchased, and thus among all commodities.

This explanation of the optimum allocation of consumer expenditures among the purchase of various goods is made entirely in terms of relative preferences for various numbers of units of goods, and avoids the use of the marginal utility concept, which implies, although it does not actually require, that satisfaction gained from particular units is measurable.

Indifference Curves and the Demand Schedule

The relationship between the price line and the pattern of indifference curves indicates the amounts of each of the two commodities which will be purchased, given the prices of the two commodities. For different possible prices for one of the commodities, given the price of the other, there will be various quantities of the two which will be purchased, as indicated by the respective points of tangency of the price lines and an indifference curve. A change in the price of one of the commodities will alter the slope of the price line, since a different amount of the commodity can be purchased with a given expenditure. If, for example, the price of X falls, the price line will become more nearly horizontal, since more units of X can be purchased than previously with a given expenditure. Likewise, at all points except the left origin (at which no units of X are being purchased) the line will be to the right of the old one. Thus the new point of tangency with an indifference curve will be to the right of the original point of tangency and on a higher indifference curve. In Figure 9 the point of tangency moves from

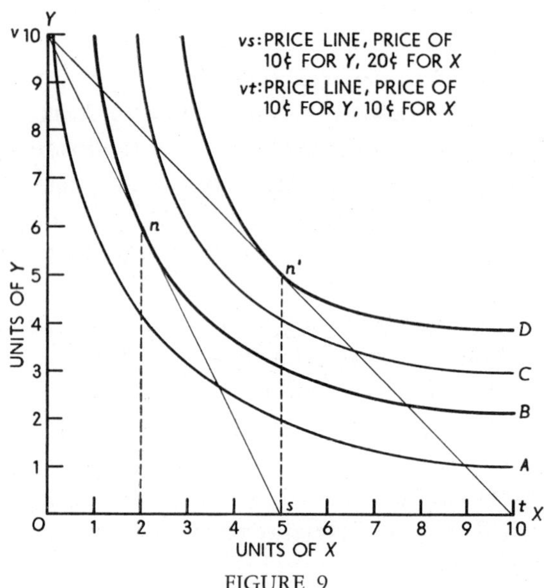

FIGURE 9

THE EFFECT OF A DECLINE IN THE PRICE OF X UPON THE QUANTITIES OF X AND Y PURCHASED

n to *n′* as a result of the decline in price of X from 20 cents to 10 cents; the quantity of X purchased increases from 2 units to 5.

Figure 10 shows a series of points of tangency of the price line with indifference curves, under the assumption of various possible prices for X (50 cents, 20 cents, 13.3 cents, and 10 cents) the price of Y remaining unchanged (at 10 cents). A line, known as the *price-consumption* curve (*CC*), may be drawn through these points of tangency, indicating the quantities of X (and Y) which will be acquired at various possible prices of X (given the price of Y). From this price-consumption curve can be derived the usual form of demand curve for the commodity. Thus from Figure 10, it can be ascertained that if the price of X is 10 cents, 5 units of X will be purchased; if the price is 13.3 cents, 3½ units will be purchased; if the price is 20 cents, 2 units

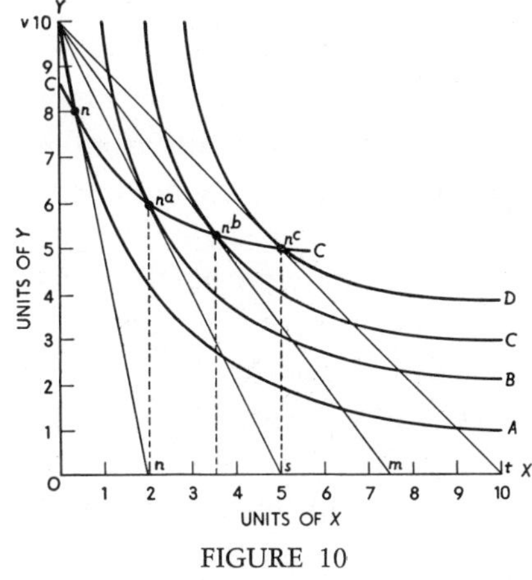

FIGURE 10

THE VARIOUS COMBINATIONS OF COMMODITIES *X* AND *Y* WHICH WILL BE PURCHASED WITH VARIOUS PRICES OF *Y*

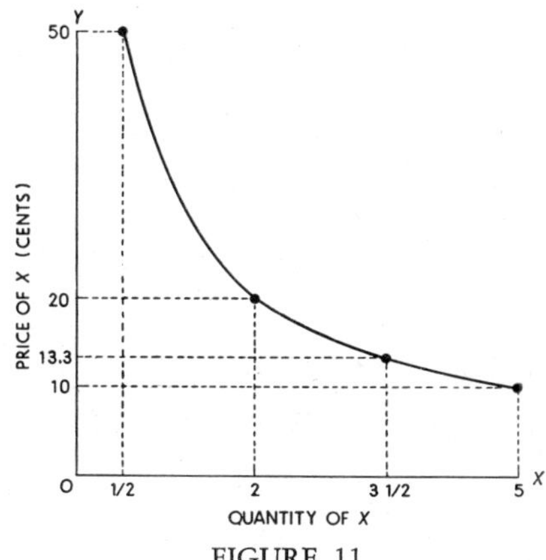

FIGURE 11

THE DEMAND SCHEDULE FOR COMMODITY *X* DERIVED FROM THE PRICE-CONSUMPTION CURVE ON FIGURE 10

will be purchased; if the price is 50 cents, $\frac{1}{2}$ unit will be purchased. This data may be plotted, as on Figure 11, in the usual demand curve form. It should be noted, of course, that on Figure 11, price of *X* is measured on the vertical axis, and quantity purchased on the horizontal axis, whereas the axes of Figure 10 show the quantities of the two commodities.

If the data shown in Figure 10 are assumed to portray the adjustment in two commodities only, the demand curve which is derived from the price-consumption curve is of limited significance, since it is based merely upon the adjustments between the commodity in question and one other, in terms of expenditures of a certain sum on the two, rather than in terms of all commodities purchased. However, if the *Y* axis on Figure 10 is assumed to represent expenditures on all other commodities, rather than on only one, and the price line to represent total expenditures, rather than those on two commodities only, the demand curve which is derived from the price-consumption curve is of the usual type, reflecting the reactions of the quantities of the commodity purchased in response to changes in the price of the commodity, with adjustments made between purchases of this commodity and all others, with a given total expenditure figure.

The Income Effect versus the Substitution Effect

With the use of indifference curves, the two ways in which a price reduction affects the quantity demanded can be distinguished more easily than in terms of the marginal utility approach to the explanation of demand schedules. When the price of a commodity declines, the *income* effect enables the person to buy more of this (or other) commodities from a given income; this is reflected by the movement onto a higher indifference curve. For example, on Figure 10, if price falls from 20 cents to 13.3 cents, the consumer is enabled to move from indifference curve *B* to curve *C*, and thus to a higher level of satisfaction. It is possible, of course, that the entire amount of purchasing power freed may be used to purchase other goods, if the marginal rate of substitution for this good drops very sharply for additional units of the good beyond the quantity purchased before the price changed. In limited cases the purchasing power freed might be used to buy better-quality substitutes for the commodity, and thus actually cause the quantity of the commodity purchased to fall. This case will be discussed in more detail in the section dealing with the effects of income changes upon demand.

The second manner in which the price decline influences the quantity demanded is the *substitution* effect; the lower price encourages the consumer to buy larger quantities of this commodity to replace units of other commodities. To the extent that this reaction is significant in a particular case, the point of tangency of the price line with the indifference curve is moved farther to the right; thus for example on Figure 10 the price line *vt* would be tangent to indifference curve *C* farther to the right than the point at which *vm* was tangent, and thus the decline in the price of *X* would lead to an increased quantity purchased even if none of the income freed by the lower price were spent. The easier the substitutability of other goods with *X*, the less will be the curvature in the indifference curve, and thus the greater the extent to which the point of tangency will shift to the right (that is, in the direction of a greater quantity of *X* purchased) as the price of *X* falls.

The substitution effect on the quantity demanded is completely distinct from the income effect, and reinforces the latter in increasing the quantity of *X* purchased as its price falls. In the case in which the income effect is negative (noted above) the substitution effect may outweigh it and cause the quantity demanded to increase, despite the nature of the income effect.

The readjustment which occurs in response to a price change may be expressed in terms of marginal rates of substitution. The reduction in the price of one good, by altering the ratio between this price and those of other goods, destroys the previous equality of price ratios and marginal rates of substitution; increased purchases of this commodity and decreased purchases of others are necessary in order to restore equality of the marginal rates of substitution with the price ratios.

This concludes the analysis of the indifference curve approach to the explanation of the nature of the demand schedules. As noted above, this approach avoids the use of the marginal utility concept with its inevitable connotation of measurability of actual amounts of satisfaction received. The statement with the marginal utility approach, for example, that optimum allocation of income requires that marginal utilities of the various goods purchased be proportional to the prices of the goods suggests that in some sense marginal utility is measurable, whereas the indifference curve approach expresses the optimum allocation simply in terms of rates of substitution of various goods for one another. The indifference curve approach also brings out more clearly the distinction between the income and substitution effects of a price change, and emphasizes the need for consumer adjustment of relative purchases of a wide range of commodities.

ELASTICITY OF DEMAND

The nature of the consumer demand schedules has been explained in the preceding sections in terms of two alternative (but not contradictory) approaches. Typically, as the price of a commodity falls, the quantity demanded will increase. But a major question remains for consideration: what determines the extent to which the quantity demanded increases as the price falls? This is the problem of *elasticity.* This term may be defined more precisely as the relationship between a given percentage change in the price of a commodity and the consequent percentage change in quantity demanded. Elasticity may be stated as a numerical expression, obtained by dividing the percentage change in quantity demanded by the percentage change in price. Thus if a 0.1 per cent change in quantity accompanies a 0.2 per cent change in price, the elasticity is −0.5 (0.1 ÷ 0.2). A minus sign precedes the figure, because price and quantity change in opposite directions. Thus the formula may be expressed as follows:

$$\text{Elasticity} = \frac{\dfrac{\text{Change in quantity}}{\text{Quantity}}}{\dfrac{\text{Change in price}}{\text{Price}}} \quad \text{or } e = \frac{\dfrac{\Delta q}{q}}{\dfrac{\Delta p}{p}}.$$

The more elastic the demand, the larger (numerically) will be the figure of elasticity, since the relative quantity change (the numerator of the fraction) will be large compared to the relative price change (the denominator of the equation). Thus a schedule with a numerical coefficient of 3 is much more elastic than one with a coefficient of 0.2. The formula given above, known as the *point elasticity* formula, is a satisfactory measure of elasticity only at a point on the demand schedule, and thus can be used only when the changes are infinitesimally small.

When the changes in price and quantity are of any significant magnitude, the exact meaning of the term *percentage change* requires interpretation, and the formula given above must be modified to indicate the precise meaning of the terms *price* and *quantity.* That is, there arises the question of whether the percentage change is figured on the basis of price and quantity before or after the change has occurred. This problem does not exist if the changes are infinitestimal, since the differences between the new and old figures also will be infinitestimal. The problem is serious, however, when the change is substantial; for example, a price rise from \$1.00 to \$1.50 constitutes a 50 per cent change if the original price (\$1.00) is used in figuring the percentage, or a $33\frac{1}{3}$ per cent change if the price after the change (\$1.50) is used. The most satisfactory solution is the use of the mid-points between the old and the new figures in the cases of both price and quantity demanded. In establishing a formula, the sums of the prices (\$1.00 plus \$1.50, in the example) and of the quantities before and after the change, respectively, may be used instead of the averages of these, since the result will be exactly the same. A fraction is not altered by dividing both the numerator and the denominator by 2. The formula thus becomes:

$$\text{Elasticity} = \frac{\dfrac{\text{Change in quantity}}{\text{Original quantity plus quantity after change}}}{\dfrac{\text{Change in price}}{\text{Original price plus price after change}}},$$

or

$$e = \frac{Q - Q'}{Q + Q'} \div \frac{P - P'}{P + P'}.$$

This formula is known as the formula of *arc elasticity,* since it measures the relative response of quantity demanded to price over an arc or segment of the demand schedule. The concept of arc elasticity is somewhat less precise than that of point elasticity. The concept is based upon the assumption that the response of the change in quantity demanded to the price change is the same over the entire price range involved. This assumption is of course not necessarily valid, especially if the price change is great.

Behavior of Total Outlay

The elasticity of demand for a commodity is reflected in the behavior of the total outlay on the commodity as the price changes. By *total outlay* is meant the total expenditure on the article at each price, that is, the arithmetic product of price times quantity purchased. When the elasticity exceeds 1 (numerically), total outlay will rise as the price declines, since the quantity demanded increases at a relatively greater rate than that at which the price falls. If a price is cut in half and the quantity demanded more than doubles, obviously more money is being spent on the commodity than before. If elasticity is less than 1, the total outlay will be less at low prices than at high, since a given price reduction will be accompanied by a proportionately smaller increase in quantity demanded. If the elasticity is 1, the relative changes in price and quantity are the same, and total outlay will be the same regardless of the price.

Classification of Segments of Demand Schedules on the Basis of Elasticity

On the basis of elasticity, particular segments of demand schedules[6] can be grouped into three major classes:

1. *Elastic* demand schedules—those with elasticity numerically greater than 1. Thus the price change is accompanied by a more than

TABLE 9

Typical Elastic Demand			Perfectly Elastic Demand	
Price (Cents)	Quantity Demanded	Total Outlay	Quantity Demanded	Total Outlay
50	8	$4.00	0	0
40	12	4.80	0	0
30	20	6.00	0	0
20	35	7.00	Infinite	Infinite
10	80	8.00	Infinite	Infinite

proportionate change in quantity demanded, and total outlay is greater at lower prices than at higher ones. The extreme limiting case of elasticity—that of *perfect elasticity*—is that in which any increase in price above a certain level causes the quantity demanded to fall to zero; at the particular price and at any lower figure the quantity demanded is infinite.[7] In Table 9 a typical elastic demand is illustrated, as well as a perfectly elastic schedule.

2. *Inelastic* demand schedules—those in which elasticity is less

[6] An entire demand schedule would rarely have the same elasticity throughout.

[7] Individual and total demand schedules cannot be perfectly elastic; the fact that incomes are limited prevents persons from buying infinite amounts of any good. The demand schedules confronting individual sellers, as discussed in Chapter 7, may appear to be perfectly elastic, from the standpoint of the sellers themselves (see pp. 107–8).

than 1. Thus the price change is accompanied by a less than proportionate change in quantity demanded, and the total outlay is greater at high prices than at lower prices. The limiting case of inelasticity is that of a *perfectly inelastic* demand; the quantity demanded is the same, regardless of the price. Individual demand schedules are often perfectly inelastic within certain price ranges; an increase in the price of gasoline, for example, from 29 to 30 cents, will not affect the volume of purchases of many buyers. A typical inelastic schedule, and one of perfect inelasticity are illustrated in Table 10.

TABLE 10

Typical Inelastic Demand			Perfectly Inelastic Demand	
Price (Cents)	Quantity Demanded	Total Outlay	Quantity Demanded	Total Outlay
50	8	$4.00	8	$4.00
40	9	3.60	8	3.20
30	11	3.30	8	2.40
20	14	2.80	8	1.60
10	19	1.90	8	0.80

3. *Demand schedules of unitary elasticity*—those with a numerical expression of elasticity of 1. In this case, the percentage change in quantity demanded is the same as the percentage change in price. For example, if price falls in half, the quantity demanded doubles. Total outlay is the same regardless of the price. It is unlikely that a demand schedule would be exactly unitary over a substantial range, the case merely constituting the dividing line between elastic and inelastic schedules. Table 11 shows a demand of unitary elasticity.

TABLE 11

DEMAND OF UNITARY ELASTICITY

Price (Cents)	Quantity Demanded	Total Outlay
50	8	$4.00
40	10	4.00
30	$13\frac{1}{3}$	4.00
20	20	4.00
10	40	4.00

In a given range of a graph, an inelastic demand will appear as a steeper curve than an elastic demand. A perfectly inelastic demand will appear as a straight vertical line, and a perfectly elastic demand as a straight horizontal line. A demand of unitary elasticity appears as a rectangular hyperbola. These are illustrated on Figure 12. Great care, however, must be taken in estimating elasticity from the slope of the curve, beyond the extreme limiting cases; when segments of curves appear on different portions of the graph, the relative slope tells nothing

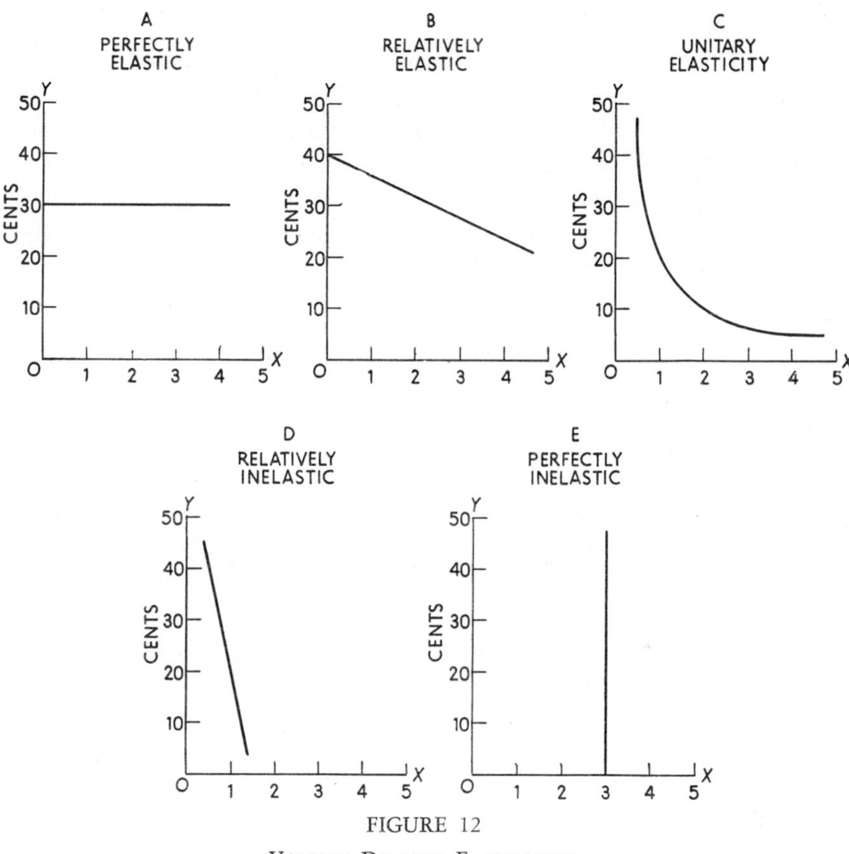

FIGURE 12

VARIOUS DEMAND ELASTICITIES

about elasticity. A straight line, sloping demand curve will change elasticity continuously along its course.

Determinants of Elasticity

The elasticity of demand for a commodity depends primarily upon the ease of substitution of this commodity for other goods in the satisfaction of wants. When several commodities are regarded by consumers as more or less equally desirable for the satisfaction of particular wants, the demand schedules for each of the goods will be elastic, since changes in their relative prices will cause substantial shifting of relative purchases of the various goods. Thus increases in orange prices will cause many consumers to purchase apples or bananas instead of oranges, and the sales of oranges will drop substantially. When no satisfactory substitutes are available, price changes will have relatively little effect upon the quantity demanded.

Elasticity is likewise affected by the satiability of the want for which the good is being acquired, or, in terms of utility, the rate of decline in marginal utility as additional units of the good are acquired. If the want is quickly satiated and thus the marginal utility—or, in alternative terms, the marginal rate of substitution—falls rapidly, the demand will be less elastic than it would be if the marginal utility fell more slowly, as the income effect on the commodity will be slight; the income freed by the price decline will be used to buy other goods. The marginal utility of bread, for example, appears to fall more quickly, for most persons, than the marginal utility of various forms of recreation. The possibility of alternate uses—that is, the ability to use the good to satisfy other wants than that for which initial units are acquired—lessens the rate of decline in marginal utility. The desire for salt is very quickly satisfied, and there are few alternate uses, under ordinary circumstances. These considerations, coupled with the fact that no direct substitutes are available, render the consumer demand for the product very inelastic.

Substitutability, and thus elasticity, are affected by the closely related considerations of durability of the product and the time interval for which the schedule is relevant. When goods can be used for a number of years, individual consumers are not in the market for additional units for a considerable period of time after they have made a purchase. But if the goods are not durable, the consumers can adjust their rates of purchase at any time and thus are more sensitive to price changes. As a consequence, demand schedules for durable goods are more elastic over a longer period of time than they are in a short interval. The demand for nondurable goods used in conjunction with durable equipment is affected in similar manner; if a person has installed a coal-burning furnace, he cannot shift from coal to oil without substantial additional expense. Thus changes in relative prices of coal and oil will not cause immediate replacement of one fuel by the other. But, once the furnace requires replacement, substitution of the cheaper fuel for the more expensive one, and of one type of furnace for the other, may occur.

Apart from the consideration of durability, the importance of habit in consumer purchasing causes the demands for many goods, durable or not, to become more elastic over a period of time than they are in a shorter period. Persons become accustomed to buying certain articles, and do not reconsider at frequent intervals the desirability of continuing or adjusting certain purchases. Thus price changes may bring little immediate response. But over a longer period there is greater chance of reconsideration of the desirability of the purchases and of seeking substitutes, and as a consequence, the effects of the changes in relative prices will become greater. Thus, if cheese falls greatly in price, most consumers at first will not consider replacing butter or oleomargarine by cheese. But if the price remains at the low level over a period of time, more and more persons may revise their purchases to take advantage of the low price of cheese. Furthermore, over a longer period, persons are more likely to become informed about the existence of the lower prices.

The elasticity of the total demand schedule for a commodity is determined by the elasticities of the various individual schedules which comprise it. The fact must be recognized, however, that, as the price of a good falls, much of the increase in quantity demanded may come from new purchasers—persons not buying the good at all at higher prices. These may be ones with relatively low incomes or ones whose preferences for the good are relatively low. For some commodities the demand schedules of individual buyers are extremely inelastic throughout most of their ranges; yet the total demand is elastic, since many additional buyers will enter the market at lower prices. Thus the demand for electric refrigerators has been relatively elastic, even though very few individuals will buy more than one regardless of the price; at lower prices many persons acquire the product who would not do so at all at higher price levels.

Substitutability and the Nature of Indifference Curves[8]

The effects of substitutability upon the elasticity of demand may be illustrated by the indifference curve technique. The greater the ease with which the commodity in question can be substituted for others (and other goods may be substituted for it), the less will be the curvature of the indifference curve; that is, the curve will more closely approach a straight line. The smaller the curvature, the greater the extent to which the point of tangency of the price line with an indifference

[8] This section should be omitted if the previous section on indifference curves has not been covered.

curve will shift to the right when the price of the good falls, and thus the greater the extent to which the purchases of the commodity will increase in response to the price reduction. If the commodity has poor substitutes, the curvature (the convexity) will be sharp, and the point of tangency will shift only slightly.

The significance of the curvature is illustrated on Figures 13 A and B. In order to show the significance of substitutability it is necessary to eliminate the income effect; this is done, graphically, by drawing a price line (p') which is parallel to the new price line (P) after the

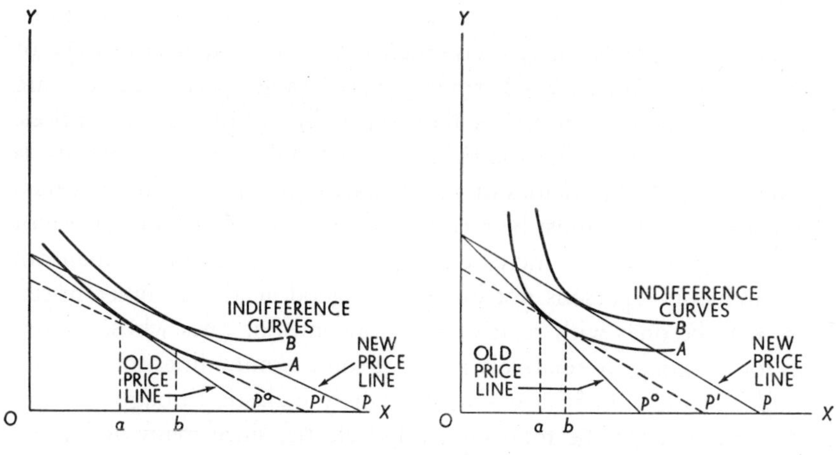

FIGURE 13

THE SIGNIFICANCE OF SUBSTITUTABILITY FOR THE RESPONSE OF THE QUANTITY OF COMMODITY X PURCHASED TO PRICE CHANGES

A — HIGH SUBSTITUTABILITY

B — LOW SUBSTITUTABILITY

price change, at a location such that it is tangent to the old indifference curve (A). On 13A, on which the curvature of the indifference curve is slight because the commodities are good substitutes, the tangency of p' (at b) is far to the right of the original tangency of p° (at a). On 13B, on which the curvature is great because the commodities are poor substitutes, the point of tangency is moved only slightly (a to b).

The same relationships may be expressed in terms of marginal rates of substitution. If this rate falls rapidly, as it will if the commodities are poor substitutes, a decline in the price of one commodity will result in only a relatively slight readjustment in quantities of the two goods purchased to restore equality of the price ratios and the marginal rate of substitution. If the marginal rate of substitution falls slowly, a much greater readjustment in relative purchases will be necessary.

THE LEVELS OF DEMAND SCHEDULES

Distinct from the questions of the nature and elasticity of demand schedules is that of the determinants of the magnitudes or levels of the schedules, and the causes of changes in these magnitudes. In general the determinants of the levels of the schedules are the "givens" upon which particular schedules are based, noted earlier in the chapter. Changes in these givens, which are assumed to remain constant in the interval for which a given schedule is relevant, cause shifts in the schedules.

Consumer Preferences

In the first place, the quantities of various commodities purchased, at particular prices, are dependent upon the intensity of consumer preferences for the commodities. Individual preference patterns are conditioned by many elements. They are dependent in part, for example, upon the customs and traditions of the period. Explanation of the development of these goes far beyond the scope of economics, and for purposes of the present analysis they must be accepted as given data. Within the general range outlined by the consumption patterns socially acceptable in the period, individual choices depend upon the reactions of individuals to various alternatives. Explanations of these reactions are likewise beyond the scope of economics. Two observations can be noted, however.

In the first place, habit is of great importance; persons becoming accustomed to the use of certain goods may not change until substantial impetus is applied, even though they have no continuing preference for the good, in the sense that they will be equally well satisfied with a substitute, once they do make the change. The reliance upon habit is not without advantage, since habit is a great saver of time and effort, allowing the time to be used for more profitable pursuits. The other observation is that individuals are subject to external influences in regard to their preferences; the latter are not iron-clad controls over behavior with which persons are born. Producers frequently find it profitable to exercise deliberate influence over consumer preferences; through advertising they seek to convince the consumer of the superiority of some commodities over others or the desirability of satisfying one want instead of another.

Since relative preferences for one good compared to those for others are of significance in determining the height of demand for the good, changes in relative preferences result in shifts in the demand schedules. A person may grow tired of one type of recreation and try another type.

Or he may become dissatisfied with the type of fuel that he is using to heat his home and shift to another variety. Changes in occupation, number of dependents, state of health, and age will alter preferences. The birth of a baby may cause a family to spend less on recreation and more on food. Illness will lessen the purchases of some commodities and increase the demand for medicine. A cold winter will increase the demand for fuel. Changes in customs and traditions will affect preferences; changing styles in clothing, for example, produce significant modifications in the demand for various types. Successful advertising campaigns will divert purchases from some products to others. Development of new products draws consumer preference away from other goods; the automobile very quickly eliminated consumers' preferences—and demand—for buggies.[9]

Incomes

A second major determinant of demand is the level of household incomes.

Changes in incomes are inevitably reflected in changes in the purchases of various goods, the degree of change varying widely with different types of goods. Some articles, such as basic necessities, show very little response, the quantities purchased being little greater if incomes are high than if they are low; with others the response is very substantial, the purchases increasing at a faster rate than income, at least within certain limits. The extent of the response of consumer purchases to an increase in consumer incomes is known as *income elasticity.* As suggested above, this elasticity for most goods is positive, since increased incomes enable persons to satisfy their wants more fully by the acquisition of additional goods.

However, there are certain commodities, known as *inferior goods,* of such character that the demand for them falls as individual incomes rise. These goods are purchased only because the buyers cannot afford higher-priced substitutes, which they would prefer for particular wants. When incomes rise, purchases of these goods are reduced, and the higher-priced better-quality goods are bought instead.[10] Thus for ex-

[9] Preferences are also subject to government control. The use of liquor or opium may be prohibited; the government may provide certain goods (education, for example) which some persons would not otherwise obtain.

[10] With the use of an indifference-curve graph, income elasticity can be illustrated by placing a succession of price lines (representing successively greater expenditures) on a given pattern of indifference curves and then drawing a line (known as the "income-consumption" or "expenditures" curve) connecting the points of tangency of successive price lines with indifference curves. For most commodities ("normal" commodities), the

ample, when persons' incomes rise, they will buy less stew meat and more sirloin steak; they will reduce their purchases of cheap clothes and buy expensive ones; they will quit traveling by bus and acquire their own cars or make long-distance trips by air or Pullman.

The influence of changes in income upon demand may not be manifest immediately after the income change. Empirical evidence suggests that expenditure patterns tend to lag behind income changes, and thus are influenced not solely by the income of the current period, but also by income of the preceding periods. Accordingly, the income elasticity of demand tends to be greater over a longer period of time than it is immediately after income has changed.

The influence of income changes upon demand is affected by the marginal propensities to save of the consumers. If the propensities are low, a large portion of additional income received will be used to purchase additional goods, and thus, in general, income elasticities will be high. If the propensities are, on the average, high, most of the additional income will be saved, and demand schedules for commodities will be affected only slightly.

Prices of Other Commodities

The third major determinant of the height of a particular demand schedule is the level of prices of other commodities. The influence of the prices of other goods is dependent upon the extent to which the latter can be substituted for the particular commodity; price levels of close sub-

---

income-consumption curve will slope upward to the right, since, with successively higher incomes and expenditures, more of the commodity will be purchased (*IC*, Figure 14).

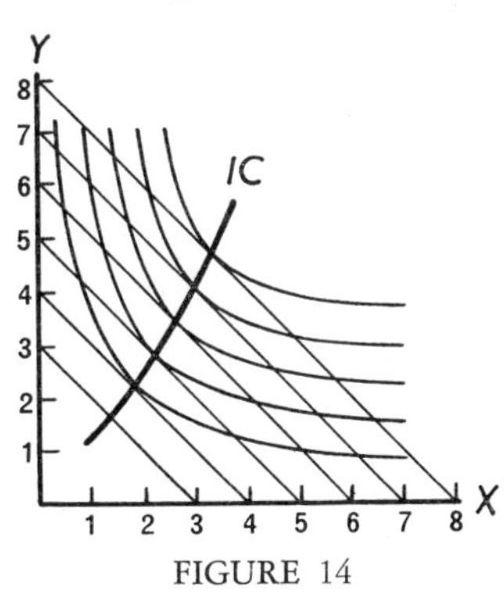

FIGURE 14

INCOME-CONSUMPTION CURVE
A "Normal" Commodity

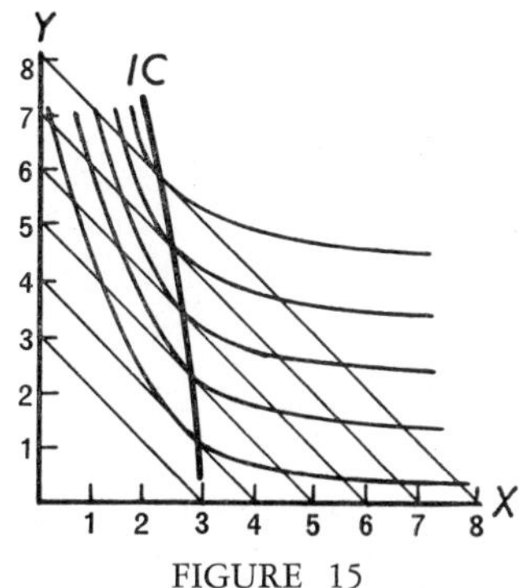

FIGURE 15

INCOME-CONSUMPTION CURVE
An "Inferior" Commodity

In the case of "inferior" goods, the curve will slope upward to the left (Figure 15). The inferior good is plotted on the *X* axis.

stitutes are far more significant than those of goods not directly substitutable. The demand for oranges is affected much more by the prevailing prices for apples than by those for theater tickets.

Shifts in the prices of other goods, especially of substitutes, will alter the demand schedule for a good; a precise measurement of the influence of the price of one good on the demand for another is provided by the concept of *cross-elasticity of demand*—the relationship of the percentage change in the quantity demanded of one good which occurs in response to a particular percentage change in the price of another good, the price of the first good remaining constant. As a formula:

$$\text{Cross-elasticity of demand for } X \text{ in terms of the price of } Y = \frac{\text{Percentage change in quantity of } X}{\text{Percentage change in price of } Y},$$

or (with the use of an arc formula)

$$expy = \frac{Qx - Qx'}{Qx + Qx'} \div \frac{Py - Py'}{Py + Py'}.$$

The nature of the cross-elasticity of demand between two goods depends upon the relative influences of the income and substitution effects. When the price of one good falls, the income effect, representing the freeing of purchasing power by the price reduction, encourages the purchasing of more units of both commodities. But on the other hand, the fact that the price of the first commodity has fallen relative to the price of the second encourages persons to substitute the first for the second, and thus to buy less of the second. If the substitution effect outweighs the income effect, the cross-elasticity is positive, and the two commodities are regarded as substitutes for each other. The higher the figure of cross-elasticity, the greater is the ease of substitution. If the articles are perfect substitutes (and thus essentially the same commodity, from the standpoint of the users) the cross-elasticity is infinite.

There are two cases in which cross-elasticity will be negative, in the sense that a decline in the price of one good will lead to an increase in the quantity of the other good purchased. One situation is that in which the income effect of the price change outweighs the substitution effect; as the price of X falls, if little substitution occurs and the demand for X is inelastic, less total purchasing power will be spent on X than before, and thus the amount of Y purchased will increase.

The other case of negative cross-elasticity is that of *complementary* goods—those of such nature that increased use of one necessitates the use of additional units of the other, as, for example, greater use of bread requires the purchase of additional butter. When two goods are complementary, a decline in the price of the one, by stimulating increased use of the good, will raise the marginal utility of the other good and increase the quantity of the latter purchased. The purchases of some other commodities (or savings) must, of course, decline to free the necessary purchasing power.

Expectations about Future Prices

The height of a demand schedule is affected by the expectations which persons have in regard to future prices. This influence is, in a sense, transitory, since consumers will not continue to buy in anticipation of future wants indefinitely, nor will they continue to postpone purchases of desired goods if expected price decreases fail to materialize. But, at any time, expectations may be of substantial importance, and changes in them may produce major shifts in demand schedules. If consumers commence to expect price increases, they may buy large quantities in anticipation of the increases and cause substantial increases in the demand schedules. If decreases come to be expected, buyers may reduce current purchases drastically. Changes in expectations *caused* by price changes have been discussed previously; these are influences affecting the elasticity of the demand schedules rather than their height.

Number of Potential Consumers

A final consideration affecting the total demand schedules is that of the number of consumers in the market. The number depends in part upon the population and in part upon the accessibility of various persons to the market. Thus population growth will increase total demand, as will reductions in import controls or similar barriers to trade, which allow more persons to enter a particular market.

Significance of Demand Schedules for the Functioning of the Economy

The full significance of consumer demand for the functioning of the economic system cannot be realized until cost-supply considerations can be considered in conjunction with demand forces. A brief summary statement is possible, however. In general, production is directed toward those commodities for which sufficient demand exists to allow profitable production; the volume of output of various goods produced must be adjusted in terms of available demand if production is to be profitable. Consumer demand exercises a major influence upon producer demand, the demand by business firms for units of factors of production, and thus affects both the allocation of factor units to various lines of production and the distribution of income among the owners of various types of factor units. Producer demand is discussed in Chapter 13.

From the viewpoint of the individual producer, total demand for the commodity which he is producing is a major influence controlling the volume which he can sell at various possible prices. The elasticity of the total demand schedule likewise affects the response of his sales to changes in his price.[11] There are, of course, other influences, such as the reactions of his competitors to his price changes.

Finally, knowledge of the total demand schedules is important for certain types of government policy. If the government seeks to lessen fluctuations in farm prices by providing information to farmers about trends of prices of various commodities, a knowledge of elasticity of demand for the product and of trends in demand are necessary for the aims of the program to be accomplished. If, wisely or unwisely, the government attempts to control directly the levels of farm prices by the purchasing of surpluses or the use of crop-control programs, knowledge of demand schedules is essential. The amount of output reduction necessary to bring a price to a certain level depends upon the elasticity of demand.

The Collection of Data of Demand Schedules

At any time a certain demand schedule exists for each commodity, in the sense that, if different various prices prevail, certain quantities will be purchased. It is impossible, however, to determine with any high degree of accuracy what the schedule actually is. In the case of most goods, the total sales in particular markets with existing prices can be ascertained; many data of this type are collected by various private and governmental agencies at the present time. But the figures of quantities that would be demanded at other prices can only be estimated with the aid of statistics of sales at various prices in the past. The greatest care must be used, however, in interpreting these statistics, since the changes in sales from one period to another are due not only to price changes but also to shifts in the various determinants of demand. Incomes, preferences, prices of other goods, and expectations are constantly changing. In part it is possible to isolate the effects of these other changes by various statistical techniques. But such techniques are by no means entirely accurate or complete. Particularly, there is no possible way of determining satisfactorily the effects on sales of changes in preferences

[11] Except in pure competition.

which occurred during the period for which data are available. Thus statistical estimates of demand schedules, of necessity, involve a substantial margin of error. But such work is of great value in providing additional information about demand behavior.

SELECTED REFERENCES

NORRIS, RUBY T. *The Theory of Consumer's Demand.* New Haven: Yale University Press, 1941.

The most complete modern study of consumer demand.

HICKS, J. R. *Value and Capital,* chaps. i and ii. 2d ed. Oxford: Oxford University Press, 1946.

A detailed presentation of the indifference-curve approach.

STIGLER, G. J. *Theory of Price,* chaps. iv and v. rev. ed. New York: Macmillan, 1952.

BAIN, J. S. *Pricing, Distribution, and Employment,* chap. 2. rev. ed. New York: Holt, 1953.

MARSHALL, A. *Principles of Economics,* Book III. 8th ed. London: Macmillan, 1936.

The classic presentation of the marginal-utility approach.

FRIEDMAN, M. "The Marshallian Demand Curve," *Journal of Political Economy,* Vol. LVII (December, 1949), pp. 463–95.

A detailed re-examination of traditional demand concepts.

MORGANSTERN, O. "Demand Theory Reconsidered," *Quarterly Journal of Economics,* Vol. LXII (February, 1948), pp. 165–201.

An advanced analysis of demand concepts.

SCITOVSKY, T. *Welfare and Competition,* chap. iii. Chicago: Richard D. Irwin, Inc., 1951.

STIGLER, G. J., and BOULDING, K. E. (editors). *Readings in Price Theory,* chaps. i–iv. Homewood, Ill.: Richard D. Irwin, Inc., 1952.

Reprints of articles on demand theory.

QUESTIONS

1. Distinguish between the terms "demand" and "quantity demanded."
2. What difficulties are encountered in establishing a precise concept of total demand for such products as refrigerators?
3. Distinguish between a "change in demand" and a "change in quantity demanded."
4. Illustrate graphically a change in demand and a change in quantity demanded.
5. Why can a decline in price not be regarded as a cause of an increase in demand?
6. From what assumptions is the Law of Demand derived?

7. What are the two general approaches to the explanation of the Law of Demand?
8. What is "marginal utility"?
9. Explain the Law of Diminishing Marginal Utility, indicating the assumptions upon which it is based.
10. Explain the rule of optimum allocation of income among the purchase of various goods, in terms of marginal utility.
11. Distinguish clearly between the income effect and the substitution effect of a price decline upon the quantity of the good demanded.
12. What does an indifference curve show?
13. What is the marginal rate of substitution?
14. Suppose that a person is now buying 6 oranges and 4 apples a week; if he buys only 5 oranges, he must buy 7 apples if he is to maintain the same level of satisfaction. What is the marginal rate of substitution of oranges for apples? Apples for oranges?
15. Why is an indifference curve convex to the point of origin?
16. Explain the Principle of Diminishing Marginal Rate of Substitution. How does it differ from the Law of Diminishing Marginal Utility?
17. What controls the convexity of an indifference curve? When will the "curve" be a straight line?
18. What is meant by the "price line," in the indifference curve analysis? Under what circumstances is it a straight line? Why?
19. Why is the optimum point for the consumer at the point of tangency between a price line and an indifference curve?
20. Explain the optimum allocation of consumer expenditures among various commodities, in terms of indifference curves and the marginal rate of substitution.
21. Explain how the traditional demand curve can be derived from an indifference curve graph.
22. Utilize the indifference curve technique to distinguish between the income effect and the substitution effect of a price decline.
23. What advantages does the indifference-curve approach to the explanation of demand have over the marginal-utility approach?
24. Explain carefully the concept of elasticity of demand, and distinguish between elasticity of demand and the slope of the demand curve.
25. On September 26, 1952, the Montreal Transportation Commission raised city streetcar and bus fares from 25 cents to 30 cents, for three tickets. In the following 20-day period, the volume of business fell to 19,250,000 from a figure of 20,580,000 for the same period in the previous year.
    a) Determine the elasticity of demand, using the arc formula, assuming that the entire loss of business was due to the fare change.
    b) Why might this assumption not be a realistic one?
    c) Why is the arc formula the appropriate one in this case?
26. With an elastic demand, does total outlay rise or fall as price falls? Why?

27. Explain the behavior of total outlay as price changes, when demand is (*a*) unitary, (*b*) inelastic.
28. Explain the concepts of perfectly elastic and perfectly inelastic demand schedules.
29. What are the primary determinants of elasticity of demand for a commodity?
30. Why is elasticity of demand for a product likely to be greater over a long-run period than it is immediately after a price change?
31. What are the primary "givens" upon which a particular demand schedule is based?
32. Distinguish carefully between the concepts of price elasticity, income elasticity, and cross-elasticity.
33. What is an "inferior" good?
34. In the depression years of the 'thirties, some city transit systems experienced an increase in business, despite unemployment and low incomes, even though the population of the area was not growing. How can you explain this?
35. Which types of commodities will have a high, positive income elasticity?
36. As a result of an increase in the price of coffee from 80 cents to 95 cents per pound, the sales of tea increase from 500,000 pounds per week to 600,000 pounds. What is the cross-elasticity of demand?
37. Under what circumstances is cross-elasticity negative? Positive and very high?
38. What are complementary goods?

Chapter 6 DEMAND FOR THE PRODUCT OF AN INDIVIDUAL SELLER

The demand schedule which influences the price and output policy of a particular firm is not the total demand for the product, as such, but the demand schedule for the product from this particular firm—the schedule of the amounts which buyers will purchase from this firm at various possible prices charged for the product. The total demand schedule is significant to the firm only insofar as it influences the demand schedule confronting this particular firm. A bakery, for example, is not concerned directly with the total demand for bread in the area, but with the schedule of the amounts which customers will buy from it, at various possible prices.

This schedule, like a total demand schedule, consists of alternative possibilities of the potential quantities which would be purchased from the firm at various possible prices charged. Thus if a bakery charges 15 cents for a loaf of bread, it may sell 750 loaves a day; if it charges 20 cents, it may sell 200 loaves. At 25 cents it might sell only 50 loaves; at a 10-cent price it might sell 3000 loaves. The seller does not know precisely the magnitudes of his demand schedule, but he must base his policies upon some estimate of them.

THE NATURE AND ELASTICITY OF DEMAND SCHEDULES FOR THE PRODUCT OF A FIRM

When an individual seller adjusts his price, changes in his sales will arise not only from shifts in total usage of the product, but also as a result of transfer of customers between himself and his competitors. The extent of this transfer, in turn, will depend in large measure upon the nature of competition in the market. The analysis of the demand schedules for the products of individual sellers, therefore, must be developed in relation to the various principal types of market situations.

The Demand for the Product of a Seller in a Purely Competitive Market

In purely competitive markets, the demand schedule for the product of a firm appears to the seller to be perfectly elastic. That is, at one price, namely, the prevailing market price, and at any figure lower than this, he can sell as much as he can possibly place on the market. But at any higher price he can sell nothing at all. Thus a wheat farmer can dispose of his entire crop at the current market price, and he knows that any change which he makes in the quantity of his output and sales will have no effect upon the price. He likewise knows that he cannot dispose of his wheat at any figure higher than the market price. The demand schedule for his product would appear as shown in Table 12, and illustrated graphically on Figure 16, assuming the current market price of the product to be $1.50. The farmer could also sell as much as he wishes at any price under $1.50, but obviously he would not sell at such a price, since he can dispose of his entire stock at $1.50. Accordingly, the quantities which could be sold at prices lower than $1.50 are not shown on Figure 16. The demand curve for the product of the firm appears as a straight horizontal line at the level of the current market price, since the firm can sell as much as it wishes (within limits of practical output expansion) at that price, but nothing at any higher prices.

TABLE 12

DEMAND SCHEDULE FOR WHEAT FROM ONE PARTICULAR SELLER

Price (Dollars)	Quantity Demanded (Bushels of Wheat)
0.50	Infinite*
1.00	Infinite*
1.50	Infinite*
2.00	0
2.50	0

* The quantities which can be sold appear to the seller to be infinite at these prices. Actually, of course, the amounts are not truly infinite, because if the seller increased output and sales far enough, eventually he would place on the market such a large quantity that price would be affected. But when this occurred the market would no longer be purely competitive. Within the realm of pure competition, the quantities which can be sold at these prices are infinite.

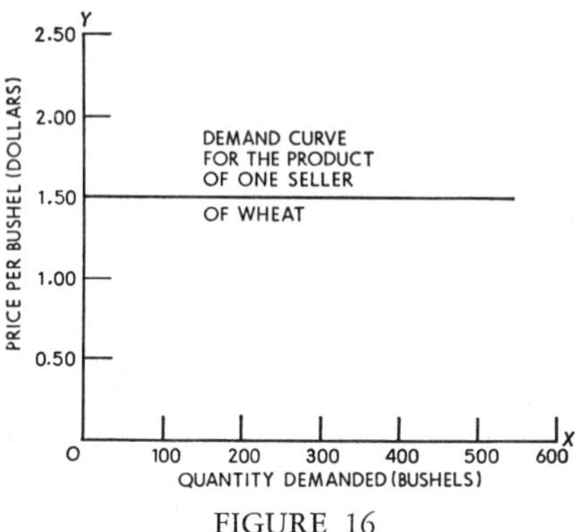

FIGURE 16

DEMAND CURVE FOR THE PRODUCT OF AN INDIVIDUAL WHEAT FARMER

How is it possible for these demand schedules for the product of an individual seller in pure competition to be perfectly elastic, when the total demand schedules for the products are not? Why is it possible for a wheat farmer to be able to sell as much wheat as he pleases without affecting the market price, when the total quantity of wheat demanded at each price is a finite amount, and larger quantities will be purchased only at lower prices? The situation is possible because of the very large number of sellers, all selling identical products. Each producer is selling such a small fraction of the total supply that a change in his own sales has such an infinitesimally small effect on market price that he does not realize that it has any effect at all; in other words, the effect is imperceptible to him. Thus his demand schedule appears to be perfectly elastic to him, over the range of output in which he could possibly produce.

The level of a firm's demand schedule in pure competition (as distinguished from its elasticity) depends entirely on the current market price. If the latter is $1.50, the firm can sell an apparently infinite amount at this price, but nothing at higher prices; if the price is $2.00, an infinite amount can be sold at a $2.00 figure. The level is completely independent of the firm's own efforts and shifts constantly as the market price changes.

The Demand for the Product of a Monopolist

When one firm possesses a complete monopoly position, the demand schedule for its product is identical with the demand schedule for the commodity, and the elasticity of the schedule is controlled entirely by the determinants of the elasticity of the total demand. The demand schedule confronting a power company is identical with the total demand schedule for electric power in the area served exclusively by the company. The firm is free of any possible shifting of customers to or from competing firms, and of any possible reactions in the prices of other firms arising as a result of price changes which it makes. No firm is completely isolated from the actions of producers of substitute commodities, and the demand schedules of monopolists are by no means perfectly inelastic, since price increases will cause purchasers to shift to substitute commodities. But the absence of other firms producing the same product, or similar brands of the same class of product, places the monopolist firm in a position in which it can act independently of any possible reactions of other firms to its policies, and renders the demand schedule for its product much less elastic than it would be if there were other firms in the industry, acting independently of one another.

The Demand for the Product of a Seller in a Market of Monopolistic Competition

Monopolistic competition is characterized by differentiation of product, with a substantial number of sellers in the industry acting independently of one another. The product differentiation has the effect of attaching some of each firm's customers to it; the differentiation by the other firms in the industry has the same effect upon their customers. However, since the various brands of the product are good substitutes for one another, these attachments are not too strong, and customers will shift, given sufficient inducement. There may likewise be numerous purchasers who pay no attention to the differentiation, being completely indifferent with respect to the brands which they buy.

Because of the differentiation, each seller has a finite demand at each particular price; no longer can an individual firm sell an unlimited amount at a particular price. Price increases above existing levels will not cause complete loss of sales, since some of the customers will continue to buy the product, despite the higher price, because of the preferences which they have for it. A price reduction will not draw all of the customers from the other firms because of the preferences of some buyers for the products of these sellers. Thus the demand schedules for the products of each firm are not perfectly elastic. However, since the various brands are close substitutes for one another, and since the firms are assumed to act completely independently of one another, the elasticity is likely to be relatively great. Any price increase will cause substantial (but not complete) loss of business to competitors, plus some reduction in consumer use, while a price reduction will draw substantial amounts of business from competing firms, as well as encouraging additional consumer use.

It is assumed, in monopolistic competition, that firms do not anticipate that price changes which they make will lead competitors to make changes as well. This assumption is based upon the fact that this type of market is characterized by such a large number of sellers that the effect of a price change by one firm upon the sales of other firms will not be sufficiently great to cause them to readjust their own prices. For example, if there are 1000 firms in an industry, and all are affected equally by a price reduction of a particular firm, a 10-fold increase in sales by the firm as a result of a price decrease would cause each competitor to lose only 1⁄10 of 1 per cent of its sales. If the effects on other firms are distributed unevenly, so that their sales are affected sufficiently that some do readjust prices, the firm will soon become aware of this, and the situation becomes one of oligopoly, discussed in the following section.

Elasticity. The exact degree of elasticity will depend upon two factors: (1) the degree of differentiation of product, or, in other words, the strength of the preferences of the consumers for the brands of particular firms, and (2) the elasticity of total demand for the product. The former determines the extent to which customers will shift among firms when relative prices change, while the latter measures the extent to which consumer use will change in response to changes in the price of the product. The degree of differentiation varies widely among different products; customers appear to be more closely attached to particular makes of cars than they are to particular brands of gasoline; to certain restaurants to a greater extent than to certain gasoline stations.

The Height of the Schedules. The height of the demand schedule confronting a particular seller in monopolistic competition, that is, the actual amounts which he can sell at various prices, depends upon several considerations. In the first place, the firm's potential sales depend upon the total demand for the product; obviously, the greater the total demand for bread, the more bread that any one bakery can sell, given the number of firms in the industry. Secondly, the potential sales by any one firm depend upon the number of competitors, given the total demand. The larger the number of sellers, the smaller the potential sales for each firm at each possible price level. Thirdly, the extent of preference of the customers for the particular brand, compared to the preferences for other brands of the product, is a factor of importance. The greater the degree of preference, the greater is the share of the total market which the firm can obtain. Finally, the prices charged by competing firms is significant; the higher the level of the competitors' prices, the more that the firm can sell at each particular price.

Changes in Demand. Changes in these determinants will of course shift the demand schedule for the product of the firm. If, for example, the total demand for bread rises, the demand schedules of at least some of the individual sellers of bread must rise. If the number of competing firms rises, on the other hand, the demand schedule for the product of the firm will fall, since the total volume of business will be spread over a large number of sellers. The entry of new firms into an industry does not in itself increase the total demand for the product, except to the extent to which some potential buyers gain sufficient preference for the product of the new firm that they will buy it, whereas they would not buy any if only the older brands were available.[1] Thirdly, increased preference for one brand will increase the demand for that brand; if one bakery, by successful advertising, convinces numbers of customers that its brand is preferable, its sales will rise. Finally, an in-

[1] For example, the establishment of a new neighborhood grocery store will lead persons to buy some additional groceries which they would not take the trouble to go to a more distant store to obtain.

crease in the prices charged by the competitors, if widespread, will inevitably increase the demand for the product of this firm, just as increases in the prices of substitutes will increase the total demand for a product.

The Demand for the Product of an Oligopolist

The primary characteristic of oligopoly is that of mutual interdependence among the various firms—a recognition by each firm that changes which it makes in its own prices are likely to produce changes in the prices charged by competing firms. Mutual interdependence, in turn, is a product of smallness of numbers. Whenever an industry is dominated by a small number of firms, any change in price by one firm has such a significant effect upon the sales of other firms that they will inevitably react to the price changes. As indicated in Chapter 4, oligopoly is very widespread in the contemporary economy; many lines of manufacturing are dominated by a few large firms, and in retailing a particular market area often contains such a small number of firms that price interdependency develops. Even if an industry contains a large number of firms, mutual interdependence will develop, at least on the part of some of the firms, if a few firms produce a large portion of the total output.

Any realization by a firm that competitors will follow price changes which it makes will reduce the elasticity of the demand schedule for its product. If a firm knows that price increases will be followed by other firms, it realizes that the increases will cause much smaller reductions in sales than would occur if competitors left their prices unchanged. If price reductions are expected to cause reductions by competitors, the firm will expect a much smaller increase in sales than would occur if the other firms did not meet the reductions. There are, of course, a large number of possible situations from the standpoint of the exact degree of mutual interdependence and thus of exact reactions expected by a firm in response to its own price changes. Only some of the major possibilities can be considered; the relative significance of these various cases cannot be assessed without further empirical study of actual conditions prevailing in various markets. These cases are presented as possible tools of analysis for use in particular situations, the applicability of a particular case in a given situation being determinable only by empirical study of actual conditions in the situation.

1. *Complete Oligopoly.* In the first place, if mutual interdependence is complete, each firm will be certain that any price change which it makes in either direction will be followed exactly by all other firms.

In such a situation, shifting of customers among firms in response to price changes would be virtually eliminated as a factor affecting elasticity, and the elasticity of the demand schedule confronting the firm would be dependent entirely upon the elasticity of the total demand schedule, as in the case of complete monopoly. It is doubtful if this case is of great importance in American industry, but it serves as a useful limiting case in the analysis.

Closely related is the case of complete oligopoly produced by collusion, in which all firms agree upon the price to be charged. In this situation, the demand schedules of the individual sellers are of no concern for price policy, since there is no independent price determination; the demand schedule which is taken into consideration by the firms as a group is the total demand schedule for the product.

2. *Price Leadership.* Secondly, and probably more commonly, mutual interdependence may be complete so far as reactions to changes by one firm in the industry are concerned, but not with respect to changes by other firms. This is the case of price leadership, in which one firm is accepted as the price leader. All initial price changes are made by this firm, the changes being followed by the other firms, which make no independent price changes of their own. As a consequence, the demand schedule for the product of the price leader, the one upon whose actions price policy of all the firms is based, has the same elasticity as the total demand for the product. The schedules of the other firms are much more elastic, since changes by these firms will not be followed by others; but these schedules are of no consequence for price determination, since price decisions are not based upon them. They merely indicate the amounts which these firms can sell at the existing price, the latter determined on the basis of the schedule of the price leader. In practice price leaders often recognize that other firms will follow only within limits, and thus only segments of their individual demand schedules have the same elasticity as the total demand. But it is these segments which are of importance for price determination, since the leader is unlikely to venture out into the range of the schedule in which some firms may not follow.

3. *The Kinked Demand Curve.* Thirdly, in some cases, the price interdependence may be greater for price reductions than for price increases. A price reduction may be followed by other firms, whereas a price increase may not be. For example, if one grocery store reduces the the price of coffee from 90¢ to 80¢ a pound, and leaves it at this lower figure, the other stores in the market area are very likely to cut. But if the first store raises the price to $1.00, it is most unlikely that the other

firms will follow. In this case the firm's demand curve will contain a sharp kink or bend at the level of the current market price, the demand being elastic above this price (since competitors will not follow the higher prices, and thus the firms will lose sales heavily to them), and inelastic below the price (since competitors will follow the reductions, and thus there will be relatively little increase in sales). This type of demand curve for the product of a firm is shown in Figure 17.

FIGURE 17

THE KINKED DEMAND CURVE FOR THE PRODUCT OF AN INDIVIDUAL SELLER

4. *Dominance of Uncertainty.* Finally, and perhaps most typically in oligopoly situations, firms may expect some reactions on the part of competitors to changes in their own policies, but they may be uncertain about the exact nature and extent of these reactions. Accordingly, they cannot estimate at all precisely the elasticity of the demand schedules for their products. For example, if a seller contemplates a price reduction, he may be aware that some competitors are likely to make reductions. But he may be uncertain about the number which will reduce, the magnitude of the reductions, and the length of time which will elapse before they make readjustments. Thus, in a sense, in such circumstances, a firm has no determinate demand schedule for its product, but, rather, several possible schedules, based upon various assumptions about competitors' reactions. Regardless of these uncertainties, however, the firm must act; it must set some price, and in so doing, must estimate the reactions which appear to be most likely to occur. But the uncertainty itself is a consideration of importance with respect to the behavior of the firm, because it makes the firm reluctant to undertake changes in policies which appear to be profitable, but may not be if competitors' reactions are different than anticipated. The uncertainty without doubt has been a major force encouraging the making of agree-

ments among firms and the adoption of pricing methods designed to minimize the effects of uncertainty.

The Significance of Differentiation in Oligopolistic Markets. The nature of the demand schedules for the products of the individual firms in oligopolistic markets is influenced by the degree of differentiation of product. Differentiation, in itself, by attaching certain customers to each firm, tends to lessen elasticity, just as it does in conditions of monopolistic competition. An increase in price will cause less serious loss in sales to the other firms, while a reduction will have a lesser effect in increasing sales. But on the other hand, the differentiation tends to weaken the feeling of mutual interdependence, and in this manner increases elasticity. Because of the product differentiation, each firm is isolated somewhat from the effects of the price changes of competitors, and there is less likelihood that competitors will react to changes made by the firm. The fact that the prices of the various firms are likely to differ somewhat lessens the chance of exact following of any price change made by one firm. Price agreements are more difficult to make, and less necessary.

When products are standardized, and the market is one of pure oligopoly, the mutual interdependence is high, since price uniformity is essential and price-cutting has disastrous effects. Thus the standardization, while in itself creating greater elasticity, almost inevitably leads to such a high degree of co-operation, explicit or implicit, that the significant demand schedule for the determination of price is the total demand for the product.

Changes in Demand Schedules for the Products of Oligopolists. The level of the demand schedule for a firm selling under conditions of oligopoly is dependent in part upon the same factors which determine the level of the schedule of a seller in monopolistic competition: the level of total demand, the number of other firms in the industry, the degree of differentiation, and the prices charged by the other firms. Changes in any of these will, of course, shift the demand curve of the firm. But in addition, the exact nature and level of particular segments of the firm's demand schedule can be altered by changes in the degree of mutual interdependence. For example, over a period of time, firms become more certain about probable competitor reactions, and thus their demand schedules take on more predictable form. A gradual reduction in the number of competing firms is likely to increase the responsiveness of competitors to the changes made by the firm, and make the schedules less elastic. Development and acceptance of various pricing policies may increase responsiveness. On the other hand, the development of excess capacity may lessen the willingness of competitors to follow increases, while severe shortages of the good will greatly increase this willingness. It is even conceivable that in periods of shortages there may be a kink in the demand schedules in the reverse direction from the type discussed above; competitors may follow price increases but not decreases, since they are unable to supply all of their customers at present prices, or can do so only at high per unit cost.

ESTIMATED VERSUS ACTUAL DEMAND SCHEDULES OF THE FIRM

While a seller knows the volume of his sales at the present price, he lacks adequate information about the remainder of the demand schedule for his product. As a consequence, his estimated schedule, the one upon which he bases his policy, may prove to be very different from the actual schedule which confronts him, and which he can discover only by changing his prices. As indicated above, the inevitable uncertainty about the reactions of competitors which characterizes many oligopolistic markets makes the task of determining the demand schedule of the firm a particularly difficult one when a firm is selling in markets of this type. But even when markets are not oligopolistic, knowledge of sales potentialities is very inadequate. If the seller's estimate of his schedule is such that he concludes that no change in price or output is desirable, he may not realize for a long period that his estimated schedule is not the same as his actual schedule, and as a consequence, he will fail to maximize profit. A firm may fear to lower prices in the belief that the schedule is inelastic to price reductions; actually, it might be elastic, but the firm may not discover this fact for a considerable period of time.[2] On the other hand, when estimated sales schedules dictate price adjustments, the firm will soon discover whether the estimate of the schedule is correct; if it is not, further readjustments will be necessary on the basis of the schedule discovered when the price changes were made. Even in these cases, however, the firm may not ascertain the actual elasticity of the schedule over a substantial range and thus may not attain the optimum price.

What means does a firm have to increase knowledge of its demand schedule? One method is the study of actual sales data when different

[2] The entrance of a new price-cutting firm into the industry may reveal the fact that the demand schedules are more elastic than anticipated.

In the 1930's the railroads discovered that the sales schedules for passenger service were more elastic than they had estimated when they were forced by the Interstate Commerce Commission to lower fares.

prices have been charged during a period. Such study must be made with great care, since other determinants of sales—consumer incomes and preferences, prices of substitutes, weather conditions, etc.—are constantly changing. Isolation of the effects of the price change from the effects of these other changes is very difficult, but careful analysis may yield some useful information. Study of sales volumes of competitors charging different prices (when obtainable) and analysis of the nature of the market to facilitate an estimate of elasticity of total demand for the product may also be of assistance. Many large firms devote considerable effort to market research, either by their own personnel or by independent firms specializing in this work. Market research today, however, is devoted primarily to such problems as estimating sales potentials in particular areas, determining new uses and outlets for the product, discovering consumer reaction to various quality changes, checking on the effectiveness of advertising and other selling campaigns, and estimating the probable response of the firm's sales to changes in national income. Little attention has been given specifically to the problem of determining price-sales relationships, primarily because of the great difficulties involved. But much of the information obtained and techniques employed in present market research are valuable in providing further information about price-sales relationships.[3]

Another approach is the use of experimentation—the making of price changes for the deliberate purpose of discovering the effects of the changes upon sales. But firms must use this procedure with great care, as serious dangers are involved. One difficulty is introduced by the possibility that the other determinants of sales may change during the period. But far more serious is the danger that, if the change proves unprofitable, the firm may be unable to return to the old price and recover its original sales volume. Competitors may meet reductions, or even exceed them, and may not follow the change back to the earlier level. Consumer resistance to the return to the old figure may be encountered; buyers may consider that the low price is the "satisfactory" one and may shift to other brands or products when the firm attempts to raise. Experimental price increases are less dangerous than decreases, since they are unlikely to produce undesirable reactions on the part of competitors. But they may drive customers away permanently to com-

[3] See C. F. Phillips, ed., *Marketing by Manufacturers* (rev. ed.; Chicago: Richard D. Irwin, 1951), pp. 75–108; J. H. Lorie and H. V. Roberts, *Basic Methods of Marketing Research* (New York: McGraw-Hill, 1951); and R. Ferber, *Statistical Techniques in Market Research* (New York: McGraw-Hill, 1949).

peting firms. A final difficulty with experimentation is the fact that the entire effect of the price change may not be manifest for a substantial period. Buyers may not shift away immediately when prices are raised but may do so over a longer period. Reductions may cause great temporary sales increases as buyers stock up in anticipation of the return of prices to the original levels. In general, because of these problems, most firms consider experimentation with price changes to be extremely hazardous; seldom will they deliberately experiment but will make changes only when they are reasonably certain that the new prices will be more profitable than the old.[4]

REVENUE SCHEDULES

The demand schedule for the product of a firm shows the potential sales which the firm can make at various possible prices. From this schedule there can be derived the revenue schedule of the firm, which shows the potential amounts of receipts or revenue which the firm can obtain if it sells various possible quantities, at the price at which each possible quantity can be sold. These revenue sums are gross, not net; they consist of the total sums of money received from the sale of various quantities. Suppose, for example, that a service station finds that it sells an average of 5 tires of a certain type per day if it charges $12, and that in order to increase its daily sales to 6, it must lower its price to $11. Thus, if it wishes to sell an average of 5 tires per day, it must set a price of $12, and its total revenue from this product will be $60 a day. If it wishes to sell an average of 6 tires, it must set an $11 price, and will have total daily revenue of $66. If comparable data are obtained for all other possible quantities, the complete schedule of revenue can be drawn up, showing, for each possible quantity of sales, the total amount of revenue taken in.

From this data can be derived figures of average revenue per unit, and marginal revenue. *Average revenue* is ascertained by dividing total revenue by the number of units and thus, in each case, is equal to the price for which the given number of units is sold. *Marginal revenue* is the increase in total revenue resulting from the sale of additional units. In the example above, when sales were increased from 5 tires a day to 6, total revenue increased from $60 to $66, and thus by $6; this figure

[4] For an extended discussion of the problem of gaining additional information on demand schedules of firms, see Joel Dean, *Managerial Economics* (New York: Prentice-Hall, 1951), pp. 180–91.

TABLE 13

DEMAND SCHEDULE AND REVENUE SCHEDULE OF A SERVICE STATION FOR TIRES, STANDARD GRADE, PER DAY

Demand Schedule for Tires from the Firm		Revenue Schedule (Dollars)			
Price (Dollars)	Number of Tires Purchased by Customers	Number of Tires Sold	Total Revenue (Dollars)	Average Revenue	Marginal Revenue
17	0	1	16	16	16
16	1	2	30	15	14
15	2	3	42	14	12
14	3	4	52	13	10
13	4	5	60	12	8
12	5	6	66	11	6
11	6	7	70	10	4
10	7	8	72	9	2
9	8	9	72	8	0
8	9	10	70	7	−2
7	10	11	66	6	−4
6	11				

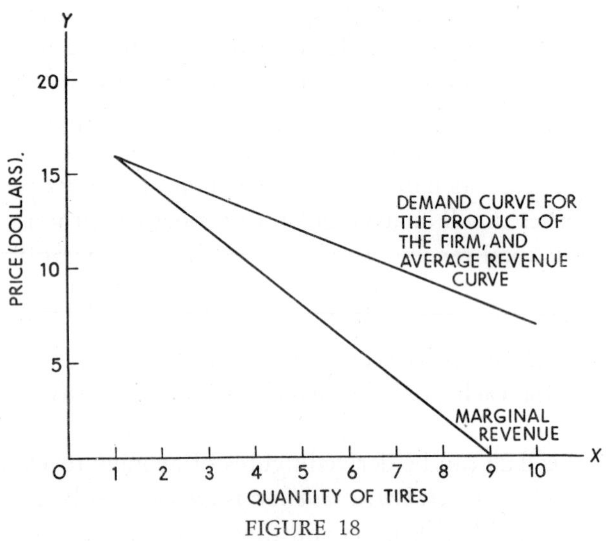

FIGURE 18

DEMAND AND REVENUE SCHEDULES FOR A FIRM SELLING TIRES

is the marginal revenue of the 6th unit. Table 13 shows the demand schedule for the product of a firm, and the revenue schedule derived from it.

The data in Table 13 are illustrated graphically in Figure 18. On the graph, the demand curve for the product of the firm and the average-revenue curve are identical, since the two schedules contain the same data, viewed in two different ways. The demand schedule shows the quantities which the firm can sell at various prices; the average-revenue schedule shows the average revenue—the price—which can be obtained from the sale of various quantities.

Revenue Schedules in Nonpurely Competitive Markets

The schedule presented in Table 13 is that of a firm selling in a nonpurely competitive market, in which the demand schedule is less than perfectly elastic. Under such circumstances, since average revenue declines as additional units are placed on the market, marginal revenue is less than average revenue for all units except the first. On the graph (Figure 18) the marginal-revenue curve is below the average-revenue curve and declines at a more rapid rate. Each additional unit sold (in the given time period) adds less to the total revenue than the price (average revenue) received for it, since the price on all units must be lowered in order to sell this unit. In the example, in order to sell 8 tires instead of 7, the firm must lower the price from $10 to $9, and thus, while the 8th tire sells for $9, it adds only $2 (the difference between $70 and $72) to the total revenue of the firm, since the 7 tires could have been sold for $10 a piece instead of $9 if only 7 had been sold.

When the demand schedule for the product of the firm is elastic (elasticity greater than 1), marginal revenue will be a positive quantity, since total revenue is greater with lower prices (and large sales volumes) than it is with higher prices (and smaller sales volumes). In other words, each additional unit sold will add a positive amount to total revenue, although, as explained in the previous paragraph, an amount smaller than the price received for it, unless the schedule is perfectly elastic. However, when a demand schedule is inelastic, marginal revenue will be a negative quantity (as with 11 tires, on Table 13), because the price reduction necessary to sell the additional unit is relatively greater than the quantity increase, and total revenue falls. The total price reduction on the units which could have been sold at the higher price exceeds the price received from the sale of the additional unit. If the demand schedule is of unitary elasticity, marginal revenue is zero. The relationship between the elasticity of the demand schedule and the positive or negative character of marginal revenue is shown on Figure 19 (page 120).

When the firm expects competitors to follow price decreases but not increases, and therefore the demand curve contains a sharp kink, the marginal-revenue curve will be discontinuous at the point of the kink, or, in terms not strictly correct mathematically, contains a vertical

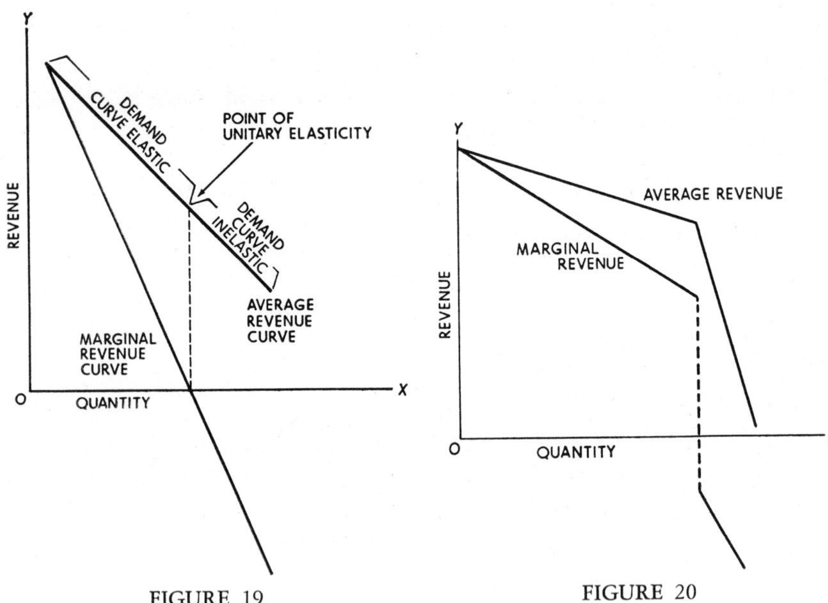

FIGURE 19

THE RELATIONSHIP BETWEEN THE ELASTICITY OF THE DEMAND SCHEDULE AND THE NATURE OF MARGINAL REVENUE

FIGURE 20

REVENUE CURVES WITH A DEMAND CURVE CONTAINING A SHARP KINK

segment, as shown on Figure 20. If the lower portion of the demand (and average-revenue) curve is actually inelastic, the lower segment of the marginal-revenue curve will be below the X axis.

Revenue Schedules in Purely Competitive Markets

The average revenue of a firm selling in a purely competitive market is the same regardless of the quantity sold, since the firm can obtain

TABLE 14

REVENUE SCHEDULE OF A FIRM SELLING IN A PURELY COMPETITIVE MARKET
(Current Market Price, $0.40)

Quantity Sold	Total Revenue	Average Revenue	Marginal Revenue
1	$0.40	$0.40	$0.40
2	0.80	0.40	0.40
3	1.20	0.40	0.40
4	1.60	0.40	0.40
5	2.00	0.40	0.40
6	2.40	0.40	0.40

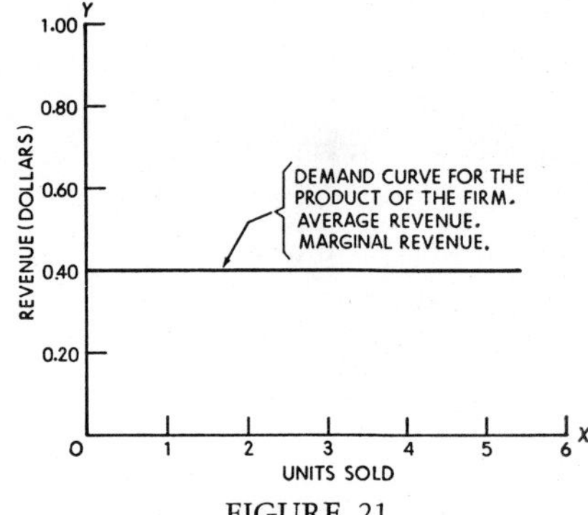

FIGURE 21

REVENUE CURVES FOR A FIRM SELLING IN A PURELY COMPETITIVE MARKET

the same price for any quantity placed on the market, and price reductions are unnecessary to sell larger quantities. Thus the average-revenue curve is a straight horizontal line at the level of the market price, and marginal revenue is identical with average revenue at all quantity levels. Since larger quantities can be sold without the necessity of reducing the price, each additional unit sold adds the full sum of the price received for it to the total revenue of the firm. A revenue schedule for a firm selling in a purely competitive market is shown in Table 14, and illustrated graphically on Figure 21.

SELECTED REFERENCES

HALEY, B. F. "Value and Distribution," *A Survey of Contemporary Economics* (ed. H. S. ELLIS), pp. 7–10. Philadelphia: Blakiston, 1948.

BAIN, J. S. *Pricing, Distribution, and Employment,* pp. 56–78. rev. ed. New York: Holt, 1953.

ALT, R. M., and BRADFORD, W. C. *Business Economics,* Part II. Homewood, Ill.: Richard D. Irwin, Inc., 1951.

DEAN, JOEL. *Managerial Economics,* chap. 4. New York: Prentice-Hall, 1951.

STIGLER, G. J. "The Kinky Oligopoly Demand Curve and Rigid Prices," *Journal of Political Economy,* Vol. LV (October, 1947), pp. 432–49.

EFROMYSON, C. W. "The Kinked Oligopoly Curve Reconsidered," *Quarterly Journal of Economics,* Vol. LXIX (February, 1955), pp. 119–36.

QUESTIONS

1. Distinguish between the total demand for a commodity and the demand schedule for the product of an individual firm.
2. What is the nature of the demand schedule for the product of an individual seller in a purely competitive market? Why is it of this character?
3. Illustrate on a graph the demand for the product of an individual seller in purely competitive conditions.
4. Under what circumstances is the demand for the product of the individual seller and the total demand for the product identical?
5. How does the demand for the product of a firm selling in a market of monopolistic competition differ from that of a firm selling in a purely competitive market? From that of a monopolist?
6. What factors determine the exact degree of elasticity of demand for the product of a firm selling in a market of monopolistic competition?
7. What effect does the entry of new firms into an industry have upon the demand schedules of the existing firms?
8. In general, what effect does the development of mutual interdependence in an industry have upon the elasticity of demands for the products of the individual sellers?

9. What is the nature of the demand schedule for the product of a firm with complete oligopoly? Of a price leader? Of a "follower" in a situation of price leadership?
10. What is meant by a "kinked demand curve"? What is responsible for this situation?
11. In what sense are the demand schedules of firms in partial oligopoly less determinate than those in other competitive conditions?
12. What methods may firms use to gain greater information about the demand schedules for their products?
13. Why are firms reluctant to experiment with price changes as means of gaining greater information about the elasticity of demand for their products?
14. Distinguish between a demand schedule and a revenue schedule. How is the latter derived from the former?
15. What is meant by average revenue? Marginal revenue?
16. Why is marginal revenue less than average revenue (except for the sale of 1 unit) in a nonpurely competitive market?
17. Why is marginal revenue negative in any range of sales in which the demand schedule for the product of the firm is inelastic?
18. Why is the average-revenue curve a horizontal line in a purely competitive market? Why, under these conditions, are average revenue and marginal revenue identical?

Chapter 7 THE THEORY OF PRODUCTION: THE RELATION BETWEEN INPUT CHANGES AND OUTPUT CHANGES

The determination of prices and the relative outputs of various commodities depends not only upon the consumer demand for final products, but also upon costs of production. Costs, in turn, are dependent upon the quantities of various factor units required to produce a given output under given technological conditions, and the prices which must be paid for the factor units. These prices, in turn, are determined by the relationship between the demands of business firms for the factors and the quantities available at various prices, as well as the nature of competition in the factor markets. The behavior of costs is dependent upon the manner in which the output of the product changes as the inputs of various factors change.

Accordingly, as a preliminary step toward an analysis of cost behavior and output levels, and as a basis for analysis of the demand by business firms for factor units (discussed in later chapters), attention must be given to the *theory of production,* which is concerned with the explanation of the nature of the *production functions*—the functional relationships between the quantities of inputs of the various factors and the quantities of outputs obtained. The actual production functions in any particular case are determined by technological considerations; economic analysis is concerned with the questions of the typical nature of the functions and the consequent significance for the selection by the entrepreneur of the optimum combination of factors, and for the behavior of cost as output is changed.

Production functions may be classified into two general groups, on the basis of whether or not the technical coefficients of production are fixed or variable. These coefficients are the quantities of particular factors necessary to produce a unit of a product. If the coefficients are fixed, certain factor combinations—and only these—can be utilized to produce a given number of units of output, and no substitution of one factor for another is possible. Cases of fixed coefficients are confined to certain chemical processes, and perhaps a few other isolated instances. Typically the coefficients of production are variable; from a technical standpoint, various combinations of the factors can be used to produce a given product, with substitution of one factor for another possible.

The discussion of the theory of production will be divided into two segments, the first being concerned with the behavior of outputs when some factors are varied and the others are held constant, and the second with the behavior of outputs when all factors are variable.

THE CASE OF VARYING PROPORTIONS

When the technical coefficients of production are variable, as they probably are in most cases, a given product can be produced with a number of different possible combinations of various factors, and thus substitution of one factor for another is possible. One type of material can be used instead of another; various fuels may be used; capital equipment may be substituted for manpower, and vice versa.

The manner in which output changes as the relative inputs of various factors, and thus the factor combinations, are changed is of importance for two primary reasons. In the first place, knowledge of the output reactions relative to input changes is necessary if the firm is to obtain the economically optimum factor combination—the one which will allow the production of the output at minimum cost. Secondly, the behavior of changes in output relative to changes in inputs when factor combinations are changed is a primary determinant of the behavior of average cost when a firm increases output in a period of time too short to allow adjustment in all of the factors employed. Accordingly, the behavior of output under such circumstances is a determinant of the supply and price in such a period of time.

The Concepts of Average and Marginal Product

Before the analysis of the relationship between changes in inputs of the variable factors and the consequent changes in outputs is undertaken, two new concepts must be introduced. By *average physical product,* or *average product,* is meant the total product per unit of the variable factor (or factors). With 10 men employed, and total output of 300 units per day, the average product per man is 30. By *marginal physical product,* more commonly known as *marginal product,* is meant the addition to total product which results from the utilization of another unit of a particular type of factor, given the quantities of the other factors. Thus if output is 70 units a day with 9 men employed, and rises to 73 units if a 10th man is employed, the marginal product of the 10th man is 3 units.

The Typical Behavior of Output as the Inputs of the Variable Factors Are Altered

Both economic analysis, on the basis of usual assumptions, and empirical studies suggest that as the quantities of one or more factors are increased (with a given quantity of fixed factors) the output will rise initially at an increasing rate, with the rate of increase in excess of the rate of increase in the inputs of the variable factors, while ultimately the rate of increase in the output will fall, ultimately falling below the rate of increase in the inputs. Typical behavior of output is shown on

TABLE 15

TYPICAL OUTPUT BEHAVIOR WITH ONE VARIABLE FACTOR

Units of Variable Factor	Total Output	Average Physical Product	Marginal Physical Product
1	12	12	12
2	28	14	16
3	52	17.33	24
4	74	18.50	22
5	91	18.20	17
6	104	17.33	13
7	114	16.29	10
8	120	15	6
9	121	13.44	1
10	115	11.50	− 6

Table 15, and illustrated graphically on Figure 22 (page 126), with units of output measured on the vertical axis and units of the variable factor measured on the horizontal axis.

Initially, the marginal product increases, since output rises at an increasing rate. Average product also rises, since output is increasing more rapidly than the inputs of the variable factor. Beyond a certain point, however, the rate of increase in total output slackens, and thus marginal product commences to decline. As long as total product continues to rise at a faster rate than the rate of increase in the variable factor, average product will continue to rise, even though marginal product is falling. Eventually, however, the rate of increase in total product will fall below the rate of increase in the variable factor, and the average product will commence to fall. At the point at which this occurs, marginal product and average product will be equal. So long as marginal product is greater than average product, the latter will rise;

once marginal product falls below average product, the latter must fall; hence the two are equal at the high point of average product, as illustrated on Figure 22.[1]

The behavior of output, as the variable factor is increased, can be separated into three stages, delimited by the broken lines on Figure 22. In the first stage, that of *increasing returns,*[2] average product is increasing, while marginal product initially rises and eventually declines. In the second stage, that of *diminishing returns,* average product declines

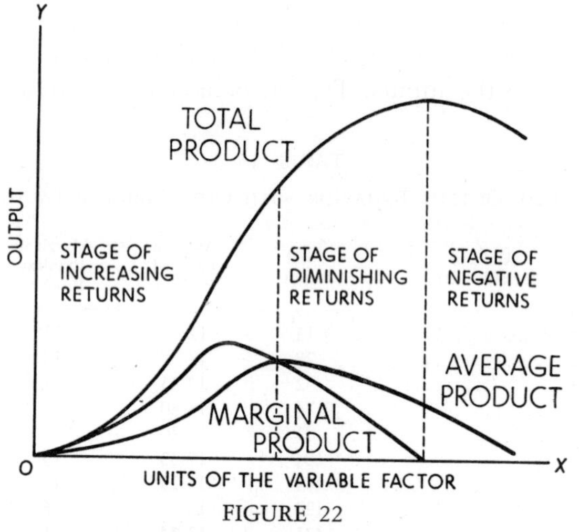

FIGURE 22

PRODUCT BEHAVIOR AS VARIABLE FACTOR UNITS ARE INCREASED

continuously, the stage extending to the point at which marginal product is zero, and thus total product has reached its maximum. The third, or *negative-returns* stage, is that in which total product is diminishing, and thus marginal product is negative.

The Explanation of the Behavior of Output with Varying Proportions: The Law of Diminishing Returns

What forces are responsible for the typical behavior of output as proportions of the factors are varied (as outlined in the preceding section)? The behavior can be attributed to two primary considerations:

[1] This represents a universal relationship of average and marginal data. As long as the marginal figure in a series—the figure being added—exceeds the previous average, the average figure must rise. Thus, if 4 is added to a series the average of which previously was 2, the new average will exceed 2. When the marginal figure is less than the average, the latter must fall. If a figure less than 2 is added to a series with a previous average of 2, the new average will be less than 2.

[2] The concept of returns relates to physical output, not profits.

1. Certain factor units are of such nature that they cannot be utilized effectively without a certain minimum number of units of other factors.

2. The operation of the Law of Diminishing Returns. The first of these considerations will be explained below in the discussion of the stage of increasing returns. Detailed attention to the Law of Diminishing Returns is desirable at this point in the discussion.

The Law of Diminishing Returns is one of the oldest and most widely accepted laws in the field of economic analysis. According to this Law, if the quantities of certain factors are increased, while the quantities of other factors are held constant, beyond a certain point the rate of increase in output, and thus the marginal product of the variable factors, will decline. Since the decline in the rate of increase in output will continue once it commences, eventually the rate of increase in output will drop below the rate of increase in the inputs of the variable factors, and average physical product will also fall.

It is essential to note that the Law is relevant only in those situations in which factor proportions are varied, that is, where some factors are increased in quantity relative to the quantities of others. If all factors are varied in the same proportion—for example, if the quantities of all factors employed are doubled—the operation of the Law is not encountered.

The Law of Diminishing Returns is based upon two premises. In the first place, a given technology is assumed; the Law is relevant to the behavior of output when inputs of various factors are varied in the framework of given available methods and techniques. For clarity of analysis, it is necessary to distinguish clearly between the effects of changes in factor proportions, as such, and those of the introduction of improved technological methods. Although, in any given period of time, both types of changes may be occurring, the effects of one are distinct from those of the other. Secondly, it is assumed that the units of the various factors employed are homogeneous, additional units added being of equal efficiency (and thus interchangeable with) the units already employed. The effects of use of factor units of varying efficiency are distinct from those of the varying of the combinations. In practice, a firm may find that additional units of the factor added are less efficient than those first employed, but the effect upon output of using successively poorer units is completely distinct from the effect upon output of the operation of the Law of Diminishing Returns.

What is responsible for the operation of the Law of Diminishing Returns? Essentially marginal physical product decreases because each successive unit of the variable factor has a smaller quantity of fixed factor units with which to work, since a given quantity of the fixed factor is being combined with larger and larger amounts of the variable factor. Once the point is reached at which the number of variable units is adequate to utilize the available fixed factor units efficiently, further increases in the variable factor will add progressively less to total product. If the principle is considered in regard to any type of business—whether it be farming, retailing, trucking, or steel production—the inevitability of the eventual decline in marginal product of any factor being added to constant amounts of the others is obvious.

With this preliminary survey of the Law of Diminishing Returns completed, it is now possible to analyze the behavior of average and marginal product in the successive stages of increasing, diminishing, and negative returns.

The Stage of Increasing Returns

The initial rise in marginal and average product as the quantity of the variable factor is increased is due in part to the operation of the Law of Diminishing Returns (working, in a sense, in reverse relative to the variable factor), and in part to the more effective use of fixed (and possibly variable) factor units as the number of the variable units is increased.

When the number of variable factors is extremely small, the Law of Diminishing Returns is essentially operating in reverse relative to the variable factor, or, in other words, in a positive way relative to the fixed factor. If the latter were increased, given the number of units of the factor which we are regarding as variable, the marginal product per unit of the fixed factor would fall, since the quantity of the variable factor would be inadequate. Or, to further clarify, the quantity of the fixed factor is so great that efficiency of operation is interfered with, and production would actually increase if some of the fixed factor units could be disposed of. If one man tried to operate a large department store alone—doing all the work of all types that was necessary in the store—his energies would be spread so thinly in so many directions that the total output (sales) might be less than it would be if he were operating a smaller store (i.e., working with less capital). As successive men were added, up to a certain number, each man would add more to total product than did the previous one. In a situation of this sort, there are simply so many units of some factors that they get in the way of the other factors, and prevent the latter from performing their tasks efficiently.

More significantly, however, the stage of increasing returns can be attributed to the greater efficiency in the use of certain fixed and variable factor units as they are combined with large quantities of the other factors. For example, certain types of capital equipment may require a minimum number of men for efficient operation, or perhaps any operation at all. With a small number of variable factors, the machines cannot be operated, or operate at a low level of efficiency. As additional variable factor units are added, the machines are brought into efficient operation, and thus the marginal product of the variable factors rises sharply.

Similarly, additional units of the variable factors may permit more effective utilization of their services.[3] There are some tasks which are inherently difficult for one person alone to perform, and the adding of a second person may far more than double output. This is true, for example, of such a task as bricklaying on the wall of a house; without a helper, the bricklayer will waste a great deal of time and energy climbing up and down with bricks. The same is true of the forking of hay into a barn; two persons can get the crop into the barn in much less than half of the time required for one person, with given equipment and techniques.

In some lines of production the stage of increasing returns may never manifest itself at all. If the variable factor units themselves cannot be obtained in small units (for example, if men cannot be hired for periods shorter than a day or a week), the first unit of the variable factor may carry production out of the increasing-returns stage, and thus the firm is never aware that such a stage exists. Only if the variable factor could be added in much smaller units would the stage be noticeable. Thus in a small store the adding of one clerk may carry operations into the decreasing-returns stage, and the marginal product of a second clerk will be less than that of the first. Likewise, if the fixed factor units are divisible into very small units, increasing returns may never be encountered, since it may be possible to set aside and ignore a portion of them, and the work of the variable units concentrated on only a small portion of the fixed factor units.

The Stage of Diminishing Returns

The second stage, that of diminishing returns, results from the operation of the Law of Diminishing Returns, once the point is reached

[3] In a sense this is an aspect of specialization discussed below. But since the primary advantages of specialization are obtained only when all factors can be adjusted, the principal discussion of this question is postponed until later in the chapter.

at which the number of variable factor units is sufficient to allow efficient utilization of the fixed factors. Further increase in the number of variable factor units beyond this point results in a decline in marginal product, because the number of fixed factor units is inadequate relative to the number of the variable units.

The exact behavior of total product, and thus the marginal and average products, and the actual output figures at which marginal and average product commence to diminish depend upon the nature of the production process and the character of the fixed and variable factor units involved. If the fixed factor consists of a large number of machines of a type which can be operated with small amounts of variable factors (materials and labor primarily) marginal product is likely to be almost constant over a substantial range as the variable factors are increased, since the additional units will be used to operate previously idle machines. Similarly, in a department store (with given physical plant), portions of the store might simply be closed off if the number of clerks was small; as more clerks were hired, additional portions of the store would be utilized. Thus, for a substantial range, each successive clerk might make possible the same increase in sales volume as did the previous clerk.

On the other hand, if the fixed factors consist of a large, indivisible, and unadaptable[4] unit—that is, if the group of fixed factors requires certain amounts of variable factors if it is to be used at all—marginal product, after initially rising rapidly, will fall very sharply, once the necessary number of variable units has been obtained. For example, if a bus company is to operate one bus run a day between two points, one driver and a certain amount of gasoline are necessary; the marginal productivity of a second employee on the bus and additional gasoline is virtually zero.[5]

The Stage of Negative Returns

The third stage, one which a firm will never knowingly allow itself to reach, is that in which the use of additional factor units will actually reduce total output, and marginal product becomes, therefore, a negative figure. In such a situation there are so many units of the varia-

[4] In the sense that the fixed factor cannot be adapted to use with small quantities of the variable factors.

[5] A good discussion of the various major situations on the basis of adaptability and divisibility of the fixed factors is to be found in G. J. Stigler, "Production and Distribution in the Short Run," *Journal of Political Economy,* Vol. XLVII (June, 1939), pp. 305–27.

ble factor that efficient use of the fixed factor units is impaired. Too many clerks in a store will make it difficult for customers to get in; too many workers in a factory will get in one another's way. In such a situation reduction in the number of variable units will increase total output, just as, in the stage of increasing returns, a reduction in the number of units of the fixed factor will increase output if the condition of increasing returns is due solely to an excessive number of fixed factor units.

OPTIMUM FACTOR COMBINATIONS

Since marginal product and average product change as factor proportions are varied, certain factor combinations are more economical than others for the production of a given level of output. A major task of the business firm is the selection of the factor combination which is the optimum, in the sense of allowing lowest cost of producing a given output. The optimum factor combination cannot be determined solely on the basis of the production functions—that is, on the basis of technological conditions and the behavior of physical output—since the relative efficiency of different combinations is also dependent upon the prices which must be paid for the various factor units. A railroad cannot decide between steam and diesel locomotives on the basis of technical performance data alone; it must know the relative prices for the two types of equipment, and of the costs of fuel and other types of factor units required with each type of equipment.

The Marginal Rate of Substitution

Explanation of the optimum factor combination can be facilitated by the use of the concept of the marginal rate of substitution as applied to factor relationships. The basic concept is the same as that introduced in Chapter 5, but is, in this instance, applied to the substitution of factors for one another by business firms instead of to the substitution of various consumption goods for one another by individual households. By the concept of marginal rate of substitution with respect to factor units is meant the number of units of one factor necessary to replace a unit of another factor and maintain the same level of output.

Let us suppose that in the manufacture of washing machines steel and aluminum can be substituted for each other. For the production of a given number of washing machines, there are various possible alternative combinations of steel and aluminum (together with given quantities of other factors) which may be used. At one extreme only steel would be used, and at the other extreme only aluminum would be used, while between these two extremes various combinations of quantities of the two metals could be employed to produce the given output. Table 16 shows various possible combinations.

If steel alone is used, 10 tons are required. If 2 tons of aluminum are used, only 3 tons of steel will be required. Five tons of aluminum will be necessary to allow production without any steel. The fact must be emphasized that these various combinations are alternative possibilities for the production of a given quantity of the product, 200 washers in the example.

TABLE 16

VARIOUS COMBINATIONS OF ALUMINUM AND STEEL WHICH WILL PERMIT AN OUTPUT OF 200 WASHING MACHINES PER DAY

Aluminum (Tons)	Steel (Tons)	Marginal Rate of Substitution of Aluminum for Steel
0	10	
		4
1	6	
		3
2	3	
		2
3	1	
		$\frac{3}{4}$
4	$\frac{1}{4}$	
		$\frac{1}{4}$
5	0	

For each quantity of aluminum which may be used, there is a figure of the marginal rate of substitution of aluminum for steel,[6] that is, the quantity of steel which must be added to allow replacement of a ton of aluminum and yet produce the same amount of output. The third column in Table 16 presents the marginal rates of substitution of aluminum for steel. For example, if 5 units of aluminum are now being used (and no steel), only $\frac{1}{4}$ ton of steel must be added to allow the elimination of 1 ton of aluminum. On the other hand, if 2 tons of aluminum (and 3 tons of steel) are now being used, 3 additional tons of steel must be added to allow reduction of aluminum input to 2 tons.

The Principle of Diminishing Marginal Rate of Substitution

As illustrated by the data in Table 16, the greater the quantity of aluminum used, the smaller is the quantity of steel which must be added to allow the elimination of one ton of aluminum. In other words, the greater the extent to which steel is replaced by aluminum, the lower will be the marginal rate of substitution—the quantity of steel necessary

[6] The term "marginal rate of substitution of steel for aluminum" might appear more logical, but the term as given represents standard terminology.

to replace a unit of aluminum and maintain output. This relationship is known as the *Law of Diminishing Marginal Rate of Factor Substitution.* It is essentially an extension of the Law of Diminishing Returns to the relationship between two factors. The Law may be stated more precisely in this manner: As the quantity of any one factor is increased relative to the quantity of the other, the number of units of the second necessary to replace a unit of the first and maintain output falls, since the marginal product of the first factor falls relative to that of the second.

For purposes of simplicity, Table 16 was set up with a diminishing marginal rate of substitution of aluminum for steel over the entire range of the table. Actually, if in a particular case, there is a stage of increasing returns for the variable factor, the marginal rate of substitution will rise initially, since the replacement of aluminum (of which there is too much) by steel (of which there is too little) will facilitate efficiency of production. As soon as the stage of decreasing returns for the factor which is being increased is encountered, however, the marginal rate of substitution will fall.

The rate at which the marginal rate of substitution falls is a measure of the extent to which the two factors are substitutes for each other. If they are perfect substitutes, that is, if either factor can be used equally well to produce the product, the marginal rate of substitution will not fall. If steel and aluminum can be used equally well to produce all of the metal parts of the washing machine, the marginal rate of substitution will remain unchanged—regardless of the extent to which substitution is carried in either direction—and the two factors are essentially identical, from the standpoint of use in production, even though they may be physically different.

At the other extreme is the case of two factors which are not substitutes at all for a particular purpose; the marginal rate of substitution is infinite, since output cannot be maintained if one factor is replaced by the other. If this relationship exists among all factors used by the firm, the factor combination employed is dictated entirely by technological conditions, and no substitution is possible. This is the case of fixed coefficients of production. If two factors are partial substitutes for one another, the marginal rate of substitution of one for the other will become infinite (if at all) only after substitution has been carried up to a certain point. Suppose, for example, that in the case of washing machines, either steel or aluminum can be used for certain purposes, but for others steel is essential because aluminum lacks sufficient strength for performing the task. In this case, once the quantity of steel had been reduced to the amount required for this purpose, the marginal rate of substitution would become infinite, since it would be impossible to replace any additional amount of steel by aluminum and maintain output. Up to this point, the marginal rate of substitution between the partial substitutes will be neither constant nor infinite, but will decline at a rate measuring the ease of substitution of the factors for each other.

For purposes of simplification, the explanation of the marginal rate of substitution and its behavior has been set up in terms of the relations of two factors. When a firm is using a large number of factors, however, there are separate marginal rates of substitution between each two factors employed, and the principles outlined apply to the relations between any two factors, and thus among all of them.

The Isoquant Graph

The various combinations of two factors which will allow the production of a given quantity of output can be illustrated graphically, by measuring the quantity of one factor required on the vertical axis of a graph, and the quantity of the other factor on the horizontal axis. The

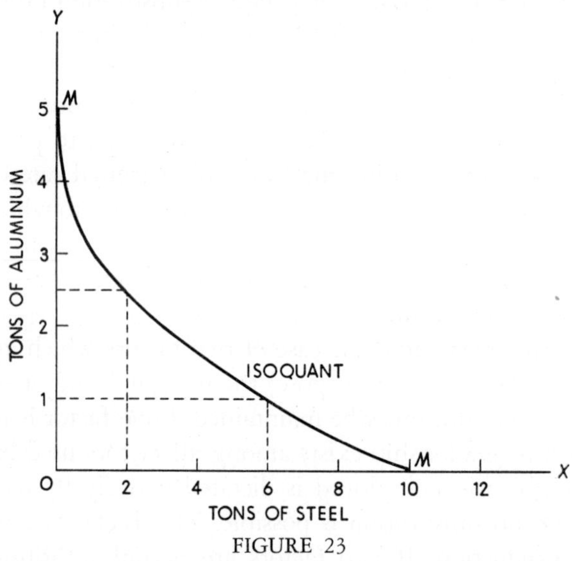

FIGURE 23

ISOQUANT SHOWING VARIOUS COMBINATIONS OF QUANTITIES OF ALUMINUM AND STEEL WHICH CAN BE USED TO PRODUCE 200 WASHING MACHINES

line showing the various factor combinations which will produce the given output is known as an *isoquant.* On Figure 23, tons of aluminum are measured on the vertical axis, and tons of steel on the horizontal axis; isoquant *MM* shows the various combinations of the two factors which will allow the production of 200 washing machines per day (with given quantities of other factors), based upon the data in Table 16.

The slope of the isoquant at any particular point shows the marginal rate of substitution between the two factors at that point. Under ordinary circumstances, the isoquant will be convex to the point of origin, because of the Law of Diminishing Marginal Rate of Factor Substitution. The greater the quantity of one factor used, the smaller is the quantity of the other factor which must be added to replace a unit of the first factor and maintain output; thus the right-hand portion of the isoquant is almost parallel to the horizontal axis, while the left-hand portion is almost parallel to the vertical axis. However, if the two factors are perfect substitutes, the isoquant will be a straight line, since the marginal rate of substitution will not fall. At the other extreme, if the two factors are not substitutes, the isoquant will contain a right-angle bend, showing that a given quantity of each factor is required to produce a given output. The more easily the two factors may be substituted for one another, the less will be the curvature of the isoquant. The isoquants are drawn in terms of two factors, but the relationships which they indicate apply between each pair of factors used, and thus among all of the factors.

The Optimum Factor Combinations

Knowledge of the marginal rates of substitution between two commodities does not, in itself, indicate the optimum quantities of each to use, in the sense of that combination which will allow the firm to produce the output at lowest cost. This combination can be determined only if the costs of the various factors are known as well as the marginal rates of substitution between them. In the washing machine example presented in Table 16, let us assume that aluminum costs $60 a ton, and steel costs $30 a ton. In Table 17 the total costs of producing the given number of washing machines are shown, with various combinations of steel and aluminum, the assumption being made that other costs are the same regardless of the combination of metals employed.

With this data, the least cost point, and thus the optimum factor combination, is attained when 2 tons of aluminum and 3 tons of steel, or, alternatively, 3 tons of aluminum and 2 tons of steel, are used. If the data were broken down in this bracket to fractions of a ton, a single combination (with fractions of tons) could be discovered which would allow the absolute minimum cost.

Examination of the data in Tables 16 and 17 will show that the range of combinations allowing the lowest cost is that in which the marginal rate of substitution is 2 to 1, and is thus equal to the ratios of the prices of the two factors (60 to 30). This relationship between the factor-price ratios and the marginal rates of substitution is essential for attainment of the least cost combination. Any deviation from this point will result in an increase in the cost of the added factor of greater magnitude than the reduction in the cost of the replaced factor, and thus in an

TABLE 17

RELATIVE COSTS OF PRODUCING 200 WASHING MACHINES, WITH VARIOUS COMBINATIONS OF STEEL AND ALUMINUM

Aluminum (Tons)	Steel (Tons)	Cost of Aluminum* (Dollars)	Cost of Steel† (Dollars)	Other Costs (Dollars)	Total Cost (Dollars)
0	10	0	300	9000	9300
1	6	60	180	9000	9240
2	3	120	90	9000	9210
3	1	180	30	9000	9210
4	$\frac{1}{4}$	240	$7\frac{1}{2}$	9000	$9247\frac{1}{2}$
5	0	300	0	9000	9300

* Assuming a price of $60 a ton.
† Assuming a price of $30 a ton.

increase in total cost. For example, on the basis of the data in Table 17, if the quantity of aluminum were cut back from 2 tons to 1, the savings in aluminum cost would be $60, whereas the cost of the additional steel required to allow production of the same output would be $90 (3 tons at $30 per ton). An increase in the quantity of aluminum from 3 tons to 4 would add $60 to the cost of the aluminum but reduce steel costs only $7.50.

Tangency of the Isoquant with a Factor-Price Line

By adding a factor-price line to the graph containing the isoquant for the two factors with a given level of output, it is possible to illustrate graphically the optimum factor combination. On Figure 24, the isoquant shown on Figure 23 is reproduced, and to the graph is added a factor-price line, showing the various possible quantities of steel and aluminum which can be purchased with a given outlay of money ($210), under the assumption that the price of aluminum is $60 a ton, and that of steel, $30 a ton. With the price line shown on Figure 24, $3\frac{1}{2}$ tons of aluminum can be obtained if only aluminum is acquired, 7 tons of steel if only steel is acquired, 2 tons of aluminum and 3 tons of steel, etc. The factor-price line is a straight line, as a matter of mathematical necessity, so long as the prices which must be paid for the factor

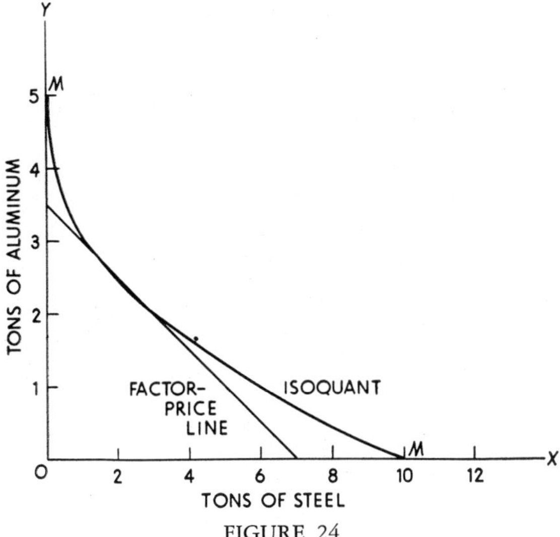

FIGURE 24

GRAPHICAL ILLUSTRATION OF THE OPTIMUM COMBINATION OF ALUMINUM AND STEEL TO PRODUCE 200 WASHING MACHINES PER DAY

units are the same regardless of the quantities which are purchased by the firm. There are various possible factor-price lines, for various outlays on the factors, the successive lines being parallel to each other. One of these lines will be tangent to the isoquant showing factor quantities necessary to produce the given output. At the point of tangency, the optimum factor combination is obtained. On Figure 24, the tangency

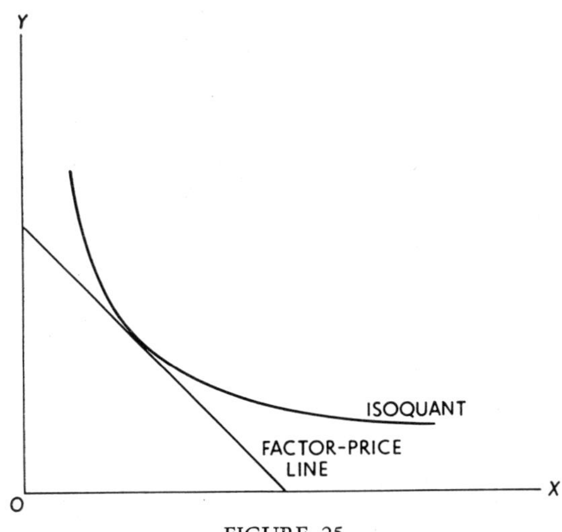

FIGURE 25

THE OPTIMUM FACTOR COMBINATION, WITH SINGLE POINT TANGENCY

is not at a single point, but over the range between 3 tons of steel and 2 of aluminum, and 1 ton of steel and 3 of aluminum; as shown above in Table 17, it is within this range that the optimum factor combination must lie. With figures for intervals within this range available, tangency would appear at a single point, as illustrated on Figure 25.

The factor-price line which is just tangent to the isoquant is that which allows the acquisition of the necessary factor units with the lowest possible outlay. Any lower line would not allow the purchase of sufficient factors to produce the desired output, while any higher factor-price line would require unnecessarily high factor costs. At any point on the isoquant other than the point of tangency, the outlay on the factors to produce the given output would be higher than that at the tangency point. At tangency, the slope of the isoquant (which is the marginal rate of substitution between the two factors) and the slope of the factor-price line (which is the ratio of the prices of the two factors) are equal, and thus the marginal rate of substitution is equal to the ratio of the factor prices at this point, and only at this point. It must be emphasized that the isoquant shows the various quantities of the two factors necessary to produce a given output, while the factor-price line shows the various quantities of the two factors which can be acquired with the expenditure of a given sum of money.

The Elasticity of Substitution of Factors

The explanation of the optimum factor combination in the preceding section has, of necessity, been based upon the assumption of given factor prices. It is possible, however, to extend the analysis to consider the relationship between changes in the relative prices of the two factors and the consequent changes in the quantities of the two factors which are acquired.

A change in the price of any factor, the prices of the other factors remaining unchanged, will necessitate a readjustment in factor proportions, since the price change will have destroyed the equality of the price ratio and the marginal rate of substitution. The readjustment will continue until this equality is restored. If the marginal rate of substitution between two factors falls slowly, the price change will cause a substantial change in the relative quantities of the two factors purchased. If it falls rapidly, relatively little change will occur, since an increase in the quantity of the factor which has declined in price will allow elimination of only very small quantities of the other factors.

In graphical terms, the change in the price of one factor changes the point of tangency between the isoquant and the factor-price line, as shown on Figure 26, and thus results in a new optimum combination. If the factors are good substitutes, and thus the isoquant has little curvature, the shift of the point of tangency will be substantial (from *oa* to *ob* on Figure 26), and the increase in the quantity utilized of the factor

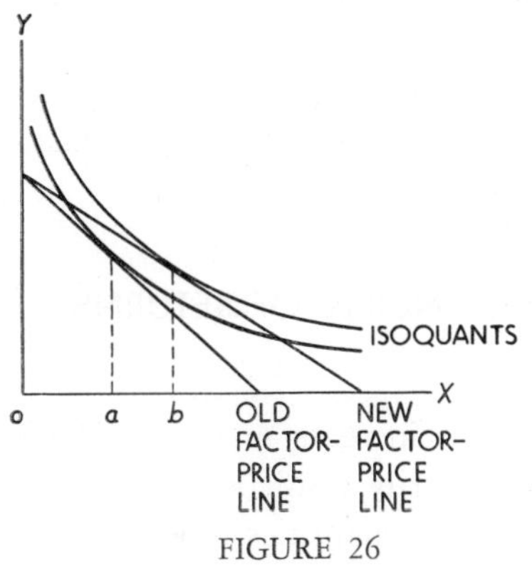

FIGURE 26

READJUSTMENT OF THE OPTIMUM FACTOR COMBINATION IN RESPONSE TO A CHANGE IN THE PRICE OF ONE FACTOR, THE TWO FACTORS BEING GOOD SUBSTITUTES FOR EACH OTHER

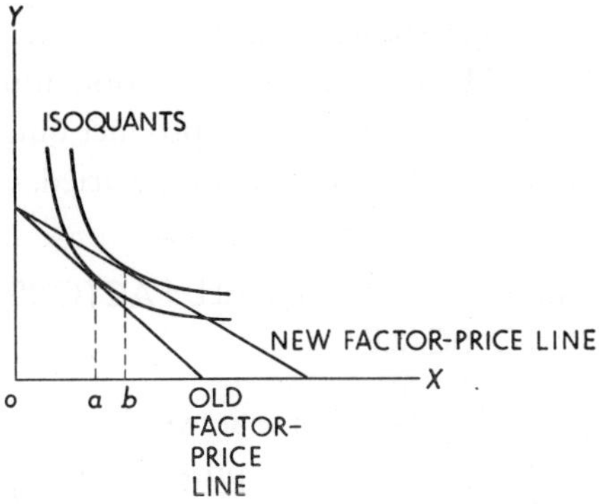

FIGURE 27

READJUSTMENT OF THE OPTIMUM FACTOR COMBINATION IN RESPONSE TO A CHANGE IN THE PRICE OF ONE FACTOR, THE TWO FACTORS BEING POOR SUBSTITUTES FOR EACH OTHER

which has become cheaper will be relatively great. If the two factors are poor substitutes, the curvature will be sharp and the shift in the quantity of the factor acquired relatively slight (*oa* to *ob* on Figure 27).

The Scope of Applicability of the Law of Diminishing Returns

The Law of Diminishing Returns is relevant only to the behavior of output when factor proportions are varied; that is, when one factor, or several factors, are increased (or reduced) in quantity while the inputs of the others remain the same. The Law is therefore significant under all circumstances (except those of fixed coefficients of production) for relative adjustments of inputs of various factors needed to obtain the optimum factor combination, since adjustments to attain this combination necessarily involve changes in the relative quantities of the various factors used.

The Law is also relevant, however, for the behavior of total output in any situation in which it is not possible for a firm to increase all factors of production in the same proportion. As explained more carefully in the next chapter, in a relatively short period of time, some factors of production, particularly capital equipment, cannot be adjusted. Accordingly, as a firm increases output by adding additional inputs of those factors which can be adjusted, the Law of Diminishing Returns is encountered with respect to the behavior of product outputs relative to inputs of the variable factors. Accordingly, the operation of the Law is significant for the behavior of cost per unit of output as a firm increases output under circumstances in which the inputs of some factors are fixed (as shown in the next chapter).

Meanwhile, consideration must be given to the relationship between factor input and product output in a situation in which the quantities of all factor units are varied.

ADJUSTMENTS IN ALL FACTORS: THE PRINCIPLE OF RETURNS TO SCALE

At first glance it would appear that an increase in inputs of all factors by the same proportion would necessarily result in an increase in output by the same proportion. If the total quantities of all factors employed are doubled, it would appear that the output would double as well. Actually, this result may not follow, and apparently does not, at least over portions of ranges of possible variation. The behavior regarded as typical is indicated by the *Principle of Returns to Scale:* As a firm increases the quantities of all factors employed, output is likely to rise initially at a more rapid rate than the rate of increase in inputs, but ultimately at a less rapid rate. The first phase is the phase of *Increasing Returns to Scale;* the second is that of *Decreasing Returns to Scale.* Empirical studies in recent years suggest that the two may be separated by a substantial range of *Constant Returns to Scale,* in which output and inputs increase in the same proportion.

Increasing Returns to Scale

A situation of increasing returns to scale, in which a given percentage increase in inputs will lead to a greater relative percentage increase in output, can be attributed to two considerations: the indivisibilities of some factors, and the advantages of specialization.

1. *Indivisibilities.* The inability to divide certain factor units into smaller units without either complete loss of usefulness in production or partial loss in efficiency results in a relatively low output per unit of input when operations are on a very small scale. Certain types of capital goods, for example, will not perform their function if they are built on too small a scale, since weight is important in their operation. This is true of various types of presses, and equipment used in road construction. As another example, regardless of how light railroad traffic on a

line is expected to be, the weight of the rails must be at least 45 pounds per yard if standard equipment is to be operated. Yet rails on the heaviest traffic lines may not exceed 135 pounds in weight. The traffic density on a heavily used line may be 2,000,000 ton-miles per mile of track annually; on a light-density line the traffic may not exceed 20,000 ton-miles. The latter is only 1 per cent of the former; yet the rail required is 33 per cent as large. A rail of only 1 per cent of the weight of the 135-pound rail would not stand the weight of a handcar. A certain minimum right-of-way and grading are also necessary if a railroad is to run at all, regardless of traffic density.

With other types of capital equipment, small units can be made, but the output per unit of factors used to make and operate them is low. A 5-horsepower diesel engine cannot be built for 1 per cent of the cost of a 500-horsepower diesel. For physical reasons, larger machines require less material, per unit of output, for their construction, than smaller machines, and they likewise require less labor for their construction, per unit of product, since it takes little or no additional time to assemble the parts of a machine designed to produce 100 units a day than to assemble the parts of a similar machine designed to produce 50 units. If the size of the machine is very small, more time may actually be required because of the difficulty of working with small parts. When machinery is small in size, necessary precision in measurements is difficult to obtain.

Indivisibilities are not confined to capital goods, however. Labor units are not completely divisible. One operator may be required for each machine, regardless of its size. A freight train requires one engineer, regardless of the tonnage of the train; there is no way of using a fraction of an engineer on a train of light tonnage. Within limits, in small enterprises employees may be used to perform several different tasks. But, as a practical matter, there are severe limitations to such possibilities. A switchboard operator may serve as receptionist and do some stenographic work, but she can scarcely be used as an elevator operator and window cleaner. A clerk in a store may be busy only one third of the time, yet he must be paid for the entire day. In any type of business it is difficult to utilize each worker to the maximum of his productivity at all times; as an establishment grows, the percentage of labor time not utilized should fall, if management policies are effective.[7]

[7] Union rules sometimes increase indivisibilities of labor and lessen effective utilization of labor time. Thus a freight train must have a crew of a stated size, though less men may be needed in certain operations. A train crew working in line operations cannot be put to work in switching operations when a run is finished, even though the run has taken only a fraction of a standard working day.

Indivisibilities are also encountered in advertising, research work, and financing. Advertising on a small-scale basis is relatively less effective than on a large-scale basis, as explained in Chapter 10. Research activities cannot be carried on effectively on a small-scale basis. Indivisibilities are likewise encountered in the financing of a business. The cost of floating a bond issue, for example, is, to a large extent, independent of the size of the issue. Thus this method of financing—the cheapest method when large amounts of capital are to be obtained—is expensive to a firm until it has expanded beyond a certain size. The refusal of many investors to consider the bonds of any except well-known companies enhances the difficulty of the use of bond-financing by small businesses.

2. *Specialization.* The other, and closely related cause of increasing returns to scale is the advantage offered by specialization. In a very small business, employees must perform a wide variety of tasks. As the size of the enterprise increases, each employee can be used in a relatively specialized job, with consequent increase in output per worker. The advantages of specialization of labor have been recognized since the days of Adam Smith.[8] The primary advantages include the greater skill acquired with specialization, the avoidance of wasted time in shifting from one task to another, the employment of persons best suited to the particular types of work, etc. In managerial activity as well as in other phases of work, advantages of specialization are encountered. As a firm grows in size, personnel relations will be conducted by a specialist; traffic management will be in the hands of a full-time traffic expert instead of being performed by an official who also has a half-dozen other types of tasks. The owner of a small retail store selects the location for the store primarily upon a guesswork basis, placing it where he thinks his sales volume should be high or where he happens to find an empty building upon which the rent is low. In contrast, the larger chains have their store sites selected by experts who have had experience in analyzing the factors which affect the relative desirability of different sites. Specialization is also possible with capital equipment. As a firm increases the scale of operations, it becomes possible to replace nonspecialized equipment which is capable of performing a number of tasks by specialized equipment designed for various specific operations, with consequent increase in output per unit of input.

The importance of the phase of increasing returns depends in large measure upon the type of production process involved. In almost any

[8] His classic example deals with the advantages of specialization in the manufacture of pins (see his *Wealth of Nations* [Modern Library ed.; New York: Random House], pp. 7–8).

type, increasing returns are likely to be encountered to some extent when the business expands from a very small initial size, if for no other reason than because of the indivisibilities of labor. If, however, the business utilizes relatively little capital equipment and few advantages of specialization of labor are obtainable, increasing returns may very quickly come to an end. On the other hand, if a firm uses extensive amounts of capital goods of types which cannot be used efficiently on a small-scale basis, very substantial increasing returns extending over a large range of output will be encountered. Thus increasing returns are very important in steel, cement, and automobile production, while they are of less importance in agriculture and retailing.

Constant Returns to Scale

As a business continues to expand the scale of its operations, it gradually exhausts the economies which are responsible for increasing returns. A firm will eventually grow to the point at which it is using the best type of capital equipment available and is gaining full advantages of specialization of labor. Beyond this point, further increases in the scale of operations are likely to produce more or less constant returns for a substantial range of output; that is, increases in factors will cause proportionate increases in output. If the entire scale of operations is doubled, output will approximately double also.[9] It must be emphasized that the constant returns to scale are relevant only for time periods in which adjustment of all factors is possible. If a firm doubles output in a short period, with a fixed physical plant which was previously utilized to normal optimum capacity, returns per unit of the variable factors will decline because of the operation of the Law of Diminishing Returns. But if all factors are varied, as is possible over a long-run period, the Law of Diminishing Returns is not relevant.

Decreasing Returns to Scale

As a firm continues to expand its scale of operations, beyond a certain point there is apparently a tendency for returns to scale to decrease; beyond this point a given percentage increase in the quantities of all factors will bring about a less than proportional increase in output. In some types of production the decreasing-returns phase may follow directly after the increasing-returns phase, with no significant intervening

[9] Even in the phase of constant returns, small increases in scale may produce decreasing returns or increasing returns because of indivisibilities—the inability to add small quantities of certain factors. A railroad cannot build half of a new track between two points; if two tracks are inadequate, it may build a third track, which initially will not be used to capacity.

period of constant returns. It is believed, however, on the basis of limited evidence, that a long phase of constant returns may typically intervene.

Decreasing returns to scale are attributed to the increased problems and complexities of large-scale management. Continuous increases in the entrepreneurial type of labor activity beyond a certain point encounter more and more serious problems and difficulties. An increasing percentage of the total labor force will be required in administrative work, in order to provide co-ordination of the activities of the enterprise and necessary control over the large numbers of employees. A growing concern, once it reaches substantial size, encounters a fundamental problem of management; the final authority for basic policy must remain in the hands of the group of men who control the operation of the business, yet these men are far removed from the actual level of operations. They are forced to make decisions on the basis of secondhand information, on subjects with which they have no direct contact. Furthermore, substantial delay can occur in the making of the decisions, since the request for the decision, plus the necessary information, must pass up through the chain of command to the entrepreneurial group, and the decision then pass down to the operating unit.

In order to reduce to a minimum the amount of red tape, delay, and making of decisions by those out of contact with the situation, it becomes necessary to delegate responsibility for many decisions to subordinate officials. But, to the extent that such a policy is followed, the decisions are made by persons who lack the knowledge of the general business policy and the experience which the men at the top level of management possess. As a result, there arises a lack of co-ordination and unity of policy among various parts of the enterprise. Modern business management attempts to carry delegation to limits which are consistent with reasonable unity of policy. But the problem can never be eliminated; scientific management principles merely lessen its seriousness.

The growth of a business likewise increases the amount of division of responsibility and serves to lessen initiative, especially on the part of persons in lower-level jobs who are in a position to note desirable changes. With increased size comes loss of personal contact between management and workers, with consequent loss of morale and increase in labor strife.

The Validity of the Principle of Returns to Scale

The Principle of Returns to Scale has not enjoyed the general acceptance afforded the Law of Diminishing Returns. The initial increase in output per unit of factor which occurs as a firm first increases scale of operations follows as a matter of logical necessity from the assumptions of indivisibilities and the advantages of specialization—assumptions which appear, on the basis of both common-sense observations and some empirical studies, to be generally valid. The ultimate exhaustion of the economies from these sources is likewise regarded as inevitable. But whether or not an ultimate decline in output per unit of input is inevitable, or is confined to those fields (such as certain types of agriculture) in which management problems are particularly serious, is open to question. Empirical studies are very limited in scope; the major ones are noted in the next chapter.

SELECTED REFERENCES

STIGLER, G. J. *The Theory of Price,* chaps. vii and viii. rev. ed. New York: Macmillan, 1952.

LERNER, A. P. *The Economics of Control,* chaps. v–xvii. New York: Macmillan, 1947.

CASSELS, J. M. "On the Law of Variable Proportions," *Readings in the Theory of Income Distribution,* pp. 103–18. Philadelphia: Blakiston, 1946.

CARLSON, SUNE. *A Study on the Pure Theory of Production.* London: P. S. King and Sons, 1939.

QUESTIONS

1. What is the subject matter of the theory of production?
2. What is a production function?
3. Distinguish between production functions with fixed coefficients of production and those with variable coefficients. Give an example of the former.
4. Distinguish between average product and marginal product.
5. Explain and illustrate with a graph the typical behavior of total product as the input of one factor is increased, with given quantities of the other factors.
6. Why is marginal product equal to average product at the highest level of average product?
7. Why does marginal product fall if the rate of increase in total product falls?
8. Can average product be rising while marginal product is falling? Explain.
9. Explain the Law of Diminishing Returns, indicating the premises upon which it is based.
10. Distinguish between the stages of increasing returns and increasing returns to scale, and contrast the causes of the two.
11. Contrast the causes of the stages of diminishing returns and decreasing returns to scale.

12. What is meant by the stage of "negative returns"? What can be responsible for negative returns if a firm expands far enough?
13. What is meant by the term "optimum factor combination"?
14. Explain carefully the meaning of the term "marginal rate of substitution" with respect to factors.
15. Why may the marginal rate of substitution of y for x fall as the quantity of y is increased? Why may it rise initially?
16. What is the relationship between the rate of decline in the marginal rate of substitution and the degree of substitutability of the two factors for each other?
17. What is the marginal rate of substitution among the various factors in a situation of fixed coefficients of production?
18. What is an isoquant? Distinguish between an isoquant and an indifference curve.
19. Why is an isoquant convex to the point of origin?
20. How is the optimum factor combination defined, in terms of the marginal rate of substitution? In terms of the isoquant graph?
21. Explain the concept of elasticity of factor substitution.
22. Why is the elasticity of substitution between two factors high if the marginal rate of substitution between them falls slowly?
23. What is the elasticity of substitution between two factors if the marginal rate of substitution between them is constant? If the marginal rate of substitution is infinite?
24. For what circumstances is the Law of Diminishing Returns applicable?
25. In what circumstances is the Principle of Returns to Scale applicable?
26. What are "indivisibilities"? How do they result in increasing returns to scale?
27. When is a firm likely to encounter constant returns to scale?
28. What is responsible for decreasing returns to scale?

Chapter 8 THE NATURE AND BEHAVIOR OF COST

The production of various quantities of output requires inputs of necessary factor units, in combinations dictated by marginal rates of substitution of the various factors for one another and the relative factor prices. In order to obtain the factor units, the firm must compensate the owners of the units. These compensations, which constitute incomes to the factor-owners, are *costs* from the standpoint of the firms. The quantities of output which the firms will place on the market, at various prices, depend upon the relationship between the prices and the total cost, per unit of product. This cost, in turn, depends upon the quantities of inputs of the various factors necessary to produce the given output, and the prices which must be paid for the factor units. The behavior of cost per unit of output, as the firm varies output, is dependent upon the manner in which output changes as the inputs of the various factors change. Not only does the relationship between price and cost determine the output of the firm, but also the decisions with respect to undertaking of business enterprises, and the liquidation of existing enterprises. In this chapter, the concept and behavior of cost will be explored more fully.

THE NATURE OF COST

The term *cost* has a wide variety of meanings. To the businessman, the elements included in cost for the purpose of some decisions are very different from those included for other purposes.[1] As the term is used in reference to the determination of profit, "cost" includes only the usual business expenses (including depreciation), interest, rent, and taxes.[2] However, when a firm is figuring the profitability of undertaking a par-

[1] See *Cost Behavior and Price Policy* (New York: National Bureau of Economic Research, 1943), pp. 20–27; J. M. Clark, *The Economics of Overhead Costs* (Chicago: University of Chicago Press, 1923), chaps. iii, ix.

[2] In determining net income in the calculation of income tax liability, the amount of the income tax itself, of course, cannot be treated as a cost.

ticular expansion or buying new equipment, in addition to the other cost elements there is included an item of return on the money capital being used for the investment, even though the money is supplied by the owners of the business. The element of return on the owners' capital is also usually included in cost when the latter is calculated for the purpose of pricing various products.[3] On the other hand, for some purposes cost includes far less than it does for profit calculation; if a firm with an idle plant considers whether or not to accept additional orders which can be obtained only at a very low price, it may take into consideration, so far as cost is concerned, only the direct, out-of-pocket cost necessitated by the additional output. Similarly, when a railroad determines whether or not to continue operating a particular passenger train, it considers only the cost resulting directly from operation of that train and does not include the train's "share" of track maintenance, administrative expenses, interest on investment, etc.

For purposes of economic analysis, the most satisfactory definition of cost is one which is broader than the concept used in financial accounting for purposes of profit calculation but is similar to the concept as used by business firms for many purposes. Specifically, by the term *cost* is meant *the compensations which must be received by the owners of the units of the factors of production and money capital used by a firm if they are to continue to supply the units to the firm.* In order to carry on production, a business firm must obtain units of various factors. To do so, the firm must compensate the factor unit owners, since the latter have the alternative of allowing other firms to use the factor units instead of this particular firm. The compensations involved constitute costs.

Two elements in the definition require emphasis. The phrase "compensations which must be received by the owners of the units of the factors" is used rather than "payments which must be made to the factor-owners" because in some instances no formal payment, in the usual sense, occurs; when a person who is operating a business supplies a portion of the money capital himself, for example, he does not "pay" himself for the use of this money. Yet, if he does not receive a return on it equivalent to the amount which he could get by lending it to others, he will eventually liquidate the business. Likewise, the phrase "continue to supply the factor units" is used in the definition rather than "supply the factor units," since in some cases the factor-owners will supply factor units for a period of time to a firm even though they are getting little or

[3] This is not meant to imply that firms can set their prices on a basis of cost considerations alone. But cost is an element considered, and for this purpose cost is usually figured to include a "profit" on the firm's own capital.

no compensation. The firm will not be able to obtain the factor units indefinitely, however, if it cannot earn a return from the use of the units comparable to that made in other industries. The owners of a business which is not yielding a normal return on the investment will often continue to operate it for several years because they cannot quickly withdraw money capital which has been invested in specialized capital goods with a life of several years. Once the capital goods are worn out, however, the money capital will not be reinvested in the business.

From the standpoint of a particular business firm, the amount of compensation which the owners of the factor units used by the firm must receive if they are to continue to supply the units is determined by other *opportunities* which they have—specifically, by the amounts which they could obtain by supplying the units to other business firms. Thus, if the market price for bar copper is 8 cents a pound, a manufacturer who wishes to use bar copper must pay this price, since sellers of the product will not supply it to him for less when they have the opportunity of getting 8 cents from other buyers. If the current wage rate for laying brick is $18 a day, a contractor must pay $18 a day in order to obtain bricklayers. The same principle applies to factor units owned by the firm itself or supplied to it by the owners of the firm. A farmer who owns 100 acres of land might be able to obtain $1,500 a year by renting this land to a neighbor; thus a part of his own cost of production is this $1,500 sum, since he is foregoing the opportunity of renting the land for this amount by using the land himself. A businessman who invests $20,000 in his own business could have bought stock—perhaps in General Motors, for example—for this sum and received $800 a year in dividends. This sum constitutes a cost for which his business is responsible. The importance of opportunity in determining cost to a firm has led to the frequent use in economic analysis of the term *opportunity cost* in place of the word *cost* alone. In general, the cost of any factor unit in a particular production use is the maximum amount which the factor unit could earn in alternative uses.

EXPENDITURE AND NONEXPENDITURE COSTS

There are two types of elements in total cost: (1) those such as wages which take the form of contractual payments by the business firm to factor-owners and are designated as *expenditure* or *outlay* costs, and (2) those which, when covered, accrue directly to the firm itself, or its owners, with no contractual obligations for payment involved. The second type may be called *nonexpenditure* or *implicit* costs.

Expenditure Costs

The first group consists of the items, except depreciation, usually treated as costs in financial accounting. The major elements include wages and salaries paid; payments for raw materials, fuel, and goods purchased for resale; payments for transportation, utilities, advertising, and similar services; interest on borrowed capital; rent on land and capital equipment leased; and taxes. Not all payments, however, made by business firms are costs. Those made for the purchase of capital equipment involve merely a change in the form of the firm's assets and hence are not costs. They are charged to capital account, and a depreciation charge—which is a nonexpenditure cost—is set up to recover the amount paid over the period of years in which the equipment will be used. Payments of dividends to stockholders are not considered to be costs,[4] but merely withdrawals of profits from the firm by the stockholder-owners.

Nonexpenditure Costs

Nonexpenditure costs—those which do not involve contractual outlay by the firm to other persons—arise when the factor units and money capital are owned by the firm itself or the owners of the firm. In this situation the firm is not obligated to make a contractual payment in order to obtain the factor units. But, as indicated above, the units are responsible for costs, since they could be supplied to other producers for a contractual sum if they were not used in this business.

In the typical large-scale enterprise operated under the corporate form of organization, the two major nonexpenditure costs are depreciation and an average or "normal" return on the money capital supplied by the stockholders. Depreciation charges, which will be discussed in greater detail in Chapter 16, consist of the sums which must be recovered in each period of time over the life of a capital good to maintain intact the capital sum invested in the good. A firm buys a new truck for $4,500. Five years from the date of purchase, the vehicle will require replacement and will have a salvage value of $300. Thus, over the life of the truck, $4,200 must be recovered if the money capital of the firm is to remain intact. The depreciation charges are not contractual obligations and the sums involved may be used by the firm for any purpose.[5] But the charges constitute costs and must be earned if the firm is to continue to operate indefinitely.

[4] As indicated below, a normal return on the funds invested by the stockholders is a cost of the nonexpenditure type.

[5] Depreciation charges are not normally accumulated as cash reserves.

Likewise, the owners of the firm must earn a "normal" rate of return on the money capital which they have supplied, that is a rate equal to that obtainable from other investments of comparable risk. If the owners of a firm have invested $10,000 in the business, they are foregoing a return on this money which they could otherwise have made by lending the money, directly or through the purchase of bonds, or by purchasing stock in other corporations, or by buying land or buildings, etc. If they had not expected to make as great a return on the $10,000 from this business as that available from other investments, they would not have started the business initially. Once the business is undertaken, they will eventually liquidate it if they cannot make a return equal to that available elsewhere. As will be explained later, the time which will elapse before the liquidation is completed may be considerable, because of the difficulties of realizing cash invested in specialized capital equipment. But it will eventually occur if the business cannot yield an average rate of return. The concept of a "normal" return will be discussed in greater detail in Chapter 19.

In smaller businesses, especially those operated with the partnership or proprietorship form of organization, an additional nonexpenditure cost may be important; namely, the wage which the owner of the business could make by hiring himself out to another business instead of running his own establishment. A grocer must be able to earn as much from his own store as he could from working for a chain store or, more exactly, the wage he could get less the value which he attaches to the privilege of working for himself. A person is often satisfied with a somewhat smaller return from his own business because of his preference for being his "own boss." But this preference has a definite value to the person; if the differential between the earnings of the store and the available wage exceeds a certain figure, the latter alternative will become preferable.

When a firm is earning an amount in excess of all costs, including those of the nonexpenditure nature, the additional amount constitutes "excess profit" or "economic profit" and is not in any sense a cost, since the business will be operated on a permanent basis whether any such excess sum is earned or not.

THE ADJUSTABILITY OF COSTS IN RESPONSE TO CHANGES IN OUTPUT

Of fundamental importance for cost behavior is the extent to which a firm is able to adjust the inputs of various factors as it varies output, and thus the total magnitudes of the various cost elements. This, in turn, is affected by the length of time involved. Over a long period of time, the quantities of all factors can be adjusted, and thus all costs are *variable,* in the sense that they change in amount as output changes. They do not necessarily change in total, however, in the same proportion as the output change. The concept of the *long-run period* is used in economic analysis with reference to a period of time sufficiently long to allow the quantities of all factors to be adjusted. It must not be considered as a certain time period (in months or years) typical of all industries, but rather as a conceptual period, the actual length of time involved varying with different firms and industries according to the length of life of the capital equipment, the ability to obtain additional skilled workers and managerial personnel, and the extent to which the capital goods are specialized, that is, usable (without substantial modification) only by the particular firm. In general, the type of factor which requires the longest period for adjustment is the specialized and relatively indivisible form of capital equipment—blast furnaces, dies used in the making of automobile parts, railroad tracks, hydroelectric plants, steamships, grain elevators, etc.

In contrast, in a shorter period of time, some factor units are not adjustable in amount. The term *short-run period* is used for this time interval. New capital equipment cannot be obtained or built over night. Often, additional skilled labor and management personnel can be secured only by training new men. Likewise, in the case of a downward adjustment, specialized capital equipment cannot usually be sold for the amount of money invested in it; the firm has the alternative of suffering a heavy loss of invested funds or using the equipment over a long period at a low return. The latter alternative is often the better one. Interest must be paid on borrowed funds until they are repaid; if the funds have been invested in fixed capital, the firm as a rule cannot make immediate repayment. Primarily, the fixed factors—those not readily adjustable, consist of capital equipment and top-management personnel. As a consequence, the term *plant* is often applied to the group of factors which are fixed in the short-run period. Thus a short-run period is one in which the plant is given, the firm being able to adjust output by changing the quantities of the variable factors, such as labor and materials, used, but not being able to adjust its plant, in the sense in which this term is employed.

Fixed Costs

The costs for which the plant—the fixed factor units—are responsible are known as *fixed costs,* while those arising from the use of the variable factors are known as *variable costs.* More precisely, fixed costs may be defined as those which are the same in total amount regardless of the volume of output, even if the latter is zero. Even if a firm produces nothing at all, the fixed costs continue unchanged. The various cost items which are usually fixed in a short-run period may be classified into two major groups, those of a *recurrent* nature, involving actual outlay of money during the period, and *allocable* fixed costs, those consisting of the share allocated to the period of outlays (such as for the purchase of capital goods) incurred at one time for the benefit of production during several time periods.

The recurrent fixed costs include interest on money borrowed; taxes which are independent of output, such as capital stock taxes, flat-sum occupation levies, and, to a large extent, the general property tax; the portions of heat, utility, and insurance costs which are independent of output; most rent; and the portions of labor cost that are not affected by output changes. Even if the plant produces nothing at all, some labor will be necessary; watchmen, maintenance employees, clerical and accounting personnel are required, and portions of the administrative staff will be retained. These recurrent fixed costs give rise to cash outlays; the firm must obtain the funds from some source—current revenue, accumulated cash surplus, disposition of noncash assets, or borrowing—if it is to continue to remain in existence.

In contrast, the allocable fixed costs—those arising from past outlays for factor units usable over several years—do not usually necessitate cash outlays during the period, and the firm can continue to operate for a time even if they are not covered. Nevertheless these items constitute costs in the sense that they must be covered over a period of time if the firm is to continue permanent operations. One major example of this type of fixed cost is the portion of depreciation, often the bulk of the total, which is a function of the passage of time rather than of usage. To a large extent the economic life of capital equipment is independent of the actual extent to which the equipment is used, being controlled by the rate of development of new techniques, which render the old equipment obsolete. The portion of depreciation which is dependent upon the rate of usage is a variable cost, but many firms make no effort to separate the time and usage elements in total depreciation, and assign the entire amount on the basis of time alone. As a consequence, the sum allocated to the output of each year is independent of the volume of output, and is treated in its entirety as a fixed cost.

The other major allocable fixed-cost element is the normal return on the capital supplied by the owners. This sum does not have to be earned or paid out in any particular period, but it must be earned over a longer period of time if the firm is to continue in operation. Given the normal return rate and the quantity of money capital invested by the owners, the normal profit sum is the same for each year, regardless of the volume of output. The actual profit earned fluctuates widely, but the necessary return figure is essentially a fixed cost.

Variable Costs

The costs for which the variable factors are responsible, and thus are dependent in total magnitude upon the volume of output, are known as *variable costs.* Variable costs may be defined as those which are eliminated if production is not carried on, and which vary with the rate of output. In a long-run period all costs are variable, since all factors can be adjusted in amount, but in a short-run period only those costs which arise from the factors which are adjustable in amount are variable. The concept of "variable" with respect to these costs items refers to the behavior of the costs when output changes and has no relation to changes in cost figures due to variations in wages, costs of material, and other factor costs per unit of factor.

The major short-run variable costs are the amounts paid for materials, fuel, electric power, and transportation; most wages, especially those for work in direct physical production; and taxes of the types which vary with output, such as those levied upon sales and gross receipts. But, in addition, other cost items which are frequently fixed costs may also be partly variable. Depreciation, for example, is in part a variable cost if the actual rate of depreciation is affected at all by usage. Interest charges on funds borrowed to buy additional materials or stocks of goods for resale are likewise variable costs, even though most interest charges are fixed costs.

A distinction is sometimes made between *direct variable costs*—those, such as raw-material costs, which vary more or less in proportion to output—and *constant variable costs,* those variable costs which change relatively little as output changes. The latter resemble fixed costs but are distinguished from them by the fact that, if production is temporarily suspended, they can be eliminated, whereas fixed costs continue unchanged even if nothing is produced.[6] Constant variable costs arise out of indivisibilities of variable factor units; once an indivisible variable factor unit is acquired, it is not fully utilized until output is increased substantially, and thus the variable-cost item for which it is responsible

[6] Under a broader definition of fixed costs sometimes used, the concept includes costs treated here as constant variable costs.

does not increase in proportion to output. For example, if a railroad is to operate freight service at all on a line, a certain train crew—perhaps four men—will be required. As volume of traffic on the line increases over a very substantial range, the same crew will be required and wages will remain approximately the same. With a small volume of traffic the potential services of the crew are not utilized fully; hence for a substantial range of increase in output the costs for which the crew is responsible do not increase significantly as the volume of traffic handled by the train increases. The wages of the crew are variable costs, however, rather than fixed costs, since they are not paid if the train does not operate at all.

As indicated above, the distinction between fixed and variable costs is significant only in a short-run period, since over a longer period all factors, and all costs, are variable.

COST SCHEDULES

A cost schedule presents the data of costs of producing various alternate volumes of output and thus shows the response of cost to changes in output. There are separate cost schedules for various time intervals. A short-run schedule is relevant to a situation with a given plant, while a long-run schedule shows the costs of producing various amounts of output in a time interval sufficiently long to allow adjustments in all factors necessary to obtain the optimum factor combination for each output level.

Determinants of Cost

For a particular time period, the actual data in a cost schedule—the magnitudes of cost of producing various amounts of output—depend primarily upon three considerations: the technique of production, the efficiency of the factor units employed, and the prices paid for the factor units, including the necessary compensation for factor units owned by the firm.

If a firm is to maximize profit, it must employ the particular technique of production which will allow the optimum combination of factors, as explained in the previous chapter. In a short-run period the optimum combination is the best one possible with the fixed factor units which the firm has and is likely not to be the absolute optimum one possible if all factors could be adjusted. The short-run optimum combination is therefore influenced by the nature of the fixed factor units which the firm has at the particular time. Over a longer period, however, all factors can be varied, and the firm is free to select the combination which is the absolute optimum, in terms of existing technological conditions and factor prices.

Cost levels are affected not only by the nature of the available methods of production but also by the efficiency of the factor units—the quality of the natural resources employed, the types of capital goods available, and the skill of all types of labor, including managerial personnel. The better the quality of the resources, for example, the greater will be the output obtained from a given quantity of resources at the optimum factor combination, and the lower will be the cost of production.

Finally, the prices paid for the factor units will influence the cost in monetary terms. As indicated earlier in the chapter, from the standpoint of any one producer, the cost to him of a particular factor unit is the price which the owner of the unit could obtain from making it available in the next-best use.

Since these considerations determine the actual magnitudes of the cost data, any particular cost schedule is based upon the assumption that these determinants are "givens" and thus constant, except to the extent that a factor price may be changed as a consequence of a change in output by the firm. When a change in one of these determinants does occur, the entire cost schedule of the firm will be shifted. An increase in factor prices, for example, will raise the cost schedules; the development of new methods of production, the discovery of better-quality resources, or increased training of workers will lower the cost schedules. It is essential to distinguish clearly between a shift in a cost schedule caused by a change in one of the determinants and a movement within a schedule in response to a change in output by the firm. The former is represented graphically by a shifting of the curve, the latter merely by movement along the existing curve.

The Nature of Short-Run Cost Schedules

A short-run cost schedule for an individual firm shows the behavior of cost when output is varied with a given plant, or group of factors which is not adjustable in the short run. In Table 18 a short-run cost schedule for a particular firm is illustrated. Total cost is separated into its two elements, fixed and variable cost. The former is, by definition, the same, regardless of the volume of output. For most purposes of analysis, the use of unit cost data is more convenient than total cost data. *Average cost*[7] is determined by dividing total cost by the number of units

[7] For simplicity, the term "average cost" is used rather than "average total cost."

TABLE 18

DAILY COST SCHEDULE OF A PRODUCER

Units of Output	Total Fixed Cost	Total Variable Cost	Total Cost	Average Fixed Cost	Average Variable Cost	Average Cost	Marginal Cost
0*..................	$20	$ 0	$ 20	....	...	.....	....
1..................	20	30	50	$20.00	$ 30	$ 50.00	$ 30
2..................	20	56	76	10.00	28	38.00	26
3..................	20	75	95	6.67	25	31.67	19
4..................	20	80	100	5.00	20	25.00	5
5..................	20	105	125	4.00	21	25.00	25
6..................	20	132	152	3.33	22	25.33	27
7..................	20	182	202	2.86	26	28.86	50
8..................	20	320	340	2.50	40	42.50	138
9..................	20	720	740	2.22	80	82.22	400
10..................	20	3,000	3,020	2.00	300	302.00	2,280

*If no units are produced, total fixed cost is the same as it would be if production were carried on. No variable costs are incurred. The unit-cost columns are blank for 0 units because the concept of cost per unit has no meaning if no units are produced.

of output; just as is the case with total cost, it can be separated into two elements, *average fixed cost* (total fixed cost divided by the number of units of output) and *average variable cost* (total variable cost divided by the number of units of output). Since all cost items are, as matter of definition, either fixed or variable costs, average cost is the sum of average fixed costs and average variable costs.

The last column in Table 18 presents data of *marginal cost*—the increase in total cost which results from the production of an additional unit of output. For example, with 5 units of output, total cost is $125; with 6 units it is $152. Thus the marginal cost of the sixth unit—the amount which the production of the sixth unit adds to total cost—is $27 ($152 − $125). Marginal cost consists solely of variable cost; since total fixed cost remains the same regardless of the volume of output, any increase in cost which occurs is necessarily in a variable-cost item.

The data in a cost schedule can be illustrated graphically, with cost measured on the vertical axis and output on the horizontal axis. Total cost data are usually not plotted, since they are unnecessary for illustrating price and output determination. A typical pattern of cost curves for a firm is shown in Figure 28 (page 158).

SHORT-RUN COST BEHAVIOR

In the development of the analysis of short-run cost behavior, several assumptions are usually made:

1. Certain factors used by the firm are fixed in quantity, and there-

fore certain cost items are fixed in total. This assumption is of course a corollary of the nature of the short-run period.

2. The fixed factor units require a certain minimum quantity of variable factor units for efficient operation, but have at least some degree of adaptability for utilization with varying quantities of other factors.

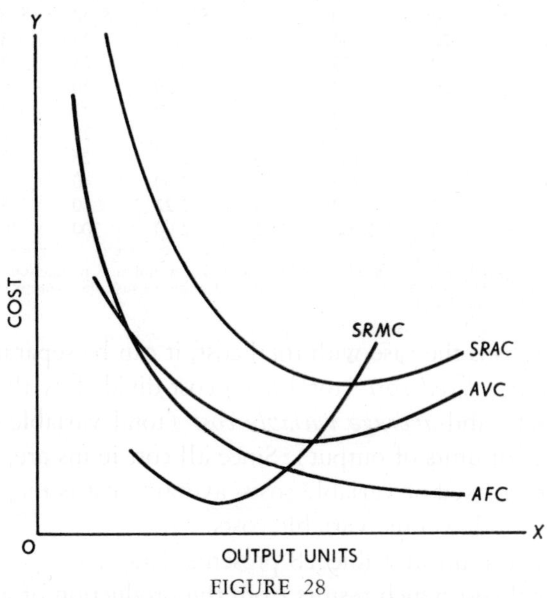

FIGURE 28

SHORT-RUN COST CURVES OF A PRODUCER

3. Some types of variable factors cannot be acquired in infinitesimally small units. For example, workers often cannot be hired for periods of less than one day.

4. Technological conditions and factor prices are given.

5. Successive variable factor units are of equal efficiency.

Under these assumptions, as output is increased, average cost will decline initially, and ultimately increase—the over-all curve being U-shaped. The reasons for this behavior can be explained in terms of the reactions of the component parts of average cost—average fixed cost and average variable cost—to the changes in output.

Average Fixed Cost

As output increases, average fixed cost declines continuously, since a given sum of total fixed cost is being divided over a successively larger volume of output. The rate of decline in average fixed cost is initially very rapid and eventually slackens, for purely arithmetic reasons.

Average Variable Cost

Under the assumptions made, average variable cost will decline initially and ultimately increase. Its precise behavior is dependent upon the behavior of average physical product per unit of the variable factors, assuming given prices for the factor units. If average physical product increases as more units of the variable factors are added, average variable cost will fall, since, as each additional unit of output is produced, the quantity of variable factors required per unit of output falls. On the other hand, if average product of the variable factor falls, average variable cost must rise. If average physical product is constant, average variable cost will be unaffected by output changes. These relationships are illustrated in Table 19. Each unit of the variable factors (consisting, perhaps, of one worker plus a certain quantity of materials and electric power) is assumed to cost $20. As average product of the variable factor rises when the number of such factors is increased from 1 to 3, total variable cost rises at a slower rate than output, and thus average variable cost falls. In the range from 3 to 5 units of the variable factor, average product per unit of the variable factor remains constant; total variable cost and total product rise at the same rate, and thus average variable cost remains constant. With 6 units or more of the variable factors, diminishing average returns are encountered; average product falls, and average variable cost rises.

TABLE 19

RELATIONSHIP OF THE BEHAVIOR OF AVERAGE PRODUCT OF THE VARIABLE FACTORS AND AVERAGE VARIABLE COST

PRODUCTIVITY SCHEDULE			SCHEDULE OF VARIABLE COST		
Units of Variable Factor	Output	Average Product per Unit of Variable Factor	Output	Total Variable Cost	Average Variable Cost
1	5	5	5	$ 20	$4
2	15	$7\frac{1}{2}$	15	40	2.67
3	30	10	30	60	2
4	40	10	40	80	2
5	50	10	50	100	2
6	54	9	54	120	2.22
7	56	8	56	140	2.50
8	57	$7\frac{1}{8}$	57	160	2.81

Under the assumptions made, average variable cost will pass through three successive phases as output is increased:

1. *The Phase of Declining Average Variable Cost.* Under the assumption that the fixed factor units cannot be used effectively with-

out a certain minimum quantity of variable factor units, the average physical product will rise as additional variable units are added, since more effective use is made of the fixed factor units. Thus average variable cost will fall, since the rate of increase in output exceeds the rate of increase in variable factor units. For example, a plant may have a certain set of machines which require 5 men for efficient operation; with only 2 or 3 men hired, the machine can be used only very ineffectively, and the output per man will be relatively small. But as the 4th and 5th men are hired, operation of the machinery reaches a high level of efficiency, and the output per man is higher and variable cost per unit of product is lower.

The tendency for average variable cost to rise will be increased if the variable factors must be acquired in relatively large indivisible units. It is difficult, for example, to hire workers for only a few hours, or to use particular men on a large number of different tasks. Accordingly, when output is low, a portion of the manpower will not be utilized fully, and a particular percentage increase in output will not require an equivalent percentage increase in labor employed. Thus output per worker will rise, and average variable cost will fall. Extreme examples arise in various service industries. One bus driver is required whether one passenger or fifty are carried in a bus, and as the load increases, the manpower cost per passenger falls. A theater must have at least one cashier on duty regardless of the number of customers, so long as the theater is open.

2. *The Phase of Constant Average Variable Cost.* Once the inputs of variable factors have reached such levels that the fixed factors can be employed effectively, and each variable factor unit is likewise being fully utilized, further increases in output, over a considerable range, may be made at more or less constant average variable cost. Through this range of output, a doubling of the variable factors will more or less double the output, and thus the average physical product and the average variable cost per unit of output are constant. This stage will be encountered at relatively low levels of output if fixed factor units are divided into small units, so that only a small number of variable units are required to operate each fixed unit. If a plant consists of a large number of small identical machines (such as those used in some lines of textile production), efficient operation of those machines in use with a small volume of output can be obtained with only a small labor force. As output is increased more men are added and more machines brought into use, and variable cost will be more or less constant per unit of output.

If the nature of a production process is such that operations can be carried on in three shifts of eight hours in length, output can be tripled, more or less, from the quantity at which the plant was fully utilized on an eight-hour basis, without any significant change in average variable cost. The ability to vary the speed at which production is carried on likewise increases the range of constant average variable cost.

Empirical studies of cost functions in recent years have confirmed the belief that the phase of constant average variable cost is an important one. The phase is not necessarily encountered in all cases, however. If the fixed capital is of such nature that a certain number of variable units is required for efficient operation, yet further increases in the number of variable factor units will increase output very little, the initial phase of decreasing cost will be followed directly by the phase of increasing average variable cost.

If the assumptions that the fixed factors require a certain minimum quantity of variable factors for efficient operation, and that variable factors cannot be obtained in very small units are abandoned, the phase of constant average variable cost could be encountered initially, with no previous phase of declining average variable costs. It is widely believed, however, that these assumptions are realistic ones, although their significance undoubtedly varies widely in different lines of production. The more divisible the units of both fixed and variable factors, the less significant will be the stage of declining average variable cost.

3. *The Phase of Increasing Average Variable Cost.* Eventually, in any type of business, as output is increased with a fixed plant, average variable cost will commence to rise because of the decline in average product of the variable factors which results from the operation of the Law of Diminishing Returns. The plant is designed for a certain volume of production; when output is carried beyond this level, the increase in the variable factors necessary to produce the additional output will be relatively greater than the output increase, and average variable cost will rise. In some production processes the increase will be gradual, as equipment will be used longer hours than intended and machinery will be operated at a faster rate. Obsolete equipment kept in reserve will be placed in use. These adjustments will involve some increase in average variable cost, since maintenance costs are certain to rise more than proportionately when machinery is run at a higher than optimum rate, and the use of older equipment will necessitate higher variable costs. But adjustments of this sort do make possible further increases in output without tremendous changes in cost. In other lines of production, however, it will be almost impossible to produce more than the quantity for

which the plant was designed, and average variable cost will rise rapidly as great increases in the quantities of the variable factors are required to produce a few more units of output. Once absolute capacity[8] is reached, average variable cost for larger volumes of output is infinite, since such quantities cannot be produced with the given plant.

The Behavior of Average Cost

Since average cost is the sum of average variable cost and average fixed cost, its behavior reflects the combined influence of the changes in the two constituent elements. As a firm first increases output, average fixed cost must necessarily fall, and under the assumptions indicated above, average variable cost will also fall. As a consequence average cost must fall as well, as illustrated in Table 18 and Figure 28. The rate of decline will depend upon the relative importance of the fixed and variable cost elements, the extent to which the fixed factor units consist of large, unadaptable units which require several units of variable factors for efficient operation, and the extent to which the variable factors can be obtained only in large units. The rate of decline in average cost will be particularly great in large manufacturing establishments with heavy fixed costs and equipment of such nature that effective operation requires a relatively large labor force.

If average variable cost does not decline initially, or becomes relatively constant once output has reached a certain level, average cost will still decline because of the fall in fixed cost per unit, but the rate of decline will be very small once output has expanded to the point at which fixed costs are a minor element in the total costs.

If production is carried far enough, average cost must eventually rise. Average variable costs will commence to increase once the optimum plant capacity output is reached, and this rise will eventually offset the continuing decline in average fixed costs. The speed at which average variable cost and average cost rise will depend primarily upon the nature of the production processes, and particularly upon the flexibility of the fixed plant—the ability to expand production beyond the optimum capacity level without substantial increases in the quantities of the variable factors required.

Thus, in summary, the average-cost curve is U-shaped or, more appropriately, ‿ -shaped when average variable cost is more or less constant over a substantial range of output. Figure 29 illustrates the latter case more precisely. Figure 30 illustrates the opposite case, in

[8] The term "capacity" is sometimes used in reference to the "optimum" or "low-cost" level of operation, in other cases to the absolute maximum output level possible with the plant.

which average cost falls and rises sharply, because the capital equipment is of such nature that a substantial number of men is required for efficient operation; yet once the equipment is brought into effective

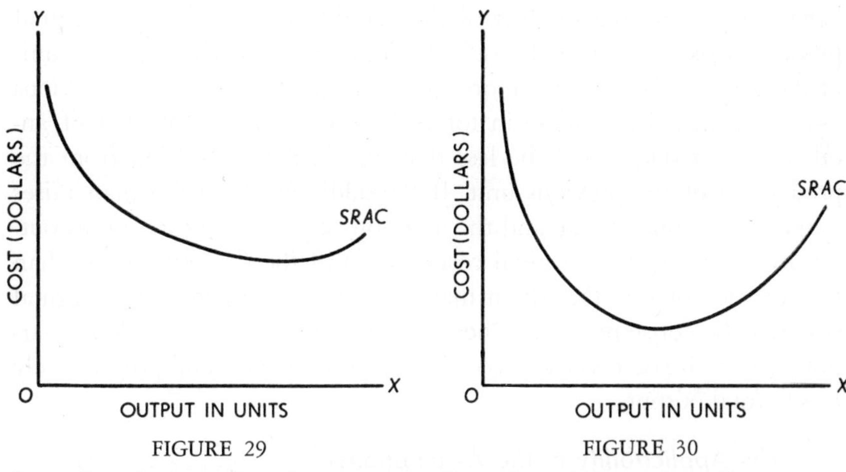

FIGURE 29
SHORT-RUN AVERAGE COST CURVE, WITH FLEXIBLE PLANT

FIGURE 30
SHORT-RUN AVERAGE COST CURVE, WITH INFLEXIBLE PLANT

operation additional output beyond this figure cannot be obtained, except with very substantial additional amounts of variable factor units.

The Behavior of Marginal Cost

Since the behavior of marginal cost depends upon that of total cost, its determinants are the same as those of average cost. Certain relationships between marginal and average cost should be noted, however. When average variable cost is falling, marginal cost must be less than average variable cost (but not necessarily falling); likewise, when average cost is falling, marginal cost must be less than average cost. On the other hand, when average variable cost is rising, marginal cost will be greater than average variable cost; when average cost is rising, marginal cost must exceed it. Marginal cost is equal to average variable cost at the lowest point of the latter and is equal to average cost at the point of lowest average cost. Thus the marginal-cost curve intersects the average variable cost curve and the average-cost curve at their respective low points. This relationship is one of mathematical necessity; when a number (the marginal cost) being added into a series is less than the previous average of the series, the new average will be lower than the previous one; when the number added is greater than the average, the latter will rise.

When average variable cost is constant, marginal cost and average variable cost will be identical, since the production of an additional unit adds the same amount to total cost as the previous average of the variable cost.

The behavior of marginal cost bears a definite relationship to the behavior of marginal product of the variable factors. When marginal product is rising, marginal cost is falling, because each successive unit of the variable factors adds more to total product than did the previous unit, and thus the increase in total cost due to the production of another unit of output will be less than the increase resulting from the production of the previous unit. If the addition of a sixth man raises output by 45 units a day and the addition of a seventh man raises output by 65 units, the marginal cost of each of the 65 units is less than that of each of the 45. When marginal product is constant, marginal cost will be constant also. When marginal product is declining, marginal cost will rise because successive factor units will add progressively less to total output.

The Applicability of the Assumptions

The usefulness of the short-run cost analysis depends, of course, upon the applicability of the assumptions to actual situations. The first assumption, of certain factor units being fixed in quantity, follows from the definition of a short-run period, and is typical of the situation which confronts firms in relatively short time intervals, since the quantities of some factors cannot be adjusted quickly.

The second and third assumptions (page 158) relate to the nature of the fixed and variable factor units; it was assumed that a certain minimum quantity of variable units is required to utilize the fixed factor units effectively, and that at least some of the variable factor units, especially manpower, cannot be obtained in very small units. The assumption about fixed factors is relevant to many types of capital equipment in various lines of manufacturing; an automobile assembly line, for example, cannot be utilized at all unless a certain minimum amount of manpower is used. In other lines of production, however, this consideration is of much less importance; in retailing for example, there is typically no equipment that requires a substantial number of workers to operate. In the latter type of industry, therefore, there is less likelihood of an increase in average physical product, and thus an initial decline in average variable costs from this cause. Average fixed costs will, of course, fall.

The assumption that variable factor units cannot always be obtained in very small units is more likely to be universally realized. It is not possible, for example, to hire one half of a man, or, in many cases, to hire a man for less than a day, or perhaps even a longer period. Accordingly, the time of the first units of manpower added will not be fully utilized initially, and as output is increased, proportionate increases in inputs of variable factors will not be required, and average variable cost will fall. From this consideration alone, average variable cost will tend to decline initially, even if the fixed plant is entirely flexible. But the consideration is likely to be much greater in some lines of production than in others.

The fourth assumption was that of given technological conditions and factor prices. The assumption that technology and methods of production are given is necessary to distinguish the effects upon unit cost of changes in output from those resulting from technological change. Since the methods are "givens" of a particular cost schedule, changes in the methods will result in an entirely new schedule, rather than a shift within the existing schedule. The same considerations apply to price changes caused by external forces. But in some instances the prices paid for various factor units will change *as a result of* changes in output by the firm; hence the changes are relevant for the nature of a particular cost schedule. When materials are purchased in larger quantities, lower prices are often obtainable. Rate schedules for electric power often provide lower rates for larger quantities than for smaller amounts. The ability to ship in carload and truckload quantities greatly reduces freight costs per unit. When "quantity discounts" of these types are available, the net cost per unit of the variable factors falls as more units are acquired, and the decline in average variable cost due to the initial rise in average physical product per unit of the variable factors is reinforced. In retailing and some other lines of business, the quantity discount feature is of particular importance and is likely to be of greater significance in bringing about an initial decline in average variable cost than the behavior of average physical product, because of the relative unimportance of capital equipment in these lines of business.

As a firm continues to expand, however, eventually all available quantity discounts will be obtained, and a point may ultimately be reached at which further increases in factor purchases may drive factor prices upward. For example, if a large firm is the principal employer of skilled labor in a certain area, it may eventually exhaust the local supply of this type of labor, and further increases in output will necessitate the payment of higher wages to draw workers from other plants or from more distant areas. To the extent that factor prices are increased as output increases, average variable cost will tend to rise. This effect will reinforce the increase produced by the decline in average physical product.

Not only may factor prices rise as a firm increases output, but the additional factor units may be less efficient than the previous; the assumption of homogeneous factor units is by no means necessarily realized in practice. Presumably a firm will hire the most efficient workers first; as additional men are hired, the successive workers are likely to be less skilled and less capable. Thus the decline in average physical product and the rise in average variable cost will be greater than it would be on the basis of the operation of the Law of Diminishing Returns alone, unless the prices paid for the less efficient factor units are proportionately lower than those paid for the better units. But, particularly in the case of labor, this may not be true.

Empirical Studies of Short-Run Cost Behavior

The actual determination of the data in the cost schedule of a particular firm is a difficult task, far more so than might appear at first glance. A firm usually has a reasonably accurate knowledge of average cost at existing output levels but nothing more than a rough estimate of costs at other output levels. Frequently, no serious attempt is made to ascertain this data, and even if an effort is made, the difficulties involved in doing so prevent the results from being entirely accurate. The firm must, however, base its policy upon some estimate of cost behavior. Various studies of business policy suggest that in many cases firms do not attempt to ascertain marginal cost, as such, but seek to determine optimum price and output levels with the use of total and average cost and revenue data. On the whole, however, it is likely that firms have a much better knowledge of their cost schedules than of their demand schedules, since the latter are dependent upon often unpredictable reactions of customers and competitors.

In recent years a number of independent studies have been made of cost schedules of various firms, primarily for the purpose of determining whether the pattern of cost behavior which had been developed by economic analysis is typical of actual cost schedules. The problems which such studies have encountered are, however, very serious. One major problem arises out of changes in other determinants of cost—factor prices, techniques of production, etc.—during the period for which the study is made. An attempt must be made by statistical techniques to isolate the changes in cost due to output changes from the changes due to shifts in the determinants. Entirely satisfactory results are not possible, however. Also, in any particular period, costs may be affected by the rate at which output changes; a sudden increase may cause temporary additions to cost which can be avoided once production is adjusted to the higher volume. Changes in the size of orders may affect costs materially in some lines of manufacturing. The problems of the time periods in which costs are recorded give rise to difficulties. Raw materials may be purchased in large quantities and charged as expenses in a period in which output is low (but an increase is expected), while in the later period, when output actually does rise, few materials purchases may be made. The measurement of units of output likewise is a source of difficulty. Most firms produce more than one type of product, and the relative importance of various types produced is likely to change during the period. Finally, the range of output may be relatively narrow, and only a small segment of the schedule can be computed; the data obtained cannot safely be projected into ranges of output for which no data are available.

The most important discovery which has been made by the studies is that of the importance of the phase of constant average variable cost. Within the ranges of output for which data were available, average variable cost and thus marginal cost were usually found to be constant. Therefore the typical average variable cost curve would appear to contain an extensive horizontal section rather than being U- or V-shaped. But the difficulties encountered in the studies were so great that too much significance cannot as yet be attached to the conclusions; it is commonly believed that the statistical techniques employed created a certain bias in favor of constant average variable cost.[9]

[9] An excellent survey of the various studies and the problems encountered is to be found in the book by Joel Dean, *Managerial Economics* (New York: Prentice-Hall, 1951), pp. 272–96.

A study by W. J. Eiteman and G. E. Guthrie, "The Shape of the Average Cost Curve," *American Economic Review,* Vol. XLII (December, 1952), pp. 832–38, sought to discover, by questionnaire, the businessman's typical belief about the nature of his short-run average-cost curve. The largest number reported average-cost curves of the types illustrated on Figures 31 and 32 below. In Figure 32, the curve would, of course, rise if carried beyond the "capacity" line. Unfortunately the authors of this article drew completely unwarranted conclusions from these findings, as noted in a series of comments in the September, 1953, issue of the *American Economic Review.* It is by no means clear whether the respondents to the questionnaires interpreted the term "capacity" to mean "optimum operating capacity," or "absolute capacity."

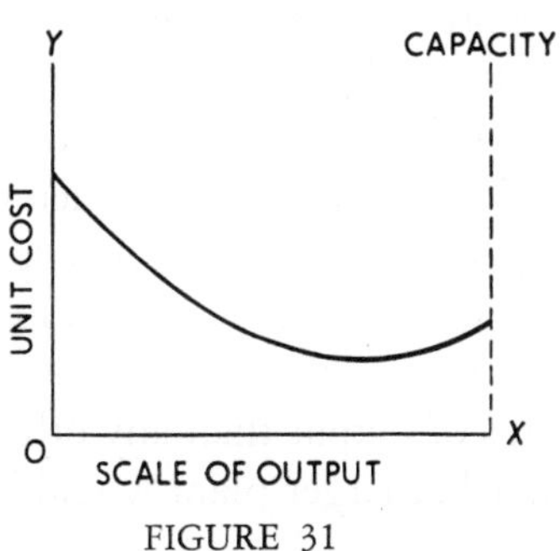

FIGURE 31

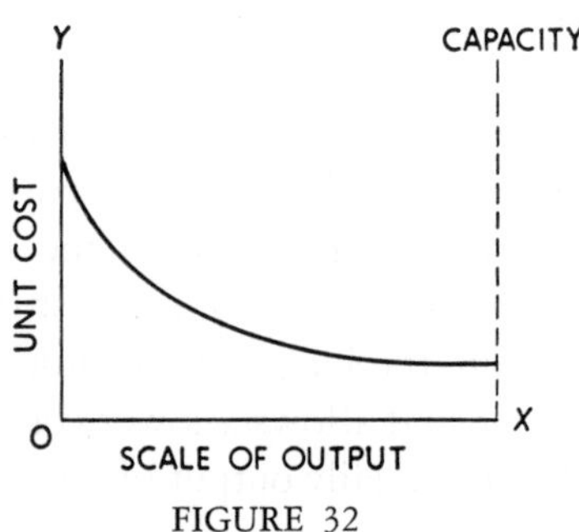

FIGURE 32

COST SCHEDULES OVER A LONG-RUN PERIOD

As indicated above, the long-run period is defined as a period sufficiently long that the business firm can make desired adjustments in all factors of production employed. The actual time interval depends upon the nature of the productive processes and particularly upon the extent to which specialized types of capital equipment requiring a substantial period to construct and having a life of a number of years are utilized. The time necessary to allow adjustment of all factors is much greater for a steel mill or a railroad than it is for a service station or a grocery store. Over a long-run period, since all factors are adjustable, all costs are variable; the factor units which are fixed in the short run and which are responsible for some costs being fixed in this period are adjustable over a longer period.

The Nature of the Long-Run Cost Schedule

The long-run cost schedule shows, for each level of output, the *lowest possible cost* of producing the particular amount of output, given a sufficient time interval that all factors can be adjusted and the absolute optimum factor combination for the particular output level attained. In Table 18, the total cost of producing 10 units is $3,020, with the particular plant. But this plant was designed for a much smaller volume of output (4 units per day); with the plant best suited for 10 units, one considerably larger than the one whose cost data are presented in Table 18, the total cost of producing 10 units per day might be $190; this figure, since it is the lowest possible cost of producing 10 units, is the appropriate cost figure for this level of output in the long-run cost schedule. Similarly, for other levels of output there are certain figures of lowest possible total cost, with the plant size—the combination of all factors—best suited to the particular output levels. A typical long-run cost schedule for a firm is illustrated in Table 20. The data are obtained from a number of short-run cost schedules, one for each possible size of plant. From each of the short-run schedules, the data taken for the long-run schedule are the cost figures for those levels of output for which the particular plant allows the most satisfactory factor combination and the lowest cost. From the short-run schedule shown in Table 18, the cost data for 4, 5, and 6 units of output might go into the long-run schedule, since the plant is designed for this output range and allows a lower cost for such figures of output than any other. But for a daily output of 7 or 8 units, a somewhat larger plant would be

TABLE 20

TYPICAL LONG-RUN AVERAGE-COST SCHEDULE OF A FIRM

Units of Output	Total Cost	Average Cost	Marginal Cost
5	$125	$25.00	....
10	190	19.00	$13.00*
15	263	17.35	14.60
20	340	17.00	15.40
25	418	16.72	15.60
30	498	16.60	16.00
35	579	16.54	16.20
40	664	16.60	17.00
45	751	16.69	17.40
50	845	16.90	18.80

* The increase in total cost of $65 resulting when 5 additional units are produced, divided by 5.

more suitable, and the long-run cost figures, taken from the short-run cost data for the larger plant, would be lower than the figures for producing these amounts of output with the smaller plant. For output of 3 units or less a day, a plant smaller than that for which the data are given in Table 18 would allow lower cost.

Long-run average cost for any output level is determined by dividing the figure of long-run *total cost* for this output by the number of units of output. Long-run average cost may be defined as the lowest possible average cost of producing a particular amount of output, with the optimum plant size, and thus factor combination, for that particular amount of output. Since in the long run all factors are adjustable, there are no fixed costs, average variable cost and average cost being identical. The concept of long-run marginal cost refers to the increase in total cost which occurs when shift is made to a one-unit-higher scale of production, with optimum factor combinations obtained before and after the change. Since changes in scale cannot ordinarily be made economically in such small increments, long-run marginal cost may be regarded more realistically as the increase in total cost which occurs when transition is made from one scale of output to the next-highest scale, divided by the number of units of increase in output which results. That is, if with a scale of plant designed for 20 units per day, total cost is $340, and with the next-largest feasible scale, one designed for 25 units, total cost is $418, the long-run marginal cost is $15.60 a unit ($78 increase in total cost divided by 5 units increase in output).

The graphical presentation of the long-run average-cost schedule should facilitate an understanding of the concept. A firm has a large number of alternative possible scales of operation, or plant sizes, which it may build and operate. For each scale or plant size there is an appropriate short-run average-cost schedule and curve. The pattern of these, for various scales of operation, may be drawn on a single graph, as illustrated in Figure 33, which, for simplification, shows the cost curves for only seven possible scales, with the assumption (not unrealistic for many industries) that indivisibilities of some factor units prevent the use of scales of operation intermediate to those whose curves are plotted. Certain relationships between the successive curves should be noted. For output of 10 units or less, average cost is lowest with plant size *A*. Costs with *B* (and larger) plants are relatively high for these

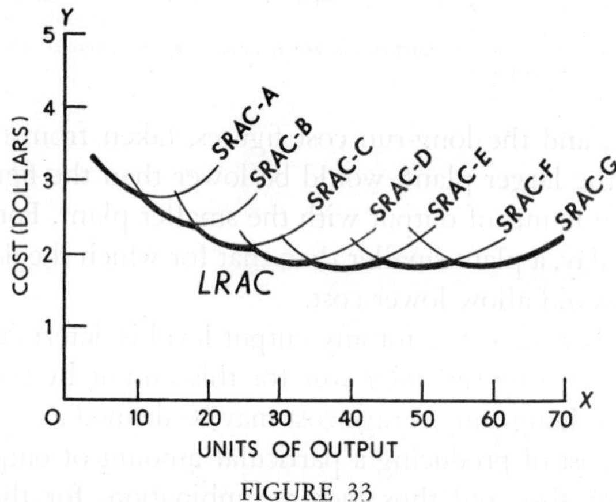

FIGURE 33

THE RELATIONSHIP BETWEEN THE POSSIBLE ALTERNATIVE SHORT-RUN AVERAGE-COST CURVES OF THE FIRM AND ITS LONG-RUN AVERAGE-COST CURVE

levels of output because the plants are far too large for the particular level of output, and machinery, buildings, etc., would be poorly utilized. But beyond 10 units of output, costs with plant size *B* become lower than those with *A*. If 18 units were produced with plant *A*, the plant would be operated beyond designed capacity, and average variable cost would be high. In contrast, plant *B*, designed for a larger volume of output, would be operating close to optimum capacity with 18 units. Beyond 19 units of output, cost is lower with plant *C*, since production of this volume with size *B* would carry it beyond designed capacity, whereas *C* is suitable for a larger volume.

For each level of output, long-run average cost is represented by the appropriate point on that short-run average-cost curve which reaches the lowest level for the particular output. If a perpendicular line is extended upward from the output figure on a graph containing the various short-run average-cost curves for different-sized plants, the point at which it first strikes a short-run average-cost curve indicates the long-run average cost for that output level. Thus in Figure 33, for 5 units of output the lowest average cost point is on curve *SRAC-A;* for 22 units it is on *SRAC-C,* etc. Thus the long-run average-cost curve is identical with *SRAC-A* up to 10 units of output (the intersection of *SRAC-A* and *SRAC-B*); it is identical with *SRAC-B* up to the point at which the latter intersects *SRAC-C,* etc. The entire long-run average-cost curve (for the output range covered) is indicated in Figure 33 by the heavily shaded line. If the long-run average-cost curve is plotted directly from a long-run average-cost schedule, such as that presented in Table 20, the only portions of the short-run curves which will appear are those which

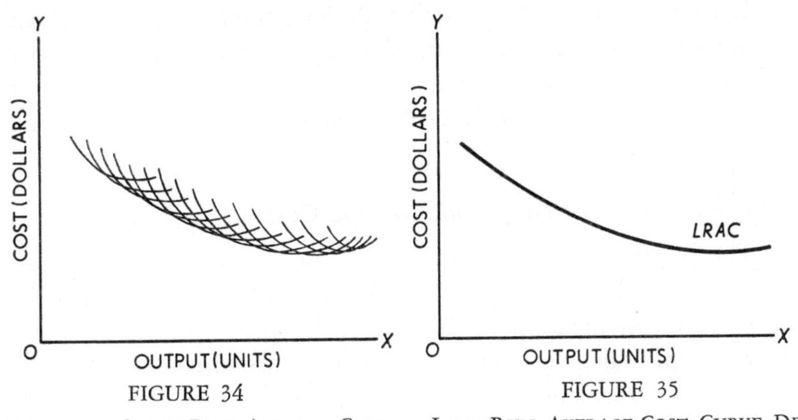

FIGURE 34

Pattern of Short-Run Average-Cost Curves, When All Factors Are Divisible

FIGURE 35

Long-Run Average-Cost Curve Derived from Short-Run Cost Curves in Figure 34

comprise portions of the long-run curve itself. It is important to note that the long-run schedule contains no data which are not to be found in the various short-run schedules of the firm; the long-run curve is the envelope of the pattern of short-run curves.

When all factors are divisible into small units, the successive scales of operation will be close to one another, as illustrated in Figure 34, and the long-run average-cost curve will be a smooth curve, as shown in Figure 35. When indivisibilities prevent small adjustments in plant scale, the short-run curves will be farther apart, and the long-run curves will be irregular, as illustrated in Figure 33 above.

The long-run average-cost curve is often called the *planning* curve, since it represents the cost data which are relevant to the firm when it is planning policy in regard to scale of operations, output, and price over a substantial period of time. At any particular time a firm already in operation has a certain plant and must base its current price and output decisions upon the cost schedule with the existing plant. But when the firm considers the possibility of adjustment in scale of operations, long-run cost data are necessary. For example, suppose that in a particular case a producer now operating to the designed capacity of his plant, with an average cost figure of $5.00 a unit, knows that he could sell a substantially greater volume of output, but he cannot produce more with his present plant without raising cost materially. Accordingly, he considers whether or not he should expand his plant in order to be able to produce the larger volume without substantial increase in average cost. His decision in regard to the expansion is obviously influenced by his estimate of the level of average cost with the larger plant.

It is important to recognize that the long-run average-cost schedule does not consist of historical data showing what cost has been in the past with various-sized plants; it shows alternative possibilities at the present time—what cost would be for various levels of output if various-sized plants were built.

The Behavior of Long-Run Average Cost

The behavior of long-run average cost in response to changes in output is controlled by substantially different considerations from those which affect cost behavior with a particular plant. Short-run cost behavior is conditioned very largely by the presence of constant quantities of some factors, which are responsible not only for certain costs being fixed in amount but also for the nature of the reactions of variable costs to output changes. In a period of time sufficiently long for the scale of operations to be adjusted, all factors are adjustable, and the consideration of fixed factors is no longer relevant for cost behavior.

The analysis of long-run cost behavior is based upon the following assumptions:

1. All factors are variable in quantity.

2. Certain factors are indivisible, in the sense that they cannot be obtained in infinitesimally small units, or are relatively inefficient if reduced in size below a certain figure.

3. An increase in the quantities of all factors allows greater specialization in the utilization of particular factor units.

4. The managerial factor cannot be multiplied in the same manner as other factors because of the need for maintaining unified control over the entire enterprise.

5. Technological conditions and factor prices are given.

6. Successive factor units are of equal efficiency, in the sense of being interchangeable without loss in output.

Given these assumptions, the primary determinant of the behavior of long-run average cost is the manner in which the Principle of Returns to Scale operates in the particular type of production activity, and thus the behavior of changes in output as the inputs of all factor units are changed. As indicated in the previous chapter, a firm typically experiences increasing returns to scale as it expands the scale of its operations initially, in part because of the indivisibilities of some factors, especially capital equipment, which make operation on a small-scale basis inefficient and costly; and in part because of the advantages of specialization of labor. As a consequence, since output rises at a faster rate than the rate of increase in the factor units, total cost rises at a slower rate than output, and average cost falls. Typically, as a firm expands, short-run cost curves for successively larger plants will be lower, in the range of output for which the plant is designed, than the cost curves with the smaller plants in the output ranges for which these were designed. In other words, the low-cost points for the cost curves for successively larger plants will be progressively lower. This is illustrated in Figure 33; the low segment of *SRAC-B*—the segment which constitutes a portion of the long-run average-cost curve—is lower than the low segment of *SRAC-A,* and that of *SRAC-C* is lower than that of *SRAC-B.* Hence the long-run average-cost curve slopes downward from left to right in the initial stage.

Eventually, however, if the firm expands far enough, the economies of large-scale production will be exhausted. The best available types of capital equipment will be employed and utilized to capacity, and full advantage will be gained from specialization. The advantages of the latter do not extend indefinitely; once the point is reached at which all workers are performing tasks sufficiently limited in scope, further increases in output merely require additional men doing the same tasks. When output reaches the level at which the stage of increasing returns to scale is succeeded by that of constant returns, total cost and output will increase at the same rate, and average cost will be constant. Especially in industries in which little capital equipment is used, and thus few economies of large-scale production are available, the stage of constant average cost may be encountered at relatively low levels of output and is likely to extend over a very substantial range. In instances in which there are important indivisibilities and gains from labor specialization, constant average cost will be encountered only after a long phase of decreasing cost.

Eventually, if expansion is carried far enough, decreasing returns to scale, caused, as explained in Chapter 7, by the complexities of large-scale management, will cause long-run average cost to become progressively greater for successively larger output levels. This rise is likely to be very gradual, however, and is not at all comparable with the rapid rise in average cost in the short run, when expansion of output beyond the designed capacity causes a sharp increase in variable cost and therefore in average cost.

The necessity of selling in a progressively wider market, covering a greater geographical area, may also tend to raise average cost as output expands. As a firm increases its output, the additional sales must frequently be made to buyers at greater distances from the plant. As a consequence, transportation costs increase and raise the average costs of production. The firm may seek to avoid this by building additional plants in other areas, but, if the original location was the one most suited to the particular type of production, costs will be higher in the new plants.

In summary, under the assumptions made, typically the long-run average cost of a firm will initially decline because the indivisibilities of various types of factors, especially capital equipment, are overcome, and greater advantages of specialization are obtained, with consequent increase in returns to scale as factor inputs are increased. The use of larger and more efficient types of capital equipment and the advantages of greater specialization in management and labor are perhaps the most important specific causes of increasing returns to scale. After expansion is carried to the point at which these economies are exhausted, a substantial range of approximately constant average cost is likely to follow, in turn to be succeeded, if the scale of operations is increased far enough, by a stage of gradually rising average cost, brought about by the complexities of large-scale management and, in some instances, by the necessity of selling in a geographically wider market. Under these assumptions, the long-run average cost curve is ◡ -shaped, the rate of decrease in the left-hand portion being much greater in some industries than in others, the rate of increase in the right-hand portion being very gradual. The exact shape of the curve in any particular case depends primarily upon the manner in which the Principle of Returns to Scale operates—that is, the extent to which economies of large-scale production are available, the level to which output must be expanded before the economies are completely exhausted, and the extent to which complexities of large-scale management are encountered. Thus, in some industries, the lowest possible cost can be obtained with a small volume of output, and the industry will be characterized by the presence of a large number of small firms. In other cases low cost is obtained only when output reaches a substantial figure, and, as a consequence, firms tend to grow large in size, with small firms having difficulty in remaining in the industry.

The Significance of the Assumptions

This traditional analysis of long-run cost behavior is based upon several assumptions noted at the beginning of the section. The significance of the analysis, therefore, depends upon the applicability of the assumptions in typical conditions. Each of the assumptions will be examined briefly.

1. Variability of factors. The assumption that all factors can be varied in the long-run period is valid except in rare cases of unique, specialized resources.

2. Factor indivisibility. The assumption that small units of certain factors cannot be obtained, or are relatively inefficient, appears to be applicable in many lines of production. It is not possible, for example, to build many types of capital equipment on a small-scale basis; in other cases, while they can be built, they provide relatively low output per unit of input. Manpower cannot be obtained in many cases in very small units, such as man-minutes. While these considerations are more important in some lines of production than in others, both casual observations and more careful empirical studies suggest that some indivisibilities are encountered in virtually all lines of production.

3. Gains from specialization of factor units. It is likewise generally recognized that economies are obtained by utilization of labor and other factor units in relatively specialized fashion.

Despite the obviously extensive validity of assumptions 2 and 3, it must be recognized that if, in a particular instance, neither assumption is valid, long-run average cost cannot be expected to decline.

4. Adjustment of the managerial factor. The assumption that the managerial factor cannot be adjusted in the same manner as other factors, with consequent increasing complexities and cost of management as an enterprise grows, is subject to greater question. The problems of large-scale management are, of course, very real. But as business firms grow in size, great attention is given to the development and application of the principles of scientific management in an effort to overcome these problems. By this means firms may succeed in preventing an increase in average cost for a very substantial range of output. Whether this increase can be prevented indefinitely as output is extended farther and farther is doubtful. But there is by no means conclusive evidence that an eventual rise in average cost is inevitable.

5. Given technological conditions and factor prices. The assumption of given technological conditions is necessary in order to distinguish between the effects upon cost of changes in output and those arising from technological change; the assumption does not lessen the significance of the analysis, but actual technological changes occurring do render more difficult any empirical studies of actual long-run cost behavior in response to output changes.

The assumption of given factor prices is open to greater question, because changes in factor inputs by a firm may result in changes in factor prices, as noted above in the discussion of short-run cost behavior. So far as factor price changes caused by extraneous factors are concerned, their exclusion from the discussion of the behavior of the cost schedule is designed merely to isolate the effects of the various influences affecting the actual cost. But when changes in factor prices which the firm must pay result directly from changes in quantities of the factors purchased by the firm, this reaction must be taken into consideration in the analysis of the behavior of long-run average cost in response to output changes.

As a firm first increases its size, it is likely to be able to obtain some factor units, particularly materials, power, and freight service, more cheaply; these quantity discounts, which are in part encountered even with expansion with a given plant, as explained on page 165, but may not be exhausted when output is extended to absolute capacity of the smaller plants, will tend to accentuate the initial decline in long-run average cost which arises from the operation of the Principle of Returns to Scale.

On the other hand, as expansion is extended farther and farther, the point may be reached at which the firm will find it necessary to pay higher prices for various materials and manpower, as the quantity available at existing prices is exhausted. Any firm will encounter this phenomenon if it expands so far that it is using a significant portion of the total supply of any particular factor.

6. Equal efficiency of factor units. Finally, the assumption of equal efficiency of factor units may not be realized in practice. The firm will presumably acquire the best factor units initially, and find that additional ones acquired are less efficient. If the difference in efficiency is offset by price differences, there is no effect on the behavior of average cost. But if the prices are the same for the poorer units as for the better ones, as is often the case with labor, especially when unions are strong, this feature will tend to raise long-run average cost beyond a certain point.

Empirical Studies of Long-Run Cost Schedules

In general, it is likely that producers have only very remote ideas of the data of their long-run cost schedules. Only a small segment of the schedule is of direct concern to a producer at any time. He knows that costs with a very small plant would be prohibitively high, but he does not care exactly how high they are. A seller in nonpurely competitive markets knows that there is no need for considering the costs with a plant ten times the present size, as he is aware that he could not possibly sell the increased output at a profitable price. A small segment is relevant for decisions relating to expansion or contraction of plant; if a producer suspects that such changes might be desirable, he will attempt to figure the cost with various scales of operation, aided by engineering estimates, and data, if obtainable, of costs of other firms with larger or smaller scales of operation than his own. Once a plant adjustment is made, the decision is irrevocable for a period of time, especially if the change has involved an expansion, even if the cost estimate upon which it was based proves to have been erroneous, since further changes cannot be made profitably, or at all in some cases, except over a considerable period of time.

Some general empirical studies have been made of long-run cost behavior, but the results have not been at all conclusive. The problems encountered are even more serious than those which arise with short-run cost studies. Any attempt to determine the actual long-run cost function of a single firm from observations of cost with different scales of operation over a period of time is almost entirely futile. Because of the length of the time period necessary to get any substantial number of observations, other determinants of cost—particularly, methods of production—change so much that statistical adjustment for them is impossible. As a consequence, the actual studies, for the most part, have taken cost data for several firms of different sizes at a particular time, in an effort to build up a cost schedule typical of the firms in the industry. This approach itself encounters serious problems. Some firms will be operating closer to capacity than others, and thus the cost differences will reflect variations in the degree of utilization of plant, as well as variations due to differences in plant size. Differences in age of equipment, quality of product, management efficiency, cost-accounting methods, and prices paid for factors will prevent exact attainment of the desired results, since the effects of these differences cannot be adequately eliminated.

The most recent survey of empirical studies in the field concludes that while there is clear evidence that long-run average cost declines as the scale of operations is increased from a very small size, there is little evidence to prove (or disprove) the thesis that average cost must eventually rise as scale of operations is expanded because of increased complexities of management and consequent decreasing returns to scale.[10] There is some evidence that long-run average cost does eventually rise as operations are expanded, but primarily as a result of the tendency of prices paid for factors and distribution costs to rise.

COST CONDITIONS OF THE INDUSTRY

The preceding sections have considered the behavior of cost of the individual firm, as the firm changes its output under various conditions, with the assumptions that the prices paid for factor units are given, except insofar as they may change as the output of the firm itself changes. Completion of the analysis must take into consideration the situation in which a significant change in total combined output of the various firms in an industry will alter factor prices, or alter the efficiency of the factors employed by the various firms. In other words, the height of the cost schedule of each firm may be affected by changes in the output of the entire industry. The term *cost conditions of the industry* is given to the nature of the relationship between changes in total output of the industry and changes in the height of the cost schedules of the individual firms in the industry.

There are three possible industry cost conditions. An *increasing-cost* industry is one in which the long-run cost schedules of the firms rise as the total number of firms and the total output of the industry increase. A *decreasing-cost* industry is one in which the cost schedules of the firms fall as the output of the industry rises. A *constant-cost* industry is one in which the cost schedules of the firms are not affected by changes in total output in the industry. Each will be considered in turn.

Increasing-Cost Industries

In increasing-cost industries, expansion of the total output of the industry—the sum of the outputs of the individual firms comprising the industry—will raise the cost schedules of each firm. In the example in Table 21, if the total output of the industry is 1 million units, the long-run average-cost schedule is at such a level that the figure of lowest cost

[10] See C. A. Smith, "Survey of the Empirical Evidence on Economies of Scale," *Business Concentration and Public Policy* (Princeton: Princeton University Press, 1955), pp. 213–39. See also the discussion of the problem by Joel Dean, *Managerial Economics* (New York: Prentice-Hall, 1951), pp. 296–312.

is 25 cents per unit; this figure, therefore, may be regarded as the average-cost figure, from the standpoint of the industry, with a total industry output of 1 million units. The cost curve of the typical individual firm is plotted on Figure 36, as *LRAC* (low point of 25 cents), and this low-point figure of 25 cents is plotted on Figure 37 as the average-cost figure, from the standpoint of the entire industry, when

TABLE 21

INDUSTRY COST SCHEDULE, INCREASING-COST INDUSTRY

Total Output of Industry (Physical Units)	Figure of Lowest Average Cost for Each Firm, with Various Levels of Output for the Industry (Cents)
1,000,000	25
2,000,000	30
3,000,000	35
4,000,000	40

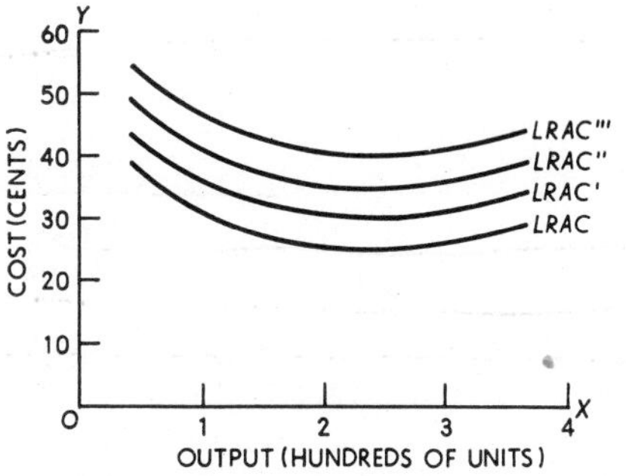

LRAC‴—industry output of 4 million units
LRAC″—industry output of 3 million units
LRAC′—industry output of 2 million units
LRAC—industry output of 1 million units

FIGURE 36

AVERAGE-COST CURVES FOR THE INDIVIDUAL FIRM, WITH VARIOUS LEVELS OF OUTPUT FOR THE ENTIRE INDUSTRY, INCREASING-COST INDUSTRY

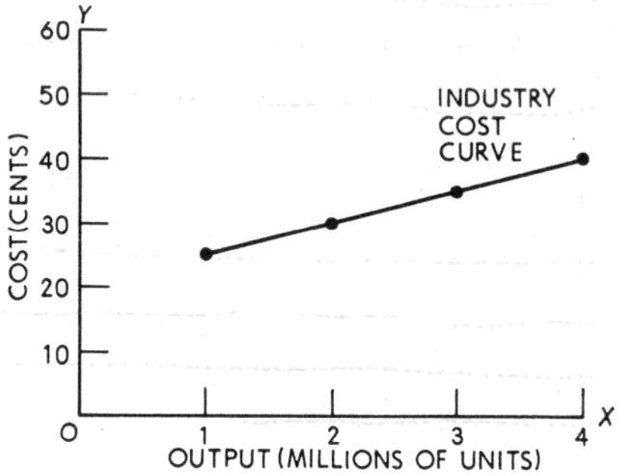

FIGURE 37

COST CURVE FOR AN INCREASING-COST INDUSTRY SHOWING LOCATIONS OF THE LOWEST AVERAGE COST OF THE FIRMS, FOR VARIOUS LEVELS OF OUTPUT FOR THE ENTIRE INDUSTRY

industry output is 1 million bushels. It must be emphasized that Figure 36 shows the cost curve of the individual firm, while Figure 37 reflects the situation of the industry as a whole; the scales on the horizontal axes of the two graphs are substantially different. If both graphs were drawn to the same scale, Figure 36 would be invisible.

If the total output of the industry rises to 2 million units, the cost schedules of all of the firms will rise, since the industry is one of increasing-cost conditions; the new figure of lowest average cost for each firm is 30 cents, and the new short-run average-cost curve for each firm is at the level of *LRAC′* on Figure 36. This situation is represented on Figure 37 by a point at an output of 2 million units showing the lowest average cost figure of 30 cents. Similarly, with outputs of the industry of 3 million and 4 million units, respectively, the figures of lowest average cost are 35 and 40 cents. When the various points on Figure 37 are connected, the industry cost curve is obtained, showing the figures of lowest average cost for the various possible levels of output for the industry.

Causes of Increasing-Cost Conditions. Increasing-cost conditions result from *external diseconomies* of large-scale production, primarily increases in factor prices which occur as larger quantities of factors are employed in the industry. As indicated in previous sections, in some instances an increase in output by one firm alone may raise the prices of the factors to the firm. But when a significant increase occurs in the output of the entire industry, either through the entry of new firms or through expansion of output by existing firms, the likelihood of factor price changes is much greater. When an industry utilizes a large portion of a factor whose total supply cannot be increased readily or at all, factor price increases are inevitable. As a consequence, the industries in which increasing-cost conditions are typically found are the "extractive" industries, such as agriculture, fishing, mining, and lumbering, in which large portions of the total supply of specialized natural resources are utilized in the industry. As the output of such an industry expands, the increased demand for the resources, such as land or mineral deposits, raises the prices that must be paid for their use. Since additional resources cannot be produced, greater supplies can be obtained (if at all) only by taking them away from other industries, or by using lower-quality (and thus higher-cost) resources. Wheat production is a typical example of an increasing-cost industry; as the output of wheat increases, the demand for land suitable for the production of wheat rises, and thus the price paid for the use of land and the sale value of the land increase. In the case of farmers owning their own land prior to the output increase, their expenditure costs do not rise, but their total costs increase just as much as those of tenant-farmers; the opportunity cost of using the land in their own production instead of renting it to others is now greater than before.

In some instances, increasing-cost conditions arise from reduced efficiency of production that occurs as total output of the industry increases. In an agricultural section irrigated from wells, for example, increased production—and pumping of water—will lower the water table and increase pumping costs for all farmers in the area. Similar problems arise in oil production; an increase in the number of wells in a field will lessen the pressure and increase the difficulty and cost of getting the oil to the surface.

Decreasing-Cost Industries

In a decreasing-cost industry, the cost schedules of the firms fall as total output of the industry increases. Such a case is illustrated in Figures 38 and 39. Such conditions are due to *external economies* of large-scale production—economies, in the sense of cost reductions, which no one firm can gain by its own expansion but which accrue to all the firms as

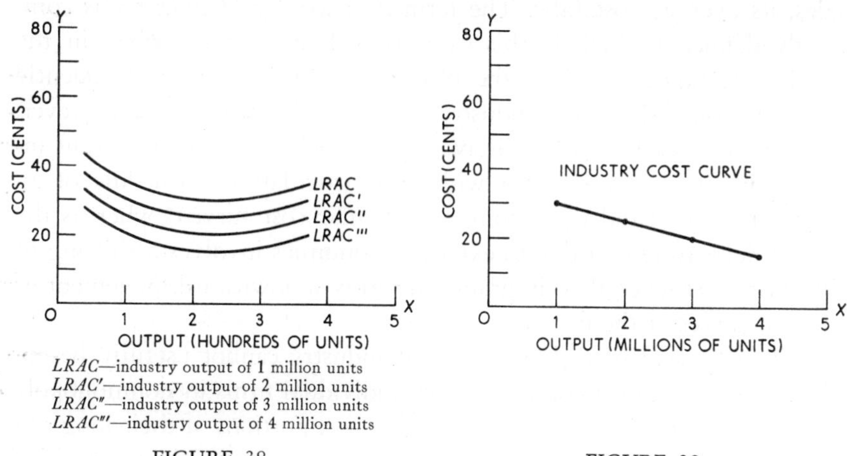

FIGURE 38

SUCCESSIVE AVERAGE-COST CURVES FOR A FIRM, AT VARIOUS LEVELS OF TOTAL INDUSTRY OUTPUT, DECREASING-COST INDUSTRY

FIGURE 39

COST CURVE FOR A DECREASING-COST INDUSTRY

the total output of the industry increases. For an illustration, consider the case of a new mining region, developed in an area remote from railroad facilities in the days before the availability of trucks. As long as the total output of the mines was small, the ore had to be hauled long distances by wagon—an extremely expensive form of transportation. But when the number of mines increased and the total output of the region rose substantially, it became feasible to construct a railroad into the area. The construction of the railroad lowered transportation costs and reduced the cost schedules of all the firms. No one mine could possibly have increased its output sufficiently to warrant the building of a railroad; but, when the total output of the industry increased sufficiently, construction of the road became profitable.

As a practical matter, however, external economies are rarely encountered, from all indications. Some industries may operate under decreasing-cost conditions in short intervals of output expansion, when continued growth makes possible the supplying of materials or services at reduced cost. But it is impossible to find examples of continued expansion in a range of decreasing-cost conditions over a long range of output.

When one firm produces the entire output of a product in a particular market and possesses a completely monopoly position, the firm may find it most profitable to operate at a volume of output less than that of lowest average cost. As a consequence, if the firm increases its sales, its average cost falls. The term *decreasing-cost industry* is commonly defined to include this case, as well as that described in the previous paragraphs. Thus the electric power industry is frequently called a "decreasing-cost" industry. It should be recognized, however, that in this case the decline in average cost which occurs as output increases involves a movement within a particular cost schedule of an individual firm (and thus along a particular cost curve), whereas the case of decreasing cost due to external economies involves a shifting of the entire cost schedule—in graphical terms, a downward movement of the cost curves of the firm.

The concept of a decreasing-cost industry cannot usefully be applied, however, to situations in which individual firms in nonmonopoly situations are operating on the decreasing-cost portions of their long-run average-cost curves, as may be typical in many nonpurely competitive fields. Likewise the concept of a decreasing-cost industry is not used in reference to a situation in which average cost declines over a period of time because of the development of new methods of production. This is merely a historical cost change resulting from a shift in one of the determinants of cost.

Constant-Cost Industries

The case of constant-cost conditions, in which the cost schedules of the firms are not affected by changes in the output of the entire industry, is the dividing line between the two other cases. An industry using only a small fraction of the total quantity available of various factors employed can increase output materially without noticeably affecting the prices of the factors used. The industry cost curve in a constant-cost industry is a straight horizontal line, as illustrated in Figure 41, since the location of the lowest point of the long-run average-cost curve of each firm is unaffected by changes in the output of the industry, as shown in Figure 40.

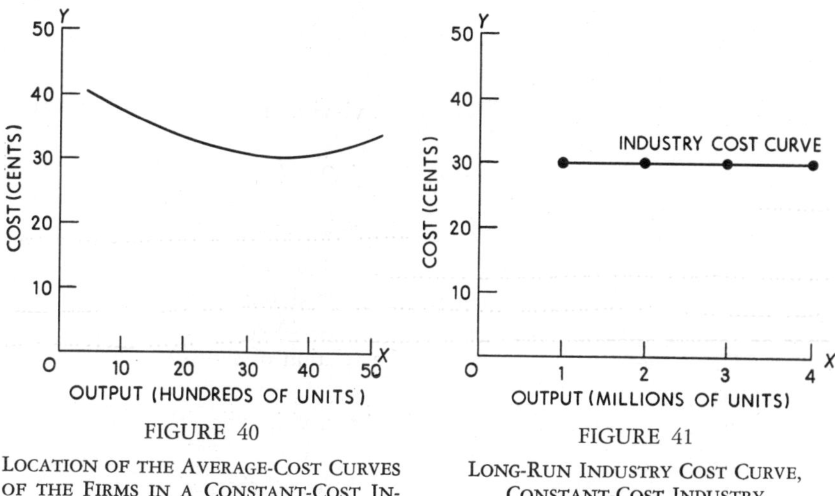

FIGURE 40

LOCATION OF THE AVERAGE-COST CURVES OF THE FIRMS IN A CONSTANT-COST INDUSTRY, AT ALL LEVELS OF TOTAL INDUSTRY OUTPUT

FIGURE 41

LONG-RUN INDUSTRY COST CURVE, CONSTANT-COST INDUSTRY

FURTHER COMPLEXITIES OF COST

The cost analysis of this chapter has been based upon two simplifying assumptions; effects of changes in certain cost elements upon demand schedules for the product have been ignored, as well as the fact that firms frequently produce more than one product. The cost elements for activities which affect sales are known as *selling* costs, in contrast to *production* costs, those arising from the actual production of the goods. Selling costs are incurred for the purpose of influencing the choice of the buyer with respect to the product which he buys or the firm from which he makes the purchase. Their existence creates an interrelationship between cost schedules and demand schedules, which will be considered in Chapter 10.

The production of more than one product by a firm—a practice which is almost universal—gives rise to *common* costs, those which are incurred for the production of two or more products, no one of the latter being responsible for any particular part of the cost. Thus the cost of maintenance of a railroad line is a common cost for freight and passenger traffic. The cost of clerk hire in a grocery store is a common cost for the various goods handled. The concept of average cost for each product is no longer precise when common costs exist; the average cost depends upon the way in which the common costs are allocated among the various products produced. The significance of common costs for price determination will be considered in Chapter 10.

SELECTED REFERENCES

STIGLER, G. J. *The Theory of Price,* chaps. vi–viii. rev. ed. New York: Macmillan, 1952.

CLARK, J. M. *Studies in the Economics of Overhead Costs,* Chicago: University of Chicago Press, 1923.

One of the most significant and complete analyses of cost.

VINER, J. "Cost Curves and Supply Curves," *Readings in Price Theory* (ed. G. J. STIGLER and K. E. BOULDING). Homewood, Ill.: Richard D. Irwin, Inc., 1952.

The pioneer work in clarifying the relation of short-run and long-run cost schedules.

BOWEN, H. R. *Toward Social Economy,* chaps. viii, xvii. New York: Rinehart, 1948.

BAIN, J. S. *Pricing, Distribution and Employment,* chap. iii. rev. ed. New York: Holt, 1953.

BOULDING, K. E. *Economic Analysis,* chaps. xxvii and xxviii. 3rd ed. New York: Harper, 1955.

LERNER, A. P. *The Economics of Control,* chap. xiv. New York: Macmillan, 1944.

ELLIS, H. S., AND FELLNER, W. "External Economies and Diseconomies," *American Economic Review,* Vol. XXXIII (September, 1943), pp. 493–511.

The most complete discussion of a neglected problem.

Cost Behavior and Price Policy. New York: National Bureau of Economic Research, 1943.

A discussion of the problems and conclusions of empirical cost studies.

"The Variation of Costs with Volume," *N.A.C.A. Bulletin,* Vol. XXX (June 15, 1949), pp. 1215–18.

Cost behavior in response to output changes, as viewed by the accountant.

QUESTIONS

1. Explain the meaning of the concept of cost, as used in economic analysis.
2. Distinguish between expenditure and nonexpenditure costs, and give examples of each.
3. What payments made by business firms are not regarded as costs at all?
4. Which implicit cost is treated as a business expense under usual accounting principles?
5. Distinguish between the concepts of short-run and long-run periods.
6. Distinguish between fixed costs and variable costs. The latter are variable with respect to what?
7. List the major fixed and variable cost items.
8. Why are all costs variable in a long-run period?

9. Distinguish between direct-variable and constant-variable costs; between the latter and fixed costs.
10. Is depreciation a cost? Explain.
11. What is the opportunity cost to you of attending college? Of taking a vacation this summer instead of working?
12. Would you expect each of the following to be, in typical cases in the short run, fixed or variable costs?
    a) Sales taxes
    b) Property taxes
    c) Rent on a factory building
    d) Interest on money borrowed to buy additional materials
    e) Fire insurance
    f) Cost of goods sold
    g) The salary of the president of the company
13. List the major "givens" assumed in usual short-run cost analysis. Does the use of these assumptions make the analysis less realistic? Compare these with the "givens" assumed in the analysis of cost behavior in the long run.
14. A firm, with a particular plant, has daily fixed costs of $400. Total variable costs for successive quantities of output, per day, are as follows:

Output	Total Variable Cost	Output	Total Variable Cost
1	200	6	400
2	250	7	450
3	275	8	550
4	300	9	750
5	350	10	1500

    Determine average fixed cost, average variable cost, average cost, and marginal cost. Plot on a graph.
15. Why does marginal cost consist solely of variable cost?
16. Why does the marginal-cost curve intersect the average-cost curve at the lowest point of the latter?
17. If average variable cost is falling, must marginal cost be falling? Must marginal cost be less than average variable cost under these conditions? Explain.
18. Why does average fixed cost decline continuously as a firm increases output?
19. Under what circumstances will average variable cost decline initially as a firm increases output?
20. Why will average variable cost eventually rise as a firm continues to increase output?
21. Why is the short run average cost curve generally believed to be U-shaped?
22. What significance does the Law of Diminishing Returns have for the behavior of short-run average cost?
23. Why does average variable cost fall if average product of the variable factor is rising?

24. As a firm adds successive units of variable factors, costing \$50 per unit, output increases as follows:

Units of Factor	Total Output
1	8
2	20
3	45
4	54
5	60
6	63
7	64

Determine average variable cost per unit of output, for the range of output for which information is available.

25. Under what circumstances is a firm likely to experience a long range of constant average variable cost?
26. Why may average variable cost fall even though average product per unit of the variable factors is constant?
27. In what respect does the ability to operate an enterprise in more than one shift affect the behavior of average cost in the short run?
28. What difficulties are encountered in making empirical studies of short-run cost behavior?
29. Define carefully the term "long-run average cost."
30. How is the long-run cost schedule built up from the short-run cost schedules?
31. Why may the long-run average-cost curve be irregular?
32. Under what conditions will long-run average cost decline as a firm first expands its scale of operations? Compare the causes of this decline with the causes of decline in average cost in a short-run period, as a firm expands output with a given plant.
33. Under what circumstances would long-run average cost not fall as a firm first increased scale of operations?
34. What may cause an eventual increase in long-run average cost if a firm continues to expand?
35. Why has relatively little empirical work on the nature of the long-run average-cost curve been done?
36. Explain the concept of cost conditions of the industry.
37. Under what circumstances will an industry be one of increasing-cost conditions?
38. What is the long-run industry cost curve? How is it derived from the cost curves of the individual firms?
39. Distinguish between external economies and internal economies.
40. What are common costs?
41. Under what cost conditions is it likely that the following industries operate?

    a) Lumber
    b) Silver mining
    c) Rubber-band
    d) Fishing
    e) Parsnip
    f) Corn

42. Does the fact that automobile prices declined greatly from 1910 to 1930 show that during those years automobile production was a decreasing-cost industry? Explain.
43. Distinguish between "selling costs" and "production costs."
44. Assume that you have a weekly streetcar and bus pass entitling you to an unlimited number of rides and costing $2.25. If you take 23 rides, what is the average cost per ride? What is the marginal cost of the twenty-third ride?
45. You consider taking a 1,000-mile vacation trip in your car. What elements would you include in figuring the marginal cost of this 1,000-mile trip, per mile? What elements would you consider if you wished to figure the average cost per mile? Which would be the significant factor in determining whether to take the trip—the average cost or the marginal cost? Explain.
46. Why is the marginal cost to a railroad of carrying one additional passenger on a train not operated to capacity almost nothing?

Chapter 9 PRICE AND OUTPUT DETERMINATION UNDER CONDITIONS OF PURE COMPETITION

With the analysis of demand and cost considerations completed, it is now possible to proceed to the explanation of the determination of price and output under various competitive conditions. The next five chapters will be devoted to the explanation of price and output levels of consumption goods, while those in Part III will consider the question of the prices of the factors of production. Chapter 20 contains a synthesis of the entire price-output analysis in terms of the general equilibrium of the economy as a whole.

In this chapter, the analysis is directed to the case of pure competition—the situation in which neither individual buyers nor sellers have direct, perceptible influence upon price. The case of pure competition is based upon two primary assumptions, as explained in Chapter 4; the numbers of buyers and of sellers are large, and the products are standardized, with no preferences on the part of buyers for the products of any particular seller, or preferences on the part of sellers for dealing with particular buyers.

The Usefulness of the Purely Competitive Model

Markets in which conditions are sufficiently similar to the assumptions upon which the purely competitive analysis is based to make the analysis useful for study of market behavior are confined largely to ones for the major agricultural products. Even in these markets in recent decades, the government farm price-support programs have lessened the similarity between the actual markets and the purely competitive model, but nevertheless the analysis can still be applied usefully in these fields. While these industries comprise only a minor segment of the entire economy, they are nevertheless not unimportant. They provide the basic raw materials in the production of food and clothing, and the prices of these materials are important elements in the prices of many finished products. The influence of these prices extends into still other fields because of their importance in the cost-of-living indexes, and thus their influence upon wage levels, and the costs and selling prices of a wide range of products. An understanding and evaluation of the various government agricultural-aid programs requires a knowledge of the functioning of the markets for farm products. Furthermore, in some forms of monopolistic competition, the extent of deviation from conditions of pure competition is sufficiently slight that the principles relating to the latter have some relevance. In the markets for securities, whose prices are significant for interest-rate determination, conditions approximating those of pure competition are found.

Study of the principles of price and output determination under purely competitive conditions is also necessary as a basis for evaluating the extent to which price and output levels in nonpurely competitive markets deviate from those which allow optimum economic welfare (as discussed in Chapter 24).

Finally, analysis of purely competitive conditions is relatively simple and allows a clearer presentation of basic economic relationships than does analysis of other competitive conditions, in which the complexities involved tend to obscure the more fundamental considerations.

The General Nature of Price Determination in Pure Competition

The actual selling prices—the market prices—in pure competition are determined by the interaction of supply and demand forces operating in the markets for the goods. No individual buyer or individual seller has any control over price; each bases his behavior upon the assumption that the price is "given" in the market and beyond his control. The combined but independent actions of the large numbers of buyers and sellers—by determining the relationship between the total quantities which buyers seek to purchase at various price levels and the total amounts which sellers offer on the market at the various price levels —control the actual level of the market price. Most markets to which the purely competitive analysis is applicable are characterized by the existence of central wholesale markets, such as the Chicago Board of Trade in the case of grain and the wholesale egg and produce markets in the larger cities, in which large numbers of buyers and sellers make purchases and sales; the prices determined in these central markets serve as the basic price for a large area, in some instances the entire country. Wheat prices, for example, are not determined separately in each locality by local supply and demand conditions. The local prices in various communities are simply the Chicago prices plus or minus transportation costs to or from the Chicago market.

The market prices, determined by current demand and supply conditions in the various markets, tend over a period of time toward certain levels known as normal or equilibrium price levels. In a short-run period, that is, a time interval sufficiently long that firms can adjust output but not plant capacity, the market price tends toward the *short-run equilibrium level,* while in a long-run period, sufficiently long to allow adjustments in all factors, the market price tends toward the *long-run equilibrium level.* Actual equality of the market price with the short-run and long-run equilibrium figures may never be attained because these levels themselves are subject to change, and may shift before the market price reaches them. But at any one time the direction of change in market price is controlled by the relationship between the existing price and the equilibrium figures. If, for example, market price is temporarily above the short-run equilibrium figure, it will tend to decline to the latter level. Knowledge of the determinants of the equilibrium levels is essential for an understanding of price adjustments over a period of time, and the final reactions of prices to such changes as technological developments, tax increases, and wage changes. In the succeeding sections, the determinants of market price and the short-run and long-run equilibrium levels will be analyzed, as well as the process of adjustment of the market price to these equilibrium levels.

MARKET-PRICE DETERMINATION

The Concept of Supply

The demand forces affecting price determination have been analyzed in detail in previous chapters. But little has been said as yet about supply. The *supply schedule,* or *supply,* of a good from a particular seller may be defined as the schedule of the various quantities of the good which the seller is willing to offer on the market at various alternate prices, in a situation in which he has no control over price. Thus at a $2.00 price, a certain wheat farmer may be willing to sell 15,000 bushels; if the price were $2.50 instead of $2.00, he might offer on the market 20,000 bushels; if it were $1.00, he might be willing to sell only 3,000 bushels. The supply schedule, just like the demand schedule, consists of various alternate possibilities at a particular time—of the alternate amounts which the seller would sell if the various prices existed—rather than a list of amounts which a person actually sells over a period of time at different prices. The supply schedule which is directly relevant for the price of a particular good is the *total* supply schedule existing at the particular time in the market, that is, the sum of the schedules of all of the individual sellers.

The concept of *elasticity* is applicable to supply schedules as well as to demand schedules. The elasticity of a supply schedule is the measure of the relative change in quantity supplied in response to a relative change in price. Supply is elastic if a change in price is accompanied by a more than proportional change in quantity supplied; it is inelastic if the change in quantity supplied is less than proportional to the change in price. A supply schedule is perfectly elastic if an infinite amount will be supplied at one price and at all prices higher than this, and nothing at all at lower prices. Supply is perfectly inelastic if the quantity supplied is the same regardless of the price.

A change in supply occurs when larger or smaller amounts will be supplied at various prices than were previously offered on the market at those prices. Graphically, an increase in supply results in a new curve to the right of the original; a decrease results in the new curve to the left of the old. A change in price cannot produce a change in supply, in the sense of the supply schedule relevant during the market period, but merely in a change in quantity supplied on the basis of the existing supply schedule.

Supply Schedules in the Market Period

The term *market period,* that in which the actual market price is determined, is defined as one in which there is a fixed stock of goods on hand. The time interval is too short to allow production of additional units, and sales can be made only from a fixed stock. In industries in which production is a continuous process, additional output is coming forth from production at all times, the rate of production is quickly adjustable, and the market period is very short. Market price adjusts immediately to the short-run equilibrium level, and the dichotomy between market price and the short-run equilibrium is of little significance. Actually, however, in most agricultural industries, including many of those for which the purely competitive analysis has the greatest applicability, crops are harvested during a short period of the year, and no additional output is possible for another year; hence the period in which only a fixed stock is available and additional output is impossible is relatively long.

With a given stock of goods on hand, a seller has only two practicable alternatives: he can sell the commodity, or hold it for possible future sale. A typical supply schedule of an individual in a time interval relevant for market-price determination is shown on Table 22. If the price is 25 cents, the seller will hold his entire stock for future sale. If it is 50 cents, he will sell 800 units in the particular time interval; if it is 75 cents, he will sell 1,200 units. At $1.50 and each price higher than this he would sell his entire stock of goods, 2,200 units. The schedule is illustrated graphically in Figure 42.

Determinants of Supply. The actual quantities which a particular seller would place on the market at the various possible prices depend

TABLE 22

SUPPLY SCHEDULE OF AN INDIVIDUAL SELLER FIXED STOCK OF GOODS ON HAND

Price (Dollars)	Quantity Supplied
0.25	0
0.50	800
0.75	1,200
1.00	1,600
1.25	2,000
1.50	2,200
1.75	2,200

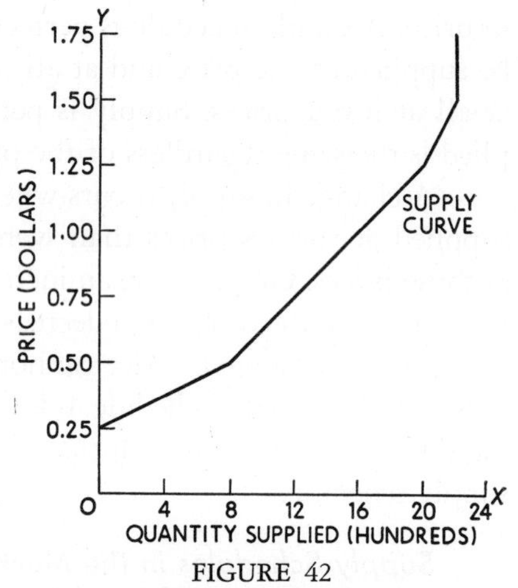

FIGURE 42

MARKET PERIOD SUPPLY OF AN INDIVIDUAL SELLER

upon the amount which he has on hand (under the assumption of a time interval insufficient to allow the production of more units) and his *reservation prices*—the prices below which he will hold, rather than sell, particular parts of his stock of goods. A seller obviously cannot sell more than he has at a particular time; a wheat farmer, on a day in October, cannot sell more wheat for delivery now than he has on hand from this year's harvest. But he will not necessarily sell all that he has available; whether he does or not, at a certain price, depends upon the relationship between the market price and his reservation price. The latter is controlled primarily by his estimate of future prices. If he believes that prices are going down, his reservation price will be low, since he wishes to dispose of his crop now while prices are relatively high. On the other hand, if he expects prices to rise, his reservation price will be high. Expectations about future prices are affected by many considerations—past experience, current reports on price and business trends, views of other persons, pure guesswork, etc. When sellers become accustomed to receiving prices within a certain range over a period of years, they are likely to regard any price below this figure as unreasonably low and will expect a price rise; unusually high prices are frequently regarded also as being only temporary.

Reservation prices are also influenced by the costs of storage including rental, interest, and depreciation of the goods; the higher these costs, the lower will be the reservation price. If a commodity is highly perishable, the costs of storage are prohibitive, and the reservation price is extremely low. The seller will prefer to realize something from the good rather than have it spoil. Likewise the seller's need for cash is significant. If he needs money immediately, his reservation price will be relatively low, regardless of the other considerations. If he does not need cash quickly, he is much more likely to take a chance that prices will rise.

Nature of the Supply Schedule of the Individual Seller. As illustrated in Table 22, in the typical supply schedule greater quantities will be offered at higher prices than at lower prices. The higher the price, the greater is the expectation that the price will fall and the smaller is the likelihood that it will go still higher. Accordingly, at successively higher prices sellers will be willing to part with successively larger portions of their stocks, since they become less certain that the price will go still higher and are more afraid that a decline will occur. Furthermore, the higher the price, the greater the likelihood that the price will exceed the figure to which the seller has become accustomed. Finally, at relatively high prices, the sellers can obtain the necessary cash to meet expenses through the sale of only a portion of their stock.

Total Supply Schedules. The sum of all the individual supply schedules in the market constitutes the total or market supply schedule. The nature of this is the same as that of the individual schedules. At successively higher prices, additional amounts will be placed on the market by those who would make some sales at lower prices, and additional sellers whose reservation prices are so high that they will sell nothing at lower prices will offer units for sale. Substantial variations exist among the schedules of the individual sellers, due to differences in stocks of goods on hand, storage facilities, need for cash, and expectations about the future trends in prices. It is impossible to generalize about the elasticity of the typical supply schedule, beyond noting that perishability is significant; when a good cannot be stored at all, the entire stock will be offered for sale regardless of the price, and higher prices will bring forth no larger quantities in the time period under consideration.

Market-Price Determination

The market price comes to the level at which the quantity supplied and the quantity demanded are equal. In a perfect market, with complete knowledge on the part of buyers and sellers about market conditions, the market price would adjust instantaneously to this level of equality of quantities supplied and demanded, and the actual selling price and the equilibrium market price would at all times be identical. Where imperfection exists, a certain delay is inevitable. Thus the actual selling price may deviate temporarily from the equilibrium market price. However, the principal wholesale markets for the goods sold under conditions approximating those of pure competition are relatively well organized, with imperfections at a minimum. Therefore the adjustment usually requires only a very short period, and accordingly, equilibrium market price and the actual selling price are usually considered to be identical.

No other price than that at which the quantity supplied and the quantity demanded are equal could remain. If the actual price was temporarily higher, some of the sellers could not dispose of the number of units which they wished to sell, since the quantity demanded would be less than the quantity that the suppliers wished to sell. Consequently the sellers would offer to sell for slightly less in order to dispose of this excess. As a result, market price would fall until the buyers were willing to buy the same number of units that the sellers wished to sell at the new price. The temporary inability of some sellers to sell does not contradict the principle that each seller in pure competition can sell as much as he desires to sell at the market price. The latter statement applies to the equilibrium market price, not to the price level which may exist temporarily during the process of adjustment of price to the market equilibrium. If the price were lower than that at which the quantity demanded and the quantity supplied were equal, buyers would desire to buy more units of the good than sellers would be willing to sell. Accordingly, the buyers would offer to pay more in order to get the desired number of units, and the market price would rise until equality of quantities supplied and quantities demanded was attained.

The supply schedule in the market period is greatly influenced by expectations of future prices; even the demand schedule is influenced to a certain extent by the same consideration. Therefore, market price is subject to very frequent change as expectations constantly shift.

It should be noted that cost has little direct influence on market price. Once a good is produced, there is no way of obtaining any money from it except by selling it. A seller may not wish to sell below cost, but it is better for him to do so than to allow the product to spoil. The only immediate influence which cost has upon price is its effect upon the figure which the seller expects to receive and thus upon his reservation price and the amount that he is willing to supply at various prices.

The determination of the market price is illustrated in Figure 43. The line *DD* indicates the total demand, *SS* the total supply. Price will adjust to *p,* the level at which the quantity demanded and the quantity

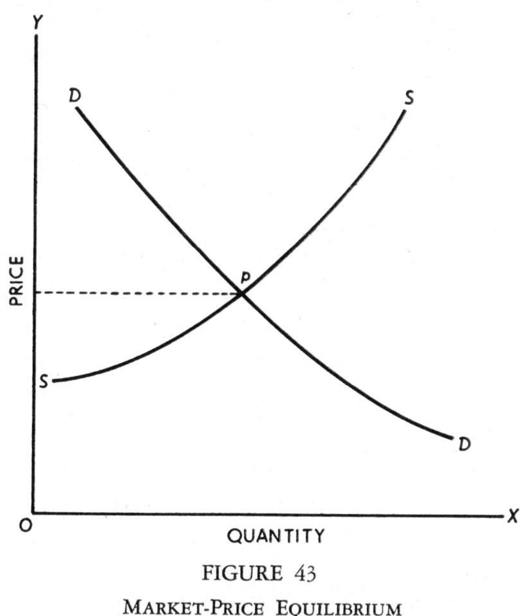

FIGURE 43
MARKET-PRICE EQUILIBRIUM

supplied are equal. If price were above *p,* the quantity supplied would exceed the quantity demanded; if price were below *p,* the reverse would be true.

OUTPUT AND PRICE IN THE SHORT-RUN PERIOD

The market price in pure competition depends upon the interaction of demand with supply forthcoming from an existing stock of goods on hand. But over a short-run period, in which firms are able to adjust the volume of output with their existing plant, market price will tend toward the figure of the short-run equilibrium level. Firms will determine output on the basis of the relationship between their costs and the market price, and changes in the market supply based upon this output adjustment will bring the market price toward the short-run equilibrium. Movement of the current market price toward the equilibrium comes about solely because of changes in output and market supply, which occur when the market price differs from the equilibrium figure. The short-run equilibrium figure itself is determined by the relationship between demand and short-period supply—the schedule of amounts that would be offered on the market at various prices during a given time interval, once the firms have had adequate time to adjust output with existing plant facilities. Demand considerations are, in general, the same, regardless of the time period.[1]

Short-Period Supply

The ability of firms to adjust output in the short-run period introduces a new determinant of supply that is not directly significant for market supply forthcoming at a particular time from an existing stock of goods—namely, costs of production.

The firm will not produce at all unless the price obtainable at least covers *average variable cost;* these costs will cease if production is suspended, and thus operation at a price which does not cover them increases the losses of the firms. If a firm cannot obtain as much from the product as the direct wage, raw-material, and power costs necessary to produce it, each additional unit produced will increase the total loss and either reduce the firm's capital or increase debt. Even if the owners of the business desire to continue operation under such circumstances, they cannot do so very long, unless large cash reserves are available, as funds will not be obtainable to pay for the necessary factor units. The only case in which firms will operate if price is below average variable cost is that in which the owners are certain that prices will rise in the near future. Temporary operation may be preferable to closing and then reopening the plant because there are various costs involved in closing and opening a business, and experienced personnel may be lost permanently.

At price levels equal to and in excess of lowest average variable cost, a firm will produce in the short-run period even if average cost is not completely covered. If the firm suspends operations, the fixed costs continue, yet nothing will be earned toward them. If price is above average variable cost and production is carried on, a portion of the fixed costs will be covered by earnings. It is obviously preferable to earn a

[1] Demand in the short-run period—the amounts that would be purchased at various prices in each time interval over a short-run period—differs from demand at any one time primarily through the lessened significance of speculative buying. If price is very low, for example, temporarily some buyers will purchase in anticipation of future need or for speculative purposes. But if price remains at the low figure over a period of time, additional purchases for these purposes will cease.

portion of these costs rather than nothing at all. Immediate liquidation of the business is usually not feasible; money capital invested in specialized capital equipment cannot be withdrawn quickly, since used capital goods, as a rule, have little sale value.

In the range of prices at which production will be carried on—at those equal to or above lowest average variable cost—the firm will adjust output to the level at which the *marginal cost* with the existing plant is equal to the *marginal revenue* received from the sale of the product. At this point marginal cost is also equal to price, which in

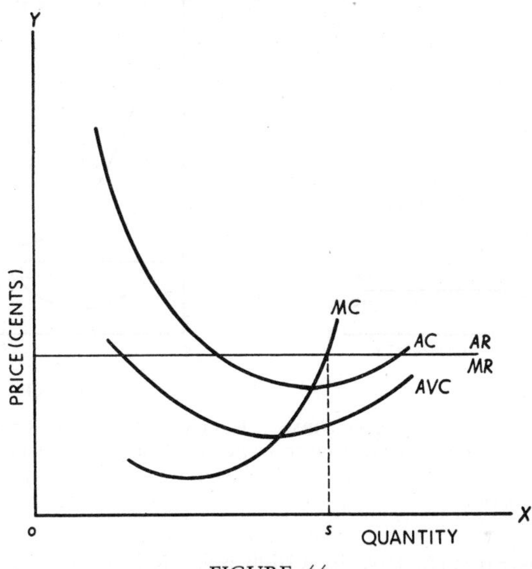

FIGURE 44

ADJUSTMENT OF OUTPUT OF THE INDIVIDUAL FIRM IN THE SHORT RUN

pure competition is identical with marginal revenue at all levels of output. Until this volume of output is reached, each additional unit produced results in a greater addition to the total revenue of the firm (marginal revenue) than the amount of the addition to total cost (marginal cost) which results from its production, and hence is profitable to produce, provided that price covers average variable cost. If output is carried beyond the level at which marginal revenue and marginal cost are equal, additional units will add more to total cost than to total revenue and will thereby either reduce profits or increase losses.

The level of operation of a firm in pure competition in the short run is illustrated in Figure 44. The short-run cost schedule, comparable to those discussed in the previous chapter, is plotted on the same chart with the revenue schedule. The average-revenue curve is a horizontal line at the level of the current market price, since the firm can sell as much as it wishes at this figure. This line also indicates marginal revenue, which is identical with average revenue in pure competition. Since, in this illustration, price is in excess of average variable cost, the firm will operate; it will produce such a number of units (*os*) that marginal revenue and marginal cost are equal. This point is indicated on the graph by the intersection of the marginal-cost and marginal-revenue curves. Price in this particular case is also in excess of average cost.

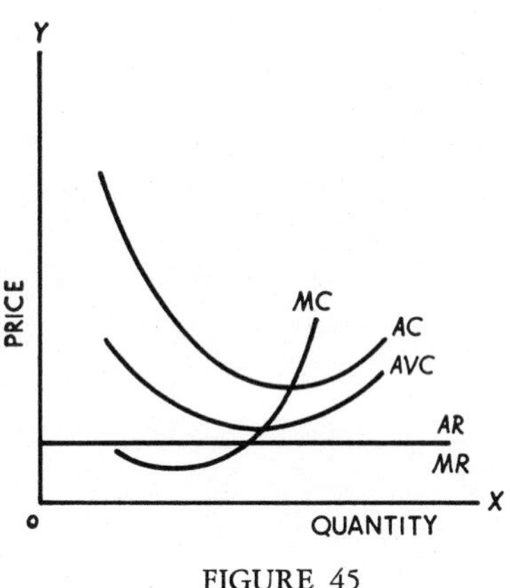

FIGURE 45

REVENUE AND COST CURVES OF A FIRM IN A SHORT-RUN PERIOD, WITH PRICE LESS THAN LOWEST AVERAGE VARIABLE COST

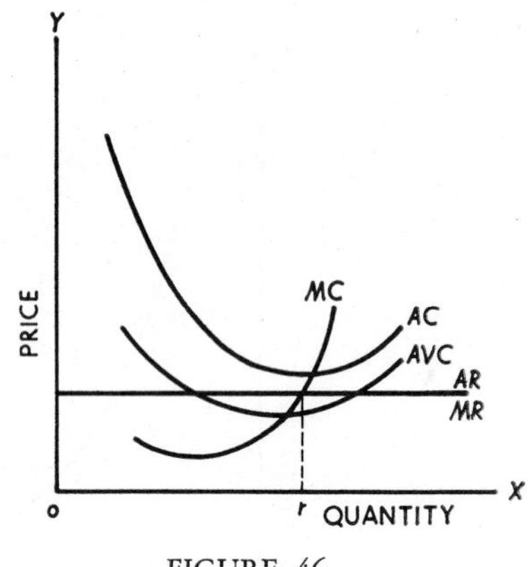

FIGURE 46

REVENUE AND COST CURVES OF A FIRM IN A SHORT-RUN PERIOD, WITH PRICE ABOVE AVERAGE VARIABLE COST BUT BELOW AVERAGE COST

Figure 45 illustrates the case in which price is less than average variable cost at all ranges of output; hence the firm will not produce. Figure 46 shows the situation in which price is less than average cost but in excess of average variable cost (*or* units will be produced).

The Short-Run Supply Schedule

At each possible price above the level of lowest average variable cost, the firm will place on the market such a number of units that the marginal cost is equal to the price. Thus the firm's supply schedule is derived directly from its marginal-cost schedule, as illustrated in Table 23. The right-hand portion of the table indicates the supply schedule of the firm, on the basis of the cost data presented in the left-hand portion of the table. At any price below 20 cents nothing would be produced, since average variable cost would not be covered. A price of 20 cents would cover average variable cost, and therefore the firm would operate; 4 units would be produced, since, with a price of 20 cents, marginal cost and marginal revenue are equal at an output of 4 units. At a 25-cent price, marginal cost and marginal revenue are equal with an output of 5 units. If the price were 27 cents, 6 units would be supplied; if it were 50 cents, 7 units; and so on. For prices intermediate to these, interpolation would give an estimate of the quantity that would be supplied. If the price were 26 cents, it would be reasonable to assume that $5\frac{1}{2}$ units would be produced.

In graphical terms the portion of the marginal-cost curve above its intersection with the average variable cost curve indicates the firm's

TABLE 23

SHORT-RUN COST SCHEDULE AND SHORT-RUN SUPPLY SCHEDULE OF A FIRM SELLING IN A PURELY COMPETITIVE MARKET

Daily Cost Schedule				Daily Supply Schedule	
Units of Output	Average Variable Cost (Cents)	Average Cost (Cents)	Marginal Cost (Cents)	Price (Cents)	Quantity Supplied
1	30	50	30	12	0
2	24	34	18	20	4
3	20	26.67	12	25	5
4	20	25	20	27	6
5	21	25	25	50	7
6	22	25.33	27	138	8
7	26	28.86	50		
8	40	42.50	138		

supply curve. As a cost curve, this curve shows the marginal cost of producing various amounts; as a supply curve, it shows the amounts that the firm would supply at various price levels. Thus, in Figure 47 (page 200), the portion of *MC* above its intersection with *AVC* is the supply curve. The declining portion of the marginal-cost curve has no significance in regard to supply, because greater profit can be made by extending production to the quantities for the respective prices on the rising portion of the curve (all units of output in the intervening range will add more to total revenue than to total cost).

Since, beyond the point of lowest average variable cost, the marginal costs of successively larger amounts of output are progressively greater, larger and larger amounts will be supplied only at successively higher price levels. The absolute maximum that the firm can supply, regardless of the height of the price, is the maximum quantity that can be produced with the existing plant.

The total short-run supply schedule is the sum of the schedules of all of the individual firms in the industry. By definition, the short run is too brief a period for new firms to commence production, and therefore the number of firms is given, and the total schedule is the summation of the individual schedules of the existing firms. One modification to this rule arises from the possible effect of higher levels of output of the industry in raising the prices which must be paid for factor units

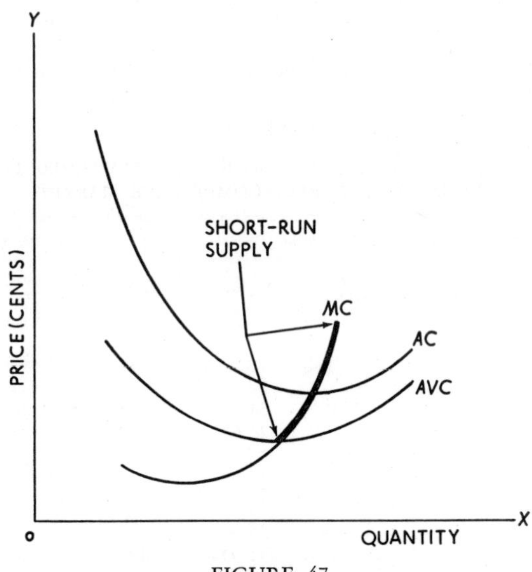

FIGURE 47

SHORT-RUN COST CURVES AND SUPPLY CURVE OF AN INDIVIDUAL FIRM

used by the firms. If this occurs, the quantities supplied at higher prices will be somewhat less than they would appear to be on the basis of a summation of the existing individual schedules.

The Short-Run Equilibrium Price Level

The short-run equilibrium price level is the figure at which the demand for the product and the short-period supply of the product are equal. At this level the total amount which sellers will produce and place on the market in each interval of time with a given plant is equal to the amount which buyers will purchase in the same time interval at that price. Once sufficient time has passed for firms to complete output adjustments with their given plant capacities, the market price will reach the short-run level (apart from possible effects of market imperfections noted in subsequent sections). If market price temporarily exceeds this level, the output of the firms will rise to a figure in excess of the quantity demanded at the existing market price, and thus the market price will fall. If market price is temporarily less, output will fall to an amount less than the quantity demanded at that price, and as a consequence market price will rise. Only at the short-run equilibrium level will the volume of output coming on the market, with the given plant capacities, equal the quantity demanded. This equilibrium position, one from which there is no tendency for market price to move away unless the determinants of the situation such as demand and cost change, is

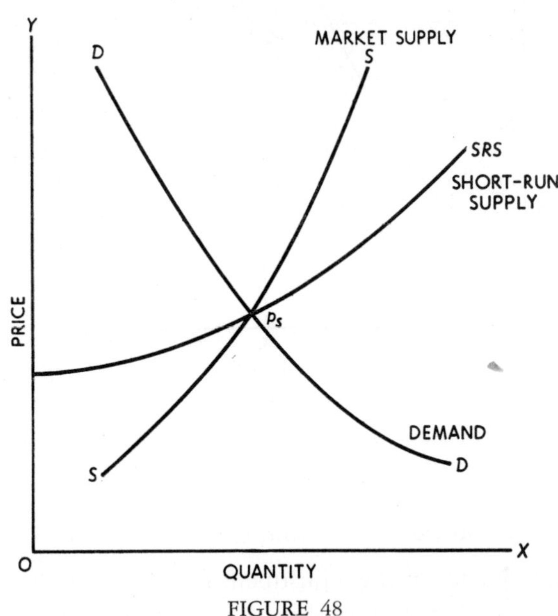

FIGURE 48

ADJUSTMENT OF MARKET PRICE AND SHORT-RUN EQUILIBRIUM PRICE IN A PURELY COMPETITIVE INDUSTRY

illustrated on Figure 48. The short-run equilibrium level is at p_s; once short-run adjustments have been completed, the market supply curve will be at the level *SS* and will intersect the demand curve (*DD*) at the same point as that at which the latter is intersected by *SRS*—the short-period supply curve. Figure 49 illustrates the case in which market price (p) initially exceeds the short-run level (p_s), because market supply (*SS*) is relatively low. With a price of p, however, firms will quickly adjust output, since at p, marginal cost is less than price. Consequently, as market supply increases, the market-supply curve moves to the right until it reaches the level *S′S′*; with this market-supply curve, the quantity sold will be *ot*, and market price will equal the short-run equilibrium figure (p_s).

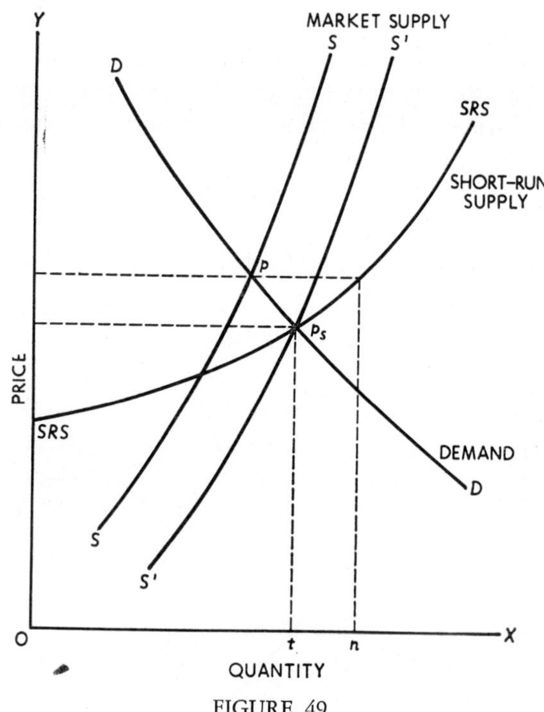

FIGURE 49

ADJUSTMENT OF MARKET PRICE TO THE SHORT-RUN EQUILIBRIUM LEVEL, IN A PURELY COMPETITIVE INDUSTRY

The Relation between Price and Cost in the Short-Run Period

As a consequence of the adjustment of output by the firms in the short-run period, certain relationships exist between price in this period (once adjustments are complete) and cost:

1. The price must equal marginal cost of each firm which is producing the product, if the firms are actually maximizing profits.

2. The price must at least cover the lowest average variable cost figures of the firms which are operating, since the firms will cease production if they are not able to cover their variable costs. If market price temporarily goes below variable cost, some firms will cease production and the price will rise again to the variable cost level.

3. The price may be less than average cost, and thereby fail to cover average fixed cost. As long as the firms earn a portion of fixed cost, they will produce, since the fixed costs will continue even if production ceases. If price goes below average cost, it will remain at the lower level until long-run adjustments have been made. The time necessary for completion of these long-run adjustments may be considerable.

4. The short-run normal price level may be higher than average cost. Since the short run is not sufficiently long for new firms to enter the industry, excess profits may remain.

The actual short-run equilibrium figure in a particular case depends upon the relationship between demand and short-period supply, as indicated above. If the demand is sufficiently great, the price will be above average cost; if it is at a relatively low level, price will be in the range between average cost and lowest average variable cost. Price can, of course, equal average cost in the short-run period, but it does not necessarily do so. In any case, actual market price will adjust to the short-run equilibrium level as soon as firms have completed their output adjustments.

OUTPUT AND PRICE IN THE LONG-RUN PERIOD

The long-run equilibrium price level is the figure toward which market price and the short-run equilibrium price level tend in a period of time long enough to allow (1) the completion by the firms of all desired adjustments in factor units, (2) the entry of new firms, and (3) the departure of old ones. At any one time, adjustments in output with existing plant are tending to bring the market price to the short-run equilibrium figure, as described in the previous section. But over a longer period—one which will allow all firms to make all adjustments in plant which they wish, and allow new firms to be established and unprofitable ones to be discontinued—the various adjustments will bring both market price and the short-run equilibrium figure to the long-run equilibrium. If all long-run adjustments are actually completed, the short-run and long-run equilibrium levels will be the same, and the market price will be at this level.

The long-run equilibrium price level is determined by the relationship between demand and the long-period supply—the schedule of total amounts that would be forthcoming onto the market at various price levels, in each time interval, over a period sufficiently long to allow adjustments in the quantities of all factors used. Demand requires little further consideration. In order to isolate the effects of the adjustment of supply, it is necessary to assume that the demand schedule does not change during the period of adjustment. As indicated previously, demand schedules are typically more elastic over a longer period than they are at a given time, as buyers often will make greater readjustments to price changes in a longer time interval than they will immediately after the change has occurred. Long-period supply, however, requires more detailed analysis, since its determinants are not identical with those which control supply in the short period.

Supply Schedules in the Long-Run Period

In a long-run period, output adjustments of existing firms will differ somewhat from those made in the short run, since the ability to adjust the quantities of all factors employed alters the cost figures which affect output determination. In addition, changes may occur in the number of firms in the industry and may not only directly alter the total quantities supplied at various prices but may also affect the cost schedules and the supply schedules of the existing firms.

Long-Run Adjustments by Existing Firms. Whereas price in the short-run period need cover only average variable cost for the firms to continue production, over a long-run period price must cover all costs—and thus at least equal average cost—if firms are to continue in operation. If a firm is not covering average cost, the owners of the firm will liquidate the enterprise and reinvest in other fields. If the owners of a firm are to maximize their incomes, they must eventually shift their capital out of an enterprise which is not earning an average return into one which is.

At price levels equal to, or in excess of, average cost the firm will adjust plant capacity until long-run marginal cost and short-run marginal costs are both equal to marginal revenue and price. The plant will be adjusted to the size which will allow equality of long-run marginal cost and marginal revenue and thus will involve the lowest-cost factor combination for the most profitable volume of output. With this plant the firm will produce at the point at which marginal cost with the plant (short-run marginal cost) is equal to price. The long-run equilibrium position is illustrated in Figure 50. The firm adjusts all factors until the plant whose short-run average-cost curve is *SRAC* is attained; *Os* units of output are produced. At this level, price (and marginal revenue) are equal to both short-run and long-run marginal cost, and average cost is covered.

Adjustments in the Number of Firms. The rule that the firm will operate, after long-run adjustments have been completed, at the level at which both long-run and short-run marginal costs are equal to price is a necessary consequence of the assumption that the firm is seeking to maximize profits; under this assumption the rule is valid whether price is in excess of, or equal to, average cost. But adjustments in the number of firms in the industry will force all firms to operate at the point at which price is equal to average cost. As long as price is in excess of average cost, excess profits will be earned, and new firms will enter the industry; this process will continue until price falls to the average-cost level.

Not only is price equal to average cost in the long-run period, but it is equal to the lowest possible average-cost figure, and the firms are thus operating at the lowest points on their long-run average-cost curves. The desire for maximum profit causes the firm to operate at the point at which price is equal to marginal cost (long run). The flow of firms into the industry forces price to equality with average cost. The firm is therefore operating at the point at which price is equal to

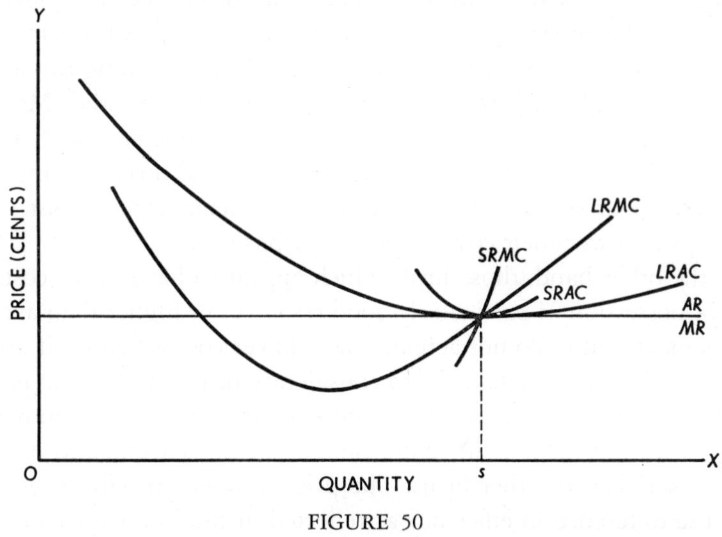

FIGURE 50

LONG-RUN ADJUSTMENT OF A FIRM SELLING IN A PURELY COMPETITIVE MARKET

both marginal cost and average cost, and these two cost figures are equal to each other only at the lowest point on the average-cost curve.

This relationship can be illustrated graphically. When long-run equilibrium adjustments have been completed, the average-revenue curve will be tangent to the long-run average-cost curve at its lowest point (as shown on Figure 50). At this point of tangency—the point at which the firm will operate—price is equal to long-run average cost (at the lowest possible figure), to short-run average cost with the optimum-sized plant, and to both short-run and long-run marginal cost. Tangency of the average-revenue and average-cost curves is essential for equilibrium, because if the curves do not touch, average cost is not covered, while if they intersect, the revenue curve cutting through the average-cost curve, there will be certain output levels at which excess profits can be earned. A horizontal revenue curve can be tangent to a ⌣-shaped average-cost curve only at the lowest point of the latter, and thus tangency is obtained at the point of lowest average cost.

Identity of Lowest Average-Cost Figures for All Firms in the Industry

Since the reasoning of the preceding paragraphs applies to all firms in the industry, when equilibrium is attained price must equal the figure of lowest long-run average cost for each firm. Because there is a single market price for the commodity, the figures of lowest average cost must be identical for all firms. The contradiction between this conclusion and the apparent variations in the cost of various firms in an industry can be explained. In any given period, in which long-run adjustments have not been completed, the conclusion is not valid. Many of the apparent cost differences are short-run phenomena, which would disappear over a longer period. Over such a period, firms having high costs because of obsolete techniques or poor management must either take steps to lower their costs or go out of business.

On the other hand, those firms which appear to have lower costs because of possession of particularly good resources or higher-than-average management ability do not actually have lower cost schedules if all implicit cost elements are taken into consideration. Because of the greater usefulness of these superior factor units, their owners can command a higher price for them than that paid for the standard-quality units if they are supplied to other firms. The price differential will, in general, equal the difference in efficiency as reflected in the lower costs of other factors required in conjunction with these. Hence the implicit costs to the firm from using the superior factor units are higher than those of the firms using standard units, and thus average cost, including both explicit and implicit elements, is not lower for the firms using the superior units. A farmer who has particularly fertile land will have lower labor and capital costs per unit of output, but he could rent the land to others at a figure based upon its yield, considerably in excess of the rent which could be obtained by the owners of poor land. The rent element in his total cost will be greater by the amount of the reduction in his other costs resulting from the use of the good land, and his average cost will be the same as that of his neighbor using poorer land. Since a particularly capable owner-manager of a business could get a substantially higher salary from other firms than that obtained by less capable managers, the implicit managerial-wage costs of his business are comparably higher than those of other firms, and thus the average cost of his product is not lower than the cost figures of other firms, when implicit as well as explicit costs are included.

Supply Schedules

The nature of the long-run industry supply schedules is dependent upon the cost conditions in which the industry operates, and separate attention must be given to the two major types of such conditions.

Constant-Cost Industries. As explained in the preceding section, once long-run adjustments are complete each firm will, of necessity, be operating at the point of lowest cost. Therefore each firm will be supplying on the market the quantity of output which it can produce at the lowest possible long-run average-cost figure. At the price equal to lowest average cost, the potential *total* supply—taking into consideration changes in the number of firms in the industry—is infinite, if the industry is one of constant-cost conditions, and thus the cost schedules of the firms are unaffected by changes in total output of the industry. With such conditions total output will increase to equal the quantity demanded at this price; should output temporarily be less than this amount, price will exceed average cost, and new firms will enter the industry. As a result the market supply will increase, and drive the market price down to the average-cost level. Hence the long-run supply curve for the entire industry (as shown on Figure 51)—the curve showing

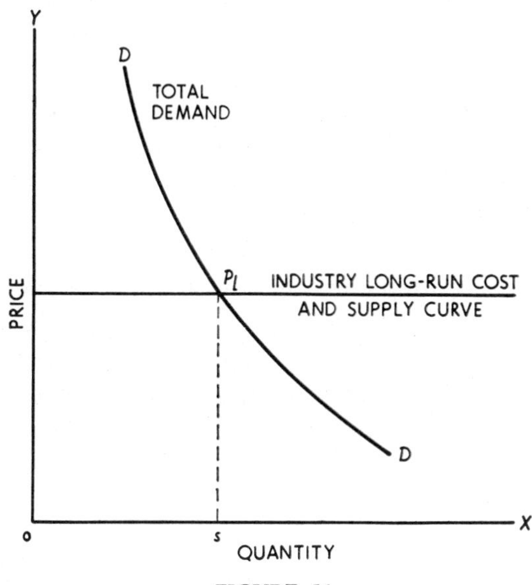

FIGURE 51

LONG-RUN EQUILIBRIUM, CONSTANT-COST INDUSTRY

the total potential amounts which will be supplied by all firms at various prices—will be a horizontal line at the level of the lowest long-run average-cost figure of the firms, for the range in which constant cost conditions prevail. At lower prices nothing will be supplied, since the firms cannot cover average cost. Higher prices are of no significance, since prices in the long-run period cannot remain above the average-cost figure, because the excess profits which would be earned would draw new firms into the industry. The industry long-run supply curve is identical with the long-run cost curve for the industry—the curve showing the locations of the lowest points of the long-run average-cost curves for the firms in the industry with various amounts of total output of the industry. The actual quantity that will be forthcoming on the market—as distinguished from the potential quantity—in each time interval after long-run adjustments have been completed is indicated by the point of intersection of the demand curve with the industry supply curve (*os*) on Figure 51).

Increasing-Cost Industries. In an industry of increasing-cost conditions, the entry of new firms into the industry will raise the cost schedules of all of the firms by increasing the prices paid for certain factor units. Accordingly, the height of the lowest-cost figure for the firms depends upon the total output of the industry, and will shift as the total output changes.

At price levels lower than the lowest figure of average cost with minimum output of the industry, nothing at all would be produced, and thus the long-run supply would be zero. At the price level equal to the figure of lowest industry average cost, and each price level higher than this, the total quantity supplied would be the amount which would allow the average cost figure to equal the price. If total output were less than this figure, average cost would be less than price, and new firms would enter the industry and increase total output until average cost rose to the level of the particular price figure. If total output were greater than this figure, average cost would exceed price, and some of the firms would leave the industry. The decline in total output would reduce average cost, until it eventually reached the price figure. It must be emphasized that the long-run supply schedule consists of the potential amounts which would be supplied at the various prices in each interval of time over a long-run period. In Table 24, the relationship between the long-run industry cost schedule and the long-run industry supply schedule in an increasing-cost industry is shown. In Figure 52 the industry cost and supply curve is illustrated.

TABLE 24

LONG-RUN INDUSTRY COST SCHEDULE AND SUPPLY SCHEDULE, INCREASING-COST INDUSTRY

Cost Schedule		Supply Schedule	
Total Output for the Industry (Units)	Point of Lowest Long-Run Average Cost for Each Firm (Cents)	Price of the Product (Cents)	Total Quantity Supplied (Units)
1 million	25	25	1 million
2 million	30	30	2 million
3 million	35	35	3 million
4 million	40	40	4 million

With this data, if the total output of the industry were 1 million units, the figure of lowest average cost for the firms would be 25 cents. Thus, if the price on the market were 25 cents, over a period of time output would adjust to the 1 million figure, since any larger quantity would result in an excess of cost over price, and any smaller quantity would result in excess profits. If the price were 30 cents, the industry output

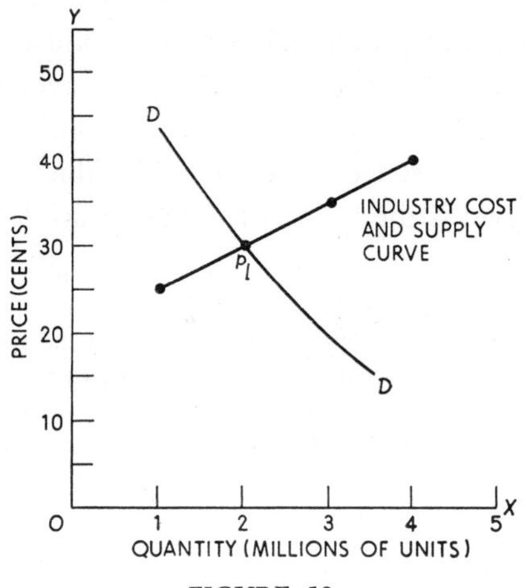

FIGURE 52

INDUSTRY COST AND SUPPLY CURVE, INCREASING-COST INDUSTRY

would adjust to the figure of 2 million because with this output average cost would be equal to the price. The same reasoning applies to the other price levels.

In this situation the industry supply curve slopes upward from left to right (Fig. 52), since the level of average cost is higher for successively larger volumes of total output. As in constant-cost conditions, the industry cost and supply curves are identical, since, at each price level, total industry supply will adjust to the level at which the average cost is equal to the price.

The third possible case is that of a decreasing-cost industry, one in which the cost schedules of the firms fall as the total output of the industry increases. However, this case is, from all indications, of no practical importance and it is not worth while to develop a detailed analysis of it.[2]

The Long-Run Equilibrium Price Level

The long-run equilibrium price level is the figure at which the quantity demanded is equal to the long-period supply, the quantity that will be supplied continuously in a given time interval after long-run adjustments are complete. At higher price figures, total output would exceed the quantity demanded; at lower price levels an insufficient amount would be produced to meet the quantity that persons wished to buy at that price level. In Figure 52, the long-run normal price level is p_l, the intersection of the demand curve with the long-period supply curve, which is, of course, identical with the industry cost curve—the curve which shows the locations of the lowest average-cost figures of the firms with various levels of output for the industry.

In terms of the cost schedules of the individual firms, the long-run equilibrium price level is the figure of lowest possible long-run average

[2] The industry cost curve (as shown in Figure 53), which slopes downward from left to right, can in this case also be regarded as a supply curve. At each point on the cost curve, the potential supply extends outward to infinity from the point on the cost curve; quantities less than the figure indicated by the point on the cost curve cannot be supplied at the particular price figure, since average cost would be higher than the price. The actual quantity that would come on the market would be determined by the intersection of the demand curve with the cost curve, and the price indicated by this intersection (p on Figure 53) is the long-run equilibrium price.

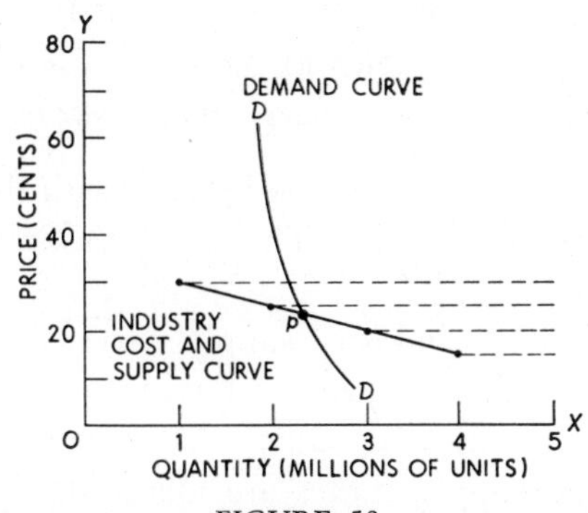

FIGURE 53

INDUSTRY COST AND SUPPLY CURVE, DECREASING-COST INDUSTRY

cost, with the cost schedule of the firm at the level appropriate to the figure of total industry equilibrium output. In a constant-cost industry the cost schedules of the firms, and thus the figure of lowest average cost, and the long-run equilibrium price level (which is equal to lowest average cost) are the same regardless of the demand for the product and the volume of output of the industry. In an increasing-cost industry, the greater the demand for the product, and thus the output of the industry, the higher will be the cost schedules of the firms, the figure of lowest average cost, and the long-run equilibrium price level. The equilibrium level is, of course, also equal to the long-run marginal cost figures of the firms, and the short-run marginal costs with the plants of optimum (lowest-cost) size.

THE ADJUSTMENT OF MARKET PRICE TO THE LONG-RUN EQUILIBRIUM LEVEL

At any particular time, market price tends, as a result of output adjustments with existing plants, toward the short-run equilibrium level. But, even if it reaches this level, further adjustments will occur, through changes in plant capacities of existing firms and in the number of firms in the industry, until market price reaches the long-run equilibrium level. In the process of adjustment, the short-run equilibrium will also become equal to the long-run equilibrium figure. The adjustment toward equilibrium can be illustrated by considering the effects upon price and output of a change in demand and a change in cost.

Readjustment to a Change in Demand

The explanation of the readjustments in response to a change in demand is facilitated if it is assumed that complete equilibrium of market price with the short-run and long-run equilibrium levels had been attained prior to the demand change (as illustrated in Figure 54, page 212), price being at the level p. The adjustment can be broken down into several steps:

1. Rise in market price. When the demand for the product increases, market price, of necessity, rises immediately, since market supply is not likely to be perfectly elastic and at the old price the quantity demanded exceeds the quantity supplied. Buyers will be unable to get as many units as they wish at the old price, and will bid the price up. Equality of market demand and market supply will be attained at p'. At this figure, the market price exceeds both the short-run and long-run equilibrium levels.

2. Increase in output and decline in market price to the short-run equilibrium level. The rise in price creates a gap between price and marginal cost. As a consequence, firms will increase output in order to re-attain equality of price and marginal cost, with their existing plants. therefore the market supply curve will move to the right, and market price will fall until it reaches the new short-run equilibrium level, p_s on Figure 54. Because of the upward-sloping nature of the short-run supply curve—which in turn is due to the fact that additional output can be produced from given plants only at higher marginal cost, since firms were previously operating at optimum capacity—the new short-

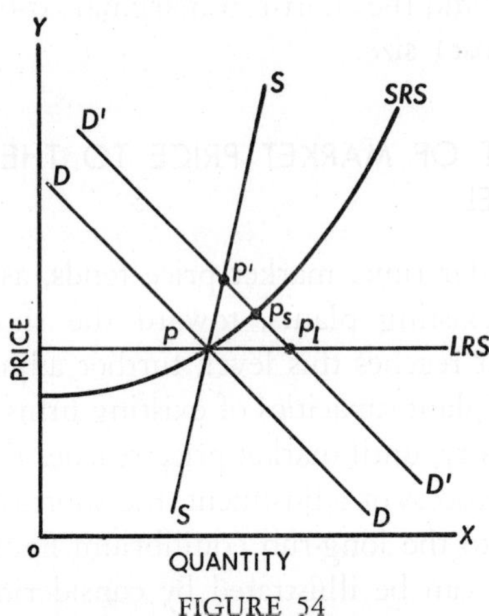

FIGURE 54

ADJUSTMENT OF PRICE AND OUTPUT IN RESPONSE TO A DEMAND INCREASE, CONSTANT-COST INDUSTRY

run normal price will be higher than the original price before the demand change. When market price reaches the short-run figure, demand and the current rate of output, with the given number of firms and plant, will be equal.

3. Increase in the number of firms in the industry, and decline in market price to the long-run equilibrium level.

Even when short-run adjustments are complete, price will exceed average cost; new firms will enter the industry, raise market supply, and bring market price down to the long-run equilibrium figure (p_l on Figure 54). The new market-supply curves are omitted from Figure 54.

If the industry is one of constant-cost conditions, the new long-run equilibrium will be at the same level as that prevailing prior to the demand increase, since the figure of lowest average cost for each firm will remain unchanged. Output of the industry will be greater, in response to the greater demand, but prices will remain the same. The adjustment shown on Figure 54 is that of a constant-cost industry.

On the other hand, if the industry is one of increasing-cost conditions, the increase in output of the industry as a whole will raise the cost schedules of the firms, and accordingly the new long-run equilibrium figure will be somewhat higher than the old, as shown on Figure 55. In such an industry, an increase in demand will lead to a permanent increase in price (given the other determinants) because of the higher average cost with the greater volume of total output of the industry.

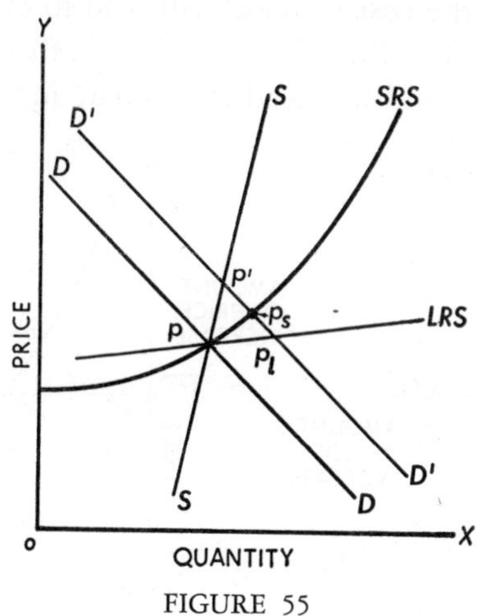

FIGURE 55

ADJUSTMENT OF PRICE AND OUTPUT IN RESPONSE TO A DEMAND INCREASE, INCREASING-COST INDUSTRY

If the demand for a commodity falls, the general process of readjustment moves in the opposite direction to that of an increase. Market price falls sharply, and firms reduce output; market supply falls, and the price adjusts upward to the new short-run equilibrium figure, which is less than the original market price. But price is still less than average cost, and thus some firms will leave the industry; market supply falls still more, and price moves back up to the long-run equilibrium. The new figure is less than the original figure if the industry is one of increasing-cost conditions, but the same as the old figure if constant-cost conditions prevail.

The adjustments outlined in the preceding sections are, of course, oversimplified. The basic determinants of cost, including factor prices, methods of production, etc., are themselves subject to change, and the long-run equilibrium figure shifts, apart from modifications arising out of changes in the rate of output. As a consequence, rarely may market price actually reach the level of long-run equilibrium, which itself is constantly changing. But nevertheless, the analysis is significant because the direction of movement in market price in any period is controlled by the relationship existing between the present market-price figure and the short-run and long-run equilibrium figures.

Adjustments to Cost Changes

When an increase in cost occurs, there is no immediate effect on market price, unless the reservation prices of the sellers are affected by the expectation that the cost increase will lead to eventual increases in price. The cost increase will, however, affect both short-run and long-run equilibrium levels and will lead to ultimate increases in price, once

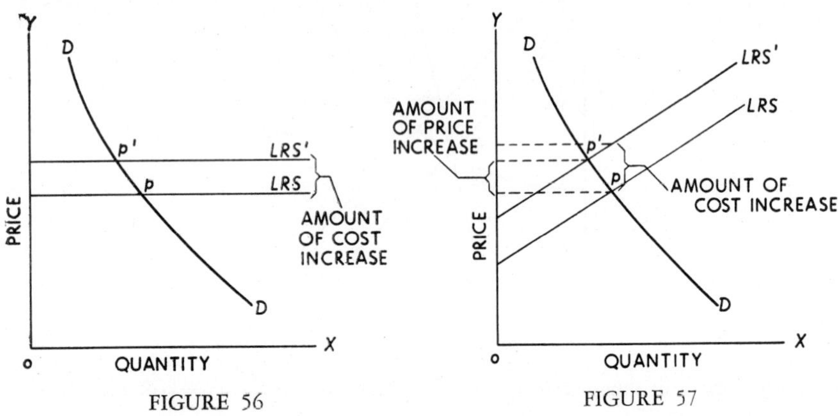

FIGURE 56

LONG-RUN ADJUSTMENT OF PRICE TO A COST INCREASE, CONSTANT-COST INDUSTRY

FIGURE 57

LONG-RUN ADJUSTMENT OF PRICE TO A COST INCREASE, INCREASING-COST INDUSTRY

adjustments in output and in the number of firms have occurred. In the short-run period, firms will contract output, since the increase in marginal cost due to the cost increase will have raised the marginal cost figure above the price. Thus the short-run equilibrium level will be higher than the old figure, but by an amount less than the cost increase per unit of product, since the reductions in output reduce the marginal cost figure. Once short-run adjustments are complete, market price will have risen by a sum less than the amount of the cost increase per unit of product. But average cost is not yet covered, and over a period of time the number of firms will decline and market price will rise until it again equals average cost. In a constant-cost industry, as illustrated in Figure 56, average cost will ultimately rise by the amount of the cost increase (per unit of output); the increase in price will equal the amount of the cost increase. In an increasing-cost industry (Figure 57) the average-cost schedules of the firms will fall as the output of the industry declines; the ultimate price increase will be somewhat less than the amount of the cost increase. In a decreasing-cost industry the rise would be greater than the amount of the cost increase. In all cases output will be less than it was prior to the cost increase; the relative output reduction will be greatest in a decreasing-cost industry and least in one of increasing-cost conditions.

IMPERFECTIONS IN PURELY COMPETITIVE INDUSTRY ADJUSTMENTS

The analysis of price and output determination in pure competition has been based, up to this point, upon the assumption of the absence of imperfections which interfere with the attainment of the adjustments. Actually, however, imperfections are likely to be of considerable significance in some instances, and delay the attainment of the adjustments.

Knowledge of Future Prices and Time Lags in Supply Adjustments

In industries characterized by large numbers of small producers, lack of knowledge of market conditions on the part of the producers, coupled with the substantial time lag which often occurs between change in inputs and actual change in output reaching the market may interfere seriously with market adjustments. Farmers, for example, must base their output plans on prices prevailing at the time the crop is planted. But they are unaware of the actions of the other firms relative to output, and thus the total increase or decrease in output made by the producers may prove to be too large or too small, relative to demand, when it actually reaches the market.

An extreme example of time lapse in the production process is in the growing of certain types of fruits. Apple and walnut trees, for example, do not reach full bearing until ten to twenty years after planting. In an industry of this type, when the market price exceeds the long-run equilibrium figure, there is a tendency for too many trees to be planted. When the crops of all the new producers reach the market, the supply will be so great that market price will fall below average cost. As a result, some of the firms will be forced to retire from business. A good example of this reaction is provided by the apple industry in the Pacific Northwest during the 1920's and 1930's. During the early 1920's, apple prices exceeded average cost. Many new orchards were developed; by the end of the 1920's the increased supply from the new orchards began to reach the market, and prices fell below average cost. The problem was greatly aggravated by the coming of the depression, which reduced demand at the same time that the increased supply reached the market.

The Cobweb Theorem

A similar reaction, but one of a recurrent nature, occurs frequently with crops which require only one season to reach maturity. If price exceeds average cost, it is very likely that such a great increase in production will occur that, when the crop is harvested, price will fall below average cost. As a result, in the following year production will be reduced so much that price will rise above average cost. This fluctuation of market price around the equilibrium level may continue more or less indefinitely. The amplitude of the fluctuations may remain constant, decrease, or, within limits, increase, according to the exact nature of the behavior of the producers in the particular situation. The statement of this type of behavior of market price is known as the "cobweb theorem."[3]

[3] The name originates from the appearance of the graphical presentation of price behavior in a situation of this sort. Figure 58(A) below illustrates the case in which the

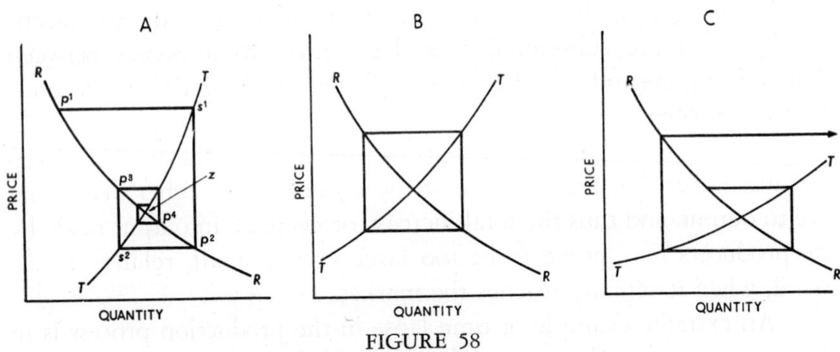

FIGURE 58

ILLUSTRATION OF THE COBWEB THEOREM

amplitude of the excessive production in alternate years is declining. The *RR* curve is similar to the usual demand curve; it shows the quantities that will be purchased at various prices in a particular year or, in other words, the prices at which various quantities placed on the market can be sold. Curve *TT* shows the quantities that will be produced and placed on the market in the second year, on the basis of various prices prevailing during the first year; it is not comparable to the usual supply curve. If, in the first year, the actual market price (determined by that year's current supply-demand relationships) is p^1, the quantity that will be supplied the next year is s^1, as indicated by the *TT* curve. But the second year, because of the increased supply, the price will fall to p^2. Supply the

For purposes of illustration, suppose that during the current year potato prices exceed average cost. As a result, next year many farmers will shift acreage from other crops to potatoes. When next year's crop is harvested, market supply will be considerably greater than it is this year. The increase may be so great that market price will fall below average cost and as a result, the following year potato acreage will be reduced substantially as farmers shift back to other crops. The reduction may be so great that prices will again rise above average cost and lead to another excessive increase in supply.

Other Imperfections

Knowledge of Cost. A source of imperfection in the markets is the lack of knowledge on the part of the sellers of their costs. The typical production unit in pure competition is small; the average farmer, for example, has very incomplete records and inadequate knowledge of his costs. As a result it is inevitable that output is frequently not adjusted to the level which will result in maximization of profit, and short-run supply is different from what it would be if farmers calculated marginal cost carefully. Production is continued for long periods when average cost is in excess of price. A common reaction to price declines will illustrate the significance of the lack of knowledge of cost. If a producer is maximizing profit, a decline in the price of a good will always make profitable a reduction in output. Yet frequently, when all farm prices fall, farmers will increase output instead of reducing it, in an effort to maintain total income at the figure existing prior to the price decline. When a farmer acts in this manner, either he was not maximizing profit prior to the price decline, or he is not doing so after he increases output. This failure to maximize profits is due primarily to imperfect knowledge of costs.

---

following year will then be s^2, and price will rise to p^3, only to fall to p^4 the next year, and so on. Eventually final equilibrium will be reached at z, since each year the amplitude of the fluctuations grows less. Figure 58(B) illustrates a case in which the *RR* and *TT* curves have the same shape, so that the fluctuations continue indefinitely at the same rate; Figure 58(C) shows the case in which the fluctuations grow in amplitude, since the slope of the *RR* curve is greater than that of the *TT* curve. There is no evidence that the latter cases will be found in practice; if there was no limit to the increase in amplification, the industry would eventually swallow the whole economy.

For further discussion see H. R. Bowen, *Toward Social Economy* (New York: Rinehart, 1948), pp. 275–76; K. E. Boulding, *Economic Analysis* (3rd ed.; New York: Harper, 1955), pp. 164–65; N. S. Buchanan, "A Reconsideration of the Cobweb Theorem," *Journal of Political Economy*, Vol. XLVII (February, 1939), pp. 67–81; M. Ezekiel, "The Cobweb Theorem," *Quarterly Journal of Economics*, Vol. XII (February, 1938), pp. 255–80.

Immobility of Farmers. Another source of imperfection is the unwillingness of small producers, particularly farmers, to abandon their farms and turn to other types of activity when they are unable to cover their costs. They frequently are not skilled in other lines of work; job opportunities may not be plentiful; personal attachment to farming may prevent them from leaving even though prices are far below average cost. Farmers will typically shift quickly from one crop to another in response to relative price and profit situations, but they are very slow to leave farming entirely. As a consequence, when prices of large numbers of farm products get below average cost, readjustment to long-run equilibrium is very slow.

Governmental Interference. A new type of imperfection has been introduced in recent years by the federal agricultural aid programs. In the case of many crops the federal government, under present law, is committed to a policy of preventing prices from falling below certain levels, by purchasing farm commodities whenever necessary to hold prices to the stated figures. Programs of this sort obviously interfere with supply adjustments and serve to perpetuate maladjustments in allocation of farm land to various crops. When production becomes excessive in certain lines, the consequent price declines should bring about a reduction in production. But, if the government artificially holds prices up by its own buying, the supply adjustment fails to occur. Other phases of the agricultural program of recent years involve even more drastic interference with long-run adjustments; in some instances the volume of output has been directly controlled.

Lack of Complete Control over Output. Finally, the influence of climatic conditions upon crop yield and the consequent inability of the farmer to control exactly the volume of his output by varying his factor inputs interfere with attainment of equilibrium prices and cause substantial price fluctuations unrelated to adjustments toward equilibrium levels.

SELECTED REFERENCES

BAIN, J. S. *Pricing, Distribution, and Employment,* chap. iv. rev. ed. New York: Holt, 1952.

BOULDING, K. E. *Economic Analysis,* chaps. iv, v, vii, and xxvii. 3rd ed. New York: Harper, 1955.

CHAMBERLIN, E. H. *The Theory of Monopolistic Competition,* chaps. i and ii. Cambridge: Harvard University Press, 1933.

STIGLER, G. J. *The Theory of Price,* chap. ix. rev. ed. New York: Macmillan, 1953.

QUESTIONS

1. Explain the concept of "supply."
2. Distinguish between a change in supply and a change in quantity supplied; illustrate the two changes on a graph.
3. What are the characteristics of the market period?
4. Distinguish between the determinants of market supply and those of short-run supply.
5. Why does the market-supply curve slope upward from left to right? Why is it perfectly inelastic above a certain point? Why may some units be supplied even at prices far below average variable cost?
6. Draw a supply curve for Christmas trees in a purely competitive market the afternoon before Christmas.
7. Explain the concept of reservation price. What determines a person's reservation price? What significance does reservation price have for the market-supply schedule?
8. Explain the determination of market price in a purely competitive market.
9. Why cannot price remain above the market equilibrium level?
10. In the short-run period, what is the relation between supply and output?
11. Why can price, in the short-run period, not remain below average variable cost? Why may it remain below average cost? Why may it remain above average cost?
12. Why is the output level at which marginal revenue is equal to marginal cost the level at which profits are maximized?
13. On the basis of the data given below, determine the supply schedule of the firm in the short-run period:

Output	Total Variable Cost	Output	Total Variable Cost
1	$22	6	$ 85
2	32	7	115
3	40	8	155
4	50	9	205
5	65	10	310

14. Why does the portion of the firm's marginal-cost curve above its intersection with the average variable cost curve constitute the firm's short-run supply curve?
15. Why does the short-run supply curve slope upward from left to right? Why does it start from the vertical axis at a higher point than the market-supply curve?
16. Explain the nature of the short-run equilibrium price level.
17. Why, in the long-run period, must price equal average cost?
18. Why, in the long-run period, must the firms be operating at the points of lowest long-run average cost?

19. Suppose that potato farming is a purely competitive industry. It would appear that farmers growing potatoes on very fertile land would be able to produce them more cheaply than those growing them on poor land, and thus would make excess profits. Why is this not the case, when long-run equilibrium is established?
20. Why is the long-run industry supply curve, in a constant-cost industry, a horizontal line?
21. Why, in an increasing-cost industry, is the long-run industry supply curve identical to the long-run industry cost curve?
22. Draw the long-run supply curve for the industry on the basis of the cost data given below.

Total Output of Industry	Lowest Average-Cost Figure for Each Firm
500,000	$47
1,000,000	52
1,500,000	55
2,000,000	59
2,500,000	63
3,000,000	66

23. What determines the actual long-run output in a constant-cost industry, as distinguished from the potential output?
24. Trace carefully, step by step, the effect of a decrease in demand upon (*a*) market price immediately after the change, (*b*) short-run equilibrium price and output and (*c*) long-run equilibrium price and output, in a constant-cost industry.
25. Why, in an increasing-cost industry, will price (over a long-run period) rise by an amount less than the amount of a tax levied on the output?
26. Under what circumstances, in pure competition, is price dependent upon demand considerations alone? Upon cost considerations alone? Illustrate graphically.
27. Explain the cobweb theorem. If you were a farmer producing a product whose price is subject to cobweb-theorem fluctuations, what could you do to increase your profits, from a long-run standpoint, provided other farmers do not do the same thing?
28. Why do the present farm programs, designed to hold farm prices up to certain percentages of "parity," interfere with the attainment of long-run equilibrium in the industries?
29. Why does wartime price control give rise to the need for rationing? Illustrate graphically.
30. Why do many farm products fluctuate greatly in price from year to year?

Chapter 10 PRODUCT DIFFERENTIATION AND MONOPOLISTIC COMPETITION

Conditions in relatively few markets today approximate the assumptions upon which the purely competitive analysis is based closely enough to allow the analysis to be useful in a study of the industries. Differentiation is widespread, and in numerous cases the numbers of firms are so small that mutual interdependence exists. Accordingly, the theory of price and output determination must be extended to cases based upon assumptions pertinent to the nonpurely competitive fields if it is to be useful for significant portions of the economy.

Such an extension is difficult, however, because of the wide range of possible assumptions which may be utilized; nonpurely competitive conditions consist not of one simple, clearly defined case, as does pure competition, but of a wide range of cases with one common bond: the individual seller (and in some cases, the buyer) exercises direct control over price. The various situations are distinguished from one another by differences in the degree of differentiation of product; the extent of mutual interdependence among sellers, and in some instances, among buyers; the types of pricing institutions; and the importance of advertising and other selling activities. Within the scope of the present study, the analysis must be limited to a few major cases, based upon assumptions which appear to have significant applicability.

GENERAL FEATURES OF NONPURELY COMPETITIVE MARKETS

Before the major cases of nonpurely competitive conditions are analyzed, certain general considerations applying to such conditions can be outlined.

Time Periods

Instead of the three time periods utilized in the analysis of pure competition, only two are required, except in rare instances, in the analysis of nonpurely competitive markets. The market and short-run periods may be regarded as identical, in most cases, since the firms adjust output continuously in conformity with current and anticipated sales, and cost elements are taken into consideration in the setting of current market prices. A firm does not ordinarily produce a large stock of goods and then decide the price at which this stock can be sold; a certain price is set, and output adjusted to the amount which can be sold at this price. In some instances, of course, a firm will discover that it has overproduced, or, in the case of a merchant, overbought, and be forced to dispose of some units, especially of perishable goods, at prices which bear no relation to cost. But these cases are not of sufficient importance to require differentiation between market and short-run periods throughout the analysis.

The distinction between the short-run and long-run periods, however, is of great importance. Just as in pure competition, price and output levels may differ substantially after long-run adjustments are completed from the levels prevailing at a given time, with existing plant and numbers of firms. There is no precise concept of a long-run equilibrium price level in nonpurely competitive conditions, but the general nature of long-run adjustments can be analyzed.

The Initiative in Price Setting

Nonpurely competitive markets may be dominated by the sellers, or by the buyers, or be characterized by bargaining between buyer and seller groups. Seller-dominated markets are most important, and primary attention will be given to these, with some reference to cases of buyer-domination, and bargaining between large buyers and large sellers.

In the typical seller-dominated market, prices are set by the action of the sellers, rather than being determined by forces of supply and demand in central wholesale markets. There is no necessary single, uniform price at which all producers must sell. The price-setting may involve nothing more than the adoption of the price of a competitor, or it may involve careful calculation of costs and demand schedules. But in any event, the actual price figure is chosen by the seller.

The setting of price involves a simultaneous determination of the volume of output. The price and output decisions cannot be made independently of one another, since the optimum-price figure is dependent upon the volume of sales which can be made; the potential sales at various prices must be estimated if price is to be set at the optimum level. At the price actually set, only a finite quantity can be sold; unlike the case of pure competition, a firm cannot sell an unlimited quantity at a particular price.

The Relationship between Price and Marginal Cost

In both purely competitive and nonpurely competitive markets, the firm must operate at the level of output at which marginal revenue is equal to marginal cost if profits are to be maximized. In pure competition, since the demand for the product of the firm is perfectly elastic, average revenue and marginal revenue are identical, and thus when the firm adjusts output to the figure at which marginal cost is equal to

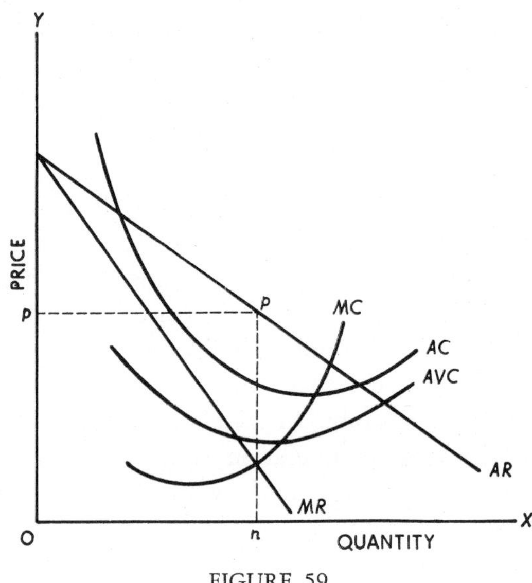

FIGURE 59

ADJUSTMENT OF OUTPUT AND PRICE IN NONPURELY COMPETITIVE MARKETS

marginal revenue, marginal cost is also equal to the price. But in all nonpurely competitive conditions, the demand schedule for the product of the firm is less than perfectly elastic, and marginal revenue is less than average revenue (price). Each successive unit sold adds less to total revenue than the price received for it, since the price obtained on the other units must be reduced in order to sell the additional unit. When the firm adjusts output to the level at which marginal revenue equals marginal cost, price will be in excess of marginal cost. On Figure 59 the optimum-output level is *On;* the price charged is *p,* which is in excess of marginal cost. The price for which the optimum-profit output can be sold is indicated by the point on the *AR* curve directly above the intersection of *MR* and *MC.* The exact nature of the firm's demand schedule will depend upon the particular form of nonpurely competitive conditions prevailing, as explained in the next section and the two following chapters.

The Relationship between Price, Average Variable Cost, and Average Cost

In a short-run period, as in pure competition, price must cover average variable cost, but need not cover average cost; it may, however, exceed average cost. If average variable cost is not covered by the most advantageous price which the firm can set, losses will be minimized by closing down, since each additional unit produced increases losses. The only exception to this rule of closing down is the case in which there are expectations that business conditions will improve; under such circumstances it may be preferable to operate for a time, in order to avoid loss of personnel, distribution channels, and customers. Temporary cessation of operations may result in dealers taking on other lines, and in shift of customers to other brands; when the firm resumes operations, some of the dealers and customers may not return to the firm. But operation at prices below average variable cost is not possible unless the firm or its owners have money which they are willing to use to cover the losses. If, on the other hand, price covers average variable cost but not all of the fixed costs, and is thus less than average cost, continued operation is desirable in the short-run period, since the fixed costs will continue whether operation is carried on or not, and it is preferable to earn something toward them rather than nothing.

Over a long-run period, however, price must, of course, cover average cost if operation is to continue. If price is temporarily below average cost, some of the firms will drop out of the industry, and the remaining firms will again be able to cover all costs. But if price exceeds average cost, there will be a tendency for new firms to enter the industry, and for prices to move toward average cost. However, as explained in subsequent sections, there are numerous obstacles to the entry of new firms in nonpurely competitive conditions, and thus the tendency of price to come down to the average cost level is seriously restricted.

Product Adjustments and Nonprice Competition

In purely competitive conditions, the products of the various firms in an industry are identical, and there is no opportunity for adjustment of product. The firm selects the general type of product (winter wheat, alfalfa, peas, canning peaches, etc.) which is believed to be the most profitable, but it cannot vary the exact quality or nature from the standard variety.[1] Likewise, because the market price is independent of the actions of the firm and the seller can sell an infinite amount at the market price, no advertising and other selling activities are necessary.

In nonpurely competitive conditions, however, in many cases firms can increase profits (or avoid losses) by the making of adjustments in their products, and by the use of advertising and other selling activities. For example, changes in body style and other features of cars are extremely important in the automobile industry in determining the sales volume which the firm can make. Furthermore, firms typically find that they can profitably increase their sales by selling activities, since the gains in additional sales (or in sales at higher prices) exceed the costs of the activities. Hence firms in most nonpurely competitive markets not only have the task of determining the optimum output and price levels, but also those of selecting the optimum product and the optimum type and extent of selling activities. Later in this chapter, the problems of adjustment of these elements will be considered.

The remainder of this chapter will be devoted to an analysis of price, output, and selling-activity determination under conditions of monopolistic competition. The following chapter is concerned with monopoly, and Chapter 12 with oligopoly.

MONOPOLISTIC COMPETITION: THE CASE OF DIFFERENTIATION AND LARGE NUMBERS OF SELLERS AND BUYERS

The nonpurely competitive case which most closely resembles that of pure competition is that of monopolistic competition, the analysis of which was first developed by E. H. Chamberlin.[2] The case of monopolistic competition is based upon three assumptions:

1. The number of sellers is sufficiently large that there is no feeling of mutual interdependence among them. Each firm acts independently, without respect to any effect which its action may have upon those of its competitors.

2. Products of the various sellers are differentiated, customers having preferences for the products of particular sellers.

[1] Standard grades are established for many farm products. By care in producing and handling, the producer will be able to get more of his output into the higher grades. But within the scope of a purely competitive market he cannot vary the nature of his product from the standard grades established.

[2] See E. H. Chamberlin, *The Theory of Monopolistic Competition* (Cambridge: Harvard University Press, 1933). There was some suggestion of the case of monopolistic competition in J. M. Clark, *Economics of Overhead Costs* (Chicago: University of Chicago Press, 1923).

3. Entry into the industry is unrestricted, new firms being able to commence production of very close substitutes for the existing brands of the product, even though they cannot make items which are exactly identical, in the eyes of the purchasers, to the existing brands.[3]

Under these assumptions, each seller will act independently, basing his policies upon his estimate of his demand and cost schedules, and accepting the policies of the other firms as given and unaffected by the policies which he follows. In practice his actions may affect the actions of the other firms, but so long as he does not anticipate such reactions, the conditions are those of monopolistic competition. Thus the seller has a determinate (though perhaps difficult to ascertain) demand schedule for his product, given the prices of the other firms.

The Nature of the Demand Schedules for the Product of the Firm

Since the products are differentiated, the demand schedules confronting each seller are not perfectly elastic, as various customers will be attached to the products of particular sellers. When differentiation develops, a seller can raise his price above the old market level without losing all his customers, since some will prefer his product to those of competitors and will be willing to pay a higher price for it. Likewise, price reductions will not bring an infinite volume of business, since other buyers will be attached to the products of competing firms. Thus at each price the firm can sell a definitely limited quantity.

Since firms do not expect competitors to follow price changes made by them, the demand schedule for the product of each firm is likely to appear very elastic to the firm. Price increases will cause substantial loss in business to makers of competing brands, while decreases will take substantial business away from the other firms. The exact degree of elasticity depends primarily upon the strength of differentiation, that is, the strength of the attachment of the customers to particular brands. If preferences are strong, price changes will cause relatively little shifting among the various brands and the demand schedules will have relatively little elasticity. If preferences are weak, substantial shifting will occur.

It is likely that in most cases the differentiation will not be strong enough to give a high degree of inelasticity to the schedule, and the discretion which the firm has in the setting of prices will be relatively limited. Any substantial increase above the optimum figure would

[3] The new brands may be physically identical to the old, but cannot bear the same brand name, and thus do not appear identical to all of the consumers.

cause a very large loss in sales, and any decrease in price would cause such a great increase in sales that the firm could not meet the demand without average cost rising above price. The firm is likely to encounter very quickly the point at which average cost ceases falling because the industries of monopolistic competition are likely to be ones requiring little capital equipment and offering few economies of large-scale production. If such economies are significant, the number of sellers is likely to become so small that the market conditions will no longer be those of monopolistic competition.

Price and Output Adjustments

In monopolistic competition, as in all situations, the optimum output level is that at which marginal cost is equal to marginal reve-

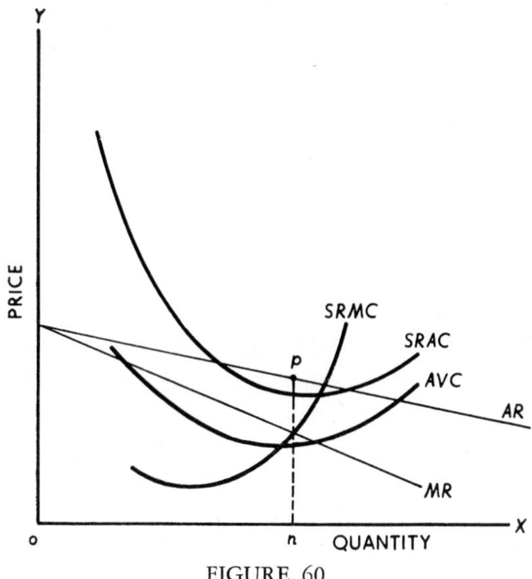

FIGURE 60

ADJUSTMENT OF PRICE AND OUTPUT IN MONOPOLISTIC COMPETITION

nue; in Figure 60, the optimum output is *on,* and the optimum price *p,* as indicated by the point on the *AR* curve directly above the intersection of *SRMC* and *MR.* This is the price figure at which the optimum-profit output can be sold. Because of the high elasticity of the demand schedule for the firm, the excess of price over marginal cost will be relatively slight, compared to the cases of monopoly and oligopoly. The prices charged by the various firms are not likely to be identical, since degrees of consumer preference, and thus the height and elasticity of the demand schedules, will differ. Firms with strongly attached customers will find a relatively high price advantageous, while new firms not yet well established may find it necessary to charge a much lower figure. Costs also will not be uniform; some plants will be larger than others, some will be more modern than others, and the extent of selling activity may vary widely.

Long-Run Price and Output Adjustments

From the standpoint of the existing firms, the adjustments over a long-run period are those which must be made to attain equality of marginal revenue with long-run marginal cost—that is, to adapt the size of the plant to the optimum in terms of the demand for the product. At any particular time, maximum profits are gained at the output level at which marginal revenue is equal to marginal cost with the existing size of plant. But over a period of time profits may be increased by a change in the size of the plant to the particular size best suited to the demand for the product. This plant may be larger or smaller than the existing one. When this long-run adjustment has been completed, marginal revenue will be equal both to long-run marginal cost and to short-run marginal cost with the plant size which is the optimum relative to the demand.

However, over a period of time, the number of firms in the industry will tend to change, assuming that free entry of firms is possible. The assumption of ease of entry is not an unrealistic one in conditions of monopolistic competition, since when such conditions prevail, capital requirements are likely to be low, and the volume of output necessary for reasonably low cost is not likely to be great. Only the established reputations of existing firms may constitute a barrier to newcomers. The rapid flow of firms into and out of the grocery-retailing and small-restaurant fields provides an excellent illustration of the relatively free entry characteristic of monopolistic competition.

To the extent that new firms enter the field, there will be a tendency for prices to fall toward the level of average cost. The newcomers may find it advantageous to set prices lower than those charged by existing firms in order to build up sales volume, and the existing firms may find it necessary to reduce their prices as their sales decline as a result of the spreading of the business over a greater number of firms. The entry of the new firms is not likely to have a significant effect on the total sales of the product, and the existing sales volume, stimulated somewhat by the lower prices, will merely be divided among more firms. Whether prices fall or not, the decline in sales which each firm experiences is likely to force operation at a point farther away from the point of lowest cost, and the excess profits will in part be eliminated by a rise in average cost.

The Tangency Case

If entry is sufficiently free so that all excess profits are eliminated, average revenue will equal average cost for each firm, and the average-revenue curves will be tangent to the average-cost curves. If the revenue curve cuts the cost curve at any point, excess profits will be attainable; if it fails to touch the cost curve, losses cannot be avoided. The adjustment is illustrated in Figures 61 and 62. In Figure 61 excess profits

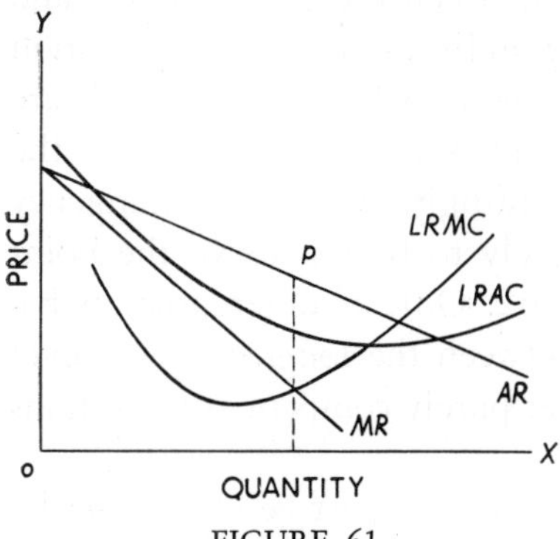

FIGURE 61
A SITUATION OF EXCESS PROFITS, MONOPOLISTIC COMPETITION

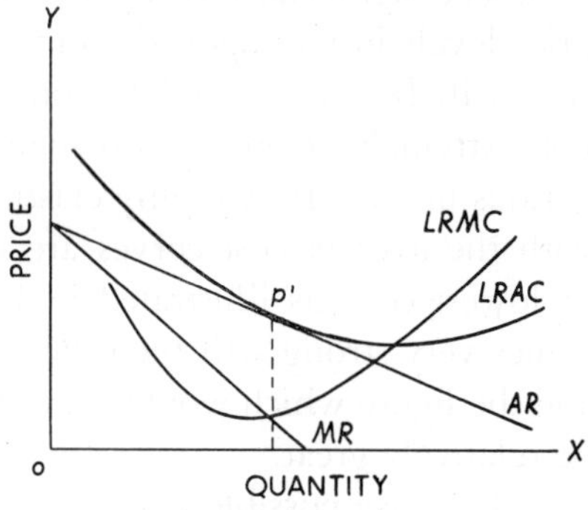

FIGURE 62
LONG-RUN ADJUSTMENT, MONOPOLISTIC COMPETITION, WITH COMPLETELY FREE ENTRY

are being earned. As a consequence new firms enter, and the average-revenue curve of each firm moves to the left, until it eventually comes to the level of tangency indicated in Figure 62. The point of tangency is, of necessity, at the same level of output as that at which marginal cost—both short run and long run—is equal to marginal revenue. At any level of output other than that of tangency of the *AR* and *LRAC* curves, price would be less than average cost, and losses would be incurred; the tangency point is thus necessarily the point of optimum profit and must be at the same output level as that at which marginal cost equals marginal revenue, since the latter relationship is essential for maximum profit.

Because of the sloping nature of the average-revenue curve, the point of tangency will not be at the lowest level of average cost. When long-run adjustments are complete, the firms will be operating at levels at which they do not attain full realization of the economies of large-scale production. The existing plant, even though the one best suited for the particular volume of output, may not be used to capacity. Any attempt to increase output to attain lowest average cost would be unprofitable, since the price reduction necessary to sell the greater output would exceed the cost reduction made possible. Thus in industries of this type there is a chronic tendency toward the existence of too many firms in the industry, each producing at a volume of output less than that which would allow lowest cost. For example there may be too many grocery stores and too many service stations, in the sense that if the total volume of business was concentrated in a smaller number of sellers, average cost and price would be less.

The significance of the difference between the long-run cost and price levels in monopolistic competition and those in pure competition can easily be exaggerated. So long as preferences for various brands are not extremely strong, the demand schedules for the products of the various firms will be highly elastic. Accordingly the points of tangency with the average-cost curves are not likely to be far above the point of lowest cost, as illustrated in Figure 62. Only if differentiation becomes very strong will the difference between the long-run price level and the figure which would prevail under purely competitive conditions be relatively great.

It is also possible that excess profits may in part be eliminated by increased expenditures on selling activities, as discussed later in the chapter.

Excessive Entry of New Firms

In industries in which the relatively low capital requirements make entry of new firms comparatively easy, it is possible that at times too many firms will enter the industry, and cause losses for large numbers of the firms. The extremely high rate of mortality of stores in some lines of retailing, especially in the first two years of operation, suggests a chronic tendency for excessive entry of newcomers. In part, the excessive entry may result when excess profits have been temporarily earned; because of the time required for operation to get under way, too many firms may commence operations, just as too many farmers plant apple trees when apple prices are very high relative to costs. But even in cases in which only normal profits are being earned, there may be a tendency for new firms to start, either because the newcomers believe that they can operate more profitably than the existing firms, or because they lack adequate knowledge of profit possibilities and are anxious to develop their own businesses.

Entry Restrictions

Adjustments toward equality of price with average cost in a situation in which differentiation is significant may be checked by the strength of the reputations built up by some firms. Those firms which are particularly successful in their selling efforts may create such strong consumer preference that newcomers—even though they are able to enter the industry freely and cover their own costs—will not take away sufficient business from the well-established firms to destroy the excess profits of the latter. Thus one grocery store in a town, which has been particularly successful in promoting customer good will, may continue to earn excess profits long after the entry of new firms has brought about equality of price and average cost for other stores. The adjustments toward a final equilibrium situation of equality of price and average cost do not proceed with the certainty that is characteristic of pure competition in which consumer preferences are nonexistent.

Industry Cost Conditions

The cost conditions in which an industry operates have the same general significance in monopolistic competition as they have in pure competition. In an increasing- or a decreasing-cost industry, the height of the cost schedules of the firms will be affected by changes in the total output of the entire industry; the actual figure of average cost to which price is equal when long-run adjustments have been completed in a situation of free entry will depend upon the total volume of output for the industry and thus, in part, upon the total demand for the product. Precise industry cost curves which would have any significance cannot be drawn, however, since the firms do not operate at the levels of lowest average cost and since costs at the actual points of operation are not uniform for the various firms, because of differences in level and elasticity of demand schedules and in cost. Likewise, the products of the various firms are not homogeneous.

ADJUSTMENTS OF PRODUCT AND SELLING ACTIVITIES

Firms in monopolistic competition have not only the task of determining price and output levels, but also of selecting the optimum variety of product, and the optimum level of selling activities. Each of these must be considered. Much of the analysis is applicable to any situation of nonpure competition, rather than to monopolistic competition alone.

Adjustment of the Physical Product

Once the firm has selected the product or products which it will produce, it must select the exact variety or quality of the product which allows maximum profit, if the profit-maximization goal is to be attained. With each potential form of the product, there is a certain cost schedule and a certain demand schedule, and thus a certain possible profit, at the level of output for the product at which marginal revenue is equal to marginal cost. In general, the higher the quality of the product, the greater the potential sales at various prices, but the greater the cost per unit for producing various quantities. Some one form of the product, with optimum price and output levels for this form, will allow the greatest profit. The price, output, and quality decisions must be made simultaneously, in the sense that one cannot be made without reference to the others.

Unfortunately, it is very difficult for the firm to estimate the sales with various forms of the product, because of the difficulty of predicting consumer reaction to various forms. Since experimenting with consumer reaction is not feasible in many cases, the firm will be forced to select the particular form which, on the basis of rough estimates, appears to yield the greatest net return. But mistakes are inevitable, and the success or failure of a firm from a long-run standpoint may depend to a very large extent on its success in guessing consumer reactions, especially in fields in which style is important. Too revolutionary a change on the one hand, and failure to keep up with changes made by other firms, on the other, may cause disastrous losses. In fields in which style is of lesser importance, the problem of quality adjustment is a less serious one and changes are less frequent.

A firm is not, of course, limited to one particular quality; firms often find it advantageous to carry several different brands of the same product, with differences in quality and price. When a firm buys out a competitor, it may continue to produce the purchased brands, particularly if they have strongly attached buyers who will be in large measure lost to the firm if the line is abandoned. The provision of several different qualities enables the firm to get a larger share of the total market, to utilize its plant more effectively, and to gain greater advantages of large-scale production, because a large share of the production facilities may be usable for the various brands. The importance of having a "full line" so that shoppers can satisfy their wishes for various types of items (colors and varieties of paints, for example) encourages the firm to carry a wider variety of qualities in some instances.

Selling Activities

The firm in monopolistic competition not only has the task of selecting the most profitable form or forms of the product, but also is likely to find that the conduct of selling activities is advantageous. *Selling activities* are defined as those designed to influence the schedule of demand for the product of the firm. Costs incurred to carry on these activities are known as *selling costs,* as distinguished from production costs—those necessary for the production of the product itself. In practice, a precise line cannot be drawn between the two classes of cost; expenses of packaging, for example, and the salaries of salesmen fall partly into each category. But the classification is useful for purposes of analysis, most costs falling clearly into one category or the other.

Selling activity, in turn, may be grouped into two major classes, quality-service competition and direct sales promotion. The former involves an attempt to increase sales of the product by increasing (or giving the impression of increasing) the quality of the product, without altering its basic nature, or by adding to the service rendered in conjunction with the sale of the product. No sharp line can be drawn between the process of selection of the optimum physical product, as outlined above, and that of adjustment of quality and service as a method of increasing sales. Both actions affect sales and cost schedules and, if successful, increase the degree of differentiation of the product. The distinction is essentially one of degree but is nevertheless useful. Most relevant business behavior can be classified into one group or the other.

Quality-Service Competition. Quality-service competition takes many forms. Packaging and branding of commodities are examples; these help to establish differentiation and serve as a basis for advertising and other forms of sales promotion, and they attract customers directly as well. Minor variations in physical product, often unrelated to efficiency but providing good features to emphasize in advertising, are common. The provision of credit and delivery service, the rendering of various free auxiliary services, such as air and water in service stations, the development of elaborate showrooms and display cases, are further examples.

A major aspect of quality-service competition is the emphasis placed upon style and the making of deliberate changes in styles designed to make existing models prematurely obsolete. Wherever style appeal can be emphasized, as, for example, in the case of women's clothing and automobiles, firms will attempt to do so and then will deliberately change styles from year to year. In large measure, in this type of industry, the successful firms are those which develop styles which meet with popular approval more satisfactorily than those of their competitors.

Sales Promotion. Almost universally in all nonpurely competitive markets, even with the relatively standardized products of many capital goods industries, firms find it advantageous to attempt to increase their sales by advertising, the work of salesmen, and other selling activities. Sales promotion, if successful, can raise the demand schedule for the product of the firm. Consequently, a greater volume can be sold at the existing price and the benefit of lower production cost per unit obtained, or price can be raised and thus the profit per unit increased. If the addition to total cost resulting from the selling activities is less than the increase in receipts (net of any change in production cost) the profits of the firm will increase.

Sales promotion is effective primarily because consumers have very limited knowledge of the quality of the goods which they are buying and their desires are subject to influence. Buyers are not aware of the existence of many commodities and frequently have no satisfactory way of judging the relative desirability of various products, or brands of products, for the satisfaction of their wants. Furthermore, the wants themselves are subject to modification. Persons have certain basic desires—to eat, to have a place in which to live, etc. But the exact nature of the wants—whether they wish to eat meat or fruit, for example—is subject to change. Many persons have incomes well in excess of the amounts necessary to satisfy the basic needs of life; great opportunity exists for producers to influence these persons in regard to the use of a portion of their income in making "luxury" purchases.

The Adjustment of the Level of Selling Activities

The adjustment of the level of selling activities is influenced by the manner in which sales react as the expenditures on selling activities are increased, or, in other words, by the "promotional elasticity" of advertising. Apparently, as a firm first increases sales effort, "returns" typically increase in the sense that additional dollars spent on advertising produce successively greater increases in sales.[4] This tendency is due to two considerations. In the first place, successful advertising requires repetition, in the sense that repeated suggestions are frequently necessary to influence the actions of the buyers. Thus if the total expenditures on advertising are small, they may have extremely little effect upon

[4] See Joel Dean, *Managerial Economics* (New York: Prentice-Hall, 1951), pp. 357–58.

sales, but a relatively limited increase may produce a sharp increase in sales because of the repetition effect. Secondly, as selling expenditures are increased, more effective means can be used. Division of labor produces advantages in selling as well as in other forms of business activity. Advertising experts can be hired, and magazines and radio and television networks with nation-wide coverage can be employed.

Eventually, however, it is inevitable that increasing returns must give way to decreasing returns, in the sense that beyond a certain point additional dollars spent on sales promotion will produce progressively smaller increases in sales. The economies indicated above will eventually be exhausted, and exploitation of the best portions of the potential market will be completed. Additional sales can be made only to persons who are less interested in the product than those who bought it initially, and greater effort will be necessary to induce them to buy. Frequently, the additional customers will be more expensive to contact. The old customers can buy additional units only by sacrificing other purchases which offer greater utility than those foregone in order to buy the initial units of the good. In order to buy one automobile, a person may need to sacrifice only a portion of the year's savings and a trip to Florida. But, in order to buy a second car, it might be necessary for him to forego some of the food and clothing to which he has become accustomed.

Attainment of profit maximization requires the selection of the optimum-profit level of selling activities, as well as the most advantageous types. This level, however, cannot be determined independently of the decisions on product, output, and price, since the level of selling activities which will maximize profit is not the same at all price levels. Likewise, price cannot be determined independently of the volume of selling activities, since the latter affects both cost and revenue schedules.

At each output level, successively larger selling expenditures will allow higher prices to be obtained but will also increase average cost. For each output level, there will be some level of selling activities at which the relationship between price and average cost will be such as to allow maximum profit. If the various possible output levels are considered, there will be one level at which, with optimum selling expenditures for that level, the greatest total profit will be obtained. This level will be the one which the firm must chose if it is to maximize profits. The price set will be the one which is obtainable with the sales expenditure which is being made. At this point marginal cost, including selling costs, will equal marginal revenue—the demand curve for the product of the firm being the one appropriate to the particular level of selling activities.

In Table 25 the profit (or loss) figure is shown for several levels of output, with various levels of selling expenditures. Thus with 1 unit of output and selling expenditures of $100, total loss will be $10, etc. Examination of the table will show that profits are maximized with 4 units of output and selling expense of $400. The price charged (not shown on the table) is that at which the 4 units can be sold, with $400 selling expenditures.[5]

TABLE 25

PROFITS WITH VARIOUS COMBINATIONS OF OUTPUT LEVELS AND SELLING EXPENDITURES

SELLING EXPENDITURES	UNITS OF OUTPUT					
	1	2	3	4	5	6
	Profit					
$100	$−10	$− 6	$− 2	$− 6	$−20	$−60
$200	−5	−1	6	12	8	−4
$300	8	18	20	40	20	−2
$400	15	17	60	80	60	10
$500	12	15	50	60	30	−5

The choice of product must also be brought into the picture; for each possible form of product, there will be an optimum price and selling-cost combination. If the maximum-profit goal is to be attained, the firm must select that form of product which, with optimum price and selling expenditures, allows the maximum profit. In building up the analysis, it has been necessary to treat price and output, product, and selling activities separately. But this procedure, which is necessary to make the analysis manageable, must not be allowed to obscure the fact that the determination of all four variables is simultaneous, in the sense that no one variable can be adjusted without changes in the others, and maximum profits can be attained only if adjustment in each is continued to the point at which no further changes in any of these variables will allow an increase in profits. Mere attainment of equality of marginal cost with a given product and level of selling activity is not sufficient; all four items must be adjusted if the absolute optimum-profit is to be reached.[6]

[5] The tabular presentation is adapted from the method used by G. J. Stigler, *The Theory of Price* (New York: Macmillan, 1946), p. 261.

[6] Diagrammatic presentation of selling-cost, price, and output adjustments is difficult with the usual two-variable type of graph. With the use of the indifference-curve technique, however, more satisfactory presentation is possible. In Figure 63 below, total selling cost is measured on the horizontal axis, the price of the product on the vertical axis. The *SC* curves, or sales contours, show the various combinations of total selling cost and price which will allow the sale of particular quantities of output; there is a separate sales con-

Imperfections in the Determination of Selling Activities

Attainment by a firm of the situation in which price, selling activities, and product are all adjusted to the levels which will allow maximum profits is likely to be extremely difficult. It is especially hard for a firm to ascertain optimum selling expenditures. The results of sales effort cannot be predicted in advance and even after these expenditures have been made, the firm cannot be sure of their exact effect upon its

tour for each output figure. Thus *SC-80* shows that to sell 80 units a week, $100 of selling cost is necessary if a price of 20 cents is set, $150 if the price is 25 cents, $200 if the price is 30 cents, etc. The *PR* lines show various combinations of price and selling costs which will allow particular amounts of production revenue (total revenue minus selling costs). The point *n* shows the maximum production revenue obtainable. For successively smaller production revenue figures, a given price with either larger or smaller selling costs or a given selling cost with higher or lower prices will be necessary; thus the successive production revenue contours will encircle *n*. The point of tangency of each sales contour with a production revenue contour shows the optimum price and selling-cost combination for the particular output volume. Line *KK* connects the points showing optimum price and sales expenditures for each volume of output. The graph does not show the optimum level of operation. The data shown in the graph, however, indicate the possible production revenues from each output level, with optimum selling cost and price; from these data a marginal production revenue curve can be drawn which, in conjunction with the marginal-cost curve, determines the optimum output. The latter thus being determined, the graph in Figure 63 shows the price that will be charged and the volume of selling expenditures.

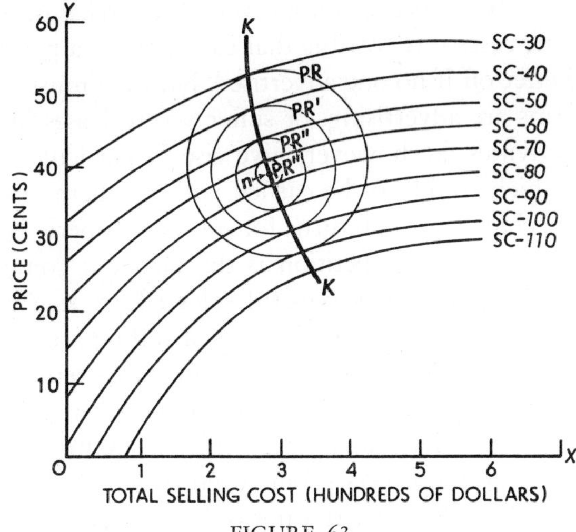

FIGURE 63

ADJUSTMENT OF SELLING ACTIVITIES

It should be noted that line *KK* shows the best way to expand from one sales volume to another (whether by price or selling-cost change or both). This presentation of selling costs is based upon the technique utilized by K. E. Boulding, *Economic Analysis,* 3rd. ed. (New York: Harper, 1955), p. 777.

demand schedule. Thus, as a practical matter, the estimate by the firm of the optimum sales effort is largely guesswork, more so than in the case of decisions in virtually any other phase of business policy. Many firms spend more or less constant amounts annually for sales promotion; others adjust sales expenditures to a certain percentage of expected gross sales; and many firms are influenced by current net-profit figures in determining their sales budgets. In recent years the so-called "objective and task" method has become widely used; the firm selects certain objectives and attempts to estimate the amount of advertising expenditure necessary to obtain them. None of these methods are likely to attain the exact optimum amount, but they are employed because of the lack of more precise techniques for accomplishing the desired goal.[7]

Selling Activities and the Rate of Profit

It is obvious that in many particular cases of monopolistic competition and other nonpurely competitive markets, each individual firm is earning a higher rate of return than it could if it carried on no selling activities. In some cases, especially when other firms are advertising extensively, any firm which did not do so might be unable to sell enough to cover its costs. This does not mean, however, that the rate of profit over a period of time is necessarily greater with the use of selling activities than it would be if such activities were not carried on at all in the industry. In some cases it is possible that each firm in a particular industry would be better off if no one advertised, but each must do so as long as the other firms are advertising, or suffer severe losses in sales.

Selling activities do, however, give rise in particular instances to excess profits which could not be earned without them and sometimes enable firms to achieve excess returns for substantial periods. One of the chief merits of nonprice competition is the fact that competitors may have difficulty in duplicating successful sales effort; as a consequence, the firms which initiate the new techniques of selling are enabled to obtain a sufficient volume of business to earn an excess return. If a firm is particularly successful in building a reputation—such as that of Coca-Cola—newcomers may have serious difficulty in taking away sufficient business to eliminate the excess profits even over a relatively long period. Thus successful sales activities not only give rise to temporary excess profits while competitors are catching up, but, by creating a barrier to the entry of new firms, may prolong the excess returns for a substantial period.

[7] See Dean, *op. cit.*, pp. 363–75 for a discussion of methods employed by firms in determining advertising expenditures.

In other cases, however, selling activities may serve as the means by which excess profits are eliminated. Suppose, for example, that in an industry with restricted entry and excess profits some firms commence sales activities in an effort to increase their profits still more. Competitors are forced to follow to protect their own sales. If the total demand for the product is not affected significantly by the sales effort, the firms will gain nothing (apart from temporary additional profits for those who started the sales promotion); their costs will be higher and their profits lower. While prices may rise, profits may remain below the level attained prior to the commencement of the selling activities. If the sales activities are expanded far enough, it is possible that all excess profits may be eliminated. No one firm can stop the selling race, and, given the conditions of monopolistic competition, neither agreements nor spontaneous co-ordination to reduce the selling activities are possible.

Selling Activities and Prices

The effect of the development of selling activities upon the prices of goods is rather complex, and generalizations are not so obvious as they might appear to be. In general, of course, the expenditures on selling activities constitute costs, which must be covered by the revenue from the sale of the product if an average rate of profit is to be earned. From the standpoint of business firms, selling costs are not significantly different from production costs. However, the selling activities will also alter the demand schedules; the combined effect of higher cost and higher sales schedules is almost certain to produce price increases. But there are possible exceptions; the sales activities may allow the firms to operate nearer the point of lowest cost, assuming that monopolistic competition existed in the industry prior to the development of the sales effort. It is possible that the decline in production cost will exceed the amount of the sales cost, per unit of product. Unless total demand for the product is affected significantly by the advertising, other firms will be forced out of business, and the sales will be concentrated in the hands of a smaller number of firms. It should be noted, however, that the new price is lower only by comparison with the price existing with conditions of monopolistic competition and no sales activity; the price cannot be lower than the figure prevailing with pure competition, since the latter is the lowest possible average-cost figure, with no selling costs included.

If entry is unrestricted, there also exists a possibility that after long-run adjustments have been completed, price may be lower with selling activities than without. While the average-cost curve is higher because of the costs of the selling activities, the point of actual operation may be nearer the point of lowest cost because each firm will have a larger volume of output. However, since firms in conditions of monopolistic competition are not likely to experience substantial cost reductions as output increases, the lower production cost can hardly be expected to offset the selling cost if the latter is at all substantial. The chances of a significant reduction in per unit cost are much greater in conditions of oligopoly, as discussed in Chapter 12.

While the selling activities may increase the demand schedules for the products of the firms, they are also likely to make them less elastic by increasing the degree of consumer preference for particular brands. This effect will tend to bring about higher prices.

The General Significance of Nonprice Competition

Nonprice competition, particularly selling activities, plays a major role in the functioning of the economy. In the first place—and most significantly—the attempts to gain business by means other than price changes influence the allocation of resources. The emphasis on new products and new methods modifies the composition of the national product. Sales activities, without question, alter consumers' demand schedules and even affect producer demand to a certain extent, and thus change the levels of output of various goods. Further influence upon output arises from the effects upon cost; cost increases lead to price increases, which will lessen the rise in output of the advertised goods. Not only does selling activity alter consumer purchase patterns because of its effect upon demand schedules and prices, but it also involves the direct transfer of some resources—manpower, materials, etc.—from the production of other goods to the production of the selling activities themselves. A substantial portion of total resources today is used to produce fancy packages and showrooms, advertising service, and direct selling activities.

Nonprice competition, and particularly selling activities, are likewise of primary importance in determining the relative share of the market for a good which each seller obtains. In pure competition the output levels of the firms are determined solely by production-cost considerations after long-run adjustments are made. Each firm will, of necessity, produce the volume of output which will allow lowest average cost. But in nonpurely competitive conditions the output of each firm depends to a major extent upon its success in the conduct of its selling activities.

Selling activities likewise play a significant part in controlling the nature of market situations. To a large extent the transition from pure competition to various forms of nonpurely competitive markets has resulted from the differentiation which selling activities created. Once nonpurely competitive conditions develop, the elasticities of the demand schedules for the products of the firms, and thus price and output levels, are controlled largely by the success of sales activities in creating strong differentiation of product.

Finally, sales activities may alter the level of national income. Selling activities very likely modify the consumption-savings ratio by increasing the percentage of income which is consumed. In a period of unemployment the net effect of this reaction will be an increase in total production and national income. But in periods in which full employment is maintained, the reduced rate of saving will necessitate a slower rate of growth of the country's stock of capital goods—and of real national income—and perhaps, as well, make more difficult the prevention of inflation.

THE SIGNIFICANCE OF THE CASE OF MONOPOLISTIC COMPETITION

The three primary assumptions upon which the analysis of monopolistic competition is based—(1) large numbers of sellers and absence of mutual interdependence, (2) differentiated product, and (3) free entry of firms—are most likely to be approximated in lines of activity in which capital equipment is of relatively minor importance in production. In these fields comparatively little money capital is required to commence production, and the economies of large-scale production are of limited importance—the advantages being attained at a relatively low level of output. Thus various lines of retailing and small handicraft production and repair would appear to be the types of activity most likely to operate under conditions of monopolistic competition.

However, study of these fields raises some doubt about the applicability of the assumptions. Despite the large numbers of retailers, each particular market area rarely has a substantial number, and feeling of mutual interdependence does not appear to be entirely absent—the firms recognizing that their policies will have some effect upon the policies of other competing retailers. The interdependence may, in some cases, be relatively weak.

The assumption of free entry is regarded by some writers as incompatible with the assumption of product differentiation; it is argued that when consumers have preferences for the products of particular firms the flow of new firms into the field is inevitably restricted, and the principle that price tends to equal average cost, with the average-revenue curve tangent to the average-cost curve at a point to the left of lowest average cost, is not valid. It is also argued that the concept of an industry in which equilibrium is attained when price equals average cost for each firm is not at all distinct when products are differentiated, and therefore the equilibrium analysis is of little significance.

Finally, it may be argued that conditions of monopolistic competition may exist only when the initial decline in average cost is of limited magnitude, and thus the principle that firms will not operate at the point of lowest average cost, once long-run adjustments have been completed, is of little significance, since the difference between price and the point of lowest average cost will be slight. Accordingly, the purely competitive analysis is regarded as applicable, even though the demand curves of the firms are not perfectly elastic.

It must be granted that these criticisms of the usefulness of the analysis of monopolistic competition have considerable merit. Few markets appear to be completely free of oligopolistic influences, and certainly established reputations are a bar to complete elimination of excess profits. However, the analysis has some use as a limiting case in analyzing situations in which interdependence is relatively weak and entry of new firms is relatively easy. The case, as all models of economic analysis, constitutes an oversimplification, but nevertheless may be of value if properly employed.

SELECTED REFERENCES

CHAMBERLIN, E. H. *The Theory of Monopolistic Competition.* Cambridge: Harvard University Press, 1933.

The pioneer analysis of monopolistic competition. Later editions of the book contain some supplementary material.

TRIFFIN, R. *Monopolistic Competition and General Equilibrium Theory.* Cambridge: Harvard University Press, 1940.

A critique and elaboration of the Chamberlin study.

BREMS, H. *Product Equilibrium under Monopolistic Competition.* Cambridge: Harvard University Press, 1951.

A study of product variation and adjustment and other aspects of monopolistic competition.

ABBOTT, L. *Quality and Competition.* New York: Columbia University Press, 1955.

A new study of quality variation.

BOBER, M. M. *Intermediate Price and Income Theory,* chap. ix. New York: Norton, 1955.

MACHLUP, F. *The Economics of Sellers' Competition,* chap. vi. Baltimore: Johns Hopkins University Press, 1952.

BUCHANAN, N. S. "Advertising Expenditures: A Suggested Treatment," *Journal of Political Economy,* Vol. L (August, 1942), pp. 537–57.

STIGLER, G. J., and BOULDING, K. E. *Readings in Price Theory,* chaps. v–ix. Homewood, Ill.: Richard D. Irwin, Inc., 1951.

A series of articles which paved the way for the development of the theory of monopolistic competition.

QUESTIONS

1. Why is price analysis in nonpurely competitive markets established in terms of two time periods rather than three?
2. In what sense are decisions on price and output simultaneous, in nonpurely competitive situations?
3. Price, in any nonpurely competitive condition, is of necessity in excess of marginal cost if the firms are maximizing profits. Why? What determines the magnitude of the gap between price and marginal cost?
4. Why may firms be more inclined to continue operations even though average variable cost is not covered if they are selling in nonpurely competitive markets than if they are selling in purely competitive ones?
5. If firms in nonpurely competitive markets are able to set their own prices, why do they not always set them above average cost, or at least equal to it?
6. What are the assumptions upon which the case of monopolistic competition is based?
7. Why is the demand schedule for the product of a firm in the restaurant business likely to be less elastic than that of a magazine stand?
8. Why is the range of possible profitable prices for a firm in monopolistic competition likely to relatively narrow?
9. Why will the prices of firms selling various brands of a commodity not necessarily be uniform?
10. What additional adjustments must a firm make over a long-run period, compared to those which it makes in a short-run period, if it is to maximize profits?
11. How can entry into an industry of monopolistic competition be free, when the products are differentiated?
12. Explain the process by which excess profits tend to be reduced and perhaps eliminated in an industry characterized by monopolistic competition.
13. If excess profits are eliminated in an industry of monopolistic competition, why can the firms not be operating at the point of lowest average cost? Illustrate graphically.
14. It is widely believed that there are too many stores of certain types in particular cities, in the sense that if the volume of business were concentrated in the hands of a smaller number, operations would be more efficient. Can

such a situation actually exist? Explain, in terms of the theory of monopolistic competition.

15. Why do firms in some cases commence operations in fields in which most existing firms are not earning a normal rate of profit?
16. Why may excess profits continue for long periods in situations of monopolistic competition?
17. Why may the rate of profit differ widely among the various firms in a situation of monopolistic competition?
18. Under what circumstances are selling activities beneficial to a firm?
19. Why are "increasing returns" likely to be encountered by a firm as it first undertakes selling activities? Why are "decreasing returns" inevitably encountered as the activities are extended?
20. Discuss the interrelationship of optimum price, output, quality, and selling-activity determination. In what sense is the determination of these variables a simultaneous one?
21. Under what circumstances will the conduct of selling activities allow the perpetuation of excess profits? Under what circumstances will these activities reduce excess profits?
22. How may the conduct of selling activities reduce prices in an industry of monopolistic competition? Why can the activities never reduce the prices below the level which would prevail if the industry were purely competitive?
23. Why is the model of price and output determination under the assumptions of monopolistic competition of somewhat limited significance?

Chapter 11 MONOPOLY

The second possible case of nonpurely competitive conditions is that of complete monopoly, the situation in which one firm is the sole supplier of a particular product. The firm thus constitutes the entire industry, and is not subject to competition of other firms producing the same product or closely related brands. Even a monopolist, of course, will be subject to the competition of firms producing substitute commodities. But so long as the product of the firm is clearly distinguished from those of other firms, or, in other words, there is no commodity which has a high rate of cross-elasticity of demand with the product produced by the firm, the case may be regarded as one of monopoly. Hence, the firm has a clearly defined demand schedule, which is identical with that of the demand schedule for the product in the market area, and it does not consider possible repercussions of its own policies upon those of other firms.

As indicated in Chapter 4, monopoly is rare outside of the public utilities field, in which the various firms normally enjoy a monopoly position in their particular areas, but are subject to regulation. However, the principles of price and output under monopoly are also significant with respect to oligopoly pricing in certain instances. The determination of unregulated prices will be considered first, and brief attention then given to regulated monopoly prices.

PRICE AND OUTPUT OF AN UNREGULATED MONOPOLIST

The expansion of price and output determination in monopoly involves a relatively simple extension of the basic rules of pricing under nonpurely competitive conditions noted in the first section of the preceding chapter. Attention will be given first to the adjustments made at any one time, and then to longer period adjustments.

Determination of Output and Price at a Given Time

If a monopolist is to maximize profit, he must adjust output to the level at which marginal cost is equal to marginal revenue, and charge the price at which this quantity can be sold. Thus the basic rule is the same as that of a firm in monopolistic competition, but the demand schedules are substantially different in the two cases. The monopolist cannot lose business to other firms in the industry by raising prices, nor gain from them by lowering prices, since he is the sole producer of

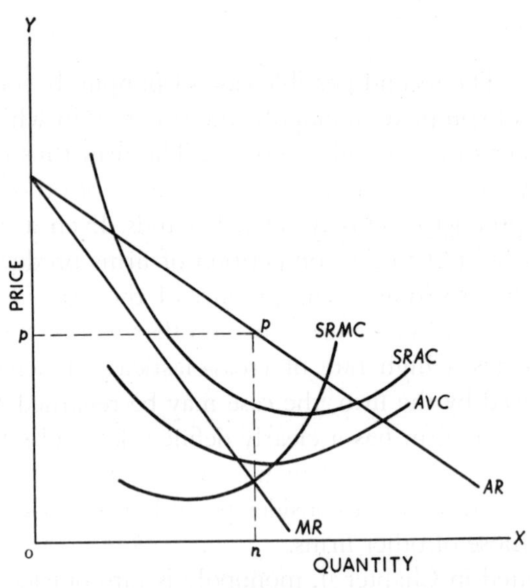

FIGURE 64

SHORT-RUN ADJUSTMENT OF PRICE AND OUTPUT BY A MONOPOLIST

the product. The demand schedule for the product of the firm is thereby identical with the total demand for the product in the market area, and its elasticity depends solely upon the elasticity of total consumer demand for the product. Unlike the situation in oligopoly, the monopolist does not need to take into consideration any effects of his price changes upon the prices of other firms, since there are no other producers of the same product, and, under the definition of monopoly employed, there is a sharp enough gap between the product and those of firms in other industries so that the latter will not be affected sufficiently by the policies of the firm to readjust their own policies.

Graphical adjustment of the firm is shown in Figure 64; the optimum-profit output level is *on* and the price charged is *op.* The *AR* curve represents both the entire demand for the product, and the demand and average-revenue curve of the monopolist. The firm may have some difficulty in determining the elasticity of the demand curve, but its problems are much less serious than those of firms in oligopolistic industries in which the elasticity of demand depends upon the unpredictable reactions of competing firms.

Long-Run Adjustments

So long as the situation remains one of complete monopoly, long-run price and output adjustments involve nothing more than readjustments by the firm designed to bring about equality of long-run marginal

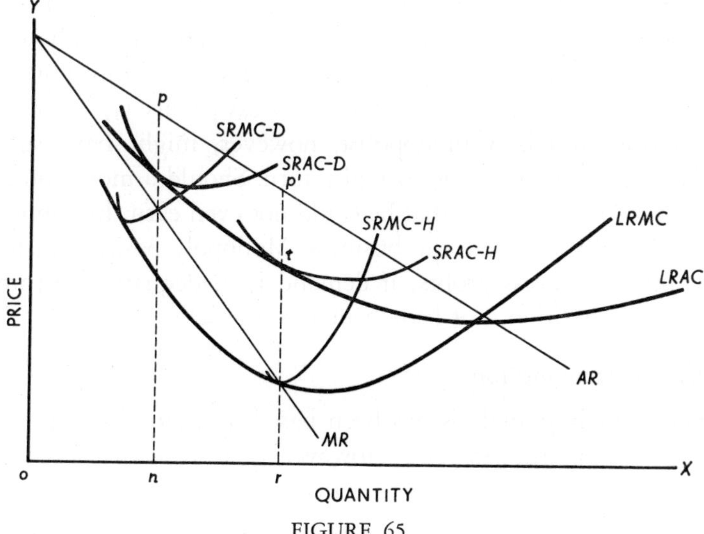

FIGURE 65

LONG-RUN ADJUSTMENT OF A MONOPOLIST

cost and marginal revenue, that is, to adjust plant to the size which is the optimum in terms of the demand for the product. Optimum profits at a given time require operation at the level at which marginal cost with the existing plant is equal to marginal revenue. But over a longer period of time it will be possible to increase profits still more by adjusting plant size (if it is not already at the optimum in terms of demand.) When this adjustment is complete, marginal revenue will equal long-run marginal cost and short-run marginal cost with the particular plant selected. The plant is not necessarily the one which would allow lowest cost, but the one best suited for the existing demand for the product. Failure to attain equality of marginal revenue and long-run marginal cost would indicate failure to complete all plant adjustments which are profitable; failure to attain equality of short-run marginal cost and marginal revenue would indicate failure to operate at the most profitable output level with the plant constructed. Figure 65 indicates the long-run adjustment; initially, with plant size *D*, the firm produced *on* units (for equality of marginal revenue and the short-run marginal cost with plant *D*) and set a price of *p*. But marginal revenue did not equal long-run marginal cost at the point of most profitable operation, since the plant size was too small, relative to the size of demand for the product. Accordingly, the firm increased the size of its plant to size H, with a new short-run average-cost curve *SRAC–H;* with this plant, marginal revenue equals both short-run and long-run marginal cost at the point of most profitable operation.

Under the assumptions of continued complete monopoly, no new firms can enter the industry, and thus no other long-run adjustments will take place. As Figure 65 is drawn, excess profits (*tp′*, per unit of product) are earned. A monopolist, however, might have sufficient potential sales to earn only a normal return. Should a monopolist have such a limited sales volume that he could not even earn this amount, he would eventually liquidate the business. Monopoly position in itself is no guarantee of excess profits; if demand is inadequate, the complete absence of competition is of little benefit to the seller.

Price Discrimination

The preceding analysis has been based upon the assumption that the firm sells at a uniform price. However, typically some purchasers of the product will buy at higher prices than others, and are willing to pay more per unit for small quantities than for larger quantities. If no buyers reacted in this manner, the demand would be perfectly inelastic. If a monopolist can devise some method of charging various customers different prices for the same product, and particular customers higher prices for some units than for others, obviously he can increase his profits over the amount which he can earn if he must charge a uniform price. Price structures designed to bring prices in particular transactions more closely in line with the maximum demand-prices of the customers result in price discrimination—the practice of charging different prices for a particular product to various buyers, the conditions surrounding the various sales being substantially similar. If one buyer is charged 7 cents a pound for sugar and another buyer, purchasing the same quantity at the same place, is charged 4 cents, discrimination exists. Discrimination also arises when, with somewhat different conditions of sale, such as quantity or place, price differences exceed differences in the costs of the various transactions. If sugar is sold for 8 cents a pound in 100-pound lots and 3 cents a pound in carload lots, while the difference in the cost of making the sale in the two types of transactions is only 2 cents, discrimination occurs. Likewise, discrimination results when costs differ for various transactions while identical prices are charged. If typewriters manufactured in New York are sold at a uniform price throughout the country, the buyers close to the point of production are paying more, relatively, than those at distant points, to which freight charges are greater.

The Conditions Necessary for Discrimination

Discrimination is possible only if monopoly exists, so that there is but a single seller, or if the members of a small group of firms follow identical pricing policies. If there are several competing firms, discrimination is impossible because the competitors will shade the prices charged in the high-price markets.

Secondly, discrimination is possible only if resale from one market to another is impossible; otherwise goods sold in the low-price market will flow into the high-price market and prevent direct sales by the producer in the latter. Transportation costs may prevent the resale; in the diagram below, the producer at *A* can charge a substantially higher price in market *B* than in market *C,* so long as the difference does not exceed the *B–C* freight rate. In the case of foreign markets, where discrimina-

B ———————— A ———————— C

tion has been common, tariff barriers may prevent the flow of the commodity back to the home market. The nature of the product may prevent resale; medical service, in the pricing of which discrimination is very common, is not transferable. Or contractual agreements forced upon the low-price buyer may prevent resale.

The Profitability of Discrimination

Discrimination is advantageous essentially because some buyers are willing to pay more for the commodity than others, and various buyers are willing to pay more for initial units than for subsequent units. One person may be willing to pay $4000 for an automobile while another buyer will buy the car only at a $3000 figure, and the first buyer may be induced to acquire a second car only if he can get it for $2000. If a single, uniform price is charged, some buyers will be pushed out of the market completely, others will buy fewer units than they would at a lower figure, and many of those buying the product at the price charged would be willing to pay more, at least for some of the units which they are buying. Discrimination is designed to gain additional revenue by varying the price in terms of the demand-price of the customers—the amounts the customers are willing to pay—in such a manner as to obtain all or a part of the full sum the buyers are willing to pay on initial units, and at the same time disposing of other units which cannot be sold at these figures at lower prices, without reducing the prices on those units for which the buyers are willing to pay the larger sums.

Discrimination may be complete, or in the *first degree,* if it obtains the maximum sum which buyers will pay on each individual unit sold; or it may be partial, or in the *third degree,* the buyers being grouped into major classes, and the prices varied according to the class.

First-Degree Discrimination

Complete first-degree discrimination is attained only if each buyer is induced to pay the maximum possible sum which he is willing to pay for each item purchased.

Suppose, for example, that a person will buy each week 1 gallon of gasoline if the price is $1.00 a gallon, 5 gallons at a price of 50 cents, and 10 gallons if the price is 25 cents. The objective of perfect discrimination is to make him pay $1.00 for one gallon, 50 cents for the next 4 gallons, and 25 cents for the last 5, and thus $4.25 for the 10 gallons instead of $2.50, which he would pay if he could obtain all 10 gallons at a 25-cent figure. In this manner the buyer's individual demand schedule becomes the seller's schedule of marginal revenue from the particular buyer, since it indicates for each quantity the amount the buyer is willing to pay for the additional unit. The optimum amount to be sold to each buyer is that at which marginal cost (assuming it to be constant in the relevant range) is equal to the marginal revenue from the sale to the particular buyer, determined as indicated in the previous sentence.

The charge set for the entire group of units to be sold the customer is the sum of the buyer-demand prices for each successive unit ($4.25 in the example above), and the buyer is required to pay this sum and take the entire amount, under an all-or-nothing bargain. The buyer has only the choice of paying $4.25 for the 10 units, in the example above, or not buying the commodity at all; the seller will not sell a smaller or a larger number of units to the buyer, since this is the figure which maximizes his profit. Or, in terms of the usual marginal revenue-marginal cost diagram, the monopolist extends production and sales up to the point at which his marginal-cost curve intersects the average-revenue (demand) curve, since he can sell the additional units at the successively lower prices without lowering his price on the initial units sold. The price charged each buyer, determined as indicated above, is much higher than the point on the average-revenue curve for the particular quantity.

Market conditions obviously do not permit first-degree discrimination to be carried out to any significant extent. An example of limited discrimination of this type is to be found in the practice of doctors of varying the charges on their customers according to their income status. A breeder of fine horses, dealing individually with various buyers in different parts of the country, with a highly imperfect market and absence of knowledge on the part of each buyer of the prices charged in the other transactions, may be able to carry on perfect discrimination to a limited extent. But apart from such isolated cases, the analysis of first-degree discrimination is useful merely in illustrating the type of discrimination which would be most advantageous to the firm if it could be employed. In practice, most discrimination takes the third-degree form.[1]

Third-Degree Discrimination

Third-degree discrimination, the only type ordinarily possible, involves the classification of buyers on the basis of the elasticity of their demand for the product, and the charging of different prices for the various classes. The buyers willing to pay a high price, but unwilling to buy more units at lower prices, will be charged a relatively high figure, while those with highly elastic demands will be charged low prices. Thus the firm is able to reach more closely the maximum demand-prices of the various buyers—the maximum amounts which they are willing to pay for various units—and to sell larger quantities than would be advantageous with a uniform price by placing a lower price on the additional units without reducing the price on the units buyers are willing to take at the higher figures. This procedure is particularly advantageous if the firm has large unused plant capacity, and the marginal cost of additional units is extremely low.

When third-degree price discrimination is possible, profits will be maximized by adjusting total output to the level at which the marginal cost of the entire output equals the sum of the marginal revenues in the various markets. Figure 66 illustrates the case of two markets; in market

[1] The term "second-degree discrimination" is used by some writers in reference to the case in which the seller sets a different price for each customer but does not fully exploit the potential demand-prices of the customers.

A the average-revenue curve is *AR–A* and the marginal-revenue curve *MR–A;* in market *B,* the two curves are *AR–B* and *MR–B,* respectively. Curves *AR–T* and *MR–T* show the sums of the average-revenue and marginal-revenue schedules, respectively, in the two markets. Total output will be *os,* if profits are to be maximized, as determined by the inter-

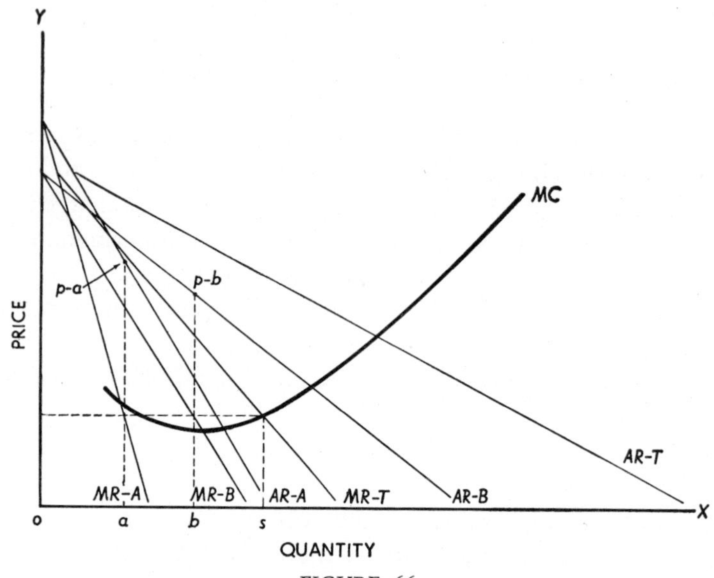

FIGURE 66

THIRD-DEGREE PRICE DISCRIMINATION

section of the marginal-cost curve (*MC*) and *MR–T,* the curve showing the sum of the marginal revenues in the two markets. The amount sold in each market (*oa* and *ob,* respectively) is the quantity at which the marginal revenue in the market is equal to the figure of marginal cost at the output level at which marginal cost and the sum of the marginal revenues are equal. This figure is indicated by the point of intersection of the marginal-revenue curve of the market with a line drawn horizontally through the intersection of *MC* and *MR–T.*[2] The price charged in each market (*p-a* in *A, p-b* in *B*) is indicated by the point on the average-revenue curve of the market directly above this intersection; it is, of course, the price figure at which the optimum-profit output in the market can be sold. The greater the difference in the elasticity of the sales schedules in the various markets, the greater will be the price dif-

[2] The output sold in each market is *not* that at which marginal revenue in that market is equal to the marginal cost of producing the particular amount of output sold in that market; the significant marginal-cost figure is that of the entire output sold in the two markets.

ference and the larger the increase in profit resulting from the discrimination policy. If the demand elasticity is the same in each market, there is no gain from discrimination.

The basis upon which the markets are segregated in various cases depends primarily upon the nature of the market conditions and the ability to prevent resale between markets; as far as possible, the seller wishes to segregate customers in such a way as to provide the maximum difference in elasticity between the various markets. In some instances the basis is that of use, when the seller is able to control the disposition of the product. Electric power companies frequently provide a lower rate for cooking than for lighting. The demand for power for lighting is relatively inelastic, while that for cooking—a use for which there are good substitutes—is much more elastic. Railroad freight rates vary according to the nature of the commodity transported.

Commonly, the basis on which the parts of the market are segregated is geographical, with different prices being charged in different areas. Since the markets are kept separate by transport costs, in general the differentials between the prices in various markets cannot exceed the amounts of the transport costs between them, or the products will be resold from one market to another. Products may be sold in a more distant area at a price lower than that charged near the site of production because more substitutes are available in the distant areas, or competition exists, and thus demand is more elastic. Suppose that a cement plant, with a monopoly position in the area near the plant, wishes to enlarge its market into more distant areas. But in the latter the cement prices will be controlled by producers in that area; the local firm must meet these prices, and will net a lower figure than in its home market. Gasoline prices are sometimes higher near refineries than in metropolitan areas to which the gasoline is shipped, because more companies are competing in the latter.

A third major basis is the direct segregation of customers on the basis of their buying preferences and incomes, by providing several brands of a product (sometimes physically identical), each intended for a certain buying group, with its price adjusted in terms of the elasticity of demand of the group. The price differences may bear little relationship to cost differences. For example, seats in various portions of a theater are priced in a manner designed to attract different income groups. If a uniform price were charged, the lower-income groups would not come at all, and those in the higher-income groups would be paying considerably less than they were willing to pay.

A fourth basis is the size of the order. Quantity discounts, which are very common, do not involve price discrimination so long as they merely reflect the differences in the costs of handling sales of different size. But when they exceed these cost differences, the large buyers being given high discounts primarily because of their strong bargaining positions and the importance to the seller of making the particular sales, discrimination arises. Essentially this form of discrimination develops because the seller believes that he cannot get this particular business unless he offers the lower price, whereas such discounts are not necessary for the remainder of the business.

Product Adjustment and Selling Activities

It may be advantageous for a monopolist to vary his product in the interests of promoting additional sales, and to carry on selling activities. The same principles for the adjustment of both product and selling activities which were relevant in conditions of monopolistic competition are relevant for monopoly. But the competitive pressures to carry on these activities are much less. A firm in monopolistic competition (and even in oligopoly, to be discussed in the next chapter) is virtually compelled to make constant variations in product to keep in line with competitors, and to carry on selling activities, especially if competitors are doing so. But the monopolist is under no such pressure; if the firm is making a high rate of profit under existing conditions, it may not take the trouble to explore various avenues of increasing sales. Nevertheless, if the firm is actually following the goal of profit maximization, it must undertake both product variation and selling activities, if these will add more to its revenue than to its cost.

Restraints upon Monopoly Price

Even in the fields in which the monopolist is not subject to regulation, there are various considerations which may deter the firm from seeking maximum profits, and cause it to set a price considerably lower than the one allowing absolute maximum gains. In the first place, the barriers against entry are never absolute; if a firm feels that there is any chance of new firms developing in the industry it may deliberately hold price below the profit-maximization figure, in order to make attempted entry less attractive and more difficult. In this case the firm is simply sacrificing temporary gains in the belief that long-term gains will be increased by so doing.

Secondly, the firm may be deterred by fear of introduction of government regulation. Especially in the United States and Canada, in which there exist long-standing policies of maintaining competition and hostility to monopoly, a firm which has a monopoly position may be extremely careful to avoid exploiting it to the full in order to ward off the danger of antitrust-law prosecution.

Thirdly, the pressures toward the goal of profit maximization are less severe on a monopolist. In any industry in which competition exists, a firm is compelled, in many cases, to seek constantly to undertake measures to maximize profit, since failure to do so is likely to lead to losses and possible bankruptcy. But if a monopolist is earning a good rate of profit, there is much less need for attempting to exploit every opportunity to increase profit—especially if the enterprise is a large, widely held corporation. Quite apart from the fear of regulation is the desire of monopolists to be "respectable"—to avoid behavior which appears to the customers to constitute ruthless monopolistic exploitation. A century ago, or even fifty years ago, this attitude was much less prevalent, as witnessed by the last-ditch exploitation of shippers by the railroads in the days prior to regulation. But today, it would appear that the desire to be regarded as "fair" in exploiting monopoly or semi-monopoly positions, just as the desire to avoid being regarded as a price-chiseler, play a significant part in moulding business behavior and in modifying the profit-maximization goal.

REGULATED MONOPOLIES

In the public utilities field, a single firm is ordinarily allowed a monopoly in its area, since in many instances provision of the service by more than one firm would not only prevent the attainment of full economies of large-scale production, but would also interfere with complete utilization of capacity (which often must be extended in advance of needs) and with provision of adequate service. However, these monopolies are subject to regulation by governmental agencies, to insure that they provide adequate service and earn only a necessary return on investment.

In terms of this goal, the aim of the regulatory agencies is to set the general rate level charged by a utility at the figure at which the rate (the price) is equal to average cost, including a "fair" or average rate of return on investment. Thus, in Figure 67, the rate (assuming no discrimination) would be set at p', the intersection of the average-revenue curve with the average-cost curve.[3] Because of the difficulties of estimating the elasticity of the demand schedule and of defining a

[3] The relevant cost curve is the short-run curve at any particular time, and the long-run curve over a longer period.

necessary return, the actual rate level would only approximate this figure.

In recent years it has been argued that the establishment of the rate at the level of average cost is contrary to the principles of economic welfare, as outlined in Chapter 24, unless the utility is operating at the point of lowest average cost, and marginal cost is equal to average cost. It is argued that optimum utilization of resources requires the extension of the output of each commodity to the point at which marginal cost is equal to price (p'' on Figure 67). If at the point at which

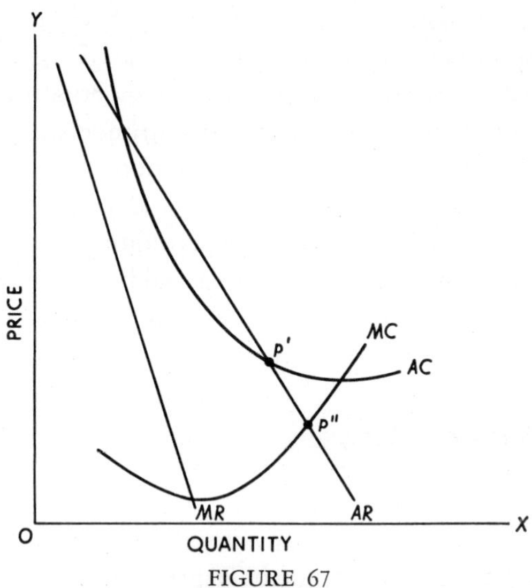

FIGURE 67

RATE ADJUSTMENTS OF A REGULATED MONOPOLY

average cost is equal to price, marginal cost is below price, as it would be if the utility is operating on the downward portion of its average-cost curve, additional units of output, up to the point at which price equals marginal cost, will add less, in real cost, to the economy than the price charged for them. Thus optimum utilization of resources requires production of these additional units.

Unfortunately, however, if price were set at the level at which it equals marginal cost, the utility will not be able to earn a normal return on its investment, or perhaps even to cover all of its explicit costs, if it is operating on the decreasing-cost portion of its average-cost curve, as illustrated in Figure 67. Hence a subsidy would be required to keep the enterprise in operation; the granting of subsidies to private enterprise by governments gives rise to various difficulties, and the taxes necessary to pay the subsidies might, themselves, interfere with resource allocation.[4] So long as the production of utility service remains in private hands, the use of the average-cost basis is almost essential.

Discrimination. The possibility and desirability of discrimination in the setting of rates greatly complicates the task of control of utility rates. From the standpoint of the average cost of the utility services and the optimum use of resources, discrimination has considerable merit; it allows the utility to gain business which it could not otherwise get, lowers the cost per unit for all of the business (assuming operations under decreasing-cost conditions), and may allow operation nearer the point at which marginal cost equals price. In some instances, especially in the case of railroads, it might be impossible for the firms to cover their costs if discrimination were not practiced. If a single uniform rate were charged on all freight, the shipments able to bear only a low rate could not move, and the shipments able to bear a high rate would be subject to a lower charge than the shippers would be willing to pay, with consequent over-all reduction in volume of business and railway revenue. But unfortunately rate discrimination raises significant questions of equity and economic effects upon the customers, for which answers are not easily attained in terms of the present state of the theory of economic welfare. Especially in the transportation field, some of the most difficult problems of rate regulation center around questions of discrimination between shippers of various commodities, shipments between different points, and shipments of various individuals. Further exploration of these questions is beyond the scope of this study.

SELECTED REFERENCES

ROBINSON, E. A. G. *Monopoly.* London: Nisbet, 1941.

The principal modern English study of monopoly.

BAIN, J. S. *Pricing, Distribution and Employment,* chap. v. rev. ed. New York: Holt, 1953.

STIGLER, G. *The Theory of Price,* chap. xii. rev. ed. New York: Macmillan, 1952.

BURNS, A. R., *The Decline of Competition,* chap. vi. New York: McGraw-Hill, 1936.

One of the best discussions of price discrimination.

ROBINSON, JOAN. *The Economics of Imperfect Competition,* chaps. iii, iv, xv, xvi. London: Macmillan, 1933.

[4] See the article by R. W. Harbeson, "A Critique of Marginal Cost Pricing," *Land Economics,* Vol. XXXI (February, 1955), pp. 54–74.

QUESTIONS

1. How does the demand curve for the product of a monopolist differ from that for the product of a firm in monopolistic competition? Of a firm in oligopoly?
2. Under what circumstances is it possible for a monopolist to gain excess profits?
3. What is meant by "price discrimination"?
4. What conditions must be present for price discrimination to be possible? Under what circumstances might price discrimination be possible, but not profitable?
5. Distinguish between first-degree and third-degree discrimination.
6. If a firm is to attain complete first-degree price discrimination, why must the bargain be an all-or-nothing bargain?
7. In the absence of discrimination, the monopolist will adjust output to the figure at which marginal revenue is equal to marginal cost, if he is to maximize profits; if first-degree discrimination is possible, the optimum-profit point is that at which average revenue is equal to marginal cost. Explain.
8. Why, in practice, is first-degree discrimination difficult to employ?
9. Explain, in terms of the analysis of price discrimination:
   a) "family" fares on air lines and railroads,
   b) low railway commuter fares,
   c) season tickets at reduced rates to football games,
   d) tourist versus first-class rates on ocean liners,
   e) the practice of some foreign professional journals of charging American subscribers much higher rates than those charged European subscribers (postal rates in no way accounting for the difference).
10. In the case of third-degree discrimination, what means are used to segregate the various classes?
11. What is the rule of (*a*) optimum output, and (*b*) optimum prices in each market, in the case of third-degree price discrimination? Why can the monopolist not simply follow the rule of equating marginal cost and marginal revenue in each market?
12. Why may a monopolist deliberately avoid setting the price which will maximize his profits?
13. What rate level is usually the goal of governmental agencies in setting public utility rates? How does this figure differ from the rate the firm would set if uncontrolled?
14. Evaluate the argument that utility rates should be set at the marginal cost level, rather than at the average cost level.

Chapter 12 OLIGOPOLY

The type of market condition which is probably of greatest importance in the present-day economy is oligopoly, characterized by mutual interdependence among the various sellers arising as a result of the smallness of the number of sellers in the particular market area. As indicated in Chapter 4, many manufacturing industries contain only a few firms or are dominated by a few. Even in retailing, in a particular market area the number of firms is rarely large enough to eliminate all feeling of mutual interdependence among the firms. Accordingly the analysis of price and output determination under conditions of oligopoly is one of the most significant portions of contemporary economic analysis. But unfortunately it is one of the most complex portions because of the importance of the specific policies followed by the particular firms for the nature of the adjustments. Oligopoly is actually not a single, clear-cut case, as is pure competition or complete monopoly; it includes a wide range of related cases, all characterized by mutual interdependence, but differing in the exact degree of interdependency and the exact policies followed by the firms.

Oligopoly, in the sense of mutual interdependence, arises whenever the number of firms is sufficiently small that a price change by any one firm affects the sales of the other firms to such an extent that readjustments are made by these firms. If there are only two or three or six producers of a product, or major producers, in an industry, oligopoly will obviously exist. But, even with a substantially larger number, firms are often aware that competitors will react to their policies. Some markets are characterized by so-called "chain" relationships; price changes by one firm will directly affect the prices of only two or three competitors, but changes made by the latter as a result of readjustments to the new price of the first firm will, in turn, lead to changes by other firms in close competition with these firms (although not with the first firm), and thus the effects of a price change by one firm may spread in a pyramiding fashion throughout the industry.

The complexities and diversities of oligopoly make it necessary to break the analysis of price and output determination in such markets into several segments. As a convenient starting place, the analysis will deal first with the case of complete oligopoly, and subsequently with major forms of partial oligopoly. The assumption will be made initially that the product is differentiated; pure oligopoly (with homogeneous product) will be considered later in the chapter.

COMPLETE OLIGOPOLY

Oligopoly may be designated as complete when relationships among the firms are sufficiently close to permit the maximization of the joint profits of the firms as a group. This condition may result merely from spontaneous co-ordination of the policies of the various firms, or, more likely, from outright co-operation on the part of the officials of the firms. This case is not fundamentally different from that of complete monopoly, except for the fact that there is more than one firm, and costs are certain to be different.

Maximization of joint profit requires the determination of the price on the basis of the total demand schedule for the product and the summation of the marginal cost schedules of the various firms. With outright agreements—necessarily secret because of the antitrust laws—the firms will attempt by collective action to estimate the demand and cost schedules and set the optimum price and output figures. If prices are set by one firm and followed by all others, this firm will attempt to price on the basis of the total schedules rather than its own immediate schedule, and other firms will abide by the decision of this firm. When collusive action is absent, maximum joint profits can be obtained only if each firm, acting independently, correctly estimates the price figure which is the optimum from the standpoint of the group, on the basis of the estimate by the firm of the total demand schedule for the product.

The manner in which the total profits are shared by the various firms in the industry depends in part upon the relative cost figures and sales of the various firms. The firms with lowest cost and those with large sales volumes will of course obtain the largest amounts. The sales, in turn, will depend in large measure upon the relative consumer preferences for the various brands. When outright collusion exists, firms may agree upon market shares, and essentially upon the division of the profits. In such cases the division of the total joint profit will depend upon the relative bargaining strength of the firms; this in turn is influenced by such factors as relative financial strength, the ability to inflict damages on the other firms if an agreement is not reached, the ability to withstand similar action on the part of other firms, relative costs and consumer preference, and bargaining skill.

Obstacles to the Attainment of Maximum Joint Profits

There are many serious obstacles in the path of actual maximization of joint profits and the attainment of complete oligopoly. The basic difficulty lies in the unwillingness of the firms to surrender all freedom of action, and the constant desire to increase their shares of the total market and thereby increase their total profit.

In the first place, the maximum joint-profit price will be optimum for each firm, as well as for the firms as a group, only if the cost and demand schedules are the same for all the firms. This is most unlikely to be the case. As a consequence, complete maximization of joint profit may require the closing down of high-cost plants and concentration of operations in the more efficient ones. But the firms are most unlikely to agree to this policy. Consequently it will prove impossible, even with complete agreement on price, to select the figure which is the optimum for the group. The figure chosen must be a compromise one which all firms will tolerate. But this figure, while tolerable for all firms, is not ideal for some of them, and there may be a tendency for some to break away from co-operative pricing.

Secondly, the problems of estimating the total demand curve will make difficult the selection of the optimum price, particularly because various firms will have different opinions about the optimum. The actual levels selected will depend upon the outcome of bargaining.

Optimum profit maximization may also at times be checked by strategical moves, discussed on page 279, designed to force other firms to take certain actions, or to discourage them from carrying out policies detrimental to the interests of the firm. Thus action may be taken to drive rivals out of business completely, or to test their strength and bargaining power.

Complete attainment of maximum group profits is also rendered difficult by the failure of firms to agree upon product changes, advertising policies, and introduction of new techniques. Typically, from all indications, agreements relate only to price, and when spontaneous co-ordination exists rather than outright agreements, firms are generally much more conscious of competitors' reactions to price changes than to changes in the other variables which affect profit. Agreement on these matters is particularly difficult because the future strength of various firms with respect to these elements cannot be discounted satisfactorily to the present. Each firm is certain that it will be able to outdo the other firms on selling activities, and therefore is unwilling to reach an agreement about them. Firms are highly conscious of the fact that price changes lead to changes by competitors and that they cannot outdo the competitors on price changes; hence agreements, explicit or implicit, on prices may be highly desirable. But the firms apparently believe that they will be able to outdo the other fellow on new methods, products, and advertising procedures. But, inevitably, profits are reduced for the group of firms by the failure to agree on these as well as on price.

A further deterrent to the setting of the maximum-profit price figure, even if co-operation among firms is strong, is the fear that such prices will stimulate the growth of new firms. Although, in most industries in which oligopoly is present, some interferences with free entry of new firms, such as the large volume of output frequently necessary for low cost, plus established reputations of existing firms, and the problems of raising large sums of money capital, are likely to be common, nevertheless new firms can and will get started. Monopoly prices, plus the consequent excess profits, not only provide great incentive to the development of new firms but likewise make such development easier. The high prices may be sufficient to cover the high initial costs of operation of the new firms, and the good profit prospects will facilitate the raising of the necessary money. As a consequence firms may deliberately hold prices below the optimum short-run maximum-profit levels, preferring instead a "reasonable" profit which will continue longer because less encouragement will be given to new firms to enter. When firms follow policies of this type, it becomes difficult to make general statements about price and output levels.

Finally, difficulties in obtaining co-ordinated action discourage the firms from making frequent price changes in light of changing conditions. Even if the price set originally was the one yielding maximum joint profit, it is unlikely to continue to do so as conditions change.

The obstacles in the path of maximization of joint profits of the group suggest that frequently, in practice, joint profits will be less than the maximum, even if mutual interdependence is strong. Furthermore, it is likely that in many situations, especially when the number of firms is somewhat large, mutual interdependence is not strong enough to permit sufficiently concerted action to bring prices near the optimum joint-profit figure. Thus consideration must be given to the cases of partial oligopoly.

PARTIAL OLIGOPOLY

The term *partial oligopoly* may be applied to all oligopoly situations in which joint profits of the group are not maximized. It is likely that such cases are characterized by spontaneous co-ordination to a certain degree, rather than outright agreements of limited scope, although the latter may be made at certain times. Under these conditions, firms set their own prices based upon estimates of their own demand schedules, taking into consideration possible reactions on the part of their competitors and their own cost schedules. The primary difference between the price setting by oligopolists and that by firms in other conditions is the importance of the influence on the firms' demand schedules of possible reactions by competitors. The general effect of expectations that some reactions will occur is a reduction in the elasticity of the demand schedule of the product of the firm below what it would be if there was no feeling of mutual interdependence. If there is any tendency on the part of competitors to follow price changes, the changes made will result in less shifting of customers among the various firms, and the demand elasticity will depend primarily upon the elasticity of the total demand for the product. As oligopoly develops in an industry, it can be expected that the prices will tend to rise, as the demand schedules of the firms become less elastic. Just as in other competitive situations, the point of optimum profit for the firm is the level of operations at which marginal cost is equal to marginal revenue.

While the mutual interdependence which characterizes oligopoly may have the tendency to make the demand schedules of the firms more inelastic, it also creates great uncertainty about their exact nature, since the firm can rarely be certain about the exact response on the part of competitors. A firm frequently knows that changes in its price will lead to reactions on the part of competitors, but it does not know the extent of the reactions. A price reduction may cause a great increase in sales if competitors reduce only slightly, or not at all, but very little increase if the competitors meet or exceed the cut. Under such circumstances the firm is in a sense confronted not by one demand curve, but by several potential ones—the appropriate one in a particular instance depending upon the exact (but unknown) reactions of competitors. However, the firm must act; it must set some price, and must accept one of the potential demand curves as the most likely one. But the uncertainty is, itself, a major influence upon the policy of the firm, and encourages firms to develop techniques of pricing which minimize the dangers of following policies based upon mistaken estimates of the reactions of competitors. The uncertainty also encourages the firms to minimize the frequency of price changes because of the possible dangers arising out of making changes from the present situation.

The Case of the Kinked Demand Curve

It is frequently suggested—on the basis of common-sense observations more than careful empirical study—that in many instances the demand curve will contain a sharp bend or kink at the level of the existing price. This kink, as illustrated on Figure 68, arises because of

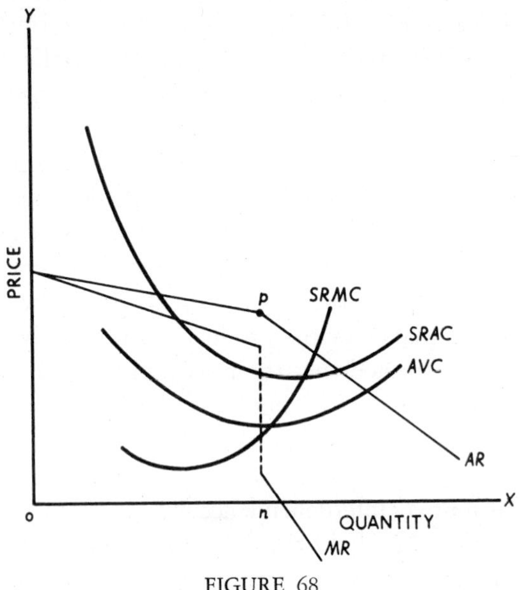

FIGURE 68

PRICE AND OUTPUT ADJUSTMENT WITH A KINKED DEMAND CURVE

the greater tendency, except in periods of severe shortages, for competitors to follow price reductions than to follow price increases. A reduction takes business away from the other firms, and forces the latter to cut prices in order to protect their sales, while an increase necessitates no readjustment, since a firm benefits from shifting of customers due to the increase made by another firm. At the point of the kink, the marginal revenue curve contains a vertical (more correctly, discontinuous) section.

The point of optimum profit for the firm (*on* in Figure 68) is almost of necessity at the output level at which the change in elasticity occurs. It is likely that marginal cost will not equal marginal revenue at a lower volume of output because the marginal-revenue curve is so nearly horizontal in this output range; at the output level of the kink, the marginal-revenue curve drops very far—perhaps to a negative figure—and almost certainly will intersect the marginal-cost curve. The price (*p* in Fig. 68) is indicated by the point on the average-revenue curve at which the latter changes slope. In a case of this sort it is likely to be obvious to the firm that any other price would be unprofitable, since increases would cause great losses in sales while reductions would gain little additional business. If product differentiation is strong, the kink is likely to be less sharp than it would be with a standardized product, since many customers will remain with the firm despite an increase, and competitors are less likely to respond quickly because the price reduction will have less immediate effect on their sales.

One important consequence of the existence of a kink in the demand curve of the firm is the possible failure of firms to readjust prices in response to cost changes. Because of the vertical section (or, technically, the discontinuity) in the marginal-revenue curve, the marginal-cost curve can move up or down over a substantial range without affecting the price or level of operation. However, if the cost increase affects all of the firms in the industry, it may bring about a movement of the level of the kink in the average-revenue curve; if all firms readjust price by the amount of the cost increase, in the belief that all other firms will do so as well, the level of the kink will be raised by the amount of the cost increase, and price will rise by the same amount. Such a reaction is especially likely in response to a cost increase which affects all firms uniformly, such as a sales tax; each firm adds the tax to the selling price and does not lose substantial sales volume because other firms follow exactly the same policy. This reaction is illustrated in Figure 69 (page 266); as a result of the cost increase, the kink moves upward from p to p'. Essentially the firms have moved closer to the optimum joint-profit level, such a shift being impossible prior to the cost increase under the existing circumstances of mutual interdependence.

While the kinked demand curve may be significant in certain cases for explaining the reactions of the sellers to various changes in the situation, the analysis of the case, in itself, contributes little to the explanation of existing price and output levels because it throws no light on the determinants of the height of the existing kink in the curve. On Figure 68, why does the kink occur at p and not at some higher or lower figure? There appears to be no general principle which can ex-

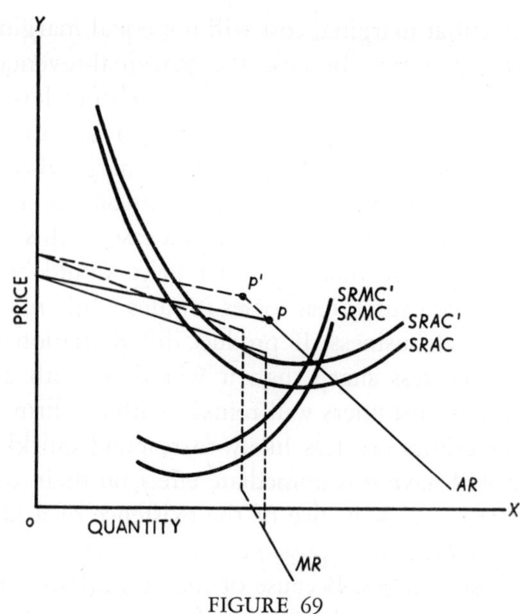

FIGURE 69
ADJUSTMENT OF PRICE IN RESPONSE TO A COST INCREASE AFFECTING ALL FIRMS, IN THE CASE OF THE KINKED DEMAND CURVE

plain this level; appeal must be made to historical trends of the price of the product in the past and the particular techniques used by the firms in the setting of prices, as noted in subsequent sections.

Price Leadership and Price Following

One method by which the firms may lessen the degree of uncertainty to which they are subject is that of making no independent price changes, but instead adopting and following the prices set by other firms, or maintaining a fixed differential above or below the other prices. If this policy is so widespread in an industry that all firms follow the prices set by one firm, the situation is known as one of price leadership. In other industries several of the firms may follow independent price policies, while others follow the price set by one or more of these firms. The policy of following the leader, of course, involves for the nonleaders the setting of price on the basis of demand conditions alone without reference to cost; the relationship between the price and the average cost, at the volume sold by the firm, determines the profit made by the firm. If this profit is not satisfactory, the firm is likely to seek to increase sales by advertising and other selling activities.

Price leadership is most likely to develop in an industry in which one firm produces a large portion of the total output, the remainder being distributed over several relatively small firms. Almost inevitably the large firm comes to dominate the pricing, the small firms perhaps being in the position of being able to sell as much as they wish at the price set by the dominant firm. The large firm may be expected to set its price on the basis of the total demand curve, less the expected amounts to be sold by the other firms, and its own cost curve; the price may approach the maximum profit figure, except insofar as it is held deliberately lower to discourage the growth of the smaller firms.[1]

In other cases, however, price leadership takes the "barometric" form; one firm in a group which includes several firms of more or less comparable size comes to play the role of price leader, not because of its dominant position in the market, but because other firms regard its actions as a suitable barometer of changing market conditions, and are willing to follow its policies in the belief that competitive disturbances are minimized by so doing. But the actual powers of a barometric price leader are greatly restricted by the fact that the firm realizes that other firms will follow only within reasonable limits, and if the firm is to retain its leadership position it must consider the effects of various changes which it makes upon the profit positions of the other firms. So long as the existing price is acceptable, it will be reluctant to make any changes except ones which will appear clearly advantageous to the other firms, such as an increase in price by the amount of a new excise tax.

Apart from the price leadership cases are those in which many firms in the industry determine their own prices individually, but some firms, particularly smaller ones, base their price policy solely upon the prices of other firms. Some may follow other prices exactly, and others, stressing quality, will maintain a certain differential above the usual figure, while the "cut-rate" firms will maintain a certain differential below the standard price figure.

"Playing Safe"

The importance of uncertainty in oligopoly, in the absence of complete implicit or explicit agreement among the firms, makes firms reluctant to take any action which offers the possibility of serious adverse consequences. Accordingly, the philosophy of "playing safe" may exercise a very important influence upon the behavior of the firms. In

[1] In some industries once dominated by one large firm, the smaller firms gradually grew in size to the point at which the domination was broken. One of the best recent discussions of price leadership is to be found in the article by J. W. Markham, "The Nature and Significance of Price Leadership," *American Economic Review,* Vol. XLI (December, 1951), pp. 891–905.

part this attitude encourages a policy of watchful waiting, of taking no action independently of other firms, of making no price variations except when other firms make changes. But particularly the importance of avoiding the creation of competitive disturbances has encouraged firms to develop various pricing techniques, usually based upon average cost, which tend to produce uniformity of action and the avoidance of setting prices at levels which will upset competitive balance.

The Cost-Plus or Average-Cost Approach

The cost-plus or average-cost approach to pricing involves the setting of the price on the basis of an estimated figure of average cost, including the rate of profit which the firm regards as "normal" or obtainable. The percentage added may be one which has proven to work satisfactorily over the years, or one which the firm knows competitors are using. The importance of cost-plus pricing was suggested in two English studies published around 1940,[2] and has been stressed by various American writers familiar with pricing practices of business firms.[3] Many writers believe it to be the most important single approach to pricing employed.

The Significance of Common Costs

Understanding of the importance of operation of cost-plus or average-cost pricing requires consideration of the fact that most business firms produce a large number of products, with a portion of their total costs common between the various products. The entire analysis, up to this point, has been based upon the assumption that each firm produces a single product; this assumption is useful for purposes of simplification, and does not destroy the significance of the results of the analysis. But for a more complete understanding of oligopoly pricing, it is necessary to develop the implications of multiple-product production and common costs.

When a firm is producing more than one product, some costs are inevitably *common* costs, that is, ones incurred for the production of

[2] See R. L. Hall and C. J. Hitch, "Price Theory and Business Behavior," *Oxford Economic Papers,* No. 2 (May, 1939), and C. Saxton, *Economics of Price Determination* (London: Oxford University Press, 1941). The Hall-Hitch study, which is widely quoted, reports the results of an empirical investigation in which businessmen were queried about pricing methods used. The sample was rather limited.

[3] See, for example, Joel Dean, *Managerial Economics* (New York: Prentice-Hall, 1951), pp. 444–54, and A. R. Oxenfeldt, *Industrial Pricing and Market Practices* (New York: Prentice-Hall, 1951), chap. iv.

several products, no one of the latter being responsible for any particular portion of the total. A traditional example is that of the costs of the steers purchased by meat packing plants; from the steers are obtained various cuts of beef, hide, ground bone, glue, gelatine, and other products. The cost of the steer is common among these various products, in the sense that no one of them is responsible for any particular portion of the total expenditure incurred. The costs of a machine used in the processing of several articles are common costs for the various articles. General administrative and selling expenses are typically common costs, as well as such items as rent and heat. Costs which are not common to more than one product, or, in other words, are amounts for which particular products are solely responsible, are known as *separable costs.* The expenditures on materials going into only one product, direct labor expenses on the product, the costs of machinery used for the processing of one good only, etc., are separable costs.

Common costs, in turn, may be classified into two types, the *joint-cost* form and the *nonjoint* form. Common costs take the joint-cost form when an increase in the output of one product necessarily results in an increase in the output of the other. For example, a sawmill cannot produce more lumber without increasing its output of sawdust; increased output of cotton brings greater output of cottonseed.

The Significance of Common Costs for Average-Cost Pricing. While the existence of common costs does not create complications in most cases for the *theory* of price determination[4] it does affect the choice of pricing *methods* employed by firms, and particularly encourages firms to use some form of average cost pricing. When a firm is producing a large number of products—perhaps thousands—the time, expense, and difficulties involved in attempting to calculate marginal revenue and marginal cost for each item make this approach impossible. Furthermore, price-setting is not a task which can be performed once and for all; the determinants of the optimum-profit price level are constantly changing, and prices must be reconsidered at reasonably frequent intervals. With multiple products and common costs, some short-cut approach to pricing is essential—an approach which makes the task a manageable one, even if it does not always succeed in maximizing profits.

[4] The chief complication is created when common costs take the joint-cost form; in this case there is no distinguishable marginal-cost figure for each of the commodities, and optimum profit output can be determined only by consideration of total cost and total revenue for the products as a group.

The existence of common costs gives rise to another and even more important reason for the development of a pricing technique which avoids direct calculation of marginal cost and marginal revenue whenever oligopoly elements are present. The existence of common costs increases the uncertainty which characterizes oligopoly situations, the danger of upset of competitive relations, and the desire of the firms to develop methods of pricing which will minimize the dangers of such disturbances developing. Unless firms distribute common costs among the various products in some more or less standard fashion, they will arrive at substantially different prices on the various lines. But, inevitably, prices on each product will tend to gravitate to the lowest figure set by any firm, and, as this occurs, the firms will be unable to cover common costs. Any attempt to employ marginal cost will be especially productive of price-cutting; on any particular line the marginal cost may appear to be very low because most of the costs, being common in nature, will continue whether this product is produced or not. Thus the firm will be encouraged to set a low figure on certain lines in an effort to increase total sales.

Consider, for example, a case in which a firm has considerable excess plant capacity capable of producing a variety of products, with a large portion of the costs being common. Further increases in output of goods now produced are unprofitable, since price reductions would be necessary on all units of the goods and the marginal revenue would be small. But if a new line of goods is taken on, a low price can be set profitably on this good without affecting the revenue from the other goods now being sold. By this means a considerable improvement in the utilization of plant capacity can be attained. But the effect of this policy on firms whose primary business is in this new line may be disastrous, and retaliation is likely to occur. For instance, if a radio manufacturer commences to produce electric stoves and sells them at prices lower than the current prices charged by other firms for stoves, in order to utilize excess plant capacity, stove manufacturers may follow the same policy with radios. In a short period of time, firms in both industries will be suffering losses. Accordingly, firms in each industry will hesitate to start such practices. Trade associations may encourage the use of policies which avoid too much attention to marginal-cost considerations in an effort to discourage this type of competition.

Under such circumstances, the use of cost-plus or average-cost pricing, with a common method of allocation of common costs among the various products, provides a very simple method of price-setting and adjustment—one which minimizes competitive disturbances, particularly if more or less uniform methods of allocation of common costs to various products are followed.

The Procedures of Average-Cost Pricing

The first step in the calculating of average cost is the determination of the separable, variable cost for which the product is responsible —materials, direct labor cost, etc. Within usual output ranges, the variable cost in many lines will be more or less constant per unit, and thus the estimate is not dependent to a great extent on the expected volume of business.

The second step is the allocation to each product of a share of the common costs. Various bases are used for different common costs, direct labor costs and direct labor hours being the most common in manufacturing.[5] For a simple example, if a firm is producing only two products and one requires twice as much direct labor as the other, this product will be assigned twice as much of the common cost as the other, or two thirds of the total common cost. Other bases used include actual machine-hours, units or weight of product, or material cost. One of the primary tasks of cost accounting is the selection, interpretation, and application of the basis of allocation.

Since common costs are made up to a large extent of fixed costs and constant variable costs, the determination of common cost per unit of output requires the use of some figure of sales. In some instances an estimate of expected sales volume will be made; as a rule, however, firms prefer to use a figure regarded as the standard or normal output volume.

In calculating average common cost, there is included in the allocated share of common cost an element to cover the rate of profit which the firm expects to be able to earn. This element is usually determined by applying the expected profit rate to the total capital investment, allocating this sum to each product according to one of the bases mentioned above, and the conversion to a per unit basis along with the rest of the allocated common cost. The expected profit rate is not the "normal" profit of economic analysis (although it might equal it in particular cases) but the rate which past experience, plus an evaluation of present market conditions, indicates to be feasible.

The average separable cost and average common cost are added to give the average cost, or "full cost." In some cases this figure is set directly as the price. Such a practice is apparently common in many types

[5] See *Cost Behavior and Price Policy* (New York: National Bureau of Economic Research, 1943), p. 183.

of contracting and in some of the capital-goods industries in which, by outright agreement or mere acceptance of the convention, the practice has become universal. It should be noted that, even if all firms follow the practice, they may not actually earn a normal return if sales are less than the volume used in calculation of average cost; on the other hand, this technique might yield the maximum joint-profit price, especially if the firms have agreed upon an "expected-profit" element in the common cost which they have selected on the basis of maximization of joint profit. It is also important to note that success of the average-cost pricing policy as an instrument for eliminating oligopolistic uncertainty depends to a large extent upon the use by all firms of the same cost-allocating bases. Some trade-association activity has been designed to accomplish this result; in other cases agreements have undoubtedly been made by the various firms in regard to the basis of allocation.

More commonly, however, average cost, determined as indicated above, serves as a guide for price-setting rather than a figure which the firms blindly set without regard to market conditions. The average-cost figure must be compared with the prices set by other firms, and a decision made with respect to the desirability of readjusting the price in terms of these other prices.[6] In some instances it is clear to the firm that market conditions permit the charging of a substantially higher price. On the other hand, firms frequently realize that some lines cannot be

[6] The following statement by H. H. Curtice, President of General Motors, before the United States Senate Committee on Banking and Currency, March 18, 1955, provides an illustration of the approach to pricing explained in the preceding paragraphs:

"Since the Committee has expressed interest in the subject of General Motors civilian product pricing practices, I shall outline them.

"General Motors pricing procedures have been set forth publicly on many occasions since the early 1920's when they were first established. While the underlying principles of these procedures are relatively simple, their application is necessarily extensive and complex in practice since they are concerned with the costs of the thousands of materials and parts which we buy and make and with the manner in which overhead costs are distributed by product lines.

"It is obvious that unless a manufacturer can sell his products for more than it costs to produce them, he will soon cease to be a manufacturer. Therefore, the determination of probable costs is most important. Direct unit costs of production (direct labor and material) must first be calculated. The indirect or overhead costs, however, even though determinable in the aggregate for any given period of time, must in the end also be reduced to a cost per unit. This means that overhead costs must be allocated to each unit sold to recover the total of all such costs.

"At this point there is a large unknown. What is the future volume of sales over which these costs must be distributed to assure their full recovery provided competitive conditions permit? In a period of low volume, a manufacturer who attempts to recover his entire overhead costs out of the unit selling price will price himself out of his market. On the other hand, if he distributes his overhead costs on the basis of a temporarily high level of demand, he will mislead himself as to his real average unit cost and thus fail to recover

made to yield an average contribution to common costs. The demand for some products is such that average separable costs can barely be covered. Certain articles are regarded as by-products, and no serious effort is made to make them contribute toward overhead.

Average-Cost Pricing in Retailing

An excellent example of average-cost pricing is to be found in the determination of wholesale and retail margins. These are important elements in the prices of consumption goods; the average wholesale margin ranges from 10 to 25 per cent of the retail selling price and the retail margin, from 10 to 40 per cent, with deviations beyond these limits. There are numerous variations among lines of retailing; margins are lowest in fields having rapid turnover (such as grocery stores) or little sales effort and large unit sales (building materials, coal). They are highest in fields such as jewelry, in which turnover is very slow.

The method of pricing in these fields will be explained with specific reference to retailing; the same methods, however, are used by wholesalers. The retail selling price is calculated by adding to the purchase price of the article (the separable cost) a figure known as the *margin.* The margin is usually calculated by applying a percentage figure, known as the *markup,* to the purchase price of the article. The figure chosen as the markup is the one which will yield sufficient gross margin on all goods carried to cover total common costs, called *overhead* in retailing, including the rate of profit which the firm expects to make. The markup percentage may be recalculated at frequent intervals by dividing the total overhead (the common cost) by the total expected

---

them. This is to say that direct costs or overhead must be pro-rated on the basis of an average volume in relation to capacity and the anticipated market.

"A manufacturer will soon be in a very precarious position if all he does is recover his total costs without making a profit on his operations. His position is further aggravated when the cost of replacing his capital equipment and tools is greatly increased by inflation. He will be unable to finance the continuous development of his product so necessary in today's markets. So it becomes essential for him to run his business efficiently not only in order to recover his costs but also to make a profit so that the business may grow and prosper.

"But no manufacturer can make the decision as to price without regard to competitive prices and the wishes of his customers. If his price is too high relative to the prices charged by his competitors, he will lose volume and slip behind in the competitive struggle. Our practice has been to set prices that are fully competitive and which we hope will be attractive to our customers. Then we try to increase profit by reducing our costs below what we had calculated they might be with no certain knowledge as to what the volume would be on each line."

Reproduced in the booklet, *General Motors Policies and Practices,* published by General Motors Corporation (Detroit: 1955).

or "normal" sales volume, or it may simply be a figure which retailers have found over the years to produce satisfactory results.[7]

Deviations from Standard Markup. In practice few retailers find it profitable to apply a uniform markup to each article carried, but vary the actual prices somewhat from the figures indicated by the application of the standard percentages. Some of the major exceptions can be noted briefly:

1. Additional separable costs. Some lines of goods are responsible for certain additional separable costs in addition to the amounts paid for the goods. For example perishable foods require refrigeration, and a higher markup may be applied to them to compensate.

2. Price lines. In some lines of retailing, such as women's clothing, it has become customary to sell only at certain price figures, called price lines, and articles whose prices based upon markup would fall at other figures are moved to the nearest price line. Prices of women's dresses almost always end in the figure of 95 cents. Men's neckties are commonly sold only at prices of $1.50, $2.00, and $2.50 (plus higher figures).

3. Resale price maintenance. The retail prices of some articles, such as many proprietary drugs, electrical appliances, etc., are set by the manufacturers, and the retailers have no discretion. The manufacturers, however, usually consider usual retail margins in setting the resale figures.

4. Demand elements. The retailer will frequently take into consideration the prices charged by other firms, and avoid prices which are far out of line with these figures. Some retailers price almost entirely on the basis of competitors' price figures. Furthermore, price competition becomes more severe on some lines than on others, and the margins frequently become depressed on these items. Considerations of elasticity of consumer demand may also influence the retailer; if he realizes that the demand is very inelastic for a certain good, he will add a higher-than-usual markup. If, on the other hand, the demand appears to be very elastic, a lower figure may be charged in order to stimulate sales.

Despite these exceptions, however, the markup system, with more or less uniformity in allocation of common costs upon the basis of pur-

[7] Note, for example, the statements of representatives of the leather footwear industry to the Canadian Royal Commission on Prices: "All three [representatives] reported that it is their practice to price their shoes by applying a fixed percentage to their laid down cost for shoes. This practice is customary in the retail shoe trade and seems to be followed almost blindly. . . . [T]he most widely used percentage is 50 per cent of cost or one-third of selling price." See *Report of the Royal Commission on Prices,* vol. iii (Ottawa: King's Printer, 1949), p. 217.

chase price of the goods handled, is very widespread and exercises great influence on the manner in which the overhead of retailers is allocated among the various products handled, and in maintaining stability of pricing in the retail field.[8]

Average-Cost Pricing and Profit Maximization

The question of the extent to which the use of the average-cost approach to pricing involves departure from the assumption of profit maximization has been a subject of substantial controversy in recent years. It is obvious that any method of pricing which involves addition of a certain percentage to variable costs can hardly maximize profits, at least in the sense of maximum joint profits for the firms as a group, except by sheer accident. It is inevitable that the manner in which overhead is distributed over various products would be different if firms approached price determination on the basis of estimates of marginal revenues and marginal costs. But nevertheless, given the circumstances of oligopoly, the average-cost method properly employed may allow the firms to come closer to maximum profit than any other pricing system. There are several reasons.

In the first place, and of greatest importance, the average-cost method is an effective device for stabilizing competition, lessening the uncertainty characteristic of oligopoly markets, and avoiding the danger of precipitate action which might cause price wars and substantial losses.[9] So long as the various firms have more or less the same average costs, and, with multiple products, use similar methods of allocating overhead among various goods, the prices arrived at will not differ too greatly.

Secondly, so long as the average-cost figure is not blindly set as the price, and some attention is given to demand considerations, the price may not differ too greatly from the one which would be selected

[8] The Canadian Royal Commission on Prices concluded: "The conventional mark-up system has become more or less a tradition, without any consideration of the effects of prices on volume of sales. Time and again the evidence before us indicated that manufacturers and retailers seemed so firmly entrenched in their policy of fixed (percentage) margins that they were unable to consider any other method justifiable." *Report of the Royal Commission on Prices,* vol. ii, *op. cit.,* p. 238.

It is likely that retailing has become somewhat more price competitive in the last five years.

[9] Fellner stresses the desire of firms to maximize safety margins as a factor leading to average-cost pricing. Since firms are uncertain about the actual optimum-profit price, they will take into consideration policies which will give them the maximum margin of safety. This requires maximum excess of price over average variable cost, which can be attained by the use of the markup system (see *Competition among the Few* [New York: Knopf, 1949], pp. 154–56).

directly on the basis of marginal considerations. The adjustments made from the average-cost figure in setting the actual price involve bringing the demand aspects into the picture, and thus reaching a price figure more closely approximating the maximum-profit level.

Thirdly, once the various firms in the industry have set their prices on a marginal-cost basis, for any one firm the price set on this basis may actually be the maximum profit one—the figure at which marginal revenue and marginal cost are equal—because the level of the kink in the firm's demand curve will be at this point. If market relations are such that competitors will follow price decreases but not increases, the level set by the other firms or some figure very close to it is the optimum price for each firm, since any increase above this would cause excessive loss in sales, and any reduction would cause the competitors to cut. The price at this level may not be the one which allows the optimum profit for the firms as a group, and may be substantially different from the figure which the firms would set if they initially approached price determination in terms of estimates of marginal revenue and marginal cost. But given the competitive relationships and the inability to gain the maximum joint-profit figure, the price arrived at by average-cost pricing may actually be the one at which marginal revenue and marginal cost for any one firm—given the prices of the other firms—are equal. The average-cost pricing technique essentially determines the level of the kink.

Apart from these considerations, the cost-plus method of pricing offers certain other advantages. Its simplicity, especially for merchants handling thousands of different items, is an important consideration; once the pricing formula is adopted, it can be applied by relatively junior personnel in the organization. No estimate of sales of particular commodities is necessary for the setting of prices. But perhaps more significantly, the procedure is regarded as "reasonable" and "fair" by many businessmen. The notions that all commodities handled should bear their "share" of overhead, and that prices should be set at a figure which includes a "fair" profit are widely accepted in the business community (although there are many exceptions). The acceptance of the fair-profit goal arises primarily because of the fear that high temporary profits will lead to increased competition, government control, or other undesirable consequences which will lessen profits from a long-range standpoint. In part also the notion of a "fair" profit does represent an actual deviation from the goal of profit maximization, as explained in Chapter 3; when this becomes the actual goal, the cost-plus system becomes a very simple method of attempting to attain the objective. But in large measure the notion of a fair profit merely reflects the view that maximizing of short-run profits may prevent attainment of highest profits over a long-run period.

While the use of average-cost pricing may in general be consistent with profit maximization in oligopolistic industries, it is clear that in some instances excessive reliance on the average-cost figure may cause the firm to sacrifice profits unnecessarily. Large potential increases in sales from relatively small price reductions may be foregone, while in other instances consumer demand may be such that increases above the average-cost figure may be advantageous. As indicated above, most business firms do consider these factors in the setting of their prices rather than using the average-cost technique alone, but some may overemphasize the significance of the average-cost figures.[10]

The Significance of Average-Cost Pricing

From the standpoint of resource allocation and reactions to demand and cost changes, the use of the average-cost pricing technique has considerable significance.

1. *Effect on Price Levels.* In the first place, the use of this technique without question results in somewhat different allocations of common cost among various products than would occur with the direct use of marginal techniques, and thus in different price levels and outputs of particular goods than would otherwise occur. In addition, apart from the common cost considerations, the technique affects the particular price figures which are selected.

2. *The Effect on Price of an Increase in Demand.* With the establishment of prices on the basis of an estimate of marginal cost and revenue schedules, an increase in demand will usually lead to price increase in the manner illustrated in Figure 70 (page 278). When demand rises from AR to AR', price rises from p to p'. But, when the average-cost approach is used, the decline in average cost consequent to the increased sales will lessen the likelihood of price increases and, in some instances, will actually lead to reductions. These would be more common if the average cost were based upon estimated sales during the coming period; the frequent use of a "standard" output volume eliminates any direct and immediate change in the calculated figure of average cost consequent to a change in sales. Likewise, when demand falls, strict adherence to average-cost pricing, with actual sales

[10] Some authorities in the field of price policy are convinced that businessmen pay inadequate attention to marginal considerations (see Joel Dean, "Research Approach to Pricing," in *Planning the Price Structure* [American Management Association, 1947]).

used as the basis of calculation of average cost, will cause price increases. But the use of a "standard" output volume figure avoids this result, at least until the standard figure is recalculated; in any event, a policy of raising prices in the face of falling demand appears contrary to good business judgment and will seldom be attempted. Typically, price will not be changed at all in response to increases or decreases in demand when the average-cost technique is employed.

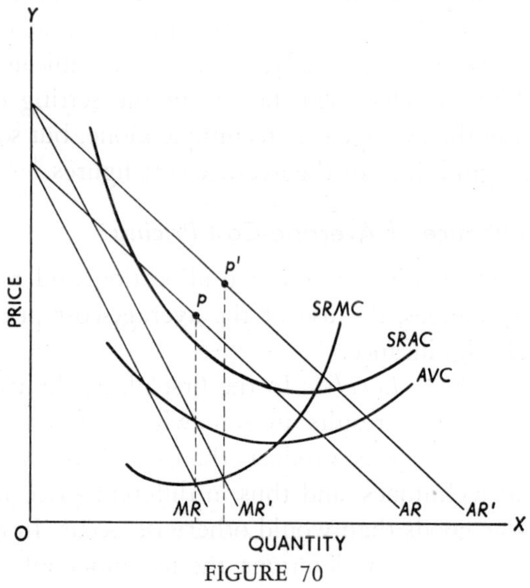

FIGURE 70

REACTION OF PRICE TO AN INCREASE IN DEMAND

3. *Reaction of Price to an Increase in Cost.* With marginal-cost pricing, price will never (except under very extreme assumptions) be raised immediately by the full amount of a cost increase. The firm will readjust output until marginal revenue and marginal cost are again equal; this involves an upward adjustment in marginal revenue by the amount of the increase in marginal cost and thus an increase in average revenue price by a smaller amount, as shown in Figure 71. Price rises from p to p', while the amount of the cost increase is the vertical distance between AC and AC'. When price is set on an average-cost basis, however, the firms are likely to raise price immediately by the full amount of the cost increase. Suppose, for example, that the wages paid by all firms in an industry increase. Average cost is raised by the amount of the wage increase per unit of output; accordingly, price is likely to be raised by the same amount. If all firms follow the same policy, all will be better off (unless they have already attained the maximum

joint-profit figure) than they would have been had they raised by a smaller amount. If the total demand for the product is at all elastic, the firms will not cover average cost despite the increase (assuming normal profit before the wage rise) but will more closely approach doing so than if they had raised price by a smaller amount. Some departure of firms will still be necessary for restoration of normal profits. It should be noted that such a price increase would have been profitable even in the absence of the wage increase. But, given the competitive situation,

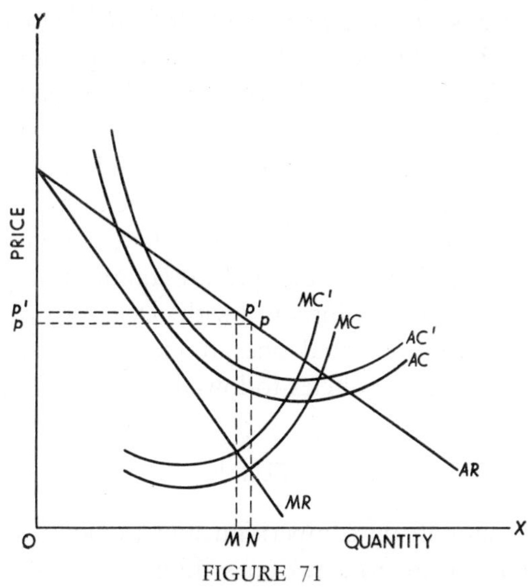

FIGURE 71

RESPONSE OF PRICE TO AN INCREASE IN COST, MARGINAL APPROACH TO PRICING

no one firm could raise because there was no assurance that others would follow. But, when a cost increase occurs to all firms, each is likely to feel that the others will raise prices if it does, and the increase takes place.

Strategical Moves in Oligopoly

In some respects a situation of partial oligopoly resembles a military campaign or a poker game; certain actions may be taken, not because they are advantageous in themselves, but because they improve the position of the oligopolist relative to that of his competitors, and may ultimately result in an improved financial position. In some instances, deliberate price-cutting, in itself unprofitable, is undertaken either to drive competitors out, or to scare them sufficiently to discourage them from undertaking certain actions contrary to the interests of the other firms. On the other hand, the desire for security, the ability to hold out against aggressive action on the part of competitors, may lead a firm to take action which is, itself, contrary to profit maximization. Thus, a firm may expand in order to increase the absolute size of its financial resources, or to insure supplies of materials or market outlets during periods of competitive struggles, even though these actions are not in themselves profitable.

In recent years, some students of oligopoly have suggested that the entire approach to oligopoly price and output policy should be recast in terms of an analysis of the behavior of the participants in a strategic game, replacing the analysis based upon the assumption of the goal of profit maximization. This point of view, first developed in the work of J. von Neuman and O. Morgenstern entitled *The Theory of Games and Economic Behavior,*[11] stresses the importance of the tendency of the various parties in such circumstances to combine in order to get the best of the opponent. In terms of this approach, there is no one single necessary solution, as implied by the profit-maximization approach, but rather a set of alternative solutions (with respect to price and output levels, for example), the actual one attained in a particular case depending upon the specific policies followed.[12]

PRODUCT VARIATION AND SELLING ACTIVITIES

In both monopolistic competition and monopoly, it may be advantageous for the firms to carry on selling activities and adjust their product in terms of consumer preferences. But oligopoly conditions provide a particularly fertile ground for the use of product variation, advertising, and other forms of selling activities. Price tends to stabilize at a certain figure; while the firm is anxious to increase sales in order to lower average cost, price reductions are not a satisfactory way of accomplishing this result because of the danger that other firms will reduce also. Thus the firms turn to various forms of selling activities as a means of increasing their sales, since these appear to be far safer methods, primarily because reactions on the part of competitors are likely to be less disastrous to the firm than possible reactions to price reductions. Time will be required for the competitors to follow, whereas they can meet price cuts almost instantly. By the time competitors have discovered the success of the policies and attempt to duplicate them, the

[11] Princeton, N.J.: Princeton University Press, rev. ed., 1947.

[12] See the article by L. Hurwicz, "What Has Happened to the Theory of Games," *Proceedings of the American Economic Association* (May, 1953), pp. 398–495.

customers may be so well attached that they do not return to the competing firms. There is always a chance that competitors may be unable to devise equally satisfactory selling methods. A price cut is a definite, conspicuous act which competitors can match or exceed if they wish. Sales activities are less obvious in their effects upon competitors. Furthermore, the widespread attitude on the part of businessmen that price-cutting is unethical encourages the use of selling activities instead of price adjustments. Even legislative action in the form of protection of resale price maintenance and restrictions upon selling below "cost" may direct competition into nonprice lines.

Mutual Interdependence in Selling Activities

While firms may fear competitors' reactions to selling activities less than those to price changes, they are not completely unaware of these reactions. Accordingly, a feeling of mutual interdependence may arise with respect to the selling activities as well as to price policy. There is a wide range of possible relationships among oligopolists with respect to product policy and selling activities, just as there is with respect to price policy. At the one extreme, there may be perfect collusion, the firms agreeing implicitly or explicitly to select the exact form of product and selling policies which will maximize the profits for the group. There is substantial evidence, however, that complete collusion on product and sales activities is rare. From all indications firms are much less willing to agree on these matters than they are upon price, and more willing to follow completely independent policies, partly because of the belief that the firm can carry on these activities more effectively than competitors, partly because the results of failure to agree appear to be less disastrous, as noted in preceding sections.

The absence of complete collusion on product and selling activities almost certainly results in a higher level of selling activities than would occur with such collusion and the adjustment of the activities to the level which would allow maximum profits for the group. Each firm attempts to increase its share of the market at the expense of other firms; since the competitors will be following the same policy, much of the activity will cancel out, and none of the firms will gain the anticipated sales volumes. All firms would be better off if all would cut the volume of advertising, yet no one firm can do so unless the other firms cut.

On the other hand, to the extent that firms do take into consideration any effects which changes in their own selling activities will have upon the policies of the competitors, the level of selling activities will be reduced below the level which would be attained without such feelings of interdependence. If a firm believes that if it starts an extensive selling campaign its competitors will do likewise, it will be less anxious to start than if it did not consider this possibility.

It is possible that in some cases competitors will follow increases in selling activities but not decreases; in this case, retreat from a high level of selling activities will be very difficult. Whether such a level is attained or not depends upon the exact policies followed by the firms.

The Significance of Selling Activities

The success of selling activities of the various oligopolists in an industry is a major consideration determining the manner in which the total market will be shared among the various competing firms. The largest shares may go to the firms which do the best selling job, rather than to those which have attained the lowest cost in manufacturing. The firms which fail may be those which make mistakes in the adjustment of product (such as the making of too revolutionary changes in style) or fall behind in selling activities. Furthermore, the tendency of firms in oligopoly situations to stress selling activities as a means of increasing sales may lead to a higher level of selling activities than would be carried on in other competitive conditions, and average cost (including selling cost) will be higher than it would be if other competitive forms prevailed in the industry. On the other hand, to the extent to which firms commence to take into consideration the effects their selling activities have upon the level of such activities carried on by their competitors, the over-all level of selling activities may be less than it would be if the market were one of monopolistic competition. Moreover successful selling activity may concentrate the total business in the hands of a smaller number of firms, allow operation nearer the point of lowest average cost, and reduce production cost per unit; this reduction could allow a lower price of the product than the one which would prevail in the absence of the selling activities (but not lower than the purely competitive price).

PRICE DISCRIMINATION

Just as price discrimination may prove to be profitable for a monopolist, so may it be profitable for oligopolists. However, discrimination is not possible unless the various firms follow uniform pricing policies, because the prices in the high-price markets would soon be pulled down to those in the lower-price markets. The firms must either agree on the prices to be charged in the various markets, or spontaneously follow the same practices. Because of the difficulties of obtaining complete co-operation, effective discrimination is less likely to occur than with complete monopoly.

Some of the most significant price discrimination in the United States has arisen from the use of devices designed to lessen price competition rather than from a pricing policy introduced to adjust prices in terms of demand elasticities of various markets. The most important of these devices has been the basing-point system, under which the price of the product in any locality was calculated by adding to the price at the basing point the freight from the basing point to the locality, regardless of the actual origin of the goods. For many years in the steel industry, prices in all parts of the country were determined by adding to the Pittsburgh price the freight from Pittsburgh, regardless of the actual origin of the steel; a Chicago buyer obtaining steel from a Gary mill would pay the Pittsburgh base price, plus freight from Pittsburgh, although the steel was shipped only from Gary. In later years several basing points were used instead of one. The single-point basing-point system provided a uniform price in each area for all firms, regardless of the location of the plant, and served as a device to lessen price competition. In recent years, Supreme Court decisions interpreting the antitrust laws have brought an end to most basing-point techniques. The use of a uniform price for the entire country, followed frequently in industries in which freight is a relatively unimportant item, also facilitates the avoidance of price differences and price-cutting.

LONG-RUN ADJUSTMENTS

In oligopoly, just as in other types of market situations, adjustments in price and output will be different over a long-run period than at any particular time, partly because of internal adjustments of the firms designed to attain the optimum-sized plant in terms of the market situation, and partly through a change in the number of firms in the industry.

Long-Run Cost Adjustments

In the first place, cost schedules will be somewhat different over a long-run period than they will be with a given plant, quite apart from any changes in external determinants such as wage and materials costs. Over a period of time the firms will adjust their plants to the sizes which are most satisfactory in terms of the current and expected demand situations. Thus long-run marginal cost, including plant as well as current operating costs, will become a primary determinant of output and price policies in both complete and partial oligopoly situations. Just as with monopoly, long-run adjustment requires equality of marginal revenue with both long-run marginal cost and short-run marginal cost with the plant which is the optimum in terms of the demand situation.

Tendencies toward the Elimination of Excess Profits

The existence of mutual interdependence is no guarantee, in itself, of the earning of excess profits. Even if the firms in an industry have succeeded in maximizing the joint profits of the group, this return may not continue to be in excess of an average rate of profit. The extent to which excess profits will disappear depends primarily upon the ease with which new firms can enter the industry.

When new firms can enter an industry, there will be a tendency for the excess profits to be eliminated. The new firms may cause a breakdown of existing pricing institutions and agreements, since they may find it desirable to cut prices below existing levels in order to establish themselves in the industry. The established firms may find it necessary to reduce prices to avoid excessive losses in sales, and the general level of prices will more closely approach the figure of average cost. If the demand curves of the firms are kinked, the action of the newcomers in setting lower prices will lower the point of the kink for all firms.

However the new firms may follow the same pricing policies of the existing firms, either initially or after a period of price cutting. As a consequence equality of price and average cost, at least for some of the firms, will be attained through an increase in average cost for the firm, rather than a decline in price. The increased number of firms results in a division of the total business among a larger number of firms and smaller sales volumes for each firm. If the loss in sales forces the firm to operate at a higher point on its average-cost curve, the excess profits may be eliminated with no price reduction occurring. This resembles the adjustment which occurs in monopolistic competition, with the exception of the fact that the demand curves for the products of the firms are less elastic in the oligopoly situation, and thus equality of price and average cost will be attained at a higher average-cost figure.

Figure 72 illustrates the elimination of excess profits through the entry of new firms; the *AR* curve moves to the left as new firms enter, until the excess profits are eliminated and *AR* becomes tangent to *LRAC* at p'. Figure 73 illustrates the similar completed adjustment in the case of the kinked demand curve. If the curve is kinked, the chances of a price reduction as the new firms enter is particularly slight; so long as

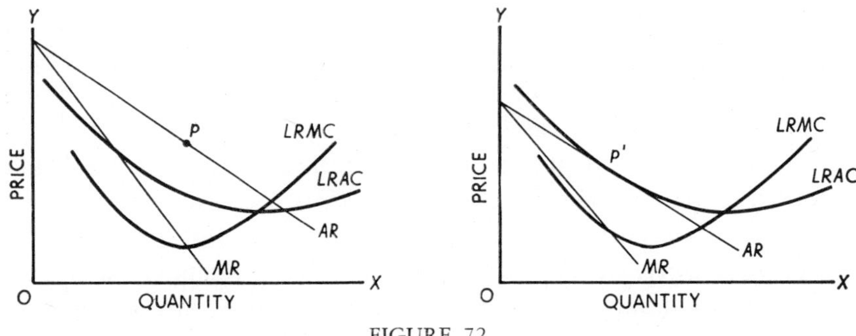

FIGURE 72

ADJUSTMENT OF PRICE TOWARD AVERAGE COST, OLIGOPOLY WITH RELATIVELY FREE ENTRY

the new firms follow the prices of the old firms, none of the firms will find a price reduction (or increase) desirable, and the point of the kink will gradually move to the left, but staying at the same horizontal level,

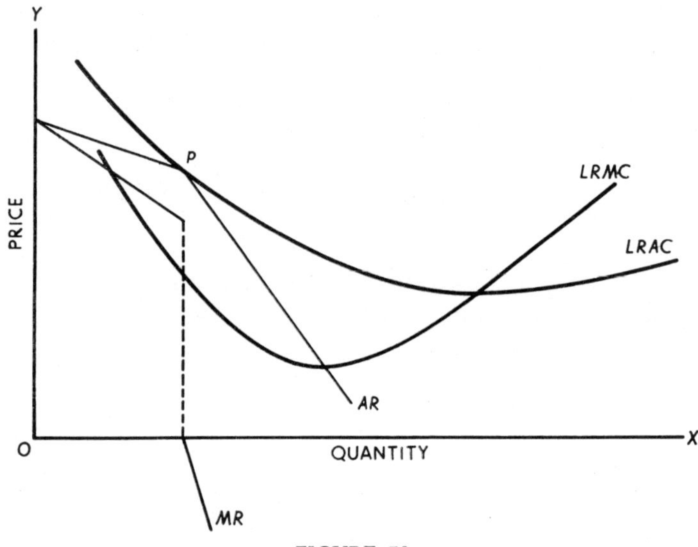

FIGURE 73

ADJUSTMENT OF PRICE TOWARD AVERAGE COST, OLIGOPOLY WITH KINKED DEMAND CURVE, AND FREE ENTRY

until it is just tangent to *AR*. The use of average-cost pricing techniques also increases the likelihood that the excess profits will be eliminated without a price cut; the declining sales volume due to the development of new firms tends to raise the figure of average cost if the latter is calculated on the basis of actual sales, and to discourage price reductions. If the average cost figure for pricing purposes is determined on the basis of a "standard" volume of sales, as is apparently common, the figure will remain unchanged as sales volume falls; price likewise will be left unaltered if the firms adhere strictly to the average-cost approach to pricing.

In some cases, excess profits may be deliberately avoided by the existing firms, which sacrifice temporary excess profits to greater long-run security. If excess profits are being earned and new firms begin entering, there is always danger that too many will commence operations, with consequent losses for a period for many of the firms. To avoid this danger, existing firms may deliberately set prices at figures which will yield only a more or less average rate of return. In this case price may be only slightly above the figure of lowest average cost, in contrast to the case in which price is initially set to yield high excess profits, and large numbers of new firms enter the industry.[13]

Common Costs and the Figure of Average Cost

When a firm is producing several products and some of the costs are common among them, there is no economically determinate figure of average cost for each product, that is, no exact average-cost figure which price must cover and to which price will fall if there is completely free entry. The enterprise, as a whole, must cover common as well as separable costs, and with free entry total receipts will equal total costs for all products, including common costs and a necessary profit. Furthermore, each particular product must sell for a price which covers its average separable costs, or the firm will cease producing it. But there is no necessary way in which the common costs must be shared among the various products, and in practice some articles may carry more than a proportionate share of overhead and others less. But it is advantageous for the firm to continue to produce items contributing relatively little to common cost, provided that they make some contribution. The actual pattern of distribution of the common costs among the various articles will depend primarily upon the techniques employed by the firms in allocating common costs, the nature of the consumer demands for the various products, and the extent of competition in the various markets.

Restrictions on Entry

While the existence of excess profits undoubtedly stimulates the development of new firms in an industry of oligopoly, there are likely to be various barriers to unrestricted entry which protect the excess profits of at least some of the firms in the industry. One of the major

[13] The importance of this line of reasoning has been particularly stressed by R. F. Harrod; see "The Theory of Imperfect Competition Revised," in his *Economic Essays* (New York: Harcourt-Brace, 1952).

sources of mutual interdependence is the technological requirement of a large volume of business for low-cost operation, which prevents the existence of a large number of firms in the industry. This same technological requirement creates obstacles to the entry of new firms when excess profits are currently earned. In mass production manufacturing industries, large sums of money capital are required for the establishment of a new firm, as well as a substantial volume of sales for low-cost operation. But a new firm may find it very difficult to gain this sales volume quickly in the face of strongly established reputations of existing firms, and persons will be reluctant to initiate new enterprises. The great difficulties which have confronted newcomers, such as Kaiser, in the automobile field, illustrate the problem.

Even in industries requiring smaller investment and volume of sales, however, newcomers may find it impossible to take sufficient business away from existing firms with good reputations to destroy their excess profits. In retailing, for example, in which new firms can start easily, those firms which have firmly entrenched reputations and strongly attached customers may continue to make higher-than-average profits for long periods. On the whole, while it may be granted that the existence of excess profits in oligopoly will tend to lure new firms into the field, it is likely that the barriers to completely free entry are so great that substantial sums of excess profits continue over long periods of time.

Elimination of Losses

The mere existence of mutual interdependence of the various firms in an industry does not insure that the firms can make even an average rate of profit. If the number of firms is so great, relative to demand, that average cost is greater than the price being charged because of the low sales volumes of the firms, losses will be incurred. In such a situation, there are two possible types of adjustments. If the price has not been at the level maximizing joint profits, increased co-operation on the part of the firms may succeed in raising the price to average cost. The NRA period of the 1930's was characterized by extensive activity of this sort, when for a short period such co-operative action was not illegal. In the absence of greater co-operation, however, restoration of price to the average-cost level necessitates the departure of some of the firms from the field. These are most likely to be the ones that fall behind in the race for customers because of poor selling efforts. They may, however, be the firms whose equipment wears out first or those whose owners are most pessimistic about the future. As some firms leave the field, the increased sales volumes of the remaining firms will allow them to cover cost (assuming that their average cost declines as they increase sales). Prices may not rise at all, as they would under similar circumstances in pure competition—the losses being eliminated entirely by the decline in average cost.

Nonuniformity of Price

Whenever differentiation exists, the prices of the various sellers in the industry are not likely to be uniform, even after long-run adjustments, whether oligopoly is complete or partial. Differentiation often involves deliberate quality differences, designed to appeal to different income levels. As a consequence, both cost schedules and the height of demand schedules will differ. Even if firms make outright price agreements, price differentials are almost essential if the low-quality firms are to remain in business. In other situations, firms without established reputations must maintain lower prices if they are to continue to sell; newcomers to an industry are often in a situation of this sort. Most of these sources of differences are not eliminated by the passage of time and long-run adjustments; even though all firms in an industry are making a normal rate of profit, the prices being charged may vary substantially.

PURE OLIGOPOLY

The analysis in the preceding sections has been used upon the assumption that the products are differentiated. It is possible, however, for oligopoly to exist even if the products are standardized, this situation being designated as *pure oligopoly.* This case is most closely approximated in the markets for various types of capital equipment, building materials, etc., which are purchased by expert buyers to meet specific uses in production. Markets for lumber, cement, brick, railroad equipment, industrial machinery of various types, steel, copper, and aluminum provide examples. Rarely, however, is differentiation completely absent, primarily because of differences in service rendered in conjunction with the sales, the personal relations of officials of the various companies, and the efforts of salesmen.

If no differentiation exists in a situation of oligopoly, the realization of mutual interdependence by the various firms and the tendency toward outright co-operation are greatly strengthened. With no differentiation at all, prices must be uniform, or the high-price firms will sell nothing. Even with slight differentiation, uniformity of price is almost essential. Accordingly, independent price determination on the part of each firm, with no attention being paid to competitors' actions, would be almost suicidal; wide price fluctuations and frequent periods of losses would be inevitable as firms sought to increase sales by price reductions. Hence, some type of co-ordinated action is inevitable—much more so than with differentiation, in which each firm has an established clientele and quality differences lessen the severity of the effects of price competition. The forms which the co-ordinated action may take are, in general, the same with standardized products as with differentiation. Price leadership or outright agreements are most likely to develop, since the use of standard pricing techniques will not give the necessary degree of uniformity.[14] Price agreements are, of course, illegal, but they nevertheless exist—their secret nature making enforcement of the antitrust laws difficult. Occasionally, upon the advent of a newcomer into the industry or in a period of severe depression, when firms are very anxious to increase sales, the established pricing institutions break down, and a period of price competition ensues. But such action is not of frequent occurrence.

The same considerations relative to price and output determination apply to pure oligopoly as those which apply to differentiated oligopoly, apart from the greater necessity of maintaining price uniformity. The greater degree of co-operation may insure closer attainment of maximum joint profits, and of temporary excess profits. The lack of differentiation makes the entry of new firms easier, but in many capital equipment industries the heavy capital investment and large volume of output necessary for low cost constitute formidable obstacles to free flow of firms into the field.

MONOPSONY AND OLIGOPSONY

Up to this point in the analysis, the assumption has been made that in all cases the number of buyers is large, and that sellers have no preferences for dealing with some purchasers instead of others. In this section brief attention will be given to the situation in which there is only one seller (monopsony) and to that in which the number of sellers is sufficiently small that mutual interdependence exists among them (oligopsony). While complete monopsony may be relatively rare, oligopsony is found in the wholesale markets for some commodities, such as those for sugar beets, canning fruit and vegetables; in the case of purchase of merchandise in large quantities by mail-order houses and chain store systems; and of parts and materials by large manufacturers.

[14] It is interesting to note that in industries of this sort the various producers will often announce price changes of the same magnitude at the same time.

Monopsony and Large Numbers of Sellers

Suppose, first, that in a certain market there is a single seller buying from a large number of small producers, the products of the various firms being identical. The buyer has a certain demand for the product, as indicated by the curve *DD* on Figure 74. If he acted without regard to the effects of his purchases upon price, he would extend purchases to the sum at which his demand and the market supply (*SS*) were equal —*on* on Figure 74. But he will, of course, recognize that the quantity

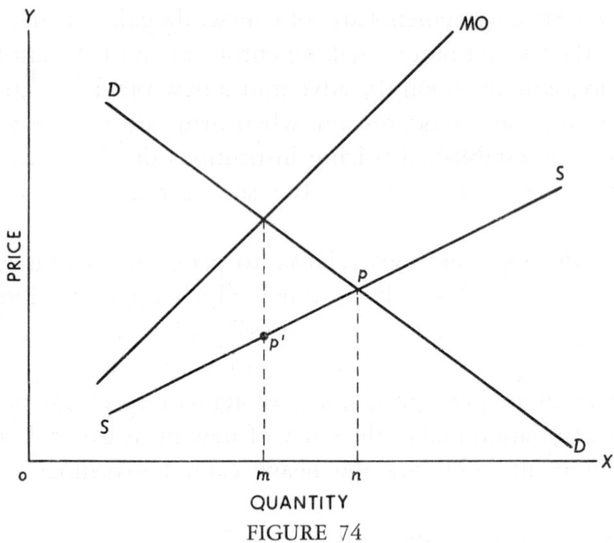

FIGURE 74

PRICE AND OUTPUT ADJUSTMENT UNDER MONOPSONY

of his purchases will affect the price; each additional unit bought will cost him not only the price paid for it, but an additional sum representing the larger amount which he must pay for all the units as a result of purchasing an additional unit. Therefore his marginal outlay on the commodity—the additional amount which he pays as a result of the purchase of another unit—exceeds the price which he must pay. On Figure 74 the marginal outlay is represented by curve *MO*. In order to maximize his satisfaction from the purchase of this commodity (or his profit, if he is buying for resale) he must extend purchases to the point of equality of marginal outlay and demand. He will thus buy a smaller quantity (*om* on Figure 74) than he would if he ignored the effect of his purchases upon demand, and the market price (p') is lower than it would be if the market were purely competitive (p).

From a long-run standpoint the effect of the monopsony power upon price will depend upon the cost conditions of production. No amount of monopsony power will allow the buyer to continue to obtain the product for less than the average cost of production year after year, as production will fall. If the industry is one of increasing-cost conditions, price will remain permanently lower than the purely competitive figure because of the smaller purchases and output. If, however, the industry is one of constant-cost conditions, the price will be the same as it would be if the market were purely competitive, since the average cost is the same regardless of the output, and the price must cover this figure. Long-run supply, in this case, is a horizontal line.

Oligopsony with Large Numbers of Sellers

If there is more than one buyer, but such a small number that each realizes that changes in the purchase price which he offers to pay will affect the purchase prices paid by the other firms, the situation is one of oligopsony. In this situation, just as with complete monopsony, the buyers will take the initiative in setting the price (assuming many sellers).

If there is little interdependence and the effects of the quantities purchased by any one firm on price are slight, the various firms may bid the price up toward the purely competitive level. On the other hand, if mutual interdependence is complete, the firms may succeed in setting the same purchase price as a monopsonist would set. If the actual situation lies between these extremes, it is difficult to make generalizations about price levels, just as it is with partial oligopoly. The greater the degree of mutual interdependence, the greater the extent of deviation between the supply price of the good and the marginal outlay of each firm, and thus the closer the price figure set will approach the monopsony figure. In somewhat less precise terms, the buyers seek to pay the minimum sum for the quantity which they desire; but this quantity, in turn, is dependent upon the price which must be paid. If the buyers are business firms, the picture is complicated by the fact that the price which the firm must pay for the purchases affects the cost of production of its product and the amount of the product which can be sold. The firms will seek to determine a purchase price which will allow maximum profit, taking into consideration the supply which they can obtain at this price, their costs with the price, and their selling prices and sales. In the case of agricultural products, the supply, of course, depends upon the size of the current crop; if the latter is large, a low price can be set; if the crop is small, the price is likely to be set at a higher level, to pull all possible supply away from alternate uses. When the supply is relatively limited, there is a tendency for the oligopsony situation to disintegrate as firms commence bidding against one another to get additional quantities of the materials.

Regardless of the power over market prices possessed by oligopsonists, they cannot ignore costs of production of the suppliers of goods purchased. In any particular year very low prices may not affect the total supply. But over a period of time prices must cover the average cost of the producers, at the equilibrium output level, if the supply is to be forthcoming. If the industry producing the product is an increasing-cost industry, the smaller volume of purchases will hold the price permanently below the purely competitive equilibrium. If, however, the industry is operating in constant-cost conditions, there will be no permanent effect on price.

Bilateral Monopoly and Bilateral Oligopoly

In the two preceding cases it has been assumed that the number of sellers was large, as is true in various agricultural industries. But it is also possible that monopsony or oligopsony on the buyers' side may be accompanied by monopoly or oligopoly on the sellers' side. Such cases are known as bilateral monopoly and bilateral oligopoly. If both oligopsony and oligopoly are complete the firms may succeed in setting a price which will maximize the gains of both sets of firms, and split the gains on the basis of bargaining. But it is perhaps more likely that differences in bargaining strength will result in the selection of a figure relatively more advantageous to the stronger party than the maximum joint-gain figure. No matter how strong the buyers are, they cannot keep the price below the average cost of the sellers, or their supply will disappear. If the sellers force prices too high, the sales of the product produced by the buyers will drop sufficiently to cut the profits of the sellers. But subject to these limits—which may be far apart—the actual price will depend upon bargaining, and no further generalization is possible. The theory of games, discussed on page 280, may prove to be useful in analyzing the strategy followed by oligopolists and oligopsonists in dealing with each other.

SUMMARY OF THE DISCUSSION OF NONPURELY COMPETITIVE MARKETS

Nonpurely competitive markets comprise a very wide range of market relationships, extending from complete monopoly, on the one hand, to monopolistic competition with limited differentiation, on the other. Certain general considerations relating to price and output determination may be offered as a means of showing the contrast with purely competitive price and output determination.

1. In both purely competitive and nonpurely competitive markets, output must be established at the level at which marginal revenue is equal to marginal cost, if maximum profits are to be obtained. In nonpurely competitive conditions, however, the price at which the optimum profit output can be sold is greater than marginal cost because of the downward slope of the average-revenue curve, which causes marginal revenue and average revenue to diverge. The gap between price and marginal cost will be slight in monopolistic competition with limited differentiation, and progressively more significant as the degrees of differentiation and mutual interdependence increase. By contrast, in pure competition, price will be equal to marginal cost at the point of operation, since marginal revenue and average revenue are identical.

2. In conditions of monopoly and monopolistic competition, each firm is faced by a determinate (although perhaps difficult to ascertain) demand schedule for its product. Under oligopoly, however, the demand schedule confronting each seller is not determinate unless the reactions of the competitors are known. The absolute optimum situation for oligopolists is complete collusion, which makes the demand schedule for each firm determinate, and allows determination of price and output on the basis of the total demand for the product in conjunction with the cost schedules of the firms. But it is likely that complete oligopoly is rarely attained. The consequent uncertainty leads to various pricing techniques, such as price leadership and average-cost pricing, designed to minimize the dangers of loss. The existence of common costs increases uncertainty and complexity of pricing and furthers the use of average-cost or markup pricing techniques. These are unlikely to maximize profits for the firms as a group, but may represent the best attainable solution; thus their use is not necessarily contradictory to the assumption that firms seek to maximize their profits.

3. In those cases in which free entry of firms is possible, there will be a tendency toward elimination of any excess profits which develop. But the process of elimination may involve no reduction in price, but merely a loss in sales volume by existing firms, with consequent higher average cost at the level of operation. If price does reach the level of average cost, the figure is likely to be higher than that of lowest average cost, because the business will be spread too thinly over too many firms.

Frequently, however, there are restrictions to entry of new firms, especially when a large volume of output is necessary for low cost and firms have reputations strongly established. In these cases excess profits may continue for long periods.

4. The prices in nonpurely competitive markets are typically set by the sellers, and in a few cases by the buyers or through bargaining between buyers and sellers, rather than by supply and demand of many small sellers and buyers in wholesale markets. There is a tendency for prices to be left unchanged for substantial periods, especially when changes might upset competitive relationships. Prices appear to be particularly unresponsive to changes in demand, so long as the change is not substantial. In contrast, cost changes of noticeable magnitude often lead to immediate price changes, especially if all competing firms are affected in much the same manner. In contrast purely competitive prices change constantly in response to changes in supply and demand, but reflect cost changes only insofar as the latter are reflected in changes in market supply.

5. Most nonpurely competitive markets are characterized by differentiation of product and emphasis upon selling activities as a means of gaining additional business. Thus firms must adjust both product and selling activities to optimum levels, as well as price and output, if they are to maximize profits. The degree of co-operation on output and selling activities appears, on the whole, to be less than that on price.

SELECTED REFERENCES

FELLNER, W. *Competition among the Few.* New York: Knopf, 1949.
The most complete study of oligopoly and bilateral monopoly.

BAIN, J. S. *Pricing, Distribution, and Employment,* chap. vi. rev. ed. New York: Holt, 1953
The best analysis of oligopoly in general texts.

DEAN, JOEL. *Managerial Economics.* chaps. vii–ix. New York: Prentice-Hall, 1951.
Pricing from the standpoint of the business firm.

OXENFELDT, A. R. *Industrial Pricing and Market Practices.* New York: Prentice-Hall, 1951.
One of the most complete discussions of pricing methods.

ROTHSCHILD, K. W. "Price Theory and Oligopoly," *Economic Journal,* Vol. LVII (September, 1947), pp. 299–320.
Reprinted in STIGLER, G. J., and BOULDING, K. *Readings in Price*

Theory. Homewood, Ill.: Richard D. Irwin, Inc., 1952.
One of the best analyses of oligopoly pricing.

MACHLUP, F. *The Economics of Sellers' Competition,* chaps. xi–xvi. Baltimore: Johns Hopkins University Press, 1952.

QUESTIONS

1. Distinguish between the concepts of pure and differentiated oligopoly; between partial and complete oligopoly.
2. If a group of oligopolists is to maximize the profits of the firms as a group, what rule must be followed in the setting of price?
3. Under complete oligopoly, what determines the manner in which the total profits are distributed among the various firms?
4. Explain the obstacles in the path of the maximization of joint profits.
5. When the demand curve for the product of a firm is kinked, what will be the optimum price and output? Illustrate graphically.
6. Why is the kinked demand curve analysis of little use in explaining the existing price and output levels?
7. For what purposes is the kinked demand curve analysis most useful?
8. Why does the existence of a kink in the firm's demand curve increase price rigidity?
9. Why is uncertainty of such great importance in oligopoly?
10. Distinguish between a dominant price leader and a barometric price leader.
11. Distinguish between common costs and separable costs; between joint costs and those common costs which do not take the joint form.
12. To what extent are the costs of maintenance of a railroad line common between freight and passenger service? Are they joint costs between the two?
13. Why does the existence of common costs encourage the use of average-cost pricing techniques?
14. Explain what is meant by the "average-cost" or "full-cost" approach to price determination.
15. What bases are frequently used by firms in allocating common costs among various products? Why are all these bases in a sense arbitrary?
16. Distinguish between the "estimated actual output" and "standard output" bases for placing cost on a per unit basis. What significance does the use of the second basis have for the reactions of prices to increases in sales?
17. Explain the manner in which retailers typically set their prices.
18. What are the obstacles in the path of exclusive use by a retailer of the pricing method explained in Question 17?
19. Why is the use of average-cost pricing not necessarily inconsistent with the goal of profit maximization?
20. What significance does average-cost pricing have for the response of price to (*a*) an increase in demand, (*b*) an increase in cost, and (*c*) the extent

to which the entry of new firms into an industry results in a decline in prices?

21. Discuss the "strategical tactics" approach to oligopoly pricing.
22. Why are selling activities particularly important in industries characterized by oligopoly?
23. Why are firms less likely to agree, explicitly or implicitly, on selling activities than on prices?
24. Why does the development of mutual interdependence with respect to selling activities reduce the level of selling activities carried on?
25. How might the conduct of selling activities in an oligopolistic industry result in a lower price for the product?
26. Why is price discrimination more difficult under oligopoly than under complete monopoly?
27. What was the basing-point system?
28. Does the existence of oligopoly necessarily prevent free entry of new firms? Why, in practice, is entry likely to be somewhat difficult if mutual interdependence is strong in an industry?
29. How, in oligopoly, may the entry of new firms eliminate excess profits without bringing about any reduction in price?
30. If firms deliberately set prices below the optimum short-run profit figure in order to discourage the entry of new firms, why are they likely to be operating nearer the point of lowest average cost than the firms in a situation in which excess profits have been eliminated by the flow of new firms into the industry?
31. Why is the average-cost figure for each product indeterminate when some costs are common among several products? What rule applies to the relation between total revenue from all products of the firm and its total cost? The price of each product and average separable cost?
32. Is it desirable for a railroad to discontinue a passenger train that yields somewhat more revenue than the separable costs for which it is responsible, yet does not earn a share of common costs allocated to it on the basis of train-miles of operation?
33. What significance does the absence of differentiation of product have for price determination in oligopolistic markets?
34. It is sometimes argued that uniformity of price charged by all firms in an industry demonstrates a high degree of competition. Is this argument valid? If not, what does price uniformity demonstrate with respect to conditions in the industry?
35. Explain the rule which a monopsonist would follow in setting price, assuming that there are a large number of small sellers.
36. Why is the power of a monopsonist over price much less in a long-run period than it is at any one time?
37. What significance does the existence of mutual interdependence among a group of oligopsonists have for price and output determination?
38. Explain the relationship between the existence of monopsony and oligopsony

in the market for certain farm crops, such as fruit, and the formation of farmers' marketing co-operatives in these fields.

39. With bilateral oligopoly, upon what considerations does price depend?
40. Contrast the cases of pure competition, monopolistic competition, monopoly, and oligopoly, with respect to:
    a) The initiative in the actual setting of prices
    b) The relation between price and marginal cost
    c) The extent to which firms will operate at the point of lowest average cost, after long-run adjustments are completed
    d) The relationship between price and average cost in the long-run period
    e) The possibility of price discrimination
    f) The importance of selling activities
    g) The rigidity of prices
    h) The immediate reaction of price to an increase in demand
    i) The immediate reaction of price to an increase in cost affecting all firms
    j) Whether or not firms will operate in the short run if average variable cost is not covered.

PART III

The Theory of Factor Price Determination

Chapter 13 INTRODUCTION TO THE THEORY OF FACTOR PRICES AND INCOME DISTRIBUTION

The analysis of price and output determination in the preceding chapters has been based upon the assumption of five major constants:

1. Consumer preferences for various goods, as modified by the selling activities carried on by the sellers.
2. The nature of competitive conditions in each market.
3. The production function for each good, that is, the possible techniques of production, and thus the quantities of various factors required to produce given outputs of the various products, given the factor prices.
4. The prices of all factors of production.
5. The total volume of expenditures on consumption and investment.

The first three determinants have been discussed in the preceding chapters, but the last two require further consideration. Neither factor prices nor income flows are determined by forces external to the economic system; while regarded as basic constants or determinants in the preceding chapters for purposes of simplification of the analysis, these elements can themselves be explained in terms of economic analysis. The next seven chapters will be concerned with the determination of factor prices, and later chapters with expenditure flows.

Much of the analysis of the pricing of consumption goods is applicable to the pricing of the factors. This is particularly true of the pricing of capital goods, which are produced by business firms just as are consumption goods; hence the determinants of price on the cost-supply side of the picture are the same as those of consumption goods. With all factors, however, the direct determinants of demand are different from those of consumption goods demand, since the factor units are acquired by business firms for use in production, rather than by individuals for the satisfaction of personal wants. Furthermore, in the case of all factors except capital goods, the determinants of supply are different from those of consumption goods, since the factor units are not produced by business firms on a profit-making basis.

This chapter will analyze the determination of demand for factor units, or factor demand, and develop a general theory of factor price determination applicable to all types of factors. The following chapters will consider special aspects of the pricing of various types of factors, and money capital.

Factor Prices and the Distribution of Income

In a market economy, the prices paid for the factor units (and money capital) by the producers constitute the sources of income with which individuals purchase the output of production. Accordingly, an explanation of the determination of factor prices not only completes the analysis of the functioning of the price system and the allocation of resources but also indicates the manner in which the total income is distributed among the various groups providing factor units for use in production. Wages, for example, are costs from the standpoint of the producers but constitute incomes for the recipients and provide the means by which they can obtain consumption goods. Wage levels, therefore, not only affect costs, prices, and relative outputs of various goods but also determine the size of the share of national income which is received by the workers.

It must be recognized, however, that the explanation of factor pricing does not provide a complete description of the manner in which individuals share in the national income. It tells nothing, for example, about the manner in which the property resources are distributed among individuals and thus about the way in which property incomes are shared by individuals. Property distribution can be explained only by empirical studies of particular situations. Likewise, present-day individual incomes are greatly affected by governmental policy. Many persons share in the national income through the receipt of transfer payments—old age pensions, relief, etc.—even though they supply no factor units for use in production. Other persons lose portions of their money incomes through tax payments designed to supply the funds for the making of these transfer payments. Both these problems are beyond the scope of the present volume. The analysis of factor pricing, however, provides the basic framework of the explanation of income distribution.

The Approach to a General Theory of Factor Price Determination

In building a general theory of factor price determination applicable to all types of factors, it is necessary to make broad assumptions which will allow general applicability of the theory; since the generality of the assumptions lessens the usefulness of the theory for analysis of specific problems, in subsequent chapters the assumptions will be narrowed to bring them more closely in line with conditions affecting the pricing of particular types of factors.

The first assumption is that of pure competition in all factor markets, and therefore of large numbers of buyers and sellers in the markets, and homogeneous factor units. Departures from pure competition, which are particularly important in the market for labor service, will be considered at a later point. Secondly, it is assumed that the total demand for goods (the total figure of expenditures on consumption and investment) is given, and thus is independent of factor-price levels, and is adequate to maintain full employment. This assumption will also be modified in subsequent chapters. The goal of gain maximization on the part of factor unit owners is likewise assumed.

FACTOR DEMAND

The determinants of the nature and behavior of factor demand—the demand on the part of business firms for units of the factors of production—differ in certain respects from those of consumer demand, since the units are acquired for use in production rather than for direct satisfaction of consumer wants. The goal of the business firm is assumed to be the maximization of profits; thus factor demand is influenced by the attempt of the firms to attain the optimum factor combinations and the most profitable levels of output.

The Basic Rule of Optimum Factor Use by the Firm

If a business firm is to maximize profits, it must acquire units of of each factor up to the point at which an additional unit of the factor adds the same amount to the total cost of the firm as it adds to the total revenue, or, in more technical terms, to the point at which the marginal outlay on the factor is equal to the marginal revenue product. Each unit up to this point adds more to revenue than to cost, and therefore either reduces losses of the firm or increases its profit. Each unit beyond this point adds more to cost than to revenue, and thus either reduces profit or increases losses.

The concepts of marginal outlay and marginal revenue product require careful explanation.

Marginal Outlay

The marginal outlay on a factor is the total increase in expenditure on the factor caused by the acquisition of an additional unit of the factor. If the price paid for the factor is not affected by the quantity used by the firm, the marginal outlay is equal to the price paid per unit of the factor. For example, suppose that a firm that has been employing 8 carpenters at $16 per day, with a total daily outlay on carpenters of $128, hires a ninth carpenter at the $16 wage. Total outlay on the factor increases to $144; the marginal outlay (the increase from $128 to $144) is, of course, equal to the wage paid the ninth man, or $16.

In some cases, however, the use of additional factor units will raise the price paid for the factor, and the marginal outlay will exceed the factor price. Suppose the firm needs a tenth carpenter, but, since no more are available locally, it must offer $18 a day to induce a man to come from a neighboring town. As a result, the total outlay on carpenters rises to $180 a day, under the assumption that the wage paid all carpenters must be uniform. The marginal outlay on the tenth man is $36 even though he is paid only $18, since hiring him necessitated an increase in the wage paid the other men. If, on the other hand, the use of additional units reduces the price paid for the factor, the marginal outlay will be less than the price. The availability of quantity discounts on materials may produce this effect.

Marginal Revenue Product

Marginal revenue product (often called marginal revenue productivity, or marginal productivity) is the net increase in revenue of the firm, before subtracting the marginal outlay on the factor unit, which results when an additional unit of a factor is added. Or, in nontechnical terms, the expression refers simply to the extent to which a firm is better off financially as a result of adding an additional factor unit—an additional worker, for example—before taking into account the amount that the unit costs the firm. A producer hires an additional worker; to see whether the latter "pays for himself," the producer must calculate (or estimate) the effect which the worker has upon his revenue. He discovers that, as a result of using the man, his net revenue before subtracting the wage paid the man has increased by the sum of $8.75 per day. It is this figure which he must compare with the wage to determine whether or not it is advantageous to continue to hire the worker.

The increase in revenue which results from the adding of an additional factor unit may arise from either of two sources:

1. Increased total revenue, due to the sale of additional units of output resulting from the use of the factor unit. If, for example, an additional worker is used to increase physical output, the contribution which he will make to the firm's revenue arises from the sale of the additional units of output which his use makes possible.

When an additional unit of one factor is used, it will often be necessary, if the optimum combination of factors is to be retained, to add units of other factors as well. Thus the employment of an additional man will likely necessitate the purchase of larger quantities of raw materials. Accordingly, a portion of the increase in the firm's total revenue will be due to the additional materials rather than to the additional man; the cost of these materials must be subtracted from the increase in the firm's total revenue to find the net contribution of the worker—his net marginal revenue product. If the marginal revenue product of the materials was being determined, the wage paid the worker would be subtracted.

2. Reduced costs of other factors. If the factor unit added is used to replace units of other factors rather than to increase total output, the contribution to the firm's net revenue arises out of the reduction made possible in the expenditures on other factors. An additional worker may be utilized to reduce waste in the use of raw materials at a certain output level; the increase in revenue which the worker makes possible arises out of the reduced expenditures on raw materials. If additional steel is purchased by a producer to replace aluminum in the making of washing machines, the marginal revenue product of an additional ton of steel is the reduction in the expenditures on aluminum which is made possible by the adding of the ton of steel.

An additional factor unit may, of course, be used partly to increase output and partly to replace other factors. In each of the various alternative uses—to increase output, to replace other factors, and for various possible combinations of the two—an additional factor unit will make possible a certain increase in net revenue (as defined). The significant marginal revenue product figure is the highest of these amounts. For example, suppose that a firm which has been hiring 68 men considers hiring a sixty-ninth. If the additional man were used solely to increase physical output, his contribution to daily net revenue (before deducting the wage paid him) might be $9.50. If he were used to replace other factor units, perhaps to deliver packages previously sent by parcel delivery service, the reduction made possible in expenditures on other factor units (parcel delivery service in this case) might be $6.75. If there are no possible combinations of the two uses, involving some increase in output and some replacement of other factors, which would allow a greater increase in net revenue than $9.75, this figure is the marginal revenue product figure for the additional man. If, on the other hand, the savings in parcel delivery service cost had been $11.50, the latter would have been the significant marginal revenue product figure.

Marginal revenue product for successive factor units may be expressed in tabular form, as illustrated in Tables 26 and 27. The former

TABLE 26
SCHEDULE OF OUTPUT AND REVENUE AS THE QUANTITIES OF FACTOR A ARE VARIED
(Conditions of Pure Competition in the Market for the Product)

Units of Factor A	Total Output	Marginal Physical Product	Price of Product	Value of Marginal Product	Total Revenue	Marginal Gross Revenue Product	Changes in Costs of Other Factors	Marginal Revenue Product
1...........	25	25	$2	$50	$ 50	$50	$+2.50	$47.50
2...........	70	45	2	90	140	90	+4.50	85.50
3...........	110	40	2	80	220	80	+4.00	76.00
4...........	145	35	2	70	290	70	+3.50	66.50
5...........	172	27	2	54	344	54	+3.00	51.00
6...........	191	19	2	38	382	38	+2.00	36.00
7...........	199	8	2	16	398	16	−2.50*	18.50
8...........	199	0	2	0	398	0	−3.00	3.00

* Reflecting a $1.00 increase in materials costs minus $3.50 reduction in other costs made possible by replacement of other factor units.

TABLE 27
SCHEDULE OF OUTPUT AND REVENUE AS THE QUANTITIES OF FACTOR A ARE VARIED
(Nonpurely Competitive Conditions in the Market for the Product)

Units of Factor A	Total Output	Marginal Physical Product	Price of Product	Value of Marginal Product	Total Revenue	Marginal Gross Revenue Product	Changes in Costs of Other Factors	Marginal Revenue Product
1..........	25	25	$2.00	$50.00	$ 50.00	$50.00	$+2.50	$47.50
2..........	70	45	1.80	81.00	126.00	76.00	+4.50	71.50
3..........	110	40	1.50	60.00	165.00	39.00	+4.00	35.00
4..........	145	35	1.30	45.50	188.50	23.50	+3.50	20.00
5..........	172	27	1.20	32.40	206.40	17.90	+3.00	14.90
6..........	191	19	1.15	21.85	219.65	13.25	+2.50	10.75
7..........	199	8	1.13	9.04	224.87	5.22	−2.50*	7.72
8..........	199	0	1.13	0.00	224.87	0.00	−3.00	3.00

* Reflecting a $1.00 increase in materials cost minus a $3.50 reduction in other costs made possible by replacement of other factor units.

pertains to a situation of pure competition in the market for the product, the latter to one of nonpurely competitive conditions. For each number of factor units shown in the table, the marginal revenue product figure given is the maximum contribution to net revenue possible with the particular number of factor units, whether the optimum use of the additional unit is to increase output, to replace other factors, or partly in each of these uses. With the particular data in the tables, the additional factor units would be used solely to increase output until 6 factor units had been acquired. A seventh unit would be used partly to increase output, partly to replace other factors (as indicated by the negative "changes in other costs" figure), while the eighth unit would be used solely to replace other factor units. Prices of other factors are assumed to be given. Any autonomous changes in the prices of those factors which are required in larger quantities as the amount of the particular factor is increased will result in an entirely new productivity schedule.

The Process of Calculation of Marginal Product Data. The steps in the calculation of the data in the two tables can be outlined briefly:

1. Determine the *marginal physical product* (MPP), the increase in total physical product which occurs as an additional factor unit is added. If the optimum use of the additional factor unit is the replacement of units of other factors, MPP will be zero.

2. Determine the *value of the marginal product* (VMP) by multiplying MPP by the price of the product.

3. Determine total revenue by multiplying the output by the price of the product.

4. Determine marginal gross revenue product (MGRP) by calculating the increase in total revenue from the adding of the successive units.

If the market for the product is purely competitive, MGRP will be identical with VMP, as shown in Table 26, since the sale of the additional units of product does not necessitate a price reduction; accordingly, the value of the marginal product is reflected entirely in increased gross revenue of the firm. Thus in pure competition separate calculation of MGRP is not necessary.

In nonpurely competitive conditions, however, additional units of product can be sold only at lower prices. Therefore, MGRP is less than VMP, since the sale of the additional units of output results in a reduction in revenue on the output produced with the smaller number of factor units. MGRP can be calculated directly from VMP by subtracting from the latter the revenue reduction on the previous units which results from the price reduction necessary to sell the additional output.

5. Determine *marginal revenue product,* the net increase in total revenue from the addition of the unit of the factor, by adjusting MGRP for any increase

or decrease in the costs of other factors occurring as a result of the adjustment of the number of units of the factor.

If the increase in the quantity of the factor necessitates the use of additional units of other factors, the additional expenditure on the other factors must be subtracted from MGRP to obtain the marginal revenue product figure. Hence the hiring of additional workers may require the use of more raw materials; the cost of the additional materials must be subtracted from MGRP to ascertain the amount of increase in revenue due to the additional worker.

If the optimum use of the additional factor unit is that of replacing units of other factors, total expenditures on the other factors will be reduced; this saving must be added to MGRP to determine the contribution of the factor to net revenue. In Table 27, if a seventh factor unit is added, optimum use of this factor involves some increase in output, which yields MGRP of \$5.22 (with an increase in materials costs of \$1.00), but also some replacement of other factor units, yielding a saving of \$3.50. The increased materials cost of \$1.00 is subtracted from the \$3.50 saving in other factor costs, to give a net saving of \$2.50; this is added to the MGRP figure of \$5.22 to give a marginal revenue product figure of \$7.72. The eighth unit would be used solely to replace other factors and would allow a saving in other costs of \$3.00. Thus MGRP, which in this case is zero, plus the net saving of \$3.00 yields a marginal revenue product figure of \$3.00.

The explanation of marginal product in the preceding paragraphs has been based upon the assumption that the quantities of certain factors are fixed, and it is therefore relevant for a short-run period. The productivity concepts, however, can be utilized also in analysis of long-run periods, in which all factors are adjustable.

The Behavior of Marginal Revenue Product in the Short Run

In a short-run period, with a given plant capacity, the marginal revenue product may be expected to rise initially and then fall, on the basis of the theory of production outlined in Chapter 7. In terms of the assumptions made in the development of that theory, which, as indicated, appear to be appropriate in many circumstances, marginal physical product rises as units of the factor are first added, because of more efficient utilization of both fixed and variable factor units, and thus marginal revenue product will rise unless the price reductions necessary to sell the additional output, in nonpurely competitive markets, outweigh the effect of the rising physical product.

Beyond a certain point, however, and perhaps at a fairly early stage in the adding of units of the factor, marginal revenue product will diminish. There are several forces responsible for this behavior, the relative importance of the various forces depending upon the nature of the production processes and the type of market in which the firm is selling.

1. If the factor being added is substituted for other factors, a decreasing marginal rate of substitution between this factor and others will eventually be encountered; accordingly, beyond this point the contribution of the additional factor units to net revenue consisting of reductions in costs of other factors will diminish.

2. If the additional factor units are being used to increase output, the marginal physical product will eventually diminish for reasons explained in Chapter 7. Since some of the factors are fixed in quantity in the short-run period, the addition of further units of other factors will eventually encounter the operation of the Law of Diminishing Returns. A very rapid decline in marginal physical product may occur, if the fixed factors are of such nature that output cannot be increased significantly once all of the units have been brought into operation.

3. In nonpurely competitive market conditions, the price of the product must be reduced as greater quantities of output are placed on the market; thus as additional units of factors are added, the marginal revenue product will decline, even if the marginal physical product remains constant. If the latter is declining, marginal revenue product will decline at a faster rate than that at which marginal physical product falls. The magnitude of the price reduction necessary to sell the increased output depends, of course, upon the elasticity of the schedule of demand confronting the firm.

4. When additional units of a factor are being utilized to increase output and the quantities of other factors used are being increased, it is possible that the increased purchases of the other factors may bid up the prices of these factors. If this occurs, the deductions from marginal gross revenue product to determine marginal revenue product will rise as additional units of the factor are acquired.

Behavior of Marginal Revenue Product over a Longer Period

When the marginal revenue product of a factor is considered in terms of a period of time sufficiently long to allow the firm to adjust the quantities of all factors employed, the figures of marginal revenue product will be substantially different than they are in a period in which some factors are fixed in quantity, primarily because marginal physical product will behave in a very different manner. In general, however, in a long-run period as well as in a period in which the plant capacity is given, marginal revenue product will initially increase and then diminish. The increase results from the economies of large-scale production; the use of more efficient types of capital equipment and the increased specialization possible with all factors cause the marginal physical product of the factor to rise as additional units—together with added quantities of other factors—are employed.

Eventually, however, just as in the short run, but at a different level of output, marginal revenue product will commence to fall. In part the decline is due to the fall in marginal physical product which occurs once decreasing returns to scale, due to the problems of large-scale management, are encountered. In addition, just as in the short-run period, the diminishing marginal rate of substitution between this factor and others, the tendency of costs of other factors to rise as more units are acquired, and the necessity of reducing the price of the product to sell more units (except in purely competitive conditions) cause marginal revenue product to fall.

The Determinants of the Demand Schedule for a Factor

With the explanation of the nature of marginal outlay and marginal revenue product completed, it is now possible to continue the explanation of the determinants of factor demand. As indicated early in the chapter, each firm will add units of each type of factor until the point is reached at which the marginal outlay on the factor is equal to the marginal revenue product of the factor, or, in other words, each firm will hire additional men and add other factor units so long as they will "pay for themselves." Thus if the factor price is equal to the marginal outlay on the product, as will be assumed in most of the analysis in order to simplify the exposition, at each factor price the quantity of the factor obtained is the figure at which the marginal revenue product of the factor is equal to the factor price. At this point no further gains can be made by acquiring additional factor units, either for substitution for others, or for increases in output. If the firm extends the number of each type of factor unit acquired to this point of equality of marginal revenue product with factor price, the price ratio between each pair of factor classes will equal the marginal rate of substitution between them—the requirement for the optimum factor combination—since the marginal rate of substitution between any two factors is equal to the ratio of their marginal revenue products.

Since this rule applies to each potential factor price, the entire demand schedule for the factor is determinate, given the data of marginal revenue product. One qualification must be introduced, however: the firm will not find it profitable to operate at all unless the factor price is covered by the average revenue product of the factor—the total revenue received divided by the number of units of the factor. Unless the average revenue product covers the factor price, the average variable cost of the firm will not be covered by the price of the product.

In Table 28, the demand schedule for Factor A is derived from the productivity data given in Table 27, a portion of which is reproduced in Table 28 to facilitate an understanding of the relationship between the productivity data and the demand schedule for the factor. In graphical terms, as illustrated on Figure 75, the declining portion of

TABLE 28

THE SCHEDULE OF AVERAGE AND MARGINAL REVENUE PRODUCT OF FACTOR A AND THE DEMAND SCHEDULE OF THE FIRM FOR FACTOR A

Revenue Schedule			Factor Demand Schedule	
Units of Factor A	Average Revenue Product of Factor A	Marginal Revenue Product of Factor A	Price of Factor A	Quantity of Factor A Demanded
1	$47.50	$47.50	$35.00	3
2	60.75	71.50	20.00	4
3	53.67	35.00	14.90	5
4	46.25	20.00	10.75	6
5	40.68	14.90	7.72	7
6	36.19	10.75	3.00	8
7	32.48	7.72		
8	28.48	3.00		

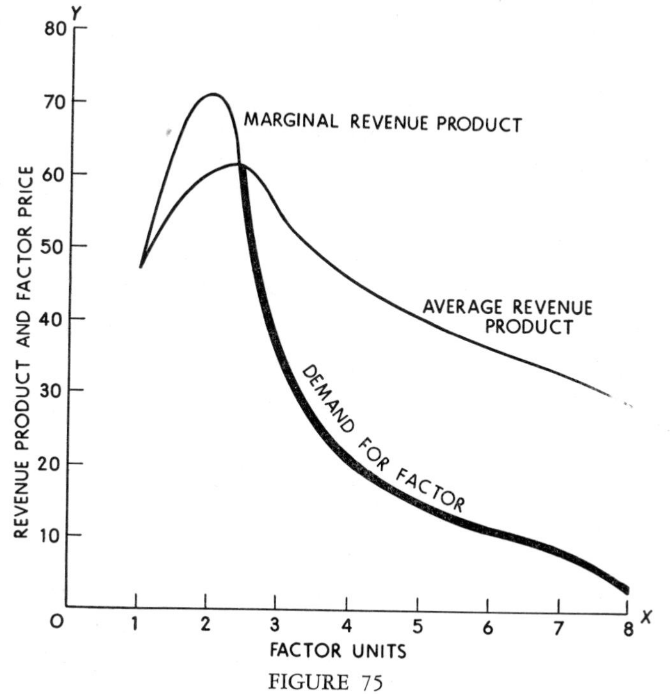

FIGURE 75

MARGINAL REVENUE PRODUCT AND THE DEMAND FOR THE FACTOR

the marginal revenue product curve below its intersection with the average revenue product curve is also the demand curve of the firm for the factor, since, at each possible factor price, the quantity of the factor which will be acquired is the amount at which the marginal revenue product is equal to that price—assuming that average revenue product is covered, and that the marginal outlay on the factor is equal to the price paid for the factor.

Divergence of Factor Price and Marginal Outlay on the Factor

When marginal outlay and the factor price are not identical, the basic principle with respect to the quantity of the factor demanded is the same, except for the fact that the point at which marginal outlay is equal to marginal revenue product is not the same as that at which the factor price is equal to marginal revenue product, and thus the explanation of the relationship between the productivity schedule and the factor demand schedule is complicated. If the factor price rises as more units are obtained, a smaller quantity of the factor will be obtained at each factor price than the amount which would be used if the marginal outlay and the factor price were equal, since the marginal outlay, which must equal the figure of marginal revenue product if profits are to be maximized, exceeds the factor price. If the factor price declines because of quantity discounts or other considerations, a somewhat larger amount will be obtained than if the price is unaffected by the quantity of the factor obtained. In all cases, however, the demand schedule for the factor can be derived from the marginal revenue product and marginal outlay schedules.

Elasticity of Factor Demand

The elasticity of the demand schedule for a factor is controlled by the rate of decline in marginal revenue product and, if the price of the factor is not equal to the marginal outlay on the factor, by the rate of change in the factor price as additional units are obtained. The demand by a producer for a factor will be more elastic to the extent that:

1. The marginal rate of substitution between this factor and others falls slowly, and thus the elasticity of substitution between this factor and others is relatively high. If steel and aluminum are good substitutes for producing a certain product, the demand by the producer for either metal is likely to be elastic. Any change in their relative prices will cause substantial substitution of one metal for the other, and a substantial increase in the purchases of the one whose price has fallen.

2. The marginal physical product declines slowly as additional units of the factor are added to increase output. If the decline is slow, and additional factor units add almost as much to total physical product as did the previous units, small factor price declines are likely to cause substantial increases in the quantity of the factor used (provided that the demand for the product is relatively elastic). If marginal physical product drops sharply, additional factor units will contribute so little that they will not be added unless the factor price falls drastically. As previously indicated, the rate of decline in marginal physical product is less over a longer period, when all factors can be adjusted, than in a shorter interval of time, in which some of the factors are fixed in quantity. Typically a factor demand schedule will be more elastic in a longer period than in a short period of time. The long-period elasticity will also be greater to the extent that decreasing returns to scale due to management problems are avoided.

3. The demand schedule for the product of the seller is relatively elastic. If the demand is very elastic, the additional output can be sold with only slight reduction in price, and declines in factor prices will lead to much greater increases in output and use of the factor than if more substantial price reductions were necessary to dispose of greater output. In the case of goods purchased by merchants for direct resale, the elasticity of the demand schedule of the merchant for the good is controlled almost entirely by the elasticity of the demand schedule for the product confronting the merchant. Substitution of this factor for others by the merchant is virtually impossible, and few important economies or diseconomies in the operation of the store are likely from a change in the volume of one product handled. Some variations in the rate of purchases compared to the rate of sales may result from the adjustment of inventory in anticipation of price changes, but these are only of temporary significance.

4. The elasticity of supply of the other factors employed is high. The less the extent of the rise in the prices of other factors required in larger quantities as the quantity of the particular factor is increased, the slower will be the decline in the marginal revenue product of the factor, and therefore the more elastic will be the demand for the factor.

Changes in Factor Demand

Shifts in the demand schedules of business firms for a factor arise, of course, from variations in the basic determinants of these schedules. Major causes of change include the following:

1. Technological changes, which increase the substitutability of

the factor with others or increase the marginal physical product of the factor. New types of machinery which increase output per man-hour and per dollar of capital invested may raise the marginal product of both labor and capital equipment.

2. Changes in the prices of other factors. Increase in the price of one factor will increase the demand for a factor which is easily substituted for it. Where two factors are not readily substitutable, the effect of an increase in the price of the other factor depends upon the relative strength of two opposite reactions. The higher price encourages substitution and an increase in the demand for the first factor; the higher cost of the other factor encourages output reduction, which reduces the demand for all factors used by the firm. A decline in the price of a complementary factor will increase the demand for the particular factor.

3. Changes in the demand for the product of the firm; increases will raise the price of the product (or allow the sale of more units at the existing price) and thus raise the schedule of marginal revenue product and the demand for the factor.

Total Demand for a Factor[1]

The total demand for a factor is the sum of the demand schedules for the factor of all producers employing the factor. However, at factor prices other than the prevailing level, the total quantity demanded will often be different than it would appear to be on the basis of the existing individual schedules. That is, if the factor price which each producer must pay actually changes to another level, the quantity of the factor which each producer finds it profitable to employ at the new price is not the same as the quantity which he anticipated that he would employ, nor the same as the amount that he actually could have employed at the new level had the change affected only the wages which he paid, and not those of the other firms in the industry as well. Suppose, for example, that the prevailing wage for a certain type of worker is $14 a day. If it falls to $12 a day for one firm, but remains $14 a day for the others, the firm may increase its labor force 10 per cent, as the lower labor cost allows it to reduce price and increase output materially. But if the wage rate falls to $12 a day for all of the firms in the industry, the firm may increase the labor force by only 2 per cent. There are several reasons why the total demand for a factor is likely to be less elastic

[1] Attention is again called to the fact that the term "factor" is being employed in reference to a particular type of homogeneous factor unit, such as labor of a certain variety, not to broad factor groups, such as labor of all types.

than the schedule of one firm for the factor, with the factor prices paid by the other firms given.

In the first place, when all firms adjust output in response to a factor price change, the demand schedules for the products of the firms will be affected. If wages fall, for example, and each firm hires more men and increases output, the demand schedules for the products of each of the firms will fall because the prices of the other firms are lowered. Thus greater price reductions than those anticipated will be necessary to sell the additional output, schedules of marginal revenue product will decline, and fewer additional men will be hired. If pure competition prevails in the market for the commodity, the price will fall as soon as the additional output comes on the market, and the schedules of marginal revenue product will drop.

Secondly, the adjustment of output and factor purchases by all firms in response to a factor price change may alter the prices of other factors and thereby modify the marginal revenue product schedules, whereas adjustment by one firm alone is not likely to produce significant modifications of this sort. A reduction in the price of a certain type of material may cause substantial replacement of other materials by this one; as a consequence, the prices of the other materials may fall and lessen the amount of substitution and the net increase in the use of the factor whose price fell initially. In other cases, reduced factor prices will cause increases in output, which will necessitate greater use of other factors and raise their prices. As a consequence, the output increase and the quantity of the factors used will be less than anticipated.

Thirdly, increased factor employment in one industry due to a decline in the factor price may be offset by consequent decreases in the use of the factor in other industries. Reduced wages in the brick industry, for example, might increase employment in that industry. However, the decline in brick prices resulting from the lower wages would increase the use of brick relative to that of lumber and reduce the demand for labor in the lumber industry.

Finally, when a broad factor group which includes a substantial portion of the total income-receivers in the economy is considered, a change in the price paid for the use of the factor units (a change in general wage level, for example) may affect the total purchases of consumption goods sufficiently that the demand schedules for the products of the firms and thus their demand schedules for factor units will be affected. If different factor-owning groups have substantially different propensities to consume, factor price changes which alter materially the distribution of income will have substantial effects on total consumption and thus upon the demand schedules for the factors. This reaction will be considered in greater detail with regard to the question of the effectiveness of general wage reductions as a means of eliminating unemployment.

The Marginal Revenue Product Principle and Business Policy

The principle that business firms adjust the quantities of each factor purchased to the level at which the marginal revenue product of the factor is equal to the marginal outlay follows as a matter of logical necessity from the assumption that business firms are seeking to maximize profit. A firm cannot be earning the maximum profit possible (or be minimizing its losses) unless the quantity of each factor employed is adjusted to the marginal revenue product—marginal outlay level. Actually, as previously indicated, this statement is merely a more precise way of expressing the generally accepted view in the business community that "a man will be hired only if he will pay for himself." But actual attainment of the principle in practice is not always realized.

In the first place, as noted in earlier chapters, it must be recognized that other motives besides that of profit maximization do influence business decisions. Pursuit of these other motives will in some cases lead to departure from the marginal outlay-marginal revenue product rule. If, at least temporarily, the firms are determining output and price on the basis of a "satisfactory" profit rather than the maximum, output may be greater than the level at which marginal cost and marginal revenue are equal, and the number of factor units acquired will be greater than that required by equality of marginal revenue product and marginal outlay. In other cases the desire to avoid taking action which will appear to aggravate a depression may cause the firm to continue to employ more men than the optimum number, if finances of the firm permit. Or unprofitable expansions, involving the adding of factor units beyond the marginal outlay-marginal revenue product figure, may be undertaken in the effort to build a greater business empire. All such considerations cause the factor demand schedules to depart from those determined on the basis outlined above. Nevertheless, the profit-maximization assumption is the best single assumption that can be made in regard to motivation of business firms; an analysis of producer demand built upon the use of the assumption, though not entirely adequate because of the exceptions noted, is more satisfactory than that built upon any other assumption, with the present state of knowledge.

But, granted the use of the assumption of profit maximization, a producer encounters very serious difficulties in actually attaining equality of marginal outlay and marginal revenue product. The determination of marginal revenue product with any high degree of accuracy is an extremely difficult task. The various steps involved in its calculation, outlined earlier in the chapter, need only be recounted for this fact to become evident. Often it is not even easy to determine the marginal physical product of an additional factor unit—an additional worker, for example. This is especially true of workers not directly involved in physical production. The firm's demand schedule, knowledge of which is essential for determination of marginal revenue product, can at best only be estimated. The various determinants of marginal revenue product, such as the prices of other factors, techniques of production, and demand schedules, are constantly changing. As a consequence of these difficulties, all a producer can hope to do is to approximate equality of marginal outlay and marginal revenue product. Nevertheless, knowledge of the principle is important in indicating the goal which producers are trying to attain in adjusting the quantities of various factors. The imperfections, however, which interfere with attainment must be recognized.[2]

FACTOR SUPPLY

In the presentation of a general theory of factor pricing, generalizations with respect to factor supply must be very broad because of the differences among the influences which affect the supplies of the various factors. In succeeding chapters the determinants of the supply of the various types of factors will be considered in greater detail.

A sharp distinction must be made between the determinants of the supply of capital goods on the one hand, and the other factors and money capital, on the other. Capital goods are produced by business firms on the same basis as consumption goods; therefore the determinants of supply are essentially the same as those of the latter, as explained in preceding chapters. Costs of production thus play the dominant role in control of supply. One difference, however, should be noted; durable capital goods last over a period of time, and once they

[2] For many years controversy has occurred over the usefulness of the marginal productivity analysis. See, for example, the attacks on the principle by R. A. Lester, "Shortcomings of Marginal Analysis for Wage-Employment Problems," *American Economic Review,* Vol. XXXVI (March, 1946), pp. 62–82; and the defense by F. Machlup, "Marginal Analysis and Empirical Research," *American Economic Review,* Vol. XXXVI (September, 1946), pp. 519–54. Note also H. M. Oliver, Jr., "Marginal Theory and Business Behavior," *American Economic Review,* Vol. XXXVII (June, 1947), pp. 375–83, and R. A. Gordon, "Short Period Price Determination in Theory and Practise," *American Economic Review,* Vol. XXXVIII (June, 1948), pp. 265–88.

have been produced the supply is essentially independent of cost of production in much the same manner as the basic factors. But over a period of time, cost is relevant, and in the pricing of new equipment coming onto the market cost plays an important role.

The other types of factors are not produced by business firms on a profit-making basis; hence cost of production has no relevance for supply. The supply is dependent upon the number of units of the particular type of factor in existence at the time, and the willingness of the factor-owners to allow their factor units to be used in production.

A few brief observations can be made with respect to the major classes of factors, and more detailed attention will be given in the subsequent chapters.

The factor class which includes land and other natural resources is, by definition, fixed in quantity at any particular time, since it consists of those factors which are provided directly by nature. Furthermore, from the standpoint of the economy, the supply of land and other natural resources is perfectly inelastic, since the owners will prefer to realize something rather than nothing, and the mere holding of idle land, in itself, offers no gain. From the standpoint of a particular industry, the supply price of land will depend upon the alternative earnings possible in the next-best uses. Even over a period of time, the supply of land is not dependent upon the return received from it because additional land, as defined, cannot be produced.

The supply of labor depends upon the number of persons in the market area, their ability to work, their skills, and their willingness to work. The actual size of the population at any one time is not determined by the current wage rate, and even over a period of time is not influenced in any significant manner by wage changes within usual limits, as explained in Chapter 14. However, the willingness of persons to work may be influenced by the wage rate; as wage rates rise some persons will be willing to work longer hours than they would at low rates, and others not working at all at low wages will enter the labor market. On the other hand other workers may work less, or even drop out of the labor market completely. Because of these conflicting reactions, the exact nature of the supply schedule of labor is difficult to ascertain. As explained in Chapter 14, it is generally believed that the supply of labor, in total, is very inelastic. The supply of any particular type of labor is more elastic, because of the possibility of workers shifting from one occupation to another.

The determinants of the supply schedule of money capital are likewise very complex. The supply depends upon the number of units of money capital in existence, and the willingness of the owners to make them available to others. An increase in the rate may have some effect—probably limited—in encouraging persons to accumulate larger amounts of money capital; it is likely to have greater effect in inducing the holders of money to part with it, making it available for use by business firms. The elasticity of the supply depends also, to a large extent, upon governmental monetary policies; the government through the central banking system can create additional units of money capital, and if it seeks to maintain a stable interest rate level, will increase the quantity supplied whenever the rate tends to rise, thus making the supply schedule highly elastic. These questions will be considered in detail in Chapter 17.

FACTOR PRICE DETERMINATION

Given the demand and supply schedules of each type of factor, the price of each factor will adjust to the level at which the quantity of the factor supplied is equal to the quantity demanded, under the assumption of pure competition in the factor markets. Given the determinants of supply of each factor, at each possible price for the factor there are a certain number of factor units available for use. At each factor price, likewise, there is a certain quantity of the factor demanded, namely, the number which allows equality of the marginal revenue product of the factor and this factor price, for each firm employing the particular type of factor. The actual price must adjust to the level at which the quantity demanded equals the quantity supplied, since at any higher level more units are available than firms can use, while at lower levels the factor price would be less than the marginal revenue product figure for various firms; thus firms will compete against each other for additional factor units and drive the price up. At the equilibrium figure the factor price must equal the marginal revenue product figure for each firm, or the firms will seek either to obtain more factor units or to lessen the number which they have, upsetting the equilibrium and causing a change in the factor price.

Or, in other words, equality of marginal revenue product of the factor and the factor price is attained because each firm adjusts the quantity of each factor employed until the marginal revenue product is equal to the price paid for the factor; once equality of supply and demand of the factor is attained, as it must be in a purely competitive market, the actual price of the factor will equal the marginal revenue product of the factor for each firm, with the available number of factor units employed. This explanation of factor price determination is known as the *Marginal Productivity Theory of Distribution* (of income).

At the equilibrium the marginal revenue product of each factor will be the same in each use to which the factor is put, apart from the effects of imperfections arising out of the difficulties involved in the calculation of marginal revenue product. Likewise, the ratios between the prices of the various factors will be equal to the marginal rates of substitution among them in all uses, since only this relationship allows the use of optimum factor combinations, and is attained once each firm adjusts the quantity of each factor to the level at which the marginal revenue product is equal to the factor price. Furthermore, under the assumed conditions of pure competition and total consumption-plus-investment expenditures adequate to maintain full employment in the economy, at equilibrium factor prices there can be no unemployment of any factor. All units whose owners wish to have them employed at the existing factor prices will be utilized. Some portions of the potential factor supply may not be used because the owners consider the present factor prices to be too low, but the units are not unemployed, however, in the usual sense of the term. Workers, for example, who prefer to remain idle because they consider the wage to be inadequate are not considered unemployed.

Deviations from Pure Competition

The actual markets for the factors are characterized by substantial deviations from conditions of pure competition. The least deviation occurs in the markets for money capital on a long-term basis, since both the number of lenders and the number of borrowers are large, the units are standardized, and the market is highly organized. As a consequence, long-term bond interest rates adjust on essentially a purely competitive basis. Rates on short-term money capital, however, are determined in nonpurely competitive markets, with the rates dominated by the principal lenders.

The market for land is characterized by the existence of a large number of local markets, with a small number of buyers and sellers in each. The average lessor has only one or a few pieces of land to rent and participates in lease transactions only on relatively rare occasions. Direct bargaining is thus significant in land-rent determination; collusive action among buyers or sellers is rare, however, and total supply-demand relationships still play a role. The total land market is further broken up into small segments because many users prefer to buy land rather than rent it; accordingly two distinct types of transactions occur. However, as will be explained later, land rents and land sale prices bear a definite relationship to each other. The practice of land purchase, plus the use of long-term leases, results in lengthy intervals between the times at which many pieces of land are subject to sale or lease transactions.

The markets for various types of labor involve the greatest deviation from conditions of pure competition. Before the development of labor unions, wages in general were dictated by employers; a very large number of small suppliers (workers) were selling their services to a relatively small number of employers, who exercised monopsonistic domination over wage levels. This situation is still to be found in some labor markets today. But, in general, the development of labor unions has transformed many of the old monopsonistic markets into ones of bilateral oligopoly (oligopoly-oligopsony) in which wages are determined by direct bargaining between unions and employers or employer groups. As a consequence, explanation of wage levels on the basis of any general principles becomes difficult, as is always true with bilateral oligopoly. There is good reason to believe, however, that the levels are different than they would be if set by supply-demand forces in a purely competitive market. Wages in nonunion industries are patterned to a large extent on union wage levels.

Total Expenditures

The second assumption utilized in the construction of the general theory of factor price determination was that total consumption-plus-investment expenditures were given, being independent of the factor price levels and adequate to insure full employment in the economy as a whole. This assumption is, of course, not necessarily applicable in all cases. Changes in factor prices may alter the level of total expenditures; for example, if wage rates fall and the demand for labor as a whole is inelastic, total wage payments will fall and reduce the total demand for consumption goods. This, in turn, is likely to reduce the volume of investment. The consequent decline in the total demand for goods may reduce the demand for labor and other factors. Implications of these changes for factor price determination are very complex, and economic analysis has not as yet dealt adequately with them. Further attention will be given to the problem in Chapter 22.

Certain generalizations, however, can be offered at this point. A particular level of factor prices, even if temporarily equating supply of and demand for the factors, cannot remain unless the factor price pattern is such that—in conjunction with the other determinants of total expenditures (to be discussed later)—the total volume of expenditures on consumption and investment[3] is equal to the current national income (the sum of the payments to the factors during the period). If expenditures are less than income, production will decline, since all the goods currently being produced cannot be sold without price reductions, and factor prices will tend to fall. If total expenditures rise above current income, the demand for factors will increase, and, with full employment, factor prices will tend to rise.

Furthermore, if the volume of planned savings tends to outrun the volume of investment in the economy at full employment levels, there may be no level or pattern of factor prices which will allow the attainment of full employment. Under such conditions national income and production would adjust to levels at which the total amount persons wish to save and the total volume of profitable investment are equal, these levels being less than ones allowing full employment. Under such circumstances, factor prices cease to be the means of adjusting total supply and total demand for the factors; instead, the factor prices adjust to figures at which the quantity of each factor which can find employment at the equilibrium level of national income is equal to the demand for the factor.

Under these circumstances, however, why does competition of the unemployed factors not pull the factor prices down and restore full employment? This question will be considered in detail in the following chapters. Apart from the effects of monopolistic elements such as labor unions which interfere with adjustments in price, it is very doubtful if general factor price reductions will actually increase the level of employment; the factor price decline is followed by a decline in the general price level and in dollar expenditures, and the net effect may be merely an over-all downward adjustment in monetary terms with no effect on the real level of incomes or output. Increased employment can result from the general factor price decline only if the pattern of the decline is such as to increase consumption and/or investment relative to national income. Further analysis of this question must await the discussion of the determination of national income levels.

SELECTED REFERENCES

MACHLUP, F. "Marginal Analysis and Empirical Research," *American Economic Review,* Vol. XXXVI (September, 1946), pp. 519–54.

One of the clearest presentations of the marginal productivity analysis.

[3] Including government expenditures.

STIGLER, G. J. *The Theory of Price,* chap. xi. rev. ed. New York: Macmillan, 1952.

BAIN, J. S. *Pricing, Distribution, and Employment,* chap. xi. rev. ed. New York: Holt, 1953.

QUESTIONS

1. Why is a separate treatment of factor pricing, distinct from the analysis applied to the pricing of commodities, necessary?
2. Why is the theory of factor pricing often called the theory of distribution?
3. Under what circumstances does marginal outlay on a factor exceed the price paid for the factor? Under what circumstances is it less than the latter?
4. Define marginal physical product; marginal gross revenue product; value of the marginal product; marginal revenue product.
5. Under what circumstances is:
   a) Marginal gross revenue product less than the value of the marginal product?
   b) Marginal gross revenue product zero, yet marginal revenue product a positive figure?
   c) Marginal revenue product less than marginal gross revenue product? More than marginal gross revenue product?
6. Complete the table below:

Units of Factor	Total Output	Marginal Physical Product	Price of Product	Value of Marginal Product	Total Revenue	Marginal Gross Revenue Product	Changes in Costs of Other Factors	Marginal Revenue Product	Average Revenue Product
1........	40	....	$1.40	....	....	....	$+4.00	....	....
2........	90	....	1.35	....	....	....	+4.25	....	....
3........	130	....	1.30	....	....	....	+5.70	....	....
4........	150	....	1.25	....	....	....	+4.40	....	....
5........	165	....	1.20	....	....	....	+3.20	....	....
6........	172	....	1.15	....	....	....	+2.05	....	....
7........	175	....	1.10	....	....	....	−2.10	....	....

7. With a given plant, why does marginal revenue product decline as units of the factor are added, beyond a certain point? Why will the rate of decline be faster if the industry is one of nonpurely competitive conditions than if it is purely competitive (other conditions being the same)?
8. Construct the demand schedule for the factor for which product data is given in Question 6 above.
9. Plot the marginal revenue product and average revenue product data in Question 6, and indicate the demand curve of the firm for the factor.
10. Why will the firm increase the number of units of a factor up to the point at which the marginal outlay on the factor is equal to the marginal revenue product if it wishes to maximize profits?
11. If marginal outlay exceeds the factor price, will the firm acquire more or

fewer units with a given schedule of productivity than if price and marginal outlay were equal? Why?

12. Indicate the effect upon the elasticity of demand for a factor of:
    a) A reduction in the rate at which the marginal rate of substitution of this factor for other factors falls, due to technological changes.
    b) A rapid decline in marginal physical product beyond a certain point.
    c) Reduced elasticity of demand for the product of the firm, due to scarcity of substitutes.
    d) Increased scarcity of materials used in conjunction with the particular factor.
13. What will be the effect upon the demand for a factor of:
    a) Increased substitutability of this factor for others?
    b) A decline in demand for the product of the industry?
    c) Increased prices of other factors?
14. Why is the total demand for a factor likely to be less elastic than the demand for the factor by any one firm?
15. Why, in practice, may firms not actually in all cases add factor units up to the point at which the marginal revenue product of the factor is equal to marginal outlay on the factor?
16. Distinguish between the determinants of the supply of capital goods and other types of factors.
17. Explain the determination of the price of a certain type of factor, under the assumption of a purely competitive market for the factor.
18. Why, under the assumptions employed in the analysis, must the equilibrium factor price equal the marginal revenue product of the factor?
19. How can the statement that the equilibrium factor price is equal to the marginal revenue product have precise meaning, when the marginal revenue product varies with the number of factor units employed?
20. It is sometimes maintained that the marginal productivity theory of distribution involves circular reasoning, by use of the following argument: "The marginal revenue product of a factor depends upon the number of factor units used. But in order to know how many factor units to acquire, the firm must know the factor price. Therefore the argument that the factor price depends upon the marginal revenue product involves circular reasoning, and explains nothing." Evaluate this argument.

Chapter 14 WAGE DETERMINATION UNDER PURELY COMPETITIVE CONDITIONS

The largest share of national income, and thus the largest element in the costs of business firms, consist of wages and salaries—the sums paid for the use of labor service. Department of Commerce figures show that in the United States in recent years about 65 per cent of national income has consisted of wages and salaries.[1] In addition, a large but unmeasurable portion of the income item reported as profits of unincorporated businesses consists of implicit wages of farmers, shopkeepers, etc. The combined figure of explicit and implicit wages, without question, exceeds 75 per cent of total national income.

The explanation of wage determination involves the elaboration of the general theory of factor price determination in terms of special characteristics of the factor labor. This general factor class is distinguished by the fact that direct human activity is involved; the factor service consists of the work of human beings, and the payments made for the services constitute directly the incomes of the persons providing the services. In a nonslave economy, the source of the service, namely, the worker, cannot be sold; only the individual worker (or, more accurately, his household) can obtain the wage income. The business firm can buy only the service, not the worker himself. Because the factor service consists of work on the part of the person, considerations of personal likes and dislikes for work are major determinants of supply schedules. The personal considerations involved also affect the nature of competition in the labor market.

Furthermore, because of the personal nature of labor service, other considerations with respect to work in addition to wages are significant to the suppliers of labor service. For example, the worker is concerned with the number of hours worked, the relative security of his income, the working conditions, pensions, vacations, etc. Detailed analysis of these considerations is not possible in the scope of this study, but their importance must not be overlooked. A substantial portion of labor

[1] See *Supplement to Survey of Current Business,* July, 1955, p. 6.

union activity is directed toward improvements along these lines, and in many instances higher wages and changes in these other elements of the job situation must be regarded as alternatives to each other.

Finally, the basic source of labor service—the population itself—is not "produced" for economic reasons; families do not raise children for the income which can ultimately be gained from their services. Trends in population and labor supply are dependent primarily upon factors other than wage rates (provided that the latter are high enough to allow persons to live) and no significant functional relationship between the wage rate and the population can be found.

In this chapter the basic marginal productivity analysis will be applied to labor service, under the assumption of purely competitive conditions in the labor markets. In Chapter 15 the significance for wages of nonpurely competitive conditions, particularly monopsony and the existence of labor unions, will be developed.

WAGE LEVELS OF PARTICULAR TYPES OF LABOR

The analysis of wage determination cannot be made directly in terms of total labor service, as such, because of the diversity in forms of labor in use, but must be made in terms of wages in particular occupations in which the labor service is more or less homogeneous; once this analysis is completed, it is possible to consider interrelationships of wage levels in various occupations and the general level of wages.

If markets for labor services are purely competitive, and the general price level and total expenditures in the economy (consumption plus investment) are assumed to be given, the wage rate for each occupation can be explained in terms of the relationship between the demand schedule for labor service of this type and the supply available at various wage rates. The money wage rate, in conjunction with the number of hours worked, determines the real wage of the workers, under the assumption of a given general price level. Both demand and supply considerations require analysis.

The Demand for Labor

The demand schedule of an employer for labor is based upon the schedule of marginal revenue product of the particular type of labor, under the assumption that the firm is seeking to maximize profit. If profits are to be maximized, at any given wage level, the quantity hired by the firm must be such that the marginal revenue product is equal to the marginal outlay on the workers, and thus is equal to the wage rate, if the latter is independent of the number hired by the firm. Imperfections in the market will interfere with the exact attainment of this optimum, but not with the basic principle involved.

The total demand for any given type of labor is the sum of the schedules of the various employers. However, in considering this total, it must be noted that with larger numbers of men hired, the marginal revenue product and thus the quantity of labor hired will be less than would appear to be the case on the basis of the schedules of the individual firms, since the use of an increased number of workers, and the consequent increased output, will reduce the price of the product, and possibly increase the cost of other factor units acquired in greater quantities.

The elasticity of demand for a certain type of labor depends, of course, upon the rate of decline in marginal revenue product as additional workers are hired. This rate, in turn, depends primarily upon the technical conditions of production, the substitutability of labor for other factors, and the elasticity of demand for the product. If conditions of production are such that, once all equipment is brought into efficient use, additional men will add very little to total product, marginal revenue product will drop sharply, and the demand will be inelastic. This is likely to be the case in the short-run period, with capital equipment of a type which requires a certain number of men for efficient operation, but yields little additional output as the number of workers is increased beyond this amount. Marginal revenue product will also drop sharply beyond a certain point if the demand curve for the product of the firm contains a sharp kink, since large price reductions will be necessary to sell additional units of output. The elasticity of demand for labor is also likely to be made less than it would otherwise be by the inadequacy of knowledge on the part of the employer of the exact data of marginal revenue product of additional numbers of workers. Lack of such knowledge makes the employer less responsive to the effects of wage changes as he can only estimate the optimum number of employees. On the basis of the assumed importance of these conditions—a sharp drop in marginal physical product beyond a certain point, limited substitutability of capital and labor in a short period of time, the case of the kinked demand curve, and lack of knowledge by employers of marginal revenue product—it is often argued that the typical demand schedule for labor is inelastic in a short-run period. Empirical evidence is not available to provide substantial confirmation for this point of view.

Over a longer period of time, the demand is likely to be more elastic because of the ability to substitute labor for capital and vice versa, and to adjust the types and quantities of capital goods in use. The ability to increase the amount of capital checks the sharp decline in marginal physical product which may be encountered in the short run with given capital equipment.

The Supply of Labor

The forces of supply of labor differ basically from those of all other commodities and factors, since the willingness to make units of labor service available depends upon the choices of individuals in the utilization of their own time as between work and leisure, and among various possible employments of their labor. Considerations of tradition, culture, and habit play a much more significant part in determining labor supply than the supplies of other factors. Furthermore, the potential supply of labor is dependent upon the level of population and the age distribution of the population, the determinants of which are almost entirely noneconomic in character.

The analysis of labor supply is also complicated by problems in the definition of the units of labor service; changes in actual effective labor supply may occur as a result of changes in the number of workers available, the hours worked, the intensity of work, and the skill of the workers. The analysis, for purposes of simplification, must be made largely in terms of labor-hours, but possible changes in the other two variables must not be ignored.

In the short-run period, the supply schedule of any particular type of labor is dependent upon the number of workers who have the necessary skills (if any) required for the work, the relative wage and nonmonetary advantages of other occupations, the availability of jobs in other occupations, the number of hours (including overtime) that persons are willing to work, and the extent to which some workers will enter or leave the labor market completely at various wage levels. If there are no unemployed workers (that is, persons willing to work at current wage levels but unable to find jobs), additional workers of the particular type can be obtained only by luring them away from other occupations, by inducing persons now idle to work, or by persuading existing workers to work longer hours.

Occupational Shifts. So far as the transfer of workers from other occupations is concerned, persons can be induced to transfer only if they are offered higher wages (the other conditions of work being assumed as given); thus the portion of the supply schedule represented by persons who may shift among occupations has the usual positive slope, higher wages in this occupation inducing more persons to move into the field. The elasticity of this element in the supply depends on three primary factors. The first is the extent to which persons in other occupations possess, or can quickly acquire, the necessary skills. Secondly, the importance of nonmonetary advantages of the various occupations, such as prestige, job security, pensions, etc., plays a part. Pension rights particularly deter persons from shifting between occupations. Thirdly, the cost involved in making the transfer affects the willingness of the workers to change occupations.

The supply of highly skilled workers may be extremely inelastic, since the number of persons in other lines of activity capable of performing the particular type of work may be very small. On the other hand, the potential supply of workers requiring little skill may be extremely elastic.

The supply of workers in any particular occupation is much more elastic over a long period than in a short period because of the greater possibility of shifting between occupations. Continued higher wages in certain occupations will lead to increased training for these fields; new workers entering the labor market are more likely to flow into the higher-paid jobs than existing workers are to retrain for them. Again, however, the long-period supply will be less elastic in fields requiring expensive and lengthy training than in those in which the training period is shorter.

The supply schedules of various types of workers are obviously closely interrelated in the same manner as the demand schedules; the supply of any one type of labor is determinate, given the prices being paid for other types of labor, but shifts in the latter may cause significant readjustments in the schedule of the particular type.

Work-Leisure Ratios. The nature of the supply schedule of any type of labor depends not only upon the possibility of persons shifting among various occupations, but also upon the effect of wage changes on the number of persons in the labor market and the number of hours that they are willing to work. This relationship is of particular significance when attention is given to the over-all supply picture for labor as a whole, with respect to the determination of general wage levels and the share of labor in national income. However, analysis of the effect of wage changes upon the total supply of labor service is difficult, in part because of the unpredictability, from any usual assumptions, of the reactions of the individuals involved. Empirical evidence with respect to labor supply is very limited.

It would appear at first glance that higher wages should bring forth a greater quantity of labor, by providing greater compensation to overcome the disutility of additional work, and to lure marginal workers into the labor market. However, the labor supply schedule differs from the usual supply situation by virtue of the fact that while work and leisure are alternative uses of a worker's time, the enjoyment of leisure is dependent upon the amount earned during the working period. A higher wage rate has two effects, which produce opposite reactions upon labor supply; these are essentially the substitution and income effects of any price change. On the one hand, the higher wage offers greater compensation for overcoming the disutility of work, or, in other words, reduces the cost of income in terms of work. This is the substitution effect, which tends to encourage substitution of work for leisure, and leads the person to work more when wages rise. But on the other hand, the higher wage allows the person to gain a given real income in a shorter period of time; this income effect encourages the person to enjoy part of the benefits of the higher wage in the form of greater leisure. The net effect is difficult to predict. If the person's demand for income in terms of (that is, in exchange for) work is elastic—if he has a strong desire to increase his level of living as much as possible—the substitution effect will outweigh the income effect and he will work more hours when wages rise. If, however, the person's demand for income in terms of work is inelastic, he is interested primarily in the attainment of a specific living level but is not much concerned about exceeding this, and the higher wage will cause him to work less rather than more. Individual attitudes, as well as general customs and traditions, are important in determining the over-all effect, as is the extent to which persons are subject to fixed financial commitments. In a society in which a customary level of living is regarded as the primary goal, and striving to do better is not considered proper, the higher wage is likely to reduce labor hours. In a society in which the accepted goal is to "get ahead in the world," the result may be the reverse.

This analysis has been conducted in terms of hours of work by a particular person. Actually the usual household often has more than one potential worker; the additional ones, beside the main wage earner, may be more or less marginal workers whose behavior is affected to a greater extent by wage changes than that of the main wage earner. A higher wage may lure into the market some of these marginal workers who do not find it worthwhile to work for supplementary income at low wage rates, especially if working results in additional costs for clothing, transportation, care of children, etc. On the other hand, higher wages for the main wage earner will render less necessary the working of the wife or children to allow attainment of the level of living regarded as essential, and cause these persons, in some instances, to drop out of the labor market.[2]

The net result of these conflicting considerations is difficult to assess. On the whole, it may be argued that the supply of labor is probably extremely inelastic in either direction within usual limits, since the average worker must seek employment to gain a living, and he has little individual choice with respect to hours of work. This point must not be exaggerated; by absenteeism and by varying the intensity of work and overtime, he does have some discretion. But the range is likely to be narrow. As wages rise, some persons will seek to work additional hours and some fewer; some persons will enter the labor market and some will leave. Whether the upper portion of the labor-supply curve is of usual shape (*SS* on Figure 76A) or backward sloping (*S′S′* on Figure 76B) cannot be established, with the present state of knowledge. The positive-sloping portion of *S′S′* is based upon the assumption that at extremely low wage levels, wage increases will induce some additional persons to enter the labor market.

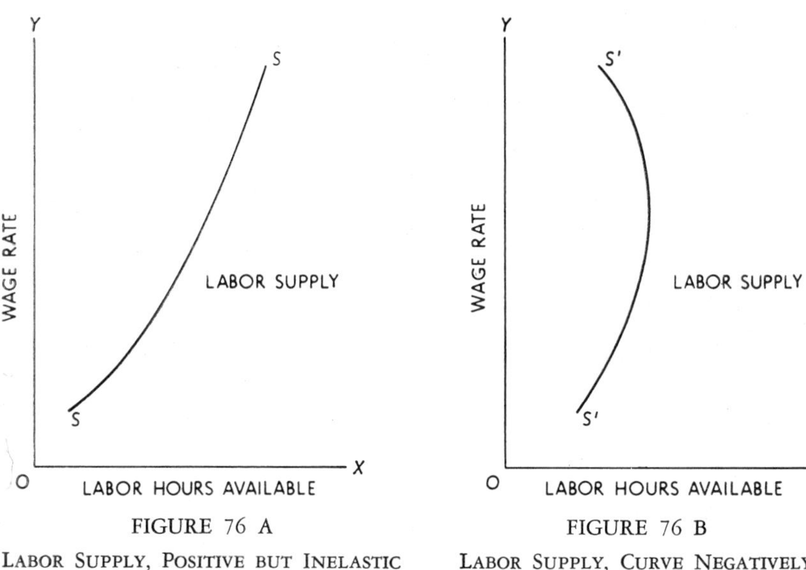

FIGURE 76 A

LABOR SUPPLY, POSITIVE BUT INELASTIC CURVE

FIGURE 76 B

LABOR SUPPLY, CURVE NEGATIVELY SLOPED IN PART

Some attempts have been made to study the nature of the supply schedule of labor empirically; while the studies are of limited scope and

[2] Wage rates may also affect, in a somewhat unpredictable fashion, the age at which persons retire and thus leave the labor market.

significance, they tend to support the hypothesis that the supply curve is either extremely inelastic or negatively sloped.[3]

Summary of Supply Conditions. The main thread of the analysis can now be resumed. The nature of the supply schedule for any particular type of labor depends upon two primary considerations: (1) the mobility of labor from other occupations to this one, and (2) the extent to which the wage level influences the number of hours persons are willing to work, and the number of persons willing to enter the labor market. The former influence produces a positive-sloped segment in the supply curve; the latter in some instances may produce a negative-sloped element. If there is any significant mobility of labor into and out of the occupation, it is likely that the former consideration will outweigh the latter. The total supply schedule for all types of labor, however, is affected only by the second consideration, and thus is likely to be extremely inelastic and perhaps negative (backward-sloping) in part.

Supply-Demand Relations and the Wage Rate

Given the demand schedule for the particular type of labor based upon the marginal revenue product, the supply of this type of labor, and market conditions of pure competition, the basic wage will adjust to the level at which the supply and demand are equal, as illustrated in Figure 77. At any higher price, some workers will be unable to find employment, and will bid down the wage level until all can be employed. If the wage level is below the supply-demand equilibrium, the demand for workers exceeds the supply, and the wage rate rises through competition among the employers for labor. When the equilibrium is established, the wage is equal to the marginal revenue product of the particular type of labor, with all of the available workers of this type who seek employment in the occupation at the given wage being employed. Given the general price level, the real wage level is determined by the money wage level.

This analysis is based upon several simplifying assumptions, which must be stressed:

1. Pure competition in the labor market, and thus the absence of labor unions on the one hand, and monopsonistic domination of wages by the employer, on the other.
2. Productivity of the workers, independent of the wage rate paid.

[3] A summary of these empirical studies is to be found in the article by George Break, "Income Taxes, Wage Rates, and the Incentive to Supply Labor Service," *National Tax Journal,* Vol. VI (December, 1953), pp. 333–52.

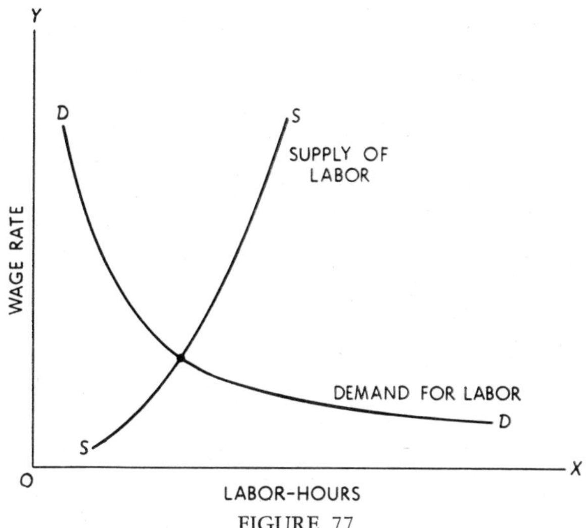

FIGURE 77

DETERMINATION OF THE WAGE LEVEL FOR A PARTICULAR OCCUPATION, WITH PURE COMPETITION IN THE LABOR MARKET

3. Positively sloping supply curve for labor.
4. Given general level of commodity prices; thus a change in money wages is accompanied by a similar change in real wages.
5. Given total demand for commodities, independent of the wage rates paid.

The assumption of pure competition is, of course, not applicable in many labor markets, and the significance for wage determination of deviations from this assumption will be considered in the next chapter. Failure of the second and third assumptions to be realized in particular cases makes possible more than one equilibrium position. If wage increases lead to greater productivity, for example, by allowing workers to maintain a better level of health and efficiency and raising morale, there may be a substantial range of equilibrium wage figures. Within this range an increase in wages will be accompanied by an increase in marginal revenue product, and the new figure may be as stable an equilibrium figure as the old.

If the supply is in part negatively sloped, there is also a possibility of several equilibria, any one of which is stable. In graphical terms, the supply curve and the demand curve may intersect at more than one point, as shown on Figure 78 (page 334).

The last two assumptions, of a given general price level and given total demand for commodities, are not necessarily realistic, and will be considered in later sections.

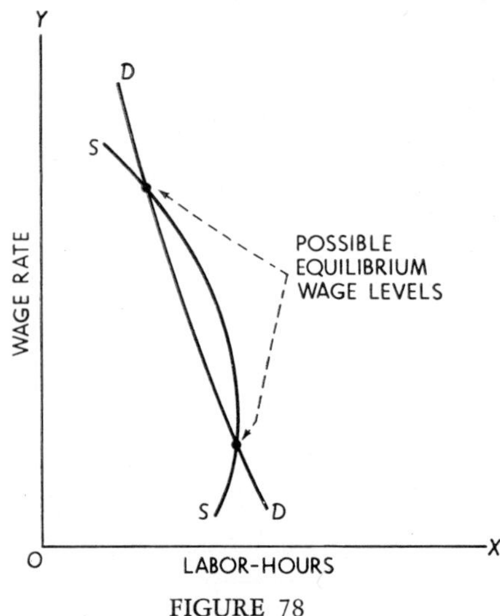

FIGURE 78

A NEGATIVELY SLOPED SUPPLY CURVE FOR LABOR AND TWO EQUILIBRIUM WAGE LEVELS

Wage Interrelationships

Before these problems are analyzed, it is desirable to note the interrelationships of wages in various occupations, under assumptions of pure competition. For each type of labor, there will exist (given the assumptions) demand and supply schedules, which will determine the actual level of wages for each occupation. But these various wage levels are interdependent, because of the substitutability of various types of labor for one another, and the possibility of the flow of labor among occupations. Accordingly, particular levels are stable only if they are mutually consistent with one another. For example, if the wages paid in one occupation rise sharply, not only would the demand for other types of labor which could be substituted for this type rise, but also the supply of workers in the other occupations would fall as workers shifted to the one in question. Thus the wages in other fields would rise, and check the flow of labor to the first occupation. Eventually a new equilibrium would be established at which there would be no net flows from one occupation to another, and no tendency for any of the wages to shift unless the basic determinants changed.

Wage Differentials. The preceding analysis can be extended to the explanation of wage differentials among various occupations, with the assumptions noted above, including that of pure competition, still being employed. The differentials at any time will depend on relative supply-demand conditions, and hence on relative marginal revenue product figures in various occupations, the tendency toward lessening of inequalities being restricted by the nonmobility of labor. At any one time, wages will be relatively high in occupations in which supply is limited relative to demand and marginal revenue product is high. The inability of other persons to move into the occupation quickly allows the high wage rate to continue for a period of time. Wages can never remain relatively high in a field in which immediate entry of large numbers of workers is possible.

Over a period of time, workers will tend to flow toward those occupations offering the greatest advantages relative to the costs of entering them, considering both monetary and nonmonetary factors. Certain occupations require longer periods of training than others, and it would be expected that the wage levels would remain sufficiently high in these to induce persons to undertake the added training. Some occupations have greater nonmonetary advantages, such as prestige, comfort of work, regularity of employment, etc., than others. Thus at equal wage rates workers would prefer these to other occupations, and differentials in money wages must remain in order to balance supplies of workers in various occupations with demand for them. Under the assumption of pure competition and lack of market imperfections, relative wages will eventually adjust to the levels at which the wage differentials exactly compensate for the higher costs of training and the monetary values of nonwage differences, so long as entry into occupations is not restricted by lack of sufficient numbers of persons with requisite abilities to perform the work involved. If there are such restrictions, the scarcity of this type of worker will maintain a higher wage differential than would exist on the basis of different training costs, etc. If the assumptions of perfect knowledge and mobility are dropped, the precise adjustments will not be attained and the adjustments will be slower, but the basic nature of the equilibrium position will be the same.

Geographical Wage Differences. Distinct from the occupational wage differentials are those among workers in given occupations in different areas. The labor market, for almost any type of labor, is not nation-wide, but covers a limited region only. At any time, the wage level in each market will depend on local supply-demand conditions, the geographical immobility of labor preventing any immediate regional equalization. Over a period of time, however, labor tends to flow to the high-wage areas, and real wages for a given occupation in various areas tend to equalize, unless workers find nonmonetary advantages of living in certain areas, such as California! Money wages, however, will not equalize when costs of living differ, as they frequently do, especially between rural and urban areas.

However, labor is by no means completely mobile, and differences which arise will continue for long periods. Moving is costly, and many persons are reluctant to move away from areas with which they are familiar, to look for jobs which they are not certain they will obtain. But the lack of labor mobility will be offset in part by mobility of other factors; industry tends to move to low wage areas, and thus to increase the marginal product of labor in these areas and to equalize the wage rates.

As noted in the following chapter, wage differentials have been modified by the development of labor unions.

THE GENERAL LEVEL OF WAGES

With equilibrium established among the wages of various occupations, the over-all pattern constitutes the general structure of wages, and the levels of the various types constitute the general level of money wages. Accordingly, given the prices of the commodities, the level of real wages and the share of labor in national income are determinate. With pure competition in all factor and commodity markets, a very precise relationship can be outlined between the wage level and the general level of prices; the commodity prices will consist of all labor costs, plus those of other factors likewise competitively determined on a supply-demand basis. With nonpurely competitive conditions in factor markets and commodity markets, the relationship between the wage level and the general price level will also be dependent upon the exact nature of competition in these other markets and the policies followed by the firms in cases of oligopoly.

The level of real wages, and thus labor's share in national income, will be dependent basically upon the marginal revenue product of the various types of labor employed. The higher the general level of the marginal revenue product of various types of labor compared to the marginal revenue product of other factors, the higher will be the over-all share of labor in the national product.

Changes in the Level of Wages

Given supply and demand schedules for various types of labor are based upon certain constants, which have been noted in the preceding discussion, and may be restated briefly:

A. Those affecting the supply and demand of one type of labor service, but not the over-all supply and demand of labor as a whole:

1. Relative skill of a certain type possessed by the workers
2. Wages paid in other occupations
3. Nonmonetary advantages of the various occupations
4. Relative preferences of workers for various types of work.

Changes in any of these will alter the demand and/or supply of workers in a particular occupation, and thus alter the wages in that occupation, and the differentials between the particular wage and those in other occupations. For example, if more workers gain a particular skill, the wages in this occupation will fall and those in others will rise. If one occupation becomes relatively more desirable (because, for example, of reduced drudgery through the development of new tools), labor supply will increase and the wages will tend to fall. Changes in these constants, however, have little or no effect on the general level of wages.

B. Those affecting the total demand for and supply of labor, as well as those in particular occupations:

1. Size and age-composition of the population
2. Over-all level of skills
3. Relative preferences of workers between work and leisure
4. Supplies and prices of other factors, and technological conditions
5. The general price level.

Changes in these constants will affect demand and supply conditions in various occupations, and alter the wages in these occupations without causing compensating changes in other fields. Accordingly the general wage level will change. The effects of changes in the second and third constants are obvious; the effects of changes in the others, however, require explanation.

Population. An increase in population will alter the labor supply, but will also affect the total demand for goods. The increase in labor supply, as such, by increasing the quantity of labor compared to the amounts of other factors, will lower the marginal revenue product of labor as a whole and reduce the average wage rate. However, the total output rises and the total real income of labor may increase, if the elasticity of substitution between labor, as a whole, and other factors is greater than one. The increased output and demand will stimulate capital formation; if the consequent increase in the amount of capital goods is substantial and if natural resources were relatively poorly utilized previously because of lack of manpower and materials, even the real wage *per worker* may increase as a net result of the various reactions produced by the population increase. Hence in an undeveloped country, population growth (through immigration, for example) may actually stimulate an increase in real wages per worker.

It was assumed thus far that the rate of population growth is an independent variable, not dependent upon the wage level. In earlier years, however, especially in the eighteenth and early nineteenth centuries, it was argued that a usual price-quantity relationship existed between wage levels and population growth. A high wage level would stimulate an increase in population, raise the labor supply, and lower wages until a subsistence level was reached; a fall below this would reduce the population and labor supply and increase wages. On the basis of this assumption, a long-run theory of wage levels (known as the Malthusian theory) was developed, which maintained that over a long-run period wages tended to a bare subsistence figure.

After the middle of the last century, however, it became evident that such a relationship between wage levels and population growth was not valid. As real wage levels rose, the birth rate tended to fall, and accordingly wages did not tend toward a subsistence level. Ultimately the assumption of a direct relationship between wages and labor supply was abandoned. However, in recent years experience suggests that there may be some correlation between continued high wage rates and full employment and a high birth rate. But so many other factors influence population trends that it does not appear feasible to establish any significant functional relationship between population and the real wage level, except perhaps in primitive economic societies in which population growth is continuously restricted by inadequate food supply.

Changes in Supplies and Quality of Other Factors. The wage level will obviously be affected by changes in supplies of other factors. An increase in the amount of capital goods, for example, will tend to increase the marginal productivity of labor and the level of real wages. However, there will be some incentive to replace labor by capital goods, and this substitution effect may increase the relative share of total income going to suppliers of money capital, if the elasticity of substitution is high. Furthermore, even though the real income of labor will rise, the demand for certain types of labor—those for which the new capital goods are a direct substitute—may fall, and these particular classes of workers, whose skills may not easily be transferable to other lines of work, may actually suffer a decline in real wages.

This decline is particularly evident when new types of capital equipment, which are labor saving in nature, are introduced. Such a change may create substantial temporary unemployment among those workers displaced by the new equipment, but unemployment will not continue unless the general determinants of the level of national income and employment, discussed in Chapter 22, are such that full employment is not possible. From the standpoint of its effect upon wages, a laborsaving invention is in a sense the equivalent of an increase in labor supply. Total output will rise and total income of the workers as a whole will rise, but the share of national income going to the suppliers of money capital will increase. As the workers initially losing their jobs are re-employed, as they will be unless at full employment total expenditures in the economy are less than national income, the real income per worker could conceivably fall, if the decline in money wages more than offsets the lower prices of goods due to improved technology. But this result is unlikely; so long as demand is at all elastic, real wages will rise, even after all of the initially unemployed find jobs again. As noted in subsequent chapters, new inventions are of great importance in maintaining adequate investment for full employment, and the advantages from this standpoint constitute an offsetting factor against the temporary unemployment which the laborsaving invention may create, just as does the higher level of output. When inventions are of a capital-saving form instead of labor saving, the relative gains to labor will be greater.

Changes in the General Price Level. A shift in the general price level will alter the demand for and the supply of labor at given prices and tend to alter the money wage level. If prices rise, for example, the marginal revenue product of labor will rise, and thus the demand for labor, at given money wage rates. If the higher prices do not affect the supply of labor, the wage rate will rise. If the increase in demand is proportional to the increase in the price level, and the supply of labor is perfectly inelastic, wages and prices will rise in the same proportion, and the general level of real wages will remain unchanged.

However, the rise in money wages may alter the supply of labor, despite a comparable increase in prices, because of the phenomenon known as the money illusion. It is widely believed that workers are influenced in their actions to a much greater extent by the money wage level than by the price level, as witnessed by the fact that workers who will refuse to work if the money wage is lowered will not even think of ceasing work if the general price level rises and lowers the real wage. Accordingly, when money wages are adjusting upward to a change in the price level, the quantity of labor may shift in the same manner as it would if money wages went up and prices stayed the same. Thus real wages will be altered.

One other effect of the money illusion is to make the supply schedule of labor particularly inelastic to changes in real wages caused by price level changes.

Unemployment and Wage Rates

The analysis thus far suggests that in the absence of departures from pure competition and market imperfections involuntary unemployment could not exist. Any excess of labor supply over demand would result in wage reductions which would allow restoration of full employment. This conclusion may be valid under the static assumptions upon which the analysis is based: a given general price level, and a given volume of total expenditure. These assumptions are not unrealistic with respect to the analysis of wage and employment determination of a small sector of the economy; if, for example, bricklayers are unemployed, and the market is perfect and purely competitive, wages paid for this work would tend to fall, and re-equate supply and demand. The lower money wage would not significantly affect the general price level or total expenditures; the real wage would fall, more bricklayers would be used relative to other factor units, and more brick houses would be sold.

Even under these assumptions, however, it is possible that peculiarities in the reaction of workers to a wage reduction may produce a type of unemployment which is in a sense voluntary, yet has many features of involuntary unemployment. Suppose, for example, that at a current wage rate of $2.00 per hour, the actual number of workers employed is 440 while 640 workers seek employment in the particular occupation. If the market is purely and perfectly competitive, and the supply curve has a positive slope, the competition of the unemployed would cause the wage rate to fall (to $1.50 per hour, on Figure 79). But there appears to be a great reluctance, in some instances, for persons out of work to accept a lower wage than the "prevailing" figure, even in the absence of union organization. This reaction is a phenomenon of psychological reactions, the explanation of which is beyond the realm of economics. In other words, the lower portion of the labor supply curve takes on the location of the broken line on Figure 79. The actual supply of labor at the wage of $2.00, when this wage has prevailed for a period of time, as indicated by the horizontal line through *W;* that is, it is perfectly elastic at the $2.00 wage figure (up to 640 workers, or *W* on Figure 79), and thus the excess supply at the $2.00 rate essentially vanishes. Or, in other words, the labor supply, at wages below $2.00, which would consist of the amounts indicated by the *SS* curve if the wage has been rising to these levels, will be zero at these figures if the wage has been at $2.00 and falls back. The wage level was set at

$2.00 in the previous period on the basis of supply-demand considerations in that period; as demand falls off, the supply contracts as well. In a sense the consequent unemployment may be regarded as involuntary. But it nevertheless is a form which is generally considered contrary to the attainment of optimum economic welfare.

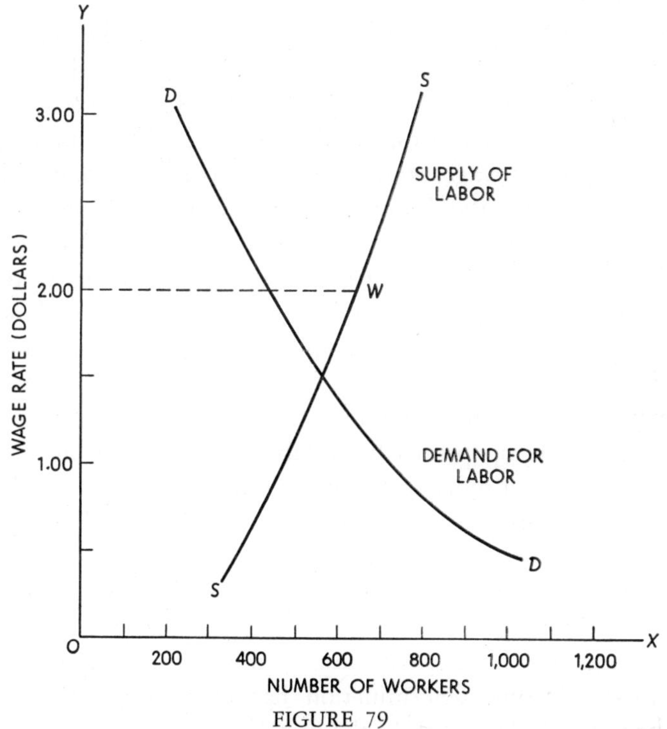

FIGURE 79

ADJUSTMENT OF THE WAGE IN THE CASE OF UNEMPLOYMENT

Even if workers are willing to accept lower-than-prevailing wage rates, imperfections in the labor market (distinct from the effects of unions noted in the following chapter) will tend to restrict the downward adjustment and perpetuate unemployment. In many cases, it is likely that the unemployed units cannot compete successfully with the employed units for jobs; the conditions of hire are such in many instances that persons out of work cannot easily underbid those who have jobs.

General Unemployment

When unemployment becomes widespread, the preceding analysis is of little assistance in a study of its causes and solutions, in large measure because of the simplifying assumptions of a given general price level and total expenditures (consumption plus investment) in the economy. Suppose, for example, that a decline in investment spending reduces total output and employment, and, as a consequence, throughout the economy in virtually all occupations supply of labor exceeds the demand at existing wage rates. Will wage rates fall, and will the decline restore full employment?

With respect to the first question, the analysis of the preceding section suggests that, at least in some instances, even in the absence of monopsony and unions, wage reductions will be slow to occur. But these may be only exceptional cases; in other instances there should be some tendency for money wages to drop, so long as purely competitive conditions prevail. But if the decline in money wages is accompanied by a comparable decline in prices of commodities, a reduction in real wages, which is essential if employment is to rise, will not occur. With purely competitive conditions in factor and commodity markets, and even with considerable deviation from pure competition in the latter, such a price decline is almost inevitable when wages fall. Since marginal costs consist primarily of wage and materials costs (which themselves are directly or indirectly made up primarily of labor costs), a decline in money wages will produce a more or less comparable reduction in prices, in a manner similar to the effect of an increase in wages noted in the preceding sections. Thus little change may occur in real wages.

Will the decline in money wages provide any stimulus to employment, even if real wages are unaffected? There are several ways in which such influences may be exerted; these cannot be explained satisfactorily until national income determination has been considered, and will merely be noted at this point. In the first place, since less money will be needed for transactions purposes at the lower general price level, the interest rate will tend to fall, and stimulate investment. Secondly, the increased real value (in terms of purchasing power) of accumulated wealth will rise, and reduce somewhat the propensity of persons to save additional amounts; the higher relative level of consumption will stimulate production. Finally, the lower wage level reduces the cost of new machinery, and, if the low wage-price level is believed to be temporary, firms will be encouraged to undertake investment. However, if the initial price decrease gives rise to expectations that further decreases will occur, firms will delay replacement and new investment, and the decline will be aggravated. It is commonly argued that if with the coming of unemployment wages fell sharply, with the expectation that the decline would not continue, employment would be stimulated, while a slow downward movement, which gives rise to expectations of continued declines, will have the opposite effect.

One final factor is the effect of the wage decline on the distribution of income, and thus upon the over-all consumption-savings ratio. The wage decline will tend to increase the proportion of total income received by the fixed income receivers, who are largely in the higher income levels; as a consequence, the over-all savings ratio may be increased, and the decline in production and employment aggravated. However, if the wage reduction does initially stimulate employment, the sharing of the wage payments over more persons may have the opposite effect. The net result is difficult to predict on any general basis.

On the whole, therefore, even with purely competitive markets, the development of unemployment, particularly on a mass scale resulting from declines in national income, is not likely to produce significant declines in the rate of real wages, partly because of the market imperfections and the reactions of unemployed workers to wage cuts, but more fundamentally because of the tendency of price changes to follow wage changes, thus restricting changes in real wages.

The usual supply-demand or marginal productivity analysis is a useful tool, so long as purely competitive conditions are approximated, in analyzing wage level adjustments in particular occupations in periods of general full employment and, in modified form, even in periods of unemployment. But it is not adequate in explaining general wage and employment behavior in periods of mass unemployment. In these periods wages do not necessarily adjust to supply-demand levels in the usual sense of the term; while, so long as profits are maximized, the wage rate will equal the marginal revenue product with the given number of workers employed, this is not the figure of marginal revenue product with all workers available at the wage rate employed, and therefore is dependent in part upon the actual volume of employment, the explanation of which must be delayed until later chapters.

Meanwhile, however, it is necessary to extend the analysis of market wage determination to consider the major cases involving departure from purely competitive conditions. On the basis of empirical observations, it is obvious that purely competitive labor markets are rare and that two major cases, (1) monopsonistic control of wages by employers, and (2) bilateral oligopoly or bargaining between unions of workers and monopsonistic employers, are the most common. A third, the domination of wages by unions, appears to be of some significance. The two major cases will be considered in the following chapter.

SELECTED REFERENCES

HICKS, J. R. *The Theory of Wages.* London: Macmillan, 1932.

The best exposition of the marginal productivity theory of wages.

ROTHSCHILD, K. W. *The Theory of Wages.* London: Macmillan, 1954.

The most complete recent analysis of wage determination under various conditions.

DOUGLAS, PAUL. *The Theory of Wages.* New York: Macmillan, 1934.

A summary of empirical studies of forces affecting labor demand and supply.

FELLNER, WILLIAM and HALEY, B. F. (eds.). *Readings in the Theory of Income Distribution,* chaps. xii–xix. Philadelphia: Blakiston, 1949.

A series of reprints of articles on wage theory. On pages 685–93 a detailed bibliography on wage theory is provided.

HALEY, B. F. "Value and Distribution," *A Survey of Contemporary Economics* (ed. H. S. ELLIS), pp. 28–38. Homewood, Ill.: Richard D. Irwin, Inc., 1948.

A survey of recent literature on wage theory.

LESTER, R. A. "Shortcomings of Marginal Analysis for Wage-Employment Problems," *American Economic Review,* Vol. XXXVI (March, 1946), pp. 63–82.

A severe criticism of the marginal productivity analysis. A similar point of view is expressed in other writings by Lester.

BREAK, GEORGE F. "Income Taxes, Wage Rates, and the Incentive to Supply Labor Services," *National Tax Journal,* Vol. IV (December, 1953), pp. 333–52.

One of the most complete reviews of the effects of wage changes upon labor supply.

QUESTIONS

1. What are the major characteristics of labor service which are significant for the determination of wages?
2. Under what conditions will the demand for labor be highly inelastic?
3. Why may the marginal revenue product of labor fall very sharply beyond a certain point?
4. List the constants upon which a given demand schedule for labor is based.
5. Why is the supply of any particular type of labor more elastic than that of labor as a whole?
6. List the major determinants of the supply of a particular type of labor at any one time.
7. Why is the supply of a particular type of labor more elastic over a long period than in a relatively short period?
8. What considerations determine the extent to which workers will shift from one occupation to another as relative wages change?

9. Distinguish between the income effect and the substitution effect of a wage increase upon total labor supply.
10. Under what circumstances will a wage increase cause persons to work fewer hours? To drop out of the labor market completely?
11. Railroads have at times discovered that increases in wages paid section hands cause a reduction in the number of man-hours of such labor available. On the other hand, it became apparent during World War II, particularly in Canada, that beyond a certain point, further reductions in take-home pay resulting from income tax increases caused a falling off in the supply of labor hours available in certain fields, especially in mining, because of increased absenteeism. Explain the difference between the two situations in terms of the analysis of labor supply.
12. What is meant by a "backward-sloping" supply curve of labor?
13. Why is the total over-all supply of labor to the economy as a whole generally believed to be highly inelastic?
14. Explain the determination of the actual wage level, with purely competitive conditions in the labor market.
15. Explain how both the supply and demand schedules of various types of labor are interrelated.
16. On what basis can wage differentials between various occupations at any particular time be explained?
17. With complete mobility of labor, to what levels will the differentials in relative wages in different occupations tend, over a period of time?
18. How would you explain each of the following:
    a) The relatively low wage level for store clerks?
    b) The relatively high hourly earnings in the building trades?
    c) Lower pay of university professors compared to that of persons of similar training and ability employed in research work by business firms?
    d) Low wages for farm labor?
    e) Lower wages for carpenters in small towns than in large cities?
19. Why do geographical wage differences, in real terms, tend to remain for long periods?
20. Under what circumstances will an increase in population increase per capita real wages? Reduce them?
21. Upon what premise was the "iron law of wages"—the theory that the wage level tends to bare subsistence—based?
22. What effect will an increase in the total quantity of capital goods have upon the per capita real wage level?
23. Why does a 5 per cent increase in the general price level (with given money wages) not necessarily have the same effect upon the available labor supply as a 5 per cent decline in money wages, given the general price level?
24. Why, even in the absence of unions, may wages be slow to adjust downward when some workers are unemployed?
25. Why, in a period of unemployment, do general wage declines probably have little effect in restoring full employment?

Chapter 15 WAGE DETERMINATION IN NONPURELY COMPETITIVE LABOR MARKETS

Numerous empirical studies of labor relations, plus everyday observations, suggest that purely competitive labor markets are very rare. In extremely few labor markets are there large numbers of small employers, all acting independently of one another, hiring nonunionized workers, with market wages constantly adjusting to maintain equilibrium between supply of and demand for labor. While much of the analysis of the previous chapter is relevant for various aspects of wage and employment determination, it is not useful for purposes of direct analysis of the determination of money-wage rates in most cases.

In some instances, to a greater degree in the past than at the present time, the employer has a superior bargaining position, and takes the initiative in setting the wage; the worker with no organization for collective bargaining has the choice of working or not working at the figure set. This is the case of monopsonistic domination of wage rates. In many cases, however, workers have formed unions which bargain for them; while in a few instances the union may dictate the wage itself, the development of unions ordinarily results in the determination of the wage by bargaining between union and employer, or employer group. This type of market is essentially one of bilateral oligopoly, or, if there is but one union and one group of employers involved, bilateral monopoly.

MONOPSONISTIC INFLUENCES IN THE LABOR MARKET

Until unions developed in strength, wages were typically set by the employer, with individual employers in many cases exercising substantial influence over the actual wage level. This situation remains in many instances today, in the case of nonunionized employees. Employer domination of wages was a product of situations in which the number of employers was much smaller than the number of workers; the workers were not highly mobile from one employer to another, and the bargaining position of the workers as individuals was inherently weaker than that of the employer. In each particular labor market which, especially in the past, has been very limited in size, the number of employers is often so small that effective competition for workers does not occur. In other markets, although the total number of employers is large, so much of the total labor force is used by a few employers that they are able to dominate the wage level. Apart from the difference in numbers, the tactical position of the employer and that of the individual worker are substantially different. In general it is much more important for a worker to obtain and hold a particular job than it is for the employer to hire the particular man. Failure to obtain a job leaves the typical worker without any source of income; as a consequence, he cannot wait for a more favorable bargain as can the employer. Labor service is perishable; the labor service of one day cannot be stored and sold on another day, whereas the property of the employer will not deteriorate in comparable fashion. The employer will not find his own income and living standard impaired by failure to hire any particular man.

The Determinants of the Extent of Employer Dominance

The influence which each employer enjoys over wages is dependent in part upon the mobility of the workers, and in part upon the extent of competition among employers for the workers. If the workers move freely from one firm to another, and if the firms act independently of one another in determining wage and employment policy, the actual control over wages by any one employer is small. But in practice, the mobility of workers is severely limited. Most workers are tied rather closely to a particular firm by various bonds, and will not move easily in response to wage differentials. These bonds include the privileges based upon seniority in the present job, such as pension and continued-employment rights, the reluctance of workers to leave one job until they find another, the preference for living in a particular locality and working with friends, and the use by employers of personnel and hiring policies which prevent effective competition between those seeking employment in the firm and those already employed. Most employers are not "job-shoppers" as long as they find their present employment reasonably satisfactory.

The control of particular employers over wage rates depends also upon the extent to which employers agree with one another upon wage policies, or take into consideration the effects of their wage-employment policies upon those of other firms. When common action, either with or without outright agreement, develops, the situation becomes one of oligopsony. Thus two cases of employer-dominated wage determination must be distinguished: the case in which each employer acts independently but immobility gives him some control over the wage level, and the case of mutual interdependence. Each case will be considered in turn.

Labor Immobility and Monopsonistic Competition

When labor is not completely mobile among firms, essentially each worker has some preference for working for a particular firm, and, therefore, assuming independence of action on the part of the employers, the situation is one of monopsonistic competition—the situation comparable, on the buyer's side of the market, to monopolistic competition. The basic feature of this type of labor market is the recognition on the part of the employer that the wage which he must pay will depend upon the number of workers hired; that is, the supply schedule of labor to him is not perfectly elastic. The less the mobility of workers among the various firms, the less elastic the schedule will be.

Since additional workers (at least beyond a certain point) can be obtained only by offering a higher wage, the marginal outlay on additional workers exceeds the wage paid; on Figure 80, the marginal outlay curve (*MO*) is above the supply curve of labor available to the particular employer (*SS*). The employer, in adding workers up to the point at which *marginal outlay* is equal to marginal revenue product, will not reach the point at which the *wage* is equal to the marginal revenue product. At each wage rate he will hire a smaller number of workers than he would if the supply schedule of labor were perfectly elastic. For example, in Figure 80 he will hire *on* workers, rather than *om.* Since the same considerations apply to all employers in the market the total demand for the particular type of labor at each wage rate will be less than it would be if the labor market were purely competitive, and thus the actual wage will be lower.

It must be emphasized that the supply price—the amount the employer must pay to get a given number of workers—depends primarily upon the exact degree of immobility of labor, or in other words, upon the alternative opportunities of the workers. Two extreme cases may be noted. If there is but one employer in a certain market (perhaps in an isolated mining town) and workers cannot move, the necessary wage would be an extremely low figure—one just high enough to induce the workers to seek employment instead of starving to death. At the other extreme is the case in which workers are highly (but not perfectly) mobile among employers; the supply schedule will be highly elastic, and competition among the employers for labor will bring the wage level close to the purely competitive figure, even though the initiative in the setting of the wage figure rests with the employer. Between these extremes there is a wide variety of possible cases, differing on the basis of the exact degree of elasticity of labor supply among firms.

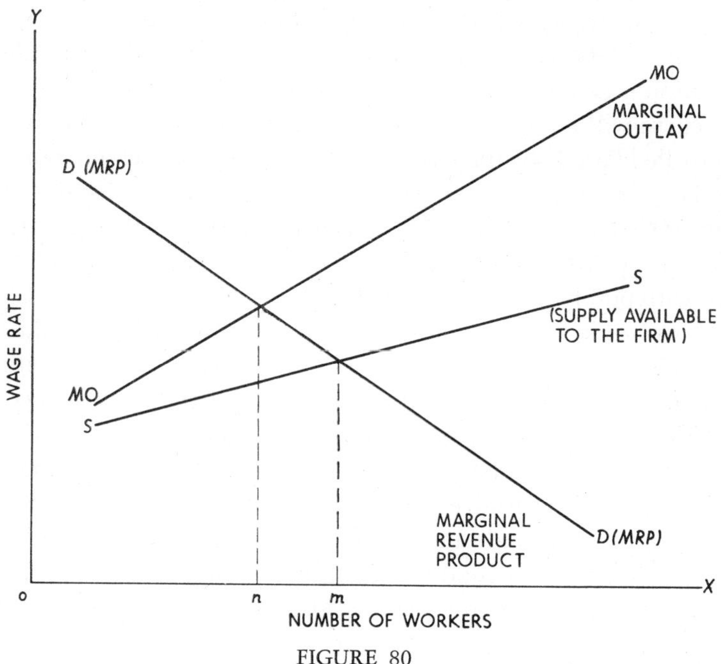

FIGURE 80

DETERMINATION BY AN EMPLOYER OF THE NUMBER OF MEN TO HIRE, MONOPSONISTIC COMPETITION OR MONOPSONY

Oligopsony

The second case of employer wage domination is that in which employers are conscious of wage interdependence; each firm realizes that changes in the wage which it pays will result in changes on the part of other firms. Whenever the number of firms in a particular labor market is small, oligopsony attitudes are likely to be common. In this situation, either by outright collusion, or merely by independent but coordinate actions, firms will avoid bidding workers away from other firms by wage increases, since they recognize that the increases will merely cause other firms to make comparable increases, and they will gain few additional workers. Under such circumstances there is no tendency for wages or even marginal outlay on labor to adjust to equality with marginal revenue product, since each firm stops hiring workers short of the point at which this equality is attained. The actual level will be in large measure a product of historical accident, coupled with the factor of current labor mobility to and from employment in the particular field. If the wages are set by outright collusion, the formal principles of setting will be comparable to those of the firm in monopsonistic competition acting independently, as analyzed above, but the marginal-outlay curve will be that confronting the firms as a group, and thus will be controlled largely by the general mobility of labor into and out of the particular labor market, and will be much less elastic than the curve confronting a particular firm. The degree of elasticity will determine the extent to which the wage level will be less than the figure which would prevail with purely competitive conditions.

However, in practice, employers may voluntarily pay considerably higher wages than the minimum figure necessary to obtain the optimum number of employees. In the first place, many employers believe that the quality of the workers which they can obtain and the productivity of their labor force will be affected by the wage level. Higher than necessary wages will be paid to attract particularly qualified workers, to maintain employee morale and efficiency at high levels, and to minimize costly labor turnover. Secondly, there is the possibility that purely noneconomic considerations, such as the ideas of the employer about the minimum wage necessary for a decent living standard, and the prestige value of paying "good" wages may lead an employer to pay more than the minimum. Some employers have been influenced by the principle that a high level of wages increases consumption and the general level of business activity. In depressions many firms are reluctant to cut wages because of public censure for aggravating the decline in incomes. An even stronger force which at present leads many employers to pay higher-than-minimum wages is the fear that the payment of lower wages will lead to unionization. Wage levels in unionized fields now exercise great influence on nonunion wage levels, largely because of this consideration. Finally, in some instances minimum wage laws will prevent payment of less than a certain figure.

Monopsonistic Power and Unemployment

The existence of unemployment in the labor markets is likely to increase monopsonistic power by reducing still further the mobility of labor. The lessened possibility of job opportunities elsewhere tends to make the worker more reluctant to leave his present employment. On the other hand, the existence of unemployment makes collusion among employers less important, since there is less danger of employers bidding against each other for workers. Apart from the effects of this latter consideration, it would be expected that in fields of monopsonistic domination of wages, sharp declines in wages would occur in depression periods as the mobility of labor falls. Actually, however, the evidence does not bear out this contention.[1]

In part the failure of wages to fall rapidly in these fields can be attributed to the insistence of workers on certain money wages if they are to work at all—an attitude found in nonunion as well as in union fields. This position, of course, can be maintained by the unemployed workers only so long as they are able to gain support from reserves or relief. But beyond this factor, the answer can be obtained only in terms of the failure of employers to act in setting wages along those lines which will allow maximum profits, or of deliberate sacrifice of short-run profits in the belief that such a policy will allow higher profits over a longer period. Rees offers several specific suggestions as to why employers do not cut wages drastically in nonunionized fields when unemployment is widespread.[2] Employers may fear public disapproval and adverse governmental action, or the development of unions, or general loss in labor morale. In the case of corporations, the fear that the wage cut may lead to a demand for lower managerial salaries may play a part in checking reductions.

LABOR UNIONS AND WAGE DETERMINATION

In most industries wages are no longer set by the employer but are determined through negotiations between unions, representing the workers, and employers or groups of employers. The significance of negotiated wages extends beyond the industries in which such methods are used; in nonunion firms today, wage rates are greatly influenced by union scales in other plants for similar work.

Employer Policies

Analysis of wage determination in situations in which unions bargain with the employers is complex, as is the explanation of pricing in any situation of bilateral monopoly or oligopoly. It is possible, however, to note the major considerations affecting union and employer policy.

[1] See A. Rees, "Wage Determination and Involuntary Unemployment," *Journal of Political Economy,* Vol. LIX (April, 1951), pp. 143–53. Other studies show similar results.

[2] *Ibid.*

The case of the employer is the simpler of the two. The employer wishes to pay no more than the amount necessary to retain the desired labor force; thus the general principle which guides his action is the same as that in the case in which unions are absent. However, the presence of the union may affect the figure that the employer is willing to pay voluntarily, without actual union pressure on wages. In some instances the presence of the union may deter him from making increases that he would otherwise voluntarily give, in order to avoid possible strengthening of the union, and to wait until the union insists upon an increase. There is danger that if he voluntarily gives an increase, the union will simply seek to obtain still more. In other instances, however, he may voluntarily give more than he otherwise would pay in order to protect the position of union officials whom he regards as less undesirable than their rivals for union power. Likewise, he may voluntarily offer relatively high wages to forestall union insistence upon other concessions, such as a closed shop or restrictive working rules.

With collective bargaining, the level which the employer will voluntarily pay is of much less significance than the maximum figure which he will not exceed. There are essentially two maxima: the figure above which the employer will not go unless forced by a strike, and the highest figure which he will pay and continue to operate. If the employer realizes that the union is sufficiently strong to make a strike completely effective and hold out until the desired wage is obtained, his two maxima are likely to be the same; he will realize that it is futile to provoke a strike and will go as high as his absolute maximum figure on the basis of negotiations alone. But commonly the employer will doubt the ability of the union to make the strike fully effective, and thus he may refuse in negotiations alone to go to his full maximum figure. Frequently, he does not know what the unions are actually willing to settle for and will refuse to go above a certain figure in the belief that the union will eventually accept it. In deciding upon this negotiation maximum figure, the employer will be influenced by several major considerations. His estimate of the strength of the union and its ability to call a strike is particularly significant, as well as his guess about the figure for which the union will actually settle. In addition, he will be influenced by the effect that the strike will have upon the business, which depends to a large extent upon the current rate of profit, the ability to meet fixed obligations in the event of the strike, the effect of disruption of operations upon good will, and the likelihood of permanent loss of customers. If current profits are low but cash reserves are high, fixed obligations small and the market is of such a nature that customers will not be lost permanently by the strike, the injury to the firm will be small. The employer's negotiation maximum will also be influenced by his views with regard to "proper" wage levels for the particular type of work. These views will be affected by wage levels of other employers. Finally, the height of the wage which the employer will concede through negotiations is influenced in many cases by his desire to ward off other union demands, such as a union shop policy; therefore, he may concede much more than otherwise in the form of wages if the union will drop these demands.

The employer's absolute maximum—the figure above which he will not go regardless of the pressure of a strike or other means—is the figure which will allow him to earn the minimum return which he regards as essential for continued operations. In a relatively short period of time, the maximum is the figure which would permit him to earn anything at all above average variable cost—subject to the modification that a firm may operate for a time even though it is not covering average variable cost if it expects an improvement. Over a longer period, the maximum wage is the figure which will allow the employer to earn an average return on investment.

The employer's negotiation and absolute maximum figures are influenced significantly by the ability to readjust prices in response to the wage changes and by the effect of the price changes upon sales. These reactions, in turn, are dependent upon the nature of competition in the industry and the scope of the wage increase. A firm in pure competition knows that it cannot adjust price at all in any direct fashion. The producers may realize that the general wage change may ultimately affect prices—if all or most firms are subject to the change—but this is likely to be viewed as a very vague and indefinite possibility. With monopolistic competition, the demand schedules for the product of each firm will appear to be so elastic that price increases adequate to shift forward the wage increase are clearly unprofitable. With strong differentiation or oligopoly, however, the chances of shifting the wage increase forward are much brighter, and the employer's maximum figures will be correspondingly greater.

The significance of a wage increase to an employer and hence the willingness of the latter to grant the increase are greatly affected by the scope of the wage change, that is, the number of competing firms affected. A wage increase universal throughout an industry is much less injurious than one applying only to the firm, since shifting forward the increase will be much more feasible. If the wage increase is universal in the industry and all firms make compensatory price increases, the injury to the employer's profits arises only from a decline in total sales of the product. The extent of the decline is controlled directly by the elasticity of total demand for the product. The behavior of profits is also affected by wage adjustments occurring in other sectors of the economy. If all —or most—industries are experiencing comparable wage increases, and thus the bulk of the workers in the economy are obtaining higher money wages, the decline in sales due to the price increases may be offset by increases in demand caused by the rise in money incomes throughout the economy.

Union Wage Policies

Analysis of union wage policy is far more difficult than the analysis of employer policy. The primary difficulty arises from the fact that the union itself is not a seller of labor but essentially a political institution representing the workers and having aims of its own distinct from those of its members. The most important of the union aims is that of union survival and growth. As a consequence, it is difficult to apply the "maximizing" approach—which has been used in the analysis of all economic behavior thus far—to the policies of unions; there is no clearly defined single magnitude which unions are seeking to maximize.[3]

What Do Unions Attempt to Maximize? The most obvious assumption which may be made with respect to union goals is that of maximization of the total wage bill, that is, the total amount of wages received by all union members. This is comparable to the profit-maximization assumption applied to business firms, and would be clearly acceptable if the unions were actually selling labor service. But, of course, this is not the case. In many instances the wage-bill maximization goal is unacceptable to the union members because the attainment of this objective would cause the unemployment of some members of the union. The wage level which would allow employment for all members of the union is not necessarily the one which allows the maximum total wage payment, and thus, if the union considers the welfare of those members who lose their jobs, it cannot pursue the maximum wage-bill goal. On the other hand, the union may be so dominated by the presently employed members that it completely disregards the interests of the unemployed members and seeks a maximum wage bill for those now employed. For example, in a particular situation in which unemployment exists, it is possible that a wage cut might allow re-

[3] The "maximization" approach to union policy is presented by John T. Dunlop, *Wage Determination under Trade Unions* (New York: Macmillan, 1944). For a criticism of this approach see A. M. Ross, *Trade Union Wage Policy* (Berkeley: University of California Press, 1948).

employment of those out of work and increase the total wage payment, if the demand for the labor is elastic. But since the incomes of the presently employed members would fall, they may refuse to accept the cut.

Pursuit of either of these goals (maximum total wage bill, or maximum wage bill for the presently employed members) requires that the union consider the effects of its wage policies upon the volume of employment available for its members. There is evidence that in some instances unions clearly consider the relationship between the wage and the job opportunities, especially when the employers are subject to strong competition in the product market, and when the industry is not completely organized.[4] However, there is substantial evidence that unions, especially in periods of full employment, tend to assume that the numbers of employees hired by the firms are determined largely by technological requirements and are independent of the wage rate, at least so long as the wage does not force liquidation of the firm—a possibility often regarded as very remote. If the unions determine their policies under the assumption of a perfectly inelastic demand schedule for labor, the goals of wage-bill maximization are meaningless, since, if the demand schedule for labor is regarded as being perfectly inelastic, there is no total finite figure of a maximum wage bill. Essentially the union is simply pursuing the goal of attaining a daily wage as high as possible. The oft-quoted goal of union leaders with respect to wages—"higher and higher, without limit"—is perhaps the most realistic single statement, although an incomplete one, about union wage aims. Unfortunately, recognition of this fact further complicates wage analysis, since in terms of this assumption the labor "maximum" is not a finite measurable magnitude.

The actual wage demands which the unions make depend not only upon the goals which the unions are seeking to attain, but also upon the tactics which the union officials believe to be the most satisfactory ones to attain the goals. These tactics, in turn, are influenced by the desire of the union officials to insure the survival and expansion of the union, and the protection of their own positions.

Union Wage Demands. In determining precise demands, the union officials are likely to have in mind two sets of figures—the one for which they are actually fighting and their initial asking figure. The former, which is the really significant figure, is influenced greatly by the increases being obtained by other unions. If a 15-cent hourly in-

[4] See G. P. Shultz and C. A. Myers, "Union Wage Decisions and Employment," *American Economic Review,* Vol. XL (June, 1950), pp. 362–80.

crease is being accepted by other unions, the union officials may feel it necessary to obtain this amount to prevent the members from becoming dissatisfied with the existing union or at least its management. As a consequence, a few wage bargains in major industries—steel and automobile production, for example—are likely to set the pattern for wage increases throughout the economy. Apart from the increases obtained currently by other unions, the officials will be influenced by their estimate of membership sentiment. The forces molding this sentiment are difficult to analyze; cost-of-living changes and wage changes of preceding years play a part. Estimates of the employers' willingness to meet demands and their ability—as determined by their present profit position and the possibility of raising prices without serious losses in sales—influence union wage goals. Finally, the unions must balance wage goals with other union aims, such as dues checkoff, union shop, pension systems, working rules, etc.; smaller wage increases may be accepted in order to obtain concessions on these matters.

The initial demands of the union almost inevitably exceed the expected gains; the amounts of the difference depend primarily upon the union's estimate of sound bargaining tactics. Most unions prefer to avoid fantastic demands which are obviously far in excess of anything which can be obtained. On the other hand, they usually ask for more than they expect to get. The possibility that a dispute over wages may ultimately be settled by arbitration increases the need for padding the original demands, since the arbitrators are likely to produce a compromise award.

Union Minimum Figures. There remains the question of the minimum figure which the union will accept. There are essentially two minima, just as there are two employer maxima; the higher is the figure below which the union will not go without calling a strike; the lower is the figure believed essential for union survival. The minimum without a strike is likely to be the actual demand figure (not the initial inflated demand), if the union feels that it has sufficient strength to carry a strike through effectively. If the union is doubtful about the effectiveness of a strike, it may accept a lower figure than the expected amount; it will not, however, go below the amount regarded as essential to the continued maintenance of the union organization. The estimates of the union officials of the figure below which they will not go without a strike are influenced greatly by the figures which they believe the employer will grant, either with or without a strike. If they are certain that the employer will not exceed a certain figure even in the event of a strike, it is foolish to strike. The absolute minimum which the union will accept is essentially the figure below which the union would disintegrate, its members drifting to other employment. If, regardless of the pressure applied to the employer through a strike, he will not accede to a wage equal to this amount, either the union will break up and the employer will set the wage, or the firm will liquidate and the workers must seek employment elsewhere. But the concept of the absolute minimum is not usually of practical significance.

In summary, union wage demands—both the initial "asking" figure and the far more significant "expected" figure, as well as the minimum figure which the union will accept—must be recognized as the product of a variety of complex factors rather than simply as the figure estimated to maximize the total wage bill or any other precise sum. Frequently, under a widely accepted union assumption that employment is not affected by the wage level, unions seek constantly to drive the money-wage figure higher, their demands in particular cases being influenced mainly by such considerations as increases being obtained by other unions, estimates of employers' profits and of the figures which the employers are willing to pay, the existence of pay differentials regarded as unwarranted, estimates of union membership sentiment, etc. Wage reductions are often fought to the bitter end, except in rare cases in which it is obvious that they are essential to prevent liquidation of the firm. In most situations wage demands are weighed against the desire for other concessions relating to working rules, maintenance of union membership, and similar considerations.

The Actual Money-Wage Level

Given the union and employer wage policies in a particular situation, the actual wage level will be determined by the relative bargaining strength of the two groups and their skill at the bargaining table. If the figure which the employer is willing to pay is close to the figure which the union is determined to get, an agreement will be reached quickly. If the union is too weak to make a strike effective, the wage is likely not to be far above the employer's minimum figure, regardless of the union's initial demands. If the union's strike minimum is above the maximum figure to which the employer will go in negotiations, a strike is inevitable; the eventual outcome depends upon the effectiveness of the strike and the employer's ability to withstand it and maintain financial solvency. The union's strength in a strike depends upon the completeness of its membership, the ability to keep strikebreakers from working and to get other unions to respect its picket lines, the adequacy of reserves to keep the members from starving, and the existence of public relief for the strikers.

In some cases governmental action plays a part in influencing wage levels. Many employers are subject to federal and state minimum-wage laws; however, at present, the figures set are so low that they exercise little influence on actual wage levels. During World War II restrictions were placed upon wage increases in order to check inflationary tendencies. Apart from these direct controls, governmental mediation plays a major part in settling many labor disputes, especially ones in which strikes have developed; in such cases the attitude of the mediators toward wage levels influences the actual figures agreed upon. In other cases governmental pressure may lead to the acceptance of arbitration or substantial pressure may be brought to bear upon one party or the other in a particular dispute to accept certain proposals.

The Effects of Unions upon Money-Wage Levels

What is the net effect of labor unions upon the structure and level of money wages? This is not an easy question to answer. To the extent that development of labor unions offsets monopsonistic influences of employers over wage levels, or gains for labor a relative bargaining advantage compared to the equal-advantage purely competitive situation, it would be expected that the money wages of the workers affected would be greater than they would otherwise be. If unions alter the flow of labor into various fields in any way, the altered supply-demand conditions may have further effects upon wage levels. Empirical studies of the effects of unions upon wages have of necessity been forced to rely upon the technique of comparing wage increases in unionized fields with those in nonunion fields. Such studies have shown that on the whole, in recent decades there has been little tendency for union wages to rise more rapidly than in nonunion fields, and some studies have even shown the reverse tendency. There appears to be greater tendency for unions to affect the relative wage levels to the advantage of union members in depressions than in prosperity periods. However, in expansionary periods, some very aggressive unions force increases in excess of those obtained in other fields. The evidence is on the whole very incomplete and conflicting.[5]

[5] A series of papers in the *Proceedings of the American Economic Association,* May, 1954, discusses at length the question of the effects of unions on wage levels, and provides additional references on the subject. See also the book by H. M. Levinson, *Unionism, Wage Trends and Income Distribution, 1914–1947* (Ann Arbor: University of Michigan Press, 1951), and the article by P. E. Sultan, "Unionism and Wage Rates, 1929–51," *Review of Economics and Statistics,* Vol. XXXVI (February, 1954), pp. 67–73. British experience is reviewed in the study by K. G. J. C. Knowles and D. J. Robertson, "Differences between the Wages of Skilled and Unskilled Workers, 1880–1950," *Bulletin of the Oxford Institute of Statistics,* 1951.

The basic limitation to this approach to the study of the effects of union activity upon wage levels is that it cannot take into consideration the effects which wage changes in unionized fields have upon wage levels in nonunion fields. The question of primary interest is: to what extent does union activity cause wage levels to differ from those which would exist if the unions were not present? No satisfactory answer can be given to this question by studying relative wage trends in union and nonunion labor markets unless the effects of the union wage levels upon the nonunion levels can be eliminated, and this cannot be done. Employers in nonunionized fields are greatly influenced in their wage policies by the union wages, not only because of the possibility of loss of labor supply in a period of labor shortages if they do not meet the union levels, but also because of the desire to lessen the danger of unionization of their workers. As noted in a subsequent section, in periods in which demand for labor tends to outrun supply at existing wage rates, the existence of unions may actually slow down wage increases below those which would be attained with purely competitive labor markets, and perhaps in some cases even below those which would be set if the labor markets were monopsonistic.

It is, therefore, difficult to generalize about the actual effect of unions on money-wage levels. In terms of the general theory of price determination employed, it is to be expected that unions may raise money wages in those cases in which they eliminate monopsonistic wage domination which holds wages below purely competitive levels, and perhaps may push the wages above the latter figure if they gain sufficient bargaining power. Much more empirical work is necessary before more positive conclusions can be reached.

LABOR UNIONS AND WAGE DIFFERENTIALS

The development of unions undoubtedly has some effects upon the differentials between wages in various firms, occupations, and geographical areas.

Interfirm Wage Differences

In the first place, widespread unionization tends to reduce wage differentials in a given occupation among various firms in an industry. These differentials, which would not exist if competition were perfect, are products of employer domination of the labor market, facilitated by relative immobility of labor. When unions develop they almost always seek to eliminate these differentials which, if continued, would threaten the security of the union itself. Workers in low-wage plants will insist that the union eliminate the differentials; high-wage employers may encourage the union to adopt a uniform wage policy. If industry-wide bargaining develops, a uniform wage policy is almost inevitable. In some cases the elimination of the differentials will merely destroy the excess profits of firms which had been able to hold wages to particularly low levels in the absence of unionization. In other cases, however, the low-wage firms were ones whose other costs were high, owing to inefficiencies in production or selling activities, poor management, or poor location. If the wage increase stimulates the firms to greater efficiency, the workers as well as the employers and society gain. If poor management or poor location is responsible, however, the high-cost firms may liquidate if they are forced to pay the uniform wage rate. If workers can shift easily to other plants, there is little loss; the sales of the other firms will increase, and society will benefit from the elimination of the less efficient firms. In some cases, however, unions encounter a serious problem: the forcing of a uniform wage rate will compel liquidation of a firm with a substantial number of employees who cannot easily transfer to other jobs. Should the firm be allowed to continue to operate at a lower wage? The employees of the plant, if certain that higher wages will actually mean liquidation, will almost always favor retention of a differential. National union officials are likely to take the opposite point of view, because pressure will develop from other firms for lower wages. Sometimes one point of view will prevail, sometimes another.

If some firms in the industry become unionized and others do not, the development of the unions may actually increase, rather than decrease, the differentials. But this effect may be less common than might be expected. Nonunion employers may fear that their plants will be organized if they do not meet union wage levels, while the existence of nonunion firms in the industry may lessen the extent to which the union will seek to and be able to drive up wages in the unionized plants. There is some evidence, however, that on the average nonunion firms pay lower wages than union firms in the same industry.

Occupational Wage Differentials

The significance of union activity for occupational wage differences is difficult to assess for reasons indicated earlier in the chapter. To the extent that unions become stronger in some occupations than others, it would be expected that the differentials otherwise existing would be modified. However, union wage levels affect nonunion levels, and the empirical evidence of the effects is very meagre and somewhat conflicting; it does suggest that unions have less significance for wage differentials than might be expected. It is inevitable, however, that particularly strong and aggressive unions may, at least for a time, raise the wages of the members of the group relative to those of persons in other occupations.

Likewise, the union may be able to limit the number of men available for employment in the industry, and prevent the competition of nonemployed persons with those who have jobs. If unions obtain closed shop agreements and limit membership, the artificial control over supply will interfere with flow of workers to the occupation and thus maintain greater differentials than would otherwise exist. Even if the union accepts all persons wishing to enter, it can ordinarily prevent newcomers from offering to work for lower wages. But this latter practice is apparently not common even in the absence of unions, and thus the presence of the unions may have little real significance.

Geographical Wage Differences

The development of widespread unionization should tend to lessen geographical wage differences. Wage differentials not offset by other differences such as variations in the cost of living create dissatisfaction among union members, and injure the competitive position of the high-wage firms. The higher-wage figures often represent a goal which unions seek to attain in lower-wage areas. For example, Canadian unions constantly refer to higher wage levels in the United States as goals for their own wage rates. The tendency toward industry-wide bargaining is likely to increase the elimination of geographical wage differences. In some instances unions may actually seek to obtain uniform money wages despite cost of living differences, and may thereby increase real wage differences.

When unions are stronger in some areas than in others, the existence of the unions may actually increase wage differentials over what they would otherwise be. Low wage levels in small towns often reflect a difference in the degree of unionization.

THE EFFECTS OF WAGE CHANGES

Understanding of the forces involved in the setting of wages and the significance of wage changes upon the economy may be facilitated by tracing, so far as possible, the effects of wage increases affecting, respectively, one firm, an industry, and the entire economy. In part this discussion involves merely a summary of points noted in the preceding sections.

Wage Increases Affecting a Single Firm

If the wage which a firm must pay is increased, while wages paid by other firms in the industry remain unchanged, there are several possible effects:

1. Stimulus to increased efficiency. The higher wage cost may stimulate the firm to improve efficiency of operations, that is, to attain more closely the least cost combination and the optimum output level.

2. Replacement of labor by capital. The higher relative cost of labor encourages the substitution of capital equipment for labor, particularly over a longer period, since changes in equipment may not be feasible in a short period.

3. The readjustment of output, and in nonpurely competitive conditions, of price. The firm must re-equate marginal revenue and marginal cost if it is to maximize profits; this requires a contraction of output to reduce marginal cost to the figure at which it again equals marginal revenue. If the demand for the product of the firm is relatively inelastic above the old price, or if it uses average-cost pricing techniques, it is likely to raise price immediately.

One effect of the wage increase will be a reduction in the profit of the firm, even if price is increased. If excess profits were earned prior to the wage increase, the wage increase will be borne largely, or perhaps entirely, from these. If, previous to the wage increase, the firm was earning only a normal rate of return, losses are inevitable as a consequence of the wage increase (unless the firm had not been charging the optimum-profit price before); the firm will eventually be forced out of the industry if the wages of other firms remain unchanged. A long period of time may elapse, however, before the firm must liquidate and, as a practical matter, almost certainly wage adjustments will affect competitors in the meantime.

What is likely to be the effect of the wage increase upon the number of men hired? As suggested in Chapter 14, it is widely believed that the demand schedule of individual firms for labor is highly inelastic, especially in the short run, up to the wage level which would force the firm to cease operations. In some instances the reduction in employment may involve different employees than those whose wages have risen; the reduced profits of the firm may cause the firm to discontinue marginal activities, such as mowing the grass around the plant, and lay off the men doing this work even though their wages are unaffected. A rise in the wages of railway locomotive engineers may result in lessened employment of track maintenance workers, since the expenditures made upon track maintenance depend, in practice, to a considerable extent upon the profit position of the company.

Wage Increases Affecting an Industry

As unions have grown in strength, to an increasing extent wage increases are not confined to particular firms but affect all or most of the firms in an industry. If the industry is purely competitive, the firms are in no better position to raise wages than in the case in which only one firm was affected, but the departure of some firms from the industry will eventually allow the remaining firms to cover their costs again. The employees of the firms which are liquidated will lose their jobs (unless the firm turns to the production of other goods). The extent to which firms cease operation depends upon the elasticity of demand for the product.

In the more typical oligopoly situation, however, the fact that the wage increase is industry-wide greatly facilitates the making of immediate price increases. With oligopoly, each firm realizes that competitors are likely to readjust their prices, provided that this firm does also, and thus a price increase will not cause loss of business to other firms in the industry. If the demand curve for the product of each firm is kinked, the level of the kink will be raised by the amount of the wage increase, per unit of output, if all firms readjust prices upward in response to the wage change. The use of average-cost pricing increases the likelihood of price rises sufficient to shift forward the addition to wages. To the extent that such price increases occur, the tendency toward substitution of other factors for labor will be lessened, although some gain from substitution remains. Likewise, the need for long-run liquidation of some of the firms will be reduced.

The price increases, however, will result in some loss in sales and in a reduction in output and employment in the industry. The extent of the sales loss depends, of course, upon the elasticity of the total demand for the product. If the demand for the product is elastic, consumers will purchase more of other products, and employment will increase in other industries. Likewise, the increase in the total wage bill in this industry, which will occur unless the demand for the product is highly elastic, will stimulate employment in other industries by increasing sales of their products. The net result of the wage increase is hence likely to be some decline in output and employment in this industry and net increases in others, with consequent altering of the composition of gross national product. A net temporary loss in total employment will likely occur.

General Wage Increases

When wage increases extend throughout the entire economy or major sectors of it, the likelihood of price increases becomes still greater, and the possibility of a net adverse effect upon employment is greatly reduced. With general wage increases, no significant reduction in sales should occur, since the total money-wage bill is greater; increased demand schedules due to greater money incomes will, in general—though not in all particular instances—offset the effect of the higher prices and allow maintenance of the old sales, output, and employment figures. In the industries in which conditions of pure competition or monopolistic competition make immediate price rises unprofitable, the increased demand due to the higher total money-wage bill will ultimately lead to price increases and will avoid the necessity of liquidation of some of the firms.

The primary result of the general wage increase is a rise in the general price level, provided necessary increases occur in the supply and/or the velocity of money. As explained in Chapter 17, under usual Federal Reserve policy such adjustments will be made. The price increases, however, will not be uniform in all industries. When the general wage level is rising, differences in the strength of unions in various industries and in employer policy and strength will produce differences in the wage increases; likewise, because of differences in competitive relationships in various markets and in the income elasticity of demand for different goods, as well as the varying importance of wages as an element in total cost, price increases will not bear the same relation to wage increases in all fields. Thus some readjustment in the composition of national product and the volume of employment in various industries will occur.

As a consequence of the general price increase, labor as a whole benefits relatively little from the general wage increase, and the real distribution of national income is not materially altered. Some net gain to labor is likely, at least in the short run, since the fixed-income receivers, particularly those gaining income in the form of interest and rent on long-term contracts, will suffer a loss in real income.

Although labor may benefit relatively little, there is no reason to believe that general wage increases will have serious adverse effects upon employment. In general, total purchasing power and prices rise more or less to the same extent, and so long as the propensity to consume and the profitability of investment are not affected, physical output and employment will remain the same. The shifting of some income from the fixed income groups to labor should increase the consumption ratio slightly, and the rising price levels may simulate investment by increasing the profit share of income, unless firms believe that the higher prices of capital goods are only temporary. The higher prices may cause some postponement of purchases of consumer durable goods.

UNIONS AND ECONOMIC STABILITY

The last two decades have witnessed substantial attention to the question of the effects of union activity upon economic stability. On the one hand, it has been charged that unions have aggravated inflation during the period after World War II and are likely to do so in the future; on the other hand, during the depression of the 'thirties the unions were charged with increasing unemployment and checking recovery by holding wages artificially high. Both arguments have been hotly contested.

Unions and Inflation

The question of the significance of unions for inflation is closely related to the question of the significance of general wage increases upon the economy. It has been argued widely since World War II that unions exert a constant upward pressure upon prices, and make impossible the maintenance of a stable price level with full employment.[6] According to this argument, the insistence of unions on continuously higher money wages raises costs and total spending and leads to a continuously increasing general price level, to the extent that the annual money-wage increase exceeds the increase in productivity of labor. By this same line of reasoning, much of the inflation of the postwar years can be attributed to union activity.

This point of view has been seriously questioned by other writers, in part on the basis of the evidence noted above, that nonunion wages have risen in much the same fashion in recent years as union wages. It is argued, furthermore, that the existence of unions actually retards increases in wages in inflationary periods, primarily because the union contracts run for lengthy periods, and increases cannot occur during the course of the contract. It is also maintained that employers may be reluctant to give increases they might otherwise offer, in order to take

[6] One of the most recent detailed presentation of this point of view is to be found in the book by C. E. Lindblom, *Unions and Capitalism* (New Haven: Yale University Press, 1949).

advantage of the concession of the increase in subsequent bargaining. Finally, the opponents of the union-induced-inflation argument maintain that the price increases are due to excessive total expenditures on consumption and investment and that the wage increases are merely consequences of the excessive demand for all factors, and would occur regardless of the existence of unions.[7]

The present state of knowledge does not permit the reaching of satisfactory conclusions on this issue of labor unions and inflation. From a theoretical standpoint it is obviously possible for widespread, union-forced money-wage increases to cause inflation, provided that necessary adjustments in expenditures and money supply take place. The argument that wage increases *cannot* cause inflation is untenable. But whether unions have in the past aggravated inflation or lessened it is an empirical matter on which available evidence is very inconclusive. Whether such effects will be encountered in the future depends in large measure upon the policies followed by unions. But from the present state of knowledge, it does not appear that the existence of reasonably full employment, price stability, and labor unions are necessarily incompatible.

Unions and Unemployment

During the depression years of the 'thirties, it was commonly argued that labor unions caused continuing unemployment because they held wages at artificially high levels, and prevented them from falling sufficiently to restore equality of the supply of and demand for labor. Superficially, this argument appears to have merit; in a sense unemployment is a surplus of supply of labor over demand, and it would appear that a reduction in the wage rate would eliminate this surplus. Actually, however, more careful examination of the argument suggests serious limitations.

In the first place, as shown in the preceding chapter, wages fell relatively slightly in nonunion fields during the depression of the 'thirties; thus it cannot be demonstrated that unions were artificially holding the wage level up. It must be granted, however, that had there been

[7] The argument that unions are not the source of inflation appears in the writings of M. Friedman, "Some Comments on the Significance of Labor Unions," *The Impact of the Union,* (ed.) D. Mc. Wright (New York: Harcourt, Brace, 1951); A. E. Rees, "Wage Levels under Conditions of Long-Run Full Employment," *Proceedings of the American Economic Association* (May, 1953), pp. 451–57; and W. A. Morton, "Trade Unionism, Full Employment, and Inflation," *American Economic Review,* Vol. XL (March, 1950), pp. 13–39.

no unions at all in the economy, the decline in wages might have been greater.

Secondly, as explained earlier, it is doubtful if declines in money wages during depression periods have much effect on real wages and therefore on the level of employment. Money wage reductions tend to produce price reductions, and essentially a general downward movement of national income in dollar terms; the decline in itself tends to depress business still more, especially if there is expectation that the decline will continue. Only indirectly, through the effects of the price level decline upon the rate of interest, the costs of new equipment, the desirability of substituting manpower for capital goods, and the consumption-savings ratio can any stimulus to increased employment be expected.

It is no doubt true that in certain particular instances, groups of workers can preserve their jobs by accepting wage reductions in a depression, especially when failure to do so will cause liquidation of the business. In other cases certain marginal types of work, such as various aspects of plant maintenance, may be continued only if wages are sufficiently low. But it cannot be argued that the general level of employment is likely to be reduced as a result of the success of unions in holding up wages in depressions, because of the general tendency in such periods for prices to follow the wage changes.

THE REAL INCOME OF LABOR

Recognition of the close relationship between money wages and prices and particularly of the tendency of prices to change as wages change brings the discussion back to the original point of departure: What determines the share of labor's real income, given the existing competitive conditions in the labor market? Does union activity, to the extent that it does affect money-wage levels, actually alter the level of real wages, and the share of labor in total national income?

The absolute level of real wages, in total, depends in part on the total level of real income, and in part upon the manner in which this total is shared between labor and other factor owners. The problem of the determination of the level of national income will be considered in detail in Chapters 22 and 23; briefly, however, the level depends upon the volume and quality of factors available, the techniques of production used, and the extent to which available resources are fully utilized. Increases in national product, in real terms, arise primarily from the development of new methods of production and the introduction of new types of capital equipment and increases in the skill of workers. Realization of this fact emphasizes the undesirable effects of policies sometimes followed by unions designed to restrict output or check the introduction of new methods of production. Such policies may aid a few individual workers, but they obviously injure the workers as a group, as well as other members of society, by restricting the growth of national income. Society cannot become richer by producing less.

Given the level of national income, the real income of the labor group is determined by the share of the total which labor receives. If all labor markets were purely competitive, the real wage of each type of labor would depend upon the marginal revenue product of the particular type of labor, and the over-all share of labor in national income would depend upon the relationship between the marginal revenue product of labor and that of other factors. With monopsony in the labor markets, the real share of labor would be reduced somewhat below this level. The development of unions allows the elimination of this monopsonistic "exploitation" of labor, and thus tends to restore real wages and the share of labor in national income to the levels which would prevail with pure competition in the labor market. However, can unions do more than this, so far as wages are concerned, and raise labor's share above the purely competitive figure? This can occur, from a long-run standpoint, only if excess profits have been made possible by restriction of entry of new firms into certain industries. It is also possible for short periods of time when union strength is sufficient to force wages up to the point at which all costs are not covered by various business firms. But eventual liquidation of some firms will occur, and destroy the temporary gains to labor. Beyond these possibilities, the real wage level cannot be forced above the figure determined by marginal productivity of labor; any increases in money wages, beyond this point, are accompanied by price changes, with no effect on the real wage level.

In recent decades the strength of unionization has greatly increased in the United States, yet the percentage of total national income which consists of wages and salaries has changed very little, as indicated in Figure 81. In depression years the percentage of income consisting of wages and salaries rose somewhat, as profits were squeezed severely. The greatest relative increase in labor's share occurred after 1952, in a period in which relative union strength grew much less than in other years in the period. The behavior of the ratio of wages and salaries to national income has been approximately the same in Great Britain as in the United States, as shown in Figure 81, despite the fact that British industry is much more highly organized. A study by Phelps-Brown of wage trends in France, Germany, Sweden, Great Britain, and the United States between 1860 and 1939 showed a high degree of uniformity of trends in real wages in the five countries, despite great differences in de-

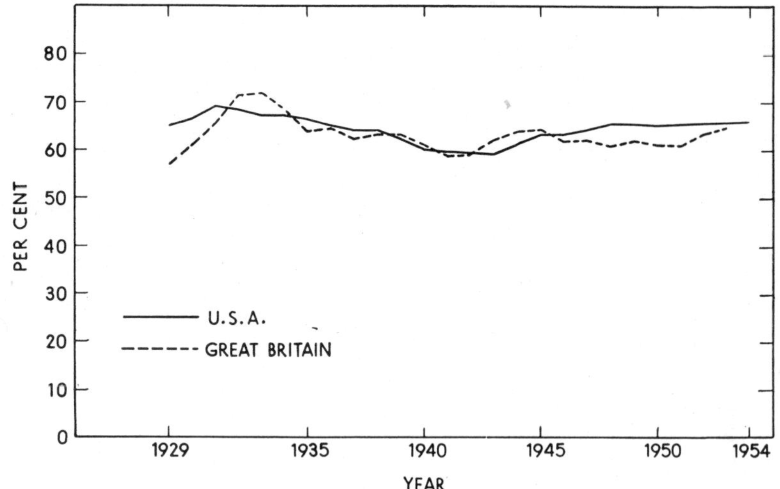

Sources: Great Britain: *The Economic Journal,* Vol. LXII, No. 246 (June, 1952), p. 277. United States: "National Income, 1954," Supplement to *Survey of Current Business,* July, 1954, pp. 162–63, and *Survey of Current Business,* July, 1955, p. 6.

FIGURE 81

WAGES AND SALARIES AS A PERCENTAGE OF NATIONAL INCOME, GREAT BRITAIN AND THE UNITED STATES, 1929–54

gree of unionization and changes in union strength over the period.[8] Studies referred to earlier in the chapter with respect to relative wage changes in union and nonunion fields serve further to confirm the point of view that unions actually have had less influence on real wage levels than might be expected.

In conclusion, however, it should be noted that unions may bring very important advantages to labor even if they have relatively little effect on real wages, beyond eliminating the effects of monopsonistic influences. They may result in improved working conditions, hours of work more closely in line with the wishes of the workers, and greater job security; perhaps more importantly, they restore to the workers a prestige and a status which the unequal bargaining position of individual workers denies them in the absence of organization.

[8] See E. H. Phelps-Brown, "The Course of Wage-Rates in Five Countries, 1860–1939," *Oxford Economic Papers,* Vol. II (June, 1950), pp. 226–96.

SELECTED REFERENCES

DUNLOP, JOHN T. *Wage Determination under Trade Unions.* New York: Macmillan, 1944.

An analysis of union wage policy and the significance of union activity for wage levels.

ROSS, A. M. *Trade Union Wage Policy.* Berkeley: University of California Press, 1948.

An analysis of the factors controlling union wage policy.

REYNOLDS, L. G. *Labor Economics and Labor Relations,* chaps. xv–xix. 2nd ed. New York: Prentice-Hall, 1954.

A clear presentation of the economics of wage determination.

REYNOLDS, L. G. "Toward a Short Run Theory of Wages," *American Economic Review,* Vol. XXXVIII (June, 1948), pp. 289–308.

FELLNER, W. "Prices and Wages under Bilateral Monopoly," *Quarterly Journal of Economics,* Vol. LXI (August, 1947), pp. 503–32.

FELLNER, W. *Competition among the Few,* chap. x. New York: Knopf, 1949.

Proceedings of the American Economic Association, May, 1954, pp. 279–401.

A series of papers on the significance of labor unions for wage determination, inflation, and geographical wage differences.

WRIGHT, D. MC. (ed.) *The Impact of the Union.* New York: Harcourt, Brace, 1951.

A symposium on wage theory by prominent economic theorists, rather than labor economists.

LEVINSON, H. M. *Unionism, Wage Trends, and Income Distribution.* Ann Arbor: University of Michigan Press, 1951.

An empirical study of effects of unions on wage trends.

See also footnote references to the discussion of the effects of unions upon wage levels and inflationary trends.

QUESTIONS

1. Why, in the absence of unions, do labor markets tend to be monopsonistic?
2. What effect does the limited mobility of labor have upon the elasticity of the supply schedule of labor available to a particular firm?
3. Illustrate on a graph the supply curves of labor available to a particular firm (*a*) when labor is perfectly mobile and (*b*) when labor is highly immobile.
4. Why in an employer-dominated labor market does immobility of labor result in a lower wage level? Illustrate graphically.
5. What effect does the presence of oligopsony in the labor markets have upon wage levels? Explain.
6. Why may employers deliberately pay higher wages than the minimum figures necessary to obtain the optimum number of men?
7. What effect should the presence of extensive unemployment have upon

the wage level in monopsonistic labor markets? Is there evidence, in practice, of this effect? If not, how can the discrepancy be explained?

8. What factors influence the wage figure the employer is willing to offer, when the workers are unionized? The maximum he is willing to pay?
9. Why are farmers typically much more hostile to the formation of unions among their workers than are manufacturers?
10. Indicate the various alternative assumptions with respect to the wage goals sought by unions.
11. Why cannot the maximization assumption in its usual form be applied to labor unions?
12. What forces influence the minimum figure a union will accept? The amount which it initially demands in a particular case?
13. Why are generalizations about the actual levels to which wages come in unionized fields difficult to make?
14. Why is it difficult to determine the actual effects which unions have had upon money-wage levels?
15. What conclusions are reached by empirical studies made of relative wage trends in unionized and nonunionized fields?
16. On what basis was it frequently argued during the 'thirties that the unions were responsible for continued unemployment? What are the objections to this argument?
17. Why do general wage reductions probably have little effect in eliminating unemployment?
18. Discuss the conflicting points of view in the argument that labor unions have been responsible for much of the inflation of the last decade.
19. Contrast the effects of a wage increase affecting one firm with those of an increase affecting an entire industry, with respect to price of the product, profits, and the volume of employment.
20. Under what circumstances can union activity actually improve the real living standard of the workers? Even if union activity does not raise the level of real wages, what other advantages may it convey to labor?
21. What are the two primary determinants of the level of real wages at any particular time?
22. Does the empirical evidence indicate that the rapid development of union strength in recent decades has affected significantly the share of labor in total national income? Explain.
23. Under what circumstances does the development of unions lessen wage differentials within an occupation? Between occupations? Under what circumstances does it increase occupational differences?
24. What is the effect of the development of unions upon geographical wage differences?

Chapter 16 CAPITAL GOODS AND INVESTMENT DECISIONS

In the most primitive societies man satisfied his wants directly by his own labor, with the assistance of the resources provided by nature. But men gradually discovered that they could obtain more goods for satisfaction of their wants if they devoted some of their time and effort to the making of tools to assist them in production of the goods. These crude tools constituted the first forms of capital goods. As time passed, such goods became increasingly important in the conduct of production, until today virtually all lines of production activity make extensive use of capital equipment.

Capital equipment is not a basic factor of production comparable to labor and natural resources, since such equipment is itself produced by the use of labor and natural resources. From the long-range standpoint of the entire economy, the use of capital equipment in production constitutes merely a particular method of use of labor and natural resources, these factors being employed initially to produce the capital equipment, which is then used in conjunction with them to turn out the final products instead of their being used directly to produce the consumption goods. A further characteristic of capital equipment is that it can be used over a period of time, rather than rendering its services at one time; furthermore, it is usually purchased outright by business firms, rather than being "hired" for limited periods as is labor. These features create special problems with respect to the determination of the quantities of capital goods which will be acquired, and with respect to the factor income which arises from the use of the equipment.

The acquisition of capital goods by business firms is known as *investment.*[1] The total sum of such goods purchased during a period of time, including any net increases in inventories or stocks of materials, other nondurable goods used in production, and finished products, and

[1] This use of the term investment must not be confused with the completely distinct meaning in reference to acquisition of securities.

including net investment outside of the country (explained in Chapter 21), is known as *gross investment.* In the analysis of national income, the value of new dwellings is included in the figure of gross investment; for purposes of the present analysis, however, the purchase of new dwellings will be regarded as a type of consumption expenditure. The investment figure includes the equipment purchased to replace old equipment wearing out or becoming obsolete, as well as purchases of equipment for expansion purposes. The portion of gross investment equal to the decline in value of existing equipment in the period due to wearing out and obsolescence is known as *reinvestment;* the remainder of gross investment, or, in other words, the excess of total investment over depreciation of existing equipment, is known as *net investment,* or more commonly *investment,* in the sense of the magnitude of the flow during a period, rather than an activity.

The first step in the analysis of the role of capital equipment in the functioning of the economy and the determination of income distribution is that of consideration of the determinants of the amount of investment which firms wish to make in any period of time. In part the general principles developed in Chapter 13 are applicable, but the special characteristics of capital equipment require some elaboration of the general principles.

THE DEMAND FOR CAPITAL GOODS

The analysis of factor combinations and factor demand in Chapter 13 was based upon the so-called static assumptions of given technology, consumer tastes, supplies of other factors, national income, and the rate of interest. The analysis of factor units acquired on a continually recurrent basis, such as labor and raw materials, in terms of these assumptions is, for most purposes, satisfactory. But this is not true for the analysis of the demand for capital equipment which lasts over a period of time, because this demand is dependent to such a great extent on dynamic forces in the economy, that is, upon the existence of change in these determinants.

As a preliminary step in the analysis, however, these assumptions will be retained; ultimately they will be discarded.

The Demand for Capital Goods in a Static Situation

The acquisition of additional capital goods allows either an increase in output or a reduction in costs of labor and other factors employed. At any time, some investment is being undertaken to allow the firm to produce a greater volume of output, while other investment is designed to allow economies in the use of other factors, particularly labor. Purchase of new locomotives by a railroad to allow it to handle additional volume of business is an example of the first; purchase of diesel locomotives to replace steam power is an example of the latter. Regardless of the exact purpose, the marginal revenue product of additional units of capital equipment can be calculated in the same manner as that of additional workers or other factors. As with other factors, marginal revenue product may rise as initial units are added, but eventually must decline. In terms of the basic rules of optimum factor utilization outlined in Chapter 13, attainment of the optimum factor combination requires the extension of the use of each type of capital equipment to the point at which the marginal outlay on it is equal to the marginal revenue product.

Despite the formal similarity of this analysis to that of the acquisition of other types of factor units, there are certain significant differences from which this general statement of the adjustment abstracts, and which must be considered if an adequate picture is to be obtained. The basic difference, as noted in the preceding paragraphs, arises from the fact that capital goods are produced by business firms on a profit-making basis, and yield their services only over a period of time, often several years, while the owners of the factors required in their production must be paid at the time of production.

The Need for Calculating Gains over a Period of Time. One consequence of these features is the need for calculating the gains from the capital equipment over the various periods in which the equipment is expected to be in use, and balancing the sum of the gains against the cost. There are two general alternative techniques: the expected gains may be cumulated to the present and balanced against the entire cost of the equipment; or the cost may be allocated to the subsequent time periods and compared with the gain in each period from the use of the equipment, the net gains then being cumulated back to the present. The latter method is the one most commonly employed. In either case the value of gains in the future must be discounted to the present.[2]

Uncertainty about Future Conditions. More significant, however, is the fact that the marginal product of the equipment can be deter-

[2] In practice business firms sometimes use a rough, rule-of-thumb alternative technique, the determination of the number of years which will be required for the capital sum of the cost of the equipment to be recovered, and the comparison of this with a certain period of years regarded as the standard; the equipment will be obtained only if the capital sum can be recovered in a period shorter than or equal to the standard.

mined only on the basis of an estimate of conditions over a substantial period of time.[3] While such estimates can be made with a high degree of confidence for a period of a few months, those made for periods of ten or twenty years are little more than guesses. A firm can never predict with any degree of assurance its demand and cost schedules over such long periods of time, or the likelihood of the development of new techniques which will render the old equipment obsolete. These uncertainties require the application of probability adjustments; in general they have the effect of lessening the extent to which investment will be carried below the amount which would be undertaken if the firm were more sure of the reliability of its estimates. Since different individuals in policy-making positions in a particular industry may have very different estimates of the future, the policies followed by various firms may differ substantially even though present objective circumstances are the same.[4]

The Need for Money Capital. The determination of the optimum quantity of capital goods is influenced by the fact that money capital is required for the purchase of capital equipment. Not only does the acquisition of this money capital cause the incurrence of certain costs, contractual or implicit, but there may be a definite limit beyond which the firm cannot obtain additional units of money capital by any means. If the firm possesses adequate money capital itself, either through prior sale of stock, through accumulation of depreciation charges on existing equipment, or by retention of earnings, the use of it does not create contractual obligations. But the firm does reduce its liquidity position, that is, its ability to meet unexpected needs for cash, and it does sacrifice possible earnings on the money capital which it could obtain through purchase of securities or other means. On the other hand, if the firm does not have the money, it cannot acquire the capital goods without obtaining more money capital from outside sources. If the money is borrowed, a contractual interest obligation is created which must be met regardless of business conditions. If additional stock is sold, future profits must be shared with the new stockholders.

Accordingly, in calculating the marginal product of capital goods, it is necessary for the firm to subtract from the marginal gross revenue product of additional units the interest cost on the money capital neces-

[3] The static assumptions noted above do not involve the assumption that present conditions are expected to remain indefinitely.

[4] A classic example in recent years was that of the great difference in policies followed by Sears, Roebuck compared to those of Montgomery Ward in the postwar period. The former increased investment substantially on the basis of optimistic estimates of the future; the latter followed exactly opposite policies.

sary for the purchase of the units, plus a compensation for loss in liquidity and for increased danger of insolvency, if the money is borrowed. This deduction is necessary whether the firm has its own capital or must borrow it, but the height of the deduction will be affected by the source of capital and the significance which the use of it has on the general financial position of the firm.

Furthermore, apart from the costs of using additional money capital, there may be an absolute limit to the amount of money capital the firm is able and willing to acquire, and this limit may be below the sum at which the marginal revenue product of all types of capital equipment is equal to the marginal outlay. Many firms are reluctant to acquire any money whatsoever from outside sources, and will limit capital investment to the funds which they have available from internal sources. If the firms are willing to seek outside funds, there are certain dangers encountered which may cause them to stop short of the amount which they could obtain. The fears of insolvency in the event of bad business conditions, with consequent loss of the business and of the reputations of the managers, will often make the firm reluctant to borrow the maximum which could be obtained. On the other hand, sale of stock beyond a certain point endangers control of the business, and will not be undertaken in many cases regardless of the potential profitability of the investment. Apart from the figure which the firm is *willing* to obtain from outside sources, there is a maximum which any firm *can* thus obtain; beyond a certain point the suppliers of money capital will fear the inability of the firm to meet obligations, and the strong acceptance of the philosophy of "eggs in more than one basket" restricts the amounts which are made available to any one firm.

Net Investment in a Static Situation. Subject to the limits of availability of money capital, the firms will adjust the amount of capital equipment in use to the point at which marginal revenue product is equal to marginal outlay on the equipment, given the constants, such as state of technology, noted at the beginning of the chapter. During the period in which a firm is making this adjustment, it will be carrying on net investment (assuming that its capital equipment was previously inadequate). But once the adjustment is attained, net investment by the firm will come to a complete end, so long as the constants remain unchanged. The firm will continue to buy capital equipment to replace units wearing out, but no new investment will be made. In contrast, the firm will continue to hire units of labor and buy quantities of materials so long as it continues to produce. The continuation of net investment for an individual firm and for the economy as a whole is possible only through the operation of dynamic forces, through continuous change in the determinants of the volume of investment. From this condition springs much of the instability which characterizes modern economies, as discussed in later chapters. In order to develop the entire picture of forces affecting investment, it is necessary to modify the assumptions with respect to the constants noted at the beginning of the chapter.

The Significance of Dynamic Forces for the Demand for Capital Goods

There are several types of dynamic forces which affect the demand for capital goods, and thus the volume of investment. These include changes in the quantities of other factors available, such as the labor supply; changes in money-capital supply; changes in national income arising from shifts in the level of employment of available factors; development of new techniques and products; and changes in expectations about future conditions. Each will be discussed briefly.

Changes in Factor Supplies. An increase in the quantities of other factors available will tend to increase the demand for capital goods. Discovery of new natural resources will lead to purchase of capital goods by firms exploiting the new resources or using the products made from them. Growth in population makes available an increased supply of labor, and requires the use of more capital equipment if the least cost combination of factors is to be maintained, provided that the increase in population does not adversely affect the supply of money capital available for investment. This qualification is particularly significant in undeveloped countries in which a high rate of population growth forces families to use so much of their incomes for consumption purposes that little money capital is available for investment.[5] In highly developed countries in periods in which there is a tendency for persons to seek to save more than the current rate of investment, the effect of the population growth in increasing the percentage of income consumed will stimulate investment by increasing the sales of consumption goods, apart from the encouragement given to investment by the effect of the population growth upon labor supply.

Changes in the Supply of Money Capital. The demand for capital goods and the demand for money capital are complementary to one another, since increased use of capital goods requires additional use of money capital. Accordingly, an increase in the supply of money capital tends to lower the interest rate and make money capital more readily

[5] If additional money capital is created by bank or governmental action under such circumstances, inflation will result.

available, and thus increases the demand for capital goods. This result will be attained, however, only if the developments which increased the supply of money capital do not simultaneously reduce the marginal revenue product of the capital goods so greatly that the profitable volume of investment falls below the figure permitted by the current supply of money capital available. If, previously, the investment opportunities had been so great that the potential investment exceeded the amount permitted by the supply of money capital, there is less danger that an increased propensity to save will reduce the profitable volume of investment below the possible level through its effects upon the sales of consumption goods. Thus in circumstances in which investment opportunties are good, an increase in the supply of money capital due to a higher propensity to save will allow an increase in the actual volume of investment. But if investment opportunities are more limited, the higher propensity to save will reduce the marginal revenue product of capital goods by reducing the sales of consumption goods, and the actual volume of investment will fall rather than rise, despite the tendency for the supply of money capital to rise.[6]

Increases in National Income Due to Lessened Unemployment of Resources. As national income rises from depression levels through re-employment of idle factor units, additional investment will be profitable because the increasing sales of products will increase the marginal revenue product of capital equipment. When recovery first commences, the effect upon marginal revenue product of capital may be slight, because firms have substantial idle capacity. But once the capacity of existing equipment is approached, sharp increases in investment are to be expected.

However, net investment due to a rise in national income will continue only so long as the increase in output (or expectations thereof, noted below) continues. As full employment is approached, the rate of increase in national income must slacken, and once full employment is attained, the rate of increase becomes limited to the rate permitted by increases in factor supplies and technological change. As a consequence, the volume of net investment must fall below the high levels possible during the period in which idle resources are being re-employed. Reinvestment will, of course, remain at much higher levels because the total stock of capital goods is much greater than it is in depression periods.

Technological Change. From a long-range point of view, the

[6] As explained in Chapter 22, the decline in national income which results from the reduced investment will curtail the sums actually saved (as distinguished from the sums persons wished to save at the old income levels), and thus no surplus of money capital will actually develop.

most important dynamic force influencing the volume of investment is technological change—the development of new *products* and *methods* of production. The development of new *products* will almost always temporarily produce new investment, although over a period of time investment for the production of goods for which they are substituted is likely to fall. If the new articles are ones requiring relatively large amounts of capital goods in their production—as, for example, automobiles—substantial net investment will occur during the period of their development, and annual reinvestment will remain at a permanently higher level. Of greater importance is the fact that a constant flow of new products on the market is likely to raise the volume of total consumption and aid in the maintenance of investment and national product at relatively high figures. The significance for capital investment of a few major new products during the last century has been tremendous; the automobile, for example, has led to great investment in factories producing automobiles and their parts and accessories (such as tires), in the oil-refining industry, in service stations, and in highways. The net effect has probably been offset only to a minor extent by consequent reduction in investment in the production of horse-drawn vehicles and in the railroad industry.

The development of new *methods* of production has significant effects upon the volume of investment. Over the last several centuries most inventions have necessitated the use of relatively more capital equipment, compared to the amounts of labor and natural resources. In general, the inventions have provided means of accomplishing with capital goods tasks formerly performed by labor directly. There have been exceptions; in recent years some technological developments have been capital-saving, in the sense that they allow certain tasks to be performed economically with less capital investment (per unit of output). The replacement of streetcars by busses in local transit service provides an example. But the general pattern of technological change has required the use of progressively more capital goods and thus has made possible continuous net investment, except in years of a sharp decline in national product. Not only have the new techniques increased investment in the industries directly concerned, but often, by freeing labor and natural resources from use in the industry, they have made possible increases in output and investment in other industries. Some developments have lessened the cost of producing capital goods and have increased the relative advantages of capital compared to units of other factors. Net investment resulting from technological change will continue only so long as the development of new products and methods continues; while the introduction of a series of new techniques will permanently increase the volume of capital goods in use and the annual volume of reinvestment, it will give rise to continuing new investment only as long as the new techniques are being introduced.

Changes in Expectations. Since capital equipment acquired in a certain period will be used over succeeding periods of time, changes in expectations about the future will affect the estimated marginal revenue product and the demand for capital goods. In a period of depression, the development of increased optimism about the future, even if based upon no tangible changes in the current profit situation, could in itself stimulate recovery. Regardless of the initial cause of a recovery movement, once it does get under way, the tendency for expectations of businessmen to improve and a general feeling of optimism to develop are likely to increase the volume of investment to a much higher level than would be justified on the basis of current sales. Changes in expectations about future technological changes can also alter present estimates of marginal revenue product of additional capital goods.

Dynamic Elements and the Optimum-Profit Level of Investment. Recognition of the significance of dynamic elements for the profitability of investment does not destroy the validity of the principle that capital goods will be acquired up to the point at which the marginal revenue product (over the life of the capital good) is equal to the cost of the capital good. But the existence of these dynamic elements greatly complicates the task of determining marginal product. Even if the present situation were static, firms could not be certain that such conditions would continue. But the fact that the determinants are in a constant state of flux greatly increases the uncertainty with respect to marginal product in the future, even over a relatively short period of time. Constant variations in national product levels, in methods of production, and in types of products make any estimates about marginal revenue product, even for a period of two or three years, hazardous. Businessmen must attempt to obtain the best estimate under the circumstances, but they must ever keep in mind the chances that anticipated conditions will not materialize. One net effect is to cause business firms to be much more cautious than they would otherwise be with respect to periods of useful life of new equipment, and to require a greater expected margin of return than otherwise before they are willing to undertake particular investments.

Investment by New Firms

Investment is not only undertaken by existing firms, but by the establishment of new firms as well. Completion of adjustment to optimum combinations of capital goods with other factors on the part of existing firms does not preclude investment on the part of new enterprises entering the industry. These may be entirely new firms, or firms which are already established in other industries which extend their activities into the particular field. The term *new firm* will be used with reference to both cases.

Under assumptions of perfect knowledge and dominance of the goal of income maximization, new firms will enter a particular industry when this field of production offers the promise of a higher rate of return than others. Even though existing firms may all have attained the point at which no further expansion is desirable, new firms will develop if the present firms are earning excess profits—a rate of return on money capital of the firm greater than that in other fields. There will be a tendency for new firms to continue to flow in so long as the excess profit situation continues, provided that they are not held out by barriers to entry.

Furthermore, if the general rate of return on money capital exceeds the interest rate which must be paid, and money capital is available, there will be a general tendency for new firms to start up throughout the economy. Even if existing firms have reached the point at which they cannot obtain additional money capital, or are unwilling to seek to do so, new firms may be in a position to obtain the necessary funds.

To a large extent, the new firms entering an industry are not completely new enterprises, but firms already established in other fields, which are extending their activities to this particular industry.[7] They may do so because of the profits to be earned from producing the particular product, independently of any effect upon their present activities. But more commonly, the adding of other products will allow the firm to utilize more efficiently the services of some factor units which it already employs, such as some of its capital equipment not now fully utilized, managerial personnel, salesmen, etc. Or the new product may allow the firm to capitalize on a reputation already established on other products. Diversification of products also offers advantages in the form of greater security against adverse cyclical or secular trends. The advantages of offering dealers a "full line" may be significant.

There is also apparently some tendency for entirely new firms to start operations in fields in which excess profits are not currently being earned. In part this is a result of a belief of the promoters that they can make a better-than-average return, even though existing firms are not,

[7] See the article by R. F. Lanzillotti, "Multiple Products and Oligopoly Strategy," *Quarterly Journal of Economics*. Vol. XLVIII (August, 1954), pp. 461–74.

because of the production of a new type of commodity, the use of new methods of production, new selling techniques, or the gaining of greater efficiency in management. As new methods are developed, old firms may be reluctant to introduce them because of doubt of their superiority, the desire to avoid loss in the value of existing capital, or sheer inertia. Very frequently, newcomers to the industry are in the best position to exploit the developments. Likewise, there appears to be a constant tendency for persons to overestimate their management abilities.[8]

In some instances in which individuals are establishing entirely new firms, they may have no expectation of making more than an average return, but they feel that they are being underpaid in their present employment or believe that their incomes will be more stable and secure from a business of their own. Many persons attach substantial importance to the ability to be their own bosses, to gain independence from working for someone else. Establishment of a new business is often occasioned by the loss of a job or failure of the firm in which the person has been employed.[9] When persons consider starting an enterprise, it is unlikely that they will actually seek out the field which offers maximum profit at the moment. A person usually has no satisfactory way of ascertaining profit possibilities in various industries; furthermore, he is virtually compelled to develop his enterprise in a field with which he is acquainted. Even though a man who has been working in a retail store knows that an iron foundry offers the best profit opportunities, he can scarcely develop an enterprise about which he knows nothing. If he starts a business, it will, almost of necessity, be in retailing or allied fields.

The Total Demand for Capital Goods

The total demand schedule for any particular type of capital good is, of course, the sum of the schedules of the various firms which can economically use this type of equipment. A portion of the demand will arise from the need for replacement of capital equipment of the same type, or similar types, which has worn out or become obsolete during the period. The total of this replacement demand will depend in part upon the volume of such equipment already in use, and in part upon the extent to which replacement has become advantageous, either because the equipment has worn out physically, or because the compara-

[8] The best evidence is the large number of failures in the first year of operation.

[9] Note A. R. Oxenfeldt, *New Firms and Free Enterprise* (Washington: American Council on Public Affairs, 1943), chap. x.

tive revenue-cost relationships between it and the new equipment are such as to make the use of the latter desirable.

Secondly, an additional element will arise from adjustments by firms to obtain the least cost combination between this type of capital equipment and other factors, either because they had not previously attained the optimum adjustment, or because the determinants have changed. Increases in national income may result in profitable installation of additional facilities to meet greater demand, or the development of new products or new methods may make the use of the equipment profitable. Shifting of demand from other products to the ones for which the equipment is needed, or increased availability of other factor units required in combination with this may increase the marginal revenue product of the equipment. A reduction in the interest rate, or increased availability of money capital will also increase the marginal revenue product. Or mere changes in expectations about the future, without any actual current changes, may have the same effect.

Thirdly, a portion of the demand will arise from new firms which are starting operations, and require units of the equipment to obtain the least cost combinations. The new firms may have been lured in by the possibility of earning of excess profits, or the advantages of including the particular product in the general line of goods carried by the firm, or merely because of the desire of the promoters to operate a business of their own in the particular field. The extent of development of new firms depends in large measure upon the relationship between the expected average rate of earnings in the industry and the current interest rate, as well as upon the availability of money capital to new firms in the field.

The elasticity of total demand is dependent, of course, upon the elasticities of the demand schedules of the individual firms for the equipment. These in turn are primarily dependent upon the behavior of the marginal revenue product of additional units of the equipment, which is controlled by the forces outlined in Chapter 13. The limit to the total amount of money capital which the firm can acquire may be a factor in some instances which affects elasticity of demand for particular types of equipment.

PRICES OF CAPITAL GOODS

The actual prices for which new capital goods are sold will depend upon the relations between cost-supply and demand considerations in the same manner as those of consumption goods, since both types are produced by business firms on a profit-making basis.

So far as market conditions are concerned, virtually no capital equipment is sold under purely competitive conditions, although some types of basic metals and other materials needed for certain types of expansions are sold in markets approaching this form. Many of the capital equipment industries are dominated by a small number of large firms, with consequent oligopoly characteristics. Since the number of buyers is often small, and the purchasers are experts at their tasks, the actual prices may be set on the bargaining basis of bilateral oligopoly. Buyers in some instances call for bids, and award the sale to the lowest bidder. The expertness of the buyers undoubtedly has some effect in lessening elements of differentiation, but these are not entirely absent. The work of salesmen is particularly important in some of these fields.

Distinct from the question of the pricing of new capital goods, but related to it, is that of the pricing of used capital goods. Further reference will be made to this question in Chapter 18, but brief consideration is possible at this point. The available supply of used capital goods being offered on the market will affect the demand for new equipment in cases in which firms have the option of the use of either. Increases in this supply will tend to reduce the demand for the new equipment. The prices of the used equipment depend almost entirely upon the estimated yield from the use of the equipment, since this consideration determines the amount the buyers are willing to pay, and thus the maximum amount the sellers can obtain. The original cost of production of the equipment has no relevance; on the other hand, so long as new equipment is freely available, the old equipment cannot sell for sums in excess of the cost of new equipment less depreciation. Only when new equipment is available in smaller quantities than the amounts which buyers are willing to purchase at existing prices, as occurs during war and immediate postwar periods, can old equipment sell for sums in excess of its replacement cost.

THE PAYMENTS FOR CAPITAL GOODS AND FACTOR INCOMES

The sums paid by business firms for new capital equipment do not, in themselves, constitute factor income payments, since the equipment has been produced by business firms; the payments serve to cover the costs, explicit and implicit, of the equipment-producing firms. The amounts involved are paid out by the equipment producers in the form of factor incomes to the persons supplying factor units to them in the same manner as amounts paid for consumption goods.

The amounts paid for capital goods by the business firms constitute costs from a long-range point of view, since the sums must be covered if operation is to be carried on indefinitely. The costs of capital equipment acquired in any one year, however, cannot appropriately be regarded as costs for which the output of the year is wholly responsible, since the equipment will be used to produce output over a period of years. Accordingly, under usual practice, the purchase price of the equipment is depreciated over the period of years of expected life, a formula being used to allocate a share of the total cost to each year. The allocation is inevitably somewhat arbitrary, since there is no way of ascertaining in any one year what the actual decline in value of the equipment for that year is, or how long the equipment can actually remain in use.

These annual depreciation charges, the form which the cost of the capital equipment takes, are, of course, not incomes;[10] they are merely the charges which reflect the decline in the value of the capital equipment, and thus represent the recovery for the firm of the money capital invested in the equipment. The sums involved are available for the repayment of loans, for replacement of old equipment, for expansion, or for increases in liquid balances or security holdings.

Hence the amounts paid for the capital equipment, in themselves, do not give rise to a distinctive form of income, distinguishable from those which would arise if capital equipment were not used. The distinctive return which arises from the use of capital equipment can be discovered only by considering the money capital which is required to obtain the equipment.

THE ROLE OF MONEY CAPITAL

The preceding analysis has abstracted in large measure from the question of the use of money capital for the acquisition of capital goods. However, since it is this use which gives rise to the distinctive return known as interest, attention must be given to the relationship between the use of capital goods and the demand for money capital. The determination of the interest rate will be explained in Chapter 17.

Investment and the Demand for Money Capital

A business firm must have some money capital if it is to operate at all. Payments for various factor units must usually be made in advance of the sale of the product, and even if capital equipment is not employed, some funds are required to meet these advance factor payments.

[10] The sums are included in gross national product, but not in national income (see Chapter 21).

But the primary source of need for money capital is for the acquisition of capital goods. These may in some instances be rented. But purchase is usually essential to insure that the equipment will be available when it is needed, and to minimize costs. Rentals usually carry a substantial risk premium which firms with good credit standing can avoid by buying the equipment outright. If equipment is rented, the lessor must have obtained money capital with which to build or buy the equipment.

Once production is under way, the flow of money from the sale of the product will meet the recurring bills for labor, materials, and other current costs, and no net additional amount of money capital for these purposes is required unless output expands, inventories increase, or the prices of goods currently purchased rise. As capital equipment wears out, however, adequate funds may not be forthcoming from current revenues to finance replacement. If depreciation charges were fully earned over the life of the equipment and have been accumulated, adequate funds for replacement will be on hand, if the prices of equipment have not risen. Actually, firms rarely accumulate the sums of depreciation charges as cash; thus when replacement is necessary the firm must obtain additional cash during the period, over and above that forthcoming from current operations. The primary need for additional money capital arises when net investment in new capital equipment occurs.

The firm's total need for money capital in any period depends, therefore, upon several considerations:

1. The amount of new investment undertaken.
2. The extent of replacement of old equipment.
3. The extent of increase in inventories.
4. The extent of increase in output, with consequent need for more working capital to pay for current purchases of materials, labor service, etc.
5. The extent of rise in price of current purchases.

Payments for the Use of Money Capital

The use of money capital requires the payment of certain costs. If the money is borrowed, the payment takes the form of a *contractual interest* payment to the lenders. If it is obtained from the owners through the sale of stock, or from internal sources such as depreciation charges earned or undistributed profits, the sum takes the form of *implicit interest,* rather than a contractual charge, represented by the return which the funds could earn if invested in other outlets involving comparable risk. These interest elements are necessary costs from the standpoint of the firm, and are distinct functional incomes to the suppliers of the money capital.

However, the money capital itself is not used in production; it is the means by which other factor units are acquired, capital equipment usually representing the chief source of need for it. Accordingly, the return to suppliers of money capital arises not from the productivity of money capital, as such, in production, but from the productivity of the factor units—particularly capital equipment—which are purchased with it. Nevertheless, the concept of marginal revenue product can be applied to money capital, being defined as the net addition to total revenue which occurs when an additional unit of money capital is used to acquire new capital equipment (the depreciation on the equipment, instead of the interest, being deducted from marginal gross revenue product in determining marginal revenue product). This figure represents the net monetary gain, before deducting interest, from utilizing additional units of money capital for purchase of capital equipment. But the productivity involved is actually that of the equipment, not of the money capital, as such, which has no product-creating power distinct from that of the factor units which it is used to purchase. The marginal revenue product in terms of the capital equipment (calculated by deducting interest from the marginal gross revenue product) and the marginal revenue product in terms of units of the money capital (calculated by deducting the depreciation on the capital equipment from marginal gross revenue product) reflect essentially the same productivity; the marginal revenue products in the two cases are in no sense additive.

While the necessary return element arising out of the use of money capital to acquire capital equipment is the interest on the necessary money capital, the actual earnings in any period once the equipment has been acquired may be substantially greater or less. This problem will be considered in the chapters on rent and profits.

SELECTED REFERENCES

DEAN, JOEL. *Managerial Economics,* chap. x. New York: Prentice-Hall, 1951.
Investment from the standpoint of the business firm.

BAIN, J. S. *Pricing, Distribution, and Employment,* pp. 573–612. rev. ed. New York: Holt, 1953.

LUTZ, F. and V. *The Theory of Investment of the Firm.* Princeton: Princeton University Press, 1951.
A high-level systematic analysis of investment by the firm.

QUESTIONS

1. Explain the difference between gross investment, reinvestment, and net investment.
2. What does investment, as an activity, consist of?
3. Distinguish between investment, as used in the analysis in this chapter, and investment as the term is used with reference to security markets.
4. What is the relationship between investment and the demand for capital goods?
5. Why would net investment be zero once equilibrium were attained in a static society?
6. In what respects does the problem of attaining equality of marginal outlay and marginal revenue product in the case of capital goods differ from that of attaining this relationship with other factors?
7. Explain the relationship between the demand for capital goods and the demand for money capital.
8. If a firm has adequate money capital from retained earnings, does it incur any type of interest cost if it uses this capital for the purchase of new capital equipment?
9. Why are firms unwilling to seek money capital beyond a certain point, even if the sum which they can obtain up to this point is less than the amount necessary to attain equality of marginal outlay on capital equipment with marginal revenue product of the equipment?
10. Explain the various possible effects of an increase in population upon the demand for capital goods.
11. Under what circumstances would an increased supply of money capital lead to increased investment?
12. Why can the rate of investment be much more rapid during recovery from depression than it can be in a continuing period of full employment?
13. When a depression is very severe, recovery may proceed for a considerable period of time without causing increased purchases of certain types of capital goods. Explain.
14. Why is technological change particularly important for the maintenance of a continuing demand for new capital equipment?
16. Do all technological changes require the use of more capital to produce a given output? Explain.
17. Why may it be advantageous for new firms to enter an industry, even if, for all existing firms, marginal outlay on capital equipment is equal to the marginal revenue product of the equipment?
18. Indicate the major elements in the total demand schedule for capital goods.
19. Why do the payments for capital goods, as such, not constitute factor incomes?
20. Is depreciation a cost to the business firm? A factor income to the recipients?
21. Under what circumstances will a firm require additional money capital in a particular period of time?

Chapter 17 THE THEORY OF INTEREST

In the previous chapter, the need for money capital on the part of business firms to acquire capital equipment and to make other factor payments prior to the sale of the products was explained. This chapter will be devoted to the question of the determination of the interest rate—the price paid for the use of money capital. This interest charge constitutes a cost to the business firm, and an income to the recipients. If the money capital is actually borrowed by the business firm, interest takes a contractual form; if it is supplied by the owners of the firm, either directly or through retention of depreciation charges or profits within the firm, the interest takes the implicit form. In addition to interest paid by business firms for the use of money capital, interest is also paid by individual consumers and by governments for the use of borrowed money.

The Origin of Interest

Persons who have accumulated money are able to obtain an interest payment, and hence a factor income, by making this money available to others. In some instances the money is borrowed (and the interest is paid) by persons who wish to make consumption expenditures which they cannot meet from their own current wealth. They are willing to make the interest payments for the privilege of spending prior to the receipt of income. Secondly, a portion of the borrowing is done by governments for various reasons which need not be discussed at this point; they are likewise willing to make interest payments in order to obtain the funds for current use by this means. But, so far as economic analysis is concerned, the most significant form of borrowing is that done by business firms for use in production. Basically the need for money capital on the part of business firms, and thus the ability of persons to gain factor incomes from making money capital available to the firms, arises from the lapse of time in production processes. If in all lines of production, the processes involved simultaneous acquisition of factor units and sale of the product, no money capital would be required. But in practice this is not possible, since time must elapse from the introduction of the input of factor units to the sale of the finished product, even if no capital equipment is used. Furthermore, efficient conduct of production requires not only the use of manpower and materials but of capital goods as well. Since these are produced in one period and yield their benefits in production over a relatively long period, a substantial sum of money is required for investment in them from the time they are produced until they have exhausted their usefulness. The productivity of the factor units in which the money is invested, and particularly of capital goods, makes possible the payment of an income to the persons who supply the money capital.

The Necessity for Paying Interest

The willingness of consumers and governments to pay interest in order to make expenditures prior to the receipt of income, and the financial gains to business firms from the use of money capital to purchase capital goods for use in production explain why the payment of interest is possible. But why is such a payment *necessary?* Essentially interest is a payment to induce persons who have money to part with it temporarily, or, in other words, to allow other persons or firms to use it. A person who has wealth in liquid form has three principal alternatives: he can spend it on consumption; he can continue to hold it in liquid form; he can make it available for use in production. The decision between saving and consumption is not directly dependent upon the interest return received from the sums which are saved; the person will not receive interest merely from saving the money, as such, and it is generally believed that the great bulk of savings would be made even if no return could be obtained from the use of the funds. But the holding of the wealth in liquid form offers significant advantages over the provision of it for use in production. The wealth is directly available for use at any time, and the risk of loss is avoided. Accordingly, persons would not part with their liquid wealth unless they received a compensation; interest therefore must be paid in order to induce the owners of money to part with their money, and thus to overcome their *liquidity preference*—the preference for keeping wealth in liquid form. Further consideration will be given to liquidity preference in subsequent sections.

In order to facilitate the transfer of money capital from persons having it to those seeking to borrow it, various financial institutions, such as banks, have developed. Since certain costs are incurred in the operation of these institutions, in part interest must be paid to cover these costs.

The Segments of the Market for Loanable Funds

The task of explaining the determination of the rate of interest is complicated by the fact that there are several distinct methods by which loanable funds may be made available. As a consequence, the market for loanable funds (including that for sums borrowed by consumers and governments) is sharply divided into different segments with widely varying techniques of payment and forms of competition.

In the first place, a very large part of all money capital used for business expansion is obtained by the firms from internal sources, particularly from earned depreciation charges and retained profits. These internal funds do not pass through a market, so long as they are used by the firm itself. But nevertheless, they constitute a portion of the total supply of loanable funds in the economy, and the use of them by the firm constitutes an element in the total demand for loanable funds. While no contractual interest return must be paid on them, the firm incurs an implicit interest cost by using them, since they could be loaned out to others.

The second segment of the loanable funds market is that in which money capital is supplied to business firms through the purchase of stock. No formal, contractual payment is promised to the supplier of money capital on this basis; he is merely promised a share of the profits in the future if they are earned. In a sense, from the standpoint of the firm as a business enterprise distinct from its owners, the cost of obtaining money by the sale of stock is represented by the current yield of the stock. Suppose, for example, that a particular issue is paying 4 per cent dividends and selling at 80, with the expectation that this rate of dividends and stock price will continue. The stock yield is 5 per cent (4/80), the percentage return the shareholders receive, and the figure which the firm must offer new stockholders if it is to obtain additional money capital from this source. Thus, at the time the new stock is sold, this is essentially the cost to the firm. However, once the stock has been issued, the firm has no fixed obligation to the stockholders; the interest element takes the implicit form, and is essentially equal to the current contractual interest return on investments of comparable risk.

It may seem somewhat illogical to use the term "loanable funds" to cover the internal funds and stock sources of funds, since in a technical sense no loan is involved. This terminology, however, has become more or less standard in the literature and will be retained.

The third segment of the money capital market is that in which money is borrowed on a contractual basis, with the promise of payment of a fixed rate of interest. This is the market in which interest as such, in a contractual form, is paid. The loan market itself consists of several segments, including the market for long-term loans represented by bonds; the market for short-term business loans; the market for long-term loans on a real estate mortgage basis; and the market for short-term consumption loans, which itself has several parts. Even within

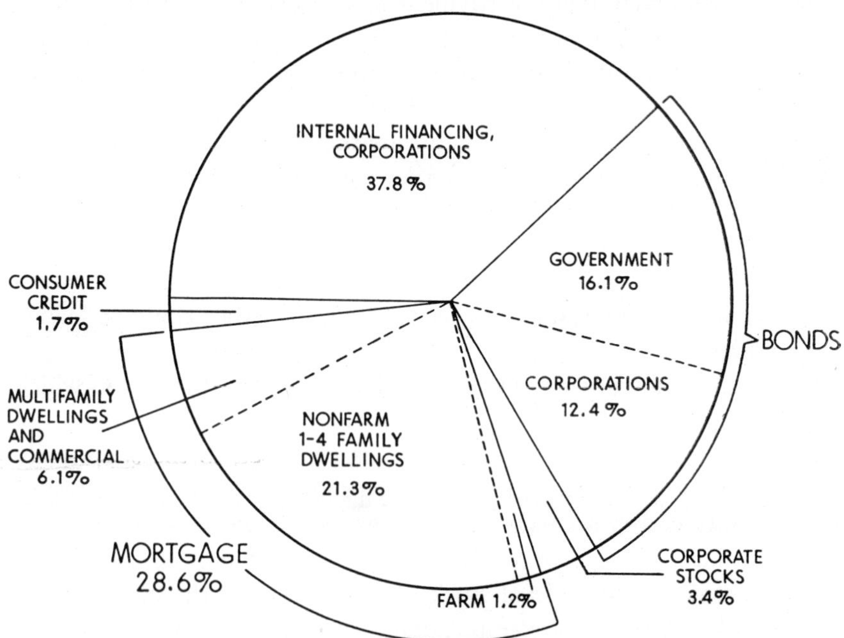

Sources: *Economic Report of the President,* January 1955, and *Federal Reserve Bulletin,* March, 1955.

FIGURE 82

IMPORTANCE OF THE VARIOUS SEGMENTS OF THE LOANABLE FUNDS MARKET, UNITED STATES, 1954
(Net New Financing)

these parts of the market, the various loans will differ from one another on the basis of the credit standing of the borrower, the costs of handling the loan, the term for which the loan is made, etc.

Figure 82 indicates the relative importance of the various major segments of the loanable funds market in the United States, in 1954.

Initially, the analysis will be concerned with the explanation of the basic rate of interest, in the sense of the figure representing the general level of the pattern of rates, contractual and implicit, in various segments of the loanable funds market. The diversities among these various markets will be overlooked, and attention focused on the total demand for loanable funds, including consumer and government borrowing, and the total supply of loanable funds. This approach to the theory of interest is known as the *loanable funds* approach.[1] Later in the chapter, attention will be given to the relationships among the rates in the various segments of the market.

The Assumptions of the Loanable Funds Approach

The loanable funds explanation is based upon several primary assumptions, some of which are relaxed in the course of the analysis:

1. Pure competition in all money capital markets.
2. A given level of national income, except as otherwise noted. As explained in a later section, the equilibrium interest rate is not a stable one unless, at the rate, the volume of planned savings is equal to the volume of planned investment.
3. The goal of maximization of gains.
4. Given time preference schedules, as between present and future consumption.
5. Given liquidity preference schedules, that is, relative preferences for keeping wealth in liquid form.
6. Given policies of the central banking system and the government with respect to credit expansion.
7. Given schedules of marginal revenue product of capital goods.

THE DEMAND FOR LOANABLE FUNDS

The demand for loanable funds is made up of three primary elements: (1) the demand for consumer credit loans by individuals,

[1] An alternative approach, known as the *liquidity preference* or *Keynesian theory* (for J. M. Keynes who developed the theory), explains the determination of the interest rate in terms of the demand for money to hold in liquid balances, and the total supply of money in the economy. This is in a sense a reverse approach to the loanable funds theory, since the sums which persons wish to hold in liquid form represent the portions of their wealth which they are *not* willing to supply to others. Also, the loanable funds theory is essentially a "flow" theory, explaining the rate in terms of the supply of and demand for loanable funds in a certain period of time, while the Keynesian theory is a "stock" or "moment of time" theory, explaining the rate in terms of the supply of and demand for cash balances at a particular instant of time. The two theories are alternative approaches, and are not necessarily inconsistent with each other if properly established.

The Keynesian approach was used in the first two editions of this book; the change has been made solely in an attempt to improve ease of exposition.

References to both theories and the relationship between them are to be found at the end of the chapter.

(2) the demand for borrowed funds by governments, and (3) the total demand for money capital by business firms, including that obtained from internal sources, from borrowing, and from the sale of stock.

Consumer Demands for Borrowed Money

The first segment of the demand for money consists of consumer borrowing. Individuals frequently wish to make expenditures prior to the time at which they have accumulated sufficient funds from income or other sources; by the borrowing of money they can accomplish this desire. Traditionally the most important purpose for which consumer loans are made has been for the purchase of homes, but in recent years

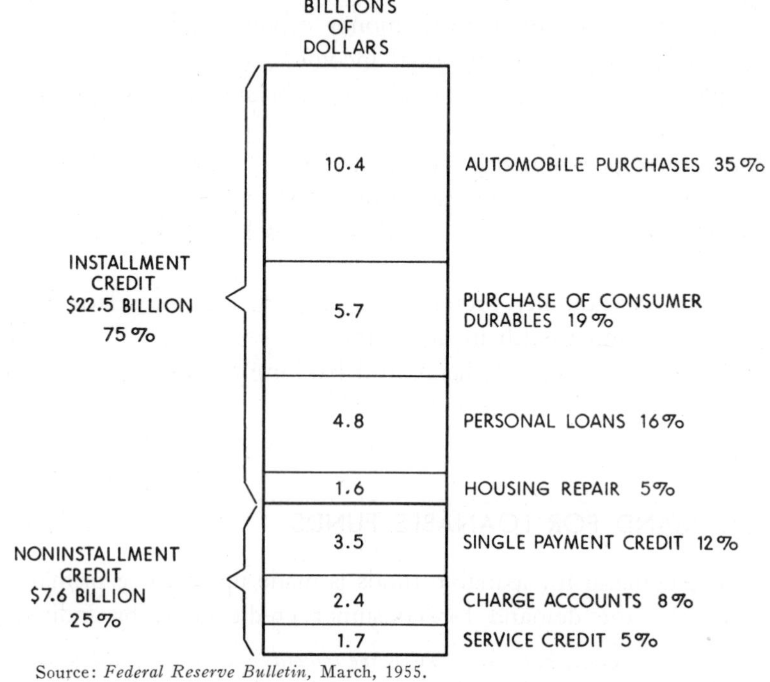

Source: *Federal Reserve Bulletin,* March, 1955.

FIGURE 83

CONSUMER CREDIT OUTSTANDING IN THE UNITED STATES, DECEMBER 31, 1954
(Excluding Loans for the Purchase of Housing)

the volume of loans for the purchase of automobiles and other consumer durables has increased rapidly. The credit may take the form of outright loans, or purchase on an installment basis—the credit being advanced by the seller. The magnitudes of various types of consumer loans are shown on Figure 83.

To what extent is the total volume of consumer borrowing affected by changes in the interest rate? It is generally believed that the schedule is highly inelastic within usual ranges of interest rates, especially the portion of the total represented by borrowing for purposes other than the purchase of homes. On loans made for the purchase of household equipment, automobiles, etc., the time period for which the loan is made is so short that the interest element in the payments is relatively small, and changes in the rate therefore have little effect upon the magnitude of the payments. On long-term loans for purchase of homes, the interest charge is more significant in the total payment, and therefore can be expected to exert more influence. However, high interest rates will be reflected in relatively high rental payments on housing accommodations, and thus the higher interest rate will have less effect in altering the relative advantages of renting versus buying a home than might first appear. High interest rates, however, may cause persons to select cheaper housing and borrow a smaller sum.

In any particular period, the significant element of consumer lending, so far as interest rate determination is concerned, is the net increase in consumer loans during the period. In large measure new loans will be made from funds obtained from the repayment of old loans, and do not represent a demand for new loanable funds.

Government Borrowing

The second element in total demand for money capital is the net amount borrowed by governments during the period, that is, gross borrowings less repayments of old debts. During wars and depressions federal borrowing becomes very substantial; in all periods state and local governments borrow significant amounts—about $3 billion net, in recent years. This borrowing is done primarily in the same markets as those in which business firms borrow, and from the standpoint of the lender there is little basic difference between a government bond and a corporation bond.

To what extent is government borrowing dependent upon the rate of interest? Federal borrowing is almost completely insensitive to interest changes, primarily because of the "emergency" purposes for which most of the borrowing is done, and the influence of other motives in borrowing policy. State and local borrowing, however, is affected to a greater extent, since higher rates not only impair the ability of self-liquidating government enterprises, for which much of the money is borrowed, to meet their obligations, but also affect the abilities of the governmental units involved, which have rather limited tax resources, to meet interest payments.

Borrowing for Business Use

The third element in the demand for loanable funds is the demand on the part of business firms for money capital for use in production, primarily for the purchase of additional capital equipment. It is this segment which is of greatest importance for the conduct of production and for distribution of factor income, since interest paid on money capital of business firms constitutes a factor income.[2]

The determinants of this demand were analyzed in the preceding chapter, and need only be summarized here. The demand on the part of each business firm is dependent upon the estimate by the firm of the marginal revenue product of additional units of capital goods (and other factors, in some cases) which can be obtained with additional units of money capital, after subtracting the depreciation cost of the capital equipment from marginal gross revenue product. The elasticity of this portion of the total demand depend, of course, upon the behavior of the marginal revenue product in the particular instances; a rapidly declining schedule of marginal revenue product results in a relatively inelastic demand for money capital. The total demand of business firms for money capital is the sum of the schedules of the various individual firms. Just as with labor, the total quantities demanded, at interest rates other than the existing one, may not be the same as they would appear to be on the basis of the summation of schedules of the demands of each individual firm, the quantities demanded by other firms being assumed as given. Expansion or contraction by other firms in response to a rate change will affect somewhat the productivity of such action on the part of each firm. There is, nevertheless, a determinate (if not ascertainable) total schedule.

In any particular period of time, the marginal revenue product of capital goods, and thus the demand for money capital, depend largely upon the operation of dynamic factors, particularly technological developments and other innovations, changes in the level of employment, and changes in the supplies of other factors.

The Total Demand for Loanable Funds

The total demand schedule for loanable funds in any period of time is the sum of the schedules of personal consumption borrowing, government borrowing, and the demand for money capital by business firms, at various possible interest rates. The third element represents

[2] Interest on loans made for consumption purposes and upon government obligations is regarded as a transfer income, rather than a factor income and an element in national income.

the total sums of money capital sought by the business firms at various interest rates from all possible sources, including borrowing, sale of stock, and internally acquired funds, such as retained earnings.

In the conception of the total of consumer, government, and business demands for money capital as a homogeneous schedule, substantial oversimplification is involved, since the money is being obtained for different purposes and in different markets. But nevertheless, the aggregate concept may be used as the basis for explaining the general interest rate level; the rate, thus determined, must not be regarded as a single, uniform figure on all loans, but as a pattern of different rates on different types of loans.

THE SUPPLY OF LOANABLE FUNDS

The total supply of loanable funds, in a given period of time, is the sum of the amounts available to consumer and governmental borrowers, and to business firms (including the amounts available through the sale of stock and from internal sources) at various interest rate levels. There are three primary sources of new money capital:

1. Individuals having personal wealth in liquid form may make it available to users. This wealth may have been accumulated during the period from current savings, accumulated in earlier periods and held in liquid form, or obtained by the sale of other forms of personal wealth. The significant figure is the net amount of money capital made available, since a portion of the gross amount may be offset by additions made to cash holdings during the period by transfer of amounts previously made available into liquid holdings.

2. Business firms having liquid wealth on hand may utilize it for their own expansion, or make it available to others. This wealth may have been acquired from saving in the form of retained earnings, from the earning of depreciation charges, from accumulations of liquid wealth made in earlier periods, or from sale of assets. Again, the net figure is significant; sale of assets from one firm to another, for example, may give rise to no additional supply of loanable funds.

3. An increase may occur in the quantity of money. Creation of new money, in the form of bank deposits, through expansion of loans by the banking system increases the amount of money capital available. So long as the banks have excess reserves, they can essentially manufacture money capital through extension of loans. Likewise, an increase in money capital can result through direct governmental action in increasing the quantity of cash.

In any period of time, the total amount of money capital in the economy available for investment of all kinds by business firms, and for governmental and consumption loans, therefore, depends upon:

1. The sum of total personal income which is saved during the period. This amount, in turn, depends upon the level of current income and the propensity to save at the current income level.
2. The volume of business profits retained in the firms.
3. The volume of depreciation charges earned.
4. The extent to which persons and business firms are willing to sacrifice liquidity of their personal wealth.
5. The extent to which the banking system and the government are creating new money.

The two variables which require particular attention are the consumption-savings ratio and the relative preference for liquid balances versus securities. These two will receive detailed treatment in the following pages; the others will be noted briefly.

The Choice between Savings and Consumption

Recipients of income have two general alternatives with respect to the use of their income: they may use it for the purchase of consumption goods, or they may save it. The sum which they save during the period is the excess of their income over their consumption during the period, regardless of the use to which the savings are put. The division which a person makes of his income between consumption and savings is dependent upon his relative time preference for the use of the income, that is, for use of the income at present rather than at some time in the future. For all persons, time preference is positive on at least a portion of their incomes; that is, they prefer to use this portion for immediate use. But for many persons, the time preference on another portion is negative, in the sense that they prefer to set aside the money for future use rather than spend it currently. There are several reasons for this negative time preference. Many persons seek to have a reserve for emergency purposes. Others wish to accumulate for old age, for the protection of their heirs, or for some particular use in the future, such as education of children, purchase of a home, establishment of a business, etc.

On the basis of the relative importance attached to these latter considerations on the one hand and the desire for current consumption on the other, each family allocates its over-all income between the two uses. Individuals will differ widely in the allocation made, on the basis of the amount of wealth already accumulated, the number of dependents, the expectations regarding future income, the amount of foresight in planning for the future, the availability of desired goods, expectations of price changes, and the extent of current windfall capital gains and losses (such as changes in the value of stock held). The level of family income may be a major consideration, as is the intensity of desire for present consumption.

The final factor which may influence the choice is the rate of return which may be obtained if the income is saved and loaned. It was long argued that the return was a major factor in encouraging persons to save higher percentages of their incomes, since the return would overcome positive time preference on a marginal segment of income and lead to a shift in the dividing line between savings and consumption. There has been great de-emphasis in recent years, however, upon the significance of the interest rate as a determinant of the volume of savings which persons wish to make at a given income level. It is obvious that the bulk of saving is made for reasons completely unrelated to the rate. In addition, many families cannot possibly save larger amounts (if any at all) because of the pressing needs of current consumption. Some savers, seeking a given annual return in dollar terms from their savings, will save more rather than less if the interest rate falls. For many families saving is largely a matter of habit, and the margin is not calculated at all closely. While the interest rate may influence some persons in the setting of their savings margins, its over-all significance is usually assumed to be slight.

Ex Post versus Ex Ante Savings. The actual sum of savings made during a period, that is, the excess of income over consumption expenditures, may be called *ex post* or realized savings. This sum may differ, in total, substantially from *ex ante* or planned savings, the amounts which persons planned at the beginning of the period to save. The two sums will be identical if all expectations are realized, that is, if incomes, prices, and other circumstances prove to be what they were expected to be. But this is not necessarily the case. For example, suppose that persons on the average commence to save a higher percentage of their incomes than they did in previous periods. If all incomes remain the same, and prices and other determinants are unchanged, the people will succeed in saving, *ex post,* the larger sum. But the general increase in the propensity to save may reduce production and incomes because of the lessened purchase of consumption goods, and the actual sum of savings during the period will be much less than the anticipated sum; the attempt to save more may thus reduce the actual sum saved—which is the source of money capital. While some individuals succeed in saving larger amounts, this is more than offset by reduced saving on the part of others, those whose incomes fell because the first persons spent less on consumption.

The Retention of Business Profits and Depreciation Policies

The total volume of new money capital in the economy also depends upon the sum of depreciation charges earned by business firms and the amount of retained profits. Depreciation exceeds the annual savings by individuals in magnitude. The amount of depreciation charges earned depends upon the amount of capital goods in use, the rates of depreciation employed, and the extent to which the receipts of the firms are adequate to cover the charges. The volume of retained earnings depends upon the current rate of profits being earned by the business firms and the decisions made with respect to dividend payments. These latter decisions, in turn, are influenced by such factors as the need for additional funds for reserve purposes, the desirability of expansion of the business, and the demands of the stockholders for dividends.

These sums are not directly dependent upon the current interest rate. The only possible influence arises in cases in which a high rate of interest encourages firms to make smaller dividend payments in order to increase earnings from additional retained earnings which are placed in income-yielding investments, and in order to finance desired expansion without the need for borrowing at high interest rates.

Liquidity Preference

Money which is saved does not automatically become available for use. Only if the individuals and business firms that have accumulated the additional wealth are willing to use it in their own enterprises or make it available to others is the supply of money capital actually increased by the additional savings. On the other hand, in any period of time the total supply of money capital can increase beyond the current rate of saving if persons release money from previously accumulated liquid balances. The net release is, of course, the significant figure; in any period of time some persons will be releasing funds from liquid balances held and others will be adding to their balances by the sale of securities. The latter sum must be subtracted from the former to obtain the net, which in some periods may be a negative figure, especially at low interest rates.

In view of the importance of liquidity preference in influencing the supply of money capital, the motives for liquidity must be analyzed carefully.[3] There are several reasons why persons will wish to hold a portion of their personal wealth in monetary form—that is, in cash or bank deposits. These include the following:

1. *Transactions Motive.* In the first place, persons need to have on hand at any time a certain amount of money for the conduct of day-to-day transactions. With both individuals and business firms, income and outgo do not balance exactly in any short period of time. A person may receive a weekly pay check and spend the money gradually during the following week. Accordingly, he will have on hand during the week the portion of the money not yet spent; he cannot conveniently lend out half the amount of the check on Saturday and obtain the money back on Tuesday. A person will also usually seek to have some margin left over at the end of the week, since he cannot calculate his expenditures exactly in advance. The average amount that a person has on hand depends on the size of his income, the interval of receipt of the income, and the practice followed with respect to payment in cash or the use of charge accounts. Business firms likewise must keep substantial cash balances to meet current payments. In some enterprises (many types of farming, for example) the entire annual receipts will be received in a very short period of time. Financial institutions must keep a substantial portion of their assets in the form of money, since they are under obligation to meet the demands of their customers at any time or on short notice.

The total amount of money required in the economy for transactions purposes is dependent upon the level of national income. As employment and output or the general price level or both rise, the total volume of money needed for the handling of transactions will, of necessity, rise. Individuals will be receiving greater money incomes and therefore holding greater average cash balances; business firms will require more money for the handling of the larger volume of transactions.

The balances kept for transactions purposes may be called *active* balances, as distinguished from the *inactive* balances held because of the remaining motives.

2. *Precautionary Motives.* In addition to the amounts needed for the meeting of routine and foreseen expenditures, individuals and business firms will keep additional sums of money on hand to provide protection in the event of emergency. The expenses of a business may rise

[3] The importance of liquidity considerations for the interest rate was first stressed by J. M. Keynes, *General Theory of Employment, Interest and Money,* chap. xv (New York: Harcourt, Brace, 1936).

sharply, or revenues may fall; failure to have sufficient money, or other highly liquid assets, on hand may cause forced liquidation of stocks or bankruptcy. An individual may suddenly experience loss of income—due, for example, to illness—or unexpected expenses; failure to have adequate funds may cause expensive borrowing, loss of a home, or resort to charity. One misfortune, both for an individual and for a business firm, may lead to another. Illness, for example, by reducing income and raising expenses, will necessitate emergency borrowing and thus impair the person's credit standing, as well as his ability to meet other emergencies. The holding of money for precautionary purposes is made particularly necessary by the "credit-rationing" policies of financial institutions; regardless of the credit standing of individuals or businesses, they are usually unable to borrow in excess of a certain sum at current interest rates. Lenders, with few exceptions, limit the amount which they will lend to a particular borrower, regardless of his credit standing. Only the largest corporations—able to float additional stock or bond issues without difficulty—are affected relatively little by this limitation.

3. *Convenience Motive.* The making of loans and the reconversion of loans into money cause both cost and inconvenience. Any type of loan, even that of making a savings deposit, results in a certain amount of nuisance and loss of time. The purchase of securities necessitates the payment of brokers' fees. Persons with relatively small amounts of savings will frequently hold them in monetary form, either indefinitely or until they accumulate a sufficient amount to warrant purchase of securities. Typically, the small saver is interested much more in the preservation of the capital sum of his savings than in any possible return; the easiest and simplest way to keep small amounts is in the form of money.

The existence of savings accounts, which in the United States, at least, are not properly classified as money since the deposits in them cannot be used directly for making payments,[4] greatly lessens the amounts of cash and demand deposits which individuals hold for both convenience and precautionary motives, since savings accounts offer most of the advantages of money itself, from the standpoint of these motives, yet earn interest. However, the placing of funds in these accounts does not automatically make them available as loanable funds; whether they enter the loanable funds market or not depends upon bank lending policy.

[4] In Canada savings deposits must be regarded as a portion of the money supply since checks may be drawn upon them.

4. *Speculative Motive.* Whenever persons expect that security prices are going to fall, and therefore that interest rates are going to rise, they will prefer to keep their wealth in monetary form at present, in order to be able to purchase securities at the lower prices in the future. If they lend now, they will be unable to realize from the benefits of an increase in interest rates until maturity of the securities purchased; if they wish to reconvert their wealth to liquid form prior to maturity, they will suffer a capital loss. When persons expect security prices to rise, they will wish to lend out larger portions of their wealth at the present time.

The Significance of the Interest Rate for Liquidity Preference. To what extent is the desire for liquidity influenced by the rate of interest? The effect is likely to be much greater than that of interest rate changes upon the savings-consumption ratio, in part because the interest rate is a direct, immediate compensation for foregoing liquidity, whereas it is not a compensation for saving, as such. At low rates the amount received for incurring the inconvenience and danger from loss of liquidity and for taking the risk of decline in the value of the securities and of nonrepayment of the principal is relatively small; as a consequence, persons will seek to keep substantial portions of their wealth in liquid form. At high rates the sacrifices of income caused by holding wealth in liquid form is great, and persons will be more willing to reduce their cash balances and suffer the consequences of loss of liquidity. If a person can receive only $10 a year from lending out $1,000, he is likely to regard this sum as inadequate for the inconvenience and risk of capital loss, and loss of liquidity. If he can receive $60 a year (on a loan with the same degree of risk), he is much more likely to consider the return as adequate to compensate for sacrificing the advantages of liquidity. When interest rates rise, even the balances held for transactions purposes will be reduced.

Furthermore, when interest rates are relatively low, there is greater likelihood that persons will anticipate an increase in rates than they will when rates are already at high levels. As a consequence, when rates are low, greater amounts will be held because of the speculative motive. Lenders of money—just like sellers of wheat—become accustomed to certain rates as being "standard"; if the actual rate rises above this figure, expectations that the rate will decline are likely to be stronger than they are when the rate is low. This principle is not necessarily valid in all cases; in some instances a decline in rates may lead investors to believe that further declines are likely. It is widely believed, however, that the principle is a significant determinant of the nature of the demand schedule. It is commonly argued that the portion of money held for speculative purposes is much more responsive to interest rate changes than that held for other motives.

Finally, when interest rates are low, the current selling prices of securities are relatively high; for example, if the interest rate level drops from 6 per cent to 4 per cent, bonds issued at 6 per cent will sell well above par. Thus the total value of a given quantity of securities held will become greater. To the extent that wealth-holders seek to maintain a balance between the current value of security holdings and the amount of their liquid balances, a relatively high figure for the former will encourage them to hold relatively larger sums of money than they would at higher interest rates. At high interest rates the current market value of bonds will be relatively low, and therefore the maintenance of a desired ratio between liquid and nonliquid wealth will require the holding of smaller quantities of money.

Creation of New Money

The extent to which new money is being created in any period depends in part upon bank lending policy, in part upon central banking policy, and in part upon governmental action in creating new cash. Bank lending policy, in turn, is dependent in part upon the extent of excess reserves which the banking system has, in part upon the demand for new loans, and in part upon the reserve ratios regarded by the bankers as adequate. The expectations of the bankers with respect to future business conditions also influence their lending policies.

Central banking policy is dependent upon the general philosophy accepted by those who determine this policy with regard to control over the interest rate as a weapon of economic stability, and their estimates of the needs for particular types of action in the prevailing circumstances. Governmental policy with respect to direct creation of new money is in general dictated by political considerations which are beyond the scope of the present discussion; the policy will merely be considered as a given, in any particular situation.

What significance will the level of the interest rate have upon the volume of new money being created? So far as banks are concerned, the higher the interest rate earned, the greater is the compensation to them for incurring the greater risks which arise from depletion of reserves. Beyond a certain limit, however, the supply of additional bank credit (in the absence of central bank policy to increase bank reserves) is extremely inelastic, since the banks cannot exceed their reserve limits, and, at least in the United States, are reluctant to obtain additional reserves by rediscounting commercial paper with the Federal Reserve System.

The significance of the interest rate for the rate of expansion of bank deposits depends in large measure upon central bank policy. If the central banking system wishes to hold the interest rate stable at a certain level, it will take measures to increase the supply of money, primarily through open market operations, whenever the rate commences to rise, and will follow opposite policies if the rate starts to fall. Commitment to a policy of a stable interest rate makes the total supply of loanable funds perfectly elastic at the interest rate which the central bank wishes to preserve. A policy of allowing flexible but reasonably stable rates will give some elasticity to the supply of loanable funds, but the schedule will not be perfectly elastic.

The Total Supply of Loanable Funds

In summary: the primary determinants of the total volume of loanable funds available in the economy at any particular time at various interest rate levels include the consumption-savings ratios of individuals, business policies with respect to retention of earnings, the sums available to the firms for depreciation charges and retained earnings, the extent of liquidity preference of individuals and firms, and the extent to which the banking system is creating new money. This final determinant may be greatly influenced by central bank policy. The total loanable funds supply is without doubt somewhat responsive to changes in the interest rate; while the consumption-savings ratio is probably affected very little by interest changes, higher rates will induce more persons to forego liquidity and release their funds for business use, and will encourage the banking system to create additional money. If the central banking system is committed to a policy of a stable interest rate at a certain figure, the supply is perfectly elastic at this figure. Any increase above it will lead to central banking action which will increase the supply of money sufficiently to restore the old rate figure. A fall in the interest rate to very low figures may have little effect in reducing savings, but it may cause a great increase in the quantities of money which persons wish to hold, and thus a great decline in the quantity of loanable funds available.

Figure 84 illustrates a typical supply curve of loanable funds under the assumption that the central banking system does not seek to exert positive influence on the interest rate; Figure 85 illustrates the case in which the central banking system will not permit the interest rate to rise above a certain figure.

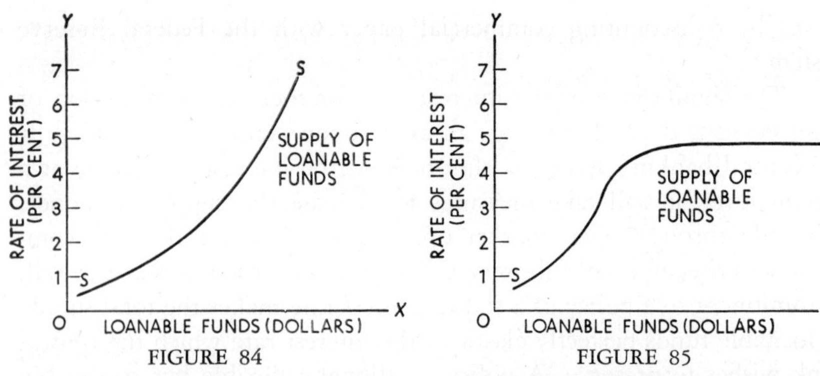

FIGURE 84

TYPICAL SUPPLY CURVE OF LOANABLE FUNDS

FIGURE 85

SUPPLY CURVE OF LOANABLE FUNDS, IN A SITUATION IN WHICH THE CENTRAL BANKING SYSTEM WILL NOT PERMIT THE RATE TO RISE ABOVE 5 PER CENT

THE INTEREST RATE LEVEL

Under the assumption of pure competition in the markets for money capital, the interest rate must come to the level at which the total

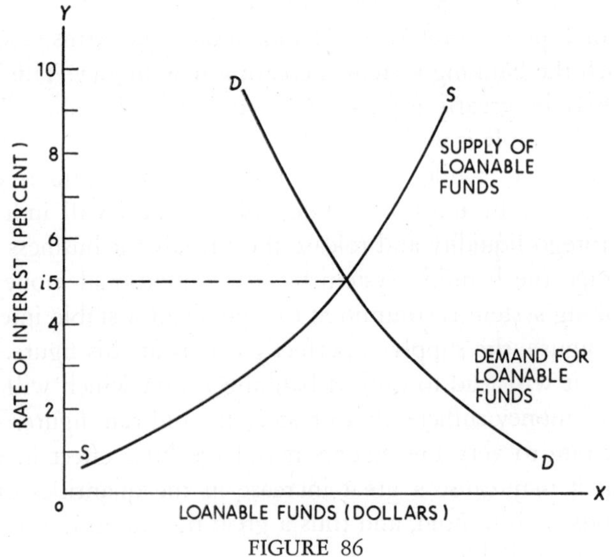

FIGURE 86

DETERMINATION OF THE RATE OF INTEREST

demand for loanable funds, consisting of consumer, government, and business demand, is equal to the total supply available. Figure 86 indicates the adjustment; the basic equilibrium rate is *oi*. This equilibrium will remain so long as the determinants remain unchanged. If the interest rate is higher than this figure, the total supply of loanable funds will exceed the demand for them, and suppliers will lower the rate; if the actual interest rate is lower, the demand for loanable funds will exceed the supply, and the rate will rise.

It is obvious that the assumption of pure competition in all parts of the money capital market is not a realistic one; in some portions the market is dominated by a relatively few firms, and in some cases differentiation is present. As a consequence, the actual rates in some instances will be higher than the figure which would be attained with pure competition. Some of the major deviations from pure competition will be discussed in the section dealing with rates on particular types of loans.

Requirements for Stability of the Market Rate

For the market equilibrium interest rate to be a stable rate, two additional requirements must be met: the total amount of money (cash and demand deposits, not the supply of loanable funds) in the economy must equal the amounts which persons wish to hold in cash balances at the stable rate figure; and the volume of investment in the economy must be equal to the volume of savings which persons wish to make, that is, the volume of planned or *ex ante* savings. Each of these will be considered briefly.

The Liquid Balances. In any one period of time, the supply of loanable funds can include sums which persons have taken from liquid balances and made available as loanable funds. But this depletion of balances cannot continue indefinitely; beyond a certain point, at given interest rate levels, persons will be unwilling to deplete their balances further, and this source of loanable funds will come to an end. If temporarily the supply of loanable funds contains an element arising from reduction of inactive cash balances, the interest rate dependent upon this supply is not a stable one, since the supply must ultimately fall (other determinants of the supply remaining unchanged) and the rate of interest will rise.

Another way of stating this requirement of stability is in terms of the relationship between the net increase in money in the economy and the additional amounts which individuals and firms are desirous of adding to their cash balances. On the one hand, all new money which enters the economy must enter the cash balances of some persons or firms, while on the other hand, persons and firms cannot hold additional sums unless a greater amount of money is available. Unless the additions to money supply are equal to the sums which persons wish to add to their balances, the supply of loanable funds will not remain stable; if, for example, persons are attempting to add greater amounts to their balances than the amount of inflow of new money, this will result in a temporary deficit of loanable funds, which will come to an end once the interest rate has moved up to the point at which persons will no longer be attempting to do the impossible—hold more money than there is. It is important to keep in mind an often neglected fact—the desire of persons to hold greater amounts of their wealth in monetary form does not increase the total amount of money available for such purposes. Attempts to hold greater amounts than are available lessen the supply of loanable funds and drive up the interest rate to the figure at which persons will cease trying to hold excess amounts. The higher rate lessens the desire for liquidity.

Savings-Investment Relationships. The interest rate can remain stable only if the level of national income is stable, since changes in income will affect both the supply and demand schedules of loanable funds, and not necessarily in such a manner that the change in one offsets the change in the other. The analysis of the determination of interest in this chapter has been based upon the assumption of a given level of national income. But, for reasons explained in Chapter 22, national income can remain stable only if the volume of planned (*ex ante*) savings is equal to the volume of planned (*ex ante*) investment. But the interest rate is one determinant of the volume of investment, and perhaps to a limited extent of the volume of savings at a given income level. Thus both the interest rate and the level of national income must adjust to levels which are mutually consistent with each other. This adjustment will be discussed more fully in Chapter 22.

Equilibrium Relationships of the Interest Rate

If complete equilibrium of the rate of interest and national income are attained, equality of the interest rate with three other magnitudes in the economy will be realized:

1. The interest rate will equal the marginal revenue product of capital (with appropriate risk premiums deducted in calculating marginal revenue product), since each producer will have adjusted the volume of his investment in capital goods to the point at which the marginal product of capital goods equals the rate of interest. The total volume of investment occurring is the amount consistent with retention of the equilibrium level of national income, once adjustments in the latter are completed, as explained in Chapter 22.

2. The rate of interest will equal the marginal rate of liquidity preference for each individual and business firm; that is, for each, the rate of interest will just balance the gains from keeping the marginal dollars of personal wealth in liquid form.

3. The rate of interest will equal the marginal rate of time preference of those persons whose allocations of income between consumption and savings are influenced at all by the interest rate available. These persons will adjust their level of savings to the point at which the marginal gain from the use of an additional dollar for present instead of future consumption is just equal to the interest rate obtainable. This adjustment probably has little significance for the adjustment of the over-all level of savings, for reasons indicated earlier in the chapter.

In practice, deviations from pure and perfect competition will interfere somewhat with the attainment of these relationships. The absence of pure competition in the money capital or capital goods markets and the difficulties of ascertaining marginal revenue product of capital goods will prevent the exact attainment of the first relationship indicated, for example.

THE STRUCTURE OF INTEREST RATES

As indicated earlier in the chapter, the market for loanable funds consists of a number of segments which, although interrelated, are rather clearly differentiated from one another. The basis upon which the loanable funds are supplied, the terms and period of the loans, and the nature of competition vary widely. Brief attention will be given to the major segments.

Long-Term Bonds

One of the most important loanable funds markets, for business firms and governments, is the long-term bond market. The great bulk of governmental borrowing is done through the sale of bonds, and corporations raise the largest portion of funds obtained from outside sources by this means. The bond market is one of the most purely (and perfectly) competitive of all markets in the economy, and thus the bond interest rate is determined directly by supply and demand forces.

The Yield on Bonds. In the bond market, the prevailing market interest rate is indicated by the current yield on existing bond issues; this yield represents the actual percentage return which lenders will receive on their investment, and the rate which companies must pay on new issues (with adjustments for differences in degree of risk). Brief explanation of the yield figure is necessary. If a 6 per cent bond issued in perpetuity (that is, with no date of maturity) and thus paying $6.00 per year per $100 of the issue price, is selling for $200, the current yield is 3 per cent, since the investor will receive $6.00 annually for each $200 he invests in the bonds. The investor then will be receiving 3 per cent on his investment, and the company will have to pay 3 per cent on any new securities of comparable type which it issues.

For simplification, this example was given in terms of bonds issued in perpetuity. Actually, in the United States bonds are usually issued with a definite date of maturity. Accordingly, in calculating actual yield at the present time, known technically as net yield to maturity, the capital gain or loss which will occur if the present price differs from the maturity value must be taken into consideration. If, for example, a person buys a 5 per cent bond at $125, he will suffer a capital loss of $25 if he holds the bond to maturity, since the redemption value is only $100. Bond-yield tables are available to determine the exact current yield to maturity on the basis of present selling prices of bonds.

Since the yield is reflected in the selling prices of existing securities, changes in these prices indicate changes in the yield. An increase in bond prices involves a reduction in the yield and hence in the current interest rate; a reduction in bond prices involves an increase in the current rate. If 4 per cent bonds issued in perpetuity rise to $200, the current interest rate falls to 2 per cent; if they fall to $50, the rate rises to 8 per cent.

Adjustment of Bond Interest. The market adjustments of the bond interest rate can be analyzed most satisfactorily in terms of the total demand for bonds, old and new, and the total supply offered for sale at various price levels. The general level of bond prices must adjust to the figure at which the quantity available for sale is just equal to the quantity which persons wish to purchase in the period. If bond prices are higher than this level, and thus the interest rate is lower than the equilibrium figure, the quantity offered on the market will exceed the quantity demanded. As a result the general level of bond prices will fall; as it does, the yield and the current interest rate rise. This process will continue until equilibrium has been attained; the figure attained will remain until the determinants of the interest rate level shift. If the bond prices are temporarily lower than the equilibrium, the quantity of bonds people wish to buy will exceed the quantity offered for sale, and bond prices will rise, with consequent decline in the interest rate.

This explanation of the market rate adjustment is made in terms of the entire market for bonds, old and new, since the current interest rate which new borrowers must pay is indicated by the rate on existing securities of comparable risk. When a corporation issues new bonds, it must set a rate on the new issues equal to the current rate if it wishes to sell them at par. If it does not set this figure, the bonds will sell above or below par to a sufficient extent that the actual rate which the company pays on the money obtained will equal the current rate figure. Since the sales of existing issues must equal the purchases of such issues, the total value of new issues sold during the period will equal the amount of new money capital made available to business firms through the sale by them of new bond issues. Therefore the bond price level and the interest rate which allow equality of the total demand for bonds and the total supply of bonds will also insure equality of the supply of new loanable funds available through this channel with the demand for them, as represented by the volume of new bonds issued.

Even within the bond market there will be substantial differences in estimated risk of purchase of various bonds, in maturity of various issues, and thus chance of capital loss, and in liquidity of particular issues, that is, the ease with which the bond may be exchanged for cash if desired. The specific interest rates on various issues of bonds will adjust to the levels which reflect the consensus of the market with respect to these differences. Accordingly, the federal government can ordinarily borrow more cheaply than any other borrower (apart from the artificial advantages of income tax exemption enjoyed by the interest on state and local bonds); corporations of the highest credit standing can borrow more cheaply than newly established or financially weak corporations. The greater the amount of debt which a company already has outstanding, the higher the rate which it must pay, other things being equal. The rate is usually higher on long-term issues than on shorter-term issues of the same corporation because the chance of loss is greater.

The Yield on Stock

An alternative method by which a corporation can obtain additional money capital is through the sale of additional shares of stock. The general level of stock prices adjusts to the figure at which the total demand for and supply of shares of stock are equal; at this point the quantity of new money capital available for stock purchase will equal the volume of new stock sold. Since bond and stock purchases represent alternative uses of money capital on the part of the lenders and alternative sources on the part of business firms the relative rates of return will adjust in terms of relative advantages. However, since the rates of dividend payments on stock are not fixed, stock prices will fluctuate in response to actual and expected changes in the rate of dividends, and the flow of money capital into this field will be greatly influenced by expectations of changes in stock prices. Thus a constant ratio between stock and bond yields will not be maintained.

Funds from Internal Sources

The most important segment of the money capital market, from the standpoint of the source of funds for business expansion, is in a sense no "market" at all; it consists of the utilization for the acquisition of capital goods of funds obtained by the firm in its internal operations, particularly from earned depreciation charges and retained earnings. In this "market" the supply and demand are simultaneous, and no contractual interest rate is determined. However, the firm which possesses such funds has the alternatives of placing them in the bond or stock market by buying securities in other companies, holding them in liquid form, or using them for expansion. Given the returns from the purchase of bonds or stock, and the advantages of holding the funds in liquid form, the firm will seek to obtain a balance between these returns and the gain from using the funds to finance expansion of the enterprise. Thus investment of the funds in new capital equipment for the firm will be extended to the point at which the marginal revenue product of the capital goods is just equal to the interest rate obtainable from lending the money to others and the marginal gains from funds held in liquid form—with differences in risk taken into consideration.

Short-Term Commercial Loans

Short-term loans to business firms are made primarily by commercial banks, although in New York some market transactions in commercial paper occur. Because of the domination of this lending by a relatively few large banks, the latter are able to set the rates in a market of differentiated oligopoly. In setting the rates, the banks are influenced primarily by the state of their reserves; the latter, in turn, depend upon the rate of expansion of loans in the preceding period and upon central bank policy. When the reserves are relatively low, the banks will raise their rates and curtail the volume of loans which they are making.[5] Short-term loans to governments are made in more highly competitive markets, and the rates are less subject to bank domination.

[5] To a large extent, banks adjust the volume of loans to the amount which they can safely lend by refusing to grant loans when their reserves are depleted rather than by interest rate adjustments. The latter are made, however, to a limited degree.

Because of the significance of bank reserves for short-term rates, these rates are subject to control by the central banking system. If, for example, the latter wishes to raise the interest rate, it will conduct open-market selling; to the extent to which the sales consist of short-term notes, the interest rate on these will be raised directly; the activity will also lower bank reserves and compel the banks to raise their interest rates on short-term notes. The central banking system will also raise its rediscount rates.[6]

The banks, in setting interest rates on short-term loans, are also influenced by their costs of operation. If they seek to maximize their profits, they must, in most cases, readjust the interest rate when their costs change.

Finally, it should be noted that short-term rates are affected directly by changes in long-term rates. If a rise in long-term rates increases the differential between the two, short-term borrowing will increase, and long-term borrowing will decrease; the banks will purchase more securities, and individuals will borrow on a short-term basis in order to buy long-term securities. As a consequence, the short-term rates will tend to rise; the increase in the funds available on a long-term basis will lower the long-term rate and lessen the differential. The reverse will occur if the long-term rate falls and lessens the differential.

Long-Term Mortgage Loans

Smaller business firms, including farmers, are not able to raise money by the sale of securities. As a consequence, long-term funds beyond those supplied by the owners or earned in the business can be obtained only on a real estate mortgage basis. Likewise, large sums are borrowed annually on a mortgage basis by individuals for the purchase or building of homes. Mortgage loans are made primarily by banks and by insurance and building and loan companies. In general, the policies followed by those institutions are similar to those of the commercial banks in setting short-term rates. However, the rates are less mobile; rates accepted as customary are held unchanged for long periods. When bank reserves run low, the banks simply refuse to make further loans rather than raise the interest rate significantly. In recent years the rates for home purchases and improvements and for farm use have been greatly influenced by direct governmental action, through the setting of maximum figures eligible for FHA and Veterans' loan guarantee, and through the farm lending program.

[6] The Federal Reserve System can also influence bank rates and bank lending by altering the reserve ratio (within the limits set by law).

Interrelationships among the Interest Rates in Various Segments of the Money Capital Market

The interest rate in particular segments of the over-all market for loanable funds are directly dependent upon the nature of the supply and demand conditions in the various parts of the market, and competitive conditions in these markets. But the general pattern of rates which develops must equate the over-all supply of and demand for money capital (apart from possible modifications from this rule caused by deviations from pure competition), and the rates in the various segments must be mutually consistent with one another. Each market segment receives a certain portion of the total supply of loanable funds at various interest rates, and a certain portion of the total demand. The relative supply, compared to the total, depends upon the relative preferences of the owners of liquid wealth for the different forms of outlets for their money, and the relative rates of return. An increase in the rate of interest on bonds, for example, will encourage persons to purchase more bonds and less stock. Increased fear about future economic conditions, on the other hand, will shift buyers from stock to bonds. The supply in any particular loanable funds market is undoubtedly more elastic than the total supply of loanable funds.

The relative demands for loanable funds in the various segments of the market depend in part upon the relative advantages of various sources of funds, the personal preferences of the borrowers, and the relative rates. For example, low bond rates will encourage the use of this method instead of the sale of stock, while inability to sell bonds at a reasonable rate will cause firms to turn to the real estate mortgage market. The strong preference on the part of many firms for the use of internal funds may cause them to limit their demand for money capital to the sum which they have available from this source; they will not seek outside funds. For the firms which are willing to sell additional bonds or stock, the amount of internal funds which they have, relative to the volume of profitable investment, will influence the extent to which they will turn to outside sources.

The general pattern of rates will adjust to the structure which will allow equilibrium of supply and demand in each of the segments of the market; thus rate differentials will develop which will allow the continuation of these equilibria. The differences will be such that there will be no net shifting of lenders or borrowers from one market to the other, and they will reflect the relative advantages, from the standpoint of both lenders and borrowers, of the various channels. Some deviation from this pattern results from the absence of purely competitive conditions in some instances, and the inability of certain borrowers to shift from one market to another. Hence the interest on personal loans is relatively high, not only because of the relatively great risk, but also because many of the borrowers have no other source of funds, and the field is dominated by a relatively few firms.

CHANGES IN THE GENERAL LEVEL OF INTEREST RATES

The basic over-all rate level will change in response to variations in supply of and demand for loanable funds. Some of the major causes of shifts in these determinants can be noted briefly.

1. A change in the willingness to part with cash balances. If persons seek to hold a smaller portion of their wealth in liquid form (but to maintain the same consumption-savings ratio), the supply of loanable funds will increase, and the interest rate will tend to fall. This fall will, of course, reduce the willingness to part with liquid balances and restore the equilibrium at a somewhat lower rate level.

2. A change in the supply of money. The creation of new money, either directly by government or central banking action or through expansion of bank loans and deposits, will make additional funds available for loans, and lower the interest rate. It is by this policy that deliberate central banking policy to control the interest rate operates. If the central banking system wishes to lower the interest rate, it will purchase securities in the open market. This action tends to raise security prices, and thus, in itself, tends to lower the rate of interest. In addition, the process increases the reserves of the member banks, and places them in a position to make additional loans. If they do so, the supply of loanable funds is increased, and the rate of interest falls still further.

However, this policy can succeed only if the individuals and the banks are willing to loan on the basis of the additional money which they receive. If all of the additional money is absorbed in cash balances, there will be no net increase in loanable funds, and the rate will not fall. Apparently there are certain levels below which it is extremely hard to drive the interest rate, because of the tendency, at very low rate figures, for any additional money made available to be absorbed in liquid balances.

Even if the rate does drop as a result of central bank action, the volume of loans and of investment will not increase unless the lower rate actually stimulates businessmen to undertake expansion. Experience suggests that, particularly in severe depressions, the volume of investment is not sensitive to interest rate reductions, since the marginal revenue product of additional capital goods is so extremely low.

3. Changes in the volume of investment. A change in the marginal revenue product of capital will alter the volume of investment and thus the demand for money capital. This increase in demand will, in itself, tend to raise the rate of interest, unless the supply of money capital is perfectly elastic (because of central bank policies). However, the increase in investment will raise the level of national income (at least in monetary terms, if not in real terms); as a consequence, the actual volume of savings and of money capital will rise. When equilibrium of national income and the interest rate is again established, the rate of planned savings and the rate of investment will be equal (since such equality is required for stability of national income), and any difference between the old and the new interest rates cannot be attributed to a change in the relationship between investment and savings, but to the effects of the rise in national income upon the amount of money in the economy and the amount required for liquidity purposes. Unless the supply of money is perfectly elastic, the higher level of national income will necessitate a somewhat higher interest level because of the larger sums required for transactions purposes.

4. A change in the propensity to save. An increased desire to save, not accompanied by an equivalent and simultaneous increase in investment, will tend to reduce the interest rate by depressing the level of national income and the amount of money needed for transactions purposes. It might appear that the increased desire to save would have a direct and immediate effect on the interest rate by increasing the supply of money capital relative to the demand for it. But this will not occur; the increase in planned savings will not manifest itself in an increase in the actual supply of money capital unless the volume of national income is maintained; this cannot occur unless investment rises simultaneously with savings—in which case there is no surplus of money capital at the old interest rate level!

FUNCTIONS OF THE INTEREST RATE

As a conclusion to this analysis of the interest rate, it is useful to summarize the major functions which interest performs in the functioning of the economy. In the first place, and of greatest importance, the interest rate insures that the flow of current savings is made available for investment in capital goods, instead of going into liquid balances and producing a deflationary effect. Or, in other words, the interest rate insures equilibrium of the supply of loanable funds with the demand for them, by inducing persons to make available their liquid wealth for business expansion and other purposes, instead of retaining it in liquid form.

In the second place, the interest rate rations the total available amount of money capital among various possible uses, to those which offer the greatest prospect of return. This rationing device does not always function perfectly, of course, primarily because some firms will undertake expansions with internally acquired capital which would not meet the tests of the market rate.

Thirdly, the rate establishes equilibrium between the amount of money (not money capital, but money in existence) in the economy and the amounts which persons wish to hold in cash balances.

Fourthly, in full employment periods, the interest rate is one factor which assists in restricting the total volume of investment to the volume of planned savings, and thereby aids in the checking of inflation. This function was once regarded as the chief task of the interest rate. But the volume of investment does not appear to be highly responsive to changes in interest rates (especially because of the importance of internal funds for financing of expansion), and the volume of savings is clearly unresponsive to the rate. As a result the effectiveness of changes in the rate of interest as a means of controlling inflation does not appear to be high; tremendous changes might be required to bring equilibrium. Thus, in recent years, when strong inflationary trends have developed, governments have sought other means to control them, rather than relying solely upon the interest rate. The latter is still regarded, however, as a useful tool for dampening mild inflationary pressures.

In periods of unemployment, the effect of the interest rate in limiting the volume of investment is detrimental to the recovery of the economy. However, this effect is easily exaggerated, since the volume of investment appears to be extremely unresponsive to interest reductions in such periods.

SELECTED REFERENCES

FELLNER, W., and SOMERS, H. M. "Alternative Monetary Approaches to Interest Theory," *Review of Economic Statistics,* Vol. XXIII (February, 1941), pp. 43–48.

A reconciliation of the Keynesian and loanable-funds theories.

HANSEN, A. H. *A Guide to Keynes.* New York: McGraw-Hill, 1953, chaps. 6 and 7.

A restatement of Keynesian and loanable-funds theories.

HICKS, J. R. "Mr. Keynes and the Classics: A Suggested Interpretation," *Econometrica,* Vol. V (April, 1937), pp. 147–59. Reprinted in *Readings in the Theory of Income Distribution.* Philadelphia: Blakiston, 1949.

The best presentation of the interrelation of interest, investment, and the level of national income.

KAHN, R. F. "Some Notes on Liquidity Preference," *Manchester School of Economic and Social Studies,* Vol. XXII (September, 1954), pp. 229–57.

A review of the motives for liquidity and the responsiveness of the demand for money to hold to interest rate changes.

KEYNES, J. M. "Alternative Theories of the Rate of Interest," *Economic Journal,* Vol. XLVII (June, 1937), pp. 241–52.

LERNER, A. P. "Alternative Formulations of the Theory of Interest," *Economic Journal,* Vol. XLVIII (June, 1938), pp. 211–30. Reprinted in Harris, S. E. (ed.), *The New Economics.* New York: Knopf, 1948.

An interpretation of the relationships of various interest theories.

METZLER, LLOYD A. "Wealth, Saving, and the Rate of Interest," *Journal of Political Economy,* Vol. LIX (April, 1951), pp. 93–116.

A recent analysis of major aspects of the theory of interest.

OHLIN, B. "Some Notes on the Stockholm Theory of Savings and Investment," *Economic Journal,* Vol. XLVII (June, 1937), pp. 221–40.

The loanable-funds theory.

OHLIN, B., ROBERTSON, D. H., and HAWTREY, R. G. "Alternative Theories of the Rate of Interest," *Economic Journal,* Vol. XLVII (September, 1937), pp. 423–43.

A critique of the Keynesian theory.

ROBERTSON, D. H. "Mr. Keynes and the Rate of Interest," in *Essays in Monetary Theory.* London: King, 1940.

One of the best-known critiques of the Keynesian theory and presentations of the loanable-funds analysis.

ROBINSON, JOAN. *The Rate of Interest and Other Essays.* New York: Macmillan, 1952.

SHAW, E. S. *Money, Income and Monetary Policy.* Chicago: Richard D. Irwin, Inc., 1950, chaps. 12, 13, 14.

QUESTIONS

1. Why are borrowers willing to pay interest?
2. Why can interest be regarded more appropriately as a compensation for foregoing liquidity preference, rather than a compensation for saving?
3. Define the term "saving" as used in economic analysis.
4. Distinguish between time preference and liquidity preference.
5. What are the three major segments of the market for money capital?
6. Under what circumstances does interest take the implicit form?
7. What are the three major elements in the demand for loanable funds? What is the relative quantitative importance of each of the three?

8. Why is the demand for consumer credit believed to be inelastic?
9. Why is the demand for borrowed funds by the federal government more inelastic than the demand by states and local governments?
10. What are the three primary sources of loanable funds?
11. Explain how the banks can create money (in the broad sense of the latter term).
12. Why is a person's time preference likely to be negative for a portion of his income? Why must it be positive for a portion?
13. Does the willingness of a person to borrow money to buy consumption goods indicate positive or negative time preference? A high or low rate of such preference?
14. Why is the schedule of savings, relative to the interest rate, likely to be very inelastic?
15. Distinguish between *ex post* and *ex ante* savings.
16. How may an increased desire to save result in a decline in *ex post* saving and the supply of money capital?
17. In what way is liquidity preference significant for the supply of money capital?
18. Indicate and explain briefly the various motives for liquidity preference.
19. Why does a decline in the interest rate increase the amounts of money which persons seek to hold because of the speculative motive? Because of the transactions motive?
20. What is the nature of the supply schedule for money capital if the Federal Reserve System follows a policy of preventing the interest rate from rising above a certain level?
21. Why was the supply schedule of money capital much more inelastic in the United States in 1900 than in 1955?
22. Why does the dislike of American banks for rediscounting reduce the elasticity of the supply schedule of money capital?
23. Why is the interest rate unstable if a portion of the supply of money capital is coming from dishoarding of liquid balances?
24. Explain the manner in which an increase in liquidity preference raises the interest rate.
25. Why does an increase in the desire to hold liquid balances not actually permit people, as a whole, to hold larger balances? What happens, when persons seek to hold larger balances than are available, to discourage them from continuing to attempt to do so?
26. Why is a given interest rate not stable unless the volume of planned savings is equal to the volume of planned investment?
27. In which portion of the money capital market do conditions approach those of pure competition?
28. If a corporation is planning to issue new bonds, what is the guide to the interest rate which it must pay? If it issues bonds at a rate lower than this figure, what will happen?

29. *a*) What is the current market interest rate if 5 per cent bonds issued in perpetuity are selling at 150?
    b) If the bond were issued for a 50 year period, rather than in perpetuity, and were selling at 150, would the current market interest rate be greater or less than the figure indicated in *a*? Why?
30. Why does a decline in bond prices indicate an increase in the current market interest rate?
31. What basic rule determines the extent to which a firm will use money capital from internal sources for expansion of the enterprise during the period?
32. How does the setting of rates on real estate mortgage loans differ from the setting of bond interest rates?
33. Why are the interest rates on real estate mortgages so very stable?
34. Explain the effect upon the rate of interest, and the reasons for the effect, of:
    a) An increase in liquidity preference
    b) Federal Reserve open-market buying of securities
    c) Under a gold standard, a large increase in the output of gold
    d) A reduction in the volume of investment
    e) An increased desire to save.
35. Why does an increased desire to save not necessarily lead to an increase in the supply of money capital, even if liquidity preference remains unchanged?
36. Why does an increase in investment tend to create, in large measure, the additional supply of money capital necessary to finance the investment?
37. What functions does the interest rate serve in the economy?
38. If the interest rate adjusts to the level which equates the supply of and demand for loanable funds, why in depression periods is there a tendency toward a surplus of money capital?
39. Why is it difficult, in a depression, to bring the interest rate down below a certain level?

Chapter 18 RENTS AND QUASI-RENTS

Attainment of the optimum factor combinations requires, in most instances, the use not only of labor and capital goods, but also of natural resources—goods provided directly by nature which are used in production. Natural resources, or land, to use the more common although less descriptive term, differ from capital goods in that no human effort is necessary to make them available. Accordingly, the supply cannot be increased by deliberate action, although the usefulness of the land for production purposes can be increased by various improvements—clearing, draining, introduction of irrigation facilities, etc.—which require labor, and constitute capital goods. Since, however, the amounts of land available for use are limited relative to demands of business firms for them, a price must be paid for their use, a price which constitutes an income to the owners in a society in which natural resources are privately owned. This return, which is not a compensation necessary to overcome any real costs in the same sense as labor, is known as land rent, or more commonly, rent.

In the last century the theory of determination of land rent played a major role in economic analysis, and some of the most bitter controversies centered around questions relating to rent. In recent decades, however, there has been a tendency to relegate rent theory to a position of minor importance. The similarities between capital goods and natural resources have been stressed, as well as the difficulties of distinguishing clearly, in practice, between the two. By many modern writers, rent is not regarded as a distinct functional return, the return from investments in land being treated simply as a form of return on money capital. At the same time, the concept of rent itself has frequently been extended to cover any return attributable to specific factor units which is not necessary to make the factor units available, either to the industry or to the economy as a whole. This concept will be considered at the end of the chapter.

This tendency to regard return on land as merely a type of return on invested money capital obscures certain basic differences between the determination of the price paid for the use of land (which is provided by nature) and that paid for the use of capital goods (which are produced), and thus the cost elements arising from the two types of factors. While in practice land and capital equipment cannot be clearly distinguished from one another, and, as noted below, in the short-run period capital goods take on certain of the characteristics of land, nevertheless separate attention to the determination of land rent is desirable. Whether this return is designated as a separate type of functional return, or merely as a form of return on invested money capital, is largely a matter of terminology.

The Marginal Productivity Analysis Applied to Land

The basic marginal productivity analysis presented in Chapter 13 can be applied to land as well as to other factors. The demand for land of a particular type is dependent upon the schedule of marginal revenue product of this type of land to various users of it; marginal revenue product declines, beyond a certain point, as additional units are added. For most business firms, the quantity of land in use is not easily adjustable in the short-run period; hence the demand may be relatively inelastic in such periods.

The nature of the supply schedule of land is conditioned by the basic characteristics of this factor; since land is fixed in quantity and cannot be increased by human activity, the potential supply to the economy is perfectly inelastic even over a long-run period. Relatively high prices paid for the use of land will of course stimulate the making of improvements such as irrigation, drainage, etc., which will increase the output on given land, but these improvements are capital goods, and the higher output is attributable to them. Not only is the potential supply of land perfectly inelastic, but so will be the actual supply offered to users at positive prices, so long as the market is purely competitive. Since the owner of land gains nothing by holding it idle, it is better for him to get the going market return for it, regardless of how low this figure is, than to get nothing at all. In contrast, the holders of money capital gain the advantages of liquidity by holding their capital idle, and workers avoid the disutility of labor by not working. But there is no gain from holding land idle.[1]

Under the assumption of purely competitive markets for the use of

[1] There are rare exceptions, for short periods; some types of land will increase in productiveness if kept out of use for a few years.

land, the rent figure for any particular type of land would adjust to the level at which the demand for and the supply of this type of land were equal. At this level, the rent would equal the marginal revenue product of the land. Because of the perfectly inelastic supply, changes in demand would produce sharp changes in rent; a substantial increase in population, for example, not offset by technological improvements in agricultural production, would result in significant increases in land rent, and thus in the share of national income going to the landowning class. It was this tendency in nineteenth-century England which led to such great interest in the theory of rent, as reflected in the writings of Adam Smith, Ricardo, and Malthus.

In the absence of imperfections in the land market, the adjustment on a supply-demand basis would be instantaneous. Actually, the land market is highly imperfect. A particular market is limited in area, with a relatively small number of tenants and lessors at any particular time. Knowledge of market conditions may be very limited, and the bargaining position of the various parties may be quite unequal. The small number of buyers and sellers prevents the markets from being purely competitive in many cases; monopolistic restriction of supply may develop, or monopsonistic influences on price. The rent may be set by direct bargaining, with results difficult to predict by general analysis. If monopoly or semimonopoly elements develop, not all the available land may come into use; it may be advantageous for the landowners to withhold a portion of land in order to maximize revenue received. The fact that much of the land may be bought outright by the owners, rather than rented, further segments the market and lessens its perfectness. When the land is owned by the users, the rent payments cease to be contractual in nature, and take on the implicit form.

The basic difference between the determination of the cost of land use and the cost of the use of capital equipment, from a long-run standpoint, is that the former depends solely upon the potential yield of the land in alternative employments, since no cost of production is involved, whereas the cost of using capital equipment is dependent upon the cost of producing the equipment, plus the interest cost element. The supply of land is perfectly inelastic, while that of capital equipment depends upon the relationship between the yield from the equipment and the cost of production of the equipment, and is thus highly elastic over a period of time. The entire sum paid for the use of land constitutes an income to the recipients, while the amounts paid for the use of capital equipment serve, from a long-run standpoint, to cover the costs of the production of the equipment.

The Selling Price of Land

Land, like capital equipment, may be purchased outright by the business enterprises using it. The selling price is dependent upon the supply of and demand for the land at a particular time (assuming purely competitive conditions in this market). The price which the buyer is willing to pay for a particular piece of land and the price at which the present owner is willing to sell are determined by the current and prospective rent (explicit or implicit) which may be gained from the land. Specifically, the selling price will tend to equal the capitalized sum of the expected rental return, the return being capitalized at the interest rate obtainable on other investments of comparable risk. Suppose, for example, that the current interest rate on such loans is 5 per cent. A parcel of land yielding, and expected to yield indefinitely, $600 a year in rent would sell for $12,000—assuming a perfect market. If the buyer paid more for the land, he would be getting a return on his investment less than he could get from other investments. If, for example, he paid $20,000, he would be getting an annual return on his investment of only 3 per cent, whereas, if he had purchased bonds, he would have earned 5 per cent. On the other hand, the present owner would not sell for less than $12,000, or he would be getting less return after making the sale than he is at present.

The markets for the sale of land, like those for its rental, are highly imperfect because the lack of an extensive market organization (comparable to the stock market, for example) and the relatively small numbers of buyers and sellers, each of whom may sell or buy land only at extremely infrequent intervals. Monopoly or monopsony conditions may be rare, but the actual price may be determined in many cases by direct bargaining because the numbers of buyers and sellers are small. Neither party can be certain about the future yield, and estimates of this figure will differ. Furthermore, in some cases the relative bargaining positions of the buyer and the seller will be different. For example, the seller may be desperately in need of cash and be forced to let the land go for a very low figure. But, except in unusual cases, the buyer would not pay more than the sum representing the capitalization of his estimate of yield; the seller would not part with the land for a figure much less than the capitalized sum of his own estimate of yield.

Care must be taken not to apply the rule as given above to real estate containing both land and buildings, since the buildings are subject to depreciation. The selling price of existing buildings and other durable capital goods is affected by the yield, but the capitalization must be based upon the limited period of expected remaining useful life, not upon permanent life as in the case of land. Furthermore, reproduction cost is significant; in general, capital goods cannot sell for amounts in excess of the cost of building new ones, provided that the construction of new units is possible, even though on a yield basis the value figure might exceed this amount.

The Differential Theory of Land Rent

The supply-demand analysis of land rent determination, co-ordinate with the explanation of other factor prices, cannot be questioned on a logical basis, under the assumptions. But for a long period an alternative approach, under which rent was explained in terms of differential returns on various grades of land, was regarded as a more satisfactory explanation of rent determination. This approach arose in part because of the wide variation in quality (and thus productivity) of different types of land, and in part from the fixed nature of the supply and the tendency, in many instances, for the producer—particularly the farmer—to regard his acreage as a permanent fixed factor, to which he adjusts quantities of other factors employed. This is not an unrealistic assumption from the standpoint of the firm in many countries in which, for reasons of law or custom, additional land cannot be purchased. From the standpoint of the entire economy, it is a realistic assumption in any country. This differential return or cost approach to the theory of rent is often called the Ricardian rent theory, for the early nineteenth-century economist, David Ricardo, who popularized it.[2]

Land Rent with Land of Uniform Quality. The differential approach can be explained most simply by assuming initially that a new area of land, a previously unknown island, is discovered and settled. In this area all land is equally fertile and equally well located. Further assumptions will be made that only one commodity is produced and is sold in a purely competitive market. When the area is first settled and all the land is not yet in use, the price of the product will equal the average capital and labor cost, with the firms operating at the point of lowest average cost. If the demand for the product increases so that the market price of the product rises temporarily above average cost, additional land will be brought into use as new firms enter production. Since the average cost for the new firms will be the same as that of the old, the supply will continue to increase until the price falls back to the original level. There is no competition among producers for land, since all are making optimum use of labor and capital on their existing land. If any

[2] See David Ricardo, *Principles of Political Economy* (1817).

one producer were not doing so, he could reach the level of lowest cost by taking up additional land. If a firm increases the amount of land being used beyond the amount which allows lowest average cost, the higher average cost will cause losses. As long as land is not scarce—as long as producers seek no more land than the amount which they can obtain by taking up idle land—there can be no rent. Price will equal average and marginal capital and labor cost.

Eventually, however, if population increases sufficiently, the demand for the product will become so great that all land will be brought into use. Further increases in demand for the product beyond this point will raise the market price, and each firm will increase its output until marginal cost is equal to the new price. This expansion will lower market price somewhat. But, so long as the demand is great enough that, at the price equaling lowest average cost, the quantity demanded exceeds the total amount that can be supplied at that price, the price must remain above this figure (at *op* on Figure 87). Thus a differential arises

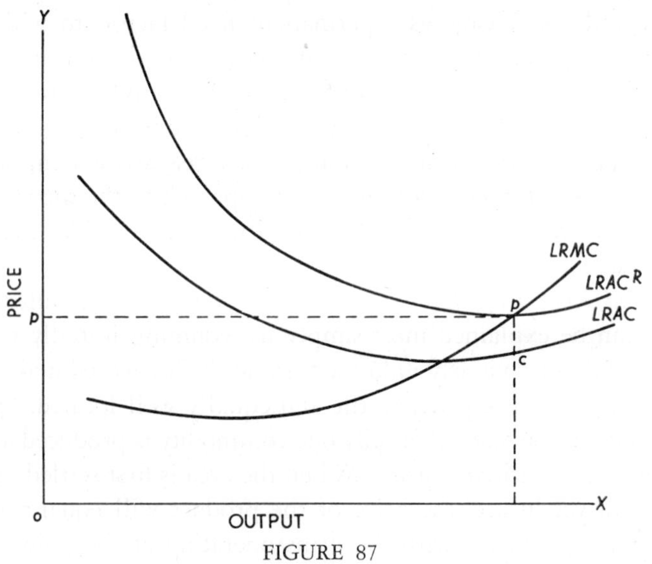

FIGURE 87

LAND RENT DETERMINATION, LAND OF UNIFORM QUALITY

between price and average capital and labor cost (*cp* on Figure 87, which cannot be eliminated by the entry of new firms, since all available land is now in use. This differential between price and average cost arises because of the scarcity of land, once the demand for the product becomes so great that the output cannot be produced on the available supply of land at the lowest figure of average cost. In order to meet the high level of demand, output must be produced at a figure of marginal cost (*op* on Figure 87) in excess of average cost; price must be high enough to cover this greater marginal cost figure, and thus exceeds average cost (exclusive of rent). The amount of this differential between price (which equals marginal cost) and average cost (exclusive of rent) is the land rent per unit of output. On a given acreage of land, the total land rent will be the amount of rent per unit of output multiplied by the annual acreage yield on the acreage. With rent included in cost, the firm's *LRAC* curve on Figure 87 is at the level $LRAC^R$.

Differences in Fertility and Location

The assumption made in the preceding section, that all land is equally fertile and equally well located, is of course an unrealistic one. Units of land in any area differ greatly in these respects.

In the case of farm land, the fertility differences are due largely to variations in the nature of the soil. With a given application of labor and capital, some types of soil will yield much more output than others because of physical differences in content. Productivity is influenced also by temperature, rainfall, and other climatic factors, as well as by drainage and ease of cultivation. Productivity differences manifest themselves in differences in average-cost figures (exclusive of rent) for the firms on various grades of land. On very fertile soil, well drained, with good rainfall and warm climate, the average capital and labor cost per unit of output will be low because of the high yield per dollar spent on these factors. The opposite will be true on poor land.

Location likewise will affect cost. The products of the various grades of land will be sold in the same market areas; firms using the more remote land and that served by poor and costly transportation facilities will have higher costs of marketing their products than those producing on better-located land. Those in poorer locations cannot sell at prices higher than those obtained by firms located close to market.

These differences do not modify the theory of rent significantly, but require some amplification of it. It will be assumed that land falls into certain definite grades, with successively higher cost schedules. In practice, land shades off gradually from the best to the poorest; but classification into grades, the assumption being made that producers on all parcels of land in particular grades have identical cost schedules, will simplify the explanation without lessening its significance.

As long as the demand for the product is small, only the very best land—Grade A land—will be used. The situation will be the same as in the initial stage of the first example above. Once the demand is great enough to bring all Grade A land into use and the demand still cannot be satisfied at the price equal to lowest average cost on Grade A land, price will remain above the Grade A lowest average-cost figure. As demand increases, market price will eventually rise above lowest average cost on Grade B land, and units of this land will come into use. The increased market supply of the product will bring market price to the level of the lowest average cost on Grade B land. Price cannot fall below this figure, with the demand at assumed levels, or all Grade B land will go out of use, and the total supply of the good will be lower than the quantity demanded at the lower price level. On Grade A land, production will be carried to the point at which price is equal to marginal cost. On Grade A land, price will exceed the old average-cost figure; the differential between price (which equals average cost on Grade B land, the marginal land) and average cost (exclusive of rent) on the Grade A land is the land rent. The firms on Grade A land will be operating at a level of output at which marginal cost is equal to price and thus at a level of output beyond that of the old low-cost figure.

If the demand for the product continues to increase, eventually all Grade B land will come into use; further demand increases will raise the market price until it covers lowest average cost on Grade C land, and the latter is brought into use. The price, which must now remain high enough to cover average cost on Grade C land if supply of and demand for the product are to be maintained at equality, will now exceed av-

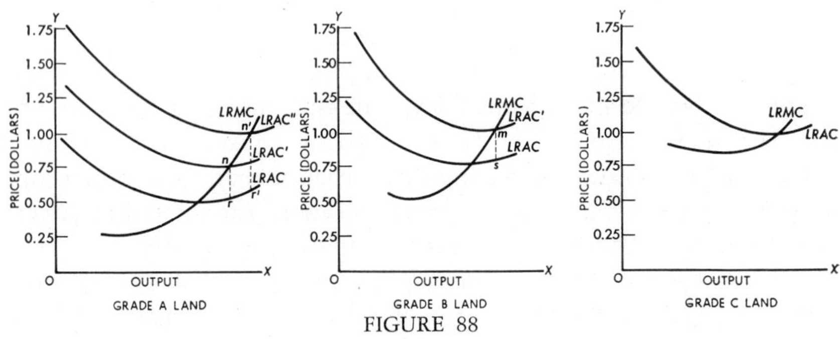

FIGURE 88

LAND RENT DETERMINATION, LAND OF VARYING QUALITY

erage cost on Grade B land, and rent will arise on the latter. Grade B land has ceased to be marginal land; Grade C, formerly submarginal, is now the marginal land. The rent on Grade A will be greater.

Typical cost curves for the firms on each of the three grades of land are illustrated in Figure 88. So long as only Grade A land must be used, price will remain at 50 cents. When demand has increased sufficiently to require the use of Grade B land to make supply and demand equal, the price must be 75 cents, or all Grade B land would drop out of use and market demand would exceed market supply. Accordingly, a differential, a rent of approximately 24 cents per unit of output (*nr* on Figure 88) arises on Grade A land.[3] When demand increases still more, so that all B land is used and C land comes into cultivation, the price of the product must be $1.00. A rent of 24 cents per unit of output (*ms*) now exists on Grade B land, and of 48 cents per unit (*n′r′*) on the Grade A land. The rent per acre would be the rent per unit of output multiplied by the average yield per acre on the particular grade.

In summary, price at any time must equal average cost on the marginal land, the poorest (in the sense of highest-cost) land which will be used in production. On better grades of land the average cost (exclusive of rent) is lower. The difference between this lower average-cost figure and the marginal land average-cost figure is the amount of land rent on the better land.

Once the land rent has arisen, it constitutes a cost from the standpoint of the individual producer. If he leases his land, he will have to pay rent to his landlord; if he owns his land, his costs include the amount which he could make by leasing the land to someone else, since he must cover this sum (along with his other costs) if he is to remain in business. Land rent may be regarded as a differential return from the standpoint of the economy but is a cost from the standpoint of the individual producer.

The analysis above, for purposes of simplification, was based upon the assumption of the production of a single product. Actually, a variety of products will be grown in any area and some land is more suited for one purpose, some for others. Each parcel of land will be used for the purpose in which it will yield maximum rent (apart from the effects of miscalculations by producers); the price of each product will equal average cost on marginal land, and the rent on better land will be a differential between this and the actual cost (exclusive of rent) on the better pieces of land. The rent yielded by the crop actually grown on each parcel of land in excess of the amount of rent which the land would yield in the next-best use is a differential rent from the standpoint of the particular industry, as well as that of the economy, but is a cost to the individual producer. The rent which the land would yield in the next-best use is a cost both to the individual firm and to the industry, but is a rent from the standpoint of the economy as a whole.

[3] The figure is less than 25 cents, since average cost rises slightly as output is pushed beyond the point of lowest cost.

Nonagricultural Production

The differential approach to land rent has been explained in terms of agricultural production. A similar analysis can be applied to other types of industries. For manufacturing, rent is a minor element in cost; in retailing, however, it is important. The cost differential in this case (as in manufacturing) arises solely out of considerations of location. Good locations in any city, which allow lower cost of operation primarily because the rate of stock-turn is greater than in stores on poorer sites, are limited relative to the demand for them. The more rapid turnover lowers capital cost, since a given amount of money capital can be invested in a greater total volume of goods during a certain period of time. Faster turnover lessens loss from spoilage and obsolescence. The good locations usually allow better utilization of personnel and greater effectiveness of advertising.

In the marginal locations for retailing, no rent will be earned over and above that which the land would yield from nonretailing use. In the better locations, the average cost of operations (exclusive of rent) will be less. This differential is the additional rent arising out of the use of the land in retailing. The landowners will be able to extract this amount (plus, of course, the amount of rent that the land would yield in the next-best use) from the retailers, since the latter can pay this amount and still earn a normal return on their own investment.

The Merits of the Two Approaches to Rent Determination

The marginal productivity and the differential theories of land rent are merely alternative explanations of the same phenomenon, and are in no sense contradictory with one another. Actually the differential theory contributes very little toward an understanding of the nature of rent, and the use of this explanation for the determination of rent while other factor prices are explained on a supply-demand basis suggests a basic difference between the rent on land and other factor prices which is not realistic. The marginal productivity analysis is adequate; the differential approach was presented in the preceding pages only because of the major role which it once enjoyed in economic theory.

Land Rent as a Distinct Functional Return

Should rent be regarded as a type of return distinct from other income, paid for the provision to business firms of units of natural resources for use in production? This point of view was long accepted in economic theory, but in recent decades its appropriateness has been questioned. The unique characteristic of natural resources is the perfectly inelastic supply, from a long-range standpoint. But from a short-run standpoint, other factor supplies, especially of certain types of capital goods, may also be perfectly inelastic, and the return therefore does not differ significantly from land rent. From the standpoint of the receiver of rent, the income is essentially a return on the money capital value represented by the selling price of the land and does not differ from the usual interest return. Because of these considerations, there has been a tendency in recent years to regard *land rent* as merely one form of return on money capital, or interest in the broad sense of the term. On the other hand, the term *rent* itself was first broadened to include short-period returns from the use of capital equipment, known as *quasi-rents,* and was then extended still further by various writers to apply to all returns which are "surpluses" over and above the amounts necessary to retain factor units in the industry, or available to the economy as a whole. But rent in this broad sense is not regarded as a distinct functional return, but rather as a surplus element in all forms of factor income.

Quasi-Rent

Over a long-run period, capital equipment must yield a sufficient amount to cover depreciation—that is, to maintain intact the money capital invested in it—and earn an average interest return (including the appropriate risk premium). If the equipment fails to do so, some units will not be replaced, and the return on the remaining equipment will rise. If the return is greater than this, additional equipment will be produced and the return will fall. The depreciation element in the return is not an income, but merely return of money capital; the interest element is a functional return to the suppliers of money capital.

In a short period of time, however, the actual receipts obtained from the use of the equipment may differ substantially from the depreciation-plus-necessary-interest figure, the actual returns to the owners of the equipment being determined solely by conditions of yield of the equipment.[4] Furthermore, from the short-term point of view, in a sense the cost to the firm arising out of the use of the equipment is not the depreciation-plus-interest-on-investment figure, but the amount which the equipment could yield in the next-best employment. It is this amount which the firm sacrifices by continuing to use the equipment in the enterprise. If the actual return in the particular firm is greater than

[4] Except as modified by the use of long-term leases of equipment.

the return from the next-best use, the additional amount is a rent, from the standpoint of the firm, attributable to the capital equipment.

From the standpoint of the economy, the entire sum of the return from the use of the capital equipment is similar to rent, since the equipment is available for use once it has been produced, whether any return is earned or not. (If the equipment will yield more in this particular industry than in others, the differential is a rent from the standpoint of this industry, as well as to the economy.) Accordingly, the term *quasi-rent* is often applied to the short-period return from the use of existing capital equipment. The similarity to land rent is strictly a temporary phenomenon, however, since over a period of time the return must cover depreciation-plus-interest.

In any particular period, the quasi-rent figure may be less than or exceed the depreciation-plus-interest return on the capital equipment. If, for example, the demand for the product produced with the equipment falls, the return from the use of the equipment will decline below the long-run necessary-return figure; the firm cannot sell the equipment or lease it out except on a reduced basis due to the lower return, and thus has no better alternative than continued use of the equipment—unless it can be used in another industry more advantageously. On the other hand, if the demand for the product and the return on the equipment rise, the return will exceed the long-run figure in the interval until additional equipment of this type can be produced and placed in operation.

The Concept of Rent as a Generalized Surplus Return

There has been a tendency on the part of many economists in recent years to expand the concept of rent to include all payments for factor units (and implicit returns attributable to specific factor units owned by the firm) which are not cost elements from the standpoint of the industry or the entire economy because payment or earning of them is not necessary to make the factor units available to the industry or the economy. In large measure these elements are costs from the standpoint of the individual firms, since the firms must make the payments to get the factor units away from other firms in the industry, except to the extent that particular factor units offer a greater yield in the one particular firm than in any other. But if the units are available to the industry whether payment is made or not because they have no use in other industries, the payments are rents from the standpoint of the industry as well as from the standpoint of the economy. If the units are not available to the industry without the making of payments, but are available to the economy as a whole whether they are made or not, the payments are costs from the standpoint of the industry, but rents from the standpoint of the economy.

Rents in this sense are not a distinct functional return, but are elements in other returns. Land rent is a rent, in this sense, in its entirety so far as the economy as a whole is concerned, and the excess earned in one industry over the amount which the land would yield in the next most-advantageous use is a rent from the standpoint of that industry as well. From a short-run standpoint, the returns arising out of the use of capital equipment are rents from the standpoint of the economy, and, to the extent that the equipment is usable (or yields a higher return) in one particular industry only, the returns are rents (entirely, or in part) from the standpoint of that industry as well. Over a longer period, however, the payments for the use of capital goods are true costs. Wages may consist in part of rents in this sense of the term; if, for example, workers have skills which are of greater value in one industry than another, the additional amounts which the workers earn in the industry, over and above the amounts which they could earn in other lines of work, are rents from the standpoint of the industry.

Boulding has emphasized the fact that whenever the supply of factor units is not perfectly elastic, a portion of the returns to the factor owners consists of rent, since the full amounts are not necessary to make all of the factor units available.[5] If the supply is not perfectly elastic, some factor units would be available at a lower return than the amount which their owners actually receive; the differential between the actual return and the one necessary to make them available is a surplus, and thus a rent in this sense. The size of this differential will be different if rent is considered from the standpoint of the industry than it would be if viewed from the standpoint of the economy, since factor supplies are typically much more elastic from the standpoint of one industry than they are to the economy as a whole because of the possibility of shifting of the factor units among various industries.

Summary

The price paid for the use of land, in the sense of factor units provided directly by nature and therefore nonreproducible, may be regarded as a separate type of return designated as land rent, or it may be regarded simply as an interest return on the money-capital equivalent of the current sale value of the land. Regardless of the designation, the

[5] See K. E. Boulding, "The Concept of Economic Surplus," *American Economic Review,* Vol. XXXV (December, 1945), pp. 851–69.

determination of the sum involved may be explained in terms of the usual marginal productivity approach applied to each type of land, or in traditional terms as a differential between the average cost (exclusive of rent) on the particular type of land as compared to average cost on marginal land. These approaches are merely alternative methods of explanation and are not contradictory with one another, but there is no particular advantage in applying a method of analysis to land different from that applied to other factors.

The distinguishing feature of land is the fact that, since it has been provided by nature and is not producible, the supply is perfectly inelastic, and the return is dependent solely upon the yield, given the supply. But in a short-run period, specialized capital equipment is likewise perfectly inelastic in supply, and cost of production is not relevant once it has been produced. Thus in a short period the return on capital goods is dependent solely upon the yield of the equipment in production, and is similar to land rent; it may be designated as *quasi-rent.* But this is a short-period phenomenon only; since capital goods are produced and wear out, over a longer period the return is dependent upon the cost of production of the equipment, and must cover this cost plus an interest return on the money capital.

In recent years, the term *rent* has been extended to cover all returns attributable to specific factors which are surpluses, in the sense that payment of them is not necessary to insure that the factor units will be available, either to an industry or to the economy as a whole. Rent in this sense is not a distinct functional return, but an element in all types of factor returns arising whenever factor supplies are not perfectly elastic.

SELECTED REFERENCES

WORCESTER, DEAN A. "A Reconsideration of the Theory of Rent," *American Economic Review,* Vol. XXXVI (June, 1946), pp. 258–77.

A review of the various approaches to rent theory.

BOULDING, K. E. "The Concept of Economic Surplus," *American Economic Review,* Vol. XXXV (December, 1945), pp. 851–69.

The concept of rent as a generalized surplus return.

ROBINSON, JOAN. *The Economics of Imperfect Competition,* chap. viii. London: Macmillan, 1933.

The broad concept of rent.

MARSHALL, ALFRED. *Principles of Economics,* book vi, chap. ix. 8th ed. London: Macmillan, 1920.

The modern version of the differential rent theory, and the concept of quasi-rent.

QUESTIONS

1. How does land differ from other types of factors?
2. What is the nature of the supply schedule of land from the standpoint of the economy? From the standpoint of a particular industry?
3. Why is the market for the renting of land highly imperfect?
4. A piece of land is yielding $650 a year rent, and is expected to continue to do so in the future. What will be the approximate selling price of the land, assuming an interest rate of 4 per cent on investments of comparable risk?
5. Why will the land not sell for more than the figure given in the answer to Question 4? For less?
6. Why will the sale price of a house not equal the capitalized sum of the figure for which it rents?
7. How, in general, does the Ricardian theory of rent differ in its approach from the marginal productivity theory?
8. Why can rent not arise when not all of the best land is in use?
9. Would rent arise if all land were equally fertile and well located, but limited in amount relative to demand?
10. Would land rent arise if the Law of Diminishing Returns did not operate?
11. Explain, in terms of the Ricardian rent theory, how the rent is determined on a particular piece of land.
12. In earlier chapters, land rent has been regarded as a cost. Yet in the Ricardian rent analysis rent is explained as a differential between rent and cost. Explain.
13. Stores in outlying areas sometimes advertise that they can sell more cheaply because they are outside the high-rent area. Is the lower rent which they pay responsible for the lower prices which they charge, or is the rent lower because they must charge lower prices to attract customers? Explain.
14. Explain the term *quasi-rent.*
15. Why, in a short-run period, are the determinants of the supply of capital goods similar to those of land?
16. Explain the concept of rent as any surplus return attributable to a specific factor.
17. How is it possible for a particular payment for factor units to be a cost from the standpoint of the firm, but a rent, in the broad sense of the term, from the standpoint of the economy as a whole?
18. Why is a portion of the returns to a certain group of factor owners rent (in the broad sense of the term) rather than a true cost, unless the factor supply is perfectly elastic?
19. If the supply schedule of a particular factor to a certain industry is perfectly inelastic, what portion of the payment to the owners of the factor unit is rent?
20. On which types of land has land rent been increased by the development of the automobile? On which types has it been decreased?

Chapter 19 THE THEORY OF PROFITS

The six preceding chapters have reviewed the manner in which the contractual payments made to the owners of the factors, or in other words the prices paid by business firms for the services of the factor units, are determined. Demand schedules for the various types of factor units depend upon the schedules of marginal revenue product of the factors; supply schedules are dependent upon the particular circumstances affecting the availability of the particular factor units, and differ widely among various types of factors. If markets are purely competitive, factor prices depend directly upon demand and supply relationships; if they are not, the actual figures will be affected by the exact nature of competition, the strength of monopoly and monopsony elements, and, in some cases, the actual bargaining policies followed. The same basic analysis has been applied to all types of factor units and to money capital; the differences in the determination of the prices of various factors can be traced to differences in supply determinants and competitive conditions. The marginal productivity analysis cannot be applied, however, to the residual income received by the owners of the businesses. The final step in the analysis of factor pricing and distribution is the explanation of the determination of this return, known as *profits.*

The first step in the analysis of profits is the clarification of the concept. The term is used in two distinct senses: (1) in the business or accounting sense, as the excess of receipts over all contractual costs and depreciation, and (2) in the sense of the excess over and above the implicit cost elements in business profits. Each will be considered in turn.

BUSINESS PROFITS AND IMPLICIT COSTS

As the term *profits* is used in accounting and in the business community generally, it refers to the sum available to a firm after all payments for factor unit services acquired on a contractual basis, other current obligations such as taxes, and depreciation charges have been covered. During a given interval of time, a firm obtains a certain sum from the sale of its products. During this period it must make various contractual payments for labor services, materials, power, etc. It must meet rent and interest obligations. Since capital equipment owned declines in value during the period, a portion of the receipts, known as *depreciation charges,* must be regarded as merely a return of capital and must be charged against receipts as a cost. Taxes must be paid. The excess of the total receipts over these various payments and charges is regarded as the profit of the business firm. In a proprietorship this sum is directly available for the personal use of the owners; in a corporation it may be paid out to the stockholders in the form of dividends, or may be retained in the business. Essentially profits, in this business sense, comprise the total share of income which accrues to the business firm, as such, and thus to its owners (although in a corporation the owners may not gain access to it).

Examination of business profits reveals that the sum of such profits is made up in large measure of implicit (that is, noncontractual) elements of other types of factor incomes, representing return on factor units and money capital provided by the owners of the enterprise. These are true cost elements, as explained in earlier chapters, in the sense that they must be covered over a long-run period if the firm is to continue in operation. They differ from contractual costs only in that no formal, legal obligation for payment of the return exists; essentially the cost elements take the form of foregone earnings from other possible uses of the factor units. Each of the major elements of implicit costs will be reviewed briefly.

Interest Return on the Money Capital of the Owners

In virtually all businesses, a portion of the money capital employed in the enterprise will have been supplied by the owners, directly in the case of partnerships and proprietorships and indirectly through the purchase of stock or through retention of earnings in the case of the corporation. Since the owners forego the advantages of liquidity or of a monetary return from the placing of the funds in other investments by placing the money in this business, a return on the money is an essential cost item from the standpoint of the business. The money would not have been placed in the business initially if a return had not been expected, and will not be retained in the business indefinitely if a return is not earned.

This necessary interest return on the money capital supplied by the owners may be broken down into two elements. The first is the pure interest return, the sum equal to the basic rate of interest on the safest investments. The second element is a risk premium sufficient to compensate, on the average, for the greater risk of loss of the capital sum from investing it in the undertaking rather than placing it in high-grade securities.

What is the capital sum upon which the implicit-interest rate must be earned? With unchanged technological conditions and price levels, the sum would be the total amount which had been placed in the enterprise by the owners, directly or through retained earnings. But both price level and technological changes alter the amount of money capital which is required to purchase equipment necessary to produce a given output. Suppose, for example, that the general price level, including the prices of capital equipment, rises. As the present equipment wears out, output can be maintained economically only if additional money capital is invested in the enterprise. Thus the necessary return must be earned on the sum required for *replacement* of the capital equipment, if continued operation is to be maintained, rather than on the sum originally invested. If general price declines or technological developments allow the replacement of the equipment at a lower cost than the original, it is not necessary that the owners earn a return on the larger original sum invested, but merely upon the new, lower amount required for replacement. The price and technological changes will essentially have destroyed, through capital losses, a portion of the money capital originally invested, but operation of the enterprise will continue so long as an average return is earned upon the smaller sum of money capital now required.

Implicit Wages

Especially in smaller firms, a portion of the business profits may consist of noncontractual wages for work performed in the enterprise by the owners. The typical farmer or small shopkeeper performs substantial amounts of ordinary labor service for which he rarely pays himself a formal wage. A large portion of the sum which he regards as his business profit is essentially an implicit wage, equal to the amount which he could obtain from hiring his services to other firms.

Closely related are implicit wages of management; in a small business typically the person or persons controlling the operation of the enterprise and making the management decisions do not compensate themselves directly for this activity. A portion of the business profit earned is a compensation for this work, equal to the amounts which these persons could earn as hired managers of other firms. In larger enterprises, likewise, a portion of business profits may represent wages of management of officials of the business, who are not paid as much as their actual contribution to the business. In this case, however, the sums do not accrue to the persons responsible for them, but to the owners, and therefore in a sense are not necessary cost elements, but a form of monopsonistic profits discussed in a subsequent section. Were the markets perfect these items would become explicit costs; they accrue to the owners rather than to the managers only because of imperfections in the market.

Implicit Rents

If rent is regarded as a distinct form of factor return arising out of the scarcity of nonreproducible assets, a portion of business profits may fall within the category of implicit rent. If the firm owns land or similar nonreproducible assets, a portion of the profits consists of the sum which this land would earn if rented out instead of being used in the business. Alternatively, an implicit interest return on the current monetary value of the property may be regarded as an implicit cost. The sums involved will be the same regardless of which approach is used.

It is sometimes argued that with respect to short periods of time, the implicit cost element arising from the capital investment of the owners should be calculated as the quasi-rent, or current rental value of the capital goods (which are nonreproducible in a very short period), rather than as a return on the money capital necessary for replacement. This point of view is defended on the grounds that in a short period the full interest return does not have to be covered for the firm to continue in operation; so long as the firm earns as much from the use of the equipment as it could obtain from leasing it out (or as much as the interest return on the salvage value of the equipment) it is advantageous to continue operations, since the money capital cannot be withdrawn. On the other hand, if the capital equipment would rent for more than the return on the money capital invested in it, because of a temporary shortage of the equipment, this higher figure should be regarded as the cost element, since the firm is foregoing this sum by using the equipment.

This approach obviously has some merit in emphasizing the elements which must be covered in a short-run period, as contrasted to those which must be covered in a longer period. However, for most purposes of analysis, it is more useful to consider implicit costs, and thus profits, in terms of long-run considerations, rather than short-run considerations, since the nonreproducible character of capital goods is only a temporary phenomenon.

THE PORTION OF BUSINESS PROFITS IN EXCESS OF IMPLICIT COSTS

Any excess of business profits over and above the various implicit costs was in the past regarded as a homogeneous return designated as pure or economic profit. More careful analysis of this return, however, has led to increased emphasis upon the fact that it consists of several diverse elements. In recent years there has been a tendency to regard only one segment of this excess as a truly distinct return, with other segments, particularly those arising from monopoly or monopsony conditions, as merely special forms of other types of factor returns, and thus in a sense implicit costs. These segments of profit will be considered first, with subsequent attention to the residual or pure profits, in the present-day sense of the term.

Monopsony Profits

The first element in the excess of business profits over the implicit costs noted above is that arising from monopsonistic influences in the factor markets. When a particular firm is able to pay factor-owners less than the competitive factor-income figure, the owners of the firm essentially receive a portion of the factor income attributable to these factor units, and thus in a sense exploit the other factor-owners. For example, if one coal mine is able to hire workers more cheaply than other mines, the firm can earn a higher-than-average rate of business profit; the excess consists simply of the wage differential which the owners of the firm have been able to appropriate for their own use because of market imperfections. Only when markets are imperfect—when factor-owners lack adequate knowledge of other possibilities, or factor units are immobile—or competition among various firms for factor units is not complete can monopsonistic profits be earned. It should be noted that if all firms in the industry gain similar advantage, the profits will tend to disappear; it is the existence of a differential advantage on the part of particular firms that enables them to earn a high rate of profit from this source.

Firms may be particularly likely to obtain monopsony profits from failure to pay top-management personnel the full contribution which they make to the enterprise. The market for such personnel is highly imperfect, and firms may succeed for a considerable period of time in compensating successful managers at a lower rate than the actual contributions of these persons, and the amounts which the persons could obtain from other firms if they sought employment with them and their abilities were known.

Monopsony profits, while constituting an excess over implicit cost elements as defined in the preceding section, tend to capitalize in the same manner as monopoly profits, and thus are distinguishable from other forms of pure profit. Capitalization will be discussed in the following section.

Monopoly Profits

When a firm is protected from entry of new firms, it will be able to earn profits over and above the implicit cost elements, provided that average revenue is, in any range of output, above average cost. This higher return arising out of entry restriction is known as monopoly profit, although the market situation may be one of oligopoly or monopolistic competition, as well as complete monopoly as previously defined.

Popular thinking attributes a large portion of "excess" profit to monopoly positions, and some economists have regarded monopoly as the primary source of pure profit. However, closer examination of monopoly profits suggests that they differ in several respects from the pure profits noted below, and should be distinguished from the latter.

Imputation of Monopoly Profits. In the first place, unlike pure profits, monopoly profits are frequently imputable, or, in other words, attributable, to certain factor units. Suppose, for example, that entry into a field is restricted because the existing firms possess patent rights, or well-established trade-marks. The excess rate of profit which continues because of the inability of new firms to enter the industry is clearly attributable to the patent right or trade-mark. The firm could lease this to other firms for an equivalent return, and thus the return is in a sense an "opportunity cost" to the firm as the owner and user of the patent, instead of being a true profit. The amount involved is essentially a rent, in the broad sense of the term, since the asset—the patent right—is not reproducible for the period in which it is valid and other firms cannot find substitutes. The return is not a necessary cost from the standpoint of the industry (assuming that the patent has no value outside of the industry) since it would have no rental value if it were freely available to all firms.

Capitalization of Monopoly Profits. In other cases, in which the restriction of entry is due to the large volume of business necessary for low cost and heavy capital requirements, the monopoly profits are less clearly attributable to particular factors. Even in these cases, however, as well as in those in which the profits are attributable, the higher rate of profit tends to capitalize, if it is expected to continue. That is, the sale value of the enterprise tends to rise by the capitalized sum of the monopoly return. Thus not only will new purchasers of the firm, or of stock in it, receive only an average rate of earnings on their money capital, but the existing owners, who could dispose of the firm or their interest in it at the higher price figure, are in a sense only earning a normal return on the money capital represented by the sale price. The monopoly profit is therefore very similar to rent, in the broad sense of the term, and from the standpoint of the firm itself has some characteristics of a true imputed cost.

An example will serve to illustrate the capitalization of monopoly profits. Suppose that a firm is established with an investment of $50,000. It succeeds in building up a strongly attached reputation which competitors cannot duplicate, and earns annual business profits of $20,000, year after year. If the firm is offered for sale, it may bring as much as $400,000, if investors regard 5 per cent as an appropriate return on investments with the particular degree of risk involved, and expect the profits to continue indefinitely. Hence the new purchasers would earn only 5 per cent on their money capital, and the monopoly returns appear to have vanished, having become an implicit cost. Actually, however, the return is greatly in excess of the sum necessary to insure continued operation of the firm; if entry barriers are broken and profits fall, the enterprise will continue to operate on a permanent basis, so long as the business profits are as much as $2,500—representing 5 per cent return on replacement cost.

Monopoly Profits Distinguished from Other Returns. As indicated, monopoly profits have certain characteristics of rent and interest returns, since in large measure they are imputable to particular factor units and they tend to capitalize. Thus they resemble implicit costs, from the standpoint of individual firms. However, they may be distinguished from true implicit costs in several ways. In the first place, they are not necessary to ration economically scarce resources among competing units; in most cases the entry-restricting factors represent artificial barriers to the establishment of new firms, rather than true scarcity factors. Patent rights could be used by all firms in an industry if the law permitted; brand names could likewise be shared. Even when limited raw material resources restrict new firms, the restriction is a product of the ownership by the existing firms of the available resources. Furthermore, the monopoly receipts are not necessary to maintain output of the industry; if the earnings of the firms drop to an average return level through the breaking of the barriers to entry, they will not leave the industry. Finally, the existence of monopoly profits gives rise to constant striving on the part of the other firms to break the entry-restricting barriers and enter production in the field. Therefore, while monopoly profits must be distinguished from pure profits, they must also be distinguished from true implicit costs even though they resemble the latter, and must be regarded either as a special form of return, or as a major but distinct species of the general category of rents.

Innovations as a Source of Pure Profits

A third source of an excess of business profits over and above usual implicit costs is the undertaking of *innovations*—of deliberate changes in production and demand functions—by business firms. Some economists, of whom the most famous was Joseph Schumpeter, have regarded pure profits as solely the result of innovations;[1] others have regarded them as one major source, rather than the sole source. Innovations may be classed into two groups: those affecting production, and those affecting the market. The first group includes all changes which alter techniques of physical production and distribution, and methods of organization and operation. If a firm is successful in introducing cost-reducing techniques, it will earn, at least temporarily, a higher rate of profit. The second type of innovation includes all changes which affect the consumer demand for the product, such as the introduction of new products, new styles, advertising techniques, etc.

The innovational profits cannot be attributed to particular factor units, as can monopoly profits in most instances, and since they are not predictable with any degree of certainty, and since those due to any one innovation cannot be expected to continue, they cannot capitalize. They constitute a type of return of different character from monopoly profits and usual implicit cost elements in business profits. They will continue only until other firms succeed in duplicating the innovations successfully. If the innovation proves difficult to duplicate, and other firms are thus in a sense restricted from entering the field, the continuing profits must be regarded as monopoly profits, since they will capitalize. Any one firm can continue to make innovational profits, as such, only by continuing to introduce successful innovations.

The innovational profits, as a form of noncontractual residual in-

[1] See J. Schumpeter, *Theory of Economic Development* (Cambridge: Harvard University Press, 1934).

come, accrue directly to the firm and ultimately to its owners. In the small firm, therefore, the persons responsible for the undertaking of the innovation in large measure reap the reward from it, and it is sometimes argued that the innovational profits are essentially a form of managerial wage and not a distinct type of income. However, the complete unpredictability of the success of innovations and their noncontinuing character suggest that they should be regarded as a distinctive and essentially residual type of income, rather than as a form of managerial wage. This approach is particularly appropriate with respect to large corporations, in which the persons responsible for the innovations typically do not receive the gains from their success. The argument that their failure to do so constitutes merely a monopsonistic absorption by the owners of gains arising from the actions of the managers obscures the basic difference between innovational gains and other managerial returns.

Uncertainty as the Source of Pure Profits

Pure profits may arise not only from deliberate innovations, but also from essentially windfall sources, that is, from unexpected changes in revenues or costs, as, for example, from unanticipated shifts in consumer preferences, declines in raw material prices, etc. If the changes are favorable, they give rise to profits; if they are unfavorable they give rise to negative pure profits, or, in other words, losses. If the concept of uncertainty is defined broadly, the outcome of innovations may be regarded as one case of uncertainty, and thus uncertainty may be regarded as the sole source of pure profits. The tendency in recent years has been to explain profits in this way, following the classic work of Frank Knight.[2] In terms of this uncertainty thesis, pure profits may be defined as the difference between expected receipts and actual receipts during a given period, although, as noted in succeeding paragraphs, the term *expected* is subject to more than one interpretation as employed in this definition. Uncertainty must not be confused with risk, which is predictable (for a group) and is insurable.

Uncertainty arises in two major realms: in circumstances directly affecting the cost and revenue schedules of the firm, and in changes in the general environment, such as national income, government policies, etc., which indirectly affect cost and revenue schedules. With respect to

[2] See Frank H. Knight, *Risk, Uncertainty and Profit* (Boston: Houghton-Mifflin, 1921). Knight's work has been extended in recent years in the work of J. Fred Weston; note the references to Weston's articles at the end of the chapter.

the former, a firm can never be certain about the behavior of sales, prices, and various cost items in the coming period, and pure profits are frequently earned because sales or prices rise, or costs fall, without offsetting unfavorable changes. Even if a firm undertakes a deliberate change, as for example by introducing a new technique or product, it cannot be certain of results; if they exceed general expectations, pure profits are earned. On the other hand, pure profits may, and without question frequently do, arise as a result of changes extraneous to the immediate circumstances surrounding the firm, as, for example, changes in the weather, increases in governmental expenditures, tax reductions, changes in government regulatory policies, changes in tariffs, etc. When the changes are adverse, negative profits are suffered.

The Concept of Expected Returns. Clarification of the concept of pure profit requires interpretation of the term *expected* in the definition given above. If by this term is meant the prediction of the firm itself, any foreseen pure profits would not be pure profits at all—since the latter are defined as the difference between expected and realized receipts. If a firm undertakes an innovation in anticipation of a certain profit and actually attains this profit, the sum would not be pure profits, in terms of this interpretation of the term *expected,* but would be an implicit cost. The concept of profits will be a more useful one, however, if the term *expected* is interpreted to mean a forecast accepted with certainty, not only by the firm but by general opinion in the market. Returns expected in this sense will be reflected in factor prices and the selling or rental price of the firm as a whole, and tend to capitalize in the same manner as monopoly profit, and thus should not be regarded as pure profit. But profits which the firm hopes to gain, but which are not accepted by the market as certain, are not capitalized, and, if realized, constitute pure profits, even though the firm may have anticipated them. Hence gains from both innovational and windfall changes which are not market-anticipated constitute pure profits. The argument of some proponents of the uncertainty theory of profits that all innovational gains should be regarded as implicit wages of management, rather than as pure profit, cannot be accepted for reasons indicated in the previous section.

The Absence of Pure Profits and Monopoly Profits in Perfect Competition

For reasons outlined in earlier chapters, neither monopoly profits nor pure profits can exist in a static, perfectly competitive market situation. Under such circumstances, business profits will adjust to the level at which necessary implicit wage, interest, and rent costs are covered—the necessary interest return being based upon replacement cost of capital equipment. The purely competitive nature of such a market insures that inflow of new firms will eliminate any temporary excess returns; if the market is truly perfect, the adjustment will be instantaneous, and there will not even be temporary pure profits in the transitional period. If conditions are static, that is, if production and demand functions remain unchanged, there will be no uncertainty, and no pure profits. Monopoly profits result from continued departure of market conditions from ones of pure competition; pure profits are entirely the results of change—of the operation of dynamic forces in the economy—which give rise to uncertainty.

Summary

The discussion of the preceding pages may be summarized briefly. Business profits consist in large measure of implicit cost elements, attributable to various factor units employed, and to money capital. These elements must be covered over a long-run period, if the enterprise is to continue in operation. Since they are not contractual obligations, however, it is not essential that they be covered in a short period. In a perfectly competitive market with static conditions, business profits would adjust to the level at which these implicit cost elements would be covered exactly, without excess. If monopolistic restrictions on entry of firms into the industry develop, firms will earn a monopoly profit if average revenue exceeds average cost. However, this monopoly return is often attributable to particular factor units, such as patent rights, and if the return is expected to continue, it tends to capitalize and comes to resemble an implicit cost from the standpoint of the firm, and thus does not constitute a pure profit. Nevertheless, for purposes of analysis, it is desirable to distinguish monopoly profits and the closely related monopsony profits (both of which arise because of departure of market conditions from those of pure competition) from other implicit cost elements.

The excess of business profits over implicit cost elements and monopsony and monopoly profits may be designated as pure or economic profits. Pure profits can be attributed to uncertainty in the economy, the undertaking of innovations being included as a major source of uncertainty. In this sense pure profits constitute the excess of actual receipts over market-expected receipts.

PROFITS AS A FUNCTIONAL RETURN

The question of whether or not pure profits should be regarded as a functional or a residual return has played an important role in the general controversy in the field of profit theory. By *functional return* is meant a compensation for the performance of a specific function in production by the recipients of the return. By *residual return* is meant simply a sum which remains to certain factor owners after all costs have been covered, accruing to these persons because of existing institutional relationships rather than as a direct compensation for performing a function. It is obvious that the portions of business profits which consist of implicit wages, interest and rent are true functional returns, accruing to factor-owners for the provision of factor units made available to the business firm on a noncontractual basis. Monopoly profit, while functional in the narrow sense of the word because it becomes a type of opportunity cost to the firm, is not functional from the standpoint of the economy, since its receipt is not necessary for continued production of the output of the industry. The controversial question has related to the functional nature of pure profit.

It was common in the past to regard pure profits, when earned, as a distinct type of functional return, which was received by the entrepreneurs of the enterprise as compensation for undertaking innovations and bearing the primary risks of uncertainty. The entrepreneurs, as owners of the business, also received the implicit cost returns and monopoly profit, if any. But the distinctive return to the entrepreneurs was considered to be the pure profit, a functional return for innovation and uncertainty-bearing.

The usefulness of the functional concept of pure profits can be seriously questioned. In the modern large corporation the separation between ownership and management causes the pure profits to accrue largely to persons other than those who perform the "entrepreneurial" functions. In such enterprises the identity of the entrepreneurs and the profit receivers is lost. Furthermore, pure profits are not *caused* by uncertainty; they arise in conditions of uncertainty when realized conditions exceed expectations, and they can best be regarded as a residual income. Even in a small enterprise in which the entrepreneur and the profit receiver are identical, the pure profits can scarcely be regarded as a reward for the performance of the function of bearing uncertainty, since the act of doing so does not in itself insure pure profits, which arise only if conditions prove to be better than expected. Even when pure profits result from innovations, they can most satisfactorily be regarded as a residual income which accrues to the owners of the enterprise, rather than as a functional return for the work of introducing the innovations. Not only does the mere act of introducing innovations not necessarily lead to pure profits, but in many cases the persons who make the decisions to undertake the innovation are not the ones receiving the profit.

The Role of Profits in the Economy

The statement that profits can best be regarded as a residual return, rather than a functional return, must not be allowed to obscure the role which pure profits play in the functioning of the economy. In the first place, the anticipation of making pure profits is an important lure which leads firms to undertake innovations of all types, and thus to maintain economic progress and investment necessary for full employment. While the pure profits actually realized cannot, particularly in the large corporation, be regarded as a functional reward for undertaking change, the possibility of making such profits is an important source of encouragement to the firms for making the innovations. Secondly, the making of pure profits constitutes a signal for the revision of behavior on the part of the firm. Failure of expected and realized profits to coincide suggests the need for revision of estimates, and in some cases, of actual policies.

Thirdly, the making of pure profits on the part of some firms leads other firms to readjust their policies. Both pure profits and monopoly profits constitute a stimulus to other firms to attempt to duplicate the policies of the successful firms which gave rise to these profits, or to attempt to develop other policies which will accomplish the same result profit-wise. In a highly competitive field, firms dare not lag behind the more successful firms or they will soon be suffering losses; the earning of pure profits by some firms constitutes a warning to other firms to adjust their policies if they are to avoid future losses. Likewise, the earning of high profits in a certain field leads additional firms to enter the industry and brings about a redistribution of allocation of resources in conformity with changes in consumer demand and other variables.

NEGATIVE PROFITS OR LOSSES

The preceding sections have been concerned with positive profits arising in cases in which actual results are better than expected results.

But actual receipts may be less than anticipated, and, as a result, pure profits are negative; in other words, a loss, from an economic standpoint, is incurred. Economic profits are negative whenever the receipts are less than the sum of contractual obligations, depreciation charges, and implicit interest, wage, and rent costs. If receipts are so low that contractual obligations plus depreciation are not covered, the situation may be described as one of *business losses,* or losses in the accounting sense; if these items are covered, but all implicit costs are not covered, the firm is earning a business profit, but is suffering negative economic profits, or an economic loss.

Certain types of losses, if expected to continue, will tend to capitalize—reducing the sale value of the enterprise by the capitalized sum of the loss. It may be argued that in such cases, the implicit cost element arising out of the investment is not the normal return on the replacement cost of the equipment, but one upon the current sale value. In other words, the quasi-rent on the capital goods, not the interest return on their cost, is the appropriate element in cost. From a strictly short-run point of view, this argument has limited merit. But for purposes of analysis, it is preferable to define losses as the excess over receipts of all cost items which must be covered if the firm is to remain in business permanently. It is a loss in this sense which is significant in determining long-range policy of the firm and the flow of resources among various industries.

The Various Situations of Losses

It is important to distinguish between those loss situations in which firms will cease operations immediately and those in which they will continue to operate over a short-run period. Several stages of losses must be noted:

1. Failure of receipts to cover explicit variable costs. If the enterprise is not taking in enough in current receipts to meet those variable costs which are explicit in nature, continued operation is obviously undesirable unless an immediate improvement is expected, and is impossible unless the firm or its owners have adequate reserve funds with which to meet the deficit.

2. Failure of receipts to cover contractual fixed costs. If receipts cover explicit variable costs, but not explicit fixed costs, of which interest is likely to be the most significant, the enterprise will go into bankruptcy, unless the reserves of the firm are adequate to meet the necessary payments, or the owners of the firm are able and willing to supply the necessary funds. Through reorganization in bankruptcy, the creditors

become the new owners of the enterprise, and explicit interest costs are reduced or eliminated; the situation thus becomes one of (3) or (4) below.

3. Coverage of contractual fixed and variable factor costs, but not depreciation charges. A firm may find itself, before or after reorganization, in the situation of being able to meet all contractual obligations involving both fixed and variable costs, but not depreciation. The firm can obviously continue operations as long as existing equipment can be used; once the equipment wears out, it will lack funds for replacement, and will be unable to obtain them unless the owners are willing to supply additional money capital. This they obviously will not do, unless an improvement in conditions is expected. Prior to the point at which substantial replacement of equipment is necessary, however, liquidation will be advantageous unless improvements are expected. If the depreciation charges reflect the actual decline in the current salable value of the capital assets during the period, failure to cover this sum warrants immediate liquidation. If the depreciation charges exceed the actual decline in the value of assets, liquidation is desirable if the actual earnings toward depreciation charges are less than the sum of the interest return on the salvage value plus the actual decline in the value of the assets.

4. Coverage of contractual costs and depreciation, but failure to earn all implicit costs. A firm may be in the position of having adequate receipts to meet all contractual factor payments and depreciation, but not enough to cover all implicit costs, the most important of which is likely to be a return on the money capital of the owners. In this case the firm *can* continue operations indefinitely if the owners wish. But it will not be advantageous for the owners to permit continued operation once the position is reached at which the actual earnings on capital of the owners is less than the interest earnings on the salvage value of the capital equipment (assuming that other implicit costs are covered). When this point is reached, it will be advantageous for the owners to liquidate the enterprise and invest their money in other outlets, unless the profit position of the firm is expected to improve.

Until this point is reached, however, it is advantageous for the owners of the firm to keep it in operation, even though they are not making an average return on their capital, since they cannot withdraw their capital from the enterprise. Once money capital has been invested in specialized capital equipment, only a small portion of it can be withdrawn quickly (the amount equal to the salvage value), and the rental value of the equipment (if rental is possible) will depend upon the earning capacity of the equipment, not its cost. So long as the owners make a return in excess of the salvage or rental value, there is nothing that they can do to improve their position until the equipment wears out.

In practice many firms operate far too long from the standpoint of the interests of the owners. In part this is a product of continuing over-optimism about the future, in part, of the dislike of persons to discontinue an enterprise with which they have long been identified, and in part because the officials of the company are reluctant to lose their positions. As a consequence, depreciation funds and such business profits as are made are utilized to maintain and repair equipment, and eventually the equity of the stockholders is destroyed. There are many examples of small railroads which operated for many years beyond the point at which the best interests of the stockholders would have been served, for a variety of reasons along the lines noted above.[3]

Causes of Losses

The sources of negative economic profits are the reverse of the causes of positive economic profits. In general losses may be attributed to uncertainty—to unanticipated events which adversely affect the cost or revenue schedules. These events may consist of general changes in the economy, such as a fall in national income or altered governmental policy, or they may be changes in the circumstances directly affecting the particular firm, such as an adverse shift in consumer preferences, rises in materials costs, etc. Or they may result from the successful introduction of innovations by competitors, or the failure of innovations attempted by the firm itself to produce desired results. In other cases they may result from mistakes, such as the failure to obtain optimum factor combinations. Where the losses are due to obvious managerial errors, it may be argued that the source of the loss from the standpoint of the firm is overcompensation of management personnel (the opposite of monopsonistic exploitation). One frequent type of mistake is that of the establishment of new enterprises under circumstances in

[3] In some cases abandonment came only when equipment had deteriorated to the point at which operation was no longer possible without repairs which the company lacked the funds to make. The Bellevue and Cascade, a short line in Iowa, ceased operations only when its last usable locomotive broke an axle and the company had no funds to repair it. The Virginia and Truckee, one of the oldest lines in the west, abandoned its Virginia City line only when a tunnel collapsed and trains could no longer operate, and continued to operate the remainder of its line for twenty years after the point was reached at which receipts no longer covered direct operating costs.

which profitable operation is impossible. This may be due to lack of adequate knowledge of revenue and cost schedules, or overoptimism on the part of the promoters.

The incurrence of losses, just as of economic profits, leads to readjustments which may bring about their elimination. Losses constitute a warning to a firm to alter its policies to obtain greater efficiency, to develop innovations, etc. The changes made may prove to be successful, and profitable operation may be restored; in other cases the firm may be unable to escape the losses, and thus must eventually liquidate. In large measure continuing losses may be regarded as the penalty for failure to adapt to changing conditions.

SELECTED REFERENCES

KNIGHT, F. H. *Risk, Uncertainty and Profit.* Boston: Houghton-Mifflin, 1921.
One of the classic analyses of the functions of the entrepreneur, with emphasis on uncertainty as the source of profit.

SCHUMPETER, J. *Theory of Economic Development.* Cambridge: Harvard University Press, 1934.
The innovations theory of profit.

TRIFFIN, R. *Monopolistic Competition and General Equilibrium Theory.* Cambridge: Harvard University Press, 1940.
A stimulating discussion of various aspects of profit theory.

KEIRSTEAD, B. S. *An Essay in the Theory of Profits and Income Distribution.* London: Basil Blackwell, 1953.
An integration of various approaches to profit theory.

WESTON, J. F. "A Generalized Uncertainty Theory of Profits," *American Economic Review,* Vol. XL (March, 1950), pp. 40–60.
An extension of the Knight approach to profit theory.

WESTON, J. F. "The Profit Concept and Theory: A Restatement," *Journal of Political Economy,* Vol. XLIV (April, 1954), pp. 152–70.
An extension of Weston's previous work.

MARSHAL, J. "The Construction of a New Theory of Profits," *American Economic Review,* Vol. XLI (September, 1951), pp. 549–65.
A profit theory which involves abandonment of the traditional implicit cost approach.

DAVIS, R. M. "The Current State of Profit Theory," *American Economic Review*, Vol. XL (June, 1952), pp. 245–64.
A review of the controversy in the field of profit theory.

GORDON, R. A. "Enterprise, Profits, and the Modern Corporation," *Explorations in Economics,* pp. 306–16. New York: McGraw-Hill, 1937.
A brief description of the three major approaches to profit theory.

The second Weston article listed above contains a very complete bibliography of recent writings on profit theory.

QUESTIONS

1. Why does a large portion of business profits consist of elements which are costs from an economic standpoint?
2. Upon what base should the necessary return on the owners' capital be figured?
3. A farmer obtains $8500 from the sale of his crop; his expenses, including taxes, were $2000. His farm would sell for $25,000. He could obtain a job for a local feed mill at $4000 a year if he wished. Determine his business profits, the implicit cost elements in the business profits, and his pure profit, if any. Use a figure of 4 per cent as an average rate of return.
4. What is the source of monopsony profits? Why will they not be attained if the monopsony powers extend to all firms in the industry?
5. Define monopoly profit. Why are monopoly profits in a sense implicit costs? Why are they not true costs from the standpoint of the economy?
6. Suppose that you buy the entire stock of a corporation that is earning, and expected to earn, monopoly profits. Will you make a higher than average rate of return on the money which you place in the enterprise? Explain.
7. Explain the meaning of the concept of innovations and give examples. How do innovational profits differ from monopoly profits? From windfall profits?
8. Why are innovational profits not regarded as a managerial wage attributable to the persons responsible for the introduction of the innovations?
9. Distinguish between uncertainty and risk.
10. If profits arising out of uncertainty are foreseen by the market as a whole, are they actually pure profits if and when they are earned? Explain. Are they pure profits if they are anticipated by the particular firm only?
11. What condition is necessary for monopoly profits to continue?
12. Why would there be no monopoly or pure profits in a purely and perfectly competitive market?
13. What are the difficulties encountered in attempting to consider pure profits as a functional return?
14. Indicate the major roles which profits play in the economy.
15. Explain the various meanings of the term "losing money."
16. Suppose that a particular firm is covering all variable costs and depreciation, but not an average return on investment. If the owners are seeking to maximize their gain, at what time will they discontinue operations? Explain.
17. Why do companies sometimes operate far beyond the optimum (from a profit standpoint) time of liquidation?
18. In several instances in the last three decades, sharp increases in scrap metals prices have led to the abandonment of railroads whose owners had intended to keep them in operation for a longer period. Explain.
19. Some railroad companies have continued to operate for many years despite the fact that they have never earned an average return on the investment. Why?

20. Indicate the major causes of losses.
21. How would you explain the following:
    a) The heavy losses, over several years in which competitors were making large profits, of the Kaiser Motors Company?
    b) Losses, despite general business prosperity in the economy, of many textile producers in the period of 1950–55?
    c) Frequent failure of small grocery stores?
    d) The extremely heavy losses of the New York subway system?
22. The following data (with some rounding of figures) on revenues and expenses of four railroads are taken from the 1951 *Statistics of Railways* volume of the Interstate Commerce Commission. Complete the table, and indicate whether each company is (*a*) making excess profits, (*b*) making business profits but not covering all implicit costs, or (*c*) suffering business losses. In the last case (*c*), what additional information would you need to determine whether or not abandonment was likely in the near future? (Assume, in answering this question, that the investment figure given reflects accurately the base upon which the normal return should be figured, that a normal return rate is 5 per cent, and that there are no other implicit costs but return on the investment. Depreciation is included in operating expenses.)

Corporation	Investment	Operating Revenues	Operating Expenses and Taxes	Operating Income	Interest	Net Income	Implicit Costs	Pure Profits
Tremont & Gulf......	$2,500,000	$ 697,000	$667,000	$ 30,000	$39,000	....	....	....
San Luis Valley So. .	90,000	43,100	46,100	−3,000	0	....	....	....
Trona RR....	1,500,000	1,175,000	964,000	211,100	4,000	....	....	....
Ferdinand RR	40,000	21,000	20,470	530	20	....	....	....

Chapter 20 GENERAL EQUILIBRIUM OF THE ECONOMY

In the preceding chapters the analysis of the determination of price and output of commodities and the prices of the factors has been established in terms of particular commodities and particular factor classes. This portion of economic analysis is, therefore, known as *partial equilibrium* theory since it deals with adjustments in particular segments of the economy in isolation with only incidental reference to interrelationships of the various segments. For most purposes the partial equilibrium theory, which developed from English classical economics, is adequate, since the simplifying assumptions do not destroy the usefulness of the analysis as a tool for the study of particular problems. In analyzing the effect of the levying of an excise tax on tobacco, for example, the assumption that other prices are given is not an unrealistic one.

However, a complete picture of the functioning of the economic system and the development of tools of analysis for studying problems with broad ramifications through several sectors of the economy requires consideration of the interrelationships of the outputs and prices of various commodities and the prices of various factors. The portion of economic theory which performs this function is known as *general equilibrium* theory. Although originally developed in the last century in the work of Léon Walras,[1] it had little impact upon the general body of economic theory until the last two decades, in which the earlier work has been revived and amplified. Some of the major interrelationships in the economy will be noted briefly before the framework of the general equilibrium analysis is presented.

[1] *Elements d'economie politique pure* (Lausanne: 1884). Recent presentations of general equilibrium theory are listed at the end of the chapter. One elementary economics textbook, that by E. T. Weiler, *The Economic System* (New York: Macmillan, 1952), follows the general equilibrium approach.

Consumer Price Interdependencies

The analysis of price and output determination of commodities in earlier chapters was based upon the assumption that the prices of other goods were given, apart from minor reference to the direct effects upon the prices of other goods which might result from the change in the price of a particular good. But this type of modification reflects only a small portion of the possible interdependencies. A change in the price of any one consumption good inevitably alters the demand for and possibly the supply of other goods. For example, a rise in the price of butter will increase the demand for substitutes, such as oleomargarine, and lead to increases in prices and outputs of these goods, if the markets are purely competitive. If they are not, the effect may be solely upon output, with a decline in price of the substitutes possible. The prices of goods complementary to butter, such as bread, may fall as the demand for them falls as butter becomes more expensive. Changes in the outputs of these other goods will affect the factor supplies available for the production of bread, and thus its cost of production and supply, while the shifts in the prices of the other goods will in turn affect the demand for bread. The changes in prices and outputs of substitute and complementary goods will in turn affect the prices and outputs of other commodities.

Thus complete adjustment in the prices of all goods can occur only when the various prices and outputs attain levels which are mutually consistent with one another. Given the basic determinants of consumption goods prices, namely, consumer incomes, consumer preferences, factor price schedules, production functions, and the nature of competition in the various markets, eventually such an equilibrium will be attained. But a shift in the determinants affecting any one good may have widespread repercussions upon the prices and outputs of other goods—a reaction which is obscured by partial equilibrium analysis.

The Relationship of the Prices of Consumption Goods and Factors

In the analysis of the pricing of consumption goods, the factor price schedules were assumed as given, while in the discussion of the determination of factor prices, for the most part the consumption goods prices were assumed to be given. Actually, of course, the two sets of prices are mutually dependent upon one another. For example, a major element in the costs of consumption goods is labor cost, and therefore the wage level is a significant factor in determining the prices of the products. But the demand for labor, and thus the wage rates, are dependent upon the marginal revenue product of various types of labor, which in turn is dependent upon the levels of consumer goods prices. No circular reasoning is involved in the analysis, as is sometimes claimed, but both wage (and other factor price) levels and commodity price levels must adjust to figures which are mutually consistent with one another, because until this situation is reached there will be a tendency for one set of prices or the other to shift.

THE FRAMEWORK OF GENERAL EQUILIBRIUM THEORY

General equilibrium theory presents an over-all framework of the basic price and output interrelationships, including both commodities (produced goods) and factors, for the economy as a whole. It demonstrates mathematically that, given the basic determinants (factor supply schedules, consumer preferences, production functions, forms of competition, and the determinants of the level of employment), the prices of all commodities and factors, and the outputs of the various commodities, will adjust to levels which are mutually consistent with one another. Given the levels of the determinants, these price and output levels will remain stable once they have been attained, and changes in the determinants will produce a widespread pattern of readjustments until mutually consistent sets of prices and outputs are again attained.

The mathematical explanation is based upon the following assumptions, several of which are designed to keep the analysis as simple as possible:

1. Given consumer preferences
2. Given factor supplies, independent of factor prices
3. Given techniques of production, with fixed coefficients of production; in other words, fixed proportions of various factors are required to produce a unit of output
4. Purely competitive commodity and factor markets, and attainment of equality of price and average cost for each commodity, equality of supply and demand for each factor, and equality of supply and demand for each commodity
5. Incomes derived solely from the provision of factor units
6. Spending of all incomes upon consumption. This assumption insures the attainment of full employment.

In the mathematical exposition, the following symbols are employed:

$x_1, x_2, \ldots\ldots x_n$	indicate quantities of various commodities
$p_1, p_2, \ldots\ldots p_n$	indicate prices of the respective commodities
$y_1, y_2, \ldots\ldots y_m$	indicate the quantities of various factors available
$w_1, w_2, \ldots\ldots w_m$	indicate the prices of the respective factors
$a_{11}, a_{21}, \ldots\ldots a_{n1}$	indicate the quantities of various factors necessary to produce a unit of a commodity
$MU_1, MU_2, \ldots\ldots MU_n$	designate the marginal utilities of various commodities to a consumer

The Demand Equations

On the demand side of the picture, there are two basic sets of equations:

(1) The budget equation, showing, for each person, the equality between his factor income (the price paid him per unit for each factor unit which he supplies, times the number of such units which he supplies) and his expenditure (which consists of the sum of the quantities of each good which he purchases, multiplied by the prices of the goods):

$$y_1w_1 + y_2w_2 + \ldots\ldots + y_mw_m = x_1 + x_2p_2 + \ldots\ldots + x_np_n$$

x_1 is the commodity in terms of which the values of all other commodities are expressed, and thus has no price of its own.

(2) The allocation-of-consumption-expenditures equation, showing, for each consumer, the equality of the ratios of the marginal utilities of all commodities to their prices, under the assumption that all persons allocate their incomes among various commodities in such a way as to maximize satisfaction:

$$\frac{MU_1}{p_1} = \frac{MU_2}{p_2} = \frac{MU_3}{p_3} \ldots\ldots = \frac{MU_n}{p_n}$$

The number of equations of the second type, for each consumer, is one less than the number of commodities $(n - 1)$, since one commodity (x_1) serves as the unit of measurement of the prices of the others. However, if the equation (1) above is included, the number of equations is equal to the number of unknowns—the amounts of the various commodities—and the purchases of the various commodities by each consumer are determinate, given the prices of the goods, the factor prices, and the quantities of the factor units possessed. Since there is a separate set of such equations for each possible price level for each good, the demand schedule of the person for each good is determinate. The demand is thus a function of the price of the good in question, the prices of all other consumption goods (although the significance of many of these is negligible), and the prices of the factors (given the amounts of the factor units supplied). The factor prices and quantities determine the person's income and total expenditures. This demand function may be expressed as follows for each commodity and each consumer, x being the quantity of the commodity demanded:

$$x_2 = f_2(p_2, p_3, \ldots\ldots\ldots\ldots p_n, w_1, w_2, \ldots\ldots\ldots\ldots w_m)$$

There are similar equations for each commodity, and for each consumer. In other words, the quantity of the good demanded is shown to depend not only upon the price of the good, but upon the prices of all other commodities as well, and upon the factor prices, which determine the person's income. Given the quantities of the factors owned and the consumer preference schedules, these equations are determinate.

The total demand functions are the sums of the functions of the individual consumers; for each commodity the equation can be expressed as follows (capital letters being used to designate total quantities):

$$X_2 = F_2(p_2, p_3, \ldots\ldots\ldots\ldots p_n, w_1, w_2, \ldots\ldots\ldots\ldots w_m)$$

In the case of commodity x_1, which is the measure of value of all other commodities, an equation can be derived from the budget equation showing that the amount of x_1 demanded is equal to total income minus expenditures on the other goods. The equations thus derived for each consumer can be summed for all consumers to give the total demand function for X_1:

$$X_1 = Y_1w_1 + Y_2w_2 + \ldots\ldots + Y_mw_m - (X_2p_2 + X_3p_3 + \ldots\ldots + X_np_n)$$

Including this equation, the number of demand equations is equal to the number of commodities (n).

The Supply Equations

On the supply side of the picture, there are two basic sets of equations. The first relates price to cost of production; under the assumptions of a purely competitive market and fixed production coefficients, the price of each good is equal to the sum of the figures obtained by multiplying the price of each factor used to produce the commodity times the quantity of the factor required to produce a unit of the commodity:

$$p_2 = a_{21}w_1 + a_{22}w_2 + \ldots\ldots\ldots\ldots + a_{2m}w_m$$

There is a similar equation for each commodity, and therefore as many equations as there are commodities (n). In the case of commodity x_1, the equation is also equal to 1, since this commodity is the common denominator of value of the others.

Secondly, there are equations showing the equality of the total quantities of the various factors used to produce the various consumption goods with the total quantities of these factors available, under the assumption of attainment of equality of factor supply and demand. Hence, for each factor, the quantity available (Y_1) must equal the sum of the quantities of the factor used in the production, per unit, of each consumption good, multiplied by the number of units of output of the consumption good:

$$Y_1 = a_{11}X_1 + a_{21}X_2 + \ldots\ldots\ldots\ldots\ldots + a_{n1}X_n$$

There is one such equation for each factor, and thus m equations.

Solution of the Demand and Supply Equations

In total there are three sets of equations:

n equations relating the quantities of various commodities demanded to commodity prices and factor prices (the latter, in conjunction with given factor quantities, determining incomes), including the equation for X_1 (which serves as the common denominator of value), showing that the quantity of this commodity demanded is equal to the total income received less expenditures on all other commodities.

n equations relating the prices of all commodities to the costs of producing them (quantities of factor units used multiplied by factor prices).

m equations relating the supplies of various types of factors available to the total quantities of the factors used in the production of the various commodities.

The total number of equations equals twice the number of commodities plus the number of factors ($2n + m$). The number of unknowns is equal to the number of commodities (n), the number of commodity prices ($n - 1$, since one commodity is used as the unit of measurement of the values of the others), plus the number of factors, or $2n + m - 1$. Thus the number of equations appears to be one more than the number of unknowns. But one equation can be eliminated, since if the prices of all commodities are known, as well as quantities of all except one, the quantity of the latter can be deduced without a separate equation. With this adjustment, therefore, the number of equations and the number of unknowns are the same $(2n + m - 1)$, and the system of equations is thus solvable, and the general equilibrium system is determinate. Given the consumer preferences, the supplies of factor units, and the production functions, the prices of all commodities and factors, valued in terms of commodity x_1, are determinate, under the assumptions (with respect to pure competition, etc.) noted above, as well as the quantities of output of the various goods, and the allocation of factor units among the production of various goods. If the data of factor supplies, consumer preference schedules, and production coefficients were actually known, all prices and outputs could be calculated. As a matter of fact this information is not obtainable. But the system of equations indicates that under the assumptions, there is one, and only one, set of commodity and factor prices and outputs of commodities in which the various elements are mutually consistent with one another and which is therefore stable. In other words, under the assumptions made, commodity and factor prices and commodity outputs will adjust simultaneously to levels which are consistent with one another.

The Simplifying Assumptions

Several of the simplifying assumptions made in the preceding analysis can be abandoned without destroying the determinateness of the system. The assumption of given production coefficients can be replaced by the more realistic one of given production functions of a character permitting substitution of various factors for one another, together with the assumption of given marginal rates of substitution among the various factors. Secondly, the assumption of pure competition may be replaced by one of varied but given forms of competition in the various markets, with given policies followed by firms in oligopoly and oligopsony positions. Thirdly, the assumption of given (perfectly inelastic) factor supplies may be replaced by an assumption of given factor supply schedules, relating the quantities of each factor available to the prices of the factors. Finally, the assumption that all income is spent on consumption may be replaced by one of a given set of consumption-savings ratios at various levels of national income. This latter assumption, together with one of a given schedule of investment at various levels of national income,[2] make the actual level of national income and employment a variable in the system, replacing the assumption of full employment. These various adjustments, which are necessary to bring the mathematical system more closely in conformity with actual conditions, greatly complicate the exposition and any attempt to establish magnitudes in the system. But they do not destroy its determinateness, and the system thus modified is a much more complete explanation of interrelationships and a more useful tool of analysis, despite its complications.

The Usefulness of General Equilibrium Theory

General equilibrium theory is of greatest value in stressing the interdependence of various portions of the economic system, which is easily lost sight of in the use of partial equilibrium analysis. Failure to recognize this interdependence is responsible for many errors in popular reasoning on economic questions. For example, tariff policy is often considered only in terms of its effect upon output and employment in the particular industry protected, with no consideration of the effects of the tariff in reducing exports and thus output and employment in exporting industries. The theory calls attention to the fact that changes in one portion of the economy may have widespread repercussions in other segments, and that commodity and factor prices are mutually interdependent; wage changes, for example, will inevitably affect prices. Finally, the theory provides an important contribution in demonstrating that the over-all system is determinate, that is, that, given the basic determinants of the system, there is only one set of prices and outputs in which the various elements are mutually consistent with one another, and equilibrium attained in one sector is stable only if it is consistent with the maintenance of equilibria in other sectors.

Limitations to General Equilibrium Theory

The general equilibrium theory is subject to two major limitations. First, it is essentially static in nature, defining the over-all equilibrium in terms of given determinants. While it offers a tool for studying the effects of specific changes in determinants, as illustrated in the following section, it is of limited value in study of general trends of economic development. Closely related is its inadequacy in analyzing the determi-

[2] The assumption of a given schedule of investment may be replaced by one of given determinants of the schedules of marginal revenue product of capital goods, and of the supply of and demand for loanable funds, which determine the interest rate; by this adjustment the level of investment becomes an element in the system, rather than an autonomous variable.

nants of the level of national income, and processes of change in national income. While the simplifying assumption of full employment can be replaced by one of the determinants of the level of employment, the system does not provide useful tools of analysis of national income adjustments, in part because of the limited attention given to the nature and role of money in the economy.

In recent years increased effort has been given to the attempt to remedy these inadequacies, by further analysis of the role of money in the general equilibrium system, and to the development of a dynamic general equilibrium theory, but much more work is required along these lines before the analysis becomes a useful tool of study of dynamic situations. Most national income theory, as outlined in Chapter 22, has developed independently of general equilibrium theory.

The second limitation is a more practical one relating to the actual body of the theory as it stands, namely, the difficulty of estimating the quantities of the various magnitudes so that the equations may be solved in quantitative terms, and the theory used to predict precise quantitative results of various changes and policies. The tremendous complexity of the system and the inadequacy of data make this very difficult, although in the last decade various attempts have been made to do so with a simplified model, as explained in the last section of this chapter.

CHANGES IN THE DETERMINANTS

Changes in any of the basic determinants of the system may have widespread repercussions in the system, as suggested in previous paragraphs, and will lead to the establishment of a new equilibrium pattern. The effects of several major sources of change will be considered briefly.

Changes in Consumer Preferences

Consumer preferences constantly change as styles and tastes and needs vary, partly as a result of deliberate efforts on the part of business firms, partly from autonomous causes. Increased relative preference for one good (A) relative to that for another good (B) increases the demand for the former and reduces the demand for the latter. Accordingly, business firms will find it advantageous to increase output of A, while output of B will fall. Thus some resources will be shifted from the production of B to the production of A. If all factors involved are equally productive in the production of either good, factor prices may not change. But this is unlikely; some factors will be more efficient in the production of A and others in the production of B. Hence the prices of factors best suited for the production of A will tend to rise, and those best suited for B will fall, and as a consequence the incomes of the owners of the former set of factors will rise and those of the owners of the latter group will fall. Over a longer period the factors will shift from one use to another more easily than in a shorter period.

Techniques of Production

New inventions produce continuous changes in available techniques of production. These changes alter the production functions, the quantities of various factors required to produce a unit of output of particular commodities in the optimum fashion, and the prices of the finished products. As a consequence, the allocation of factors to the production of various commodities is affected, as well as the prices of the commodities and the factors (and the distribution of income). For example, suppose that a new technique is developed for the production of glass tableware which lessens the amount of man power necessary per unit of output, but increases the amounts of certain chemicals required. The reduction in the cost and the price of the glassware stimulates increased consumer use, and greater use by the producers of the various ingredients. The quantities of the chemicals and silica and other factors not affected by the technological change will increase; the quantity of labor used will decrease unless the increased sales more than offset the substitution of chemicals for manpower. The suppliers of the chemicals and other materials will receive increased incomes, at least temporarily, and the owners of nonproducible specialized resources used in their production will gain permanently higher incomes. Workers replaced by the new processes will experience declines in wages, unless their skills can be transferred to other industries. The net effects upon factor prices and income distribution will be greatly affected by the ease of transference of factor units from one line of production to another.

The increased use of glassware will also affect the sales of other products. Sales of direct substitutes, such as plastic dinnerware, will tend to fall, with consequent repercussions on output and factor prices. If the demand for the glassware is relatively inelastic, less money will be spent on the product, and purchases of other unrelated products will rise—with further repercussions on prices, outputs, and factor prices.

Technological changes which make new products available likewise produce modifications in the general equilibrium system. Such products alter consumer preference patterns, the output of substitute and complementary goods, and relative factor prices. The development of the automobile, for example, has had tremendous effects upon the economy. The demand for and output of complementary goods, such as highways, gasoline, tires, etc., have increased greatly, together with facilities to produce them. The demand for and output of substitutes, such as horses, buggies and wagons, and short-haul railway travel have declined. The pattern of location of retail stores and of dwellings has been greatly altered, as well as the nature and location of places of amusement and recreation. Incomes of owners of factors of particular importance in the production of automobiles and the other complementary goods have risen, while those of factor units used primarily to produce the substitutes, and not adaptable to other uses, have fallen. The owners of land containing oil have experienced great increases in their incomes, while owners of land primarily suited to the growing of hay for horses have experienced declines in incomes. The relative incomes of the owners of completely adaptable factors have not been affected by the change.

Changes in Factor Supplies

Changes in factor supplies, either in quantity or in quality, have much the same effects as technological developments. An increase in the quantities of one factor available compared to those of others will alter relative factor prices, optimum factor combinations, and prices and outputs of consumption goods. The prices of goods using relatively large amounts of the factor which has increased in supply will fall relative to those of other commodities, and consumption and output will increase. The price, per unit, of the factor which has increased in supply will tend to fall, but the total share of income going to the owners of this factor may rise. For example, a growth in the supply of capital goods, relative to the quantities of other factors, will increase the prices paid for labor and the incomes of the workers, and increase the relative outputs of goods requiring relatively large amounts of capital goods for efficient production.

Changes in Competitive Relationships

Changes in competitive relationships will produce modifications in the equilibrium system. For example, if strong oligopoly replaces pure competition in a particular commodity market, the relative price of the article will rise and consumption and output will fall. The demand for other commodities will rise if the demand for this commodity is elastic, and will fall if it is inelastic. The owners of the firms producing this commodity will obtain greater incomes, as long as they are protected from the entry of new firms into the industry. The reduced employment of other factors in the industry will lead to readjustments in factor prices, and in costs, and thus outputs, of other industries. Changes in competitive relations in the factor markets will alter relative factor and commodity prices and the relative outputs of various goods.

Theories of Change in the Determinants of General Equilibrium

In the preceding paragraphs, the types of readjustments which occur when the basic determinants of equilibrium change as a result of forces autonomous to the economic system have been indicated in a general way. Relatively little attention has been given to the question of whether or not a theory of change in the determinants, relating this change to certain forces within or external to the economy, can be developed. A few such attempts have been made. T. R. Malthus, for example, developed a long-term relationship between wage levels and population growth, of such a nature that growth in population and thus labor supply were limited to the rate of increase in subsistence available to the workers.[3] This theory was accepted and developed by various English classical writers subsequent to Ricardo.[4] Joseph Schumpeter attached great importance to the rate of change in the introduction of innovations as the primary factor determining the rate of economic development and hence the rate and pattern of change in the determinants of the equilibrium system.[5] One of the most complete theories of economic development was that of Karl Marx; his basic principle of economic change was the thesis that each form of economic system develops within itself internal inconsistencies, which manifest themselves primarily in struggles between various groups in the economy. These ultimately destroy the particular form of economic system, which gives way to a new form, which in turn develops its own internal inconsistencies.

In recent years renewed attention has been given to the establishment of theories of economic change and development, particularly with respect to the causes and processes of changes in the level of employment, and with respect to the determinants of the rate of long-term economic growth, in both undeveloped and more highly developed countries. Further reference will be made to this analysis in Chapter 23.

[3] T. R. Malthus, *Essays on Population* (London: 1798).

[4] Note the summary in W. J. Baumol, *Economic Dynamics,* chap. ii. (New York: Macmillan, 1951).

[5] Joseph Schumpeter, *The Theory of Economic Development* (Cambridge: Harvard University Press, 1934).

INPUT-OUTPUT ANALYSIS

The general equilibrium theory emphasizes the basic interrelationships among the various sectors of the economy, but its complexity and its high degree of abstraction limit its usefulness as a tool of analysis in specific cases. As a result, in recent years an attempt has been made to develop a simpler version of the theory to which empirical content can be given, with statistical estimates of the magnitudes in the equations, so that it may serve as a useful tool of analysis, particularly in the study of problems relating to economic mobilization for war. The new version of general equilibrium theory is known as *input-output analysis.* The work was initiated largely by Harvard economist Wassily Leontief.

The Theoretical Framework

There have been two steps in the development of the analysis, namely, the establishment of the theoretical framework, and the determination of the actual magnitudes for the various categories in the framework. The first step has consisted in large measure of a simplification of the general equilibrium mathematical system. The economy has been divided into a relatively small number of segments, each including industries producing closely related products (from the standpoint of factor inputs). Equations are then established relating the output of each industry to the outputs of the industries using the product of this industry, and to final, autonomous demand.

In order to make the system manageable, several simplifying assumptions are made:

1. Given coefficients of production, or, in other words, the assumption of a given combination of quantities of various factors necessary to produce a unit of output of a commodity.
2. Linear character of the production equations; thus a certain percentage change in the output of one product will cause the same percentage change in the inputs of the various factors used to produce it.
3. Given factor supplies, consumer demands, and prices. Prices are not a variable in the system, which is concerned solely with output adjustments.

Given these assumptions, the output of each sector will depend directly upon the outputs of all sectors which utilize this product, and final consumer and government demand. The assumed linear nature of the equations insures that, for example, an increase in 10 per cent in the output of all industries using steel will result in an increase of 10 per cent in steel input, and thus in the output of steel, provided, of course, that the maximum figure of steel output is not reached. Since there is one equation for each sector-product relating the output to the outputs of other sectors, there is the same number of equations as there are unknowns (the outputs of each sector), and the system is mathematically solvable. If the available factor supplies and final consumer demands, as well as the production functions, are known, it is possible to determine the magnitudes of outputs of all sectors by a system of simultaneous equations. There are various possible combinations of levels of output of the various sectors which are mutually consistent with one another; one of these sets of combinations will be consistent with the actual factor supplies and consumer demands which exist at a certain time.

Empirical Content

The second and more difficult step in input-output analysis has been that of giving empirical content to the theoretical framework, by the determination of the actual magnitudes in the various equations. A substantial amount of work of this type has been done in the last decade, partly by government agencies or under government auspices, and partly by nongovernmental research organizations. The task is a tremendous one, partly because of inadequacy of data, but progress has been made. As the elements in the equations are given magnitudes, it becomes possible to trace the quantitative effects upon various sectors of changes in the determinants, such as consumer demand, factor supplies, or governmental purchases. Particular use has been made of the analysis in estimating the reductions in output of civilian goods which would be necessary to allow a given output of military equipment in case of war, and the extent of production for military purposes which would be possible with a maximum feasible reduction in output of goods for civilian use.

Limitations to the Analysis

Despite its contributions, input-output analysis as it now stands is subject to serious limitations. The basic problem is that of the development of equations which are simple enough to be manageable, yet sufficiently refined to reflect to an adequate extent the actual behavior of the economy. The assumption of linear equations, relating outputs of one industry to outputs of others in a unique fashion, is obviously somewhat unrealistic. Increases in output do not in many cases require proportionate increases in input, mainly because of the indivisibilities of various factors. The assumption of fixed production coefficients precludes the possibility of factor substitutions. Even in a short-run period some substitutions may be possible, and over a longer period the opportunities for substitution are likely to be relatively great. As a result it is possible to maintain outputs of some goods at higher levels than would be possible on the basis of given production coefficients when materials currently used in the production of these products are diverted in part to other uses. For example, during World War II it was possible to maintain production of office filing cabinets by making them from wood when steel supplies were diverted to war production. Theoretically, of course, the equations could be redesigned to introduce the possibility of factor substitutions, but to do so would tremendously complicate the task of establishing the magnitudes in the equations.

The assumption of fixed relationships between outputs of various sectors likewise precludes the possibility of increases or decreases in inventories; as a consequence, changes in inventories which actually occur as production levels change will prevent the attainment of the exact results anticipated on the basis of the analysis. The time factor—the lag between inputs and outputs—is also ignored. This is of little consequence in the continuous flow of a static situation, but is significant when changes in the rates of output occur. The fact that different firms in a sector will employ diverse production techniques is also a complicating factor, since changes in outputs by the various firms will have different effects upon the inputs of particular factors. Finally, the treatment of investment demand is a troublesome one. It is obvious that the inputs of capital goods are not related in a proportionate fashion to changes in outputs of the products. Some attempts have been made to develop a relationship between investment input and the *rate of change* in the outputs of the products, on the basis of the acceleration principle explained in Chapter 22, but this task is by no means simple. More commonly, the input-output analysis has been based upon the assumption that investment is an autonomous variable, a procedure which simplifies the system but lessens the significance of its results.

Actual progress in the development of the analysis is of course retarded by the lack of adequate data of consumer demand functions and production functions; knowledge of both is necessary for satisfactory determination of actual magnitudes in the system.

SELECTED REFERENCES

CASSEL, G. *Theory of Social Economy,* book i, chap. iv. trans. New York: Harcourt, Brace, 1932.

A simple presentation of the general equilibrium model.

PHELPS-BROWN, E. *The Framework of the Pricing System.* London: Chapman and Hall, 1936.

A more elaborate presentation of general equilibrium theory.

STIGLER, G. *The Theory of Price,* chap. xiv. rev. ed. New York: Macmillan, 1952.

A brief statement of general equilibrium theory.

HICKS, J. R. *Value and Capital,* chaps. iv-viii. Oxford: Oxford University Press, 1938.

The most recent presentation of general equilibrium theory.

LEONTIEF, W. W. *The Structure of American Economy, 1919–1939.* New York: Oxford University Press, 1951.

The basic conceptual and empirical framework of the input-output analysis.

LEONTIEF, W. W. *Studies in the Structure of the American Economy.* New York: Oxford University Press, 1953.

A survey of the development of input-output analysis in recent years.

DORFMAN, R. "The Nature and Significance of Input-Output," *Review of Economics and Statistics,* Vol. XXXVI (May, 1954), pp. 121–33.

An excellent brief review of the nature and development of input-output analysis.

QUESTIONS

1. Distinguish between partial and general equilibrium theory.
2. Trace the probable effects of an improved variety of orange, which allows a great increase in yield per acre, upon:
   a) The price of apples (immediate, and long run)
   b) The production of apples (immediate, and short run)
   c) The income of the owners of land best suited for (1) the production of oranges (2) the production of apples
3. Trace some of the probable effects of the development of nylon, dacron, and orlon shirts upon the prices and outputs of other commodities, and factor prices.
4. When will a change in consumer preferences *permanently* alter factor prices?
5. Explain the budget equation and the allocation-of-consumer-expenditure equation, and explain how the usual demand function is derived from them.
6. What are the two basic general equilibrium equations, from the supply standpoint?
7. Explain why there is one excessive equation in the general equilibrium system, as it is initially set up, and how it is eliminated.
8. How is a demand equation obtained for commodity x_1, the one used as the common denominator of value?
9. Why is the general equilibrium system mathematically determinate?

10. Note the various assumptions upon which the simplified general equilibrium system is based, and indicate the extent to which these may be modified.
11. What are the advantages and limitations of general equilibrium theory?
12. In what sense is the general equilibrium theory a static theory?
13. Trace the effects on the economy of an improved method of producing helicopters, which would allow the sale of them for $3000, and would make them as safe as automobiles.
14. Explain the nature of input-output analysis.
15. How do the equations of input-output analysis differ from those of general equilibrium theory?
16. Are prices, or quantities, or both variables in the input-output analysis? Explain.
17. What are the major limitations to input-output analysis?

PART IV

National Income

Chapter 21 THE MAGNITUDES OF NATIONAL INCOME

The preceding portions of the book have been concerned with the allocation of given resources among the production of various goods, and the distribution of the output of production among the owners of the factor units. The analysis, therefore, has been directed towards the question of the composition of total output of the economy and its relative distribution to various factor owners, rather than to the question of the magnitude of total output. To this latter problem attention must now be given. Economic well-being of society is obviously influenced by the volume of total output as well as by the composition of the output and the relative size of the shares received by various groups. The portion of economic theory which deals with the determination of total output is known as national income theory, or, alternatively, as aggregative or macro-(as distinguished from micro-) economics. Although this portion of economic theory, in various forms, has been a portion of the general body of economic theory for centuries,[1] only in the last 25 years has it received systematic development and come to play a role in economic analysis co-ordinate with value and distribution theory.[2]

The analysis of national income will be divided into three parts, dealing, respectively, with the concepts or magnitudes of national income; the basic framework of the theory of determination of the level

[1] Many of the early economists, such as Adam Smith, were concerned with the determination of the real level of national income (Smith's work was entitled, *An Inquiry into the Nature and Causes of the Wealth of Nations*). In the period between 1900 and 1930, national income theory consisted almost solely of a study of the nature and causes of business cycles and other economic fluctuations; business cycle theory is now recognized as merely one aspect of national income theory. Since 1950, greatest attention has been given to the portion of national income theory concerned with economic growth.

[2] The interest was, of course, greatly stimulated by the depression of the 'thirties, World War II, and, at the theoretical level, by the work of J. M. Keynes, *The General Theory of Employment, Interest and Money* (New York: Harcourt, Brace, 1936).

of national income; and the nature and causes of change in national income. This chapter will be concerned with the first problem, and Chapters 22 and 23 with the second and third.

The Development of National Income Accounting

The general concept of national income or national product as a measure of the total output of the economy during a given period has long been utilized. But only since the 1930's has there developed the use of a systematically established set of concepts relating to the magnitudes of output of the economy, and extensive efforts to ascertain the data of these magnitudes, both on a current basis and for past years. World War II particularly emphasized the importance of the study of these magnitudes and compilation of data, and the science of national income accounting made its most rapid advance between 1940 and 1950. In the United States the bulk of the work has been done by two groups, the National Bureau of Economic Research, particularly by Simon Kuznets who is affiliated with that organization, and the Department of Commerce. Current data is compiled by the Department, and published in the July issues of the *Survey of Current Business.* The terminology and procedures used by the Department of Commerce have been generally accepted in the United States, and will be used in this chapter, although certain objections to them will be noted. Comparable work has been done in other countries, although both terminology and procedures frequently differ from those in the United States, and thus the international data are not fully comparable. Current data for all countries is published in the *Monthly Bulletin of Statistics,* issued by the United Nations.

The Concept of National Income

The basic magnitude of importance in measuring the output of the economy during a given period is *national income,* which may be defined as (1) the value of the output of the period which is available for direct utilization by individual consumers or which constitutes a net increase in the economy's stock of real wealth; or (2), alternatively, as the sum of the incomes earned during the period from the supplying of factor units for use in production. As suggested by these two alternative definitions, national income may be calculated in either of two ways. The first, known as the *product approach,* involves the summation of the values of the various goods produced during the period. The second, known as the *income approach,* involves the summation of all factor incomes received during the period. As explained in subsequent sections, the magnitude will be the same regardless of the approach to its calculation; the two approaches involve essentially the measurement of the same flow at different points, the product approach at the point of sale of the physical units of output, the income approach at the point at which the amounts received by the business firms become incomes to the factor unit owners.

THE PRODUCT APPROACH TO NATIONAL INCOME CALCULATION

The product approach requires initially the determination of *gross national product* (GNP), the total market value of all *final* products produced during the interval of time. Final products may be defined as end products, as distinguished from *intermediate* products, those produced and consumed during the period in the production of other goods. For example, during the year iron ore may be mined and utilized to make pig iron, which is in turn converted into steel. The steel is fabricated into automobile frames, which are incorporated into automobiles. The iron ore, the pig iron, the sheet steel, and the frames are intermediate goods, since they are directly used up in the production of other goods; if their values were included in gross national product, the same item would essentially be counted several times. The values of the intermediate goods are incorporated into the value of the final product; only the latter is available for consumption use or as an increase in the stock of the nation's physical wealth.

The line between final and intermediate goods is somewhat arbitrary, of course, especially with respect to the distinction between capital equipment which can be used only a few years (but is regarded as an end product) and dies or similar articles which are used a number of times in the productive process but have a useful life less than one year. But the distinction is a workable one, particularly because it coincides with the standard accounting practice of drawing an arbitrary line at one year between items charged as current expenses and those regarded as capital equipment, charged to capital account, and depreciated.

The Elements in Gross National Product

Gross national product may be classified into four major groups, each of which will be discussed briefly.

1. *Consumption Goods.* The bulk of the total of gross national product—about two thirds—consists of consumption goods, those directly utilized in the satisfaction of personal wants. This item, as illus-

trated in Table 29, is designated in the Department of Commerce tables as *Personal Consumption Expenditures.* The category includes both services and physical commodities, and durable as well as nondurable items, with one exception: the values of new homes produced during the period are excluded, and treated as an element in the investment category below because of the long life of the average home, and the tendency of persons to regard the purchase of a home as an investment rather than as a consumption expenditure. Rental payments, plus an estimated annual rental value of owner-occupied homes, are included in the consumption goods category. Similar procedures could be applied to automobiles and other consumer durables, but are not, partly because of the difficulties of estimating annual use value, and partly because the purchase of these goods, rather than their annual use, is of primary concern with respect to the determination of the level of national income.

Gross national product does not include the value of secondhand goods purchased, since these items are not a part of current production. The total does include purchases from government-operated commercial enterprises, such as water and electric power systems. Governmental services which are not sold to the users are not regarded as a portion of the consumption category, but are treated separately in item 4 below.

Goods produced and consumed by the same persons, such as produce grown and consumed by a farmer, should logically be included in gross national product, since these items constitute a portion of total output, and failure to include them causes the figures of national income to change when the relative extent to which persons purchase goods instead of producing them for their own use changes, even though the same total output is produced. Thus under present procedures, if more persons eat in restaurants instead of at home, and send out their clothes to laundries, the figures of national income will rise, even though no more goods are produced. But with the sole exception of produce of farmers utilized for their own consumption, no attempt is made to include home-produced items, partly because of lack of data, partly because of the difficulties of drawing the line between activities which are carried on for the purpose of gaining the product and those which merely represent a pleasurable use of leisure time.

2. *Capital Goods.* The second category, labelled *Gross Private Domestic Investment* in the Department of Commerce tables, consists of those capital goods produced during the period which are final products. There are three primary elements in this category: durable capital goods, increases in inventories of all goods held by business firms, regardless of the nature of the goods, and new homes, whether built for

use by the owners or for rental. The inventory change figure may, of course, be negative. The capital goods item in gross national product includes both capital equipment acquired for replacement of old equipment, and that used for expansion. Capital goods produced by firms for their own use are, of course, treated in the same manner as if they were purchased. The values of increases in physical inventories, whether intentional or the product of overestimates of potential sales, are included, since they constitute a contribution of the production of the current year toward consumption in the future. The increase in inventory is valued on the basis of the cost of purchasing or producing the goods involved. All other goods in the capital goods category are valued at their actual selling prices, or, if user-produced, at the amounts at which they would have sold had they been placed on the market. Mere increases in the monetary value of inventories due to price changes, and capital gains in the value of fixed assets held are not included in gross national product, since they are not the results of production activity.

3. *Net Exports and Net Amounts Earned Abroad.* The third category, labelled *Net Foreign Investment* by the Department of Commerce, consists of the net gain to the economy arising out of international transactions during the year; it may of course be a negative figure. International transactions affect GNP in several ways:

a) Goods produced for export, although not available for domestic use, constitute a portion of the current output of production and give rise to claims against foreigners which can be used to obtain foreign-produced goods for domestic use. Accordingly, the value of exports must be included in gross national product.

b) Goods imported do not represent a contribution of domestic production; accordingly, they must not be included in national product. But the consumption- and capital-goods items (1 and 2 above) include all goods purchased, regardless of whether they have been imported or produced domestically, and the government services item (4 below) may include imported goods. Accordingly, in order to keep imports out of the total, it is necessary to subtract their total value; under Department of Commerce procedure, this item is subtracted from the exports item, and the net figure (which may be a negative quantity) is included in gross national product.

c) Because national product is defined in terms of the production arising from the activity of residents of the United States, it is necessary to determine the contribution of Americans to foreign production and the contribution of foreigners to American production and to include the excess of the former over the latter in gross national product. This difference may, of course, be a minus quantity. The contribution of Americans to foreign production is measured by the amounts paid to Americans (primarily in the form of interest and dividends) by foreign producers; the contribution of foreigners to American production is measured in a comparable manner. The item of the excess of American contributions over foreign contributions constitutes a claim by Americans against residents of foreign countries, which can be converted to goods for domestic use.

The net figure of adjustments in gross national product arising out of international transactions is designated as *net foreign investment* by the Department of Commerce, since the figure represents the net increase, during the period, in claims of Americans against foreigners. On the basis of the assumption that these claims can eventually be converted into goods for American use, they are regarded as constituting a form of investment—a contribution of current production toward want-satisfaction in future years.

4. *Governmental Services.* The final category of gross national product consists of the value of governmental services, other than those sold by government commercial enterprises to the users and included in categories 1 and 2 above. Governmental services require factor units for their production, give rise to factor incomes, and convey benefits to the people of the community. Essentially the governments are merely special forms of business firms, primarily providing services which convey their benefits to the community as a whole rather than separately to individuals. Because of the community nature of the benefits, and accepted principles of equity in the distribution of the burden of the cost of providing the services, the services are not sold to the users in most cases, but instead are financed by taxation or other means. As a consequence, the determination of their value gives rise to special problems.

Since the services are not sold, they cannot be valued on the basis of their selling prices, and an alternative method of valuation must be used. The actual method involves determination of their value on the basis of the costs of the goods and services purchased by the governments to render the services; thus the label *Government Purchases of Goods and Services* is applied to this category in the Commerce tables. This method of valuation is not entirely satisfactory, since the amounts the community would be willing to pay for the services might be more or less than the costs of rendering them. But since these amounts cannot be determined, there is no satisfactory alternative.

This fourth category does not include the purchases of goods and services by governmental commercial enterprises, since the values of the services rendered by these enterprises are directly included in national product. Furthermore, government transfer expenditures, those which are essentially gifts, such as old age pensions, are excluded from GNP since they do not reflect the production of goods or services, but merely the transfer of purchasing power.

The inclusion of the value of all governmental services in gross national product involves the treatment of such services as final products, even though business firms are benefited by many of the services. It may be argued that such a procedure is illogical, and that the value of those services which are directly beneficial to business firms in production should be excluded from GNP. But this argument is not valid; the basic reason for excluding intermediate goods from GNP is the fact that their values enter into the values of the finished products. But this is not true of those intermediate goods which are provided by governments to business firms without a direct charge; they are essentially free goods, from the standpoint of the firms benefiting from them, in the same manner as air. It is true, of course, that business firms pay taxes, but there is no direct correlation between the taxes paid by particular firms or business in general, and the services received. The problem of business taxes is a completely distinct one, which will be considered in subsequent sections.

In summary: gross national product is made up of four major categories: consumption goods, capital goods or domestic investment, net foreign investment, and governmental services. The relative importance of the four in 1954 is shown in Table 29.

TABLE 29

NATIONAL PRODUCT ACCOUNT, 1954
(Millions of Dollars)

Category	*Amount*
Personal consumption expenditures	236,532
Gross private domestic investment	47,248
Net foreign investment	−266
Government purchases of goods and services	76,960
Total gross national product	360,474

Source: *Survey of Current Business*, July, 1955.

The Usefulness of the Magnitude of Gross National Product

The magnitude of gross national product is not merely a steppingstone in the process of determining national income by the product approach, but has certain uses in itself. The GNP figures, which include the values of all final products produced during the period, are better measures of total output of production and the extent of utilization of resources than national income, which reflects output net of depreciation of existing equipment. Changes in national income data from prosperity to depression, for example, tend to overstate the actual decline in output and employment, since they do not include the portion of production which serves to maintain intact the current stock of capital goods. Furthermore, the GNP figures are more accurate, since the adjustments made from them to obtain the national income figures must be based upon estimates of depreciation, and arbitrary assumptions about the shifting of certain taxes.

However, GNP figures overstate the actual contribution of production during the period toward consumption and increase in the stock of capital goods; major adjustments are required in GNP figures to obtain from them the figures of national income. Or, in other words, GNP includes certain items which do not become factor incomes, and thus must be excluded if a magnitude is to be obtained in the product accounts which is comparable to national income as determined by summing factor incomes. Two principal groups of items must be subtracted from GNP to obtain the figure of national income, namely, depreciation and indirect business taxes. Each will be discussed briefly.

Adjustment for Depreciation

The first adjustment which must be made is the subtraction from GNP of depreciation—the decline in the value of existing capital equipment during the period. GNP figures show total output of final products, including the output of capital equipment for replacement purposes, with no adjustment for the using up of existing equipment. But a portion of total output constitutes neither a sum available for current consumption or a net addition to the stock of capital equipment, since it merely serves to maintain intact the capital goods which existed at the beginning of the year, or, in other words, to offset the decline in the value of existing equipment. Accordingly, it is not a portion of national income, as that concept is defined. It does not constitute a factor income, but merely a change in the form of wealth, and thus has no counterpart in the income approach to the calculation of national income.

Accordingly, in the product accounts, the sum of depreciation is deducted from GNP, as a step in the calculation of national income; the term *net national product* is given to the magnitude obtained by this deduction (together with the subtraction of the minor items noted in the next paragraph). Unfortunately, of course, the actual depreciation can never be determined in any one year; in the calculations it is necessary to use the reported depreciation charges, which in many cases do not reflect the actual decline in the value of the capital assets. Hence the figures of net national product (and national income) are somewhat arbitrary.

Two other minor adjustments are made in determining net national product. Accidental damages to durable capital goods, such as those resulting from fire or storm, are subtracted from gross national product; these damages reduce the existing stock of capital goods and require a portion of the current output of production to offset them. When a house is destroyed by fire and a new one constructed to replace it, no consumption has occurred, nor has the total stock of capital goods increased. The other adjustment is the subtraction of capital outlays on such items as tools, which are charged by business firms to current expense; since they have been included in the item of capital goods purchased, but no depreciation charges are set up for them, a deduction is necessary to avoid overstating net national product.

The sum of depreciation plus these two items is designated as capital consumption allowances in the national income tables.

Deduction of Indirect Taxes

The second major deduction from GNP in the determination of the figure of national income by the product approach is that of indirect business taxes, taxes levied upon business firms but presumably shifted to the consumers of the products in the form of higher prices. Sales and excise taxes, and the portion of the property tax collected from business firms are the chief taxes of this type. The deduction is based upon the argument that the sums of these taxes essentially enter into GNP twice—as elements in the prices of final products produced by the business firms, and in the total figure of the value of governmental services. The taxes, as such, do not become factor incomes directly, but only when the sums are paid out by the governments. Failure to deduct the taxes in determining national income by the product approach would result in a difference between national income determined in this manner and the sum of factor incomes,[3] and would result in a shift in the reported figures of national income whenever governments shifted their relative reliance upon indirect and direct taxes, even though no real change in national income had occurred. This shift

[3] The sums could, of course, be added to national income calculated as the sum of factor incomes to make the two magnitudes equal.

could be offset in the figures of national income adjusted for price level changes by appropriate modifications of the price index numbers, but the usefulness of the unadjusted figures would be lessened. By contrast, no such adjustment is required for direct taxes borne by individuals, since they do not affect (it is assumed) the prices of the products, and the sums involved enter into national product only once—when they are used by the governments to pay for goods and services.

Under the assumptions that the indirect business taxes are shifted forward in the form of higher prices, while other taxes, including the corporation income tax, are not shifted, the present procedure is satisfactory. But the assumptions are not necessarily valid in all cases. In some instances sales, excise, and business-property taxes are probably not shifted forward, resting essentially upon the owners of the business firms, or upon other factor owners.[4] In other instances taxes regarded as direct, such as the corporation income tax, are probably shifted, at least to some extent. Accordingly, the present procedure gives a somewhat distorted picture of national income, and shifts by governments between various tax sources will cause artificial changes in data of national income. But with the present state of knowledge, it does not appear possible to devise a more satisfactory procedure. Some writers, however, favor the procedure of making no deductions of taxes, and adjusting the figure of national income derived from a summation of factor incomes instead.

Two other minor adjustments are made in obtaining the figure of national income by the product approach. The first is the subtraction of business transfer payments, that is, amounts paid by business firms for purposes other than the acquisition of factor units. The chief examples include gifts by businesses to individuals and nonprofit institutions (charitable organizations, etc.); these amounts are reflected in the prices of the products but do not represent the results of production activity. The amounts of bad debts are also subtracted; the sums involved represent essentially gifts by the business firms to the purchasers, gifts whose costs (over a period of time) are covered by the prices on goods sold and paid for.

A final adjustment involves the addition of subsidies paid by gov-

[4] There has developed in recent years one school of thought which maintains that sales and excise taxes are not borne by consumers; see E. R. Rolph, *Theory of Fiscal Economics* (Berkeley: University of California Press, 1954), chaps. vi, vii. This argument is based upon a very restricted concept of tax incidence and narrow assumptions which greatly reduce the significance of the conclusions.

ernment to business firms and the subtraction of the operating profits of government commercial enterprises; as the national product accounts are set up, a single item—the excess of the first over the second—is entered. Subsidies are added because they cover a part of the costs of the goods produced by the firms receiving them but, of course, are not reflected in the prices of the products, nor do they enter into government purchases, the measure used of the value of government services. The surpluses of government commercial enterprises constitute receipts of revenue to the government which are used to make purchases; accordingly, just like indirect taxes, they enter twice into net national product and must be subtracted.

Summary of the Product Accounts

As viewed from the product accounts, national income may be regarded as the total value of all final goods produced during the period, less: (1) the depreciation of existing capital equipment, (2) indirect business taxes, which enter into the prices of the products but do not become factor incomes, and (3) other miscellaneous items noted above. The national income figure derived in this manner represents the value of the output of the period which is available to the economy for consumption use (including the consumption of government services) or as a net increase in the economy's stock of capital goods available for future use. From the standpoint of output, this is the most satisfactory measure of the contribution of the period toward the economic well-being of the society.

Table 30 represents the data of adjustments in gross national product to obtain national income, for 1954.

TABLE 30

DETERMINATION OF NATIONAL INCOME FROM GROSS NATIONAL PRODUCT, 1954
(Millions of Dollars)

Gross national product		360,474
Less: Depreciation and other capital consumption allowances		30,034
Equals: Net national product		330,440
Less: Indirect business taxes	30,252	
Business transfer payments	1,221	
Statistical discrepancy	−814	
	30,659	
Equals		299,781
Plus: Government subsidies minus current surplus of government enterprises		−108
Equals: National income		299,673

Source: *Survey of Current Business*, July, 1955, p. 6.

THE INCOME APPROACH TO THE CALCULATION OF NATIONAL INCOME

The magnitude of national income may be ascertained directly from the data of factor incomes received, in what may be described as the income approach, as well as from data of output. Or, alternatively, as the basic tables published by the Department of Commerce are set up, the factor incomes may be regarded as charges or claims against national income as determined through the product approach.

In the presentation of national income data, factor incomes—those received for the supplying of factor units for use in production—are classified into five groups:

1. *Compensation of employees:* amounts received, directly or indirectly, by employees for work performed. This item is the sum of (*a*) wages and salaries paid and (*b*) supplements to wages and salaries, such as contributions of employers to social insurance systems and private pension plans, compensation paid in the case of injuries, etc.
2. *Income of unincorporated enterprises:* the net earnings of proprietorships, partnerships, and co-operatives, excluding capital gains and losses. This item is a "mixed" type of income, since the owners of the businesses usually supply more than one type of factor unit. Ordinarily, they supply their own labor and management activity, units of money capital, and often land.
3. *Rental income of persons:* the rentals received by individuals for real property (both land and improvements) which they rent to others, rental value of owner-occupied homes, and royalties. Rent received by corporations is excluded, as it enters into corporation profit.
4. *Corporation profits before tax:* the net earnings of corporations, before deduction of corporation income and excess profits taxes. The latter are regarded as contributions of the owners toward support of government. Corporation profit is included in national income, whether it is held in the enterprise in the form of undistributed profits or paid out to stockholders in the form of dividends.

   One adjustment, known as the *inventory valuation adjustment,* is made in the total figure of corporation profit; this consists of the subtraction from profits of the element consisting of gains from changes in the value of inventories during the period due to price changes. As profits are usually calculated, inventory value increases are included; these do not represent factor incomes arising from production and thus are eliminated in the calculation of national income.
5. *Net interest:* interest payments received by individuals from private business. Interest received from governments is not included, under the assumption (only partially valid) that government borrowing has been undertaken for consumption purposes (war financing and the meeting of current deficits in

depression periods primarily) and therefore does not affect current production. The amount of government interest received by corporations is subtracted in calculating net interest, since it has entered into corporation profit, and will appear in national income unless subtracted.

Factor income data for 1954 are shown in Table 31.

TABLE 31

NATIONAL INCOME AS THE SUM OF FACTOR INCOMES, 1954
(Millions of Dollars)

Compensation of employees:		
Wages and salaries	196,244	
Supplements	11,657	
Total		207,901
Income of unincorporated enterprises		37,876*
Rental income of persons		10,539
Corporate profits:		
Corporate profits tax liability	17,082	
Dividends	10,008	
Undistributed profits	6,952	
Total	34,042	
Less: Inventory valuation adjustment	227	
Total		33,815
Net interest		9,542
National Income		299,673

* After inventory valuation adjustment
Source: *Survey of Current Business*, July, 1955, p. 6.

Exclusion of Transfer Incomes

National income includes only factor incomes; transfer incomes, those received without factor units being supplied by the recipients, are excluded, since these incomes do not reflect the conduct of production activity, and have no counterpart in the data of output. The payment of direct relief, for example, is not a result of the production of goods, but merely constitutes a transfer of purchasing power from one person to another. The major transfer incomes include old age pensions, unemployment relief, social security benefits, and government bond interest.

The failure to consider government bond interest as a factor income has been subject to considerable controversy. The present procedure is followed primarily because the bulk of government debt outstanding was incurred for purposes of war and depression financing, and does not reflect investment in capital goods used in current production. The increase in government interest payments which results from a war in no way manifests a real increase in national income, and the inclusion of the interest in national income would artificially inflate the latter. However, logically, the portion of government interest on funds borrowed for capital improvements used directly in the provision of government services, such as highways, schools, hospitals, etc., should be treated as a factor income, since interest on funds invested by private businesses for similar purposes is included. However, if this procedure were followed, the figure of national income would be affected by the extent to which governmental capital improvements were financed by borrowing rather than by other sources. This problem could be avoided by including not only the interest paid, but an imputed interest return on governmental capital investment financed by other means, a procedure followed in part in Canada. But the difficulties of obtaining a satisfactory estimate of the amount of this imputed return are substantial.

From the standpoint of the recipient of interest income, there is, of course, no basic difference between governmental and corporate bond interest, and the treatment of the latter but not the former as a factor income is somewhat anomalous. This has led some students of the problem to argue that all interest payments, as such, be regarded as transfer incomes, in the same manner as dividends.[5]

The Relationship between the Income and Product Approaches to the Calculation of National Income

As explained in the preceding sections, national income may be calculated from data of output or data of income. National income, as the sum of factor incomes, is of necessity equal to national income as the value of all final products less depreciation, indirect taxes, and the other minor items noted previously. In other words, in any period of time, the sum of all factor incomes is equal to the value of all final products produced during the period, after the adjustments for depreciation, etc., have been made. Every dollar of the value of final goods (net of depreciation and business taxes) must appear as factor income to someone; a portion is paid out as wages and salaries, interest, rent, etc., and the remainder constitutes a profit income for the owners of the firm. On the other hand, there is no source of factor income except the value of goods produced during the period. Since the entire sum of the value of final goods produced (after the adjustments noted have been made) must appear as factor income, and since factor incomes can arise only from the value of goods produced, the two magnitudes are necessarily equal; the same figure will be obtained for national income (apart from statistical discrepancies arising out of incomplete data) regardless

[5] See Rolph, *op. cit.,* chap. iv.

of whether one method or the other is used for calculation of it. This is illustrated in Table 32, with data for 1954.

This identity between the sum of factor incomes and the value of final products less depreciation and indirect taxes is of substantial importance in the explanation of the level of national income and changes in national income, as will be noted in the following chapter. It was once widely believed that as business activity expands, income tends to lag behind output—resulting in general "overproduction," in the sense that persons are unable to buy all goods produced. This is, of course, untrue; output and income of necessity increase together, and incomes (together with depreciation charges and indirect tax revenues of the government) are always adequate to buy the entire output. They may not be entirely used for this purpose, and in practice, in some periods purchases may lag behind output. But the difficulty arises out of the manner in which the income is used, not because it is inadequate, in total.

TABLE 32

CALCULATION OF NATIONAL INCOME BY THE TWO ALTERNATIVE APPROACHES, 1954
(Millions of Dollars)

INCOME APPROACH (*Read downward*)		PRODUCT APPROACH (*Read upward*)	
Wages and supplements	207,901		
+ Income of unincorporated businesses	37,876		
+ Rental income	10,539		
+ Corporate profits	33,815		
+ Interest	9,542		
= National income	299,673	= 299,673	National income
		− 30,767	Indirect business taxes and minor adjustments
		= 330,440	Net national product
		− 30,034	Depreciation, etc.
		360,474	Gross national product

Source: Date from *Survey of Current Business*, July, 1955, p. 6.

Personal Income

The figure of national income is the most satisfactory measure of the output of the production system in any given period. But for purposes of analysis of the use of income by individuals, the national income figure is not entirely satisfactory, since not all of the income reaches the hands of individuals and some factor income is shifted through transfer payments from the original recipients to others. Decisions with respect to the use of the income are made by the latter rather than by the former. Thus the concept of *personal income* has been introduced; this magnitude is the sum of all incomes received by individuals—but only by individuals—from all sources, including transfers, during the period. Personal income is calculated from national income by making the following adjustments (which are illustrated, for 1954, in Table 33).

1. There is subtracted from national income those items which do not become personal incomes of individuals during the period. These include:

a) Undistributed corporation profits.
b) Corporation income taxes and excess profits taxes.
c) Payments by employers and employees into social insurance funds.
d) Corporation inventory valuation adjustment. Net inventory losses are subtracted (and thus net inventory gains are added). In determining the corporation profit element in national income, an adjustment was made to exclude the effect of inventory value changes, which are reflected in corporation profit data but do not affect national income. Since these inventory value changes do affect income received by individuals, an adjustment is made to restore the item eliminated in calculating national income.
e) Excess of wage accruals over disbursements for the year.

2. There is added to national income the sum of all transfer incomes of individuals. As previously noted, these consist primarily of

TABLE 33

CALCULATION OF PERSONAL INCOME FROM NATIONAL INCOME, 1954
(Millions of Dollars)

National income		299,673
Less: Undistributed corporation profits	6,952	
Corporate profits tax liability	17,082	
Corporate inventory valuation adjustment	−227	
Contributions for social insurance	9,617	
Excess of wage accruals over disbursements	0	
Total	33,424	
		266,249
Plus: Net government interest payments	5,165	
Government transfer payments	14,997	
Business transfer payments	1,221	
Total	21,383	
Equals: Personal income		287,632

Source: *Survey of Current Business*, July, 1955, p. 10.

pensions, relief, unemployment compensation and other social security and related benefits, and government bond interest. Gifts between individuals and bequests are omitted, largely because of difficulties of obtaining data, as well as capital gains, which for purposes of the national income accounts, are not treated as income at all.

It should be noted that while transfer payments are included in personal income, the tax payments necessary, in many cases, to finance them are not deducted. Thus in a sense the figure of personal income exaggerates somewhat the purchasing power actually available for use for the purchase of output of the private sector of the economy, or for saving.

Disposable Income

The figure of personal income shows the total income received by individuals during the period. But a portion of this sum is taken away from them in the form of direct tax payments; the sum which is available to individuals to use as they wish is a considerably lower figure, known as *disposable income.* The magnitude is calculated by subtracting from personal income all personal tax payments made, including sums withheld under the personal income tax. Contributions to social security systems are deducted in determining personal income and are not subtracted again in calculating disposable income.

Table 34 shows the magnitude of disposable income, as derived from the figure of personal income, for 1954.

TABLE 34

DISPOSABLE INCOME, UNITED STATES, 1954
(Millions of Dollars)

Personal income		287,632
Less: Personal tax and related payments:		
Federal	29,138	
State and local	3,680	
Equals: Disposable income		254,814

Source: *Survey of Current Business,* July, 1955, p. 10.

It must be emphasized that only personal direct taxes are deducted at this point; indirect business taxes, such as the sales tax, are deducted in the determination of national income.

Disposable income in the hands of individuals may either be spent for the purchase of consumption goods, or may be saved. In 1954, for example, personal consumption expenditures totaled $236,532 million, and personal savings $18,282 million; thus about 93 per cent of all disposable income was spent on consumption and 7 per cent was saved.

REAL VERSUS MONETARY MAGNITUDES

National income and related magnitudes must be measured in monetary terms. The actual output of the economy consists of a wide variety of commodities and services; because of the diversity of units, it is impossible to sum together the physical quantities of output in any meaningful way, and any attempt to use such a procedure would ignore the relative importance of the various goods in the functioning of the economy. Any use of physical units, such as weights, would abstract completely from economic value; a ton of coal and a ton of beef steaks are not of the same importance to the economy, in an economic sense. However, the monetary measure of changes in the various magnitudes is by no means entirely satisfactory, especially in an unadjusted form, because of changes in the general price level, and thus of the measuring stick of value. National income in 1954 was about 4½ times the 1939 figure—in monetary terms—but the general price level had roughly doubled during the same period. Therefore the real increase in output was much less than 4½ times.

In order to obtain a more satisfactory measure of real changes in national income, it is necessary to adjust the data to eliminate the effect of price changes, so far as is possible. This process of adjustment is known as "deflation"; it involves the use of index numbers of price level changes, figures reflecting the general change in the price level and thus in the value of money over the period. The numbers are compiled by determining the average change in the prices of a large number of commodities over the period, and expressing the figures for the various years in terms of one year selected as the base year, and represented by 100. Thus if, on the average, prices had doubled between 1939 and 1954, the price index number for 1954 would be 200, in terms of 1939 as a base year. In the preparation of the index, the prices of the various commodities must be weighted in terms of the relative importance of the commodities in the economy.

The absolute figures of national income for the various years are divided by the respective price index numbers for those years to eliminate the effect of the price change. For an example, the unadjusted national income figures for 1939, 1947, and 1954 were, respectively, 72, 197, and 299 billions of dollars. The wholesale price indexes for these years were 58, 100, and 120 (1947 being used as the base year). Accordingly, the adjusted figures of national income, in terms of constant (1947) dollars, were 124, 197, and 249 respectively. Thus the national income, in real terms, approximately doubled between 1939 and 1954.

The Limitations to Deflation Procedures

The deflation of the absolute data by price index numbers, however, cannot give entirely satisfactory results. In the first place, the index number must be based upon a sample of commodities, which may not reflect the over-all picture with complete accuracy. There is no single "price" for many commodities; the task of collecting representing price figures is substantial, as is that of obtaining data of sales of the various commodities, necessary for weighting of the commodities according to their relative importance. But the more fundamental problem, often called the "index number problem," is that of the changing importance of various commodities over the years. During a war, for example, many peacetime goods are no longer produced, and outputs of war material increase greatly. Even in peace times, new products are developed, others increase in popularity, and others decline. Quality of the products may increase greatly (or decrease). There is no satisfactory way of adjusting for these changes; if the index number weights are changed from year to year, the figures will reflect the weight changes as well as the price changes. Accordingly, the figures of national income adjusted for price changes, of necessity, involve arbitrary elements, and an increase in the figures does not necessarily show an improvement in the real level of living. But particularly in periods of rapid price changes, the adjusted figures are more satisfactory measures of real changes than the unadjusted figures.

SELECTED REFERENCES

RUGGLES, RICHARD. *An Introduction to National Income and Income Analysis.* 2nd ed. New York: McGraw-Hill, 1955.

This volume contains a detailed statement of national income concepts.

SHOUP, C. S. *Principles of National Income Analysis.* Boston: Houghton, Mifflin, 1947.

A very careful study of the problems involved in measurement of national product and income.

SHOUP, C. S. "Development and Use of National Income Data," *Survey of Contemporary Economics* (H. S. Ellis, ed.), chap. viii. Homewood, Ill.: Richard D. Irwin, Inc., 1948.

National Income: Supplement to Survey of Current Business, July, 1954.

A description of the terminology used by the Department of Commerce in presenting output and income data.

KUZNETS, SIMON. *National Income: A Summary of Findings.* New York: National Bureau of Economic Research, 1946.

A statement of the income concepts as developed by the National Bureau of Economic Research.

MAYER, J. "Proposals for Improving Income and Product Concepts," *Review of Economics and Statistics,* Vol. XXXVI (May, 1954), pp. 191–201.

A discussion of some of the current controversies in the field.

BOWMAN, R. T., and EASTERLIN, R. A. "An Interpretation of the Kuznets and Department of Commerce Income Concepts," *Review of Economics and Statistics,* Vol. XXXV (February, 1953), pp. 41–50.

A discussion of the two principal approaches to the problem.

POWELSON, J. P. *Economic Accounting.* New York: McGraw-Hill, 1955.

A survey of the relationship between corporate and national income accounting.

QUESTIONS

1. Where will you find current national income data for the United States?
2. Define and explain carefully the difference between gross national product, national income, personal income, and disposable income.
3. What are the two alternative approaches to the calculation of national income?
4. Distinguish between final products and intermediate products. May a particular good sometimes be a final product and sometimes an intermediate product? Explain.
5. Find the figures of national income for the United States for 1929, 1932, 1945, and 1955 (when available). Find the national income figures for Canada for the same years.
6. What are the four categories of gross national product? Roughly, what is the relative importance of each category?
7. How are homes classified with respect to these categories?
8. What special problems arise in the determination of the value of governmental services? What procedure is followed?
9. What advantages does the magnitude of GNP have in measuring the results of the functioning of the economy? What limitations does it have, compared to national income?
10. How is net national product calculated?
11. Why is depreciation deducted from GNP in determining national income by the product approach?
12. Why are indirect business taxes deducted from GNP in determining national income? What objections may be raised against the present procedures with respect to deduction of taxes?
13. What are transfer incomes? Why are they not included in national income?
14. Why is government bond interest regarded as a transfer income? What objections can be raised against this procedure? What are the obstacles in the way of more logical treatment of government bond interest in the national income accounts?
15. Why is national income, calculated as the sum of factor incomes, of necessity equal to the figure of national income calculated via the product approach? Explain.
16. Explain the adjustments which must be made in national income to obtain the figure of personal income.

17. How is disposable income determined from personal income? Of what use is the concept of disposable income?
18. Why must national income and related magnitudes be measured in monetary, rather than real, terms?
19. What is a price index number? How is it formed? How are the items used in the formation of the index number weighted?
20. National income in 1931 was $59 billion, in 1949, $216 billion. Ascertain the wholesale price indexes for these two years, deflate the national income data to a common base, and indicate the percentage increase in national income in real terms from 1931 to 1949.
21. What is the "index number problem"?
22. Where can you find the most recent description of the procedures followed by the Department of Commerce in calculating national income and related magnitudes?

Chapter 22 THE LEVEL OF NATIONAL INCOME

The level of national income attained in the economy is obviously a factor of utmost importance for the economic well-being of society as a whole; the level of output not only determines the total volume of goods available for the satisfaction of wants, but also controls the extent to which all resource owners are able to find employment for their factor units. Failure of national income to attain the maximum possible level, designated as the full-employment level, results in unemployment of resources—one of the most undesirable occurrences in an economic system, as explained in Chapter 24.

The analysis of the determination of the level of national income has two major segments. The first is concerned with the equilibrium level, the level which is stable under given magnitudes of the determinants. The second is concerned with the highest level attainable with given resources, or, in other words, the full-employment level, with which the actual equilibrium level at any time may or may not coincide. These questions will be considered in this chapter.

THE EQUILIBRIUM LEVEL OF NATIONAL INCOME

The theory of the equilibrium level of national income which is widely accepted at the present time is based upon the work of John Maynard Keynes, *The General Theory of Employment, Interest and Money,* first published in 1936. Keynes, of course, drew heavily upon the work of others, but his presentation was the first systematic analysis of the determinants which control the equilibrium level of national income, and he was the first to demonstrate why the equilibrium level might be below the full-employment level. For some years, the theoretical framework of Keynes's system was confused with his policy recommendations, and persons opposed to the latter tended to reject his theoretical analysis regardless of its merits. But as time has passed, the prejudices have been largely overcome, and his analysis has become a basic segment of the general body of economic theory.

The Concept of Total Expenditures or Aggregate Demand

The first step in the explanation of the basic theory of national income is the introduction of the concept of total expenditures or aggregate demand. Expenditures may be defined as the purchases of final products (including net excess of exports over imports). In the interests of simplification, international transactions will be ignored in the succeeding sections; they can easily be fitted into the general framework of the theory, however. Expenditures consist of three major classes:

(1) Consumption expenditures by individuals
(2) Net investment expenditures by business enterprises
(3) Purchases of goods and services (but not transfer expenditures) by governments.

The sum of these constitute total expenditures, or, in other words, aggregate demand, in the economy. The sums involved are those which persons, firms, and governments seek to spend in each period out of given income levels, not necessarily the sums which were actually spent in a past period.

The Schedule of Aggregate Demand

In order to analyze the determination of national income, it is necessary to consider the schedule of total expenditures or aggregate demand at various levels of national income. As is typically the case with demand schedules, it is not possible to ascertain the data of aggregate demand at various income levels, but the schedules nevertheless exist. A hypothetical schedule is shown in Table 35. The nature of the behavior of each of the three segments of the schedule will be explained in subsequent sections.

The data in this schedule are plotted on Figure 89. National income is measured on the horizontal axis, and the various expenditures on the vertical axis. Curve C indicates the level of consumption expenditures at various magnitudes of national income, curve $C + I$ is the curve of consumption plus investment (investment itself being represented by the vertical distance between C and $C + I$), and curve $C + I + G$ indicates the sum of consumption, investment, and governmental expenditures. On this graph, an additional guide line, not used on previous graphs, is employed, namely the 45° line. So long as equal distances on

TABLE 35

HYPOTHETICAL SCHEDULE OF TOTAL EXPENDITURES (AGGREGATE DEMAND) IN THE ECONOMY, AT VARIOUS LEVELS OF NATIONAL INCOME
(Billions of Dollars)

National Income	Consumption Expenditures	Investment Expenditures	Government Expenditures	Total Expenditures
50	60	2	28	90
100	100	4	28	132
150	140	6	28	174
200	180	8	28	216
250	220	10	28	258
300	260	12	28	300
350	300	14	28	342

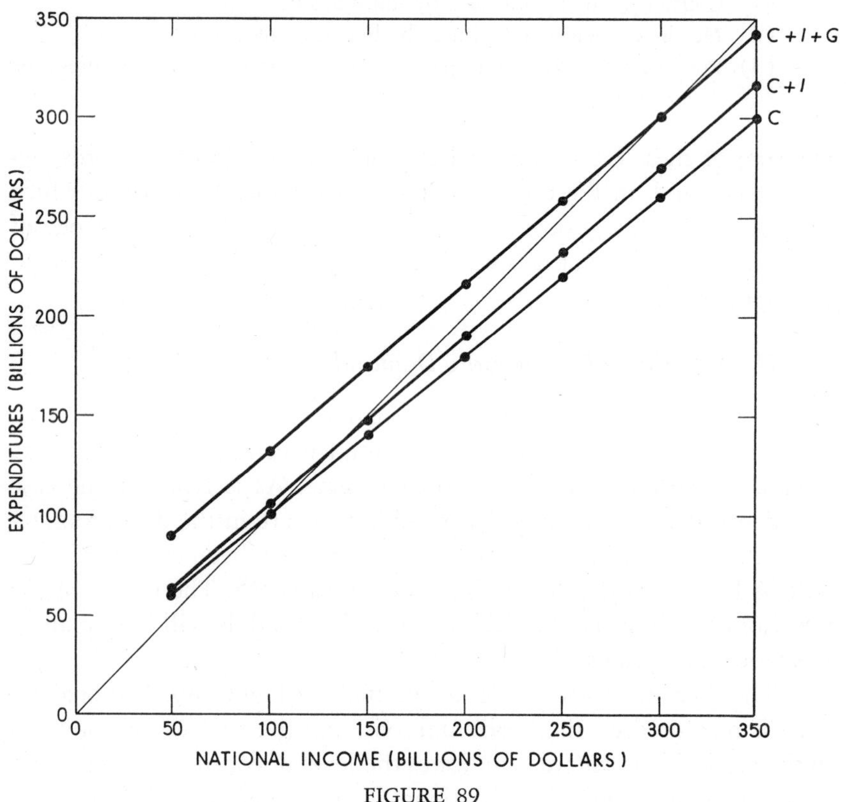

FIGURE 89

THE EQUILIBRIUM LEVEL OF NATIONAL INCOME

the horizontal and vertical axes measure equal sums, at any point on the 45° line, the sum of expenditures (measured vertically) will be equal to the figure of national income (measured horizontally).

The Equilibrium Level of National Income

Given the schedules of the amounts of expenditures at various levels of national income, the equilibrium level of national income is determinate; it is the level at which the total volume of expenditures $(C + I + G)$ is equal to the figure of national income (which may be regarded as aggregate supply), or, in terms of Figure 89, at the point at which the total expenditures curve $(C + I + G)$ crosses the 45° angle line. Equilibrium of national income can be maintained only at the level at which the total volume of expenditures—consumption, investment, governmental—is equal to the total national income figure. At any higher level of national income, expenditures would be less than income, and thus some of the current output of final products (which, as indicated in the previous chapter, is identical with national income) could not be sold. Hence business firms would be receiving back from the sale of products less than they paid out to the factor-owners, and they would curtail production. As national income fell, equilibrium would eventually be attained at $300 billion national income.

If, on the other hand, national income were less than the equilibrium figure—$200 billion, for example—total expenditures which persons would seek to make out of this income would exceed current output. Inventories would be depleted, and business firms would increase output. National income would continue to rise until it reached the $300 billion figure.

Explanation of the Equilibrium in Terms of Savings and Investment

Alternatively, the equilibrium level of national income can be explained in terms of savings and investment relationships. Savings constitute the excess of national income over consumption and government expenditures. Investment represents the excess of expenditures over consumption and government spending. Since the consumption and governmental items are the same whether viewed from the standpoint of income or expenditures, national income and planned total expenditures can be equal only when savings which persons seek to make out of their incomes are equal, in total, to the volume of planned investment. Table 36 shows the data of savings and investment, based upon the data in Table 35, and Figure 90 illustrates the savings-investment relationships graphically. With the data given, savings and investment are equal only at a level of national income of $300 billion (as on Table 35) and the respective curves intersect on Figure 90 at the $300 billion level. Table 36 and Figure 90 are merely alternative methods of presentation to those given in Table 35 and Figure 89; they show no additional relationships.

The relevant investment figure, it should be noted, is net investment, that is, gross investment less depreciation, since depreciation is deducted from GNP in determining national income. If the analysis were established in terms of gross investment and savings-plus-depreciation, it would give identical results. Since the investment figure is the net figure, it will be negative if depreciation exceeds gross investment.

TABLE 36

EXPLANATION OF NATIONAL INCOME EQUILIBRIUM IN TERMS OF SAVINGS AND INVESTMENT
(Billions of dollars)

National Income	Planned Savings	Planned Investment
50	−38	2
100	−28	4
150	−18	6
200	−8	8
250	2	10
300	12	12
350	22	14

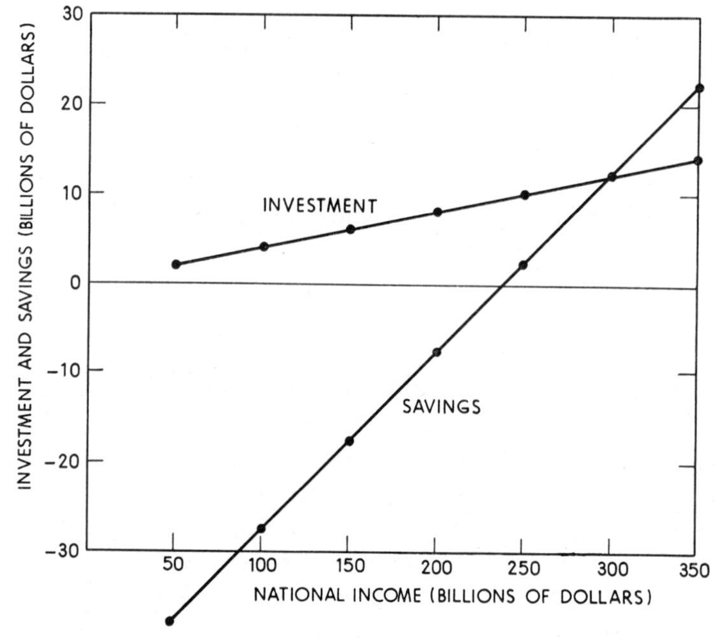

FIGURE 90

EQUILIBRIUM LEVEL OF NATIONAL INCOME IN TERMS OF SAVINGS-INVESTMENT RELATIONSHIPS

These schedules represent planned or *ex ante* savings and investment—the sums which persons and firms seek voluntarily to save and business firms seek to invest, at various income levels. In any past period of time, the actual volume of savings made must of necessity equal the actual volume of investment made. This can most easily be demonstrated by reviewing the nature of these magnitudes and their relation to national income:

(1) Actual savings is the excess of the sum of factor incomes (national income) over consumption and governmental expenditures during the period.

(2) Investment is the excess of national income (viewed from the product approach, as the total value of all final products, less depreciation and indirect taxes) over consumption and governmental expenditures.

(3) Since national income as the sum of factor incomes is identical with national income as the value of the output of final products less depreciation and business taxes, and since consumption and governmental expenditures represent the same magnitudes in (1) and (2) above, actual savings and actual investment in any period must be equal.

However, the figures of actual savings and investment made during the period may differ from the intended amounts; the level of national income is stable only if the planned or intended savings is equal to the planned volume of investment. Otherwise, behavior will change in such a manner as to cause a shift in national income.

The Determinants of National Income

In light of the preceding analysis, it is now possible to summarize the determinants of national income. The primary determinants include:

(1) The consumption function, that is, the division of national income between consumption and savings, at various levels of national income.

(2) The volume of investment that is undertaken at various levels of national income. This, in general, is dependent upon:

   (*a*) The rate of interest, determined as explained in preceding chapters

   (*b*) The marginal revenue product of capital goods, or, to use the term commonly employed in national income analysis, marginal efficiency of capital.

(3) The level of governmental spending, at various income levels.

Given the magnitudes of these determinants, national income will adjust to an equilibrium level, which will be stable so long as the determinants remain unchanged. A shift in any one of the determinants will cause a movement in the equilibrium level of national income, as explained in Chapter 23. Each of these determinants requires further consideration.

The Consumption Function

The consumption function has been defined as the functional relationship between income and consumption, at various levels of national income. The nature of the function depends, therefore, upon (1) the propensity to consume of individuals relative to their disposable income, and (2) the relationship between national income and disposable income. These will be considered in turn.

Disposable Income and the Propensity to Consume. The nature of the schedule relating consumption to disposable income is not precisely known, despite various efforts in recent years to discover its nature by means of statistical studies. It has generally been believed, however, largely on common-sense grounds, that as disposable income rises, on the average a greater percentage of the income will be saved, and thus a smaller percentage will be spent on consumption. With low incomes persons have little or no margin above absolute minimum amounts required for subsistence. As their incomes rise, the margin available for savings rises; persons are enabled to enjoy the luxury of savings which they are denied at lower income levels.

In recent years, however, various empirical studies have raised some doubt about the tendency for the percentage of income saved to rise as income rises. The work of Kuznets has shown that over a long period of time aggregate saving has constituted a relatively constant percentage of national income. The studies of Margaret Reid and Modigliani on savings by income group suggest that at any given time, the percentage of income saved appears, on the whole, to be independent of the income level, except when income has changed sharply.[1] There is a definite lag in consumption behind income as the latter changes; therefore as income rises, for a short period the percentage saved rises sharply, and as income falls, saving is squeezed severely.[2] But, in terms of these studies, the long-run consumption function would parallel the 45° line on Figure 89, instead of having a steeper slope.

The height (as distinguished from the nature) of the schedule of consumption relative to disposable income depends upon a number of factors, some of which have been noted in previous chapters. These will be summarized briefly:

[1] See M. Reid, *Savings in the Modern Economy,* (Minneapolis: University of Minnesota Press, 1953), p. 219; and F. Modigliani and R. Brumberg, "Utility Analysis and the Consumption Function," *Post-Keynesian Economics,* K. Kurihara, ed., (New Brunswick: Rutgers University Press, 1954).

[2] See J. S. Duesenberry, "Income-Consumption Relations," *Income, Employment and Public Policy* (New York: Norton, 1948).

1. The relative preference for present, compared to future, use of funds. This in turn depends upon such considerations as the intensity of present desires, the attitudes toward the desirability of accumulating for the future, the availability of social security benefits which lessen the need for accumulation, etc.

2. The extent to which durable goods have been previously acquired. Immediately after a war period, the propensity to consume tends to be very high, because of the great depletion of the stock of durable consumers goods.

3. Existing monetary and security holdings. The greater the extent to which persons have already acquired cash and other liquid investments, the less will be their feeling of obligation to save large portions of their incomes. The possession of liquid assets also enables persons to dis-save, if they wish, by spending more than their incomes.

4. Expectations of future prices and availability of consumer goods. Fear of approaching shortages leads to an increased propensity to consume. Expectations of price declines will have the opposite effect.

5. The pattern of income distribution. To the extent to which persons in the higher income groups save relatively high percentages of their income, the more equal the income distribution, the lower will be the percentage of income saved. It is now recognized, however, that transfer of income from the wealthy to the poor will have less effect upon consumption than was once believed.

6. The availability of credit and the interest rate. To a large extent consumer durables are purchased upon credit. Accordingly, the availability of the credit exercises a major influence upon consumer purchases of these goods and thus upon the consumption function. The interest rate itself probably exercises relatively little influence (within usual ranges of rate changes), either in encouraging persons to save more in order to earn a larger interest income, or in discouraging them from buying on credit.

7. Expectations of future incomes.

Shifts in any of these determinants will cause a shift in the propensity to consume, and lead to a change in national income.

The Relationship between Disposable Income and National Income. The consumption function, in the sense of the relationship between consumption and national income, depends not only upon the propensity of individuals to consume out of disposable income, but also upon the relationship between national income and disposable income. Savings are made not only by individuals out of disposable income, but also by corporations out of undistributed profits. The larger the size of this sum of undistributed profits, the larger will be the gap between national income and disposable income, and the lower will be the consumption function, other things being the same. As explained in earlier chapters, the volume of undistributed profits depends in part upon the rate of profit earned, and in part on the policies followed by corporation management with respect to the distribution of the profits. These, in turn, depend upon the estimates of returns to be made from retaining the profits and using them for expansion; the need for additional liquid funds; and the demands of the stockholders for dividends.

The consumption function, relative to national income, depends also upon the nature, magnitude, and effects of transfer incomes received, and the effect of the taxes (other than indirect business taxes, which are deducted in calculating national income) collected by government to finance its activities. Transfer payments, as such, represent additions to disposable income, over and above factor income; thus, in themselves, they tend to increase consumption to the extent to which they are used for this purpose. It is generally argued that transfer payments benefiting the very poor, such as relief payments, will have greater effect on the consumption function than those payments, such as interest on the government debt, primarily benefiting the higher income groups.

On the other hand, all personal and direct business taxes constitute subtractions from national income, and, in themselves, tend to reduce the consumption function. The higher the tax levels, the greater will be the excess of national income over disposable income, and given the propensity to consume, the lower will be the volume of consumption. In part the tax collections will be used to finance transfer payments, and the negative effects of the former will be offset, so far as consumption is concerned, by the positive effects of the latter. In part the taxes will be used to finance governmental expenditures on goods and services. Thus, even though total consumption expenditures may fall as a result of the governmental tax and expenditure program, total expenditures (consumption-plus-investment-plus governmental) may not. The exact effects of the taxes upon consumption will, of course, be influenced by the type of tax imposed; without doubt some taxes are absorbed out of savings to a greater extent than others.

The Determinants of the Volume of Investment

The other key determinant of the level of national income is the volume of investment, in the sense of the purchase of new capital equipment. The determinants of investment were discussed in detail in

Chapter 16, and need only be summarized here. The volume of investment which any firm will undertake will depend upon the marginal revenue product of additional capital goods, relative to the rate of interest; as indicated in Chapter 16, the interest rate is believed to exercise relatively little influence on most investments. The marginal revenue product of capital equipment depends, in turn, in large measure upon the expectations of businessmen about the future, and thus is subject to considerable variation as future prospects change. Marginal revenue product is also influenced by innovations, as previously explained, and upon the extent to which capital equipment has already been acquired.

The interest rate, as explained in Chapter 17, is dependent upon the supply of loanable funds, relative to demand for them, or, alternatively, may be explained in terms of the relationship between the supply of money in the economy and the demand for it for liquid balances.

Can a functional relationship be developed between the level of national income and the volume of investment? It is obvious that, in general, an increase in national income causes a rise in investment, especially if plant capacity is largely utilized. But in large measure the additional net investment will disappear if national income stabilizes at the higher level; it is the shift to the higher level, rather than the latter itself, which calls forth the additional new investment to provide capacity to meet the larger demand for consumption goods.

The Acceleration Principle. From this relationship there has been developed the *acceleration* principle, designed to show a close functional relationship between national income and investment. According to this principle, the volume of investment, given the other determinants, such as the rate of interest and the extent of innovations, is proportional to the *rate of change* in consumption. Suppose, for example, that a firm is producing 1000 automobiles a day, and requires 20 machines for this output. With an average life of 10 years, 2 new machines, on the average, would be purchased each year. If automobile production increases 10 per cent to 1100, the firm must acquire 2 additional machines, and the annual machine purchase doubles, the net investment rising from 0 machines to 2. But the firm will continue this net investment in 2 machines per year only if the daily output continues to rise by the sum of 100 units. If output stabilizes at the higher figure, replacement investment will remain higher, but net investment will vanish.

However, the acceleration principle is subject to serious limitations. It is not valid at all so long as the firm has idle machines, as is often true in periods of depression. It assumes a constant ratio of capital and labor, which is not necessarily valid. And the additional machines will not be purchased unless the firm believes that output will stay at the higher level.

In view of the limitations of the acceleration principle and the failure to develop other explanations, it is impossible with the present state of knowledge to establish a satisfactory functional relationship between national income and investment; the latter, like governmental expenditures, must be regarded as an exogeneous variable, an external determinant rather than an element determinable within the system of theory. The assumption upon which the investment data in Table 35 were based, that investment is permanently higher at higher levels of national income, may be completely erroneous; it is based upon nothing more than the belief that a high level of national income offers more opportunities for the introduction and development of innovations and of laborsaving devices than does a lower level.

Depreciation Policies and Investment. In the analysis of national income, the relevent investment figure is that of net investment—gross investment less depreciation charges. Therefore, the actual figure of investment in any period depends, in part, upon the total sum of depreciation charges, since this represents the deduction made from gross investment in determining net investment. But the actual depreciation charges in any particular year depend upon the policies followed by firms with respect to depreciation, because of the impossibility of determining the actual decline in value of existing assets during the year. If firms follow policies which result in relatively high depreciation charges, but do not alter their replacement programs, the amount of net investment in the economy will be less than it would be if depreciation charges were lower, other circumstances being given. Accordingly, national income will be lower. But GNP, and employment, will not be lower, unless the amount of the additional depreciation charge would otherwise have been paid out as dividends, and used by the recipients for consumption, or unless the higher reported figure of profits would have led the firms to undertake a higher level of investment.

Government Expenditures

The third element in total expenditures consists of those made by governments. These expenditures must be taken as exogeneous, or independent, variables in the system, since they cannot be explained in terms of economic factors. It is impossible to develop a satisfactory functional relationship between government expenditures and the level of national income, although the acceptance of a policy on the part of the government of eliminating unemployment by the use of fiscal devices tends to produce an inverse functional relationship; as the level of national income falls, the volume of federal government expenditures tends to rise. On the other hand, state and local governments tend to reduce their expenditures as incomes and tax receipts fall, and thus offset in large measure the action of the federal government in increasing expenditures to eliminate unemployment. In Table 35 (page 498) a constant amount of government expenditures at all income levels was assumed.

The making of expenditures by the government may or may not cause an equivalent reduction in consumption or investment expenditures. If the government expenditures are financed by taxation, and the collection of the taxes reduces consumption or investment by the equivalent amount, no net increase in total expenditures occurs from the undertaking of the governmental program. But if the government expenditures are financed by taxes which do not cause equivalent decline in consumption or investment (as for example if they are borne out of saving without an equivalent effect upon investment), or if they are financed by borrowing (without an equivalent repressive effect on private investment), or by printing of paper money, total expenditures will be greater as a result of the conduct of the governmental activities.

Mutual Equilibrium of National Income and the Interest Rate

In Chapter 17, in the analysis of the determination of the interest rate, it was indicated that the demand for and supply of loanable funds were dependent upon the level of national income. In the preceding sections of this chapter the rate of interest has been noted as one determinant of the level of national income. Consideration of the interrelationship of these two elements is necessary.

To the extent that they exert influence upon each other, national income and the rate of interest must adjust to levels which are mutually consistent with each other. Suppose, for example, that temporarily the basic interest rate level is at 5 per cent. With this figure, given the other determinants of national income, suppose that national income adjusts to the $250 billion level. But at this level, the demand for loanable funds may be such, relative to supply, that the interest rate rises to 6 per cent. This rate may be incompatible with the maintenance of national income at $250 billion, because investment is curtailed. Thus national income and the interest rate must fall until they reach levels which are consistent with each other; when these levels are reached, the interest rate will not interfere with stability of the national income figure, and the latter will be such that no shift in the interest rate will occur.

This interrelationship can be demonstrated graphically by a method based upon the work of J. R. Hicks. In Figure 91, national income is measured on the horizontal axis, and the interest rate on the vertical axis. The *LL* curve shows the interest rate which will prevail at each level of national income, given the determinants of the rate, that is,

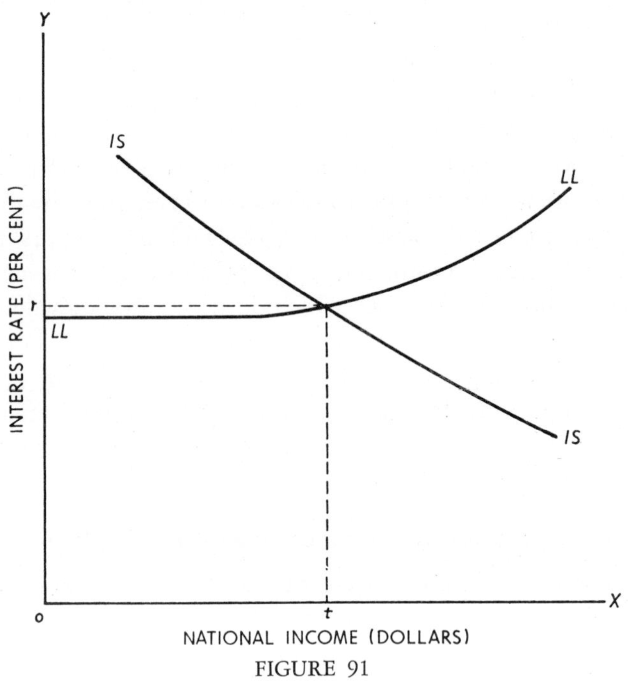

FIGURE 91

SIMULTANEOUS ADJUSTMENT OF THE INTEREST RATE AND NATIONAL INCOME

the various factors influencing the supply of and demand for money. The curve slopes upward from left to right, beyond a certain point, unless central bank credit policies insure a perfectly elastic supply of money capital, because the higher levels of national income will require larger amounts of money for transactions purposes, and will cause the supply of money capital to lag behind the demand. The left-hand portion is believed to be more or less horizontal, because once the interest rate falls below a certain level, any additional amount of money freed through the reduced volume of transactions will merely enter idle balances, rather than the active supply of money capital.

The *IS* curve, on the other hand, indicates, for each level of national income, the interest rate figure which is consistent with the maintenance of the particular level of national income, that is, the rate which will allow equality of planned savings and planned investment. If, as national income rises, planned investment tends to lag behind planned savings with a given interest rate, the curve will slope downward from left to right—a lower rate being necessary at the higher levels of national income to raise investment up to the planned savings level. The actual location of the curve depends upon the consumption function and the behavior of marginal revenue product of capital goods. If investment is relatively unresponsive to interest rate changes, as is believed to be the case, the *IS* curve will be very steep, and may cut below the horizontal axis at a fairly low level of national income.

The point at which the *LL* and *IS* curves cross is the point at which the interest rate and the level of national income are mutually consistent with each other. On Figure 91, the equilibrium interest rate figure is *or,* and the equilibrium level of national income is *ot.* At any higher level of national income, with the determinants as given, the interest rate would be raised by the need for additional funds for transactions purposes to a figure too high to permit continuation of this level of national income. At any lower level of national income, the interest rate would be too low; the stimulation to investment would raise the level of national income.[3]

This analysis is significant only if (1) the rate of interest is free to move, rather than being maintained at a certain level by central bank action, and (2) the interest rate does exercise some influence on the volume of investment. If the interest rate is maintained at a given level, *LL* will be a horizontal line (as shown in Figure 92, p. 510), and the actual rate is thus independent of the level of national income. If investment is not affected by the rate of interest, *IS* is a vertical line, and the actual level of national income is not affected by the height of the interest rate (as shown in Figure 93).

The Relationship between the Actual and Full-Employment Levels of National Income

The actual level of national income cannot, of course, exceed the full-employment level—the level permitted by available resources and technology, as explained below. But it is recognized today that the equilibrium level may be less than the full-employment level, as was

[3] See J. R. Hicks, "Mr. Keynes and the Classics: A Suggested Interpretation," *Econometrica,* Vol. V (April, 1937), pp. 147–59. This is reprinted in the *Readings in the Theory of Income Distribution* (Philadelphia: Blakiston, 1949).

See also the treatment in W. J. Baumol and L. V. Chandler, *Economic Processes and Policies* (New York: Harper, 1954), chap. xi.

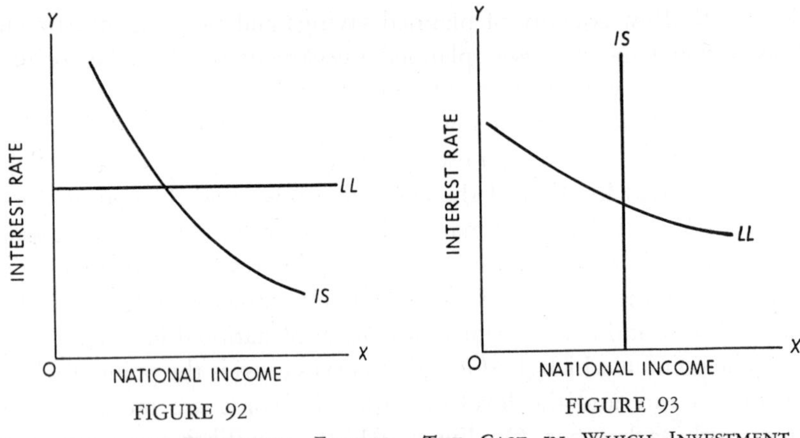

FIGURE 92

THE CASE OF PERFECTLY ELASTIC MONEY SUPPLY

FIGURE 93

THE CASE IN WHICH INVESTMENT IS NOT DEPENDENT UPON THE INTEREST RATE

true, for example, during the 'thirties. If, at the full-employment level, the total volume of investment is less than the total volume of planned savings, total expenditures will be less than national income, and output and income will fall. As income falls, the percentage of income saved will fall—as a result of the basic nature of the consumption function—and eventually equilibrium will be restored, at the level at which planned investment and planned savings are equal. This equilibrium will continue—so long as the determinants of total expenditures remain unchanged—despite the fact that all resources are not fully employed. Full employment can be maintained only if, at full-employment levels, investment is adequate to absorb the volume of planned savings which persons wish to make at that level of income. Savings and investment are undertaken in large measure by different groups of persons for substantially different motives; there is no absolute necessity that the magnitudes be equal at the full-employment level of national income.

Factor Price Changes and Restoration of Full Employment. It was once widely argued that an equilibrium at less than full employment was not a stable one, because factor prices, especially wages, would tend to fall and restore full employment, particularly if factor markets were perfectly competitive. But it is now recognized that a decline in factor prices, even if it occurs, does not necessarily restore full employment. As factor prices go down, the commodity prices will tend to fall in much the same proportion, and total purchasing power will, of course, fall as well. Total expenditures will not rise, relative to income, except for the effect of the two forces noted below. In general, all that happens is a general downward movement in monetary terms with little real change. As noted in Chapter 14, a reduction in money wages does not necessarily bring the reduction in real wages necessary to increase employment.

However, the decline in factor prices and the general price level will produce two types of reactions favorable to the lessening of unemployment. These may be called the Keynesian and the Pigou effects, for the persons who first explained them.

The Keynesian Effect. Keynes, who more than any other writer developed the thesis that wage cuts would not restore full employment, granted that the price declines would tend to stimulate investment slightly by lowering the interest rate. Given the supply of money, a decline in prices lessens the demand for money necessary for the conduct of transactions. Hence more money is available for meeting of demands for passive liquid balances, or, in other words, the supply of loanable funds tends to rise. But Keynes, in company with many others, did not believe that the interest decline would have significant effect upon employment, particularly because of the "stickiness" of the rate below certain levels.

The Pigou Effect. The English economist Pigou developed the thesis that the increasing real (purchasing-power) value of fixed assets which occurs as the price level falls tends to increase the percentage of income consumed and thus to aid in restoring full employment. As the price level falls, the real value of those assets which yield fixed returns, such as bonds, and of cash itself rises. Persons holding such assets will tend to consume a higher percentage of their incomes, since they will consider additional saving to be less urgent.

The significance of the Pigou effect is doubtful; motives which influence savings are very complex, and the effects of the increase in real value of existing holdings may be negligible. Even when both effects are taken into consideration, tremendous factor price reductions might be necessary to restore full employment—reductions which in practice could never be realized. Furthermore, during the process of reduction, aggregate demand might be reduced still more. If prices commence to fall, and persons believe that they will continue to fall, both consumption and investment will be delayed in anticipation of the lower prices. A sudden sharp once-and-for-all cut would not produce this effect, but even purely competitive conditions will not bring about this type of a reduction.

Expenditures in Excess of Income at Full Employment

The preceding sections have been concerned with the cases in which total expenditures are equal to total national income (and planned savings are equal to planned investment) at levels of full employment or less than full employment. But it is possible that at full employment, total expenditures may be greater than income; that is, the sum of consumption, investment, and governmental expenditures which persons seek to make is greater than the level of national income. Since production cannot rise (except slowly, over time, as productivity rises), the entire effect of the excessive demand manifests itself in a rise in prices; thus inflation, an increase in the general price level, results. This is the situation which has been commonly encountered in war and immediate postwar periods. Figure 94 portrays this situation graphi-

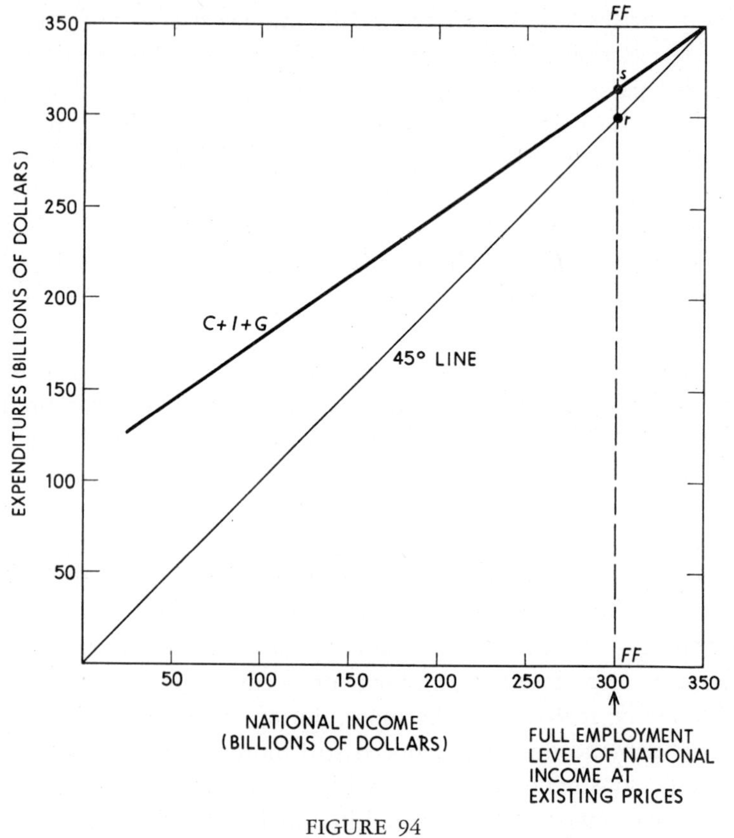

FIGURE 94

THE CASE OF INFLATION

cally; when full employment (indicated by *FF*) is reached, total spending is still in excess of national income; the difference between the two magnitudes at full employment may be called the inflationary gap (*rs* on Figure 94).

Under such conditions, will the price increases which result bring about a stable equilibrium, as suggested on Figure 94, on which the total expenditure curve $(C + I + G)$ crosses the 45° line at $350 billion? As the general price level rises there are several influences which tend to eliminate the inflationary gap. In the first place, with a tax system in which income taxes play an important role, tax collections tend to rise faster than income (because of fixed exemptions and progressive rates), and thus restrict consumption and investment; aggregate demand will fall, relative to income, unless government expenditures rise by the amount of the additional tax collections.

Secondly, the increasing demand for money for transactions purposes will tend to raise the interest rate and check bank lending, unless the central banking system makes the supply of money perfectly elastic.

Thirdly, if, after a certain point is reached, individuals and business firms become convinced that prices will fall, purchase of consumer durables and investment will slacken in anticipation of lower prices.

Finally, the Pigou effect operates as the real value of cash balances and of wealth in the form of fixed-return securities, such as bonds and mortgages falls; persons are likely to attempt to increase their rate of savings in order to maintain the real value of their liquid and semiliquid wealth. A $1,000 savings deposit kept on hand to meet emergency medical expenses, for example, may be regarded as inadequate as costs of medical care increase. The sum accumulated to allow retirement on a reasonable income will become completely inadequate if the cost of living doubles, and persons will attempt to save additional amounts.

However, these forces may not be adequate to stop the inflation, especially if it is caused by a very heavy level of government spending.

THE REAL LEVEL OF NATIONAL INCOME

The savings-consumption ratio, the volume of investment, and the volume of governmental spending determine the equilibrium level of national income, which may be one which allows full employment, or may be less than this figure. But analysis of these determinants tells nothing about the actual real output of goods—about real income, in the sense of goods and services consumed and new capital equipment built—which comprise the full employment, or less-than-full-employment, level of income.

The Real Full-Employment Level

Let us consider first the determinants of the real content of the full-employment level of national income. The first is, of course, the quantity of various resources available. The greater the supply of labor, the various types of natural resources, and capital equipment, the higher will be the level of output, other circumstances being given. Secondly, output will be affected by the available techniques of production, which affect the nature of the capital equipment available, and the processes of production which are employed. Thirdly, the skill of labor and management will affect the level of output. Finally, the general economic, political, and social environment will affect the efficiency of the conduct of production and the level of output. Social relationships influence worker and employer morale; governmental controls may drastically reduce (or in some cases, increase) the efficiency of the conduct of production. Over a period of time, the real level of full-employment income magnitudes will depend primarily upon changes in these determinants, particularly the development of improved techniques, the introduction of better types of capital equipment, the gaining of greater skill on the part of labor and management, etc.

Real Income at Less than Full Employment

If national income stabilizes at a less-than-full-employment level of income, the actual level of real income will depend upon the percentage of total resources which are employed, the relative efficiency of the employed and unemployed resources, and the effect of the reduced level of output upon the general efficiency of the conduct of production. Since the unemployed resources are likely to be the less efficient units, a 10 per cent reduction in employment is not likely to be accompanied by a 10 per cent reduction in output.

SELECTED REFERENCES

The volume of literature on the determination of national income in the last twenty years has been tremendous. Only some of the major studies are listed.

KEYNES, J. M. *The General Theory of Employment, Interest and Money.* New York: Harcourt, Brace, 1936.

The basic work upon which much of the recent income analysis has been built.

DILLARD, D. *The Economics of John Maynard Keynes.* New York: Prentice-Hall, 1948.

A simplified statement of Keynes.

HANSEN, A. H. *A Guide to Keynes.* New York: McGraw-Hill, 1953.

An explanation of Keynes, by his most famous American disciple.

MCKENNA, JOSEPH P. *Aggregative Economic Analysis.* New York: Dryden Press, 1955.

A concise general statement of national income theory.

RUGGLES, RICHARD. *An Introduction to National Income and Income Analysis.* 2nd ed. New York: McGraw-Hill, 1955.

An analysis of the determinants of national income and the process of adjustment.

KURIHARA, K. K. (ed.). *Post-Keynesian Economics.* New Brunswick: Rutgers University Press, 1954.

A series of essays on various aspects of national income theory, in light of contemporary analysis.

HELLER, W. W. (ed.). *Savings in the Modern Economy.* Minneapolis: University of Minnesota Press, 1953.

A series of studies on questions relating to savings and investment.

Income, Employment, and Public Policy: Essays in Honor of Alvin H. Hansen, Part I. New York: Norton, 1948.

A series of essays on national income and related questions.

HARRIS, S. E. (ed.). *The New Economics.* New York: Knopf, 1948.

A series of studies by various authors of the Keynesian approach to national income and related questions.

FELLNER, W. "Economic Theory and Business Cycles," and VILLARD, H. H., "Monetary Theory," in ELLIS, H. S. (ed.), *A Survey of Contemporary Economics.* Homewood, Ill.: Richard D. Irwin, Inc., 1948.

A survey of recent literature in the fields of national income and monetary theory.

QUESTIONS

1. In the traditional economic analysis, some consideration was given to the determinants of the full-employment real level of national income, but none at all to the equilibrium level of national income. Why?
2. What is meant by the term "expenditures" as used in national income analysis? What are the three types of expenditures?
3. What is the significance of the 45° line on Figure 89?
4. Explain the equilibrium level of national income in terms of (a) aggregate expenditures and (b) savings and investment relationships.
5. Suppose that the equilibrium level of national income is $250 billion, and that temporarily national income is at $300 billion. Explain exactly why national income will fall back to $250 billion.
6. Suppose, on the basis of the data in Question 5, that temporarily national income falls to $200 billion. Explain the process by which it will return to $250 billion.
7. Why, at levels of national income in excess of the equilibrium, will firms be getting back less from the sale of the products than they are paying out in factor incomes?
8. In the previous chapter, national income was explained as being equal, at all times, to the sum of consumption, investment, and governmental expenditures (plus net foreign investment). In this chapter, the argument is advanced that the equilibrium level of national income is determined by the

levels of these expenditures. If national income is always equal to the sum of these magnitudes, how can it be determined by them?

9. Why in any past period of time must the magnitudes of savings and investment be equal? Why are the planned or intended magnitudes in any coming period not necessarily equal?
10. Summarize the determinants of national income.
11. Why is it generally assumed that the percentage of income consumed falls as income rises?
12. What is meant by the term "consumption function," with respect to national income? With respect to disposable income?
13. Explain the effect upon the consumption function of:
    a) A general rise in stock prices
    b) Anticipated shortages of commodities
    c) Introduction of guaranteed annual wage programs
    d) Increased down-payment requirements on installment purchases
    e) A tendency on the part of corporations to retain larger percentages of profits in the firms
    f) Increased old age pension payments, financed by borrowing by governments
    g) Increased income taxes to finance higher defense spending
14. Restate the determinants of the volume of investments.
15. What is the acceleration principle? What important relationship does it stress? What weaknesses does it have as a means of establishing a functional relationship between national income and the volume of investment?
16. Why is investment greater during a period when national income is rising to a new level than it is after national income has stabilized at the higher figure?
17. Why cannot a satisfactory functional relationship be established between national income and government expenditures?
18. Under what circumstances could government expenditures increase without an equivalent decline in consumption and investment spending?
19. Why must national income and the rate of interest adjust to levels which are mutually consistent with each other?
20. Under what circumstances can full employment not be maintained?
21. Why do factor price reductions, if they occur, not necessarily restore full employment?
22. Distinguish between the Keynesian effect and the Pigou effect of general price declines, and evaluate the importance of each.
23. Suppose that, at full employment, total expenditures exceed national income. What will happen? Why? Will this process continue indefinitely, or will an equilibrium eventually be attained? Explain.
24. Explain the determinants of the real level of national income at full employment.

Chapter 23 CHANGES IN NATIONAL INCOME

In the previous chapter, the determinants of the equilibrium level of national income were outlined, together with reference to the factors which control the real content of full-employment and less-than-full-employment levels of income. This chapter will be devoted to questions relating to change in national income, including the possible causes of change, monetary versus real change, the patterns of recurrent change, the growth in national income, and deliberate stabilization policy.

POSSIBLE CAUSES OF CHANGE IN THE EQUILIBRIUM LEVEL OF NATIONAL INCOME

Directly and immediately, any change in the equilibrium level of national income can be explained in terms of a shift in total expenditures, relative to the current level of output and income. The primary causes of shifts in the equilibrium figure of national income are (1) a change in the volume of investment, (2) a change in the consumption-savings ratio, and (3) a change in government spending (provided, of course, that a change in one of the determinants is not accompanied by an equivalent change in the opposite direction in one of the other determinants). The three primary causes will be considered in the order listed.

Changes in Investment

Since investment is one of the segments of total spending, any change in investment causes a change in aggregate demand, and thus a shift in national income. Except in periods such as wars in which government expenditures change sharply, investment is usually regarded as the element in total expenditures most likely to change significantly and thereby the most important source of variations in national income.

Consumption is generally assumed to be relatively stable at particular levels of national income, changing in total largely as a result of changes in national income. But the volume of investment is subject to change from autonomous causes at any time. New technological developments will increase the profitability of additional capital equipment, as will the discovery of new resources. Mere changes in expectations of businessmen about sales and profits in the future will alter the volume of investment which they regard as profitable.

An increase in investment will lead to increased output of capital goods, and thus greater factor incomes originating in this sector of production. As these factor incomes are in part spent, output of consumption goods will rise, and will create additional factor incomes in this field; as these are spent, output will increase still more. On the other hand, reduced purchases of capital goods will reduce incomes earned in this sector; as the factor-owners experience reduced incomes, they will buy fewer consumption goods, and thus output and income in the latter fields will decline as well.

The Investment Multiplier. The concept of the investment multiplier has been developed as a more precise expression of the relationship between an increase or decrease in investment and the consequent increase or decrease in national income. Specifically, the investment multiplier is the numerical relationship between a change in the volume of investment and the consequent change in national income. If a $2 billion increase in investment leads to a $10 billion increase in national income, the multiplier is 5.

The multiplier is the reciprocal of the *marginal* propensity to save—the proportion of additional income which is saved. Suppose, for example, that on the average, given the present level of national income, persons will save one fourth of any additional income they receive. If so, the multiplier will be 4—the reciprocal of ¼. Thus a $3 billion increase in investment will cause a $12 billion increase in national income. If the marginal propensity to save is ⅒, the multiplier will be 10; if it is 50 per cent, the multiplier is 2. The marginal propensity to save must be distinguished from the average propensity to save, discussed in the previous chapter. The latter refers to the proportion of the total income which is saved; the former refers to the proportion of additional income received which is saved. A person may be saving only 5 per cent of his total income, but may save 25 per cent of additional income.

What is the reason for this relationship between the marginal propensity to save and the multiplier? As explained in the previous chapter, national income can be in equilibrium only if the planned volume of savings in each period is equal to the planned volume of investment. Therefore, when investment rises by a given sum, savings must rise by the equivalent sum for equilibrium to be restored. If the marginal propensity to save is 25 per cent, savings will rise by the amount of the investment increase only when national income has risen by 4 times the amount of the investment increase. If persons are, on the average, saving 25 per cent of the income which they receive, their incomes must increase by 4 times the amount of the new investment if they are to save an amount equal to the latter. This is illustrated on Figure 95; an increase in investment of I′ (an increase of $25 billion) moves the equilibrium level of income from $200 to $300 billion, or by $100 billion. To simplify the exposition, government expenditures are combined with consumption expenditures on Figure 95, and in order to

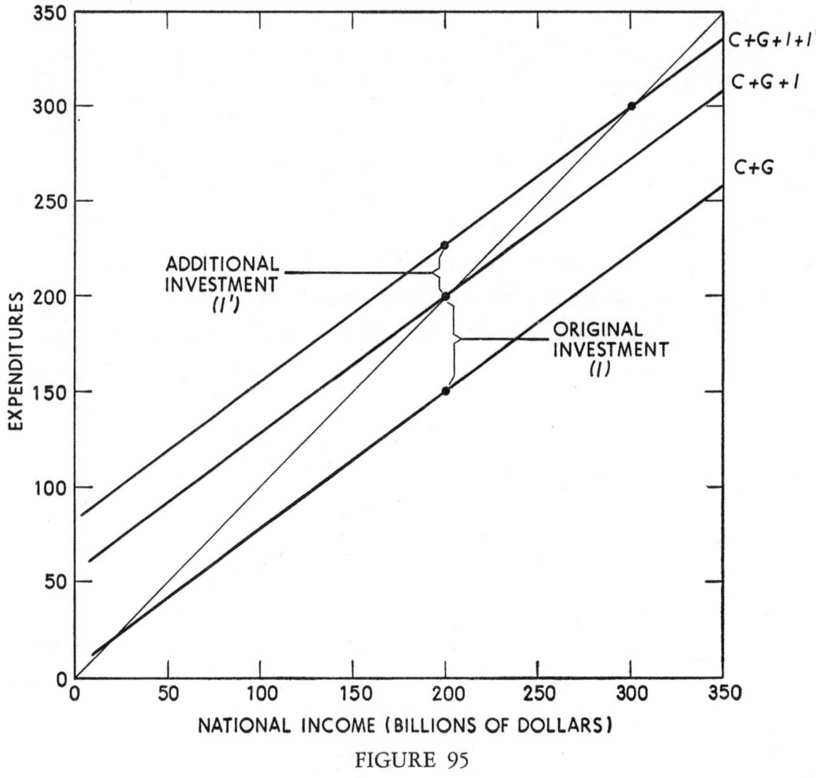

FIGURE 95

THE INVESTMENT MULTIPLIER

isolate the multiplier reaction, the volume of investment is shown to be independent of the volume of national income. The multiplier, as such, does not take into consideration the induced investment arising from the increase in national income.

Limitations to the Multiplier Analysis. There are several important limitations to the significance of the multiplier analysis, which presents an oversimplified picture of the reactions to an increase in investment. In the first place, as noted, it ignores induced investment caused by the rise in national income. As the latter rises, the increased outputs will increase the profitability of investment in many lines, and thus a certain amount of induced investment will be undertaken (assuming, of course, that initially the amount of idle plant capacity was not so great that no additional capacity was needed as output rose). Hence during the period of increase, total income can be expected to rise to a higher level than that indicated by the multiplier. But since the additional investment is due to the *increase* in national income, as such, rather than to the *higher level* of national income, it will slacken as the national income stabilizes at the higher figure.

Secondly, the multiplier is of little use in analyzing monetary changes in national income in periods of full employment. If additional investment merely produces an increase in the general price level, the new equilibrium level of national income cannot be explained in terms of the multiplier.

Thirdly, the analysis, as given, assumes that the marginal propensity to save does not change as national income rises. If it does, the task of estimating the new equilibrium level is complicated.

Finally, the point must be stressed that the multiplier reaction is effective only to the extent to which the additional investment represents a net increase in total expenditures. As national income rises, increases in imports (relative to exports) and more-than-proportional increases in tax collections tend to check the increase in total expenditures and thus in national income. If the rise in the volume of transactions raises the interest rate, as will occur unless the supply of money capital increases in proportion to the rise in the demand for it, the net amount of new investment will be reduced.

The multiplier principle, of course, also operates in reverse; a decline in investment will cause a decline in national income of a magnitude dependent upon the marginal propensity to save.

On the whole, despite its limitations, the multiplier is a useful tool of analysis, if properly employed, with full recognition of the necessary qualifications. Together with the acceleration principle, it plays a major role in the more important recent theories of the business cycle, noted below.

Changes in the Consumption Function

While the consumption function is generally assumed to be relatively stable, it is recognized that autonomous forces may cause shifts in it, with consequent changes in the level of national income. Suppose, for example, that persons commence to spend higher percentages of their incomes, because of the development of a belief that certain goods will be scarce in the immediate future. Such a belief was widespread, for example, following the outbreak of war in Korea in 1950, and led to a sharp increase in consumption spending. As purchases increase, temporarily inventories are depleted, and the increase in consumption is in part offset by a decline in net investment (in the form of reduced inventories). But producers will increase output (assuming that resources are not fully employed) and national income will rise until it again equals the volume of expenditures which persons wish to make.

The reactions may be expressed in terms of consumption-savings relationships. An increase in the propensity to consume involves an equivalent reduction in the propensity to save. Therefore at the original level of national income the volume of planned savings is less than the volume of planned investment, and national income must rise until the two are again equal. Thus the concept of a consumption multiplier, relating the increased consumption (and hence the gap between planned savings and planned investment) to the consequent increase in national income, could be employed. In practice, however, the concept of the multiplier is employed primarily with respect to the effects of changes in investment and governmental expenditure.

The direct effect of the increased consumption upon national income will be supplemented by the effect of the rise in national income upon the volume of investment. The additional investment induced by the rise in national income will be subject to the multiplier, and will cause a secondary increase in total production.

The Paradox of Saving. A decline in the propensity to consume (or, in other words, an increase in the propensity to save) will lead to a reduction in national income (other determinants being given), and produce this peculiar paradox: an increased desire to save on the part of the community as a whole, not accompanied by an equivalent increase in investment opportunities, will result in a decline in the actual volume of savings. As the savings function rises, temporarily some of the output forthcoming cannot be sold, and initially investment rises (as inventories rise). But this increase in investment is involuntary, and firms will commence to reduce purchases and output. Thus incomes will fall, and precipitate still greater reductions in output. As national income falls, the absolute volume of savings falls, until equilibrium of savings and investment is again restored. Society cannot save more merely as a result of an increased desire to save; real saving can increase in total only as a result of increases in investment in new capital goods.

However, in a period in which investment opportunities are very high and investment is tending to outrun planned savings (with consequent inflation), an increased propensity to save will permit a higher level of investment and a more rapid rate of capital formation. This is likely to be the typical case in a country whose resources are relatively undeveloped and investment opportunities are very good. Dangers arise from an increased propensity to save only when investment opportunities are not adequate to absorb the increased savings.

It was once argued that under all circumstances an increase in the volume of savings would directly and immediately increase the volume of investment by raising the supply of money capital and thus lowering the interest rate. As a consequence, no decline in national income would occur. There are two deficiencies in this line of reasoning. In the first place, as noted in previous chapters, the volume of investment does not appear to be highly responsive to interest rate changes. In the second place, no "surplus" of money capital may ever appear. Simultaneously with the increase in the propensity to save there occurs a decline in the sales of consumption goods, and accordingly output and incomes fall at once. As a consequence of the reduction in incomes, persons will not have larger sums of money capital to offer for business expansion. Once again, the mere increased desire to save does not actually produce an increase in the volume of savings. It is true that as national income falls, the lessened need for money for transactions purposes tends to reduce the interest rate. This tendency will slow the decline in national income but can scarcely prevent it, since the rate falls only because of the decline in transactions.

Increases in Governmental Spending

The third element in total expenditures consists of governmental spending. An increase in this magnitude, without a corresponding decline in private spending, will cause national income to rise. The numerical relationship between the initial increase in government spending and the consequent rise in national income is known as the governmental multiplier. In practice the term *multiplier* alone is often used with respect to both the investment and governmental multipliers. The latter, like the former, is the reciprocal of the marginal propensity to save. A rise in governmental spending, without an offsetting decline in private spending, creates a gap between planned savings and planned investment in the same manner as an increase in investment; as a consequence, national income must rise by a multiple (dependent upon the marginal propensity to save) of the increase in government spending in order to restore equality of planned savings and planned investment.

In practice, an increase in governmental spending is likely to have some restrictive effect on consumption, investment, or both. If it is financed by taxation, both private consumption and investment are likely to be reduced, to an extent dependent in part upon the type of tax used and the reactions of the taxpayers to the taxes. Only if the tax revenues come out of sums which would otherwise have been saved, the collection having no adverse effect upon investment, will there be no offsetting decline in private spending. If the government obtains the necessary funds from borrowing, particularly from the commercial banks or the central banking system, there will be less restrictive effect upon private spending than if taxes are used. But the growth of the national debt may reduce investment somewhat if it creates fears about future financial stability of the government and the economy.

Later in the chapter, attention will be given to the question of deliberate efforts on the part of governments to obtain economic stability by adjusting expenditure and tax policies.

REAL VERSES MONETARY CHANGES IN NATIONAL INCOME

In the preceding paragraphs it has been assumed that the monetary and real levels of national income change in like manner, a given change in the monetary level reflecting a proportional change in the real level. This relationship is valid only so long as the general price level remains unchanged. To the extent that changes in expenditures produce changes in the general price level, the real change will be relatively less than the monetary change. For example, when full employment is reached, further increases in national income which may occur from increased expenditures are purely monetary changes (apart from real increases permitted by increased productivity).

The general price level—the over-all pattern of prices as measured by price index numbers—will shift whenever a change in aggregate demand for goods is not accompanied by an equivalent change in total output and supply. Thus the general price level will rise if an increase in expenditures is not followed by an equivalent increase in output. The exact extent of the response of the general price level to changes in expenditures will be affected by the presence or absence of full employment.

Nonfull-Employment Situations

So long as idle resources are available, it can be expected that a rise in total expenditures will primarily affect output, rather than prices. Firms, in general, will meet the increased demand with greater output, since they will either have excess capacity or can increase plant easily because of the availability of idle resources. Average-cost pricing practices will increase the tendency to leave prices unchanged. New firms will develop with the use of unemployed resources.

However, even prior to the attainment of full employment, there will be some tendency for the price level to rise. In the first place, in agricultural industries, the products of which are sold in highly competitive markets, there will be relatively little readjustment of output, and so prices will tend to rise. The output of individual farm crops will increase in response to a demand increase, since land will be shifted from other crops. But, when a general increase in the demand for farm products occurs, there is not likely to be much increase in output. Farmers are inclined to use their land fully even at low prices, since, as a rule, they can maximize their own individual incomes by so doing. The increase in farm prices in itself raises the general price level and also leads to increases in costs—and thus in prices—of other goods.

Secondly, far short of full employment, "bottlenecks" are likely to develop in various industries; shortages of skilled labor, of natural resources, or plant capacity of a type which requires an extensive period for readjustment will check increases in output and result in price increases in response to the increasing demand. If the steel industry reaches its maximum output, for example, the expansion of other industries using steel may be checked seriously for a period of several years while steel producers are expanding capacity.

Thirdly, increased expenditures and national income are almost certain to raise wages. Unions will grow in strength as unemployment lessens and will seek wage increases, arguing for them on the basis of increased cost of living and increased business profits. As wages are pushed upward, firms will adjust prices to cover the higher costs.

Finally, despite the usual policy of business firms of increasing output rather than price when sales increase and idle capacity is available, some firms are almost certain to make price readjustments in response to the increase in demand. In periods of low output, some prices will be depressed by the increase in the severity of price competition. As national income rises, firms will be able to push these prices upward to more profitable levels.

Despite these forces tending to raise prices, however, so long as unemployment remains the increased expenditures will primarily result in output increases. For example, from 1933 to 1939, national income rose from $39 billion to $81 billion;[1] the general price index rose only from 65.9 to 77.1.[2]

Full-Employment Situations

Once full employment is reached, further increases in total expenditures will exercise their entire influence on the general price level, apart from the increases in output which result from improvements in productivity. For example, suppose that with full employment, planned investment increases beyond the level of planned savings. Total expenditures will exceed national income and the volume of output at current prices; since output cannot rise significantly, almost the entire effect will be upon the price level. During the boom periods of the last century, almost certainly planned investment tended to outrun planned savings at full employment, with consequent tendency toward inflation until shortages of money capital brought the expansion to a halt.

The most significant inflations, however, have been during war and immediate postwar periods in which government expenditures reached such high levels as to cause planned total expenditures to outrun national income after full employment had been attained. In a major war, governmental and consumption expenditures alone may tend to outrun output at current prices; thus total planned savings is negative, yet investment is a positive figure. Therefore prices tend to rise sharply unless prevented by direct price controls, which essentially prevent the excessive demand from bidding prices up and force persons to save more than they wish.

If total expenditures commence to outrun national income at full employment, there is the possibility that runaway inflation may develop. As explained in the previous chapter, when the general price level rises, there are certain factors which tend to check the rise and allow attainment of an equilibrium. These include increases in tax collections, a tendency for the interest rate to rise, reduced real value of savings, and the development of expectations that prices will fall. But if the excess of expenditures over national income is very great, and no effective

[1] *Survey of Current Business,* July, 1949, p. 10.

[2] 1926 = 100, U.S. Bureau of Labor Statistics index of wholesale prices.

effort is made by the government to check inflation, the rate of increase in prices may become so great that persons lose all confidence in the future value of the money; spending increases still more rapidly as persons seek to exchange money for goods before prices reach still higher levels. The final result may be runaway inflation, with the money becoming almost worthless. This was the experience of a number of countries after World Wars I and II.

Declining Expenditures and the General Price Level

When planned investment drops below planned savings and thus total expenditures on consumption and investment decline, both price and output will tend to fall, whether full employment exists at the time or not. In agricultural industries, with large numbers of small producers, the primary reaction will be a decline in price, since producers will make relatively little adjustment in output and may in some cases increase it.[3] Present government price-support programs will materially check the price reduction, however, on commodities to which they apply. In other lines of production, producers will typically reduce output rather than make drastic price reductions; the use of average-cost pricing greatly increases this tendency. Some price reductions are inevitable, however, as some firms commence price-cutting, and others are forced to follow. The decline in agricultural prices, by lowering costs, will lead to downward readjustments in other prices. But, primarily, the declining expenditures will affect output. Between 1929 and 1933, for example, the price index of nonfarm prices fell from 91.6 to 71.2, while gross national product declined in about half, from $103 billion to $55 billion.

As total expenditures fall, prices would drop much more if wages readjusted downward as a result of the development of unemployment, since wage payments represent the major cost item. Wage rates, however, are notoriously sticky. Unions fight reductions bitterly; even when unions are absent, usual personnel policies make the competition of unemployed workers with those who have jobs difficult. The extent of the decline in wages which actually occurs, more than anything else, determines the extent of price reductions and the monetary value of the new equilibrium level of national income; as explained in Chapters 14 and 15, however, the behavior of wages probably has little significance for the volume of employment.

[3] The difference in the reaction of farmers to a general decline in the price of farm products and a decline affecting only one or a few goods must be emphasized. In the latter case production will be shifted to other crops, and the output will decline rapidly as the price falls. When prices of all farm products are falling, however, there will be little reduction in the output of any of the crops, since the farmers will have no better alternatives (at least in the short run) than to continue producing.

Cost Changes and the General Price Level

While changes in the general price level are generally attributed to changes in total expenditures relative to output, they may also occur from forces whose initial impact is upon the cost of production of a number of commodities. Rapid technological change, affecting many industries and allowing lower cost of production, will lower the price level. National income will increase in real terms, in the sense that more goods are being produced, provided that unemployment does not increase, but the level of national income in monetary terms may remain more or less unchanged. A widespread reduction in output, due, for example, to a severe drought affecting most agricultural production, could increase farm product prices and thus the costs of producing other goods.

The most likely cause of a general change in cost, however, is a change in the wage level. As indicated above, changes in national income due to expenditure changes will cause some readjustments in wages, which will reinforce the initial effects of the expenditure change. But, apart from this case, a general change in the wage level may occur from independent causes, such as increased strength of unionization. As a consequence of a general wage increase, firms will tend to readjust prices upward; the increased total money-wage figure will allow more or less the same volume of goods to be sold, despite the higher prices. In pure competition, while the higher costs will not directly allow producers to increase prices, the greater total demand (in monetary terms) for goods will tend to raise the prices of the products immediately, without the necessity of a supply readjustment. A general wage decrease would, in general, lower the price level. But such decreases—apart from ones of limited magnitude arising in periods of severe decline in business activity—do not occur.

The Quantity Theory of Money

An alternate approach to the explanation of general price-level changes, the *quantity theory of money,* emphasizes changes in the quantity of money as the primary cause of price-level changes.[4] The principle, in its more rigid form, is based upon the assumptions of full employment of resources and of a relatively constant ratio of cash balances held to incomes received. Under the latter assumption, additional money entering the economy will increase spending, and thus, with a situation of full employment, prices will rise. The assumption of relatively con-

[4] For an extended analysis see A. H. Hansen, *Monetary Theory and Fiscal Policy* (New York: McGraw-Hill, 1949).

stant cash balances may be stated in terms of the *velocity* of money (the average number of times a dollar changes hands during a period); if cash balances maintain a constant ratio to income, the velocity of money also remains constant. The quantity theorists, of course, recognized the fact that over a period of time the volume of transactions would increase as the economy developed and that the velocity of money would adjust as the customs of individuals and the procedures of businesses with respect to the use of cash changed. But the velocity was assumed to be relatively stable over shorter periods of time, and hence price level changes were attributed primarily to variations in the amount of money in the economy.

In the exposition of the quantity theory there was developed the equation of exchange: $MV + M'V' = PT$; M and M' represent the amounts of cash and of bank deposits and V and V' their relative velocities; P the average price; and T the physical volume of transactions.[5] Since V and V' are assumed to be relatively constant and T is assumed to be the full-employment volume of transactions, P—the general price level—depends primarily upon the amount of money, and changes in the latter will be reflected directly in changes in the price level.

Under these assumptions, the validity of the quantity theory cannot be questioned. The full-employment assumption, however, restricts its applicability; in its usual form it is of little use in explaining price changes at nonfull-employment levels. But, more seriously, the assumption of relative constancy of velocity of money—and thus of cash balances relative to income—is of doubtful applicability. The motives for holding cash are very complex, as indicated in previous chapters. Persons' relative desires for holding wealth in monetary or security form vary with changes in expectations about future conditions and with the rate of interest. An increase in the amount of money will have little or no effect on the price level if the money is simply added to idle balances, as it may well be, particularly when the interest rate drops to low levels. The increase in M is offset by a decrease in V. Or, with a given supply of money, an increase in expenditures (manifesting itself as an increase in V) will raise prices.

Today, as a rule, persons preferring the quantity-theory approach

[5] This equation is often called the "Fisher equation" after its popularizer, Irving Fisher.

An alternative approach to the explanation, commonly called the "cash-balances" approach, developed by Alfred Marshall and refined by D. H. Robertson and others, uses the equation $M = KTP$, in which M is the supply of money, T the volume of transactions, K the fraction of money income which persons wish to hold as cash balances, and P the average price.

take into consideration variations in velocity, as well as in the volume of transactions. But, when this change is made, the theory loses precision and presents an approach to price-level changes that is less satisfactory in emphasizing the significant factors in the changes than is the alternate approach presented above. Changes in the supply of money will in some cases affect the price level, but in other situations they will not do so; likewise, price-level changes may occur without a change in money supply. If the supply of money increases, the price level will be affected only if consumption, investment, or government expenditures are affected. If the government makes expenditures with newly printed paper money or finances its activities by means of borrowing from the commercial banks, the spending of this money will raise the level of national income and, if full employment has been attained, cause significant effects upon the price level. But it is much more realistic to attribute the price increase directly to the increased total expenditures rather than to the increase in money supply as such.

If additional money enters the economic system in exchange for other wealth, as occurs when the Federal Reserve System conducts open-market buying, it is unlikely that persons will either spend the additional money or use it for expansion of business. The attempt of the persons holding the additional money to exchange it for securities will drive up the price of bonds and lower the rate of interest; as a result, there may be some slight effect upon investment. Apart from the indirect effect through the interest rate and some possible influence which the size of persons' cash balances have on their propensity to consume, in this case the increase in money supply will have no effect on the price level. The frequently repeated statement that inflation occurring between 1939 and 1950 was due to the great increase in money in circulation is very misleading; the inflation can be explained much more satisfactorily in terms of the high consumption, investment, and governmental expenditures during these years. Explanation of the price changes solely in terms of monetary changes completely obscures the nature of the process by which they occurred.

RECURRENT CHANGES IN NATIONAL INCOME: THE BUSINESS CYCLE

The first section of this chapter outlined the various possible causes of change in national income. Autonomous changes in any of the determinants of aggregate demand may occur at any time, and produce shifts in the level of national income. Many of the changes in recent decades can be explained primarily in terms of these autonomous forces. The sharp rise in output between 1939 and 1942, and the general price rise in the subsequent ten years can be explained in terms of the increase in government spending in preparation for and the conduct of World War II. The sudden, sharp rise in the general price level in 1950 can be explained in terms of an increase in purchases of consumer durables and an increase in business inventories resulting from fears of scarcities and rationing. It is obvious also that important technological changes, such as the development of the automobile, can cause significant rises in national income.

However, it has been widely believed for many years that there are forces which operate within the economic system which tend to produce recurrent upward and downward movements in national income. Economic activity has shown considerable tendency toward alternating periods of prosperity and depression, known as *business cycles.* Although the cycles have varied substantially in both length and amplitude of the changes in production, prices, income, and employment, the constant recurrence of change from prosperity to depression and back to prosperity suggests that random causes alone have not been responsible; that, regularly, in a period of prosperity there develop forces which cause a decline in national income; and that, similarly, in depression periods forces arise to start recovery on its way. In other words, the economy, instead of adjusting toward an equilibrium position and remaining stable at that position, tends constantly to move upward and downward because each time an equilibrium is reached, on the basis of the determinants outlined in the previous chapter, forces develop which shift the determinants.

The Cumulative Nature of Expansion and Contraction

Once an upward or downward movement has started, the source of the cumulative nature of the change is relatively clear. As business activity commences to rise, through increased output in some industries, incomes earned in these industries rise. As a consequence, sales of other industries increase as persons spend the additional incomes. This, in turn, gives rise to increased income and production in still other fields and reinforces the initial expansion in the industries first affected. The general expansion in sales raises the profitability of investment throughout industry. The increased confidence on the part of businessmen which develops as national income rises greatly increases their willingness to undertake business expansion. The increasing output and gradual price increase raise profits, as some costs lag behind, and further stimulate business expansion and the feeling of confidence. In the terminology of national income analysis, in the period of expansion the multiplier effect operates on all increases in investment, and, because of the acceleration principle, increases in consumption purchases bring about increased investment. The two reactions reinforce each other to make expansion cumulative; their direct effect is strengthened by the increased optimism and confidence in the future which develops among both consumers and business firms.

Likewise, once a period of contraction starts, it can easily become cumulative. As some industries reduce output, men are laid off, and incomes fall. As a result, sales and output in other industries also decline; incomes earned in these industries fall and accentuate the contraction. Costs lag behind price, and sales decline. The consequent squeezing of profits, coupled with the excessive plant capacity which develops as sales decline, causes investment to fall drastically, and the multiplier effect pulls national income down still farther. Business firms reduce inventories, and their purchases—and the output of manufacturers—fall more rapidly than consumer purchases. The optimism of prosperity gives way to general pessimism. The unwillingness of lenders to advance funds checks investment still more. Bankruptcies of business firms increase the feeling of pessimism.

General Explanation of the Downturn

Explanation of the turning points is much less obvious than that of the cumulative processes of expansion and contraction. In general terms, a decline will commence when total consumption and investment expenditures fall below current national income,[6] or, in other words, when planned savings commence to outrun planned investment. The decline in total expenditures—and hence the divergence between planned savings and planned investment—may arise either because planned investment begins to drop or because it fails to keep pace with a rising volume of planned savings. The impetus to the decline may be a curtailment of investment as the profitability of the introduction of new capital goods commences to fall, or a decrease in the rate of consumption and thus a relative increase in the volume of saving.

There are certain conditions which tend to develop in a period of expansion which make continued expansion less profitable and render the economy vulnerable to a decline. The first is the tendency for costs

[6] Government expenditures are omitted from this discussion, which is concerned with nonautonomous forces.

to rise. As full employment is approached,[7] less efficient workers are hired. There may be difficulty in maintaining efficiency when workers have less fear of losing their jobs. Obsolete machinery and equipment may be brought into use. Workers are paid overtime wages. Material costs rise, especially when the output reaches capacity figures.

Secondly, at least in the past, there has been a tendency for interest rates to rise and for the banks to curtail loans as they reach reserve limits. Essentially, the supply of money has not kept pace with the rising monetary volume of transactions.

Finally, as expansion continues, increased output of goods made possible by the investment in capital equipment occurring during the period of recovery begins to reach the market. As a consequence, firms are likely to experience increasing difficulty in raising prices to meet cost increases. Likewise, the profitability of additional investment may fall, once the new capital goods actually come into use.

General Explanation of the Upturn

Just as the downturn develops as a result of a decline in total expenditures below the current level of national income, so recovery starts when total planned expenditures commence to rise above national income or, in other words, planned investment commences to outrun planned savings. This change, in turn, may arise from increased profitability of investment or from increased consumption, which lowers the volume of planned savings.

Several developments in the later period of the depression facilitate recovery. In the first place, costs, which lag behind the decline in output and prices, may eventually commence to fall and place the firms in more favorable profit positions. Prices of raw materials, sold frequently in purely competitive markets, drop more than finished product prices. Less efficient firms are eliminated, and poorer workers are released. Costs dependent upon long-term contracts are gradually revised downward. Financial obligations are reduced through corporate reorganizations.

Furthermore, replacement of capital goods cannot be postponed indefinitely; eventually, replacements and repairs must be resumed if firms are to continue production. The reductions occurring in inventories—a major factor aggravating the decline—will eventually cease, since there are certain minimum stocks which must be carried if operations are to be continued.

Investment is also facilitated by low interest rates and the willing-

[7] It is possible, however, that the downturn will occur before full employment is attained.

ness of lenders to advance funds, once they have assurance that improvement in conditions is likely. Low construction costs also encourage firms to undertake investment projects lasting over a long period of years. Corporate reorganization facilitates the acquisition of new funds. The invention of new techniques likewise facilitates recovery of investment.

Theories of the Business Cycle

The discussion of the preceding section is, for the most part, noncontroversial; the cumulative nature of expansion and contraction and the analysis of conditions in prosperity and in depression which facilitate a change in business activity are generally accepted. But many explanations of the reasons for the actual change from prosperity to decline and from depression to recovery have been developed.[8] Some theories have stressed single causes; others have recognized that a number of considerations may play a part. In the following paragraphs several of the major types of theories will be outlined briefly. Those presented should be regarded, however, only as typical approaches; there are great numbers of variations in explanations.

The Interaction of the Multiplier and the Acceleration Principle

Much of the recent writing in the field of business-cycle theory has centered around the interaction of the multiplier and the acceleration principle. During a period of expansion, these two forces interact to bring about an expansion in national income. A rise in investment generates, through the multiplier, a substantially greater rise in national income; the rise in the latter, in turn, through the operation of the acceleration principle, gives rise to induced investment, upon which the multiplier operates. However, as expansion continues, the rate of growth in national income slackens—of necessity when the ceiling of full employment is reached, but perhaps before. When this occurs, the opera-

[8] The literature of business-cycle theory is very extensive. There are two general lines of approach to the problem: one involves empirical study of changes in the economy during the periods of fluctuation; the other attempts to develop by deductive reasoning the causes of cyclical fluctuations. The former approach, pioneered in the United States by W. C. Mitchell, has been developed particularly by the National Bureau of Economic Research. Note, for example, A. F. Burns and W. C. Mitchell, *Measuring Business Cycles* (New York: National Bureau of Economic Research, 1946). Various theories developed by those utilizing primarily the deductive approach are summarized by J. A. Estey, *Business Cycle Theory* (rev. ed.; New York: Prentice-Hall, 1950), and G. von Haberler, *Prosperity and Depression* (rev. ed.; Geneva: League of Nations, 1939). Asher Achinstein, in *Introduction to Business Cycles* (New York: Crowell, 1950) surveys both the empirical and the deductive approaches. One of the most recent surveys of the literature is that by M. W. Lee, *Economic Fluctuations* (Homewood, Ill.: Richard D. Irwin, Inc., 1955).

tion of the accelerator causes the volume of induced investment to fall, and the action of the multiplier then brings down the total volume of national income. The accelerator and the multiplier then interact to push down the level of investment until an upturn is finally reached as a result of dis-saving and the continuation of a certain volume of autonomous investment. In other words, it is difficult for the economy to stabilize from a period of rapid expansion, because a portion of the investment arises out of the expansion itself, and this portion vanishes once the national income commences to stabilize.

The slowing down of the rate of expansion may result from the attainment of full employment, in what Hicks calls a "strong cycle"; if expansion has gone on at a very rapid rate, permitted by the unemployment of resources, it must slow down to the rate of real growth in national income (permitted by technological change, etc.) once full employment is attained. But the turning point to this slower rate of growth is difficult to make without collapse.

In other cycles, called by Hicks "weak cycles," the turning point is reached short of full employment, as a result of some type of change in the figures of the multiplier and the accelerator. For example, a shift in relative income toward persons with high propensities to save will reduce the multiplier. Or, time lags may play an important part; expenditures of the current period, based upon the income of the previous period, may be inadequate to sustain the higher level of income.[9]

Older Theories of the Cycle

In general, modern versions of cycle theory recognize the possibility of more than one immediate cause of the upturn and the downturn. In previous analyses, there was a much greater tendency to attribute the cycle to one factor exclusively. Some of these will be reviewed briefly.

The Underconsumption Approach. One of the oldest approaches to the explanation of business cycles has stressed the tendency toward inadequate consumption—and thus excessive savings—in periods of prosperity. In the earlier forms of this theory, the coming of depressions was attributed to the failure of income to rise as rapidly as output during expansion; as a consequence, all goods being produced could not be sold, and a decline was inevitable. This theory was attacked on the basis

[9] Note the Hicks and Harrod studies listed at the end of the chapter, and the article by S. S. Alexander, "Issues of Business Cycle Theory," *American Economic Review,* Vol. XLI (December, 1951), pp. 861–78, which reviews the literature of this approach to cycle theory.

of the argument that income of necessity rises at the same rate as output, as every dollar of the value of final output becomes income to someone.

As a consequence of this criticism, the underconsumptionists shifted their emphasis to an inadequacy of consumption, rather than income, as the source of depressions. They argued that too large a proportion of income was saved to allow output to remain at high levels, the excessive saving, in turn, being attributed to unequal income distribution. The poor, who consume most of their income, receive too little of the total while the wealthy, who save large amounts, receive an excessive portion. In recent years some underconsumptionist writers have stressed the tendency for the marginal propensity to save to rise as expansion continues. Other writers have stressed inadequate investment opportunities relative to the volume of saving after prosperity has continued for a period of time. As additional goods, made possible by the earlier investment, reach the market, investment opportunities fall, essentially because consumption is not great enough to absorb all of the additional output made possible by the larger stock of capital goods. If consumption were greater, investment opportunities would remain high and production would not fall.

In the underconsumption approach, recovery is usually attributed to the extreme decline in savings which occurs as the depression becomes severe. Many persons live on accumulated savings and even the wealthy find their savings margins drastically reduced. Some underconsumptionists, however, regard recovery as more or less accidental and consider depression to be the normal state of economic activity.

The Overinvestment Approach. Another major approach to the explanation of business cycles stresses the tendency for investment to increase during the period of expansion to a level which cannot be maintained because of the eventual development of shortages, either of money capital or of materials and labor resources required for further expansion.[10] During the period of recovery from depression, investment increases to a very high figure; profits are high, idle resources are available, and the banks, having excess returns, are able to expand loans rapidly. Eventually, however, bottlenecks will be encountered. The banks will approach their reserve limits and will be forced to curtail lending. Interest rates will rise as the money supply becomes inadequate

[10] Some writers have stressed the money-capital shortage, others the "real" shortages. The former version of the theory is often called the "monetary overinvestment" version, the latter the "real overinvestment" approach. Among the best-known overinvestment theorists have been Gustav Cassel and F. A. von Hayek.

for the large volume of transactions. Shortages of skilled labor and various materials will check expansion. As a consequence, the actual volume of investment will fall and will start the downward movement in national income. Basically, the difficulty is attributed to overinvestment, in the sense that the volume of investment reaches a figure which cannot be maintained, once the banks reach reserve limits and full employment of resources is attained.

Recovery is attributed to the decline in interest rates which occurs as business activity contracts and to the decline in labor and material costs. These changes encourage investment, which eventually will increase sufficiently to start recovery.

Closely related to the overinvestment analysis is the purely monetary approach, which stresses changes in bank credit expansion as being solely responsible for the cycle. When the banks have excess reserves and lend freely, business activity expands; when the banks come to their reserve limits and contract lending, business activity is, of necessity, slowed down. Change in inventories of business firms in response to interest rate changes is stressed by this approach rather than change in investment in durable goods. Likewise, the drain of cash from bank reserves into circulation, which occurs as the national income rises, is considered to play a major part in forcing banks to raise interest rates and curtail lending.

These explanations, as well as others, indicate logically possible causes of cyclical movements in business activity. But any attempt to find a single explanation of cycles by deductive reasoning is futile; the various theories warrant consideration as models useful for guidance in the examination of data in particular situations. There is no reason to believe that there is one, single cause of all cyclical changes; a satisfactory explanation of the behavior of national income in particular cycles is possible only on the basis of the interpretation of empirical studies of the actual situations. The theories are useful in facilitating this interpretation.

SECULAR GROWTH IN REAL INCOME

The preceding sections of this chapter have been concerned with short-term fluctuations of national income below the full-employment level, the various possible causes of such fluctuations, and the possibility of recurrent changes due to forces developing within the economy itself. But of equal or greater importance are long-term trends in the full-employment level of real income, as these determine the extent of improvements in the real standard of living of the people.

In the previous chapter, the determinants of the level of real income prevailing at any particular time were outlined. Changes in these determinants represent the basic forces responsible for real growth in national income. The major changes can be outlined briefly:

1. Increases in population. The growth of population gives rise to increased labor supply, and thus to increased output. Whether per capita income will increase or not depends upon the relationship between the labor supply increase and the income increase; this depends in large measure upon the factors noted below.

2. Increases in availability of land and resources. Over the past centuries, factors making possible continued growth in national income were the discovery of new resources and the development of transportation and other facilities allowing the exploitation of additional land areas. Even today new discoveries—of oil, copper, iron ore, uranium, etc.—are constantly being made.

3. Increased rate of capital formation. In general, an increased supply of capital goods makes possible a growing rate of output. In undeveloped countries today, in many instances, low incomes are being perpetuated by the inability to obtain sufficient capital goods to raise output levels. Under such circumstances, an increased rate of savings, by making possible a faster rate of capital formation without inflation, facilitates a rise in the level of national income. An increased rate of saving becomes detrimental only when the volume of savings tends to outrun the volume of profitable investment, and national income falls below equilibrium levels.

4. The rate of technological development. Growth in real income is influenced to a very large extent by the rate of development of new techniques of production, new methods of organization and new procedures for distribution of goods. These changes often allow the production of better quality goods, and the production of given output with fewer resources—thereby freeing resources for the production of other goods.

5. Skill and incentives of labor and management. Increased skill of workers and managers of business enterprises plays an important part in economic growth, as do improvements in incentives to undertake economic activity and to increase efficiency.

6. General environmental factors. The general social, political, and economic environment influence production, and changes in this

environment favorable to production can result in increases in output. The industrial revolution in nineteenth-century England would have been seriously impeded if the old mercantilist regulations of economic activity had not been swept away, for example.

Economic growth can, of course, give way to economic decay; secular trends in real income are not always upward. Entire economies may decline through exhaustion of natural resources, devastation of material resources and population through war, and other sources. The economic decline of the Roman Empire as the political structure collapsed, and the decline in Spain and Portugal in the sixteenth and seventeenth centuries provide outstanding examples.

THE THEORY OF EQUILIBRIUM RATES OF GROWTH

In the last decade, substantial attention has been given to a neglected problem of national income theory, that concerned with equilibrium rates of growth, particularly, the question of the maintenance of a balance in the various growing magnitudes of the economy so that the rate of growth may be a stable one, and one permitting full employment.

The Nature of the Equilibrium Rate of Growth

Explanation of the equilibrium rate of growth requires consideration of the relationships between aggregate demand (total expenditures) in the economy and aggregate supply as national income increases. On the demand side of the picture, there are the three elements discussed in the previous chapter: consumption, regarded as a function of income; investment, dependent in part on autonomous forces such as inventions, and in part on the rate of growth in output; and governmental expenditures, determined by autonomous forces. On the supply side of the picture the basic element is the capacity to produce, dependent upon labor supply and skill, the rate of capital formation, etc. The precise definition and measurement of this side is difficult; labor supply, multiplied by some measure of increase in productivity, has commonly been employed. Capital input has been suggested by others as the best measure, and some combination of the two by still others.

Given the determinants of aggregate demand and aggregate supply, the basic problem of the theory of growth is the ascertainment of the pattern of relative rates of growth of the various segments of aggregate demand and aggregate supply which will permit a stable, continuing rate of growth in national income, with neither unemployment nor inflation. Such a rate can be maintained only if the rate of increase in potential output, made possible by the growing labor force, increased capital formation, and technological development, is matched by an equivalent increase in aggregate demand—consumption plus investment plus governmental expenditure. Investment is dependent in part upon the growth in the labor force; if this is too slow to allow a volume of investment sufficiently great to insure that aggregate demand equals output, unemployment will result. If labor supply increases so rapidly that investment causes demand to outrun output, inflation will result. The effect of other variables, such as government expenditures or technological change, can be analyzed in like manner.

The Harrod Model

The English economist R. F. Harrod, one of the first to develop a systematic treatment of the requirements of a stable rate of growth, has stressed the difficulties encountered by the economy in maintaining this objective. The rate of investment is, according to Harrod, dependent in large measure upon the rate of increase in national income. Savings, on the other hand, is believed to be a more or less constant percentage of national income. Since planned investment and planned savings must rise at the same rate if the equilibrium rate of growth is to be maintained, national income must rise at an ever-increasing rate or investment (which depends on the rate of increase in income, not on the magnitude of income) will lag behind savings. The higher that income goes, the faster must be the rate of increase—yet the faster the rate of increase, the higher will be the level of income in the next period. Furthermore, argues Harrod, if the equilibrium rate of growth is not maintained, the economy will fall back into a depression, as any slackening in the growth of national income will result in an absolute, cumulative decline, for reasons noted earlier in the chapter. Thus failure to maintain the equilibrium rate of growth means not a small amount of unemployment, but a setback into a depression.

One of the basic reasons why it is difficult for the level of national income to rise at a sufficiently high rate to insure equality of planned investment and planned savings is the fact that once full employment is attained, the growth in the equilibrium rate of national income cannot exceed the real rate of growth, as determined by technological improvements, increases in labor supply, etc. The rate of real increase in national income may be less than the rate required to maintain investment at high enough levels to equal planned savings.

The Harrod model is offered as one of the best-known models of the explanation of the equilibrium rate of the economic growth. Others have been developed, and considerable attention is currently being given to this field, along with the related field of the determinants of the actual rate of growth in undeveloped countries. Further advances in the theory of growth may allow substantial improvements in other segments of economic theory, which have typically abstracted from considerations of growth.

Depreciation and the Equilibrium Rate of Growth

One particular factor affecting the ability to maintain an equilibrium rate of growth that has attracted interest in the last few years is that of the relationship between depreciation, replacement, and economic growth. As first recognized by Domar and Eisner,[11] in a period of economic growth, the volume of replacement investment of necessity lags behind the volume of depreciation, at a stable price level. If, each year, a certain volume of new investment is undertaken, the depreciation in each succeeding year will exceed the value of capital goods requiring replacement. There is no "catching up"; the gap continues so long as the volume of investment continues at a high level. This is obviously a destabilizing factor; while the excess depreciation charges may, of course, be used to finance new expansion, or loaned to firms which will so use them, there is danger that this may not occur.

The excess of depreciation charges over replacement constitutes a supplement to the volume of net savings during the period, and thus new investment must be higher by this sum than it would otherwise need be to maintain full employment. The gap can, of course, be eliminated by price increases, which bring the cost of the replacement equipment up to the sum of depreciation on the old equipment, but there are obvious objections to such increases. The longer the life span of the capital goods, and the more rapid the rate of growth of investment, the greater will be the excess.

The Theory of Secular Stagnation

During the decade of the 'thirties, well in advance of the modern theories of economic growth, there developed widespread acceptance of the theory that as an economy "matures," the maintenance of full employment becomes increasing difficult, with a tendency toward "secular

[11] See particularly R. Eisner, "Depreciation Allowances, Replacement Requirements and Growth," *American Economic Review,* Vol. XLII (December, 1952), pp. 820–31; and E. Domar, "Depreciation, Replacement and Growth," *Economic Journal,* Vol. LXIII (March, 1953), pp. 1–32.

stagnation"—periods of continuing unemployment. Thus national income tends to remain for long periods below full-employment levels.

The possibility of the attainment of equilibrium at less than full employment was indicated in the previous chapter, without any argument that such a situation was likely to occur. The adherents of the stagnation thesis, however, claimed that such a situation is inevitable as an economy becomes highly developed. The basic difficulty was attributed to inadequate investment opportunities, relative to the high volume of savings which persons wish to make at full-employment levels of income. During a period of rapid development of a new area with unexploited resources, and during periods of rapid technological development, full employment can be maintained. But, it was argued, eventually a point is reached at which investment opportunities are no longer adequate, as large segments of the economy have reached a high stage of development. The difficulties are aggravated by the tendency for the rate of population increase to decline, by the absence of new frontiers to exploit, and by the laborsaving character of many modern technological changes. England during the 'twenties and 'thirties, and the United States during the latter decade were noted as examples of secular stagnation.

Serious objections have been raised against the stagnation thesis. There is no evidence that the percentage of income saved rises as an economy grows, nor that the rate of technological change is in any sense slowing down. Population trends have been sharply reversed since World War II—perhaps only temporarily so, of course. The experience since 1945 has greatly weakened the case for the stagnation thesis; a high level of investment and rapidly increasing levels of national income have been maintained for a long period. It cannot be denied that secular stagnation is a possibility, but there is no logical proof that such a situation in inevitable. Only time will tell whether the thesis has any significance or not.[12]

In the postwar years, there has been greater fear of secular inflation than of secular stagnation: of a tendency toward a continuous upward spiral of wages and prices. With high levels of government expenditures, widespread acceptance of a philosophy that governments

[12] This thesis was developed in J. M. Keynes, *The General Theory of Employment, Interest and Money* (New York: Harcourt, Brace, 1936); it has been popularized particularly by A. H. Hansen (see his *Full Recovery or Stagnation?* [New York: Norton, 1938]). A severe criticism of this point of view is to be found in G. W. Terborgh, *The Bogey of Economic Maturity* (Chicago: Machinery and Allied Products Institute, 1945).

For a more recent analysis see B. Higgins, "Concepts and Criteria of Secular Stagnation," in *Income, Employment, and Public Policy* (New York: Norton, 1948).

must prevent unemployment in the future, and strong labor unions, it is feared that there will be a tendency for wage increases to outrun productivity increases, and thus for the general price level to rise continuously. It is likewise impossible to assess, at present, the likelihood of such a trend.

GOVERNMENT STABILIZATION POLICY

The recurrence of unemployment, on the one hand, and inflation on the other, has led to extensive discussion of deliberate governmental intervention to attain economic stability and an equilibrium rate of growth. Limited action along these lines has been taken for many years, but significant action dates back to the severe depression of the mid-thirties and the inflationary periods of the war. It is beyond the scope of this book to analyze the policies in detail; a few lines of approach will be suggested. Three general types of policies have been undertaken (the third being relevant only to inflationary periods): monetary policy, fiscal policy, and direct wage and price controls.

Monetary Policy

The traditional weapon against economic instability has been monetary or credit-control policy, the effort, through the central banking system, to control the interest rate and the rate of credit expansion by the banks. In the United States, when the Federal Reserve System wishes to check credit expansion, it sells securities in the open market, raises its rediscount rate, and raises reserve requirements. As a consequence interest rates tend to rise and the ability of the banks to lend is reduced. Thus investment—one of the major elements in aggregate demand—is reduced.[13] On the other hand, when unemployment exists, the Federal Reserve System buys securities in the open market (thereby increasing bank reserves) and lowers rediscount rates and reserve requirements, as a means of facilitating the expansion of loans.

Monetary policy undoubtedly aids in the maintenance of stability, and particularly in the avoidance of periods of financial stringency common in the last century. But it has several limitations as an instrument of stabilization:

1. In periods of depression, the placing of the banks in a position in which they can make additional loans does not insure that the loans

[13] The Federal Reserve System also exercises control over consumption expenditures by regulating down payments and periods for repayment of consumer credit loans in inflationary periods.

will be made. The banks tend to be cautious, and most business firms are not interested in borrowing, regardless of how low the rate is, because they have excess plant capacity.

2. The interest rate apparently does not fall easily below certain levels, because of the tendency of persons to hold any additional amounts of wealth in liquid form, once the compensation for foregoing liquidity drops below a certain figure.

3. In periods of inflation, such a large amount of investment is financed by retained earnings that the interest rate and bank policy is less effective in checking the expansion than it once was. In war and postwar inflationary periods, investment may represent only a small segment of the excessive total expenditure, and checking of the forms of investment which lead directly to increased output of scarce materials may aggravate the inflation.

4. In the post-World War II period, the large amount of government debt outstanding raised a serious practical obstacle to effective monetary policy: a sharp increase in interest rates would have greatly increased the government's interest burden.

Fiscal Policy

Fiscal policy consists of deliberate adjustments in governmental tax, expenditure, and debt policies for the purpose of gaining greater economic stability. In part, fiscal policy operates directly upon the governmental element in the aggregate expenditure picture; in part, it operates upon consumption and investment spending.

In a period of unemployment, fiscal policy would be directed toward an increase in total expenditures. There are two general approaches; the government can directly increase its own expenditures in such a manner that private expenditures do not fall by an equivalent amount, or it can seek to increase private spending. The former involves such programs as the development of public works, or increases in governmental services, financed either by borrowing or by taxes which tap idle funds and do not cause an equivalent decline in private spending. The second objective can be attained by cutting taxes (with expenditures at given levels) and by increased transfer grants, such as relief or old age pensions, which increase private spending.

These various alternative methods have particular advantages and disadvantages, which have been discussed in detail in the literature in the field. Public works provide results of direct gain to society; in addition to aiding recovery, they maintain the skills of the unemployed, and they avoid the morale problems of direct relief. But they are probably less effective, dollar for dollar, than relief, because the money concentrates in the hands of fewer people. The delays in getting such projects under way lessen their effectiveness with respect to recovery. Direct relief on the other hand gives the money directly to persons who most need it and will spend it, but is regarded as destructive of morale. Tax reductions avoid the difficulties and administrative wastes of all governmental expenditure programs, as well as the increase in the sphere of governmental activities, but they provide no direct assistance for the unemployed, and they are likely to be less effective than other programs, dollar for dollar, because a higher percentage of the money is likely to be saved, without an equivalent increase in investment.

In inflationary periods, opposite policies would be followed. Reduction of government expenditures curtails total spending, and increases in taxes reduce private consumption and investment. Some forms of taxes are more effective than others; reduction in income tax exemptions is probably one of the best means of checking consumption expenditure. Sales taxes would be relatively effective were it not for their tendency to enter into cost of living indexes, and thus produce wage increases.

An intelligent, carefully designed program of fiscal policy, coupled with a co-ordinated monetary policy should be capable of increasing economic stability. But there are serious obstacles to the complete success of such a program:

1. In a depression, the methods of financing the fiscal program are likely to cause some offsetting decline in private spending. If taxes are used, disposable income is reduced; if borrowing is utilized, the fear of the rise of the national debt may have adverse effects, especially on investment.

2. The problems of timing are serious. Time is needed to get the programs under way, and with the present state of economic forecasting, it is difficult to know, at any one time, where the economy is headed. There are further difficulties in determining the appropriate magnitudes of tax or expenditure changes to be employed. Excessive tax increases in inflationary periods, for example, could precipitate unemployment.

3. The political obstacles to the conduct of an effective program are substantial. This is particularly true in inflationary periods, since tax increases are always unpopular politically.

4. The task of finding suitable projects for government expenditures is a serious one. The government is faced with a basic dilemma: the most useful projects are those which will most likely involve competition with private enterprise and thus check private investment; those

doing least harm to the private sector are the least useful projects.

5. In inflationary periods, the basic problem is that of curtailing spending without interfering with incentives to carry on production. Particularly in a war period, tax rates sufficient to check inflationary spending might interfere seriously with the willingness of persons to work and firms to carry on production.

6. Any recovery from periods of unemployment arising from a governmental spending program may be lost as soon as the program is slackened, as the multiplier works downward as well as upward. Only if the recovery can stimulate sufficient optimism to lead to a significant increase in private investment is there much chance of its being permanent.

Direct Controls

Direct wage and price controls attempt to prevent price increases by restricting prices (and usually wages) to certain levels—in the case of World War II to levels prevailing at the outbreak of the war. Such a program, if successful, essentially forces persons to save more than they wish by preventing their bidding up prices on scarce commodities. In these programs investment is usually likewise restricted by allocations of materials and new equipment.

These direct controls represent extreme measures, designed to supplement monetary and fiscal measures when war and semiwar conditions render the latter inadequate. If rigidly enforced, they can accomplish their goals, as demonstrated during World War II, in large measure. But likewise, obstacles to effective operation of the programs are serious:

1. The holding of prices below the levels at which demand is equal to output results either in queues and inequitable distribution, or rationing; the latter is troublesome, hard to enforce, and also likely to be inequitable.

2. Price controls themselves offer serious enforcement difficulties, since it is in many cases to the advantage of both the buyer and seller to avoid them.

3. When the controls are lifted, there is danger that sharp inflation may occur, as was the case in 1945 and 1946.

4. The controls interfere with the basic guiding mechanism of the economy; continued application can resort in serious distortion of resource allocation, loss of incentives, and perhaps breakdown of the whole economy. Direct controls are necessary weapons in a period of all-out war, but their use for any period of time in nonwar condition,

represents a basic interference with the functioning of the capitalist economy.

Continuing Unemployment and Stabilization Policy

If the economy is subject only to recurrent periods of unemployment and inflation, with maintenance of stable economic growth during much of the time, the monetary and fiscal policies need be utilized only for limited intervals. But if the economy has a tendency toward secular stagnation, or a tendency for the equilibrium rate of growth to be at less than full-employment levels, the task of the government is much more serious; the same is true if inflation tends to continue. If there is a chronic tendency toward unemployment, the government must seek some method of holding aggregate expenditures to higher levels. To do so by a permanently higher level of government expenditures financed by borrowing would result in a continuous growth in the national debt which could have serious psychological, if not other, effects—yet no other alternative may prove to be more satisfactory. Avoidance of taxes which particularly depress either consumption or investment would be desirable, as well as policies which tend to increase the over-all propensity to consume. On the other hand, if the difficulty should prove to be one of continuing inflation, opposite policies would be needed; the maintenance of a continuing governmental surplus is, politically, an extremely difficult feat.

SELECTED REFERENCES

Most of the references included at the end of the previous chapter are also pertinent to this chapter. Note also:

HARROD, R. F. *The Trade Cycle.* London: Oxford University Press, 1936.
One of the modern theoretical studies of the cycle.

HARROD, R. F. *Toward a Dynamic Economics.* London: Oxford University Press, 1948.
The best-known model of the theory of growth.

BAUMOL, W. J. *Economic Dynamics.* New York: Macmillan, 1951.
One of the very few general studies of dynamic economics and the theory of growth.

DOMAR, E. D. "Economic Growth: An Econometric Approach," *Proceedings of the American Economic Association,* May 1952, pp. 479–95.
A review of the theory of economic growth.

HICKS, J. R. *A Contribution to the Theory of the Trade Cycle.* London: Oxford University Press, 1950.
One of the most recent analyses of economic fluctuations.

HANSEN, A. H. *Fiscal Policy and Business Cycles.* New York: Norton, 1941.
One of the first detailed analyses of fiscal policy.

MAXWELL, J. A. *Fiscal Policy.* New York: Holt, 1955.
A recent review of fiscal policy.

SMITHIES, A., and BUTTERS, J. K. *Readings in Fiscal Policy.* Homewood, Ill.: Richard D. Irwin, Inc., 1955.
A collection of articles on fiscal policy.

"The Problem of Economic Instability, a Committee Report," *American Economic Review,* Vol. XL (September, 1950), pp. 501–38.
A review of current thinking with respect to stabilization policies.

QUESTIONS

1. Why are changes in investment usually regarded as being more significant causes of changes in national income than changes in consumption?
2. Suppose that the marginal propensity to consume is 60 per cent. What will be the increase in national income which will result from a $3 billion increase in investment?
3. Why is the multiplier the reciprocal of the marginal propensity to save?
4. Under what circumstances will the multiplier overstate the increase in national income resulting from an increase in investment? Under what circumstances will the multiplier understate the increase?
5. Indicate several possible causes of change (*a*) in the volume of investment, and (*b*) in the consumption function.
6. Does the multiplier operate with respect to induced investment as well as autonomous investment, or only to the latter? Explain.
7. Distinguish carefully between the multiplier and the acceleration principle.
8. Explain the following: an increase in the propensity to save permits, but does not insure, an increase in the rate of capital formation.
9. Under what circumstances will an increase in the propensity to save reduce, rather than increase, the actual rate of savings in the economy?
10. Why does an increase in the propensity to save not necessarily increase the supply of money capital available to business firms?
11. Under what circumstances can government spending increase without an equivalent decline in private spending?
12. In nonfull-employment situations, why does an increase in total expenditures primarily affect output, rather than prices?
13. Why, even in a nonfull-employment situation, will an increase in total expenditures tend to raise the general price level to a certain extent?
14. Under what circumstances will inflationary trends ultimately stabilize? Under what circumstances will they turn into runaway inflation?
15. When total expenditures fall, does output, or the general price level, or both, fall? Explain.
16. Explain briefly the quantity theory of money, and contrast it to the explanation of changes in the general price level given in preceding paragraphs.

17. Distinguish between random and cyclical changes in national income.
18. Why does a period of expansion tend to be cumulative once it starts? What are some of the possible reasons why a period of expansion ultimately comes to an end.
19. Explain the approach to business-cycle theory based upon the interaction between the multiplier and the acceleration principle.
20. Distinguish between the underconsumption and overinvestment theories of the cycle.
21. What are some of the major causes of growth in the real level of national income?
22. How would you explain the failure of Brazil, which has excellent natural resources, to attain as high a per capita national income as the United States?
23. What is meant by the term "equilibrium rate of growth"?
24. What requirements must be met for a particular rate of growth to be maintained in a stable fashion without unemployment developing?
25. Why, according to Harrod, it is difficult to maintain a stable equilibrium rate of growth?
26. Why, in a growing economy with a stable price level, does depreciation exceed replacement investment? Why is this a destabilizing factor in the economy?
27. According to Major C. H. Douglas, founder of the Social Credit movement, continuing unemployment is inevitable, unless governmental action is taken to prevent it, because depreciation is an element in costs and prices, but is not an income; thus income and expenditures of necessity lag behind output. Evaluate this argument.
28. What was the "secular stagnation" thesis? To what causes was secular stagnation attributed?
29. Distinguish between monetary and fiscal policy.
30. Indicate various alternative fiscal policies which might be used in a depression, and the relative merits of each.
31. What are the general limitations to the effectiveness of monetary policy? Fiscal policy? Direct control of wages and prices?

PART V

Welfare Economics

Chapter 24 A SURVEY OF WELFARE ECONOMICS

The analysis thus far has been concerned with the principles which explain various relationships in the operation of the economic system, without reference to evaluation of the operation of the economy in terms of selected standards. We have been concerned only with the question of how the economy operates and why it operates as it does, not with that of whether particular features are "good" or "bad." We have considered the manner in which the price system determines relative outputs of various goods—and hence the composition of national product—without inquiring whether or not the results conform with desired standards. We have considered the forces which determine the distribution of income by factor group, without raising the question of whether or not the distribution which results is satisfactory in terms of an "optimum" pattern of distribution. This final chapter presents a brief survey of welfare economics, the portion of economic analysis which seeks to raise questions of evaluation, of "good" versus "bad," and thus to judge whether or not the manner in which the economic system operates best attains the goals which are regarded by society as desirable.

THE ACCEPTED GOALS OF THE ECONOMIC SYSTEM

In any field of study, evaluation is possible only in terms of standards of evaluation selected. The selection of these standards or goals is not a function of economics, as such. This task is a portion of the field of ethics, of the making of value judgments with respect to standards of desirability. Welfare economics can merely evaluate various features of the economy in terms of these standards; it cannot select them. For our present purposes, we shall merely assume certain goals, selecting the ones which appear to reflect most satisfactorily the attitudes of contemporary society. The fact that these goals are assumed, not determined by economic analysis, must be stressed, as well as the fact that all evaluation which follows is valid only in terms of these goals. If we were to assume other goals, the evaluation would produce different results.

Three primary goals of the economy will be assumed:

1. Maximum freedom of individual choice of action, consistent with the rights of others.

2. Attainment of optimum standards of living for the community as a whole, in terms of preferences of consumers and factor-owners, and available resources and technology. Serious difficulties are encountered in obtaining a precise definition of optimum standards of living, as noted below, but the general meaning of the term is clear: given the pattern of income distribution, each family should be able to attain the highest possible standard of living.

3. Distribution of income in conformity with the standards regarded by society as being most equitable. This goal would be replaced by one of a pattern of income distribution which would allow maximum satisfaction of wants, were such a pattern definable; since it is not, as explained in later sections, the goal must be that which is presented in the first sentence of the paragraph.

In the remainder of the chapter, these goals will be explained more fully, the conditions necessary for their attainment indicated, and a brief evaluation made of the extent to which the conditions, and thus the goals, are attained in the present-day economic system. Greatest attention will be given to the second goal listed, primarily because, with present knowledge, the most satisfactory and complete evaluations can be made in terms of this goal.

FREEDOM OF CHOICE

Freedom of choice, in the sphere of economic activity, is the right of the individual to act as he wishes with respect to choices in this field of human activity. Attainment of this goal requires that a person be free to select the commodities which he prefers for the satisfaction of his wants. He must be free to make decisions with respect to use of factor units which he owns—to make them available to business firms or not, to select the type of work and the place of work which he prefers from among the available opportunities, to divide his time between work and leisure as he pleases, to establish a business if he wishes, and to make decisions of his own choice with respect to the operation of the business. Contemporary western society regards this goal of freedom of action as inherently desirable in itself, apart from the role it may play in facilitating attainment of an optimum over-all standard of living.

It must be recognized, however, that freedom of choice is a relative matter, since absolute freedom would result in serious injury to others. Freedom of choice must be exercised within the framework established to protect the interests of society as a group, and sometimes the person himself. If all persons were free to hunt deer without restriction, there would soon be no deer to hunt, and the right to hunt would become worthless. The greatest real freedom is sometimes obtained through the establishment of certain restrictions in the interests of the people as a group. Over the years, there has been a tendency to increase the number of restrictions of this type. Yet in the capitalist form of economic system, as found in the United States and Canada and much of western Europe, as well as in other areas, a very high degree of personal freedom of choice remains. In general persons are free to buy anything they please (with a few exceptions of goods which are likely to bring serious injury to themselves or others, such as opium). They may, legally, work or not as they wish, obtain a job anywhere they can find one, and move from one area to another as they wish. People are free to start any type of business (with a few exceptions), and select products, prices, methods of production, etc., as they please.

OPTIMUM STANDARDS OF LIVING

The second goal is that of the attainment of optimum standards of living, given the pattern of distribution of income, which will be considered in a later section of this chapter. In other words, given the resources and technology, the level and the composition of the output of the economy must be such as to allow the highest possible level of satisfaction of wants. The definition of "maximization of satisfaction of wants" is not a simple one, since this satisfaction is in no sense a measurable magnitude, and comparison of satisfactions received by various persons is not possible. It is not even easy to devise a satisfactory measure of a real increase in national income as a measure of an increase in the degree of want satisfaction, because of the change which is constantly occurring in the composition of national income and the relative prices of various goods. If national income rises 5 per cent this year, after adjustment is made for price-level changes, but the composition changes somewhat (as is inevitable), the statement cannot be made with any degree of certainty that the level of want-satisfaction has reached a higher level. The more that economists have explored this question of the optimum level of want-satisfaction, the more undecided they have become about the selection of appropriate measures and criteria of the optimum, until the point has been reached at which there is a tendency to abandon the term "maximization of want-satisfaction" itself as being useless and undefinable.

In terms of present-day welfare theory, the most that can be said about the position of optimum standards of living is that the optimum is not reached so long as any changes can be made which benefit some persons without injuring others, or, that if some are injured, the persons benefiting can pay those injured a sufficient amount to compensate them for their injury and still be better off as a result of the change. This definition of the optimum does not establish a single, unique position for it, but merely establishes its boundaries; it is possible that once the point is reached at which no further changes of the types outlined could be made, there are changes which could still be made and improve economic welfare—but contemporary welfare theory cannot define them.

Despite the difficulties involved in the definition of the optimum position, it is possible to indicate a group of conditions which must be attained if the optimum over-all standard of living, given the pattern of income distribution, is to be realized. These are often called the marginal conditions; as presented below, they have been simplified somewhat from those which have been developed in the field of welfare theory.

Optimum Efficiency in the Use of Resources

In the first place, optimum standards of living cannot be attained unless resources are utilized in production with the maximum degree of efficiency. This in turn requires the attainment of the least-cost combinations in production, and thus the adjustment of factor combinations until the marginal rates of substitution of the factors are equal to the factor prices (the latter equating supply of and demand for the factors). Maximum efficiency requires the use of the most productive techniques, and the most satisfactory methods of administrative organization and physical distribution.

Furthermore, optimum efficiency requires that the firms operate at the point of lowest long-run average cost; they must not only expand plant to the size allowing lowest cost, but must also operate at the optimum capacity (lowest-cost point) of this plant.

Only by these means can maximum output be obtained from given resources; if inefficient methods are used, or plants are too small, or firms are not operating at the points of lowest cost, obviously the total output obtained from given resources is less than it could be.

To what extent is the optimum organization of production attained in a market economy? This is not an easy question to answer. With respect to attainment of least-cost combinations, the profit motive provides a continuous incentive to reduce costs—one which is, of course, strongest when competition is severe, but which is present even in a situation of complete monopoly. Yet it is probably rare that the exact least-cost combination of factors, in all respects, is attained. It is an extremely difficult task for a firm to accomplish, especially with complex industrial processes.

With respect to the attainment of operation at the point of lowest cost, that is, with the plant capacity and the level of output which allow the most efficient use of resources, theoretically this situation should always be attained when markets are purely competitive, as explained in Chapter 9. But imperfections, and particularly lack of knowledge, undoubtedly interfere with the attainment of lowest average cost. In nonpurely competitive markets with free entry of new firms, operation at the point of lowest average cost in the long run is impossible, since the downward-sloping demand curves for the products of the firms cannot be tangent to the $\smile$-shaped average-cost curves at the lowest points of the latter. Hence there are essentially too many firms in terms of the market (but too few to permit the markets to be purely competitive); resources are poorly utilized, and costs could be lower if the market were divided among a smaller number of firms. The waste, however, may be less than is sometimes argued. In these industries the demand curves of the firms are likely to be highly elastic, and thus the departure from the purely competitive optimum may not be very substantial.

In nonpurely competitive markets in which entry is not entirely free, the firms may, of course, be operating at the point of lowest cost (although price does not equal average cost), but there is no necessity that they must be. If the output of the industry is dominated by a very few large firms, they may easily expand to the point of lowest average cost or even beyond. If the typical long-run average-cost curve contains an extensive horizontal segment, as is now widely believed, the likelihood that many firms may be operating at or near the lowest average-cost figure in nonpurely competitive conditions is increased.

Whenever differentiation of product is present, a new element in cost is introduced, namely, that of advertising and other selling activities. These elements inevitably raise the cost schedules above the purely competitive levels. On the other hand, the advertising does convey certain benefits to consumers. Evaluation of the relative advantages of the higher costs and benefits is very difficult. In some instances in which the markets would not be purely competitive even in the absence of the selling activities, the development of these activities may allow the firms to operate nearer the point of lowest average cost by increasing their sales volumes.

Optimum Adjustment of Production in Terms of Consumer Preferences

The second requirement which must be fulfilled if optimum standards of living are to be attained is that the relative outputs of various commodities must be established in a manner as to conform most fully with consumer preferences. That is, the composition of gross national product—and thus the allocation of resources—must be of such a character as to best satisfy consumer preferences. For example, if consumers desire some shoes and some luggage, all of the available leather will not be used for luggage production while people go barefooted or wear wooden shoes, but the leather supply will be allocated (through the operation of the pricing system in a market economy) in such a manner that consumer preferences for the two products are satisfied as completely as possible. If consumers desire both cake and bread, all of the flour will not be used to produce bread, but some will be utilized in cake production as well.

Optimum adjustment of production can be obtained only if, for each consumer, the marginal rates of substitution between each two commodities purchased are equal to the marginal rates of transformation between the two commodities in production. The marginal rate of transformation is the number of units of one commodity that must be sacrificed if an additional unit of the other commodity is to be produced. If this relationship is not attained, consumer preferences will be more fully realized if some resources are shifted from the production of goods the output of which is excessive, relative to consumer preferences, to the production of goods the output of which is inadequate. Or, in other words, the output of each commodity must be adjusted to such a level that consumers have equal preference for the marginal output of the various goods, per unit of the factor input. For example, the relative outputs of bread and cake must be such that, given the prices and preferences, consumers have equal preference for the bread made with the marginal units of wheat going into bread production as for the cake made with the marginal units of wheat going into cake production. If the preference for bread is greater at the margin, more wheat would be used for bread production and less for cake production until a balance is attained.

This relationship between marginal rates of substitution and marginal rates of transformation will be attained only if several requirements are met:

1. Consumers allocate their incomes in such a manner that the marginal rates of substitution between all commodities which they buy are equal to the ratios of the prices of the commodities, or, in other words, that the marginal utilities of all goods purchased are proportional to their prices. Failure to accomplish this adjustment will mean that the consumer has not reached the highest indifference curve possible with his income, or, in other words, is not maximizing satisfaction.

2. Relative prices of various goods reflect the marginal rates of transformation between them, so that, provided consumers allocate incomes in such a manner that the marginal rates of substitution are equal to the price ratios, the marginal rates of substitution will equal the marginal rates of transformation.

The relative prices will reflect the marginal rates of transformation only if several requirements are met:

(*a*) Factor prices equate the supply of and the demand for the factors, and are uniform to all producers. If the factor prices exceed the supply-demand level, for example, they do not reflect the real cost involved in the production of an additional unit of a commodity, in the sense of the sacrifice of other goods necessary to obtain another factor unit for the production of the particular good. The same is true if factor prices are not uniform to all users.

(*b*) Marginal costs to the firms for the production of the product reflect all costs to the economy arising out of its production. If there are certain costs to society which do not appear in marginal cost of the firm, the price of the commodity will be too low (assuming that it equals marginal cost) and an excessive amount of the good will be produced. The traditional example is the damage done by factory smoke, which does not become a cost to the business firm operating the factory. Or, for another example, suppose that a drive-in theater is built on a narrow, heavily traveled road. As the patrons pour out as the movie ends, traffic is bottled-up on the highway for miles, accidents result, and substantial delays are caused motorists and truckers. These are real costs for which the drive-in is responsible, but which are not borne by the firm operating it and are not reflected in the prices charged the patrons.

(*c*) Prices of the commodities are equal to the marginal costs of production. If conditions (*a*) and (*b*) are realized, the marginal costs reflect the marginal rates of transformation, or, in other words, the real costs to society of producing additional units of the commodity. If, in turn, the prices of the products are equal to the marginal costs, and condition (1) above is realized, the allocation of resources to the production of various goods will have attained the optimum in terms of consumer preferences, given the pattern of income distribution. If price exceeds marginal cost, the consumer is paying more for the commodity than the figure properly reflecting the real costs to society, and therefore too little of the commodity is used (and produced), in terms of consumer desires. These units which are sacrificed as a result of the unduly high price would have been preferred by the consumers over the additional units of other goods which can be produced with the freed resources, and production has thus been misdirected—given consumer preferences and income patterns.

3. All benefits from the use of commodities accrue to the persons acquiring them. If some indirect benefits are gained by other persons, too little of the commodity will be purchased and thus produced, since the indirect benefits do not influence the action of the person purchasing the units. For example, if a person kills the dandelions in his lawn, his neighbors will benefit as well. But the person is not likely to consider the latter (unless in the interests of neighborhood goodwill!) when he makes the decision whether or not to buy the weed-killer. The more significant examples of indirect benefits arise, however, in the case of services, such as national defense, which convey their benefits to the community as a whole, rather than to individuals separately.

Realization of These Requirements. Complete attainment of these requirements would insure an optimum allocation of resources, or, in other terms, an optimum "product-mix," given the pattern of income distribution. Review of the operation of the market economy, as outlined in the previous chapters, suggests that these requirements are not fully attained, and indicates why governments have undertaken various types of activities instead of leaving them in the hands of private enterprise. The operation of the economy will be evaluated briefly in terms of these requirements.

1. Consumer allocation of incomes. It is generally assumed that individuals seek to allocate their income in such a way as to maximize satisfaction, and therefore seek to attain equality of marginal rates of substitution with price ratios. But, without question, in many cases

inadequate information about the ability of particular goods to meet various needs prevents attainment of this equality. In part, this is made inevitable by the very nature of consumer wants; a person cannot tell if he likes rhubarb life savers until he tries them, and if he does not, he has not maximized satisfaction. But the economic system does not do as an effective a job of informing the consumer as it might conceivably do. Advertising accomplishes this in part, but is by no means entirely satisfactory, and in some cases is clearly misleading. Some rules with respect to the labeling and description of contents have been imposed by the government.

2(*a*). It is rather obvious that factor prices do not always equate supply and demand; the most extreme cases of deviation from this level are those of mass unemployment. In such cases the real cost of additional units of output may be almost nil, because unemployed workers and resources can be used to produce them, but the marginal costs, reflecting existing factor prices, will be very much higher. Such situations may be explained in part by nonperfectly competitive elements in the factor markets, but primarily because factor-owners cannot easily adjust their real factor prices. If workers agree to work for lower wages, the prices of the products come down, and real wages may remain unchanged.

Similarly, factor prices are not always uniform for all users. Wages for a given type of labor may be higher in one area than in another, perhaps because of the weakness of unions in the latter, and thus uneconomic location of industry will result. Price discrimination practiced by monopolist or oligopolist producers of materials may also cause failure to attain this requirement, as well as monopsony influences exercised by buyers over price.

2(*b*). Marginal costs do not always reflect all costs for which production of additional units is responsible. Examples were given in the discussion of this requirement above; many others could be supplied. The social costs of alcoholism do not become factor costs to liquor producers, for example. If a factory is built in a residential area, the declines in the value of residential property are not borne by the business firm.

Governments have sought to meet this problem in several ways. They have prohibited the production of certain goods which have heavy social costs not borne by the producers, such as narcotics. They have placed taxes on the sale of other products, such as liquor, to shift some of the additional social costs to the users and thus reduce consumption. City zoning ordinances are primarily designed to prevent losses in property values by indiscriminate location of particular types of activities without reference to other property uses.

2(*c*). Equality of marginal costs and prices is attained so long as the firms are selling in purely competitive markets, apart from the effects of imperfections such as lack of adequate knowledge of costs by the producers. The greatest advantage of purely competitive market conditions, from the standpoint of economic welfare, is the attainment of equality of price and marginal cost.

In nonpurely competitive conditions, however, price will exceed marginal cost. Under such conditions, characterized by downward-sloping demand curves for the products of the individual firms, at the output level at which marginal revenue is equal to marginal cost, price will be in excess of marginal cost, as illustrated in Figure 96. Therefore

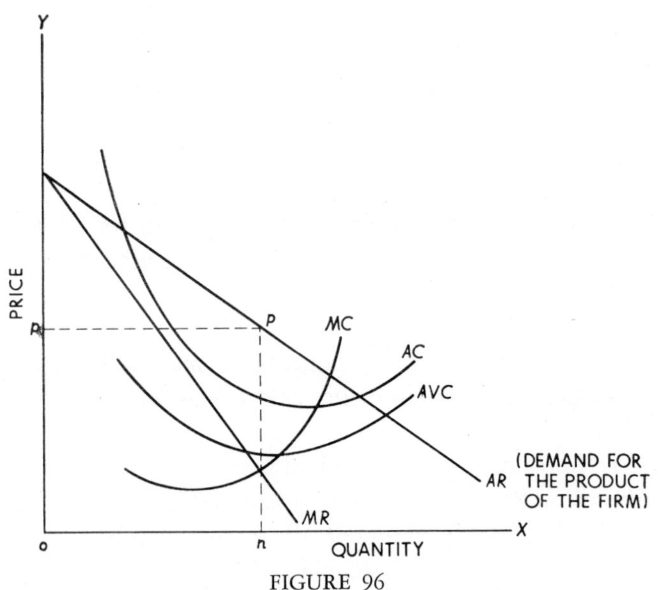

FIGURE 96

RELATIONSHIP OF PRICE AND MARGINAL COST, NONPURELY COMPETITIVE CONDITIONS

the prices of the commodities exceed the figures which reflect the real factor costs, in the sense of the sacrifice of output of other goods, and the outputs of the commodities are held to uneconomically low levels. This result is encountered whether excess profits are earned or not; the source of the difficulty is the downward-sloping nature of the demand curves for the products of the firms, which causes marginal revenue to be less than price at the point of most profitable operation.

In other cases, deviation between marginal factor costs and prices are caused by the levying of excise taxes on the sale of the particular commodities. These taxes result in prices for the commodities in excess of their factor costs—and hence in uneconomic reductions in output (assuming that the other requirements for optimum economic welfare are attained)—unless, of course, the excises reflect costs to society which are not costs to the producers. The liquor taxes may be justified on this basis.

One basic dilemma has been noted in recent years: the case in which, when price is equal to marginal cost, average cost is not covered, and thus all costs of production cannot be recovered. The most obvious case is that of a public utility enterprise which, although possessing a monopoly in the particular area, does not have sufficient market to allow it to reach the point of lowest cost. As explained in earlier chapters, in ranges of output less than that of lowest average cost, marginal cost is less than average cost. An extreme case is provided by a toll bridge not used to capacity; marginal cost of use of the bridge by another car may be nil, yet the average cost may be substantial. If prices are set at the level equal to marginal cost, the deficit must be made up by a subsidy financed by taxation. Since virtually all taxes exercise some adverse effects upon the economy, the decision with respect to pricing must be made upon the basis of a weighing of the relative disadvantages of taxes versus those of the departure from marginal cost pricing.[1]

3. There are many types of goods which yield important benefits to persons other than those who acquire them, or, yield all or most of their benefits to the community as a whole, rather than separately to individuals. National defense is the traditional example; by its nature it cannot be broken up into small pieces and sold to individuals. Education directly benefits the recipients, but yields important community benefits as well in the form of greater social and political stability and more rapid economic development.

Because of the importance of the indirect benefits from many types of activities, governments, representing the community as a whole, have found it desirable to undertake the activities providing the services to the community, and covering the costs of producing them from compulsory levies in the form of taxes. Private enterprise cannot produce many of these services at all, because they cannot be sold to individuals. Others, such as education, could be privately produced, but the total output would be uneconomically small if the production were left in

[1] The most recent survey of the marginal-cost pricing problem is to be found in the article by R. W. Harbeson, "A Critique of Marginal Cost Pricing," *Land Economics*, Vol. XXXI (February, 1955), pp. 54–74.

private hands because the indirect benefits would not influence the purchases.

Optimum Degree of Factor Utilization

The third general condition necessary for the attainment of optimum standards of living, given the pattern of income distribution, is that of an optimum degree of utilization of factors. There are several aspects of this condition:

1. Avoidance of unemployment. Optimum use of factor units requires that all factor units whose owners wish to have them employed at the factor prices which become established should find employment. Unemployment of factors obviously reduces the output of the economy below the optimum level and reduces the general standard of living below the optimum. Furthermore, especially in the case of labor, unemployment causes severe distress for the individuals concerned, since their source of income vanishes. Unemployment not only reduces output below the optimum, but causes a redistribution of income of a form particularly injurious to certain persons.

In practice full employment has not always been attained. When aggregate expenditures fall below national income at full-employment levels, unemployment is inevitable as production declines. Fortunately the resulting depressions have usually been of short duration, except, in the United States, that of the 'thirties, which continued so long that doctrines of secular stagnation and permanent unemployment became widely accepted. Because of the recognized evils of unemployment, governments have undertaken various measures—first monetary and then fiscal—to facilitate attainment of full employment.

2. Optimum division of time between work and leisure. Optimum economic welfare does not require the absolute maximum possible output, but rather the level which is consistent with the allocation of time between work and leisure which persons prefer to make, both employed workers and operators of business enterprises. As national income rises as a result of increased productivity, optimum economic welfare does not require that the entire gains be taken in the form of greater output; if persons, as a whole, prefer to take a part or even all of the benefits of greater productivity in the form of increased leisure, optimum economic welfare requires that this result be attained. The argument against shorter hours—that output will be reduced if the length of the working week is cut—is not a conclusive one; if society prefers more leisure and less output, it cannot be argued that such a choice is an undesirable one in terms of the assumed goals.

In practice, the requirements of efficient production make it impossible for each individual to decide the number of hours which he works; individuals must, in general, accept the working period which is standard in the particular line of employment, or work elsewhere. But as labor unions have grown in strength, the workers, as a whole, are in a much better position to obtain a working period which conforms with the average wishes of the workers, than in the periods in which employers dominated the labor market.

On the other hand, it may be argued that the growth in the importance of income (and commodity) taxes has interfered with the attainment of optimum division of time between work and leisure. Income taxes apply to the gains from work but not those from leisure, and sales and excise taxes apply to the gains from work to the extent that the income is spent on taxable goods. Thus the relative gains from work and leisure are altered somewhat; some persons may seek to work more because of the taxes, while others will seek to work less. It may be argued that the consequent distortion interferes with the attainment of optimum economic welfare. But the defenders of income taxation argue that the effects are not significant because the supply curve of labor is highly inelastic, and maintain that other advantages of the tax are sufficient to outweigh any possible adverse effect upon the work-leisure ratio.[2]

3. Optimum rate of capital formation. It may be argued that optimum economic welfare requires the division of total income between consumption and savings in a manner which conforms with the relative preferences for present and future consumption on the part of individuals. However, this requirement is subject to certain modifications:

(*a*) An increased rate of capital formation allows a more than proportional increase in output of consumption goods in the future. Particularly in countries with very low per capita incomes, relatively small increases in savings now might lead to very sharp rises in consumption in the future—ones not foreseen by the people of the society. It may be argued, in such cases, that a higher rate of capital formation than that permitted on the basis of present division of income between consumption and savings would greatly increase economic welfare over time.

(*b*) The preferred allocation of income between consumption and savings may prevent the maintenance of full employment and

[2] One of the best discussions of this question is to be found in the article by R. Goode, "The Income Tax and the Supply of Labor," *Journal of Political Economy*, Vol. LVII (October, 1949), pp. 428–37.

stable economic growth. If persons seek to save more at high income levels than the sums which can find outlet in investment, unemployment will develop and optimum economic welfare will not be attained. Under such circumstances a compromise is necessary between the requirement of allocation of income on the basis of choice of individuals and the need for maintaining full employment.

4. Optimum rate of utilization of scarce natural resources. Economic welfare requires an optimum rate of utilization of scarce natural resources such as petroleum and iron ore. But this optimum rate is very difficult to define because of the need for striking a balance between the relative interests of present and future generations. An extremely rapid rate of exploitation would exhaust the supplies available for the future; an excessively slow rate involves heavy sacrifice of present welfare for future welfare, one which may prove to have been unnecessary as new resources or alternative methods of production are developed in the future.

Attainment of an Optimum Rate of Economic Growth

Traditionally, the theory of economic welfare has been established in terms of static conditions—merely seeking to define the requirements for optimum welfare in terms of given determinants of equilibrium positions. In recent years, however, increased attention has been given to the significance of dynamic considerations for economic welfare. This attention has centered primarily on two elements:

1. The maintenance of an equilibrium, full-employment rate of growth. As explained in the previous chapter, an economy can continue to expand at a stable rate, without continuing or frequent recurring unemployment, only if balance is maintained among the various determinants of the rate of development. Particularly, aggregate demand must keep pace with growth in aggregate capacity to produce. The theory of economic growth has not reached a sufficient stage of advancement to be able to prescribe more fully the specific requirements for stability in growth.

2. The attainment of an optimum rate of increase in the real level of national income. The economic system must operate in such a manner as to provide maximum incentive for the discovery and introduction of new techniques, new methods of organization and operation, and new products. Quite apart from the effects of such developments upon the real level of national income, they aid in maintaining the volume of investment at sufficiently high levels to permit full employment.

One of the greatest advantages of the capitalist private enterprise economy lies in this field of development. One of the most important means by which firms can gain a rate of profit higher than the average is through the making of innovations which will allow excess profit in the period until competitors duplicate the change, and may give rise to continuing monopoly profit. The pressures of competition likewise force the other firms to meet the innovations in order to escape losses.

With respect to economic development, nonpurely competitive conditions may be somewhat more advantageous than purely competitive ones, so long as some elements of competition remain. The typical firm selling in purely competitive markets is too small to undertake the research and experiment necessary for innovations; largely for this reason, in the United States most research in agriculture has been undertaken by the federal government. It is the larger firm, in the situations of oligopoly and related cases, which is best able to develop and introduce the improvements which allow real increases in national income.

However, the pressures toward improvements and efficiency will slacken if entry of new firms into various industries is limited, and existing firms gain monopoly or semimonopoly positions. Many innovations are made by newcomers; if these cannot start, and if existing firms are already making a high rate of profit, development may be checked. Restrictions on entry of new firms may be more detrimental, from the standpoint of over-all economic welfare, than mere differentiation of product and the presence of relatively few firms in an industry. Outright agreements among firms with respect to methods of production, shares of output, etc. as permitted in the cartel systems of some countries, are likewise detrimental to economic progress.

THE OPTIMUM PATTERN OF INCOME DISTRIBUTION

The preceding analysis has been based upon the assumption of a given pattern of income distribution; if all of the requirements noted thus far are fulfilled, economic welfare may be said to be at the optimum in terms of the given pattern of income distribution—but only in terms of this distribution. The last question is that of defining the optimum pattern of income distribution, and to this question welfare theory can give the least satisfactory answers.

Maximization of Satisfaction?

If it were possible (*a*) to measure satisfaction and (*b*) to compare satisfactions received by different persons, it would, of course, be possible to define the optimum precisely as "the pattern of distribution which would allow the maximum total satisfaction." But satisfactions cannot be measured (a limitation of little significance in analyzing the behavior of individuals, since preferences for various alternatives can be compared), and, with the present and foreseeable state of knowledge, interpersonal utility comparisons—the comparisons of satisfaction received by different persons—are impossible. As a matter of practice, rough comparisons are frequently made; most persons would accept the argument, for example, that the transfer of one dollar from a millionaire to a starving family would increase the satisfaction of the latter more than it decreased the satisfaction of the former. But there is no way of proving even this extreme case; in fact the statement has very little meaning of any kind. Progressive income taxation is based in large measure on the notion that the sacrifice arising out of the loss of 10 per cent of income is less for a person with $100,000 income than for a person with a $2000 income. But no proof of this statement is possible.

The Lerner Argument

Lerner has argued that, in the absence of knowledge of the actual pattern of distribution which will maximize satisfaction, the most satisfactory assumption which can be made is that an equal distribution would be the one most likely to maximize satisfaction from a given level of national income.[3] The argument is based upon the principle that capacities for satisfaction are distributed normally around the mode of a frequency distribution, and that an equal distribution would involve only random error, whereas any other would involve a definite bias. But this assumption can be questioned, particularly because actual satisfaction may depend to a large extent upon the ability to be able to outdo other persons in consumption, or to keep up with them, in a society in which such "keeping up" is not insured by equality of distribution. Furthermore, an equal distribution is obviously not consistent with the maintenance of a high level of national income, because of effects upon incentives, nor with prevailing attitudes in contemporary Western societies.

The Attitudes of Society

The only feasible approach to the problem, but one which is not easy to apply, is based upon the principle that the optimum pattern is that which is regarded as the most equitable by the consensus of opinion in the particular society. This is a value judgment, one which cannot

[3] A. P. Lerner, *The Economics of Control* (New York: Macmillan, 1944), chap. iii.

be derived from economic analysis, but is merely noted as appearing to reflect most satisfactorily contemporary thinking on the question. It cannot be argued that the pattern determined in this manner necessarily maximizes satisfaction—a goal which is of no significance because it cannot be defined—but is simply one which accords with the concept of equity accepted in the particular society.

How can the consensus of thought on this question be determined? No precise method is possible; evaluation of legislation, as reflecting (perhaps rather imperfectly) the will of society, represents about the only tangible approach. On this basis, certain general statements about the consensus of opinion on the question are possible:

1. Excessive inequality of income is regarded as undesirable. This point of view is reflected in the use of progressive taxation, in the provision of old age pensions, relief, and aid to housing, in minimum wage legislation, etc. Opinions differ with respect to the question of what constitutes excessive inequality, but the general principle that the extent of inequality which develops in the absence of governmental interference is excessive is widely accepted.

2. The attainment of large incomes from monopolistic "exploitation" of the public is regarded as particularly objectionable, and an attempt is made to check this by antitrust legislation, public utility regulation, etc. From the standpoint of resource utilization, the basic objection to monopoly is the restriction of output below the level at which price is equal to marginal cost. But legislation on the question has been greatly influenced by the desire to eliminate monopoly profits.

3. Complete equality of income is regarded as undesirable from the standpoint of its effects upon production, and inequitable because it denies the more efficient, hard-working person the attainment of a higher reward for his skill and effort.

The difficulties in the path of obtaining a more satisfactory definition of the optimum pattern of income distribution greatly reduce the significance of contemporary welfare theory, the preciseness and strength of its conclusions, and the force of policy recommendations based upon them. For example, on the basis of welfare principles relating to optimum use of resources, it can be argued that subway fares should be higher in rush hours than in nonrush hours because marginal cost is higher in the former (when extra cars and trains must be added to carry more passengers) than it is in the latter (when trains are half empty). But the distribution of passengers by income group is not the same in the two periods, with a heavy concentration of workers in the rush hours. Thus such a fare system is condemned on the grounds of its effects on distribution of the costs of providing subway by income group, and welfare theory can offer no conclusive answer to this argument.

SUMMARY EVALUATION OF THE MARKET ECONOMY IN TERMS OF ECONOMIC WELFARE

The market economy offers significant advantages in terms of welfare theory, but likewise suffers from certain limitations, many of which have been corrected, at least in part, by governmental action.

Among the most significant advantages are the maintenance of a high degree of individual freedom and choice—a feature more difficult to maintain in any type of government-controlled economic system. Secondly, the market economy offers great incentive to the maintenance of a high degree of efficiency in production, to the attainment of the least-cost combinations, and, perhaps above all, to a rapid rate of economic development through the incentives given to the introduction of new techniques and new products. In large measure, output is directed in terms of consumer demands—given the pattern of income distribution—especially when purely competitive conditions prevail. The latter likewise insure operation at the point of lowest cost, apart from the effects of inadequate knowledge, but are probably less conducive to economic progress than nonpurely competitive conditions with free entry of firms. Finally, the market economy is able to obtain co-ordination in the functioning of the economic system and the making of the basic decisions by the independent action of millions of individuals and business firms, with no central agency of control.

On the other hand, in certain respects the economic system fails to attain fully the standards of optimum economic welfare, particularly in the complete absence of government participation in economic activity. Certain types of services, such as national defense and education, yield gains to the community as a whole, over and above those received directly and separately by individuals; thus society, through the government, must undertake their production in the interests of optimum allocation of resources. Secondly, lack of adequate knowledge on the part of consumers, business firms, and factor-owners prevents complete attainment of optimum adjustments in consumption and production and the attainment of maximum efficiency in production. Difficulties in forecasting lead at times to overproduction of certain types of goods in terms of consumer preferences. Thirdly, when pure competition is replaced by nonpurely competitive conditions, firms do not necessarily operate at the point of lowest cost, and price exceeds marginal cost. The greater the control which particular firms have over their markets, the greater will be this excess, and the greater the extent to which production is not adjusted in terms of consumer preferences. Restriction of entry of new firms aggravates this situation, and may also slow down the rate of technological change. Fourthly, at certain periods mass unemployment has developed, with consequent adverse effects upon economic welfare. Finally, the pattern of income distribution which comes about, especially if monopoly is strong, has obviously differed from that which society appears to regard as the most equitable, and various measures have been taken by governments to improve it.

The government has had considerable success in mitigating the worst of these evils. But the solution of the problem of the adverse effects of the development of nonpurely competitive conditions is difficult. In many instances technological requirements necessitate a relatively small number of large firms, preventing the markets from being purely competitive. Any attempt to break these firms up would lessen efficiency in production and check economic progress. On the other hand, financial considerations may lead to the development of firms which are much larger than is required by technology. The government has been forced to follow a policy of permitting continuation of nonpurely competitive conditions, and merely seeking to check the worst abuses, such as artificial restrictions placed upon the entry of new firms, agreements among firms with respect to price and output, the use of noneconomic methods to drive out competitors, and excessive consolidation, relative to economic considerations. With respect to the problem of eliminating unemployment, also, the success of the government has by no means been complete in the past.

The Alternative of Socialism

The most severe critics of the market economy argue that a higher level of economic welfare could be attained if capitalism were replaced by socialism with all production, or at least that in the most important spheres, being undertaken by the government. From an economic standpoint, the defenders of socialism maintain that prices under such a system would be set at levels equal to marginal costs (including all social costs) with the output levels such that output would equal demand at the price set. Thus optimum adjustment of production in terms of consumer desires would be attained. Industries would be organized in such a manner that each producing unit would operate at the point of maximum efficiency, and therefore lowest cost. Incomes would be adjusted in terms of the pattern of distribution regarded as most equitable; factor prices, set at supply-demand levels for purposes of cost determination and resource allocation, would not, as such, constitute incomes to the factor-owners, except in part, at least in the case of labor. Unemployment would cease to exist, since output would be increased whenever necessary to absorb idle resources.

However, such a system encounters significant obstacles in its efforts to maximize economic welfare. The first is the problem of maintaining incentives to insure maximum efficiency, especially in the case of managers of production units. The elimination of the profit motive would not only reduce the pressures toward efficiency, but, perhaps even more seriously, the incentives toward progress and economic development. In addition, a tremendous administrative organization would be required to co-ordinate the functioning of the various segments of the economy, and make the decisions which are made autonomously in capitalism, under the guidance of the pricing system. Personnel and other resources required for this organization would not be available for use in the production of goods. The dangers of failure to achieve complete co-ordination would be serious. The problems of delay, red tape, and shifting of responsibility—characteristic of large-scale business organizations—would be multiplied manyfold in a socialist economy. Finally, some loss of personal freedom, at least along economic lines, is inevitable. There is the further danger that the maintenance of other aspects of personal freedom and of democracy in government might prove incompatible with an economic system in which the government carried on all production activity; the goals pursued might cease to be those of economic welfare of the people as a whole, and become those of the welfare of the persons in control of the government. Over the years some of these basic problems may be solved, but they constitute significant arguments against the replacement of a market economy by one of socialism.

SELECTED REFERENCES

LITTLE, I. M. D. *A Critique of Welfare Economics.* London: Oxford University Press, 1950.

The most recent advanced-level analysis of welfare economics.

SCITOVSKY, T. *Welfare and Competition.* Chicago: Richard D. Irwin, Inc., 1951.

An extensive analysis of the significance of various forms of competition for the attainment of economic walfare.

BOULDING, K. E. "Welfare Economics," *A Survey of Contemporary Economics,* Vol. II. Homewood, Ill.: Richard D. Irwin, Inc., 1952.

A review of recent literature in the field.

BOWEN, H. R. *Toward Social Economy.* New York: Rinehart, 1948.
A clear presentation of the requirements of maximum economic welfare and the extent of their realization in capitalism.

REDER, M. W. *Studies in the Theory of Welfare Economics.* New York: Columbia University Press, 1947.
An advanced study of welfare economics.

LERNER, A. P. *The Economics of Control.* New York: Macmillan, 1944.
An extensive study of the principles of welfare economics.

SAMUELSON, P. A. *Foundations of Economic Analysis,* chap. viii. Cambridge: Harvard University Press, 1947.
An advanced analysis of the welfare problem.

PIGOU, A C. *The Economics of Welfare.* 4th ed. London: Macmillan, 1932.
A classic presentation of welfare economics.

QUESTIONS

1. Distinguish carefully between welfare economics and positive economic analysis.
2. Why cannot economics, as a scientific study, determine the appropriate goals of the economic system? How are these determined?
3. Why must welfare economics be based upon certain goals?
4. What are the three goals which are assumed in the present analysis of economic welfare?
5. Suppose that national income, after adjustment for price-level changes, rises 3 per cent between 1956 and 1957. Does this fact show that the economic welfare of society has risen by 3 per cent? Explain.
6. Why does the concept of maximization of satisfaction have little meaning when applied to the community as a whole?
7. Why does the attainment of optimum economic welfare require that firms be operating at the point at which price is equal to lowest average cost? At the point at which price is equal to marginal cost?
8. Why does pure competition, and only pure competition, insure the attainment of both of the requirements noted in Question 7?
9. Which of these two requirements can be attained in oligopoly but not in monopolistic competition? Which cannot be attained in either?
10. In what respects may the attainment of optimum adjustment of production not be attained in pure competition, despite the fulfillment of the two requirements noted in Question 7?
11. Evaluate the cobweb theorem reaction in terms of economic welfare.
12. Is the conduct of advertising necessarily contrary to the attainment of optimum economic welfare? Explain.
13. What is the marginal rate of transformation? The marginal rate of substitution?
14. In several respects the existence of unemployment interferes with the attainment of optimum economic welfare. What are these?

15. Subway lines virtually never cover their costs from operation, yet the construction and operation by governments may be fully justified, from the standpoint of economic welfare. Explain precisely why this is the case.
16. A good case can be made for subsidizing subway deficits out of gasoline-tax revenue. Explain.
17. Suppose that one firm is able to hire workers at $2.00 an hour, while another firm can obtain workers of the same type for $1.50 an hour. Why does this situation lead to distortion of resource allocation?
18. Give some examples of cases, other than those noted in the text, in which various real costs to society do not enter into the marginal costs of the firms producing the product.
19. Why does optimum economic welfare require that price equal marginal cost, rather than average cost?
20. Suppose that the costs of construction of a toll bridge become completely paid off from tolls at about the same time that the traffic on the bridge reaches a more-than-capacity level at rush hours, causing serious delays. Should the toll be taken off, and the bridge be made free, since it is now paid for? Explain.
21. What is the marginal-cost-pricing dilemma, with respect to certain public utility enterprises and similar undertakings?
22. How can the optimum division of time between work and leisure be defined?
23. The 30-hour week proposal, long regarded as an ultimate goal by labor unions, is widely condemned on the grounds that national product would be reduced were it carried into effect. Evaluate the argument, indicating the elements which must be taken into consideration in weighing this proposal.
24. Is the maximum possible rate of capital formation necessarily the optimum one in terms of economic welfare? Explain.
25. Liberal allowances for the deduction of depletion in determining income tax liability is frequently justified on the basis of the argument that this policy speeds up the rate of exploitation of natural resources. Evaluate this argument in terms of economic welfare.
26. Contrast the relative advantages of pure competition and nonpurely competitive conditions, from the standpoint of attainment of optimum economic welfare.
27. Indicate the alternative definitions of optimum income distribution, and evaluate them.
28. Why, in the present state of knowledge, can welfare theory provide little assistance in evaluating a particular scale of progression in the income tax structure?
29. Suppose that all monopoly profit could be absorbed by the government through some form of excess profits tax. Would the monopolies then be harmless from the standpoint of economic welfare? Explain.
30. Contrast the relative advantages of a market economy and socialism, in terms of optimum economic welfare.

Index

INDEX

INDEX

A

B

C

This book has been set on the Linotype in 12 point Garamond No. 3 leaded 1 point. Chapter numbers and titles are in 18 point Spartan Medium. The size of the type page is 27 by 46½ picas.